SURVEY
OF
SOCIAL
SCIENCE

GOVERNMENT AND POLITICS SERIES

Volume 3
903-1354

Indigenous Peoples' Governments—One-Party Systems

Edited by
FRANK N. MAGILL

Consulting Editor
JOSEPH M. BESSETTE
CLAREMONT MCKENNA COLLEGE

SALEM PRESS
Pasadena, California   Englewood Cliffs, New Jersey

Library of Congress Cataloging-in-Publication Data
Survey of social science: government and politics series /
edited by Frank N. Magill; consulting editor Joseph M.
Bessette.
   p.   cm.
Includes bibliographical references and index.
   1. Political science—Encyclopedias. 2. United States—
Politics and government—Encyclopedias. I. Magill,
Frank Northen, 1907-   . II. Bessette, Joseph M.
JA61.S88   1995
320'.03—dc20
ISBN 0-89356-745-0 (set)   95-30408
ISBN 0-89356-748-5 (volume 3)   CIP

CONTENTS

GOVERNMENT AND POLITICS

SURVEY
OF
SOCIAL
SCIENCE

INDIGENOUS PEOPLES' GOVERNMENTS

Field of study: Types of government

Following conquest by alien powers, the original inhabitants of territories have often been permitted to retain forms of self-government. Though the conquerors may leave the structures of local regimes unchanged, however, they invariably expect local leaders to comply with their orders in major political matters.

Principal terms

ABORIGINE: synonym for native; from the Latin words for "from the beginning," this term is most commonly applied to the original inhabitants of Australia

ALIEN: foreign or external

COLONY: territory ruled by an alien power

CHIEF: generic title commonly assigned to local rulers by alien conquerors

INDIGENOUS: adjective for native or original

NATIVE: noun for any person who has always lived in a place (as opposed to a visitor); in colonial usage, this word has become a demeaning term for a colonized person

RESERVATION: tract of land set aside, or reserved, for the exclusive use of a designated group, such as an American Indian tribe

RESIDENT: generic term for a colonial official who lives among indigenous peoples and oversees their administration

Overview

Indigenous peoples' governments have usually resulted from conquest by outsiders. Colonization and imperialism have thus been the origin of most of the semi-independent governments that conquered peoples have formed. Partly autonomous governments have appeared in almost every region of the globe, but they are particularly associated with Africa, Asia, and the Americas.

A colonizing power might have several motives for allowing a conquered region's original inhabitants to keep a measure of self-rule. For example, many of the peoples of the Iroquois Confederacy in North America allied with the British in the eighteenth century. During the American War of Independence, the Iroquois gave military assistance to Great Britain. After the thirteen American colonies became independent, many Iroquois were forced to move to Canada. As a reward for their loyalty, the British rulers of Canada allowed them to retain their own governmental system, which was based on warrior assemblies ultimately controlled by councils of elder females.

During Great Britain's conquest of India similar alliances occurred. Rulers bearing titles such as nawab, nizam, raja, and maharajah either supported the British or did nothing to hinder their progress. In the eighteenth and nineteenth centuries, they became the leaders of some three hundred "native states" over which the British exercised indirect control.

One of the most elaborate attempts to form indigenous peoples' governments occurred in modern South Africa. After 1948 the ruling white minority created a series of "homelands" for black South Africans. The resulting "independent" states, such as Transkei and Venda, were thinly disguised attempts to continue a system of racial segregation in South Africa. These homelands were only nominally autonomous and were not recognized as independent states by any established nations. The coming of majority rule to South Africa in the 1990's led to their dismantling.

Sometimes indigenous populations were small and thinly scattered over wide areas. Their home territories were frequently in barren, isolated places. For the conquering power to govern them directly would have been expensive and impractical. The conquerors' governments could safely leave such people to control their own desolate retreats. The aborigines of Australia had that experience. Scattered in the vast outback of the large island continent, they were able to maintain their own political organizations almost until the twentieth century.

During the early years of the United States, the federal government attempted to shift Indian populations to remote areas where they would not impede settlement by peoples of European descent. The forced relocation of the Cherokee from Georgia to what became Oklahoma in 1838-1839 was a large-scale example of that policy. The push to settle the western regions throughout the nineteenth century continued to restrict native Americans to small reservations, which were usually located in the most inhospitable portions of the continent. Not only were the Indians compelled to live on infertile patches of ground, but also those on the reservations were not allowed to hunt or pursue many traditional occupations. Though nominally ruled by their own leaders, they were under government agents, who really controlled the reservations.

One aspect of the reservation system in the United States did, however, eventually become a benefit to Indians, whose various groups were described in treaties with the federal government as "nations." The laws of the states in which Indian reservations were located did not apply within the boundaries of the reservations. Late in the nineteenth century, Indians realized that this fact permitted them to ignore local regulations forbidding gambling. Casinos soon began to sprout up on reservations from New York to Arizona, and some Indian groups actually began to profit from the subordinate status confirmed by their treaties with the federal government.

Within the British Empire, economic considerations were a strong motivation in the development of what the British called indirect rule. Mobilizing, transporting, and supplying large bodies of soldiers to subdue indigenous peoples was expensive. On the other hand, sending a handful of administrators to serve as residents in a region nominally ruled by local chiefs was much cheaper than outright conquest. So long as the indigenous people obeyed their residents in important political matters, colonial overlords could govern on the cheap.

Agents on American Indian reservations were often political appointees, the beneficiaries of the politics of patronage. In the British Empire, residents typically came from military backgrounds. Soldiers who showed diplomatic skill were thought to be ideal supervisors over local rulers. As army officers, they were fond of sports, such as hunting and polo—which indigenous chiefs, especially in India, also enjoyed. Residents often set themselves up as confidants and advisers to local rulers. Soldiers' presumed ability to keep cool in crises further encouraged their recruitment as agents of the dominant power.

Whether political hacks or well-trained soldier-bureaucrats, the officials of ruling governments usually shared several assumptions about the native peoples whom they administered. Such officials were typically convinced that the indigenous peoples' governments operated on unchanging traditional lines. For them, tradition meant tribal loyalty and respect for chiefs or councils of elders. Government agents thought tribes were simple organizations based on ties of blood. Tribes were, in fact, often highly fluid groups which constantly formed and reformed themselves. Kinship provided the basic political terminology of such organizations but did not necessarily imply real family connections. Tribal leaders were rarely rulers whose words were law; they were actually compromisers who had to please all the factions within their groups. In giving such leaders official status, the alien ruling states often imposed unpopular chiefs on internally restless societies.

While indigenous peoples' governments are most apparent in Asia, the Americas, and Africa, Europe itself has seen many experiments in self-government for local peoples who considered themselves to be victims of conquest by alien powers. The Basques of northern Spain, for example, have long agitated for self-government under the Spanish monarchy. They claim that as the original inhabitants of the Iberian peninsula they should have the right to control their own affairs. Old empires, such as that of Austria-Hungary, or newer ones such as that of the Soviet Union, were beset by demands from different linguistic groups for virtual autonomy. In the late twentieth century, several new nations—such as the Slovak and Czech republics—emerged from indigenous peoples' governments within large modern states (in this case Czechoslovakia). The breakup of Yugoslavia into the mutually hostile states of Slovenia, Croatia, Serbia, and Bosnia showed that violence frequently accompanied the founding of new states which had been self-governing parts of national political systems.

Applications

The British Empire provides many case studies in different types of indigenous peoples' governments. From the Middle Ages onward, the British tried several political experiments in Ireland. Those ranged from attempts to obliterate the native Irish population to the creation of a mostly Protestant Irish landed gentry, who would both control and represent the indigenous Roman Catholic peasantry. Throughout the nineteenth century, rebellions by the Irish alternated with discussions of Home Rule until the Irish Republic was created as an independent nation after World War I.

From 1757 until 1845, the British extended their control throughout the Asian subcontinent of India. Relatively few British troops (about 25,000) served there at any one time. An army of roughly 250,000 Indian soldiers commanded by British officers undertook most of the work of conquest. But even that number was tiny within a total population of 125 million. Because the British could not afford to administer directly the whole of India, many local rulers were left in charge of states whose boundaries were established by the British. In some cases, such as that of the nizams of Hyderabad in Central India, local princes ruled over extensive kingdoms. Hyderabad was about the size of France. In other cases, a native kingdom might be only slightly larger than a ranch in Montana.

The native rulers of Hyderabad retained their power by allying themselves with the British at strategic moments during the eighteenth century. Other rulers, such as the rajas of the tiny state of Dewas, ruled jungle or mountain tracts that were almost inaccessible. Outright conquest of such places would have been too costly.

Depending on the size and importance of the indigenous Indian state, one or more British residents would be assigned to act as advisers, spies and, if need be, replacements for the local ruler. A large state such as Hyderabad merited a chief resident and a small corps of assistants. Places such as Dewas had to share their residents with their equally tiny neighbors. Likewise, the honors afforded to the rulers differed according to the sizes of their kingdoms and the prestige that they enjoyed. As the highest ranked native prince in India, the nizam received a salvo of artillery as a salute on official occasions.

Indigenous rulers in India had several different ways of attaining their positions under British rule. The nizams of Hyderabad had been high officials in the former Mughal Empire. The founder of Hyderabad state bore the title "Nizam al-Mulk," which meant "organizer of the state." The first nizam had become governor of the newly conquered state of Golconda in the early eighteenth century. His descendants in the Asaf Jahi dynasty ruled Hyderabad until the area was incorporated into the modern Republic of India in 1948. The rajas of Dewas, by contrast, were more or less successful bandits who had acquired control of their territory on the eve of the British conquest.

Generally, the British respected the semi-independence of rulers such as the nizams, who followed imperial directions and remained absolutely loyal to the British. The nizams gradually reorganized their government according to British standards, and bureaus and law courts became prominent features of their state. In other native states, when a raja or nawab misbehaved—such as by treating his subjects too harshly—the resident might well remove the offending prince. The "native state" would then either be directly incorporated into the regular administration of the empire, or ruled by the resident until such time as a son or other relative of the deposed ruler became old enough to take the throne.

These indigenous rulers were not always "traditional" rulers. The nizams, for example, were Muslims who ruled a territory whose people were 95 percent Hindu. Nevertheless, the British thought of themselves as preserving native custom and believed that their conservative approach would make it easier for Indians to adjust to the progress that they believed their empire brought. In many cases, the British actually promoted political stagnation, and indirect rule hindered local adjustments to change. Modern politics did not come to many native states until they were annexed by the Republic of India after 1947.

The major lesson that the British learned from their experience in India was that the indirect system of controlling indigenous peoples was almost always cheap and effective. They applied systems of indirect rule in many other areas. The sultans of the Malay peninsula, for example, were left in control of their states under the direction of a few residents. The states of the Persian Gulf—Kuwait, Oman, and Abu Dhabi— likewise remained under the nominal control of local authorities.

Another extensive use of indirect rule occurred as the British began their conquest of West Africa. As the British subdued the Ashanti peoples of what is now Ghana, they relied heavily on local leaders whom they called chiefs. Among the Ashanti, one important mark of a chief was that he sat on a stool. Arguments and decisions about who should or should not occupy any given stool occupied the attention of many British officials. Most of those officials had either had some experience as residents of India or had read the writings of Indian officials who espoused the advantages of indirect rule in colonies.

British officials often decided rather arbitrarily who should become a chief. For example, in 1900, the governor of the Gold Coast (now Ghana) demanded that the Ashanti surrender to him the golden stool of the paramount chief. He either was unaware or did not care that the Ashanti had an elaborate system of selecting their chiefs. Also, he ignored the ways that popular assemblies of the elders and younger warriors acted as checks on the powers of the chief. Rather, he selected a chief whose primary qualification was his loyalty to the British. Other similarly qualified individuals likewise became leaders. Feeling that they had the full support of the British, these appointed Ashanti chiefs sometimes acted like petty tyrants. When discontent, especially among the younger warriors who had always had influence over the chiefs, led many Ashanti to refuse to serve their headmen, the British usually did support the chiefs they had installed.

Though ostensibly intended to preserve traditional governmental forms, indigenous peoples' governments were usually closely tied to the colonial powers. If local leaders were loyal to their overlords and followed the orders they gave about governing the people, such chiefs had a certain amount of independent power. Their use of that power sometimes did not please the majority of their subjects. Although there were a great many native states, the occasions on which colonial governments removed rulers were few. Indigenous peoples' governments, therefore, most often served the needs of the conquerors before they met any of the most vital needs of the original inhabitants.

Context

From the fifteenth through the nineteenth centuries, the peoples of Europe established ever stronger national states in their home regions. They also spread throughout the globe. Within the European national states, peoples of different linguistic or cultural traditions: The Bretons of France, the Basques of Spain, and the Scots of the

British Isles were either forcibly incorporated or given small measures of control over their own affairs.

The problems that local ethnic minorities presented to Europe's emerging nation-states were minor compared to those created by peoples whose languages, customs, and histories were completely alien to those of Europeans. Direct conquest of the indigenous peoples of the Americas, Asia, and Africa did occur, but warfare was time-consuming and costly. The idea of allowing the aboriginal inhabitants to rule themselves, at least partially, in their own enclaves often proved an expedient alternative.

In some cases, indirect rule hurt the original inhabitants. The demoralization and degradation of Native American populations on reservations in the United States was one example of how indigenous peoples derived almost nothing from the little autonomy they enjoyed. Sometimes a ruling state's award of partial autonomy did afford a few indigenous peoples slight relief from the kinds of radical change which the invaders brought. The Indians of Canada apparently fared somewhat better than those of the United States.

Throughout much of Asia and Africa, indirect rule had a mixed record of accomplishment. In a few places, such as India's Hyderabad state, the indigenous rulers proved to be both enlightened leaders and effective guardians of an older cultural system. Even so, generations of British residents did not protect Hyderabad from its eventual forced incorporation into the Republic of India. In many other cases, the preservation of indigenous peoples' governments worked to retard political change. Rather than being truly customary or traditional, such regimes were often the artificial creations of colonial officials.

Bibliography

Cartey, Wilfred, and Martin Kilson, eds. *The Africa Reader: Colonial Africa.* New York: Vintage Books, 1970. Anthology of writings about Africa by both Africans and non-Africans. Several essays discuss indigenous peoples' governments of Africa in the nineteenth and twentieth centuries.

Fisher, Michael H. *Indirect Rule in India.* New York: Oxford University Press, 1991. Though primarily concerned with the workings of the residency system in British India, this book devotes considerable time to comparing developments there with those in Africa.

Jeffrey, Robin. *People, Princes, and Paramount Power.* Delhi: Oxford University Press, 1978. Collection of essays covering most of the major regions of India and illustrating the different forms which indirect rule assumed.

Josephy, Alvin M. *The Indian Heritage of America.* New York: Knopf, 1974. Though now somewhat dated, this is a highly readable account of the many different Indian cultures that existed in North America at the time that Europeans arrived. It describes the rise of the reservation system and its detrimental impact on indigenous Americans.

Lynton, Harriet R., and Mohini Rajan. *The Days of the Beloved.* Berkeley: University of California Press, 1974. Highly readable and charming account of Hyderabad during the reign of the next to last nizam, Mahbub Ali. It seeks to portray all levels of society in Hyderabad from the nizam's court to the world of his poorest subjects.

Gregory C. Kozlowski

Cross-References

Africa: Politics and Governments, p. 21; American Indian Governments, p. 59; Asia: Politics and Governments, p. 108; Clientelism, p. 337; Colonial Government, p. 344; Colonialism and Anticolonialism, p. 351; Empires and Empire Building, p. 597; Genocide, p. 752; Hegemony, p. 817; Self-Determination, p. 1796; Tribal Government, p. 2027.

INDIVIDUAL VERSUS STATE RIGHTS

Field of study: Political philosophy

The mutual obligations of citizens to the political systems in which they live are complex. What should one do when rulers demand beliefs or actions violating one's conscience? Many consider this question to be at the core of political philosophy.

> *Principal terms*
>> CIVIL DISOBEDIENCE: deliberate and public defiance of a law believed to be unjust by one or more persons in order to invoke a conscientious appeal for justice
>> DUTY: responsibility owed by an individual or a group
>> LIBERTY OF CONSCIENCE: right of one to believe and act in accordance with one's religious or political beliefs
>> PASSIVE OBEDIENCE: doctrine that urges the performance of duties claimed by the state even when one disagrees
>> POLITICAL OBLIGATION: duty to obey the state; the limits to that duty
>> RIGHTS: claims to authority made by individuals, groups, nations, and the state

Overview

People who do not live entirely alone live within political systems, and political systems are forms of government. The relationship between the people and their government is expressed in law and custom, which spell out mutual rights and duties. The primary duties that political systems owe to the people whom they rule revolve around public safety—protection and relief from disease, disasters, and dangerous people. In addition, rulers are expected to show respect for life, liberty, and property, the sanctity of marriage, the home, customs and beliefs, and other cultural and legal traditions. People have a right to expect that the laws on these matters will be faithfully executed.

What are the duties that the people owe to the state? Citizens, subjects and even visitors to a country owe civic obedience, which includes observance of the laws, payment of taxes, armed defense of the nation if necessary, and loyalty. Citizens may also be expected to report crimes, serve on juries, and vote.

What if a state does not observe its duty to its people? Civil obedience is not owed to regimes that rule by force and fraud. If murder, rape, imprisonment, starvation, and other instruments of terror are used to subject a population, then rule by law has vanished. The law no longer has a moral foundation to give it legitimacy. Gross abuse of power is not the only basis for opposition to the laws of a state. Injustice may lead individuals or groups to oppose one or more specific laws without seeking to over-throw the state. In some governments any criticism is viewed as sedition or treason. In democratic systems dissent has been virtually institutionalized. Dissent may be expressed in protests such as marches, picketing, petitions, mass rallies, and other actions designed to show disapproval of a policy. Protesters may even use illegal actions to promote their cause.

The suffering created by injustice has long evoked political thinking about the duties of the individual to the state. Political struggles such as the American Revolution, the Civil Rights movement, and the Russian Revolution periodically revitalize the perennial problem of political obligation.

The problem of political obligation is finding correct answers to such questions as why one ought to obey the law, by what moral right political authority demands obedience, what the limits of one's duty to obey the state are, and if one has the right or duty to disobey the state when it is corrupt. The obvious answer to these questions is that anyone who does not obey the law—even for good reasons—will be put in jail, or worse. This is a prudent, but not a moral answer. It tells one what is smart and practical but does not explain the moral reasons that the state may have for demanding civil obedience. It does not explain how to respond if one believes the state does not have a morally justified reason for commanding one to kill in war, to practice racism, or to engage in other actions violating the liberty of conscience.

Throughout history, the right of states to command has been justified by might, divine right, or the consent of the governed. Justifications of one's duty to obey fall into three rather broad categories: the absolutist, the liberal, and the libertarian. Each differs in the scope it gives to the duty of the individual to obey.

The absolutist position says that duty to obey the law is absolute whether laws are just or unjust. The remedy for injustice is to appeal to the authorities for injustice, or simply to suffer the injustice. The liberal position sees the state's powers as limited by the individual's possession of inalienable rights. Governments based upon the liberal theory rule by the consent of the governed and have limited rights to control life, freedom, and property. Such governments have weaknesses; majorities, or groups of the powerful, may give their consent to be governed, but small or weak groups may be coerced. A result may be tyranny of the majority, or more commonly, tyranny of activist elites. Finally, the libertarian position sees government as barely necessary. The most extreme libertarian position is the anarchist. While this philosophy does not advocate social chaos, it sees the state—because of its use of coercion—as the source of all social ills. Abolishing the state would secure the rights of individuals.

The history of Western political theory can be summarized in terms of the tension between the rights of the individual versus those of the state. This is not the case with Eastern political thought, in which the emphasis on cooperative family and religious ties has long been influential. In China, both Taoism and Confucianism argue that a wise person becomes virtuous by living according to the Tao (insight into the ultimate nature). Lao-tzu, the founder of Taoism, counseled kings to become virtuous because doing so created a prosperous kingdom, and to follow a laissez-faire policy with respect to the people. The wise person, whether king or subject, should follow the path of least resistance, wearing away the strength of opposing forces, as water wears away stone. Kings and subjects who obey natural law endure; those that do not disappear.

Confucianism, which was the dominant philosophy in China until the twentieth century, also views government as natural and stresses the virtue of filial piety. The king should be a model of virtue for the people. Since natural disasters and political disturbances are caused by the moral failure of the emperor, lesser officials may depose a wicked ruler. In Korea, Confucianism has had an influence similar to that in China. In Japan, however, the obligations of filial piety were transferred from the individual's parents to the emperor.

In China, Korea, Japan, and Indochina, Buddhist teachings have also had a significant influence. Buddhism, originating in Hindu culture, teaches *dharma*, a spiritual framework for understanding that does not emphasize political rights. *Dharma* teaches ways to fit into the harmony of the universe by right, ethical action. In Buddhist kingdoms, the king may be considered a Buddha, and hence a man of virtue the individual may be expected to imitate. Assertions of inalienable rights of the individual were not native to the culture, but as Buddhist resistance to foreign intervention in Vietnam and to the Chinese invasion of Tibet indicate, the individual may, by Buddhist reasoning, decide that right, ethical action includes resistance to unjust power.

Hinduism's teaching on *ahimsa* (do no harm to a living creature) was developed by Mohandas Gandhi into a philosophy of nonviolent resistance. His program of satyagraha (reliance on truth) is not a doctrine of passive resistance. Rather, its basic idea is to not cooperate with unjust political orders, and to do so in such a way as to convert the opposition.

Islamic teachings tend to command political obedience. Their general rule is obedience without violating the Islamic law. When a state violates Islamic law, however, the individual has no duty to obey it. Civil disobedience is preferred to violent action.

Applications
Since ancient times a vast literature has developed dealing with the tension between the state and the individual. Some of it justifies a limit to obedience on grounds of religious duties. The Bible records the story of Shadrach, Meshach, and Abednego, who refused to obey the command of the king of Babylon to worship an idol because it would violate God's law. The Greek playwright Sophocles tells of Antigone, who disobeys her sovereign by appealing to the "higher law" of the gods. Similar justifications for resistance to tyranny were developed by philosophers who appealed to natural law. In Plato's *Apology*, Socrates tells the jury that sentences him to death that he must obey the gods rather than men. Later, in *Crito*, Socrates refuses to escape from prison because he rejects the idea of a right to violate Athenian law. Socrates' teachings on civil disobedience rest on reason, which—after religion—is the second major ground for theories about the individual's duty to the state.

The New Testament reports that Jesus was asked whether his followers should pay taxes to Caesar. His answer, "render unto Caesar the things that are Caesar's and unto God the things that are God's," established a divided loyalty in the West, since God's prior claims on the individual make Caesar's claims less than absolute. The Apostles expanded upon this by declaring that with regard to religious liberty they would obey

God rather than men. The Apostle Paul argued that the origin of government is divine, and he made obedience to civil authority a Christian duty. John the Elder, on the other hand, declared that when the state becomes a beast, making war on the saints, resistance is obligatory. These differing views, all of which appear in the Bible, stimulated constant debate over the limits of individual obedience to civil authority.

In the Middle Ages, both John of Salisbury and Thomas Aquinas conceived of political office as a trust. Their doctrines of resistance were focused on the community as a whole rather than on the individual. At the time of the Reformation, Martin Luther and John Calvin taught passive obedience as the proper Christian response to despotism. However, Calvin laid the groundwork for passive resistance by teaching that the individual had a right and even a duty to disobey both unholy and unjust laws. Lower magistrates were viewed as having a right to depose higher officials who acted wickedly. Doctrines advocating the right to violently resist rulers reached a peak with the Monoarchomachs—Protestant and Catholic writers who advocated assassination of heretical rulers. It did not matter whether the rulers acted unjustly, their heresy alone justified their removal. Writing in the era of the English Civil War, Thomas Hobbes, in his book *Leviathan*, refutes doctrines of resistance to authority based on the liberty of conscience. He teaches that personal security requires absolute obedience to the sovereign; otherwise, society would slip back into a state of nature, in which life is "nasty, brutish, and short." This is a social contract theory with the government viewed as artificial—that is, a consciously made construct among people.

John Locke wrote to justify the Glorious Revolution of 1688. His *First Treatise on Civil Government* refutes monarchial claims of a divine right to receive absolute obedience from subjects. His *Second Treatise on Civil Government* presents a social contract theory of the state that grounds its legitimacy in the rights of individuals. All are born into a state of nature with inherent rights. Government is created to protect the rights of the peaceful from those "bad souls" who do not obey the law of nature. The natural rights of man include the right of revolution.

Thomas Jefferson's Declaration of Independence follows Locke in declaring that rights are inalienable and that the purpose of government is to protect them. When the government no longer has the consent of the governed, the governed have a right to change it.

In the United States, theories of constitutionalism, states' rights, and separation of powers are used to secure liberty for the individual. In addition, lists of rights such as the English Bill of Rights and the Virginia Bill of Rights are written into constitutions, severely restricting government actions toward individuals. In the nineteenth century, Henry David Thoreau argued civil disobedience from a libertarian perspective. He was to influence the nonviolent teachings of Leo Tolstoy, Gandhi, and Martin Luther King, Jr. John Stuart Mill, in his book *On Liberty*, puts limits on the rights of both the government and society to restrict the individual. King believed there was a moral obligation to obey just laws and a moral obligation to disobey unjust laws. To overthrow legal segregation in the South, he and his followers practiced nonviolent resistance.

Context

In the nineteenth century, a widespread acceptance in the West of liberal concepts of the social contract and limited government enlarged the scope of private rights. The rise of powerful industrial interests, however, led to theories supporting the government as protector of private property, which led to the de facto reduction of the rights of many. In 1848, in many Western nations, the dispossessed revolted, justifying their actions with the concept that the individual does not owe allegiance to an unjust state.

After World War I, an age of democracies and dictatorships began. Under both forms of government, struggles of individuals or groups against injustices repeatedly occurred. Often repression was cloaked under the color of law, patriotism, or the pretended protection of individual freedoms. For example, the ravages of German fascism were justified by arguments about the German people's right to claim their homelands, protect themselves, and fulfill their destiny. Often, governments claimed that national security necessitated acts of repression.

The world wars and the Depression led to the shrinking of the sphere of private rights; in the face of war and severe social unrest, governments often acted against individual rights of speech, liberty, and even life. The rise of positivist law theories sometimes aided those parties seeking to deny individual rights. Based on a strict empiricism, positivism stressed procedural justice and denied the reality of substantive justice. At the same time, liberal and libertarian thought continued to gain acceptance, leading to popular insistence on self-determination.

The end of World War II served notice of the restoration of the idea of inalienable human rights. In 1949, the United Nations Declaration of Human Rights restated the rights of individuals in relation to the state. The Cold War era, however, produced numerous attempts to suppress human rights in the name of national security. In the United States, the struggle to end racial segregation blossomed in the late 1950's and was followed by peace movements that opposed the Vietnam War, the draft, nuclear weapons policy, and government support of repressive regimes around the world. Protest movements have developed to advance women's rights, secure safe environments, and foster other policies favoring the welfare of individuals.

The end of the Cold War and the emergence of democracies around the world have not ended conflicts between the state and the individual. They have only taken new form. Liberties that at one time were only extended to the few are now claimed by the many. The few, through history, have sought to protect their interests. With the end of the Cold War, the terms of the argument about the rights of the individual versus the rights of the state shifted. The threat of war between the superpowers no longer justified governments' broad invocations of national security as a reason to limit individual rights. The fall of the Soviet socialist republics largely ended the argument that individual liberty is subordinate to the demands of the proletarian revolution. Issues of individual liberty turned, or returned, to that of the rich versus the poor, of one race versus another, and of the minority versus the majority. Also, some Third World regimes justified attacks on human rights as a defense of tradition, since Western ideas about democracy, secular government, or the equality of women, for example, may be considered culturally imperialistic. At the same time these same Western ideas of rights have been used to create movements that seek to establish justice. The struggle for liberty and justice is ancient and universal.

Bibliography

Bowie, Norman E., and Robert L. Simon, eds. *The Individual and the Political Order: An Introduction to Social and Political Philosophy*. Englewood Cliffs, N.J.: Prentice-Hall, 1977. Selections with introductory discussions that treat many aspects of the problem of political obligation.

Confucius. *The Wisdom of Confucius*. Edited and translated by Lin Yutang. New York: Modern Library, 1938. Thoughts of Confucius, including political opinions.

Hanson, Donald W., and Robert Booth Fowler, eds. *Obligation and Dissent: An Introduction to Politics*. Boston: Little, Brown, 1971. Essays with introductions about the problem of political obligation.

Kent, Edward, ed. *Revolution and the Rule of Law*. Englewood Cliffs, N.J.: Prentice-Hall, 1971. Collection of articles debating the issue of the ethics and politics of civil disobedience.

Mayer, Milton. *On Liberty: Man v. the State*. Santa Barbara, Calif.: Center for the Study of Democratic Institutions, 1969. Essay dealing with the issues related to individuals and the rights of states.

Ramachandran, G., and T. K. Mahadevan, eds. *Gandhi: His Relevance for Our Times*. Rev. and enlarged ed. Berkeley, Calif.: World Without War Council, 1967. Collection of essays discussing many aspects of Gandhi's life and thought.

Sabine, George H. *A History of Political Theory*. 4th ed. Revised by Thomas Landon Thorson. Hinsdale, Ill.: Dryden Press, 1973. Classic history of Western political theory.

Somerville, John, and Ronald E. Santoni, eds. *Social and Political Philosophy: Readings from Plato to Gandhi*. Garden City, N.J.: Anchor Press, 1963. Rich selection of classic readings covering many elementary issues.

A. J. L. Waskey, Jr.

Cross-References

Burke's Political Philosophy, p. 171; Caste Systems, p. 203; Civil Disobedience, p. 285; Civil Liberties Protection, p. 291; Civil Rights and Liberties, p. 298; Civil Unrest and Rioting, p. 317; Confucianism and Government, p. 405; Corporatism, p. 452; Government Roles, p. 778; John of Salisbury's Political Philosophy, p. 1006; Legitimacy, p. 1105; Liberalism, p. 1118; Locke's Political Philosophy, p. 1142; Right of Revolution, p. 1744; Rousseau's Political Philosophy, p. 1756; The Social Contract, p. 1827; Spinoza's Political Philosophy, p. 1872.

INDUSTRIALIZATION

Field of study: Economic issues

Industrialization occurs when goods are mass produced in mechanized factories usually located in population centers that provide the workers required to run the factories. Their work is often performed on assembly lines, with each worker responsible for performing one small, repetitious task.

Principal terms

ASSEMBLY LINE: slow-moving belt or track along which goods pass during their manufacture, each worker being responsible for one small element in their assembly

COLLECTIVE BARGAINING: negotiations between employees, through their labor unions, and their employers regarding working conditions

DIVISION OF LABOR: assignment of specialized tasks to individual workers

ECONOMIES OF SCALE: cost savings made possible by the large-scale purchase of materials for the mass production of goods

LAISSEZ-FAIRE: policy that permits industries and businesses to determine, without outside interference, the rules by which they will operate

MONOPOLY: exclusive control of a service or product in a specific market

OLIGOPOLY: control of a service or product by a small group of businesses or industries

PRICE FIXING: artificial setting of prices by the industries or businesses in an oligopoly

Overview

A combination of inventions and the concentration of large amounts of capital in the hands of those who had dominated Great Britain's brisk world trade during the sixteenth and seventeenth centuries created the conditions necessary for widespread industrialization in England during the eighteenth century. The leader in providing much of Europe and Asia with much-sought-after commodities, Great Britain ruled the seas. One of the principal products of its trade was cloth, usually produced in the homes of artisans, who raised and sheared sheep, spun their wool into thread, and wove the thread into cloth.

In 1733, John Kay's invention of the flying shuttle provided a prototype for machines that, before the century ended, would enable one worker to produce more cloth than a hundred had previously. Lewis Paul and John Wyatt moved England a step closer to the mechanical spinning of thread with their invention in 1741 of a frame with rollers designed to accomplish that feat, even though their first, imperfect machine was of little practical value.

By the time James Hargreaves invented the spinning jenny in 1764, mechanization was beginning to dominate the textile industry. His invention, patented in 1770, permitted each worker to run eight spindles rather than the single spindle each had previously handled. Thomas Newcomen's invention in 1705 of the first steam engine held the promise of a reliable source of power to run these new inventions, although it was not until 1763 that James Watt refined the steam engine and made it practical for powering machinery.

Around 1770, Richard Arkwright invented a water-powered thread-spinning machine. By 1779, Samuel Crompton had combined Arkwright's inventions with Hargreaves' spinning jenny to produce a machine called a mule that could spin the finest and strongest thread yet available to the textile industry. Six years later, Edmund Cartwright patented his power loom.

These tentative steps toward modern industrialization occurred slowly. They aroused suspicion among people who were accustomed to working in their own cottage industries, some of whom rioted and destroyed the factory machinery they thought threatened their livelihoods. Factories, profiting greatly from the economies of scale that mass production made possible, began to flourish, nevertheless, alongside the cottage industries that survived well into the nineteenth century,

England remained the preeminent industrial nation in the world for more than a century. Following the French Revolution (1789), France, the first continental country to industrialize, was too much involved in the Napoleonic Wars (1799-1815) and the War of 1812 to mechanize rapidly. Although Samuel Slater established a textile mill in Rhode Island in 1790, and other industries developed over the next half century, the United States remained a largely agrarian society until after the Civil War (1861-1865). It was not yet poised to industrialize because it lacked the necessary accumulations of capital needed for massive industrialization.

In the Southern states, which were largely agricultural, the need for mechanization was not pressing because slave labor was readily available. In the Northeastern states, the manpower needed to build and run factories was limited because America's western expansion was siphoning off large segments of the potential workforce.

The needs of an industrialized society were regularly met by the inventions and developments that such a society necessitated. As the need for cotton increased with a growing worldwide demand for textiles, Eli Whitney invented the cotton gin in 1793, enabling one laborer to clean as much cotton as fifty laborers could clean by hand, making it possible for plantation owners in the southern United States to provide raw material for Britain's—and later America's—ravenous textile industry.

As need arose to transport manufactured goods, John McAdam and Thomas Telford, working independently, devised ways to pave roads and make them more passable. Soon, in Britain and other countries, interconnecting canals were built among the major waterways so that goods could be transported by barge. Tracks were laid and the earliest railroads, at first horse-drawn, carried over them twenty times the quantities of goods that a single horse-drawn vehicle traveling over a rutted road could convey.

When water was the chief source of power for running machinery, factories were situated beside rivers. As the steam engine was refined, however, it became a reasonable source of power that could be generated by wood, charcoal, and coal, so factories could be built where a generation earlier they would not have been feasible. As petroleum, natural gas, electricity, and nuclear power have become common energy sources, factories have been built in an ever-increasing variety of locations.

Inevitably, as factories proliferated, so, too, did the problems that industrialization causes. In the earliest days of manufacturing, however, the laissez-faire philosophy of Adam Smith, whose influential *The Wealth of Nations* (1776) advocated free enterprise without government interference, prevailed. Smith advocated that the growth of industry be regulated only by competition in the marketplace and by market conditions.

With manufacturing moving out of the home, people who had previously been their own bosses were forced to adapt to work situations in which they had to adhere to predetermined schedules and in which they were paced by the machines that moved products before them in never-ending processions. Artisans who worked in their own homes had usually worked long hours, but they established their own pace, breaking from their labors when they needed to.

Along with industrialization came urbanization, as well as the development of systems of public education designed to instill discipline, obedience, and dependability in youths who began to work in factories at early ages and received only minimal schooling. With mechanization and the division of labor in the workplace that assembly lines allowed, the physical demands of working were somewhat reduced so that many of the laborers were women and children. They often worked twelve to fourteen-hour days in deplorable conditions.

The shocking working conditions of British youth led Britain's Parliament to enact the Reform Bill of 1832 and the Poor Law Amendment Act of 1834, both aimed at alleviating the lot of downtrodden workers. These reforms led to such later legislation as child labor laws in the United States and other developed countries and laid the groundwork for the formation in the twentieth century of such protective agencies as the Food and Drug Administration, the Federal Trade Commission, the Interstate Commerce Commission, the Federal Communications Commission, the Occupational Safety and Health Administration (OSHA), and the Environmental Protection Agency, all designed to monitor industrial activities that might jeopardize the public welfare. With the enactment of such legislation, however necessary it was, governments gained substantial power.

When some industries grew into monopolies or into oligopolies, governments enacted legislation to control industries' hold upon the public and to discourage price-fixing. In the United States, the Sherman Antitrust Act of 1890 and the Clayton Antitrust Act of 1914 were both aimed at controlling monopolies and trusts, although some carefully regulated monopolies were permitted to exist in most countries among the public utilities and transportation. The automobile industry is essentially a monopoly or oligopoly in most countries where it exists.

As industrialization began to impinge upon most aspects of human existence, it was inevitable that businesses and industries be subjected to regulations laid down by governments that, with growing industrialization, became increasingly large and authoritarian. As early as 1799, Great Britain passed laws that prohibited labor organizations. These laws, however, were soon challenged as British workers successfully demanded the right to vote, which gave them a needed voice in government and advanced British society a major step toward democratization.

Labor organizations were formed originally so that dues-paying members could receive monetary relief during times of illness or unemployment. Before long, however, these organizations, through collective bargaining and strikes, pressured industry to improve working conditions. Labor strikes paralyzed the factories of unyielding managements, although governments often moved brutally to break demonstrations and strikes, as was the case in the United States in the Haymarket Riot of 1886 or the Pullman Strike of 1894.

Industrialization spurred invention which, in turn, led to further industrialization. Invention of the telegraph and telephone, electricity and automobiles, airplanes and computers, motion pictures, radio, and television all grew out of needs for products that would improve communication and transportation. As such inventions met these needs, industry grew prodigiously because of them. So important are the communication and transportation facilities of a nation that they are universally subjected to stringent government regulation.

The establishment of the sophisticated systems of roadways that industry needs is a huge undertaking and, in most places, has resulted from governments' expenditures of public funds to implement it. In the United States, the vast interstate highway system grew out of wartime necessity during the 1940's and has continued to be expanded through federal and state funding. The autobahns in Germany were also government financed, as are the railway systems of many countries, including the bullet trains in both France and Japan.

Massive industrialization is impossible without a strong and extensive banking system, which, in most cases, is federally regulated. Decisions regarding interest rates and money supply are governmental decisions that have a strong impact upon industries that have to borrow to finance their expansions.

Industrialization has created international problems that only governments in cooperation with one another can resolve. Such matters as acid rain, for example, are highly charged and can lead to strained relations between adjacent nations. Fair trade pacts and tariffs also result from international agreements between governments.

Applications

Although France was Europe's richest and most populous country during the eighteenth century, it was slow to industrialize because of internal problems that began with the French Revolution and continued through the Napoleonic Wars and past the middle of the nineteenth century. These upheavals combined with a strong protectionist policy born of an exaggerated nationalism that led to the imposition of high tariffs on imported goods that substantially limited the degree to which France could grow industrially.

Conversely, Britain and the United States, which easily outstripped France in competitive international markets, were ready to grow according to laissez-faire principles. France's industrialization involved more government control than existed at that time in the major competing nations. Such control stifled attempts for the nation to become a contender in the crafts industry, its strongest industrial component.

Historically, in both the United States and Britain, some major industrial transgressions evaded official notice or control for long periods of time, often to the detriment of workers and the public. Such a case occurred in the U.S. meat-packing industry, which was largely unregulated until 1906 when Upton Sinclair's exposé of that industry, *The Jungle* (1906), was published. Sinclair had hoped that his novel would tug at the heartstrings of Americans. As it turned out, the book hit most readers in the solar plexus instead. This novel attacked many social ills, including the exploitation of immigrants, the unfairness of laws regarding installment buying, and the shocking practices of a meat-packing industry whose chief purpose was profit at any cost.

President Theodore Roosevelt, a progressive Republican with a bent toward labor reform and a reputation for trust-busting, read Sinclair's book and was sickened by its vivid descriptions of the unsanitary conditions under which the nation's meat was then allegedly being produced. He called for a full-scale investigation of the industry and, finding much in the reports of his investigators to substantiate Sinclair's claims, he pushed for the enactment of the Pure Food and Drug Act, which Congress passed later in the same year. This act, which was still in effect in the 1990's, controls the conditions under which food and drugs are produced and distributed in the United States.

Another novel of the period, Frank Norris' *The Octopus* (1901), focuses on farmers who depend upon the railroads to transport their crops to market only to have the rates increase outlandishly just as the crops are harvested. Industrialization, through mechanization, transformed farming. This transformation, however, was accompanied by a wave of middlemen, often unscrupulous, who stood between producers of crops and consumers. These entrepreneurs frequently represented the railroads and owned the granaries, the mills, and the cotton gins without which farmers could not market their crops profitably.

The federal government, working largely through the Interstate Commerce Commission that was established in 1887, began to regulate railroad rates and to regulate the interstate transportation of goods. As industry grew and became more complex than ever before, governments throughout the world were drawn increasingly into regulating this growth with the result that enormous governmental bureaucracies were spawned to oversee such regulation. Industrialization led inevitably to larger, more authoritarian, and more regulatory government.

Context

The machinations of the early industrial leaders produced instant millionaires. In 1850 the United States had an estimated twenty millionaires; fifty years later, as industrialism flourished, it had at least three thousand—among whom several persons had net worths of more than $100 million each.

The nation's population more than doubled between 1870 and 1915. This phenomenal increase occurred largely because of immigration as the United States, now the foremost industrial nation in the world, offered jobs and, more important, hope to those who flocked to her shores. During the same period, as factories began to spring up throughout the country, city dwellers, who had in 1870 constituted one-quarter of the total population of the United States, skyrocketed by 1915 to half the total population. The rich lived lives of incredible luxury, whereas the workers, most of them crowded into tenements and living insecure existences, survived from payday to payday.

Between the rich and the poor there existed a growing middle class, composed largely of managerial employees of industry or owners of small businesses. This middle class, an offspring of the industrial age, lived comfortably, although its members were not wealthy.

As labor unions before the turn of the century began to agitate for higher wages and better working conditions as well as for such emoluments as health insurance, unemployment insurance, and death benefits, the divisions between labor and management widened, often approaching impasse. The two world wars created jobs in the defense industries for many people who had been marginally employed earlier. During and immediately after World War II, labor unions gained considerable strength despite such legislation as the Taft-Hartley Act in 1947, which was aimed at controlling them.

Recently, with softening job markets, unions, although still significant forces in industry, have lost some of their power. In many instances, government has stepped in to offer workers the kinds of protection that unions once demanded. This is particularly true of such acts as OSHA, which is designed to assure safe working conditions for labor.

Bibliography

Barnes, Thomas G., and Gerald D. Feldman, eds. *Nationalism, Industrialization, and Democracy, 1815-1914.* Boston: Little, Brown, 1972. Focuses on philosophical movements such as utilitarianism that affected industrialization and were themselves spawned by the growth and spread of industry.

Chenery, Hollis, et al. *Industrialization and Growth: A Comparative Study.* New York: Oxford University Press, 1986. Contributors to this study view the outcomes of industrialization in dominant and emerging societies. Their contrasting views are provocative and challenging. Especially strong are the book's implications of the effects of industrialization in Third World countries.

De Schweinitz, Karl. *Industrialization and Democracy.* New York: Free Press, 1964. De Schweinitz deals with industrialization in Britain, the United States, Germany, Russia, and the economies that he designates "underdeveloped." He demonstrates how, despite some oppression of the worker, industrialization has led to more representative government for the masses. His thesis is intelligently argued and convincingly presented.

Patterson, Jerry E. *The Vanderbilts*. New York: Harry N. Abrams, 1989. The Vanderbilts rose to a position of prodigious wealth largely through the railroad holdings of
Cornelius Vanderbilt, Jr. Patterson chronicles the rise of this patriarch who capitalized on westward expansion and on the country's need for a nationwide transportation system.

Rabb, Theodore, and Robert Rotberg, eds. *Industrialization and Urbanization*. Princeton: Princeton University Press, 1981. Essays examining urbanization, to which
industrialization ultimately leads, linking the move toward urbanization to progressivism and other prominent political movements that accompanied the rise of
industry. This remains one of the most cogent studies of the effects of industrialism
on society.

Smith, Henry Nash, ed. *Popular Culture and Industrialism, 1865-1890*. Garden City,
N.Y.: Anchor Books, 1967. The contributors focus on the period of greatest
industrial development in the United States, when the nation grew into a world
power industrially and militarily. The presentations are balanced and cogent.

Stearns, Peter N. *The Industrial Revolution in World History*. Boulder, Colo.:
Westview Press, 1993. Stearns both defines and interprets the Industrial Revolution.
He relates it in three specific phases to the worldwide growth of industrialism during
1760-1880, 1880-1950, and 1950-1990. He writes about industrialism in a broad
variety of countries besides Britain and the United States, including Asian and Latin
American countries.

R. Baird Shuman

Cross-References

The Arts and Government, p. 101; Bureaucracy, p. 164; Business and Government,
p. 177; Capitalism, p. 197; Civil Unrest and Rioting, p. 317; Class Conflict, p. 331;
Commerce Regulation, p. 357; Corporatism, p. 452; Government Agencies, p. 765;
International Agreements, p. 949; Labor Relations, p. 1038; Mercantilism, p. 1173;
Positivism, p. 1557; Public Utilities, p. 1640; Resource Management, p. 1718; Trade
with Foreign Nations, p. 2000; Transportation Management in the United States,
p. 2006; Urbanization, p. 2071.

INITIATIVES AND REFERENDUMS

Field of study: Law and jurisprudence

Initiatives and referendums are procedures by which voters can make laws or decide important questions of public policy directly, rather than through the state legislature.

Principal terms

DIRECT INITIATIVE: procedure by which a voter-initiated measure is placed directly on the ballot for voter approval

INDIRECT INITIATIVE: procedure by which a voter-initiated measure is first submitted to the legislature before being sent to the voters

PETITIONING: process by which a requisite number of signatures is obtained to initiate a ballot proposition

PROPOSITION: ballot measure placed before voters by either the initiative or referendum procedures

RECALL: procedure enabling voters to decide by popular vote whether a public official should be removed from office before the expiration of his or her term

REFERENDUM: procedure by which a law passed by a legislative body is presented to the voters for approval

VOTER INFORMATION PAMPHLET: popular method of informing voters on the questions that will appear on the ballot

Overview

The initiative and referendum, and their natural extension, the recall, are not used at the federal level of politics in the United States, but they are used extensively in the government of many states and their subdivisions. Also known as direct legislation, these procedures offer voters a means by which they can make laws or decide important questions of public policy directly, without interference by a legislative body. Twenty-six states allow for some form of initiative or referendum.

The initiative is of two types, direct and indirect. In the direct initiative, an individual or group may propose legislation or suggest constitutional amendments by securing a required number of signatures from registered voters via petition, and have the proposed measure placed on the ballot for adoption or rejection by the electorate. In the indirect initiative, state-wide initiative propositions must first be submitted to the legislature before being sent to the voters. Some states allow the legislature to submit a substitute proposal along with the popularly initiated one; the voters then decide which, if any, of the proposals should be adopted. Some states limit the use of the initiative. The most common restrictions are that initiatives pertain to only a single topic and that they not involve the judiciary.

The number of signatures required to propose statutes and constitutional amendments are set by law, but the figures vary from state to state. The number is either a percentage of the total vote cast in the preceding election, or a percentage of votes cast in the previous election for a particular state official (usually the governor). The number of signatures required to initiate a statute is usually from 5 to 10 percent of the electorate. The number of signatures required to initiate constitutional amendments is higher, usually from 8 to 15 percent of the electorate. Approximately half of the states allowing the initiative require that petition requirements be met in a certain number of counties as well, to guard against sectional voting and dominance by urban areas.

Most states that allow for the initiative require that voters be informed about each proposition placed before them. This is usually done in the form of a voter information pamphlet or handbook, printed and mailed at state expense to every registered voter three to four weeks before an election. The official title and brief summary of each proposition is prepared by the attorney general or other designated official. Brief arguments for and against each proposition are also included. These are usually prepared by persons chosen from among the ranks of the proponents and opponents, respectively.

If a majority of voters favors an initiated proposition, it becomes law. In some states, initiated legislation is given special status and is not subject to legislative repeal or gubernatorial veto; however, initiatives are susceptible to legal challenges and prolonged court battles. Successful initiatives usually take effect within ninety days of an election.

The twenty-one states that have adopted the statutory initiative are Alaska, Arizona, Arkansas, California, Colorado, Idaho, Maine, Massachusetts, Michigan, Missouri, Montana, Nebraska, Nevada, North Dakota, Ohio, Oklahoma, Oregon, South Dakota, Utah, Washington, and Wyoming. The seventeen states that allow for the constitutional initiative are Arizona, Arkansas, California, Colorado, Florida, Illinois, Massachusetts, Michigan, Missouri, Montana, Nebraska, Nevada, North Dakota, Ohio, Oklahoma, Oregon, and South Dakota.

There are several uses of referendums. The statutory referendum is the initiative process in reverse. Instead of creating legislation, voters are given the opportunity to nullify laws passed by their legislative bodies. A legislature may choose to submit controversial measures to the electorate, or voters (once again by petition procedure) can force a measure passed by their legislature to be referred to them for approval or rejection. Most states exclude emergency legislation, that is, laws classed as being necessary for the preservation of the public health, peace, or safety, and appropriations from the referendum. To prevent abuse of the emergency classification, laws so designated usually require the approval of at least a two-thirds majority in each house of the legislature. The number, percentage, or geographic distribution of signatures required to invoke a referendum is generally the same as that set for the initiative. If voters reject a measure passed by the legislature and placed before them, the law then becomes null and void.

The referendum is also used in some states as part of the process of calling a constitutional convention to effect a general revision of a state constitution. A majority vote is always required to call a convention. In some states, this is defined as a majority of those voting on the proposition, while in others it is defined as a majority of those voting in the election.

Every state except Delaware requires its legislature to submit all proposed constitutional revisions to the electorate for their approval. This is known as a constitutional referendum. Advisory referendums are also allowed in some states to reflect public opinion or to recommend legislative action. The twenty-five states that have adopted the referendum include all those states using statutory initiative, plus Illinois, Kentucky, Maryland, and New Mexico.

The arguments for and against initiatives and referendums are varied. Proponents claim that these procedures reduce the power of political parties, machines, and bosses; reduce the influence of special interests on the legislature; reduce voter apathy and popular dissatisfaction with government; educate the voters and increase citizen interest and civic responsibility; bring public policy decisions closer to the people; force a quicker resolution of controversial issues; and guard against legislative irresponsibility.

Opponents argue that these procedures further empower special interest groups, not the people; create ballot confusion with an excessive number of complex or trivial measures; place an added burden on voters who are ill-prepared to deal with many complex issues; undermine representative government by taking policy-making decisions away from elected representatives; and fail to educate voters or increase civic responsibility. Critics also argue that opportunities exist for misleading voters in the wording of ballot propositions and in the media and publicity processes.

The recall is a device by which voters can, again by signing a petition, call a special election to determine whether an elected public official should be removed from office before his or her term has expired. The procedure was intended to allow voters to remove public officials who violate the public trust. Some states and localities place restrictions on the use of the recall so that it may not be used immediately after an individual is elected to office, nor used repeatedly against any one official. Some states exclude judicial officers from the recall. The number or percentage of signatures required to invoke the recall varies, but the requirement is more stringent than for either the initiative or the referendum, typically 25 percent of the electorate. A majority vote by the electorate is usually sufficient to remove an official from office. Proponents argue that the recall allows the electorate continuous control over public officials, and opponents contend that the recall weakens the independence of public officials by making them vulnerable to public passions. The fifteen states that allow for the recall of state officials are Alaska, Arizona, California, Colorado, Georgia, Idaho, Kansas, Louisiana, Michigan, Montana, Nevada, North Dakota, Oregon, Washington, and Wisconsin. Thirty-six states permit the recall of local officials.

Applications

Voters have used the initiative to address a wide range of issues, such as nuclear power, school busing, deposit fees for nonreturnable beverage containers, casino gambling, state lotteries, minimum drinking age, antismoking ordinances, rights for homosexuals, the death penalty, rent control, education vouchers, abortion, and taxation.

California's property tax initiative (Proposition 13) which appeared on the ballot in the California primary election in June, 1978, offers an illustration of how voters in one state bypassed the legislature to make their own law. As a result of the rapid inflation in home values, taxes on California homes had tripled in the decade prior to 1978. Not only were homeowners upset but also many voters believed they were not receiving adequate services in exchange for the money that the state collected in taxes. Reports that the state anticipated a $4 billion surplus in conjunction with their added tax burden further angered voters and made them receptive to direct action.

Using the initiative process to achieve property tax relief was the idea of Howard Jarvis, a conservative tax reform advocate, and Paul Gann, head of People's Advocate Inc., a conservative taxpayer group with ten thousand members in California. They proposed a constitutional amendment to limit property taxes to 1 percent of assessed value, allow tax bills to increase only 2 percent annually, and prohibit any new state or local taxes on real property. Under Proposition 13, the average property tax bill would be cut by 57 percent. Despite warnings that a major reduction in property taxes would endanger schools, colleges, parks, libraries, and numerous public services, voters were receptive to the idea.

Like all initiative petitioners in California, proponents of Proposition 13 followed established procedures. To meet state restrictions, they limited their proposal to a single subject, met a preliminary petition filing requirement (a one thousand dollar deposit to be refunded if their proposition qualified for the ballot), and filed their petition at least 130 days before the next election. The state attorney general then prepared a ballot title and summary of the proposition and placed that information at the top of an official petition. A designated state official had the petition forms printed at public expense. Once this process had been completed, volunteers started collecting signatures.

California is one of several states that allow petition-drive groups to employ signature-collection firms that pay solicitors to collect signatures when volunteer efforts have either lagged or fallen short of their goal. Direct-mail consulting firms have also entered the signature-collection business. Since the late 1970's, these companies have designed and managed computerized mail solicitation campaigns, and have been effective at collecting both signatures and funds. Initiative petitioners in California are required to collect signatures from a number of registered voters sufficient to meet the state's petition requirements for statutory and constitutional initiatives: 5 percent of the total vote in the preceding gubernatorial election for statutes and 8 percent for constitutional amendments. After obtaining 1,264,000 signatures, proponents of Proposition 13 had their completed petitions verified by the secretary of state. Verification permitted Proposition 13 to appear in California's official voter pamphlet. To help manage their political campaign, the Jarvis-Gann forces hired a consulting firm. The firm raised money, prepared campaign ads, and solicited endorsements. Proponents of Proposition 13 were ultimately successful. Sixty-five percent of the electorate voted in favor of changing the state's property tax law. This was well above the simple majority of those voting on the proposition required for it to pass.

Proposition 13, like many successful initiatives, was challenged in court. In 1978, the California Supreme Court upheld the constitutionality of the law. In 1979, 1980, 1981, and 1982, however, various California courts allowed for the levying of special assessments, fees for land use regulatory activities, school impact fees, and new sales taxes. Proponents of Proposition 13 have argued that such legal decisions have undermined the effectiveness of their original ballot initiative.

Context

The popular movement to establish initiative and referendum procedures in the United States dates to the 1890's, when growing numbers of Americans became dissatisfied with the system of representative government. Special interest groups seemed to have gained control over legislators and to be using legislative privilege to act against the public interest. A number of reformers advocated changing the political system to give the people more power, and political parties, interest groups, and legislators less. Their suggestions included the secret ballot, the direct primary, the vote for women, direct election of senators, nonpartisan state and local elections, and the initiative and referendum.

The first state to pass an amendment to its state constitution allowing for the initiative and referendum was South Dakota, in 1898. The idea increased in popularity during the Progressive period, and by 1920, twenty-two states allowed for some form of direct legislation. Only four states, however, joined the list of states allowing for initiatives and referendums after 1920. The procedures have been more popular in the Western half of the United States. Of the twenty-three states that permit some form of the initiative, only six are east of the Mississippi River. The greatest number of initiatives reached the ballot between 1912 and 1920. There was a general decline in usage during the 1920's, followed by an increase in the 1930's, and then another decline until 1968. After 1968, the number of ballot initiatives increased dramatically. A survey of state-wide initiatives shows that voters placed 1,326 initiatives (754 statutes and 572 constitutional amendments) on state ballots between 1898 and 1979, approximately half of them after World War II. Voters approved 38 percent (289) of all statutes and 34 percent (193) of all constitutional amendments before 1979.

Initiatives and referendums have become important in state and local politics, and polls show that public support for both is strong. Overall, the procedures have served to complement representative government rather than undermine it. Through use of the direct initiative, voting groups have been able to set the agenda for state politics. Indirect initiatives can force legislators into action, but they can also encourage legislators to avoid taking action on controversial issues in the hope of voters' settling those issues for them. Initiatives and referendums have contributed to the weakening of political parties but have not eliminated special interests from politics. Initiative campaigns have become increasingly expensive, however, as signature-collection agencies, media blitzes, and legal appeals require most groups to be well funded.

Bibliography

Cronin, Thomas E. *Direct Democracy: The Politics of Initiative, Referendum, and Recall*. Cambridge, Mass.: Harvard University Press, 1989. Includes some discussion of the origins of direct democracy, but is more concerned with recent applications of direct ballot initiatives. Provides useful information on voter tendencies, the influence of money and the media on ballot initiatives, the impact of direct democracy on minority rights, prospects for a national initiative and referendum, and ways in which the techniques of direct democracy might be improved.

Magleby, David B. *Direct Legislation: Voting on Ballot Propositions in the United States*. Baltimore: The Johns Hopkins University Press, 1984. Examines the initiative and referendum as forms of decision making. Uses statistical analysis to discover regularities in voting behavior on ballot propositions, assess voter rationality and competence, and gauge the effectiveness of direct democracy. Excellent bibliography.

Munro, William Bennett, ed. *The Initiative, Referendum, and Recall*. New York: D. Appleton, 1916. Essays on the development of direct legislation in the United States, written by leading politicians and educators during the first two decades of the twentieth century. Includes case studies on the practical use of the initiative, referendum, and recall during that period.

Oberholtzer, Ellis Paxson. *The Referendum in America*. New York: Charles Scribner's Sons, 1900. First comprehensive study of the origins and operation of the referendum in the United States. Provides a detailed survey of how specific states and localities first used the referendum to decide important questions of public policy. Includes a chapter on the early use of the initiative.

Schmidt, David D. *Citizen Lawmakers: The Ballot Initiative Revolution*. Philadelphia: Temple University Press, 1989. Examines arguments for and against the initiative, and uses a series of case studies of initiative campaigns in the 1970's and 1980's to illustrate how conservatives and liberal activists and environmentalists have used the process. Offers instructions on how to place an initiative on the ballot and how to plan a successful campaign. Lengthy appendix details the history of the initiative in each state.

Sullivan, J. W. *Direct Legislation by the Citizenship Through the Initiative and Referendum*. New York: True Nationalist, 1893. Based on personal observations of the operation of the initiative and referendum in Switzerland and a study of the town meeting tradition and constitutional amendment process in the United States, this was the first book to argue that direct legislation could bring about a peaceful political revolution in this country. Served as catalyst for the direct legislation movement in the United States.

Zimmerman, Joseph F. *Participatory Democracy: Populism Revived*. New York: Praeger, 1986. Examines the various forms of citizen-directed decision making in the United States. Includes description and analysis of the New England town meeting, the initiative, referendum, and recall, and the relatively new actions of community school boards and community boards as methods of enhancing citizen governance at the neighborhood level. Excellent bibliography.

Steven L. Piott

Cross-References

City Government in the United States, p. 266; Political Participation, p. 1479; Public Policy, p. 1633; Self-Interest in Politics, p. 1802; State Government, p. 1891; Town Meetings, p. 1993; Voting Behavior in the United States, p. 2109; Voting Processes, p. 2123.

INSURGENCIES AND COUPS D'ÉTAT

Field of study: Military

Insurgencies and coups d'état are extralegal means of altering political systems, usually with the goal of changing the leadership. An insurgency involves a prolonged armed struggle by a relatively large group, while a coup d'état is a sudden attempt carried out by a small group.

Principal terms

COUNTERINSURGENCY: military and political action taken by a government to defeat insurgents

COUP: short for coup d'état

GOVERNMENT: people or institutions that administer or control the affairs of a territorial unit, such as a nation

GUERRILLA WARFARE: violent conflict where at least one side is made up of irregular soldiers engaged in surprise raids and hit-and-run attacks

LEGITIMACY: state of being considered politically lawful, just, moral, or acceptable

REGIME: type or form of government

TERRORISM: use of violence, or threats of violence, especially against an innocent population, in order to achieve political goals

Overview

Both insurgencies and coups are forms of unlawful political behavior, involving violence or the threat of violence, with the goal of overturning the existing government or political leadership, or undermining it to the point where it will acquiesce to its opponents' desires. A coup d'état ("stroke, or blow, of state" in French) is a distinct, planned operation conducted by a small group with the aim of gaining control of crucial political organs and institutions through the sudden, forcible removal of political leadership by the use or threat of force. In its simplest form, a few individuals conspire, eliminate the head of state, and assume leadership themselves.

An insurgency also involves a nonconstitutional or extralegal force from outside the government. Insurgents engage in some form of struggle, almost always violent, against the ruling authorities, brought on because they question the legitimacy of the ruling authorities or their policies. Therefore, many insurgencies have the goal of overturning the government and replacing it, as all coups do. One basic difference between a coup d'état and an insurgency is duration. A coup may require only a few hours to complete, or fail, and last a few days at the most. An insurgency, on the other hand, usually involves a prolonged struggle that may last years without resolution. A second basic difference is the size of the groups. Coups almost always involve small numbers of individuals, often based within the machinery of the state—usually the military—forcing change from the top. For an insurgency to have any chance of success, it must eventually have a broader numerical base of support and participation. Insurgencies often have thousands or tens of thousands of participants, although they are often much smaller when they begin.

Insurgencies and coups share certain basic characteristics. Both require the use or threat of force. In this sense, any change in government leadership or policy brought about by the actions of insurgents or coup leaders must be contrary to established procedures and occur against the wishes of the political leadership. When a coup or insurgency with the goal of transforming the government is successful, the government is replaced by the leaders of the coup or insurgency or their designated agents. A successful coup or insurgency does not always result in a regime change, such as from dictatorial to democratic government, since many coups and insurgencies simply replace one set of dictatorial leaders with another, for example.

Leaders of insurgencies and coups must be able to overcome the natural advantages of the state, in terms of political resources such as budgets, personnel, and military power. Organization is, therefore, important to both insurgencies and coups. The conspirators in a coup attempt need to be able to act very quickly, and usually with surprise on their side. Coup leaders often seek to cultivate sympathetic allies in other vital institutions, or actors outside the nation's borders. Insurgents need a strong organization to mobilize large segments of the population on behalf of their cause. The organizations for both need to be cohesive, that is, not subject to significant internal factions or divisions.

In terms of the use of violence and force, coup leaders must have at least the acquiescence of some part of the military, if not their direct cooperation, in order to gain control of key strategic sites, such as telecommunications centers, military or police headquarters, the presidential palace, or the legislature, as well as to confine, arrest, or assassinate powerful members of the government.

Insurgents usually rely on guerrilla tactics to combat the superior numerical and material resources of the government. Guerrilla warfare involves mobile tactics used by small, lightly armed units who aim to harass the government, rather than defeat it outright on the battlefield. Terrorism also is used at times by insurgents when the group is particularly weak compared to the government. Terrorism may involve acts of violence against innocents, or acts of violence committed against the government or the installations and resources important to it, such as bridges, roads, or factories. Some insurgents also engage in conventional warfare, direct confrontation by large, regular, organized military units in the field.

Both coups and insurgencies require a certain degree of popular support. This support may be either passive or active, but no coup or insurgency can succeed without either support or else extreme acquiescence and indifference by the population. Support is often pursued from external actors, specifically other nations. This support can be moral, such as sympathy for the cause; political—public statements that a change of regime, however brought about, would be tolerated, for example; or material, providing sanctuaries for insurgent forces, weapons for coup conspirators, or even direct intervention.

There are many types of coups and insurgencies, usually dependent on the goals of the group. A restorational, or reactionary, coup or insurgency is one that seeks to replace the existing regime with a government dominated by the values and structures of a recent political order. The noncommunist partisans in the Nazi-conquered nations during World War II would fall into this category.

A conservative, or traditional, coup or insurgency is one that seeks to maintain the existing regime, usually in the face of pressures on authorities to change it. The Muslim Brotherhood in Egypt and other Middle Eastern nations, which has fought to keep Western influence and values out, is an example of this type of insurgency. The many coups in Latin America since the mid-nineteenth century also are of this type, where leadership might change, but no real change in policy occurs, or where the military takes power to preserve the existing order in the face of governmental ineffectiveness.

A revolutionary coup or insurgency is one that seeks to impose a new regime based on egalitarian values with the goal of radically restructuring society. The Sandinistas in Nicaragua, with their Marxist ideology, were this type of group. Modernizing coups, such as Brazil's in 1964, which include goals associated with reducing the developmental gap between their own society and the modern world, would also fit into this category.

The reformist coup or insurgency has the goal of providing more political, social, or economic benefits to a particular group, without necessarily rejecting the entire political community, the regime, or its leadership. This type of insurgency or coup, like the Anayanya guerrillas in southern Sudan, often is concerned primarily with discriminatory policies. Peru, in 1968, also experienced a reformist coup, characterized by the themes of change, a worker-managed economy, and the expansion of state influence and control, but without the radical transformation of government and society that occurred in Nicaragua after 1979, for example.

The secessionist insurgency involves a rejection of the existing political community with the goal of withdrawing completely from the unit and establishing a new, autonomous community. The United States revolution was an example of this type of insurgency, as were the activities of the Palestine Liberation Organization against the government of Israel in the West Bank of the Jordan River.

Applications

Political upheavals in Angola and Chile provide examples of the workings and effects of insurgencies and coups.

In 1961, the National Liberation Front of Angola (FNLA) began a revolutionary insurgency against the Portuguese colonial government. They were soon joined by the Popular Movement of Angolan Liberation (MPLA) and the National Union for Total Angolan Independence (UNITA). This insurgency was revolutionary because these groups sought to replace all Portuguese-dominated political values and institutions with values and institutions based on strong Angolan nationalism, political independence from Portugal, an African-centered society, and egalitarianism.

The Portuguese responded by nominally changing Angola from a colony to a "province," deploying military units and recruiting Angolans to the military cause, and attempting to resettle rural populations. As long as the insurgent organizations had external support, sanctuaries for their forces to rest and train unhampered (either outside the borders or in isolated geographic areas), and the will and popular support to continue, the Portuguese could not completely defeat them. So the Portuguese quit and left.

Because they held the capital city of Luanda and a few key political positions, the MPLA became the default government of independent Angola. The MPLA was helped immensely by the presence of thousands of Cuban troops and significant material support from the Soviet Union. UNITA, led by the charismatic Jonas Savimbi, continued to fight, now against the MPLA government. This movement was partly secessionist because UNITA was located primarily in southern Angola and received much of its support from the Ovimbundu people, partly reformist because UNITA claimed simply to want a greater share of political power and rejected the Marxist ideology of the MPLA, and partly revolutionary because military success would almost certainly mean the end of the MPLA government as it currently existed.

UNITA used both selective terrorism, targeted against the Cubans, and indiscriminate terrorism during its struggle against the MPLA. These insurgents repeatedly struck important railroad ties to Zambia and engaged in significant industrial sabotage, designed to weaken the government by undermining its ability to promote economic growth and development, thus eroding the government's popular base. UNITA also engaged in a significant amount of direct military action with the government, eventually gaining control of much of the rural areas of Angola.

This insurgency provides examples of several important characteristics, not the least of which is the strength of insurgent groups, given the right circumstances. When insurgents can maintain geographical and organizational isolation from the government, it is difficult for the government to completely defeat them. Furthermore, the tactics employed in each insurgent movement, guerrilla warfare, for example, were typical of this type of warfare. Support from outside actors was critical both before and after independence, as Angola became a battleground in the Cold War between the United States and the Soviet Union.

Prior to September 11, 1973, Chile had experienced one of the most durable and progressive democratic regimes in Latin America. In 1970, Chile became the first nation in the Western Hemisphere to choose a socialist as president in free elections. Popular Unity candidate Salvador Allende Gossens, who received 36 percent of the vote, proceeded to lead a government that expropriated major means of production and promoted massive redistribution of wealth to the rural and urban working classes. Workers were mobilized into unions and the political system for the first time.

These policy changes, combined with some actions by the U.S. government, led to severe economic dislocations, rampant inflation, escalating class conflict, and highly polarized political divisions. Following Chilean congressional elections in March, 1973, which produced a legislature dominated by opponents of the government, a stalemate between the president and the legislature occurred.

On September 11, 1973, the military, led by the commander in chief of ground forces, Augusto Pinochet, and encouraged by certain civilians, removed Allende from power in a coup d'état. Allende was either killed or committed suicide, and many officials of the Popular Unity government, as well as party leaders and activists, were harassed, imprisoned, or executed. The party was outlawed and its assets confiscated. Labor federations were disbanded, congress dissolved, and censorship imposed.

This coup provides examples of many of the common characteristics of coups and insurgencies. The coup was at least passively supported by the upper classes, substantial portions of the middle class, and even some members of the working class who were supporters of the opposition parties. These groups all felt they were profoundly threatened by the policies of the Popular Unity government and by the climate and rhetoric of confrontation, violence, and disorder these policies seemed to create. Therefore, this coup was a conservative or reactionary coup. Organization was also very important to the success of this coup, because commanders loyal to the government were forced to resign or were neutralized by their subordinates before the coup took place. All significant governmental actors in Chile, including elected local officials, were replaced after the coup, almost all by military officers.

Context

Insurgencies and coups d'état have been one of the most common sources of regime or government change since the creation of organized political communities. Roman armies were well aware of the hazards of fighting insurgents, given their experience in Gaul and Judaea. The first modern coup took place on November 9, 1799. Napoleon Bonaparte convinced the members of the governing councils of the First French Republic to meet at St. Cloud, a suburb of Paris, supposedly for security against a Jacobin plot. Once in St. Cloud, the councils were surrounded by soldiers and dissolved, making Napoleon the de facto ruler of France.

From World War II to 1985, the developing nations experienced approximately one hundred successful coups, and almost the same number of failed coups. In much of Africa and Latin America, coups have been the most common form of political change. Every region of the world has experienced coups, which had affected two-thirds of the world's countries by 1987. Almost all the large-scale violence in the world in the late twentieth century has been in the context of internal wars and insurgencies. Although the world had not seen any major war since World War II, millions of lives and billions of dollars in resources were still being lost to armed conflicts, guerrilla wars, and terrorism as the twentieth century ended.

There is little reason to believe that insurgencies and coups d'état will cease to be significant sources of regime changes, given the continuing problems in the Third World that provide an environment in which coups and insurgencies can flourish. The military often is the most powerful institution in underdeveloped nations, and because of its superior organization, centralized command structure, and use of violent means, military coups are likely to continue to be used to resolve difficult situations. Problems that are likely to continue to plague the developing world include the lack of political participation in the state; weak public commitment to political institutions; the effects of rapid change because of industrialization and urbanization on society; and generally low economic, social, and political development. All these factors, which showed no signs of disappearing by the end of the twentieth century, will continue to enable insurgents or coup leaders to find motivation for change, and afford them the possibility of success.

Bibliography

Anderson, Jon Lee. *Guerrillas*. New York: Times Books, 1992. A journalist looks at what it is like to be a guerrilla in today's world. Based on individual contacts with five different groups; provides an interesting glimpse at the lives of insurgents.

Decalo, Samuel. *Coups and Army Rule in Africa*. 2d ed. New Haven, Conn.: Yale University Press, 1990. Discusses the strife in five French-African nations, and the dynamics impelling armies into politics. Selected bibliography.

Joes, Anthony James. *Modern Guerrilla Insurgency*. Westport, Conn.: Praeger, 1992. Five well-written historical case studies are used to provide lessons learned for U.S. policy. Good for the perspective of possible actions by outside actors in these conflicts.

O'Neill, Bard. *Insurgency and Terrorism*. Washington, D.C.: Brassey's, 1990. Highly readable study that includes an excellent overview of insurgency in the world, with focus on the types of insurgencies, their strategies, organization, and other important topics.

Rice, Edward E. *Wars of the Third Kind*. Berkeley: University of California Press, 1988. Good discussion of the problems nations face in responding to insurgent movements. Good case studies.

Wickham-Crowley, Timothy P. *Guerrillas and Revolution in Latin America*. Princeton, N.J.: Princeton University Press, 1992. Rigorous analysis of the causes of guerrilla success and failure. Scholarly, but rich in detail and explanation of theories.

Eduardo Magalhães III

Cross-References

Africa: Politics and Governments, p. 21; Asia: Politics and Governments, p. 108; Civil Wars, p. 325; Class Conflict, p. 331; Colonialism and Anticolonialism, p. 351; Marxism-Leninism, p. 1155; National Liberation Movements, p. 1255; Nationalism, p. 1268; Political Violence, p. 1539; Revolutionary Governments, p. 1725; Revolutionary Parties, p. 1731; Revolutions, p. 1738; Secessionism, p. 1790; Terrorism, p. 1962; Underdeveloped Nations, p. 2039.

INTEREST GROUPS

Field of study: Politics

Interest groups are organized groups that share values and that attempt to influence public policy. In order to achieve their goals, interest groups may lobby government officials, donate money to political candidates, organize political marches, or engage in many other forms of political activity.

Principal terms

ELECTIONEERING: trying to influence public policy by seeking to determine which public officials get elected or appointed

LOBBYING: trying to influence governmental policy

PLURALISM: theory or practice of numerous groups' competing within the political system; public policy is often a result of competition among groups

POLITICAL ACTION COMMITTEE: committee set up to handle the collection and spending of money for political campaigns

PUBLIC INTEREST GROUP: organization whose purpose is to serve the interests of society as a whole. Defining the public interest, however, is often a subject of heated debate

SOFT MONEY: donations made by political party organizations for state and local party-building activities that are not subject to contribution limits but can be used by the parties to assist candidates to political office

Overview

Interest groups are organizations that seek to influence the development of public policy. They are composed of individuals who share a common interest, whether it be saving Chesapeake Bay, removing gun control legislation, or lobbying against abortion. Interest groups differ from political parties, whose primary goal is to get their candidates elected into office. While interest groups may campaign or donate money on behalf of a candidate, they do so only with the overall objective of seeing their goals enacted into public policy.

National interest groups did not emerge in the United States until the 1830's. Many of these groups were deeply rooted in the Christian revivalism then sweeping the nation. An example is the Young Men's Christian Association, which was founded in Boston in 1851 to reach out to the children of immigrants and the poor in order to assimilate them. The other major type of interest group during this period was the trade association. Agricultural groups such as the Grange and Railroad groups were formed after the Civil War, using the communication networks that had been formed during the war.

The 1880's saw a second wave of interest group activity as the young nation struggled to deal with problems caused by rapid industrialization and influx of immigrants into the United States. It was during this period that labor organizations developed to protect the rights of workers. Many businesses also formed their own interest groups to counteract the organized labor forces. The 1880's also saw the creation of many settlement houses such as Hull House in Chicago in 1889. These were community centers that provided child care, job training, and lessons in the English language. They also provided room and board for progressive activists, many of whom went on to form some of the most prominent interest groups today, including the National Association for the Advancement of Colored People and the American Civil Liberties Union.

The largest growth in interest group activity, however, occurred after the 1960's. While labor, professional, and business groups continued to develop, the largest growth came in the area of public interest groups. Public interest groups seek to serve the interest of society as a whole. Groups commonly classified as public interest groups include Common Cause, Public Interest, and many others. This period also saw the growth of groups such as the National Organization for Women (NOW), environmental groups, and abortion groups. In 1960 there were fewer than five hundred national interest groups; by 1992 the number of interest groups had grown to more than six thousand.

Individuals join interest groups for many reasons. Many may seek the benefits that interest groups offer. Interest groups commonly offer magazines, bumper stickers, insurance discounts, or merchandise discounts to attract new members. For a nominal fee (five dollars in 1994), those over fifty can join the American Association of Retired Persons (AARP), the largest interest group in America, with over twenty-six million members. The AARP attracts new members not only by its low fee, but also through its low-cost pharmacy service, monthly magazine, discounts at travel establishments, and special insurance programs. Individuals also join interest groups so that they may influence public policy. This is the most common reason, for example, for joining an environmental group such as the Sierra Club or Greenpeace. Individuals may also become members of interest groups to seek companionship with other like-minded individuals. Many social organizations such as the Parent Teacher Association or fraternities fall into this category.

Group membership in the United States is not equally distributed among the socioeconomic classes. As political scientist E. E. Schattschneider has noted, the interest group system has a decided class bias. Only about 10 percent of the United States' population has joined an interest group. The members of interest groups share several common characteristics. They tend to be middle class, with higher levels of income, education, and occupational status. Those who are poor typically do not join interest groups. Individuals who join interest groups tend to have a strong sense of civic duty and personal confidence.

Interest groups perform several major functions in politics. First, they provide a simple way for people to become involved in government. Joining an interest group can be as easy as mailing a check or showing up at a local demonstration. By joining a group, people can get their interests heard by representatives, possibly have policy goals met, and learn about the government. Second, interest groups provide a counterbalance against the major political parties. Elected officials must pay attention to numerous special interest groups, not merely to party directives. In making public policy, this can be both advantageous and disadvantageous. While interest groups allow more interests to get represented, they may also make it more difficult to make public policy, particularly if many interest groups disagree on a single issue.

Interest groups typically use many different methods to get their needs translated into public policy. First, they attempt to persuade public officials. To do this, most interest groups employ lobbyists. Lobbyists may either be paid professionals or members of the organization who are hired to represent an interest group's goals in government. Often former members of Congress or former officials in the White House will later be hired by various interest groups to represent their interests. Former public officials are often effective as lobbyists because they have worked in the organization that they are lobbying. Lobbyists often contact public officials directly to inform them of their groups' interests. Interest groups may also speak at legislative hearings, present research, and stage events or demonstrations. On the illegal side, although more rare, interest groups may also engage in threats, bribery, or violence.

Second, interest groups might attempt to influence who gets elected or appointed to public office. These offices can include state legislators, the Congress, the courts, and the White House. Sometimes the best way for groups to be heard is to make sure that they have officials in public office who are sympathetic to their interests. Interest groups employ many means to make sure that their desired candidates get elected. They make financial donations to campaigns, hold fund-raisers, or do grassroots work for candidates. Interest groups may also engage in negative electioneering as well. Sometimes they seek to defeat candidates opposed to their views by using negative advertising or other means.

Finally, interest groups seek to influence public opinion. By communicating directly with the public, interest groups can not only recruit new members but also convince individual citizens to support their causes. If enough citizens are motivated, they might contact their public officials, thus possibly changing public policy. Interest groups have often used televised appeals, newspaper advertisements, and press conferences to ensure that their views are heard.

In order to be effective, interest groups must have certain resources. One resource that is particularly useful is money. Money cannot buy everything, but in interest group politics it can help to pay for leaders, political consultants, advertisements, bumper stickers, telephone lines, and other needed resources. The financial resources of a group are a sure measure of its political effectiveness. Another resource that can help a group is its size. Larger groups tend to have more influence in politics because there is the assumption that they speak for all members. This is particularly the case if the group represents a large share of its population. This is one of the reasons why the American Medical Association (AMA) has been a powerful organization; about 70 percent of all doctors belong to the AMA. The organization can truthfully say that it speaks for most doctors. An interest group must be careful, however, that it does not get too large. Large organizations can become unwieldy as a result of disunity among members. This was the fate of many labor organizations in the 1980's, although they continued to have a great influence in American politics. Interest groups that want to succeed should also have a strong leadership, good marketing capability, and clear goals.

Applications

Many interest groups have been able to gain influence in American politics. One of the most effective groups in American politics has been the American Association of Retired Persons (AARP). With thrity-three million members in 1994, the AARP is omnipresent in American politics and a force to be opposed only with great care. The AARP has active programs in more than three hundred congressional districts and overwhelms its opponents through the sheer number of its members. Besides age, one thing that AARP members have in common is that they were all recruited by direct mail. The AARP has been very successful in preventing attempts to reduce Social Security, Medicare, and Supplemental Security Income benefits. Much of its success can be attributed to the size of its membership. Senator Pete Domenici could certainly attest this influence. When working on the budget in 1992, he received a clipping on the Social Security issue from the AARP with a handwritten note from his mother asking that he read it; his mother happened to be a member of the AARP and was lobbying. Beyond its ability to send millions of letters to members of Congress, the AARP also has an in-house research firm that conducts studies of how each piece of legislation passed by the Congress will affect senior citizens.

Another effective group is Common Cause. This group was established in 1970 after its first chairman, John Gardner, posted an advertisement in *The New York Times* asking for members. Common Cause is a public interest group that is devoted to reform and accountability. It seeks to clean up government by making public officials accountable for their actions. In the early 1970's, for example, Common Cause lobbied members of the House to pass reforms that would have committee chairmen elected by the party caucuses and not appointed by the party leadership. Common Cause argued that these reforms would remove some corruption in government by eliminat- ing the secrecy that surrounded some appointment decisions. This interest group has also been one of the primary advocates of campaign finance reform, arguing the campaign finance process should also remove its veil of secrecy. Since its creation in 1970, Common Cause has consistently lobbied for federal funding of all federal campaigns, bans on political action committees, (PACs), and limits on donations to candidates, PACs, and political parties.

To achieve these aims, Common Cause does not give money to political candidates, unlike the AARP and many other interest groups. Instead, it steadily pressures members of Congress and other public officials into agreeing with its goals. Although this group is about one-hundredth the size of the AARP, it has been effective as an organization because it has learned to use other resources. One of its most effective techniques is to use the media to change the tide of public opinion. Common Cause has launched numerous campaigns over the airwaves to publicize the names of members of Congress who received hefty contributions from interest groups, as well as to fight to get the members to deny themselves pay raises. Common Cause also uses grassroots lobbying tactics and publicizes the voting records of members to achieve its objectives.

Not all organizations need to have extensive financial resources or successful publicity campaigns to be effective. Sometimes smaller interest groups can be equally effective in American politics if they are able to mobilize enough grassroots support or can encourage other groups to join them in a coalition. Many of these groups use grass roots and indirect lobbying techniques to achieve their goals. Instead of contacting members of Congress directly, they try to influence them through other means. In 1994, a group of small businesses formed to lobby Congress to protect their interests when creating a new health care policy. Ordinarily, an individual small business would not carry much political clout on Capitol Hill, but by joining together they were able to gain political influence. Smaller interest groups may also use other lobbying methods. For example, several environmental groups boycotted a major fast food restaurant chain after finding out that it used beef from Central America, where dangerous ranching practices damaged rain forests. After a 13 percent drop in sales during the boycott, the chain announced that it would no longer use rain forest beef.

Context

Interest groups and their activities are sometimes thought to have a negative influence over politics. As recognized early by the Framers of the Constitution, including James Madison, the problem is that a small group of individuals may be able to subvert the public good. A small group might be able, in other words, to thwart the democratic process. In a democratic government, representatives of the people should rely on their own views, the views of their constituents, and their sense of the national interest when deciding on public policy. Some critics have argued that interest groups seek to intervene in this process.

Such fears are not unfounded. One of the perennial debates about members of Congress is whether interest groups have an influence on politicians' votes. Several interest groups such as Common Cause and Public Interest have suggested that interest groups and their political action committees do buy votes. Their recommendation is that campaign finance reform should be enacted. Specifically, there should be federal funding for congressional candidates as well as a ban or further limits on donations to candidates from political action committees. Many political scientists have not accepted this argument that interest group money buys votes, however, pointing out that it is difficult to prove scientifically that money from interest groups and their political action committees has an effect on members' votes. Instead, interest groups may be getting better access to government officials. Access in this age of information may sometimes, however, be just as important.

Questions have also been raised about whether interest groups subvert the democratic process by arguing only for special interests. Critics of interest groups point out that several of the wealthier groups, such as the National Rifle Association or the AMA, have been able to push for legislation that might not have the full support of the American people, at least as judged through public opinion polls. These groups typically respond by either showing their own polls which show that their interests do have support or by holding public press conferences to sway public opinion. What is clear, however, is that interest groups are likely to endure. While they allow for greater participation by citizens and provide more access to the government, they will always have their critics.

Bibliography

Birnbaum, Jeffrey H. *The Lobbyists: How Influence Peddlers Get Their Way in Washington.* New York: Times Books, 1992. Behind-the-scenes examination of corporate lobbying in Washington, D.C., during the 101st Congress.

Cigler, Allan J., and Burdett A. Loomis, eds. *Interest Group Politics.* 4th ed. Washington, D.C.: Congressional Quarterly Press, 1995. Articles on several types of interest groups.

Hrebenar, Ronald J., and Ruth K. Scott. *Interest Group Politics in America.* 2d ed. Englewood Cliffs, N.J.: Prentice-Hall, 1990. One of the best overall books on interest groups. It examines the various theories on interest groups, their size, structure, and lobbying activities in various institutions.

Petracca, Mark P., ed. *The Politics of Interests: Interest Groups Transformed.* Boulder, Colo.: Westview Press, 1992. A more theoretical book than the others listed, offering an excellent bibliography.

Schattschneider, E. E. *The Semisovereign People.* New York: Holt, Rinehart and Winston, 1960. One of the early books on interest groups, claims that interest group representation had an upper-class bias.

Wittenberg, Ernest, and Elisabeth Wittenberg. *How to Win in Washington: Very Practical Advice About Lobbying, the Grassroots, and the Media.* 2d ed. New York: Basil Blackwell, 1994. The title describes the book.

Jan Carol Hardt

Cross-References

INTERGOVERNMENTAL RELATIONS

Field of study: Functions of government

Intergovernmental relations encompass all executive, legislative, judicial, administrative, and political interactions among all elected and appointed officials working in national, state, and local government organizations. Due to the expansion of the roles of governments, intergovernmental relations affect almost all aspects of daily life in the United States.

Principal terms

BLOCK GRANT: financial assistance from a grantor who defines broadly the grant's purpose to a recipient who is given considerable discretion as to how it will be spent

CATEGORICAL GRANT: financial assistance from a grantor who defines specifically the grant's purpose to a recipient who is given little discretion as to how it will be spent

CROSS-CUTTING REQUIREMENT: procedural, administrative, and fiscal requirements, designed to cause specific outcomes, which are a part of every type of financial assistance offered by one level of government to another

FEDERAL: formed by a compact between political units that surrender their individual sovereignty to a central authority but retain limited residual powers of government

FUNGIBILITY: ability to use one part in exchange for another part in the satisfaction of an obligation

GENERAL REVENUE SHARING: return to a state of a percentage of the federal income tax receipts collected within that state

GRANT-IN-AID: financial assistance paid by one level of government to another for particular purposes articulated in legislation or administrative regulation

GRANTSMANSHIP: attempt by officials to obtain as many grants as possible for their organization

IGR: acronym for intergovernmental relations

Overview

To visualize intergovernmental relations (IGR) in the United States, one might visualize a large map of the country on which one places a dot for each elected or appointed public official in every town, city, state capital, and the nation's capital. For each contact an official makes with officials in other local, state, and national government organizations, one might draw a line joining the officials. These lines of communication, influence, and interaction would represent intergovernmental relations.

Although such lines of communication generally are unseen by the public, IGR wields growing influence on the daily lives of all U.S. citizens. This influence occurs because governmental policies, that is, intentions and plans for action, and policy implementation are often developed through interactions between public officials. Two important features of these interactions are complexity and conflict.

Complexity is fostered by the sheer volume of government responsibilities, government units, and IGR participants. The responsibilities of the U.S. government have expanded from defense, trade, and territorial expansion during the early years of the nation, to include welfare, education, transportation, labor, medicine, agriculture, insurance, housing, environment, space exploration, research, energy, and many others in the 1990's. Ideology, war, economic pressures, and social conditions have encouraged this growth. The assumption of increasing responsibilities by national, state, and local governments explains the large number of government units and employees.

At the national level, government units include the president, Senate, House of Representatives, Supreme Court, and all federal departments, agencies, and commissions. Executive, legislative, and judicial organizations constitute the state level. Regional and county governments, municipalities, townships, special districts, school districts, and civic or volunteer citizen organizations make up the local level. Seven major public interest groups are also active in IGR; the Council of State Governments, National Governors' Association, National Conference of State Legislatures, National Association of County Officials, National League of Cities, United States Conference of Mayors, and International City Management Association. In an abstract sense, these organizations interact, but in reality, people, not organizations, do the interacting. Since the members of government organizations and related public interest groups number more than fourteen million, the actual number of interactions among them is enormous.

The nature of the federal system, the size of government, competition for resources, and perceptual differences make conflict inherent to IGR. Within the federal system, each organization or public official has the capacity to initiate independent actions. These actions are numerous because of the size of government. No centralized tracking, communication, or coordination of these autonomous actions exists; therefore, they are fragmented and often in conflict.

Because of the size of government and concomitant number of participants in IGR, differences of opinion are assured, and conflict is the frequent result. It is a challenge to achieve consensus, agreement, or compromise in IGR. In a federal system, national, state, and local governments all compete for a share of the revenues collected from the public. This is another source of conflict in IGR. Studies have shown that officials at each level of government perceive themselves to be broad-minded and circumspect, while perceiving officials at other levels as narrow and parochial. These perceptions foster distrust, further contributing to conflict.

As all these factors fuel conflict over power and resources, negotiation, regulation, mandates, political maneuvering, and coercion are the mechanisms used by IGR participants to cope with such conflict. Since the strongest participant will often experience the least cost and most benefit, identifying the strongest participant can help to predict the outcome of IGR conflict.

Some people have contended that national, centralized control would enhance the efficiency and effectiveness of government. This perspective was not the dominant view in the United States when it was founded, but it gradually garnered support until the late 1800's, when it was more widely accepted. This belief fosters greater expectations and dependence on the national government for direction, control, and money, thereby making the national government the strongest IGR participant.

Regulations, mandates, court decisions, and fiscal transfers have institutionalized the expectations of and dependence on government. Regulations are government rules and requirements that govern or prescribe a course of action. Mandates are authoritative rules or orders in written form, designed to protect the public, businesses, and governments. They may be industry-specific, such as banking regulations, or generalized, such as occupational safety regulations. Although regulations are created at all levels, national regulations have the most far-reaching impact.

General revenue sharing, loans, and grants-in-aid are three types of fiscal transfers. General revenue sharing is the return to each state of a fixed percentage of the federal income tax collected from that state. Because of restrictions on debt at the state and local level, the majority of funds transferred between governments are transferred using the grant system rather than loans. Grants are funds that are given to a lower level of government by a higher level for a particular purpose. The acceptance of these funds subjects the receiving government to the conditions specified by the grantor government. Grants thus are used to gain control.

Three administrative mechanisms in grants foster the centralization of control at the national level. Cross-cutting requirements are established in all grant programs by the U.S. Congress for specific purposes, such as to prevent discrimination. Crossover sanctions are instituted by Congress to withhold funds from one program if requirements are violated in another program. Partial preemption enables national programs to be instituted in areas where states may be reluctant to comply, by giving states discretion over the extent of their participation. The Clean Air Amendments of 1970 exemplified a national program that sets regulatory standards for an aspect of life over which individual states are reluctant to assume regulatory responsibility.

Other examples of using fiscal transfers to implement national priorities by centralizing control at the national level include establishing minimal standards for government services; redistributing resources from rich states or localities to poor states or localities; introducing comprehensive solutions to problems that are prevalent in more than one area; increasing public services without, ostensibly, increasing the size of government; and improving the quality of government services.

There are several methods for classifying the types of grants: administrative discretion, availability, and matching requirements. Administrative discretion is the extent to which the grantor government designates the purpose for which the funds can be used. Block grants, for example, are given for relatively broad purposes, while categorical grants are given for specifically designated categories of expenditures.

Availability gauges how accessible a grant is to recipient governments. Formula grants use statutory or administrative formulas to determine the amount of funds that are equally available to all qualifying units. Project grants are allocated on a competitive basis. There are more formula grants than project grants, but project grants account for twice as much money disbursed as formula grants. Competition for project grants has fostered grantsmanship, that is, calculated strategic behavior designed to acquire as many grants from as many grantors as possible.

The classification of grants using matching requirements refers to the ratio of matching funds that the recipient government must provide. Some grants require no matching funds at all. For those grants that do, ratios can range from lows of one to two, to highs of two to one.

The centralized control promised by the grant system presents several problems to some IGR participants. Yielding greater control to the grantor government can diminish local initiative. The priorities of the recipient government become distorted to reflect those of the grantor government. In addition, although a comprehensive solution is the intended result, jurisdictions vary in their compliance with and implementation of grantor requirements. Also, successful grantsmanship requires professional skill. For example, fungibility, which refers to the shifting of funds received for one purpose to another purpose, requires extensive knowledge of assistance-related regulations. More affluent jurisdictions are enabled to receive more grants because they can afford to obtain the specialized, professional help needed to conduct grantsmanship successfully.

Finally, coordinating the application for and, upon receipt, the implementation of grants, can be complicated and disruptive to recipient governments. A jurisdiction can receive more grants than it can effectively administer. The funds needed to maintain regular services of the recipient government can be redirected to satisfy matching funds requirements.

Some scholars argue that during the late twentieth century state and local governments increased their resource base and, thereby, their power and independence from the national government. The preponderance of court decisions favoring centralized power, and the continued flow of funds and regulations from the national to the state and local levels, generates little empirical support for this conclusion, however. States had more significant autonomy for only a brief period after the enactment of the Constitution. In the intervening years, state and local governments have become increasingly dependent on and directed by the national government.

Applications

Two periods in the history of the United States provide examples of IGR complexity and centralization: President Franklin D. Roosevelt's New Deal and President Lyndon B. Johnson's Great Society. Known by a campaign slogan used by Roosevelt in the 1932 election, the New Deal is associated with the massive government effort to combat the effects of the Great Depression, the economic collapse dating from 1929 to 1941. The threat to the survival of the nation encouraged state and local officials to cooperate with efforts initiated at the national level. During the Depression, funds were made available to the states through formula grants to provide services such as old age assistance, health services, and aid to dependent children. The National Resources Planning Board was created by the national government in 1933 to stimulate policy planning at the state and local levels. The national government offered states a tax offset in 1935 in exchange for the development of state-administered programs providing unemployment compensation.

The Great Society was a slogan invoked by President Johnson in the mid-1960's. It represented the ideology that advocated the centralization of objectives, supervision, and control for the ostensive benefit of all. In 1961, there were 40 existing grant programs. By 1969, the avalanche of Great Society fiscal transfers that had been enacted included 150 major grant programs, four hundred specific legislative authorizations, and thirteen hundred federal assistance activities. Cross-cutting requirements were instituted in these fiscal transfers to achieve national objectives in the area of planning. Because of the many administrative and fiscal requirements of these programs, extensive red tape was involved in applying for and administering these grants.

The administrative chaos generated at the state and local level by the proliferation of Great Society grants initiated pressure to reverse the trend of expansion. Consolidation of grant programs began in the 1970's to reduce the complexity of the grant system and to attempt to ensure that grant implementation would accomplish the intended objectives.

Context

The question of how power is to be distributed is such a fundamental aspect of government that it is the basis by which governments are classified. In unitary systems of government, power is totally centralized, and regional governments are branches or representatives of the central government. In federal systems of government, power is not centralized, and regional governments are autonomous units that share power with the central unit. The regional governments agree to subordinate their power to the central unit only in common affairs; the central unit allows the regional governments to retain their power in all other affairs. True federal systems are routinely confronted with conflict, because the determination of what powers are reserved for the regional governments and what powers belong to the central government is an ongoing process, not a permanent decision.

The U.S. Constitution enumerated the powers of the central government and implied that the remaining powers were reserved for the states and people. Advocates of strong central government have interpreted the language in the Constitution to support the supremacy of the national government in any area in which it desires to take initiative or have control. Advocates of strong regional governments argue that the Constitution specifically limits the central government from asserting sovereignty or control in areas not specifically enumerated as belonging to the central government. Acting as an arbiter between these two ideologies, the court system, primarily the

Supreme Court, has more frequently supported increasing the power and control of the central government.

The allocation of power is an important issue for intergovernmental relations, because the nature of the relations between government entities is based on the allocation of power between them. Chief Justice John Marshall, who served on the Supreme Court from 1801 to 1835, viewed the Constitution's supremacy clause (Article 6, section 2) as granting the national government with authority in any area in which it wanted jurisdiction, regardless of whether prior jurisdiction had been vested in the states. Marshall's influence on IGR formed the basis for the centralization of power still in effect today. Chief Justice Roger B. Taney, who served on the Supreme Court from 1836 to 1864, viewed the Tenth Amendment (powers reserved to the states) as limiting national power. In *Hoke v. United States* (1913), Supreme Court Justice McKenna expressed the view that both states and the nation represent one people and have powers to promote the general welfare. If, when two parties are negotiating or bargaining, one party has overwhelmingly more power than the other, the stronger party always has greater control of the outcome of the interaction than the weaker party. Increasingly, therefore, intergovernmental relations are characterized more by the control of the central government than by the control of the regional governments.

Bibliography

Gordon, George. *Public Administration in America*. 4th ed. New York: St. Martin's Press, 1992. Contains an overview of intergovernmental relations with primary emphasis on grant-in-aid programs.

Perry, James, ed. *Handbook of Public Administration*. San Francisco: Jossey-Bass, 1989. Relevant essays in this volume include a lively discussion of the increasing capacities of state governments by James Conant and an examination of the new roles assumed by the federal government under the Carter and Reagan administrations by Eugene McGregor, Jr.

Rabin, Jack W., Bartley Hildreth, and Gerald J. Miller, eds. *Handbook of Public Administration*. New York: Marcel Dekker, 1989. Useful chapters in this volume include Deil Wright's excellent survey of the history of the fluctuations in power between the national and state and local governments in the United States, with special attention to court cases and decisions affecting IGR. A chapter by Richard Leach examines the ideologies of federalism from constitutional, states' rights, administrative, centralized, and "new" perspectives.

Riker, William. *The Development of American Federalism*. Boston: Kluwer Academic Publishers, 1987. Comparison of Dutch and U.S. federalism that makes interesting use of such unusual measures as political party strength to determine how national centralized power is.

Rivlin, Alice. *Reviving the American Dream*. Washington, D.C.: Brookings Institution, 1992. Contains a historical overview of the centralizing and decentralizing influences on intergovernmental relations. Includes discussion of the values and beliefs about the role of government pertinent to IGR.

Starling, Grover. *Managing in the Public Sector*. 4th ed. Belmont, Calif.: Wadsworth, 1993. Contains a chapter that approaches intergovernmental relations from the managerial perspective. Identifies skills and knowledge public managers need to have to function effectively.

Stillman, Richard, ed. *Public Administration*. 5th ed. Boston: Houghton Mifflin, 1992. Introduction discusses the constitutional issues underlying the allocation of power between the national and state governments.

Wright, Deil S. *Understanding Intergovernmental Relations*. 2d ed. Monterey, Calif.: Brooks/Cole, 1982. Thorough and straightforward text covering all aspects of intergovernmental relations. Contains glossary and appendices with government documents relevant to IGR.

Santa Falcone

Cross-References

INTERNATIONAL AGREEMENTS

Field of study: International government and politics

International agreements are undertaken by states and other entities such as international organizations. Such agreements are intended to address some mutual concern that reaches across national boundaries, such as international relations, pollution, and trade.

Principal terms

CAMP DAVID ACCORDS: Interim agreement between Egypt and Israel made in September, 1978, in the presidential retreat at Camp David, Maryland

GENERAL AGREEMENT ON TARIFFS AND TRADE (GATT): International agreement binding its signers to follow certain rules to reduce artificial barriers to trade

HELSINKI ACCORDS: name commonly given to the Final Act of the Helsinki meeting of the Conference on Security and Cooperation in Europe in 1975

PACTA SUNT SERVANDA: Latin term meaning "agreements must be kept"

STRATEGIC ARMS LIMITATION TALKS (SALT): negotiations held between the United States and the Soviet Union between 1969 and 1985, attempting to limit strategic weapons

Overview

"International agreements" is a general term including many kinds of agreement. Treaties are the best-known type of international agreement and have particular features. They are usually discussed separately from other forms of international agreements, which include accords, agreed minutes, conventions, charters, covenants, final acts, pacts, and protocols. What all these agreements have in common is that they are forms of contracts between or among states.

International agreements are subject to common international understanding on the basis of the Vienna Convention on Treatises concluded in 1969. This convention includes many of these agreements that are not called "treaties," because it defines a "treaty" as "an international agreement concluded between states in written form and governed by international law." Thus, only verbal agreements and the establishment of international organizations are excluded from the convention's regulation.

Nations enter into international agreements primarily because international society has no legislature analogous to the legislature of domestic society to make laws regarding matters of mutual interest and concern. International agreements are a primary means through which chief transnational actors—states and international organizations—attempt to bring order into a disordered world. They are usually negotiated by professional diplomats, although various amateurs and retired politicians may at times become active players. Personalities may sometimes be key ingredients in the character and success of agreements. For example, President Franklin D. Roosevelt undertook personal negotiation with Winston Churchill to create the 1940 lend-lease agreement between Britain and the United States.

Many aspects of international life have been the subject of agreements among states. Agreements of various kinds regulate international aviation, postal service, communications, and other matters. Agreements dealing with war are among the most significant for dealing with the breakdown of order among the world's states.

A number of war conventions were agreed upon in the nineteenth century and the first half of the twentieth. Among them are conventions agreed upon in Geneva, Switzerland, and The Hague, The Netherlands, between 1846 and 1949 to regulate the conduct of war. An 1864 agreement ratified by many countries, for example, was a convention for the amelioration of the wounded in time of war. Initially applicable only to land wars, the convention was extended to naval warfare in 1899 and 1907.

Several Hague conventions added to a growing body of international agreements dealing with war. International conferences at The Hague in 1899 and 1907 tried and failed to place limitations on nations' armaments, but the conferences succeeded in creating conventions that defined a state of war between states and regulated other customs concerning land and sea warfare. These conventions prohibited the use of poison gas and of expanding dum-dum bullets, and, in the pre-airplane era, the dropping of explosives from balloons. In addition, the 1899 Hague Conference adopted a convention for the "pacific settlement of international disputes" and set up a permanent court of arbitration. The 1907 Hague Conference adopted further important conventions dealing with the conduct of war, such as the rights and duties of neutrals during wartime and the status of enemy commercial shipping.

An important consequence of the success of the conferences in creating internationally acceptable conventions was establishment of the principle that international problems should be submitted to international conferences for resolution. This principle influenced the founding of the League of Nations after World War I. The league was the predecessor of the United Nations, founded in 1945.

Later agreements attempted to deal with dangers to world peace. One such agreement in the early 1970's was an interim agreement between the United States and the Soviet Union on the subject of strategic arms. The Strategic Arms Limitation Talks (SALT) were begun in 1969. By 1972, the negotiators had concluded their first major agreement, the Anti-Ballistic Missile Treaty. At the same time, they were able to conclude an interim agreement for limiting strategic nuclear missiles. This agreement was the basis for the SALT II negotiations of 1973-1979.

Another agreement that had significant effects on international politics, especially in Europe and between the superpowers, was the Helsinki Final Act of the Helsinki Meeting of the Conference on Security and Cooperation in Europe (CSCE), better known as the Helsinki Accords. The CSCE that produced the accords was a grouping of North Atlantic Treaty Organization (NATO), Warsaw Pact, and other European nations that began meeting in the mid-1970's. The accords were signed by all participants except Albania. The Soviets viewed the CSCE as a means to reinforce and guarantee the geopolitical status quo in Europe, affirming their hegemony in Eastern Europe. The West wished to guard the foundations of peace in Europe by regularizing talks with the Soviets and to press them on human rights questions, a glaring communist weakness.

The Helsinki Accords were divided into three categories or "baskets," concerning security issues, economic issues, and human rights. The human rights agreement turned out to be the most significant and influential aspect of the accords. The agreement called for each participant to publish the full text, making it available to its citizens. The accords also provided for a series of follow-up conferences. These provisions focused attention on the human rights abuses of the Soviet bloc.

Within the Soviet bloc, publication of the text of the accords respecting human rights had the effect of stimulating a number of courageous individuals to dissent actively from their countries' repression of fundamental rights. Movements to monitor implementation of the accords' human rights provisions sprang up in several Eastern bloc countries. Although these movements were crushed, they served to spotlight the unsavory and hypocritical behavior of communist authorities.

After President Jimmy Carter took office in 1977, the United States used the first follow-up conference to assume leadership of the West in calling the Soviet bloc to account for failing to live up to the accords' human rights provisions. Soviet bloc governments responded by attacking the West for alleged human rights violations. After Mikhail Gorbachev came to power in 1985, the Soviets began to accept human rights principles, and by 1989 Soviet-instigated human rights abuses in Eastern Europe had nearly ended.

A second troubled area in which international agreements have played a constructive role is the Middle East. International violence in the area centers on the Arab-Israeli conflict. After the Six-Day War of 1967, Israel occupied Palestinian lands, including the Gaza Strip and the area west of the Jordan River known as the West Bank. In addition, Israel occupied the Sinai Peninsula, part of Egypt.

Israeli occupation of Gaza and the West Bank was bitterly opposed by Palestinians, represented by the umbrella organization of various groups known as the Palestine Liberation Organization (PLO). In attempts to further its cause, the PLO resorted to numerous terrorist acts, galvanizing Israeli public opinion against giving up lands won during the 1967 war. Having failed to have their lands returned peacefully, Egypt and Syria attacked Israel during the Jewish Yom Kippur celebrations of October, 1973. Although the Arab sides recaptured some occupied lands, Israel was able to reclaim most of the Arab gains.

The United States led attempts at peacemaking. The United States was concerned because a Middle East war could bring confrontation with the Soviet Union, which championed the Arab cause. The Americans therefore supported a December, 1973, Madrid conference sponsored by the United Nations.

When the Madrid conference broke up in disarray after two days, the United States began a process of diplomatic negotiations among Syria, Egypt, and Israel. Through the mediation of Secretary of State Henry Kissinger, three agreements were hammered out to bring about the disengagement of the armed forces of the three countries.

Nevertheless, peace eluded the area. The greatest stumbling block to peace between Egypt and Israel lay with Israeli occupation of the Sinai Peninsula. In 1977, however, Egyptian President Anwar el-Sadat suddenly announced his willingness to visit Jerusalem for peace talks with Israel. Initial talks were unsuccessful, but President Carter invited Sadat and Israel's Prime Minister Menachem Begin to Washington to continue the talks. During grueling thirteen-day marathon negotiations at the presidential retreat at Camp David, Maryland, Carter was able to broker an interim agreement between the parties. This key agreement formed the basis of the peace treaty signed later in Washington.

A further step easing the Arab-Israeli conflict was the agreement between Israel and the PLO, represented respectively by Prime Minister Yitzhak Rabin and PLO Chairman Yasir Arafat, signed in Washington in August, 1993. A key symbolic moment of the agreement came when Arafat and Rabin, who had been mortal enemies for decades, publicly shook hands in a White House ceremony. This important agreement called for PLO recognition of Israel and peace between the PLO and Israel in exchange for Israeli withdrawal from the Gaza Strip and part of the West Bank. Although this agreement by no means settled the Arab-Israeli conflict, it was a milestone on the road to permanent peace.

Applications

After the end of the Cold War, Western political analysts called attention to the extent to which the international scene was wracked by disorder. A dangerous and sometimes chaotic world requires an agreed set of rules and the means to enforce them. International agreements play important roles in a number of spheres of international life in efforts to shape a semblance of world order. Two key areas in addition to peace can be singled out for attention.

One area concerns agreements governing military, commercial, and other use of the earth's oceans. Oceans and seas have always been both sources of resources and means of transport. Rules developed primarily by European powers in the seventeenth to nineteenth centuries became outmoded as the world's supply of fish became scarce and as the means to exploit oil and minerals beneath the ocean were developed.

A United Nations Conference on the Law of the Sea convened in 1958 and was followed by a second conference two years later. Although four international conventions were produced, they did not resolve the several key issues, including the extent to which coastal states governed the waters that bordered them, the definition of how far the continental shelf extends into the ocean, and the extent to which coastal nations could control fishing.

Other questions arose. In 1967, the Mediterranean island of Malta proposed that the deep seabeds of the world's oceans be declared "the common heritage of mankind" and an international agency be established to control mining of the ocean floors. This proposal precipitated a third United Nations Law of the Sea Conference (1973-1982).

This conference drew up a compromise allowing coastal nations to control the use of resources within two hundred miles of their shores. They could not, however, exclude any state's ships from navigating within these waters. In addition, the conference declared the ocean floor to be humanity's common heritage and proposed an international monopoly on exploitation of the ocean floor. A new international agency, the International Seabed Authority, was to administer this monopoly for the benefit of all nations.

Not all nations agreed to these provisions. Developed nations, including the United States, refused to agree to the provisions regarding ocean bed mining. Moreover, the conference's provisions did not cover all maritime matters requiring regulation, and critics argued that some parts of the convention are ambiguous.

A second significant area in which international agreements are applied in the contemporary world is trade. To negotiate rules on trade, many of the world's nations participate in the General Agreement on Tariffs and Trade (GATT). The purpose of GATT is to increase international trade by lowering tariffs and reducing other barriers to trade.

GATT was formed in 1947 in the aftermath of World War II, when more than twenty countries signed a founding agreement. Western democracies wished to reform trade relationships that had led to the disastrous tariff barriers that characterized the Depression era of the 1930's. GATT provisions were intended to loosen the hold of domestic restrictions on trade. Domestic producers typically wish to protect their home markets by excluding foreign competitors. They do so by pressuring their governments to place high tariffs on competing goods from abroad. Such practices are known as protectionism. The Depression illustrated that a regime of worldwide protectionism can harm everyone involved.

Besides seeking to reduce tariff barriers, GATT seeks to promote the idea of nondiscrimination among trading partners. Nondiscrimination means that a state does not favor one partner over others. This principle is embodied in the rule of "most favored nation" that applies to all GATT signatories. Each member of GATT must apply the same tariffs to other members that it applies to its "most favored" trading partner.

From the late 1940's to 1967 there were six rounds of GATT negotiations. The early rounds took place in circumstances of world economics that varied widely from those of later rounds in the 1970's and 1980's, when fears were voiced that the world's most important economic powers were dividing into trading blocs. In addition, the trading scene was complicated by the fact that multinational companies assembled products whose components might be imported from around the world instead of producing entire products in single nations. Moreover, the United States had lost dominance as an economic power. GATT negotiators faced new issues of trade managed by national governments, the rise of industrialization in Southeast Asia, global concerns about pollution, and migration of industry in search of low-cost labor. These issues and others reached across international boundaries, making international agreements such as GATT desirable.

Context

International agreements are binding because they are legitimate promises of states. The Latin term *pacta sunt servanda* ("agreements must be kept") embodies the fundamental idea that states must keep their promises to one another if there is to be a modicum of order and certainty in the world. There is, however, a school of thought, originated by seventeenth century English philosopher Thomas Hobbes, that holds agreements to be binding only if the means exist to enforce them. In this view, international agreements—and international law in general—create legitimate obligations only to the extent that the parties effectively can be called to account for infractions. The consequence of this perspective is that humanity can expect little more than the rule of the powerful in world affairs. International agreements can do little to alter the fundamental fact that the international scene is one of anarchic, competitive individualism.

Other views are based on the perspective of seventeenth century Dutch legal philosopher Hugo Grotius and point to the influence in world affairs of an international community. In this community, world opinion plays a significant role in moderating the behavior of most states, including the powerful. In such a world, international agreements stand as countervailing forces to sheer military or economic might. In this view, in a world drawing ever closer through sophisticated means of communication, powerful and weak states alike find it increasingly in their interest to abide by the agreements they make.

A third view of the possibilities of the international world is derived from the thought of German philosopher Immanuel Kant. In his *Perpetual Peace* (1795), Kant outlined the principles and conditions under which an international community could achieve something more than uneasy peace punctuated by war. Kant postulated that a world federation of free states could be established. It would be a "union of nations," but not a world state, and would be established gradually through international agreements freely accepted by the nations of the world. The United Nations might be seen as a step in this direction, but the nations of the world remain far from unified.

Bibliography

Jackson, John H. *Restructuring the GATT System.* New York: Council on Foreign Relations Press, 1990. A comprehensive account of GATT negotiations and the place of this key international agreement in the future of the world economy.

Janis, Mark W. *An Introduction to International Law.* 2d ed. Boston: Little, Brown, 1993. A comprehensive introductory text presenting the basic ideas of international law in a clear style. Uses the term "treaties" to cover all international agreements and should be read accordingly.

Kissinger, Henry A. *Years of Upheaval.* Boston: Little, Brown, 1982. The former U.S. secretary of state presents the inside story of negotiating a number of international agreements, sparing no detail.

Nathan, James A., and James K. Oliver. *Foreign Policy Making and the American Political System.* Baltimore: The Johns Hopkins University Press, 1994. Informative discussion of international agreements in American foreign policy. The chapter on the increasing role of executive agreements that are not subject to congressional approval is particularly helpful.

Walzer, Michael. *Just and Unjust Wars: A Moral Argument with Historical Illustrations.* 2d ed. New York: Basic Books, 1992. Includes extensive treatment of war conventions and other aspects of international agreements as applied to war. Gives thorough attention to ethical dimensions of abiding by international conventions and other agreements during wartime.

Charles F. Bahmueller

Cross-References

Alliances, p. 47; Ambassadors and Embassies, p. 53; Arms Control, p. 95; Diplomacy and International Negotiation, p. 552; Human Rights and International Politics, p. 848; International Law, p. 956; International Monetary Fund, p. 963; International Relations, p. 969; Leagues, p. 1072; Sanctions, p. 1777; Superpowers and World Politics, p. 1916; Treaties, p. 2020; The World Bank, p. 2153; The World Court, p. 2161; World Government and Environmental Protection, p. 2167; The World Health Organization, p. 2180.

INTERNATIONAL LAW

Field of study: International government and politics

International law comprises the obligatory customs, treaties, and principles by which governments agree voluntarily to limit their sovereignty and to regulate and facilitate their interrelations.

Principal terms

CODIFICATION: process by which law is legislated, centrally collected, and systematically developed

CUSTOMARY LAW: legally binding practices that, having evolved in a general, uniform, consistent, continuous way over a significant period of time, are regarded by states as obligatory

RECIPROCITY: principle that the acceptance by states of obligations and assertions of rights under law apply mutually

SELF-HELP: principle that states may take action independent of collectively sanctioned responses against states threatening their sovereignty, territorial integrity, or independence

SOVEREIGNTY: principle that no authority exists above nation-states, whose governments have exclusive jurisdiction and control over their own territories

SOURCES OF INTERNATIONAL LAW: means by which international laws are created or interpreted, including customs, treaties, general principles, judicial decisions, and expert writings

Overview

All political systems, whether local, national, or international, being composed of different parts with varying interests, require some principles of law to enable their orderly interaction. At the global level, international law helps to bring a degree of order to interstate relations as governments pursue their interests in an arena where no centralized authority exists over and above them. International law recognizes the principle that states are sovereign, that is, they are the highest international legal authorities. No state may be told how to conduct its domestic or foreign affairs. International law is primarily a coordinative process of interaction between states rather than a subordinative process of governmental adherence to centralized institutional authority, which is weakly developed at the international level.

International law is routinely observed by the vast majority of governments throughout the world, despite the lack of effective centralized mechanisms for its legislation, execution, and adjudication. This is so because states realize that enjoyment of the fruits of international trade, commercial activity, travel, scientific and cultural exchange, and technological diffusion cannot take place without some measure of order and regulation. From the earliest times, governments have realized that to have reasonable contact with other nations, they would have to respect the safety and dignity of diplomatic representatives of other countries, according them special legal status and immunities. A law of diplomatic privileges and immunities thus developed as legally binding custom among nations over centuries of international relations. The law emerged from a sense of the need for reciprocity. That is, if a government expected its diplomats to be protected by other governments, it had to extend the same courtesy to diplomats it received from these governments. Much of the customary law developed over time was rooted in this recognition of reciprocity and in the long-established practices that helped to lend stability and order to international relations.

International law is still created by customary means, but it is increasingly legislated by treaties, which make it possible for governments to spell out their obligations to one another more quickly and concisely. The United Nations General Assembly often stimulates international negotiations and conferences that produce drafts of multilateral treaties, which may then be ratified by states. This rather loose, state-driven form of legislation does result in the creation of new legal norms. Treaties, however, only bind those states who explicitly agree to be bound. Thus, the legislative mechanism in international law is a weak one. It must recognize the most fundamental principle of all international law: States are sovereign.

If legislative functions are decentralized and flow from governmental calculations of interest and reciprocity, executive functions are similarly weak and unsystematic. The U.N. Security Council has the power to enforce its decisions to impose sanctions on or otherwise punish aggressors and violators of international law. Its capacity to do this depends, however, on its ability to attain consensus among the five permanent members, and such consensus is often fragile. Where international institutions fail to maintain order, individual governments may choose to do so, especially when their own territorial integrity or political interest is directly involved. When U.N. bodies fail to respond to aggression, states have routinely resorted to self-help to protect themselves and punish violations of international law.

A customary law of retaliation, or *lex talionis*, limits how states may seek to punish illegal actions by other states. It is presumed that warlike actions, blockades, shows of force, bombardments, occupation, or invasion are to be undertaken only against states that have committed a prior illegal act, and that such acts of retaliation against aggressor states must be proportional to the original offense. Because it is often difficult to assess where wrongdoing has occurred, who is responsible for it, and whether a retaliatory action is truly proportional, this law of retaliation is not a certain exercise, and the executive functions of international law are therefore not always effective or dependable.

Judicial functions in international law are also broadly decentralized. The International Court of Justice (ICJ), the sole global court, lacks compulsory jurisdiction except in cases in which states have explicitly granted it. As a result, the court remains a largely passive actor, which states may use as their political interests dictate. Even when the ICJ rules on a case, it has no power to create binding precedent, unlike the high courts within many nations. Only governments of states can make international law. Courts have the power only to interpret and apply the specific elements of treaties and customary law to a particular case. Although there is no overarching international judicial body with compulsory jurisdiction, the high courts of the various nations do serve an international judicial function by interpreting and applying international law in cases involving foreign nationals, interests, and subjects. This decentralized, nationally rooted system of adjudication is not systematic or always consistent, but it reflects both the need for international coordination and the fact of international sovereignty.

Unlike many domestic legal systems, international law is not centrally codified. Its main sources, including state-made customs, treaties, and general principles, are often preserved by foreign ministries and legal bodies of individual governments. Secondary sources of the law—those not originating with states—such as judicial decisions and the writings of highly respected experts, writers, and jurists, help to interpret these principles, but such opinions are often contradictory. Efforts to codify international law include the development of lawmaking multilateral treaties, which identify and explicitly articulate existing customary law, and efforts by the United Nations to encourage states to register treaties with it. The latter is not a mandatory activity, nor does failure to register and publish treaties with the United Nations nullify them, but no state may cite unregistered treaties before bodies of the United Nations.

International law must provide some degree of continuity so that governments can know with confidence what their obligations are. The *pacta sunt servanda* principle that treaties must be observed is one norm that states recognize as a means of accomplishing continuity. Law also must be flexible enough to respond to changing times. In treaty law, this is reflected in the *rebus sic stantibus* doctrine, which holds that a state may be relieved of its treaty obligations when the legal and factual circumstances surrounding the promulgation of a treaty have changed so fundamentally that the treaty can no longer be expected to apply. Most treaties contain provisions for amendment, termination, renegotiation, or withdrawal as means of anticipating future change. Even customary law can change, sometimes over rather brief periods of time, when an international consensus recognizes the evolution of new principles.

States are generally considered the main subjects of international law. Normally individual persons cannot bring suit in international courts; only the government of their citizenship or nationality may sue foreign governments. To have access to justice at the international level, a person first must seek redress within the legal structures of the state of residence or nationality.

Applications

International law is an indispensable means of determining or resolving territorial disputes; rights of title to land; human rights; jurisdiction over and treatment of aliens, refugees, and asylum seekers; regulation of transnational trade; communication and travel; resolution of disputes; exploitation and use of the sea; and regulation of the use of force during times of conflict or war. Issues concerning aliens and asylum seekers, human rights law, and the applications of the laws of war can be used to illustrate the workings of international law.

Customarily, governments have recognized that aliens should be protected and given equal rights of access to the judicial process. Aliens generally are not entitled to be treated better than the population of the host country. Standards of justice vary widely, however, leading some states to claim that a minimum standard of justice pertains to all people. Although this concept is not universally accepted, there is wide agreement among governments about the fact that they have a responsibility toward aliens. This customary law of state responsibility clearly calls upon states to afford aliens the rudimentary protections and opportunities for redress of grievances afforded to citizens. If an alien has suffered injury, and if the injury is attributable to the failure of the state to exercise due diligence in protecting the alien's rights, or if the state has directly violated those rights, then the government can be held responsible for this wrongful injury. The alien must exhaust all domestic legal remedies available before seeking redress through their own country of nationality. The latter is free to take up its national's claim against the offending state or to ignore it.

A different issue arises when a state treats its own citizens so brutally as to shock the rest of the world. Many people believe governments should be held accountable for violating the human rights of their own citizens. In a system based on the concept of state sovereignty, however, assertions of human rights are problematical. Human rights ultimately are enforceable only by governments in respect to their own citizens and subjects or by other governments exerting political pressure on offending states to abide by human rights standards.

Several nonbinding U.N. declarations have asserted what general rights of human beings should be observed. One of these, the Universal Declaration of Human Rights, was later given greater legal status by many nations that incorporated its provisions into their constitutions or legal statutes. Subsequently, conventions relating to civil, political, economic, social, and cultural rights were negotiated, ratified, and entered into force for ratifying parties. In general, the enforcement provisions in these treaties are weak; the treaties rely on the good will of governments for enforcement. No universal right exists for the individual to sue his or her own state or government, although political pressure is often brought to bear on governments by other govern-ments and human rights advocacy organizations to ensure compliance with human rights principles.

The issue of asylum is closely related to the growing body of human rights principles and to the law of state responsibility toward aliens. Governments have no obligation under current international law to admit into their territories all aliens who desire to enter. Passport and visa regulations reflect governmental practices in controlling immigration, whether for travel, business, studying, or employment. Persons who illegally enter into a state's jurisdiction may be legally deported. The one exception to this that is recognized by the international community concerns asylum seekers. Individuals who have been persecuted by their state of nationality and flee it, or having left it have a well-founded fear of persecution should they return, may seek asylum from other states. No state is obliged to grant asylum to asylum seekers, but they are obliged, on finding that the asylum seeker's fear of persecution is genuine, not to repatriate the person against his will to his home state when this will invite his persecution or threaten his safety. When a state refuses asylum in such cases, it should seek out a third state willing to receive the asylum seeker.

The international law of war is an old and venerable feature of customary international law. It is based on the notion that governments must distinguish between innocent civilians and combatants. It places limits on how war may be fought, insisting that civilian areas and hospitals should be free of bombardment as much as possible. Soldiers or combatants must operate in an effective chain of command, wear uniforms, carry weapons openly, and obey the laws of war. Individuals or groups not adhering to these criteria have committed war crimes.

Modern guerrilla warfare directly challenges this classic conception between citizen and soldier. So does the concept of nuclear or total war, which does not distinguish between friend and foe, soldier and civilian. Thus, the classic distinction that gave the traditional law of retaliation and war its character has been greatly eroded by modern warfare. Attempts to overcome this have been undertaken by the International Committee of the Red Cross and Red Crescent Societies (ICRC), which provides training for governmental security forces to ensure that they know the existing human rights principles and how to abide by and protect them. The ICRC also has promulgated numerous Geneva Conventions in the hope of convincing states to respect the rights of civilians in time of civil conflict and strife.

Context

International law, in one form or another, has existed between and among nations and peoples throughout the centuries. The ancient Greek city-states were concerned about regulating war, promulgating treaties, determining the status of aliens, protecting diplomats, and providing asylum to suppliants and exiles. The Romans, in developing the concept of *jus inter gentes*, the law among nations, saw the need to regulate nationalities under the empire. The *jus inter gentes* conception provided the foundation for modern international law.

The modern state system derives from the Peace of Westphalia in 1648. Although the Peace of Westphalia was rooted in principles of state sovereignty, territorial integrity, and independence, it anticipated the need for international law as a means of sovereign autolimitation. Together with the growing role of international organizations, expanded global commerce, rapid technological advances, and the growth of private voluntary agency and corporate business activity abroad, international law has remained a necessary feature of regulating interstate affairs.

Because international law is not imposed on states, but agreed to by them out of a sense of mutual self-interest, it can be expected that most of this law will continue to be routinely observed. Only the most flagrant abuses of international law make news. War does break out, but even when it does there are customary laws of war that regulate state behavior during times of conflict. Genocide does happen, but governments have, on more than one occasion, responded by punishing the offending government.

The future development of international law faces several challenges. One is the rapid pace of technological change, which customary law, and often treaties, are ill-equipped to address in a timely fashion. Another problem is the dilemma of human rights in connection with state sovereignty. Finally, the growth of nationalistic fervor has unsettled the state system and given rise to wider claims for self-determination and to resulting civil conflict that often have grave international implications. The traditional rule of nonintervention in the affairs of sovereign states is challenged under these circumstances, especially when the civil conflicts that result are coupled with gross violations of human rights and the traditional laws of war. Although numerous challenges face the application and functioning of the international legal order, there can be little doubt that this coordinative body of law has served as a major steadying influence in the affairs of nations, and that it should continue to be a critical element of stability in a world still marked by significant conflicts and variable national interests.

Bibliography

Brierly, James. *The Law of Nations: An Introduction to the International Law of Peace.* 6th ed. Oxford, England: Clarendon Press, 1955. Still valuable and insightful treatment of the fundamental principles of international law, this book examines the origins of international law, its chief sources and modern structure, questions of jurisdiction, and mechanisms for regulating the use of force.

Falk, Richard, Frederick Kratochwil, and Saul Mendlovitz. *International Law: A Contemporary Perspective.* Boulder, Colo.: Westview Press, 1985. This edited volume contains thirty-eight scholarly and critical essays on the history and modern development of international law.

Glahn, Gerhard von. *Law Among Nations: An Introduction to Public International Law.* 6th rev. ed. New York: Macmillan, 1992. Thorough contemporary treatise on international law. Provides detailed analysis of every major area of the law together with case briefs and case studies.

Grotius, Hugo. *The Law of War and Peace.* Translated by F. W. Kelsey. Indianapolis: Bobbs-Merrill, 1925. Known as the father of international law, Grotius, in this classic text of the seventeenth century, provides the intrepid reader with a sense of how international law in its formative stages was interpreted by one of its foremost commentators.

Henkin, Louis, et al. *Right v. Might: International Law and the Use of Force.* New York: Council on Foreign Relations, 1989. Short but engaging collection of essays examining the legal role of force and self-help in a world where collective use of force is often problematic.

Jessup, Philip. *A Modern Law of Nations: An Introduction.* Hamden, Conn.: Archon Books, 1968. Superb analysis of the relationship of the individual to the state in an international legal order dominated by the latter, as well as a critique of modern international law. This book, although dated in some respects, is alive with uncommon wisdom and insight that still applies.

Robert F. Gorman

Cross-References

Ambassadors and Embassies, p. 53; Arms Control, p. 95; Conflict Resolution, p. 397; Diplomacy and International Negotiation, p. 552; Genocide, p. 752; Human Rights and International Politics, p. 848; Immigration and Emigration, p. 868; Immigration Regulation, p. 875; International Agreements, p. 949; International Relations, p. 969; Jurisprudence, p. 1019; Nationalism, p. 1268; Naturalization, p. 1275; Sanctions, p. 1777; Supranational Government Institutions, p. 1922; Treaties, p. 2020; United Nations, p. 2045; War, p. 2129; The World Court, p. 2161; World Political Organization, p. 2186.

INTERNATIONAL MONETARY FUND

Field of study: International government and politics

The International Monetary Fund (IMF) was established in 1944 to promote global economic growth, stabilize currency exchange rates, and expand international trade in the aftermath of World War II.

Principal terms

CONDITIONALITY: economic reforms required by the IMF as a precondition for added loans and/or rescheduling assistance

EXCHANGE RATE: price at which two currencies can be exchanged for each other

GOLD STANDARD: value of a nation's currency expressed as a fixed worth in gold

LESS DEVELOPED COUNTRIES (LDCs): countries whose per-capita income is below that of the developed nations

PEGGED EXCHANGE RATES: early IMF agreement, by which all members' currencies were expressed as a certain value in terms of the dollar, which, in turn, was expressed as a certain value in gold

QUOTA: one nation's contribution of funds, relative to total contributions; proportional to the importance of that nation's economy in world trade

SPECIAL DRAWING RIGHTS: initiated by the IMF in 1970 as a means of increasing worldwide liquidity, issued in proportion to a member's quota; also known as "paper gold"

WORLD BANK: sister organization to the IMF, established in 1944 to provide long-term loans to developing economies

Overview

The International Monetary Fund (IMF) resulted from an agreement reached at Bretton Woods, New Hampshire, in 1944, to foster worldwide economic recovery and development through monetary cooperation and exchange rate stabilization. In 1944, World War II was still proceeding and much of Europe was devastated, while the United States had emerged relatively unscathed as the premier economic and military power. More than any other nation, the United States was instrumental in the establishment of the IMF, with Great Britain an important, though junior, partner. By 1993, the Fund had grown from 35 to 177 members.

The founding philosophy behind the IMF stretched back to the period between World War I and World War II. Policy planners weighed the havoc caused by war reparations imposed on Germany by the Treaty of Versailles and the not-coincident rise to power of Adolf Hitler. They also considered the negative effects of currency depreciation and the Smoot-Hawley Tariff on domestic and international economies. The impact of onerous debt burdens and "beggar-thy-neighbor" trade policies had proven to be expensive lessons. On the other hand, the opportunity to restructure and solidify a world order torn apart by war, facilitated through currency convertibility and expanded trade, seemed at hand. The signing of the Bretton Woods accord signaled the full evolution of U.S. external policy from isolationist to internationalist.

The broad goals of the IMF, as stated in the Articles of Agreement in 1944, remained largely intact in the 1990's. They are: to expand trade and growth through currency convertibility; to stabilize exchange rate fluctuations as a means of improving convertibility; to provide an international forum for monetary issues; and to increase international liquidity and provide short-term loans to members as a means of promoting trade and growth while reducing the need for debilitating instruments such as higher tariffs and forced currency depreciations.

Initially, the IMF adopted a system of adjustable-peg exchange rates for member currencies. Each currency was pegged to the dollar at a rate specified and maintained by each central bank. In turn, the dollar was equal to a set amount of gold (thirty-five dollars equalled one ounce of gold), and dollars held by foreign central banks could be redeemed in gold at this rate. Members were required to maintain their currency in a narrow deviation from the peg-rate, although countries with a proven fundamental disequilibrium in their exchange rates could receive IMF approval to adjust the dollar peg, up or down. Because the U.S. dollar stood as the key currency, held as reserves by virtually every foreign nation, foreign central bankers were required to buy and sell dollars in order to maintain the proper relationship between the domestic currency and the dollar.

The adjustable-peg system proved a viable mechanism into the 1960's. Initially, rebuilding foreign nations held few dollars, and U.S. gold stocks were ample to satisfy foreign central bank demand. As the 1960's proceeded, however, the Vietnam War and Great Society welfare programs pushed the United States into trade and budget deficits. Foreign holdings of dollars increased and U.S. gold stocks shrank. By 1965, U.S. gold stocks were no longer sufficient to redeem all foreign holdings of dollars. One option for U.S. monetary authorities was to raise the dollar price of gold, effectively depreciating the dollar against all currencies. To limit speculation in gold, however, major industrial nations established a two-tiered gold system, where gold flows between central banks would maintain the thirty-five-dollar-per-ounce price of gold, but gold could be traded as a precious metal in commodity markets for a market-determined price. This became the first major step in the demonetization of gold.

Early in the 1970's, foreign holdings of dollars soared, and it became clear that the link between gold, the dollar, and world currencies would have to be completely severed. In August, 1971, President Richard Nixon suspended the redemption of foreign-held dollars for gold. On January 1, 1975, gold ceased to serve as the standard of value for world currencies. The IMF began to sell its stock of gold at market-set prices. The movement toward managed, floating exchange rates had become a reality.

In 1969, in a move to increase world reserve assets and enhance liquidity after the modified gold standard had been abandoned, the IMF instituted a new asset, Special

Drawing Rights (SDR), to be used to settle balances owed in foreign currencies. SDRs were literally created by a stroke of the IMF pen and were apportioned among members according to the relative sizes of their IMF quotas. At first glance, it might appear that the IMF was acting like a bank and creating money through new credits for international trade; SDR credits allowed a nation to borrow up to 50 percent of its IMF quota in the foreign currency of choice. SDRs are not the equivalent of money, however, because their issuance is limited by quota size and they are exchanged only between governments and central banks.

Nevertheless, SDRs became an internationally controlled reserve, replacing gold to a large extent, and the dollar to a much lesser extent. SDRs are more stable in supply, being tied neither to production (gold) nor to variable U.S. trade deficits (foreign dollar reserves). The price of the SDR initially was pegged at one U.S. dollar, but dollar devaluations and the unlinking of currencies with gold resulted in a new approach to SDR valuation. In 1994, the SDR valuation basket included the currencies of the United States, Germany, Japan, Great Britain, and France.

The IMF evolved from a credit union configuration, in which members subscribed and drew on their own subscriptions, to one more closely resembling an international bank. The IMF has periodically borrowed from its stronger members, under the General Agreements to Borrow, to improve liquidity and increase the overall pool of loanable funds. The IMF allows credit, above and beyond quota level, for members experiencing chronic cash flow problems in financing international trade. Typically, deficit nations borrow from the IMF by purchasing needed foreign currency with their own currency, replacing that amount in a set period of time with a "hard" or internationally acceptable currency.

The changing nature of the IMF mission was reflected in its role in the international debt crisis of the 1980's. During the 1970's, oil and other commodity prices had spiraled upward. Organization of Petroleum Exporting Countries (OPEC) nations, flush with dollars, maintained huge sums in U.S. and European banks. The banks, in turn, loaned large amounts of their surplus cash to less developed countries (LDCs) under the assumption that ever-rising commodity prices would enable repayment.

The decade of the 1980's brought falling commodity prices, rising interest rates, and recession. Many LDC loans had flexible interest rates; as worldwide interest rates climbed, so did the costs of debt service. With exports to industrialized nations declining because of recession, many developing nations found themselves unable to repay loans. Major money-center banks in the United States and Europe then found themselves pushed toward bankruptcy, as failing LDC loans reduced assets relative to liabilities. The flow of new loans to capital-starved LDCs soon dried up.

Sensing a financial crisis of truly international proportions, the IMF, along with the banks and government agencies, initiated a program of containment. Between 1983 and 1985, more than seventy separate agreements were hammered out among LDCs, banks, and the IMF to reschedule loan repayments. Generally, the new accords included postponements of principal repayment, while maintaining interest payments, and extended loan maturities. Bridge loans were made by the IMF and the U.S.

Treasury to help debtors with critical, short-term fiscal needs. As a condition for access to IMF loans and rescheduled loan terms, nations were required to undertake basic, often painful, economic reforms.

Applications

The debt crisis of the 1980's redefined and elevated the role of the International Monetary Fund in the world economy. The conditions imposed by the IMF on countries seeking loan rescheduling established the organization as a global, economic traffic cop. Generally, as a nation sought more in terms of IMF loans or intervention in a debt issue, it was subject to increasing levels of IMF supervision and policy constraints. This conditionality has been a subject of ripe controversy in many LDCs. On one hand, accepting International Monetary Fund conditions may provide the only pipeline to foreign capital and, thereby, economic growth. On the other, the economic costs imposed on LDCs by IMF conditionality can be severe.

The economic rationale backing IMF-imposed conditions on nations seeking debt relief is threefold. First, disciplined, often painful, economic policies are necessary to restore a nation's ability to service debt and thereby maintain IMF liquidity. Second, as an outside agency, the IMF can objectively control for external effects and best affect the collective welfare. Finally, the IMF has a level of experience, expertise, and information second to none, and thereby is more likely to propose an effective policy prescription.

The IMF conditionality package generally has contained some or all the following elements: reductions in the annual excess of government spending over revenues; reduction or elimination of subsidies to consumers and producers; devaluation of an artificially high price for the domestic currency, to encourage exports; throttling back the growth rate of the money supply; lowering of barriers to freer international trade; allowing the marketplace to set prices and value resources while reducing the government's role in administering prices; and reducing the annual rate of inflation and wage growth.

During the international debt crisis of the 1980's, and into the 1990's, LDCs have been vociferous in their complaints over the constraints imposed by IMF conditionality. They contend that reductions in deficit spending and food subsidies disproportionately affect the poor and thereby increase the inequality of income distribution and the costs of social unrest. LDCs argue that the deflationary medicine prescribed by the IMF negatively affects their employment and consumption, but has no impact on those who helped create the problem: the OPEC countries that forced up oil prices, and the United States, which drove up interest rates. Furthermore, LDCs contend, deflation spreads. Nations that traditionally buy LDC products have less income for imports.

The International Monetary Fund has responded that conditionality provisions must be strict if the IMF is to convince private, risk-minimizing banks that new loans will be repaid. In the 1970's, more LDC assistance came in the form of direct governmental aid and government-subsidized loans. Also, making an LDC curb excessive domestic spending is less costly if done sooner, rather than later. The IMF has argued that the conditionality package may be harsh, but it is the sole means of reopening the pipeline to foreign capital flows. Without an inflow of foreign capital, conditions are likely to become even worse. Finally, the IMF has proposed that LDCs could reduce defense expenditures rather than programs that directly affect the poor.

Context

Along with its sister organization, The International Bank for Reconstruction and Development—commonly known as the World Bank—the International Monetary Fund was instituted to restore and improve the world economic order in the aftermath of World War II. Specifically, the role of the IMF was to foster trade and thereby economic growth through a system of stable, convertible currencies and an international pool of loanable funds.

After 1944, the scope of IMF operations increased markedly, while its mission continued to evolve. The abandonment of the international system of fixed exchange rates and a modified gold standard in the early 1970's, and its replacement by floating exchange rates, freed the IMF from one of its watchdog tasks. Nevertheless, facilitating currency convertibility as the means for enhancing trade and development remains at the heart of the IMF mission. As the IMF increased its membership and subscription quotas were raised (to approximately SDR 150 billion in 1993), the pool of internally loanable funds grew. However, the demand for IMF financing has paralleled the increase in the capital base.

How large the IMF may become is, in part, a function of future economic events that affect both the current (spending) and capital (investment) side of nations' balance of payments. Certainly, the debt crisis of the 1980's made private sector banks reluctant to make loans to many LDCs. Therefore, the IMF has been the only recourse for poorer nations who failed the creditworthiness test in the private sector. It is possible that the International Monetary Fund will function in the future as the central bank of the global economy—the lender of last resort. While this transition would constitute a quantum leap in the mission and scope of the IMF, the momentum toward a global economy could fuel a need for it to expand its function in this direction.

In a local economy, a depositor "run" to withdraw money from a single bank will quickly deplete that bank of ready reserves to meet depositor demand for cash. While the bank may be solvent in terms of asset/liability management, it will suffer a liquidity crisis in not being able to convert sufficient assets to cash in a short time. Prior to establishment of a central banking system (such as the Federal Reserve) this bank would have failed. A central bank, however, would provide the bank with a cash loan sufficient to sustain the run.

If a similar panic were to occur at a national level, with all the lenders to a certain country deciding to withdraw their funds, the IMF could step in to provide sufficient liquidity to prevent economic collapse and reassure banks that the economy remains viable. While national liquidity runs have occurred, for example, in Mexico in 1982, the most serious problem facing many poorer nations is one of long-run insolvency and inability to repay foreign debt.

Loans to already insolvent LDCs might be justified by imposing strict conditionality rules. Many of the fiscal woes of LDCs can be traced to poor national economic policies. The IMF has the expertise and experience to propose proper changes in policy. It also has more institutional leverage than commercial banks and the ability to make unpalatable policy prescriptions stick. On the other hand, LDC compliance with conditionality agreements has been weak. The existence of a large stock of foreign-owed debt may discourage compliance. Given such "debt overhang," a significant part of the expanded export income induced by conditionality will go to service foreign-held debt, providing little or no stimulus to economic growth. Thus, the role of world lender of last resort is not without peril.

Bibliography

Acheson, A. L. K., J. F. Chant, and M. F. J. Prachowny, eds. *Bretton Woods Revisited.* Toronto: University of Toronto Press, 1972. Contains the annals of the conference convened to honor the twenty-fifth anniversary of the Bretton Woods accord. The articles, largely by individuals who had a hand in the original accord, provide insight into the political and economic forces that shaped the agreement.

Hogendorn, Jan S. *Economic Development.* New York: Harper & Row, 1987. Solid overview of the development problems facing less developed countries and potential solutions.

Kenen, Peter B. *Financing, Adjustment, and the International Monetary Fund.* Washington, D.C. Brookings Institution, 1986. Author does an excellent job detailing the activity and philosophy of the Fund, particularly with respect to its role in the "debt crisis" of the 1980's. Would benefit from the inclusion of a few more tables and charts.

Sachs, Jeffrey D. "Conditionality, Debt Relief, and the Developing Country Debt Crisis." In *Developing Country Debt and Economic Performance*, edited by Jeffrey Sachs. Chicago: University of Chicago Press, 1989. Excellent insight into conditionality and the debt service problems faced by LDCs provided by the leading authority on economic rehabilitation.

Scammell, W. M. *International Monetary Policy.* New York: John Wiley & Sons, 1975. Thorough and detailed account of Fund operations under the fixed exchange rate system of monetary organization.

John A. Sondey

Cross-References

Debts and Deficits in the U.S. Federal Budget, p. 489; International Agreements, p. 949; Trade with Foreign Nations, p. 2000; Underdeveloped Nations, p. 2039; The World Bank, p. 2153; World Political Organization, p. 2186.

INTERNATIONAL RELATIONS

Field of study: International government and politics

International relations is a branch of political science which studies how countries interact with one another. These interactions occur in the realms of economics, politics, diplomacy, and warfare. As the flow of material goods, information, money, and people has grown among countries, the world has become increasingly interdependent.

Principal terms

BALANCE OF POWER: condition in which the military and economic strength of competing countries or alliances is approximately equal

DIPLOMACY: communication between states through formal channels according to established rules

IDEALISM: theoretical perspective that holds up a set of concepts as worthy of practical emulation

INTERNATIONAL POLITICAL ECONOMY: branch of international relations that focuses on economics

LEVEL OF ANALYSIS: particular way in which one disaggregates the international system for the purpose of analysis

MULTINATIONAL CORPORATION: business with operations in more than one country

NATION-STATE: country whose population constitutes a single nation, or people

REALISM: theoretical perspective that views states as coexisting in a condition of global anarchy and thus are motivated by the logic of self-help

SOVEREIGNTY: principle that an entity (usually a national government) is the authority over its designated territory

Overview

Countries interact in a number of ways, both cooperatively and in conflict, in the realms of diplomacy, economics, and military engagement. The important first principle of international relations is that the world's countries coexist in a condition of global anarchy. That is, there is no global government to rule over the various national governments. Countries, in other words, are sovereign, answering to no higher authority.

This condition of global anarchy is akin to the "state of nature" by which the seventeenth century philosopher Thomas Hobbes characterized a hypothetical condition of humanity without government. Just as people would arguably find themselves in a war of everyone against everyone without a government to maintain order, countries must fend for themselves in a world without a global police force to enforce laws which might regulate the behavior of countries. For Hobbes, a person's life in the state of nature would be "solitary, poor, nasty, brutish, and short." International relations explores the extent to which this is true for countries' "lives" as well.

Several factors speak against drawing a direct parallel between people in a state of nature and countries in a state of global anarchy. First, countries are not people; they do not have wills of their own and do not act as unitary entities. Indeed, in a sense countries do not exist at all. Rather, they are fictions upon which people agree. To a country are attributed the actions of government policymakers, diplomats, armed forces, and others who serve on behalf of an organized group in a defined territory. Additionally, although there is no world government, there do exist international laws and international institutions (such as the United Nations) that attempt to have a say in countries' policy choices. Finally, although countries do go to war, a significant number of international relationships are based on peaceful cooperation rather than violence. For many countries life is by no means "solitary, poor, nasty, brutish, and short."

How, then, should interactions among countries be described and explained? How can people and countries best coexist in the international environment? International relations addresses both the factual questions of how countries interact, as well as the normative questions about how leaders should develop foreign policies. A broad range of answers and opinions on these questions has been offered. They can be loosely grouped into two categories, each of which may be assigned a label: "realism" or "idealism."

Realism is a theoretical perspective of international relations that focuses on the anarchic aspects of the international system. It assumes a parallel between the international system and the Hobbesian state of nature. States are assumed to compete over a number of finite resources in the world, from territory to market share to control over strategic waterways. Conflict is thus seen as inevitable. Because it views the international system as a free-for-all, realism counsels that states pursue their interests while preparing to defend themselves against outside threats. For these reasons, realists have been seen as taking a pessimistic view of human nature. Realists also have been accused of amorality—although realists would counter that, while human beings are expected to act according to moral precepts, morality cannot be expected of states. Thus a leader who acts on behalf of a state should base his or her actions on state interests rather than morality.

Idealism, as its name implies, takes a more optimistic view of possibilities for cooperation in the international system. Idealists acknowledge the absence of a global authority to impose order on international relations, but they believe that global anarchy and war are not givens. Many idealists look to international organizations such as the United Nations as nascent world governments, with some anticipating the eventual development of a world federation. Idealists therefore focus on the commonality of human interests rather than competition over finite resources. They tend to see states as an obstacle to global cooperation, so idealists question the legitimacy of state interests. It follows that policies made on behalf of a state must be held to a moral standard. The most optimistic idealists believe that if decision makers would abide by an understood universal morality, conflict could be eliminated.

International relations is also approached from different levels of analysis. A level of analysis is a particular way of viewing the world as a collection of parts for the purpose of studying various aspects of international relations. At the broadest level of analysis, the world can be viewed as a single system, comprising states whose individual differences are less important than their similarities. At this level, state behavior is explained as a result of the system's structure and the state's role in it. A bipolar system (group A versus group B) might incline states to act conservatively and inflexibly, while a multipolar system (many different countries acting various ways) might incline them to act quite differently. At the opposite extreme of levels of analysis, international relations can be viewed as the interaction of individuals who act on behalf of particular states. Viewed this way, state behavior is a function of the particular motivations, biases, and perceptions of individuals. Of course, any number of levels of analysis between these two extremes can be described: regions, blocs, alliances, hemispheres, and so on. What is important about levels of analysis is that one's understanding of international relations is colored by the level at which one chooses to view the system. For example, systems-level inquiry might find an imbalance of power among systems as a primary cause of war. An individual-level analysis might find an individual leader's pride or paranoia as leading a country to war. Scholars of international relations remain divided regarding which level of analysis to work on. Much depends simply on preference for particular levels of analysis and on sympathy toward realist or idealist assumptions.

International relations can be classified by the nature of state interactions chosen for study. Traditionally, international relations has studied the realm of diplomacy, which includes treaties, agreements, and embassies. Countries that cannot resolve differences diplomatically move into the realm of military engagement—wars and other uses of force. Other manifestations of diplomacy include arms races, alliance formation, and blockades.

Of ever-increasing importance are economic interactions among countries. These include the trading of goods and services, coordination of currency exchange rates, lending of capital, provision of humanitarian aid, and other transfers of money. The continuing increase in the number and type of interactions of an economic nature among states has led many to speak of a complex interdependence among nations. Some idealists expect that this interdependence may develop to the point where warfare becomes obsolete.

Applications

For four decades after World War II, the international system was viewed as bipolar, with the United States and the Soviet Union each marshaling resources and allies in a Cold War of ideological and military competition. The field of international relations blossomed during this time, and many of the theories and explanations of international behavior were influenced by the Cold War. As a result, much of what was written then gives the sense that the bipolar, ideologically charged nature of the international system was to be a permanent feature of international relations. Yet the deterioration of the Soviet sphere of influence in the late 1980's, the subsequent disintegration of the Warsaw Pact, and the disaggregation of the Soviet Union threw many of the verities of international relations theory into question.

Scholars of international relations therefore began to search for a model which better fit the evolving post-Cold War political order. A central question concerned the number of poles, or centers of power, in the international system. Was the world system now unipolar, with the United States unrivaled as the world's superpower? Was it still bipolar, with a large and nuclear-armed Russia taking the place of the Soviet Union? Or was it multipolar, with Western Europe, Japan, and perhaps China rivaling the United States with an amalgam of economic and military power? Various international relations scholars have advocated each of these models, among others. One popular approach replaces the old three worlds paradigm of the Cold War (democratic West, communist East, and underdeveloped South) with a two worlds scheme, whereby the international system is divided between a developed North and an exploited South. This model suggests that, with the demise of Marxism-Leninism as a workable ideology, the industrialized countries of East and West can now recognize their shared interests. Similarly, it suggests that the disparate countries of the South hold shared interests as a result of their relative deprivation, and that the two worlds are opposed on numerous issues of policy, trade, and environmental concerns.

A more radical vision for the post-Cold War international order focuses on forces in the international system that are not states: multinational corporations, international interest groups, terrorist organizations, trade blocs, factions within states, and numerous others. This burgeoning category of nonstate forces is seen as crowding out the traditional (and, some say, antiquated) model of states as the prime forces in international politics. That these nonstate forces are becoming increasingly powerful in international relations is beyond question. One still may legitimately ask, however, whether states are truly being marginalized as the primary actors of the international system. If so, the most established theories about international relations must be rethought. The realists' assumptions about interest-focused sovereign states, the condition of global anarchy, and the inevitability of conflict deserve close examination, for example.

Whatever the particular forces that predominate in international relations, unquestionably they are becoming increasingly interlinked. Nowhere is this more obvious than in the realm of economics. Currency markets are linked electronically, with even the smallest financial developments transmitted instantaneously around the world. Increased specialization of products and booming consumer demand require that countries import more than ever before.

The reduction of trade barriers through the World Trade Organization, the European Union, international free trade areas, and other institutions has increased the volume of trade dramatically. Free movement of capital pushes unemployment and wage differentials among countries to converge. International organizations such as the World

Bank and the International Monetary Fund lend member countries' money to promote development and international economic stability.

Another category of global forces highlights international interdependence in a different way: Global environmental challenges, worldwide disease and drug epidemics, and international political threats such as terrorism transcend national boundaries, and thus perhaps are best addressed with coordinated, multilateral policies. To the extent that various threats to humanity are in fact best addressed by the "human polity" as a whole, the idealists' view of international relations is supported.

Nevertheless, the new world order anticipated by George Bush at the end of the Cold War has not come to pass. This is especially clear regarding nuclear arms proliferation. During the Cold War, the enormous nuclear arsenals of the Western and the Eastern blocs were somewhat stabilized by a condition known as mutual assured destruction (MAD), in which each bloc had the capability to destroy the other, even after suffering an initial attack. Now, with the Eastern bloc defunct, the nuclear arms of the Soviet Union dispersed among its successor states, and various countries from North Korea to Iraq seeking to build their own nuclear arsenals, the logic of MAD no longer holds. As a new world system develops in the wake of the Cold War's political order, scholars of international relations assess prospects for containing these growing threats.

Context

International relations is one of several fields of political science, which include politics, comparative government, law and jurisprudence, local and regional government, and political philosophy. Although relatively new as a field of academic study (becoming fully established only after World War II), international relations has developed rapidly.

The growing number of politically independent countries since the World War II and the increasing economic integration among countries have multiplied the sheer number of international relationships and interactions. This has developed the need for theories about international behavior, analysis of the international system, and prescriptions for guiding foreign policy. Much of the analysis conducted during the Cold War might seem to have less relevance than formerly, but the study of international relations continues to build upon the experiences of the past as well as on the observations of the present. In this way, international relations scholars seek to discover rules of international behavior that apply regardless of the particular configuration of the international system. There is, however, no laboratory in which to conduct international experiments. The developing and validating of theories remains a complex, confusing, and disputatious process, and the debate between realists and idealists does not lend itself to easy resolution.

Bibliography

Fukuyama, Francis. *The End of History and the Last Man*. New York: Free Press, 1992.
Popular description of the post-Cold War order, arguing that Western liberalism has

emerged as the virtually universal ideology of modern civilization.

Kennedy, Paul. *The Rise and Fall of the Great Powers: Economic Change and Military Conflict from 1500 to 2000*. New York: Random House, 1987. Argues that all great powers, including the United States, must decline and be superseded—a view that provoked an intense debate about the "decline" of American hegemony.

Morgenthau, Hans J. *Politics Among Nations: The Struggle for Power and Peace*. 5th rev. ed. New York: Alfred A. Knopf, 1978. Morgenthau has been called the "father of realism." This work represents one of the first and, for some, best explications of a theory of international relations.

Rosenau, James N., ed. *Linkage Politics: Essays on the Convergence of National and International Systems*. New York: Free Press, 1969. Concerned with the interdependence among countries and the extent to which actions in the international sphere affect countries' domestic policies.

_____. *Turbulence in World Politics: A Theory of Change and Continuity*. Princeton, N.J.: Princeton University Press, 1990. Attempts to account for the demise of the post-World War II international order and to offer insights into future developments.

Singer, J. David. "The Level-of-Analysis Problem in International Relations." *World Politics* 14 (October, 1961): 77-92. Classic article describing the level-of-analysis problem.

Viotti, Paul R., and Mark V. Kauppi. *International Relations Theory: Realism, Pluralism, Globalism*. 2d ed. New York: Macmillan, 1993. Examination of various theories of international relations. Includes glossary, extensive notes, subject index, and suggested readings.

Waltz, Kenneth. *Theory of International Politics*. New York: Random House, 1979. Attempts to build upon Morgenthau's realism with an improved theory called "structural realism."

Steve D. Boilard

Cross-References

Alliances, p. 47; Ambassadors and Embassies, p. 53; Arms Control, p. 95; Conflict Resolution, p. 397; Diplomacy and International Negotiation, p. 552; Foreign Relations, p. 718; Hegemony, p. 817; Hobbes's Political Philosophy, p. 836; Idealism, p. 855; International Law, p. 956; Islam and Government, p. 994; National Security, p. 1261; Peace, p. 1390; Realpolitik, p. 1668; Supranational Government Institutions, p. 1922; Trade with Foreign Nations, p. 2000; United Nations, p. 2045; War, p. 2129; World Government Movements, p. 2174; World Political Organization, p. 2186.

INVISIBLE GOVERNMENT

Field of study: Political philosophy

Certain critics theorize that the visible governments of the industrialized societies, especially of the United States, are less important than an invisible government of elites in corporations, Wall Street, think tanks, foundations, the armed forces, and other centers of power. Invisible government is often believed to dominate the visible government.

Principal terms

ELITE: the few people who hold positions of power, influence, wealth, honor, merit, or other measure of high status in government, the arts, business, education, or other valued pursuits

EXECUTIVE COMMITTEE OF THE RULING CLASS: term used by Karl Marx to describe those holding formal political power in a capitalist state

POWER ELITE: sociologist C. Wright Mills's term for those who occupy the principal centers of power in the United States, who he believed to act as a single entity

UNSEEN HAND: term used by Adam Smith to describe the operation of a free market in which each actor intends only his own good, but the public good results as if guided by "an unseen hand"

Overview

Ideas about "invisible government" are common among human cultures. Some religions believe that there are unseen governments, whether they be the "Great Spirit" of American Indians, the Yahweh of the Hebrew Bible, or the Christian God. The idea of an invisible government within modern industrial societies, however, is an exclusive creation of Western civilization.

The roots of this idea can be traced to the ancient Greek philosopher Plato. In his dialogue *The Laws* (c. 340 B.C.E.), he imagines a society with few contacts outside of its borders and that is deliberately isolated from other societies in order to shield it from cosmopolitan temptations such as luxury and the excitement of novelty. Nevertheless, Plato imagines that this society must have a means of taking note of the external world so that it can adopt changes when they would be beneficial. To this end, Plato institutes in his imaginary society a shadowy ruling group known as the "nocturnal council," so called because it meets at night. More to the point, it meets secretly, receiving reports of developments in the outside world. It meets secretly because the reports it hears are forbidden to the populace at large, who might desire harmful changes if they are dazzled by the luxuries and fleshpots available elsewhere. Thus, the secrecy maintained by this imaginary Platonic government is a means of ensuring that democracy—a disastrous rule of the ignorant—could never take power.

In later centuries, Christianity outlined another version of invisible government. Most powerfully expressed in Saint Augustine's *The City of God* (426 C.E.), this vision of the government of the cosmos divides reality between an earthly, material existence and a spiritual, otherworldly existence. In this life, the spiritual existence of believers is mixed with the material world in the earthly city; but after death, the believer reaches fulfillment with an eternal life in the heavenly city, the City of God. The material world is transient; more real than this temporary reality is the invisible reality, the kingdom ruled by God. Here is the Christian version of invisible government. Rulers on earth may war and sin, causing grievous suffering of humanity. But the invisible government of the deity, represented on earth by the Church, is more real, more dependable, and more just than its visible counterpart.

This positive account of invisible government continued in secular form during the Enlightenment of eighteenth century Europe. One of the most striking and long-lived versions of invisible government was that of Adam Smith in *The Wealth of Nations* (1776). To portray the desirable results of the operation of a free market, in which no one can control the supply of products and determine their quality and price, Smith invented the idea of an "invisible hand." Although each producer follows his own self-interest in order to maximize his profits, the free market advances the public welfare, as if "led by an invisible hand." Although there was no literal invisible hand governing the collective outcome of numerous individual decisions, the free market behaved as if it were invisibly governed, with positive results for everyone.

A second version of the invisible government idea was put forward in the eighteenth century by the English legal reformer and utilitarian philosopher Jeremy Bentham. In his model, invisible government is quite literal. Bentham devised a system of management for institutions such as prisons, factories, and hospitals that were built to be circular in shape. At the center of each would be an inspector who could not be seen by those whom he watched because he would sit within an enclosure. By turning around and peering out from slits in the enclosure, he could see whether inmates, workers, or staff were behaving properly. But since the inspector would be shielded from their view, those who were expected to follow prescribed rules could not know if they were being watched at any given moment. Government would thus be literally invisible to them. Bentham expected that when inmates discovered that their misdeeds were instantly punished, they would avoid the pain of punishment and voluntarily control themselves. The result would be that there would be no punishment. Thus, invisible government was, in this view, a most useful invention.

Bentham adapted this arrangement of invisible government, known as the "Panopticon principle" (Greek for "all seeing"), to society at large. To Bentham, the governments of this day were thoroughly corrupt because they were unaccountable for their actions. To make them accountable Bentham proposed to subject political power to a potent form of invisible government. This "invisible" government would be the public opinion of a democratic electorate. The means to make the actions of the actual government visible to the "invisible government" of public opinion would be a free press combined with open government offices and actions, both of which would be subject to the scrutiny of the press, and when desirable, officeholders could be voted from office by an aroused public.

These essentially positive models of invisible government were soon eclipsed by perhaps the most powerful negative account of invisible government in modern times. This was the version articulated by Karl Marx in the nineteenth century and by his followers, as well as many less directly influenced by his ideas. In Marx's view, the political system of any country is a direct consequence and is dependent upon its economic system. The real powers in any society lie in the hands of those who own or control the means of production and distribution. This is the economic base, from which all culture arises. Although the institutions of parliamentary democracy pretend to be true democracy—rule of the people—they are in fact a sham. Behind the facade of democratic institutions, the real government—which is invisible to the untutored eye—makes the decisions that count. In the industrializing societies of the nineteenth century, this group comprised the people controlling industry who were known to Marx by the French word for middle class, "bourgeoisie." Since the real government was the invisible bourgeoisie, in Marx's view, those in government who appeared to hold political power were merely "the ruling committee" of the bourgeoisie.

In one form or other, Marx's ideas that the "real" power of a society lies with those who control its economic power have been enormously influential. Non-Marxists as well as Marxists have given credence to this idea. By the 1920's and 1930's the idea of "invisible government" was being freely applied to the United States. Thus, a 1928 book was titled simply *The Invisible Government*, and the subtitle of the 1934 work *Who Rules America?* was *A Century of Invisible Government*. The latter book purported to show that the influence of money and finance on American government stretched from the administration of George Washington through the 1920's.

By the beginning of the Vietnam War era, a negative version of invisible government had become the stock-in-trade of a section of the political Left in many of the Western democracies, especially in the United States. Adherents to this idea also believed that "invisible government" was "hidden government," operating throughout the nation's corporate boardrooms. A source of uncontrolled and unaccountable power of special concern to critics was the power of multinational corporations, which exercised more control over international enterprises than individual national governments.

Applications

The question of the extent to which "invisible government" is an accurate and valuable notion for analyzing the power of industrialized democracies is controversial. In the middle and latter decades of the twentieth century the arguments of several individuals have been most influential in reviving the invisible or hidden government idea. Foremost among them was the American sociologist C. Wright Mills, whose book *The Power Elite* (1956) attempted to strip bare the ideals of American democracy that located ultimate power in "the people." Rather than the people, Mills found an all-embracing elite exercising significant powers and influence in the most important holders of political power, the military, high society, top corporate executives, "the corporate rich" (those within the upper reaches of corporate salaries), the super rich, "war lords" (generals and admirals), and other influential groups.

Mills rejected the simple economic determinism that characterized some Marxist thinking, such as the notion that political power was in the hands of key capitalists through a "ruling committee" who held formal office. Instead, Mills argued that those at the commanding heights of business, military, and politics each have a large measure of autonomy and rule in intricate ways through coalitions to make and carry out the most important political and economic decisions.

Mills admitted that there are factions among these elites and that the policies of these factions sometimes conflict. But the internal discipline and community of interests among these elites bind them together. Thus, in his view, the fact that the power elite is not a seamless monolith does not undermine the basic power elite idea.

Other American radicals have held varying views similar to those of Mills. Linguist Noam Chomsky has written extensively on his ideas of the corruption of the American polity and the unchecked power of elites to control the direction of American society. Chomsky's radical views took hold during the U.S. war in Vietnam. Among his principal complaints was the role that intellectuals played in promoting loyalty to the U.S. government at a time when, in his belief, American military power was being grievously misused abroad.

Among those applying the idea of invisible government in a somewhat different context is consumer advocate Ralph Nader. By the 1990's, his chief concern was the unchecked power of American and multinational corporations operating behind closed doors with consequences that might injure the public. Nader and his associates found these injuries to be far too frequent. In the context of American politics, they regard Washington as overly influenced by the unchecked power of special-interest lobbies. Their solution is to organize active and informed citizens to oppose special interests at all levels of government.

Many of the interest groups and lobbies influential in Washington are hardly "invisible." The gun lobby, labor unions, certain foreign lobbies, older persons, and others are highly visible, in some cases quite publicly attempting to unseat members of Congress who fail to support them. Nevertheless, the day-to-day means of influencing the operation of government often does occur imperceptibly, lending credence to the view that popular government is being undermined.

The question of determining whether hidden forces do exercise some control over public policy in democracies is exacerbated by secrecy in government. In theory, democratic government is "of, by, and for" the people, so nothing should be secret. The people have a right to know what is being done for them and in their name and how the money they pay in taxes is spent. In practice, however, democratic governments have legitimate need of secrecy for national security. This was especially true in the West during the Cold War, but it remained true afterward. Governments have tended to use national security as a cloak to hide many questionable policies and practices. To the extent that government is conducted in secret, it is indeed "invisible government." Citizens can only respond by pressuring governments to make public their reasons for their secrecy, using both citizen and legislative watchdogs to ensure compliance and to keep secrecy to the minimum necessary for the public good.

It should be recognized that many of the notions of "invisible government" discussed here are viewed skeptically by some students of politics. While no one can deny that significant power is exercised behind closed doors, few political scientists accept the idea that political decision making is done by an "invisible government" as suggested by Marxist writers. Similarly, few believe that it makes sense to conceive of elites as a single entity, a "power elite," whose factions are less important than its overall unity. Most Western political scientists believe that elites must be seen in the plural, not in the singular. They argue that elites, especially political, financial, and business elites, actually compete with one another, and that political elites in particular are influenced by popular demands. In this conception, power is fluid and, to a significant extent, decentralized in that it does not lie solely or principally in a single cohesive group.

Nevertheless, this critique does not drain the "invisible government" idea of all meaning. Whether or not it constitutes an "invisible government," substantial power is exercised within government bureaucracies, corporate offices and boardrooms, and elsewhere away from public sight. It should be recognized that in a free society this must always be the case, for the complete public control of such decisions is part of the very definition of tyranny. Yet it is equally true that in a free society the public consequences of those actions must be scrutinized. This is so precisely because so many individuals and organizations seek power, and, in Lord Herbert Acton's apt formulation, power tends to corrupt.

Thus, the location and character of decision-making power that has important public consequences is always of concern in a free society. Informed citizens must judge the extent to which elites act for the public interest. When elites are found to be deficient in promoting the public good, it is the place of democratic citizens to decide what corrective action, within constitutional limits, is appropriate.

Context

The study of how modern societies are composed and how this composition affects how they are governed is an important aspect of sociology and political science. In one of their roles, political scientists are concerned to locate where political power is exercised, to determine the forces that influence political decisions, to describe the process of decision making, and to determine the extent that their findings are consistent with the legal, political, and philosophical norms of society. These norms demand, at a minimum, that the exercise of power in the political process bear a close semblance to the idea of the rule of law and that processes that purport to be "democratic" be more than mere shams.

Democratic norms demand that government be open and visible to the public, unless pressing needs of national security or similar constraints force some government activities behind closed doors. Carried to any length, secrecy is abnormal in modern Western democracy. Long experience has taught democratic theorists as well as a skeptical public that power that operates behind closed doors is especially liable to be abused. The idea of an open society, which is a fundamental principle of liberal democracy, is deeply opposed to the operation of governing powers that are invisible to the public eye. Even if the operation of a government appears to be largely open, the question arises whether other, unseen, forces affect the exercise of political power and whether such forces are sinister, self-serving, or otherwise opposed to the public good. It is in this context that the subject of "invisible government" is relevant. To the extent that "invisible government" truly exists, it may undermine the moorings of a free society.

Bibliography

Chomsky, Noam. *Necessary Illusions: Thought Control in Democratic Societies.* Boston: South End Press, 1989. Typical Chomsky vision of the Western world as an evil place controlled by unaccountable and unacknowledged powers.

Dahl, Robert A. *Who Governs?* New Haven, Conn.: Yale University Press, 1961. Classic study of the government of New Haven, Connecticut, by one of America's foremost political scientists. Opposing a "power elite" idea, Dahl argues that in the beginning of the republic the three main determinants of political power—numbers, wealth, and inherited high social standing (birth)—were mainly in the hands of one group, but they are now in the hands of different groups.

Domhoff, William G. *The Power Elite and the State: How Policy Is Made in America.* New York: A. de Gruyter, 1990. Updated version of the author's 1967 work *Who Rules America?*, which defends C. Wright Mills's thesis.

Mills, C. Wright. *The Power Elite.* New York: Oxford University Press, 1956. The classic work in the field, arguing that a series of elites acts as a single entity to control U.S. policies and destiny.

Rothacher, Albrecht. *The Japanese Power Elite.* New York: St. Martin's Press, 1993. Detailed study of the two thousand most powerful people in Japan. Argues that Japan's power structure is not substantially different from other Western democracies.

Stead, William Thomas. *Satan's Invisible World Displayed; Or, Despairing Democracy.* New York: Arno Press, 1974. Reprint of a work originally published in 1897 that examines the existence of invisible government in greater New York.

Charles F. Bahmueller

Cross-References

Accountability in U.S. Government, p. 1; Capitalism, p. 197; Democracy, p. 513; Government Roles, p. 778; Interest Groups, p. 936; Intergovernmental Relations, p. 942; International Agreements, p. 949; Power in Politics, p. 1584.

IRON TRIANGLES

Field of study: Politics

Iron triangles are the relationships that develop among members of Congress, interest groups, and bureaucratic agencies on particular issues or policy areas. They provide numerous benefits for the political actors in the triangle, but may not be the best way to make policy.

Principal terms

APPROPRIATION: provision of funds for specific policy programs authorized by a bill reported out by the appropriations committees of Congress

DISTRIBUTIVE BENEFIT: reward that is shared; "something in it for everybody"

INTEREST GROUP: organized group that seeks to influence public policy

ISSUE NETWORK: web of loosely interrelated actors knowledgeable about and interested in some policy; can include government authorities, legislators, business people, lobbyists, academics, and journalists

LOBBYING: act of trying to influence governmental policy decisions or legislation

PLURALISM: theory of government that argues that numerous groups compete in the U.S. political system for widely scattered resources; public policy often results from the competition among these groups

POLITICAL ACTION COMMITTEE (PAC): special committee set up to collect and spend money for political campaigns

SUBGOVERNMENT: narrow and autonomous sets of actors that operate virtually without interference in making routine policy in a policy area

SYMBIOTIC RELATIONSHIP: relationship between two or more groups of individuals in which each partner in the relationship receives benefits from the other(s)

Overview

In attempting to describe how public policy is made, political scientists and journalists have often relied on the concept of subgovernments. The main assumption of the subgovernment model is that policy within particular issue areas is routinely made by small sets of political actors that operate virtually without interference from the president or legislators. The most typical form of subgovernment is the iron triangle.

An iron triangle can exist in any specific policy area. It consists of three sets of actors linked together by a common interest. First, there are the members of Congress who sit on the relevant committees or subcommittees. These members will eventually vote on legislation dealing with that interest. Second, there are interest groups, which perform many functions in government. Not only do they allow more people to participate in the political system, but they also provide information to members of Congress. They might give members a sense of how the public feels about a policy, or they might provide information about legislation they want in the future. The third set of actors in the triangle comes from the bureaucracy. The relevant bureaucratic agencies are important, because these agencies will implement the legislation passed by Congress.

The "iron" in the phrase "iron triangles" refers to the fact that the relationships among the three actors are strong, for several reasons. First, the relationship among the triangle's actors is symbiotic, or mutually reinforcing; each actor in the triangle gains substantial benefits from participating in the triangle. Members of Congress, for example, receive information necessary to develop their legislation from both bureaucratic agencies and interest groups. Members often rely on this information, because most policy legislation is complex and they need outside expertise. They also may receive financial support from the interest groups. Interest groups often set up political action committees (PACs) so they can give money to members of Congress for their campaigns.

The interest groups also benefit from this relationship. They need Congress to pass legislation that serves their interests. Those members of Congress who sit on the committees that service their interests are in the best position to pass that legislation. Not coincidentally, members of Congress often pick committee assignments that will meet the needs of their constituents, thus strengthening the triangle. Interest groups are also dependent on the bureaucratic agencies who will implement the legislation. For example, Congress may pass a bill that helps the trucking industry, but the legislation will be handled by the Department of Transportation.

Finally, bureaucratic agencies also benefit from the iron triangle. Once the money for policy programs has been appropriated by Congress, it is spent by the various agencies. The larger the program passed by Congress, the more that the agencies will have to administer. As a result, various departments have a stake in making sure that the projects passed by Congress are as large as possible so that they will have more to administer in the future.

The ties binding the members of an iron triangle are further strengthened by the fact that iron triangles often receive little public scrutiny. The public is often unaware that members of Congress receive information from interest groups to write their bills, nor are they aware that all members of the triangle have an incentive to continue the relationship. Public scrutiny would focus attention on that particular policy issue and possibly cut off funding or cause other drastic action. Thus, the triangle's participants usually try to keep the issue from public scrutiny.

Finally, these triangles are often made even stronger by the exchanges of personnel that take place among the triangle's actors. Former bureaucrats and congressional staffers have capitalized on their expertise by moving to the private sector to work as lobbyists. They usually receive more money as lobbyists, and their services often are highly sought after because they have worked closely with key policymakers. This is known as the "revolving door" syndrome, because the face-to-face nature of lobbying means that people are popping into and out of their familiar haunts in about as much time as it takes to go through a revolving door; only their job titles change.

The iron triangle concept is not new. In the 1950's, journalist Douglas Cater studied the sugar subgovernment and showed that an iron triangle had been created between the House Agriculture Committee, the Department of Agriculture, and various farm groups. Iron triangles also have been used to describe the acquisition of benefits for the elderly (involving the House Subcommittee on Aging, the Social Security Administration, and senior citizens' groups) and for veterans (the House and Senate veterans' committees, the Department of Veterans Affairs, and the American Legion and Veterans of Foreign Wars).

In looking at these three policy areas, the sugar industry, older persons, and veterans, one can find commonalities that explain why certain issues are more likely to become the subject of iron triangles. These issues not only had low salience, but also involved distributive policies with tangible benefits, ranging from more favorable legislation for the sugar industry to better health benefits for veterans. Iron triangles are more likely to arise in areas that involve distributive benefits, because such benefits help all members of the triangle, thus maintaining the symbiotic relationship. Members of Congress get benefits that help their constituents, interest groups get services for their members, and bureaucrats get more programs to administer.

In the late 1970's, political scientist Hugh Heclo argued that the iron triangle model did not accurately describe public policy-making. He believed that it was best described by issue networks instead. Issue networks can be defined as communications networks of those knowledgeable about policy in some area, including government authorities, legislators, lobbyists, and journalists. These networks start with the premise that as issues become more specialized, more actors need to get involved.

Issue networks differ from iron triangles in several important aspects. First, they assume that more than three actors are involved with every issue. Issue networks consider the role of the President, Washington, D.C., law firms, the media, and other actors. Health care in the 1990's has been an example of this. Not only were interest groups, members of Congress, and the bureaucracies involved, but the fate of universal health care also depended upon President Bill Clinton and First Lady Hillary Rodham Clinton, who made health care a key issue in the first year of the Clinton Administration. Other actors included the media, who covered the debate on this issue, and Washington, D.C., law firms who helped to write the legislation. The health care debate also consumed the resources of hundreds of interest groups, including the American Medical Association, the American Nurses Association, insurance groups, and several grassroots organizations.

The iron triangle may be too simplistic to describe most policy issues. It not only underestimates the number of actors, but also makes several unnecessary assumptions. It assumes, for example, that the number of actors in each leg of the triangle is relatively small, and that the actors are all focused on the same goal when making policy. A small number of actors and a unified goal would make it easier for the triangle to maintain the symbiotic relationship. In looking at numerous policy issues, however, it is clear that the number of actors has not been small nor have these actors been unified. An attempt to pass the Clean Air Act in 1990, for example, involved many interest groups, ranging from groups interested in preserving the environment, such as the Sierra Club, to those representing the industries charged with causing the pollution.

Applications

The telecommunications industry provides an interesting example of how public policy was made originally through an iron triangle, which by the 1980's had become an issue network. The bureaucratic actors and congressional actors remained the same: The bureaucracy involved was the Federal Communications Commission (FCC), responsible for regulating the industry; the primary congressional actors were the communications subcommittees of the House Committee on Energy and Commerce and the Senate Committee on Commerce, Science, and Transportation. What changed, however, was the level of interest group attention.

Prior to 1968, the telecommunications picture was relatively simple. American Telephone and Telegraph Company (AT&T) and its affiliated Bell System had a government monopoly. The monopoly was easy for AT&T to justify: It provided low-cost, reliable service to residential customers, had an extensive network for businesses, and was part of the defense communications system. Telecommunications policy was thus noncontroversial; an iron triangle was created because all three actors had a stake in maintaining the status quo and the symbiotic relationship.

The status quo began to change substantially after 1968, with a series of court decisions that challenged the monopoly held by AT&T. In 1968, other companies were allowed to produce telephones to be used on AT&T's lines. In 1969, MCI was allowed to begin long-distance service to business clients. In 1975, the U.S. Department of Justice brought suit against AT&T, charging it with running a monopoly. In the early 1980's, as a result of this suit, AT&T lost its right to own local telephone service. This service was split among eight regional companies, which were all independent of AT&T. AT&T was still allowed to continue its long-distance service, but now there would be open competition, with many new carriers able to compete against AT&T.

With these court decisions, telecommunications policy could no longer be made through a simple iron triangle. An issue network had emerged. Now, numerous actors sought to influence both Congress and the FCC. These actors included the eight new regional companies, and the long-distance companies that had entered the market, such as Sprint and MCI. This confusing array of telephone companies led to the founding of many new interest groups, such as the Organization for the Protection and Advancement of Small Telephone Companies and the National Telephone Cooperative Association. To eliminate some of this confusion, the government created more bureaucracy, adding a National Telecommunications and Information Agency within the Commerce Department to govern the new industry.

Context

Studying iron triangles raises many questions about how public policy is made: Do iron triangles allow each political actor to work freely in the political system? Do they allow members of Congress to represent their constituents? Do they allow interest groups to provide for their members? Are they the best way to make policy, or are issue networks better?

The answers to these questions are complex. With almost every iron triangle, one can see advantages and disadvantages to these relationships. There are advantages for the actors, all of whom receive benefits from participating in the triangle. Iron triangles also make it easier for participants to become experts in their respective policy areas. If members of Congress, bureaucrats, or interest groups know that they will be working in a given policy area and receiving benefits from that work, they will become specialists in their fields. Participants in the iron triangle also establish working relationships with one another, making it easier to communicate when policy changes are needed.

This symbiotic relationship among the three actors, however, may not be good for the nation as a whole, and many of these advantages can also be seen as disadvantages. First, since all actors receive benefits from the system, they have a stake in maintaining the status quo or even enlarging the program. This may not be the best public policy to follow. Iron triangles have tended to increase the rising deficit that has plagued U.S. politics since the early 1980's. Second, there is no guarantee that the public wants the services or benefits provided by the iron triangle. Since these triangles are often conducted away from public scrutiny, the public is usually unaware of the amount of information or campaign dollars being exchanged by the political actors. Iron triangles decentralize public policy-making by including more actors than the president and Congress, therefore making public policy more difficult to control.

Nor is it clear that issue networks offer more advantages. Issue networks are even more decentralized than iron triangles. Although the symbiotic relationships may be weaker because of the larger number of actors, it is almost impossible for politicians to control the overall policy with so many actors. The resulting policy is usually a compromise that accommodates the numerous actors, but which may not be the best public policy. Competing actors each receive a piece of what they want in terms of the policy, and the size of the piece is determined by the amount of their influence in the political system.

Despite these problems, both iron triangles and issue networks are expected to continue to play an important role in public policy-making. After all, both of these models are pluralism at work. Both models show that U.S. public policy is not made simply by the three branches of government, but by many other actors in the political system, including the bureaucracy, interest groups, the media, and other actors. Both also help to meet many of the goals of these political actors.

Bibliography

Adams, Gordon. *The Iron Triangle: The Politics of Defense Contracting*. New York:

Council on Economic Priorities, 1981. Detailed case study that examines the operation of iron triangles by looking at several major defense contractors and the extent to which they received contracts from Congress.

Cater, Douglass. *Power in Washington: A Critical Look at Today's Struggle to Govern in the Nation's Capitol.* New York: Vintage Books, 1964. The first book to refer to subgovernments using the iron triangle concept, looking at the sugar industry in the 1950's.

Fritschler, A. Lee. *Smoking and Politics: Policy Making and the Federal Bureaucracy.* 3d ed. Englewood Cliffs, N.J.: Prentice Hall, 1983. First published in 1969, this was one of the early attempts to apply the iron triangle concept to a specific policy area, in this case the tobacco industry.

Gais, Thomas L., Mark A. Peterson, and Jack L. Walker, Jr. "Interest Groups, Iron Triangles, and Representative Institutions." In *Mobilizing Interest Groups in America: Patrons, Professions, and Social Movements*, edited by Jack L. Walker, Jr. Ann Arbor: University of Michigan Press, 1991. One of the most often cited works on iron triangles; argues that iron triangles no longer govern policy-making, if they ever did.

Heclo, Hugh. "Issue Networks and the Executive Establishment." In *The New American Political System*, edited by Anthony King. Washington, D.C.: American Enterprise Institute, 1978. Influential work in the field of interest groups, because it was one of the first to argue that the concept of iron triangles was outdated in explaining how public policy is made by interest groups and the Congress.

McCool, Daniel. *Command of the Waters: Iron Triangles, Federal Water Development, and Indian Water.* Berkeley: University of California Press, 1987. Case study of iron triangles examining the development of water-producing plants in Indian territories.

Mahood, H. R. "Administrative Policy Making: New Relationships and Actors." In *Interest Group Politics in America: A New Intensity.* Englewood Cliffs, N.J.: Prentice Hall, 1990. As part of a good introductory text on interest groups, this chapter has a large section on iron triangles and how bureaucrats and interest groups use them to make public policy.

Jan Carol Hardt

Cross-References

Clientelism, p. 337; Commerce Regulation, p. 357; Congress, p. 412; Elitism, p. 591; Funding of Government, p. 724; Government Agencies, p. 765; Interest Groups, p. 936; Legislative Functions of Government, p. 1098; Lobbying and Lobbyists., p. 1130; Pluralism, p. 1402; Policy Development and Implementation, p. 1414; Political Action Committees, p. 1420; Public Policy, p. 1633.

IRRATIONALISM IN POLITICS

Field of study: Political philosophy

Irrationalism in politics refers principally to political messages, ideologies, loyalties, and forms of participation that reject reason in favor of a predominant or exclusive reliance on the emotions.

Principal terms

ELITISM: belief that a small class of superior persons should have the power to rule or dominate the rest of an entire society

EMOTIONALISM: behavior or belief based on abstract feelings, rather than tangible reasons

FASCISM: intensely nationalistic ideology that glorifies a corporate, authoritarian state that has the right to control every aspect of citizens' lives

IDEOLOGY: set of beliefs or attitudes concerning the proper role and form of government

McCARTHYISM: political style characterized by public hysteria over communism; named for U.S. senator Joseph R. McCarthy, whose broad public accusations that communists were infiltrating American institutions dominated American politics from 1952 until McCarthy's death in 1957

RATIONALITY: behavior based on reason or objective, rather than understanding

REASON: sound basis of an explanation or logical argument—such as hard evidence, rather than emotion or mystical belief; in a related sense, reason is also the power to think rationally

Overview

Irrationality has always been a factor in politics. Although Aristotle called man a "rational animal"—that is, an animal capable of reason—man is also an irrational one. The irrational side of human nature has never ceased playing a role in human affairs. While certain aspects of the irrational may be positive, students of politics are generally agreed that irrationalism has undesirable consequences. During the twentieth century, some of these consequences were catastrophic. Within politics, irrationalism has generally taken the form of accepting leaders whose messages and ideologies defy rationality. This defiance of reason may take the form of flatly opposing objective scientific evidence, or it may appeal to human emotions to the detriment or exclusion of rational thought and inquiry.

It is useful to compare irrationalism in politics with nonrational factors. The foundations of every modern democracy contain at least one important nonrational element. For example, democracy is predicated upon the idea that political authority ultimately derives from "the people." Who are "the people"? The answer to this question is based at least partially on the loyalty of a set of people to one another and to the polity that they mutually agree to support. Political loyalty is based in part on love of country as well as on rational calculations of interest. Loyalty contains emotional ingredients that cannot be reduced to rational ideas and principles. Common, everyday loyalty may be said to have nonrational (as well as rational) elements, while extreme forms of allegiance such as ultra-nationalism and xenophobia are more accurately described as irrational because they make claims for the state that cannot be rationally supported.

For millennia, accounts of politics have included evidence of the role of the irrational. In modern Europe, appreciation of the problem of the irrational in politics became apparent as early as the seventeenth century. In his treatise *Leviathan* (1651), the English philosopher Thomas Hobbes reacted to the violent excesses of the English Civil War by denouncing language that he considered irrational. He argued, for example, that because theological terms such as "eternal now" are meaningless, strict definitions of words and control of their use in public speech would help prevent the breakdown of authority and the advance of irrationalism.

Another English philosopher, John Locke, was similarly appalled by the role of ideological religious fervor in inducing the violence of the English Civil War. His *Essay Concerning Human Understanding* (1690) included a section on "enthusiasm." Hoping to damp down the fires of irrationalism, Locke argued that enthusiasm is not a legitimate basis for knowledge. Locke—unlike the religious zealots of his day— found knowledge difficult to obtain.

A famous instance of the outbreak of irrationalism occurred in the next century's French Revolution during the "*grande peur*" or "Great Fear" that occurred between July and August, 1789. After the razing of the Bastille in Paris and widespread attacks on the homes of the aristocracy, the French peasantry believed that counterrevolutionary soldiers were about to attack them. A mass panic spread from village to village; it encompassed some areas, while leaving others completely untouched.

No one who has witnessed modern political rallies, with their gesticulating orators and often frenzied crowds can doubt the element of irrationalism in politics. Perhaps more important, however, is irrationalism as a political doctrine and as a formula for political action.

As a political doctrine irrationalism first erupted into the political arena in twentieth century Europe in the form of fascism and then spread to other parts of the world. Perceptive observers, however, saw the roots of the politics of the irrational in nineteenth century European culture. For example, in his novel *The Brothers Karamazov* (1879), Fyodor Dostoevski sets a parable in the time of the Spanish Inquisition, when Christ returns to earth. As a threat to established authority and institutions, Christ must be killed. The Grand Inquisitor defends Christ's execution because the mass of common people are weak and need someone to whom they can submit. Unable to tolerate liberty, they place their freedom at the feet of the Church and its leaders, consumed by mystery and submission.

Before Dostoevski, the ideas of Joseph de Maistre foreshadowed the abandonment of reason in politics. Reacting to the French Revolution and its terror, de Maistre saw dogmatic faith, inflexible social hierarchy, and unbending authority as foundations of social order. Throne and altar—monarchy and church—were the twin pillars of his social edifice, which anticipated modern fascist doctrine. A supreme elitist, he rejected reason in favor of mystery and the irrational. He also demanded total submission of the individual to the state; he glorified violence and the divinity of war, with its "five or six kinds of intoxication"; and he repudiated the free expression of ideas.

Later in the century, the German philosopher Friedrich Nietzsche was among the most powerful and prescient analysts of the decadence of European culture and the coming of an age of unreason and of the unlimited tyrannies that fascist regimes represented. Europe, in Nietzsche's view, had spiritually lost its way. So much of Europe no longer believed in the traditional Christian God that Nietzsche proclaimed, "God is dead." He saw Christian values and beliefs as providing the moral foundations of social and political order that resulted in democracy—a weak system of government led by shallow men. Without competent leadership and a culture that believed in itself, Europe could become prey to degenerate political doctrines and a new class of thugs who spread political poison. Nietzsche was particularly scathing about German culture, with its anti-Semitic fringe. He regarded liberalism—as the inheritor of the Enlightenment's belief in the power of reason—as powerless to prevent Europe's eventual political ruin. Only the rise of a superior, value-creating set of cultural leaders—whom he called *"ubermenschen"* (often misleadingly translated as "super-men")—could save Europe from its fate. Adolf Hitler and Benito Mussolini were not, however, what Nietzsche had in mind.

Contributing further to the nineteenth century background to fascism were racial doctrines and anti-Semitism. Writers such as France's Joseph Gobineau and Great Britain's Houston Chamberlain popularized doctrines of Teutonic racial superiority combined with anti-Semitism and demands for "racial purity." These ideas helped form Nazi racial doctrines.

Other currents of ideas at the turn of the century such as elitism and vitalism contributed to the acceptance of political irrationalism. Among the important theorists of elitism was the Italian Vilfredo Pareto, who argued that elites inevitably rule every society. Such ruling classes have their own values, which they express in myths that cannot be proved or disproved.

"Vitalism" saw some version of the "life force" as a central philosophical category. The "life force" took precedence over reason and intellect. Vitalism and glorification of the role of myth formed an important part of the thought of French theorist Georges Sorel. In His *Reflections on Violence* (1908), Sorel championed a new dynamic working class against a waning and sterile bourgeoisie. The working class required irrational myth to achieve its historical task of making revolution. Sorel identified the myth that energized the working class as the myth of the "General Strike," which occurs when all workers simultaneously strike. Sorel's theory was influential among radical socialists, including the Italian dictator Mussolini, who was a socialist before turning to nationalism.

Applications

From an anti-intellectual cultural climate fostered by these ideas and from the European social breakdowns that followed World War I, fascism arose. Mussolini was elected to the Italian parliament in 1921; the following year, after his black-shirted followers marched on Rome, he was invited to form a cabinet. By the late-1930's, fascist governments controlled much of Europe: Poland, the Baltic republics, Romania, Spain, Germany, Italy, and elsewhere. Meanwhile, some of the democratic regimes that still survived were pressed by fascist movements. Even Britain—the bastion of democracy—had a fascist movement led by Oswald Mosley.

From its beginnings, fascism—as the incarnation of the irrational in politics—had little or no program. Its message lay in its appeal to base human instincts, especially violent aggression. Young men joined youth movements that reveled in total obedience to leaders, who encouraged them to terrorize sections of the population. Mussolini had his blackshirts; Hitler's Nazi regime had its brown shirts and its elite black-uniformed SS (*Schutzstaffel*) army troops.

Fascism focused on the glorification of the nation and its leader—Il Duce in Italy and Der Fuhrer in Germany. Nazi torchlight parades and giant rallies epitomized the fascist appeal to the irrational. Songs celebrated fervent nationalism and the bonds of the people to their leaders. The free expression of ideas was suppressed. Thought was denigrated at the expense of action. Prior to the outbreak of World War II, the pinnacle of the Nazi principle of violent action came on November 9, 1938, when Nazi thugs throughout Germany attacked Jewish shops and homes, burning, looting, and killing. The event became known as "*Kristalnacht*," or the night of breaking glass. Such action was only the prelude to a deeper and more appalling expression of the irrational, the Holocaust, in which millions of human beings were systematically rounded up and killed for reasons societies ordinarily regard as unthinkable.

Fascism's embracing of irrationalism can be usefully compared to communism. Communism also had its irrational element in the blind faith that many Soviet citizens placed in the authority of the Communist Party. In addition, the carnage of Joseph Stalin's great purges of the 1930's, in which millions of falsely accused victims lost their lives and more millions their freedom, embodies more than the irrational paranoia of a bloodthirsty dictator. Because such events required the active cooperation of thousands of accomplices, they constituted a social phenomenon of supreme irrationalism. Even when the peril of the Soviet Union became increasingly apparent on the eve of World War II, Stalin had much of the top leadership of his army destroyed.

Nevertheless, communism did differ from fascism in its attitude toward irrationalism. Communism's principal message—however questionable in itself—was that its program was based upon scientific evidence of the true nature of society, economics, and historical change. Fascism, by contrast, seldom based its claims upon scientific validity. Although Nazism advanced various pseudo-scientific theories about the racial superiority of "Aryans," the main thrust of its theory and practice lay in the blind loyalty to the leader and a mystical attachment to the nation and its destiny.

Similar political irrationalism was apparent in some of the fascist movements outside Europe. In Argentina, for example, the crowds that backed the regime of Juan Perón exhibited mass hysteria similar to Perón's European counterparts. A cult formed around his first wife Evita, a minor actress, whose fiery oratory helped ignite the popular emotionalism upon which the regime depended.

Context

Political irrationalism of a different sort occurred in the United States during the mid-1950's. Joseph R. McCarthy, a U.S. senator from Wisconsin, encouraged public fears of the influence of communists by claiming that communists infested the U.S. government (especially the State Department), institutions of higher learning, the film industry, the labor movement, and elsewhere. Public hysteria over domestic communism grew for several years, and traces lingered throughout the decade.

No widely respected political philosophy or party in the modern world openly champions irrationalism, such as the advocacy of instinctive action to the exclusion of thought. Nevertheless, outbreaks of irrationalism occur regularly in many parts of the world. In Iran, for example, the fundamentalist Islamic revolution led by the Ayatollah Khomeini was accompanied by prolonged outbursts of irrationalism. Both a political and a religious leader, the Ayatollah was virtually worshiped by multitudes stirred by frenzied adulation. When he died, enormous crowds were overcome with a delirium unknown in the West since the 1930's.

In the economically developed world, apart from the emotional enthusiasm and attachments that are part of normal political life, irrationalism in politics often takes more subtle forms. Chief among them is the use of "hidden persuaders" in political advertising calculated to play upon the fears and hopes of democratic citizens. Some of the devices used by political advertising today were analyzed in the 1930's by the Institute of Propaganda Analysis (IPA). These include such time worn methods as "glittering generality" ("man of the people"), "bandwagon" ("everyone's doing it"), and personal endorsements. To these older means of seeking to influence the emotions, new ones have been added, especially those that appeal to fear. These have been especially prominent in the United States, where negative political advertising has been most fully developed. A notorious example occurred in the 1988 presidential campaign, in which the nominee of the Democratic Party was depicted as condoning the release of murderers from jail so that they could kill again, illustrated by a released convict named Willie Horton. Playing upon the fears of viewers, the advertisement (which was quickly removed from the airwaves) was believed to be effective.

In these and other cases, irrationalism is not explicitly supported or condoned by those who seek political benefit from emotional manipulation. Since irrationalism is hidden, only those who are aware of its methods can shield themselves from its influence. Political messages that seek to take advantage of the irrational side of human nature may take the form of media advertising of party doctrine, or the form and content of political rhetoric. To the extent that they are successful, all players in the struggle for political power may be forced to adopt similar methods. Whether the citizens of modern democracies living in the age of mass electronic communication receive reliable information and rational argument or whether they are systematically manipulated through electronic and print media is a continuing problem that can only be met with rigorous civic education.

Political movements in the twentieth century have often taken on a macabre, blood-chilling aura on account of their violent and destructive tendencies or characteristics. Whole societies appear to have been overcome with self-destructive urges. Tens of millions of lives were lost on account of the aggressive policies of nations such as Nazi Germany and Soviet Russia. Cults of personality were encouraged and grew up around figures such as Hitler, Stalin, and the leader of Chinese communism, Mao Tse-tung. Otherwise rational individuals, as well as whole nations, succumbed to extreme nationalism and to a desire to lay their will and critical powers of reason before political leaders and parties claiming total power.

It is in this context that the question of irrationalism in politics has arisen in its most urgent form. If the forces of unreason—of darkness itself—can descend upon apparently advanced parts of the world, then what is to stop them from reappearing to bedevil humanity?

Bibliography

Bullock, Alan. *Hitler: A Study in Tyranny*. New York: Harper, 1952. Rigorous dissection of the German dictator's rise and fall by a much respected Oxford University historian.

Conquest, Robert. *The Great Terror*. New York: Macmillan, 1968. A distinguished British historian's work on Stalin's purges of the 1930's in the Soviet Union.

Freud, Sigmund. *Civilization and Its Discontents*. Translated by James Strackey. New York: W. W. Norton, 1961. The inventor of modern psychoanalysis discusses the results of the repression of human instinct by the forces of civilization and argues that civilization's burden may become too great.

Fromm, Erich. *Escape from Freedom*. New York: Farrar & Rinehart, 1941. Classic work that examines the characteristics of German society and the psychology that allowed Hitler and the Nazis to come to power.

Jamieson, Kathleen. *Packaging the Presidency*. New York: Oxford University Press, 1984. A leading analyst of the use of political advertising presents a history and criticism of the use of advertising to persuade the American public in presidential campaigns from 1952 to 1980, with a look at earlier campaigns.

Meisel, J. H. *Pareto and Mosca*. Englewood Cliffs, N.J.: Prentice-Hall, 1965. Collections of writings by two Italian theorists of elitism.

Nolte, Ernst. *The Three Faces of Fascism*. Translated by Leila Vennewitz. New York: Holt, Rinehart and Winston, 1965. A German historian's acclaimed analysis of fascism.

Charles F. Bahmueller

Cross-References

Communist Parties, p. 377; Conservatism, p. 419; Dictatorships, p. 546; Existentialism, p. 642; Fascism and Nazism, p. 656; Nationalism, p. 1268; Political Myths and the Philosophies of Mosca and Pareto, p. 1474; Radicalism, p. 1661; Revolutionary Governments, p. 1725.

ISLAM AND GOVERNMENT

Field of study: Religion and government

With more than a billion adherents worldwide who equal one quarter of the world's population, Islam is second only to Christianity in numbers of followers. Although one in five Muslims resides in the Middle East, Islam has emerged as a major force in world politics generally and it is the second largest religion in the United States.

Principal terms

ALLAH: Muslim name for the one God, the supreme being

KORAN (QURAN): collection of Allah's revelations to the Prophet Muhammad; the basic Islamic scripture

MUHAMMAD: Allah's messenger on earth, the last of the prophets

MUSLIM: adherent of Islam; also a synonym for Islamic

PILLARS OF ISLAM: five basic tenets governing the practice of Islam

SECULAR: relating to the nonreligious world, as a government free of direct religious influence

THEOCRACY: nonsecular government or state whose ultimate authority is God

Overview

What is the relationship between Islam and modern world governments? What distinguishes governments in Islamic societies from those in non-Islamic societies? How does Islam help shape relationships between Islamic and non-Islamic governments? What are the primary differences among governments within the Islamic world? Answers to these questions can be acquired by examining the principal characteristics of governments in Islamic societies and the effect of a modern Islamic resurgence (*tajdid*) on world societies and governments alike. But before conducting such an examination, a brief review of Islamic history is required.

The Prophet Muhammad Ibn Abdullah was born around the year 570 C.E. in Mecca, a prominent commercial center for the caravan trade in western Arabia. Long before the arrival of Islam, Mecca was also a religious center for Arabs who worshiped pagan gods and goddesses under a chief deity called Allah. The religious center at Mecca contained a shrine called the Kaaba that attracted pilgrimages annually from all over the region. A deeply religious man, Muhammad was moved by social injustices and corruption in Mecca's religious establishment. He often spent nights in meditation and prayer in the mountains near Mecca. In the year 610, on a night that Muslims commemorate as the "Night of Power and Excellence," Muhammad is believed to have received the first in a series of revelations from God through the angel Gabriel. He then preached a message of religious and social reform based on strict monotheism, belief in God's prophets, belief in the spiritual world of "the unseen," judgment day, and the hereafter.

Muhammad's first converts were from among the poor, the young, the enslaved, and his own relatives. The Meccan establishment saw his doctrine of strict monotheism as a threat to their control of the Kaaba and to the rich profits that they earned from pilgrims who visited it. They also felt that Muhammad's social prescriptions challenged the status quo.

Following the death of his wife and his uncle in 619, Muhammad retired to the town of Taif, where he hoped to find a more receptive community. However, in Taif he once again met insult and mockery and was even stoned by a mob. He returned to Mecca in despair but before reentering the city, he married another widow, Sauda, and became engaged to Aisha, a young daughter of Abu Bakr. Muslims believe that during this difficult period, God summoned Muhammad on a nocturnal journey during which the Prophet traveled from Mecca to Jerusalem and Heaven and back in a single night. While in Jerusalem, Muhammad met and prayed with Abraham, Moses, and Jesus. The instructions that Muhammad received from God during this journey confirmed his prophethood and established Jerusalem as one of Islam's three holy cities.

For some time the town of Yathrib had been torn by violent tribal conflicts. Impressed by his reputation, local tribes invited Muhammad to arbitrate in their disputes. Muhammad seized this opportunity by secretly sending two hundred followers to the town, into which he soon arrived with his father-in-law Abu Bakr. Muhammad was so enthusiastically welcomed at Yathrib that the year following 622 became the starting point for the new Muslim calendar. Muhammad's memorable flight from Mecca to Yathrib is known as the Hijra, the Arabic word for migration. Yathrib became known as the city of the Prophet: Madinat al-Nabi, or Medina for short.

The move from Mecca to Medina transformed Muhammad from a leader of a persecuted minority to a statesman, governor, and principal Arab authority. Yet conflicts continued to emerge in Medina. Consequently, Muhammad launched a series of preemptive raids on rich caravans traveling in and out of Mecca that successfully challenged the political authority and economic power of Mecca. In 630, he returned victorious to Medina, where he continued to receive revelations and to direct Muslim military campaigns. He performed his last pilgrimage to Mecca in 632; his conduct became the model for future pilgrims. He died on June 8, 632, leaving no heirs or appointed successors.

Since Muhammad's time, Islam has rested on five basic tenets, or "pillars." The first and most important of these states, "There is no god but God and Muhammad is His messenger." The second pillar is prayer (*salah*), which should be done at least five times daily. The giving of alms is the third tenet; this can be done either in the form of obligatory payments (*zakat*) or fixed taxes in money or services. Obligatory payments are traditionally collected by the state, while voluntary payments are normally collected by the community. The fourth pillar is fasting (*sawm*), which requires abstaining from food, drink, and sexual activity during daylight hours in the month of Ramadan. The final pillar is the pilgrimage, or *Hajj*, to Mecca that every physically fit Muslim must undertake at least once in a lifetime.

A primary difference between Islamic and other modern world governments is that

Islamic governments minimize and often avoid distinctions between religion and government. For Muslims, no aspect of life is devoid of religious significance because the Islamic notion of religion (*din*) is more akin to a whole way of life than it is to a set of formalized rituals assigned to particular days of the week, places of worship, or aspects of life. By contrast, a clear separation of church and state has become a fundamental feature of modern life, especially in the West. Thus Islamic government is ideally nonsecular, while most modern world governments are secular. When an Islamic government tries to base itself entirely on religious law (*sharia*), it represents what is formally known as a theocracy. Islamic theocracies differ from the European theocracies of the Middle Ages in eschewing priestly authority. Whereas authority in European theocracies derived mostly from a priestly class, authority in Islamic theocracies derives from the community (*ummah*) as a whole. It is exercised through mutual consultation (*shura*) and consensus (*ijmah*). Among Sunni Muslims, who represent 90 percent of the world's Muslims, the idea of a priestly class does not even exist. The smaller number of Shiite Muslims differ from Sunnis in giving an important role to prayer leaders (*imams*) and other religious officials.

For the vast majority of Muslims, the Islamic state ideally derives its democratic character from the authority that it receives from the community as a whole rather than from a clergy. Thus, in classical Islamic practice, there is an absence of hierarchical authority that in many ways reflects the independent spirit and culture of early bedouin Arabs. Some scholars call this form of government a "theo-democracy." The governments of Iran, Saudi Arabia, and Sudan attribute their authority directly to Allah through Islamic law (*sharia*). The notion of an Islamic government derives from several basic Islamic principles, the most important of which is the belief in the unity and sovereignty of Allah (*tawhid*). This belief provides the foundation for the Islamic social and moral system and shapes the relationships between Islamic governments and what Westerners would call their subjects. However, the Islamic principle of *tawhid* rejects Western notions of basic distinctions between "rulers" and "subjects" or between "church" and "state." Indeed, the Koran clearly states that "all authority belongs to God alone."

Islam's distinctive philosophy and values have produced a dramatic impact on the character of government in predominantly Islamic societies. Islamic governments have several dominant characteristics. The first of these is the principle that no person, class, or group—not even the population of the state as a whole—can lay claim to sovereignty; God alone is the sovereign and all others are His subjects. A second principle is that because God is the true law-giver, absolute authority rests with Him alone. Muslims thus can neither enact totally independent legislation nor modify God's laws, even by unanimous consent. Finally, an Islamic state must in all respects be founded on God's law, as revealed by his prophets. If an Islamic government disregards God's law, it forfeits its moral authority to govern. As the chief agency responsible for enforcing God's laws, an Islamic government is also entitled to obedience. Indeed, the Prophet Muhammad reportedly said, "Listen and obey even if a negro is appointed as a ruler over you."

A modern resurgence in Islam seeks to re-establish the true foundation of democracy in Islam which the Prophet Muhmmad articulated in the statement "Everyone of you is a ruler and everyone is answerable for his subjects." Also two fundamental points emerge from the Islamic theory of the state. Islam uses the term "viceregency" (*Khilafa*) rather than sovereignty, and the power to rule over the earth is promised to the whole community of Muslim believers. Finally, liberal Muslim thinkers believe that the structure of Islamic legislation rests on the twin pillars of personal judgment (*ijtihad*) and collective thought (*ijma*). However, conservative Muslim thinkers who assign a greater significance to the authority of religious scholars (*ulema*) afford considerably less legitimacy to the value of personal judgment (*ijtihad*) in matters related to Islamic legislation.

Throughout history, Islamic leaders who have been accused of wandering astray from Islamic principles have been targets of retaliation by injured parties. Indeed, three of the four immediate successors to the Prophet Muhammad—the caliphs Umar, Uthman, and Ali—were killed by assassins. Abu Bakr, the Prophet's immediate successor, escaped assassination; however, his brief reign planted the seeds of the basic Sunni-Shia sectarian split among Muslims that has lasted for fourteen centuries.

While the Sunni-Shia division is perhaps the most conspicuous reflection of differences between Muslims and their governments, other factors, such as history and political experiences, have produced differences. For example, Muslim/non-Muslim conflict in Malaysia, Mauritania, Nigeria, and Sudan has produced more restrictive government policies affecting religious minorities than in countries such as Jordan, Senegal, and Morocco where Muslim/non-Muslim conflict has been less acute.

While religion represents the central organizing principle in these Islamic theocracies, their strong and often uncompromising stance on international political issues frequently places them in direct conflict with most other governments of the world. In addition to being associated with human rights violations, state-sponsored terrorism, and religious—as opposed to secular—perceptions of world events, these states have been principal combatants in conflicts in Afghanistan, Europe, and the Middle East.

Applications

By the late nineteenth century, most of the world's Islamic peoples were under the rule of either Turkey's Ottoman Empire or European colonial powers. The removal of alien rule began with the raising of Islamic consciousness. Afghan journalist and political activist Jamal ad-Din al-Afghani (1838-1897) is widely regarded as the father of modern Pan-Islamic political movements. He tirelessly agitated against European colonialism in the Islamic world and became a focus for Muslim radicals and nationalists throughout the Islamic world. After World War I saw the dismantling of the Ottoman Empire, most of Turkey's former Middle Eastern territories underwent periods of transitional rule under European protectorates mandated by the League of Nations. By the end of World War II, most of the Islamic countries of North Africa, the Middle East, and South Asia were completely free of alien rule. The following decades saw the political liberation of many additional Islamic societies in sub-Saharan Africa.

Most governments in predominantly Islamic societies—such as Afghanistan, Egypt, Indonesia, Jordan, Malaysia, Mauritania, Morocco, Pakistan, and Senegal—are not theocracies in the strict sense. Nevertheless, their laws and policies are influenced by Islamic principles and practices. Even Arab nationalist governments—such as those in Libya, Iraq, and Syria—incorporate Islamic principles and practices to reinforce the political legitimacy of their authority. Such efforts generally fail, however, to conceal the fact that many such governments—especially in Africa and the Middle East—lack popular support because they do not govern democratically, raise living standards, or control government corruption.

An Arab proverb states that there is nothing more pious than a ruler who seeks to serve a holy man, nor is there anything more despicable than a holy man who seeks to serve a ruler. The governments of many Islamic countries—notably Morocco, Iraq, and Egypt—often use religious leaders as their apologists. This practice is resented by Islamic purists, giving rise to what has been called "fundamentalist" opposition. The strongly entrenched positions of authoritarian Islamic governments leave opposition groups limited opportunities for expression.

Context

Neither political independence nor increased revenues from petroleum sales in the 1970's has enabled most Muslims to escape economic underdevelopment, political weakness, and cultural-spiritual decline. In response to this predicament, an upsurge in Islamic activism and revival (*tajdid*) has emerged since the 1970's. The popular media use the term "fundamentalists" to denote Muslim activists. Yet the term fundamentalism is misleading since it implies a retreat to the past and the adoption of literal interpretations of religious scripture by individuals of limited educational ability with limited ties to the modern world. Contrary to this image, Muslim activists reflect a variety of educational and social backgrounds and embrace Islamic values and principles as a positive alternative for addressing contemporary Muslim problems rather than as a retreat from modernity.

In the post-colonial era, many Muslims have strongly opposed what they see as the illegitimate authority of their secular governments. The numerous episodes of Muslim opposition to illegitimate authority include the Islamic Brotherhood's opposition to the socialist government of Gamal Abdel Nasser in Egypt during the 1960's, the overthrow of the Shah of Iran in 1979, the assassination of former president Anwar el-Sadat of Egypt by members of the radical Islamic Jihad movement in 1981, Mujahideen opposition to Soviet occupation of Afghanistan in the 1980's, opposition to Yasir Arafat by the Palestinian Islamic group Hamas in 1994, and the Chechnyan Muslim revolt against Russian authority in 1994.

The idea of an Islamic state is as old as Islam itself. Indeed, the first examples of an Islamic state can be traced to the life of the Prophet Muhammad and to the early years of Islam following his death in 632 C.E. Efforts since the late 1970's to establish an Islamic state reflect an Islamic revival aimed at purifying Muslim practices and addressing major political, economic, and spiritual challenges facing modern Muslims.

A primary thrust of the modern Islamic revival can be traced to the overthrow of the shah of Iran and the subsequent emergence of an Islamic state there in 1979. Since that time, numerous events underscore the role of Islam as a major world force. For example, Islamic influence has measured prominently in the Arab-Israeli dispute since 1948, as well as in the defeat of former Soviet forces by Afghan rebels in 1989, and the rise in Muslim terrorism since the 1970's.

These events have led some to view Islam as the new primary threat to international peace and stability. The tendency to view Islam and Muslims as a monolithic and menacing threat underscores the need for a greater understanding of Islam and its true impact on the governments and politics of the Islamic and non-Islamic worlds.

Bibliography

Barboza, Steven, ed. *American Jihad*. New York: Doubleday, 1993. The first comprehensive and popular guide to the Islamic faith as practiced in the United States.

Donohue, John J., and John L. Esposito, eds. *Islam in Transition: Muslim Perspectives*. New York: Oxford University Press, 1982. Valuable collection of essays, including a first-hand discussion of Islamic government by the leader of Iran's Islamic revolution, the Ayatollah Khomeini. Other selections include an essay on the political theory of Islam by Abdul-Ala Mawdudi, a Pakistani Islamic activist, and Fazlur Rahman's essay on the Islamic concept of state.

Esposito, John L. *The Islamic Threat*. New York: Oxford University Press, 1992. Excellent overview of the role of Islam and government by one of the most prolific writers in the field.

Moyser, George, ed. *Politics and Religion in the Modern World*. New York: Routledge, 1991. Contains an important essay on Islam in Egypt and Iran by Glenn E. Perry.

Rahman, Fazlur. *Islam*. 2d ed. Chicago: University of Chicago Press, 1979. Detailed overview of Islam for advanced readers.

Sabini, John. *Islam: A Primer*. Rev. ed. Washington, D.C.: Middle East Editorial Associates, 1990. Clear and concise account of the religion and civilization of Islam.

Samory Rashid

Cross-References

Autocracy and Absolutism, p. 127; Church and Government in History, p. 230; Comparative Government, p. 384; Geopolitics, p. 759; Hinduism and Government, p. 823; International Relations, p. 969; Legitimacy, p. 1105; Modern Monarchy, p. 1209; Nomadic Peoples' Governments, p. 1306; Religion and Politics, p. 1685; Revolutionary Governments, p. 1725; Terrorism, p. 1962; Theocracy, p. 1968.

ISOLATIONISM AND PROTECTIONISM

Field of study: Political philosophy

Isolationism is a belief that a country should minimize its involvement in the affairs of other countries and in disputes between countries. Protectionism seeks to promote a country's domestic industries and economic base through trade barriers. Both philosophies are rooted in a commitment to state interests.

Principal terms

AUTARKY: policy of minimizing a country's dependence on other countries for security, trade, and important resources

AUTONOMY: ability of a state to be independent in the making and implementation of policies, especially those that apply to the domestic arena

BALANCE OF TRADE: difference between the amount of money a country receives through exports and the amount it spends on imports

MERCANTILISM: policy of governmental intervention to promote exports and discourage imports, so as to increase the country's wealth

MONROE DOCTRINE: U.S. policy of opposing European intervention in the Western Hemisphere that was articulated by James Monroe

TRADE BARRIER: obstacle (such as a tariff or quota) to the free movement of goods and services across state boundaries

ZERO-SUM GAME: situation in which a gain for one country (in terms of wealth or power) derives from a corresponding loss by another country

Overview

Protectionism and isolationism are doctrines concerned with maintaining or augmenting the power of the state in a perilous international environment. Both place state interests above the interests of the international community as a whole. Both view foreign policy as an appropriate and effective tool for promoting state interests. Both view the interests of foreign countries without compassion and their motives with suspicion. While isolationism and protectionism focus upon different aspects of state interests, many of those who subscribe to one of these doctrines tend to sympathize also with the other.

Isolationism posits that a state's interests are best served by isolating it from the vicissitudes of the larger world. A conservative doctrine, it counsels against reliance on other states for security (as through alliances), against intervention in foreign conflicts, against offering foreign aid to needy countries (especially if no direct national interest is apparent), against taking part in international ideological movements, against participation in global institutions, and against joining international legal frameworks. In short, isolationism values the fullest expression of autonomy as the prerogative of sovereign nations. It is not only the right, but also the duty of government leaders to direct their efforts primarily to the promotion of their own country's interests.

Isolationism is concerned with a broad range of state interests, including autonomy and security. Protectionism is more focused on economic and trade interests. In simple terms, protectionism advocates the use of law to protect domestic industries from foreign competition. Protectionism, unlike isolationism, is defined by the actions it advocates rather than by the actions it remonstrates against. The most common tools employed by protectionist governments are tariffs (which place a surcharge on imports to make their prices less competitive with domestic products) and quotas (which limit the number of imports from a particular country). Quotas are one kind of nontariff barrier. Other nontariff barriers include more subtle (but not necessarily less effective) mechanisms such as performance standards and content requirements.

Protectionism takes its ideological heritage from mercantilism, a doctrine that was especially popular in the sixteenth and seventeenth centuries. Mercantilism held that a country's wealth and power could be increased through international trade if the government would actively and aggressively intervene to promote exports and limit imports. This classical mercantilism was especially concerned with amassing gold reserves through state-directed trade. Mercantilism viewed international trade as a zero-sum game, in which states competed over a finite quantity of power and gold. Such a conception of international trade logically led to trade wars, which sometimes led to military wars. As commerce increased considerably in the late eighteenth and early nineteenth centuries, the more combative aspects of mercantilism weakened. A more nuanced neomercantilism, which gained popularity in the 1930's, however, often is blamed as a major factor contributing to World War II.

Mercantilism and neomercantilism were largely discredited after World War II, and most countries in the capitalist world vocally supported free trade as a healthy alternative to protectionism. Yet in the postwar era protectionist sentiment has continued to rise whenever countries experience domestic economic difficulties—and particularly when they are experiencing a negative balance of trade (more money being spent on imports than is received through exports). As did mercantilism, protectionism continues to view the international economic system as a zero-sum game. Money that goes out of the country for the purchase of imports is considered lost, and therefore trade is discouraged if it involves a negative balance. Protectionism rejects the liberal argument that trade increases the overall quantity of goods and services produced in the global economy, and hence that absolute gains can be had by all participants.

Placing national interests above global interests, isolationism and protection are imbued with nationalism, and in their more extreme variants extend to chauvinism and even xenophobia. If their normative assumptions about the relative priority of state interests is accepted, isolationism and protectionism are open to criticism that they are ultimately self-defeating. It has not been firmly established that isolationism truly increases a state's security or that protectionism truly increases a state's wealth.

Applications

The United States has been characterized as a traditionally isolationist country. When President George Washington delivered his farewell address, he approvingly embraced America's "detached and distant situation" and urged his country to remain isolated from "the toils of European ambition, rivalship, interest, humor, or caprice." Washington spoke for many Americans in suggesting that his country was exceptional, essentially above the petty conflicts and amoral diplomacy that characterized European politics. Protected by two broad oceans and blessed with militarily weak neighbors, the United States could afford to be isolationist. Isolationism was more explicitly stated as official U.S. policy by President James Monroe in 1823, when he declared that the United States would remain uninvolved in European affairs, and that the United States in turn expected that Europe would not intervene in America's sphere of influence, which he defined as the North and South American continents. The United States continued to engage itself in foreign affairs in Latin America and the Caribbean (areas viewed as within America's sphere of influence), and it did generally avoid direct intervention in European affairs.

Eventually the United States became directly, militarily involved in Europe during the two world wars. Isolationist sentiment had not disappeared, however; the U.S. Congress initially was hesitant to intervene in those two wars. After the conclusion of World War I, the Congress rejected the Versailles Treaty and with it American participation in the newly established League of Nations. It was only after the defeat of Nazi Germany and imperial Japan in 1945 that the United States chose to remain engaged in world affairs as a matter of long-term policy—with the purpose of containing Soviet-sponsored communism. Some have suggested that America suffered from a "Munich syndrome," in which the country blamed World War II on the fact that Germany was not stopped from annexing part of Czechoslovakia in 1938, but rather was appeased at the Munich conference of that year. The Munich syndrome motivated America thenceforth to check aggression in its early stages, before it expanded into another world war. Such a task was incompatible with isolationism.

During the post-World War II period, the United States not only deviated from its isolationist tradition but also rose to become a hegemonic power with military and economic alliances that drew in countries from around the world. Over the next several decades the country actively projected its military power into the Middle East, Korea, Cuba, and most notoriously, Vietnam. It was the long, costly, and ultimately lost war in Vietnam that renewed isolationist sentiment in the United States.

After the American withdrawal from Vietnam in the mid-1970's, it became popular to replace the notion of a Munich syndrome with a "Vietnam syndrome," which counseled against intervention in conflicts from which it would be difficult for America to extricate itself or to achieve victory. Isolationism was back in the American psyche.

It was the collapse of communism in the Soviet Union and Eastern Europe at the end of the 1980's, however, that most strongly revitalized America's traditional isolationist sentiment. With the task of containment arguably completed, and with no major external threats to the United States perceived by the public, America's domestic concerns and problems became highlighted. Crime, racial conflict, homelessness, acquired immune deficiency syndrome (AIDS), unemployment, underemployment, and various other concerns came to occupy the public consciousness. Many saw the first post-Cold War presidential election in 1992 as a referendum on the relative importance of foreign policy—the bailiwick of President George Bush—versus domestic policy—upon which Democratic nominee Bill Clinton focused his campaign. Clinton won.

With the election of Clinton, it seemed that America would be able to redirect the enormous energies it had used as a global power during the Cold War to the work of improving America's domestic situation. Yet the end of the Cold War resulted not only in a virtual elimination of the Soviet threat facing the United States, but also numerous civil wars and border conflicts among peoples whose disputes largely had been contained by the bipolar order. The early post-Cold War period was defined by wars within and among the various parts of what had been the Soviet bloc, wars in the Middle East, and wars in Africa. America was not eager to address those conflicts. It preferred to look to Europe, Russia, Africa, and the Middle East to contain their own regional disputes. President Clinton engaged his country at a limited level in several of those conflicts, and by and large American public opinion wanted the rest of the world to take care of itself.

Protectionist and isolationist sentiments in the United States have tended to rise and fall in tandem. America's isolationist sentiment, for example, was doctrinally rejected by 1947's Truman Doctrine of militarily defending democratic countries, and its policy of protectionism was rejected in the Marshall Plan of the same year, whereby America sought to subsidize West European economies in order to promote mutually beneficial trade. American isolationism after World War II was discarded in the act of forming the North Atlantic Treaty Organization, the United Nations, and other organizations, while American protectionism was institutionally locked out by the General Agreement on Tariffs and Trade (GATT), an American-sponsored initiative designed to promote free trade throughout the capitalist world. Both the Marshall Plan and the GATT were largely successful; Western Europe rapidly recovered from its wartime devastation, and over the next five decades GATT succeeded in increasing international trade one hundredfold.

For much of the postwar period America enjoyed increasing prosperity and, despite the tensions of the Cold War, military security at home. The benefits of America's engagement abroad dampened America's traditional enthusiasm for isolationism and protectionism. Yet again, as America's economic fortunes turned for the worse in the mid-1970's, and again in the 1980's, America's commitment to free trade began to weaken. The country's backtracking toward isolationism was accompanied by a movement away from free trade. "Protectionism" had become something of a bad word during the heyday of GATT, the Marshall Plan, and other liberal economic institutions, so opponents of American free trade in the 1980's avoided the term. Instead they advocated fair trade as an alternative to free trade.

Japan, enjoying a large balance-of-trade surplus with the United States, and Western Europe, whose common market was perceived as an adversarial economic bloc, were singled out as especially egregious offenders. With its isolationist sentiment, America's sympathy for protectionism rose as the Cold War waned. Many Americans believed that Western Europe, Japan, and other regions had grown prosperous under America's benevolent aid during the Cold War, and now they were ungratefully engaged in unfair trade practices against the United States.

As the Cold War gave way to a new international system in the 1990's, American public sentiment and American foreign policy were returning to isolationism and protectionism. America became involved in heated trade disputes with its postwar allies. Fervent opposition arose in the Congress to presidential deployment of troops abroad, to a new GATT treaty, and to a North American Free Trade Agreement treaty (which nevertheless narrowly passed). Foreign aid and immigration quotas were substantially cut. America's adherence to liberal globalism appeared to be ending.

Context

Isolationism's and protectionism's historical roots go back centuries. The periodic reemergence of both in various countries can be attributed to a variety of factors, including domestic economic conditions and the ideological disposition of governmental leaders. External conditions also have a tremendous effect on a country's international orientation, and global developments in recent decades would seem to discourage isolationism and protectionism. The increasing interdependence of countries in the modern global economy, as well as the rising importance of transnational issues such as terrorism, overpopulation, and nuclear weapons, would suggest that the zero-sum game assumptions of isolationism and protectionism no longer add up. Yet the post-Cold War era seemed to be witnessing a renewed popularity of these doctrines, especially in the United States, Russia, and certain parts of France and Germany. It seemed unlikely that international relations would descend to 1930's-style trade wars, or that the world's national governments would retreat entirely into isolation. The post-Cold War years did, however, provide considerable reason not to anticipate the early fulfillment of the visions held by the more optimistic architects of the United Nations and the GATT.

Instead, it was thought that countries would continue to vacillate between isolationism and engagement, and between protectionism and free trade. Not all states have the wherewithal to play a significant role in international affairs; only relatively powerful states can properly be thought to have the option of interventionism. Isolationism, however, is not merely the absence of intervention, but rather an unwillingness to become engaged in any significant way with the outside world. Isolationism is the fulfillment of a wish to ignore the outside world, and to be removed from its corroding effects. Protectionism similarly tries to guard against the invidious economic policies of foreign states. Both doctrines often can seem attractive short-term options, whatever their ultimate effect on the long-term interests of the state.

Bibliography

Cole, Wayne S. *Roosevelt and the Isolationists, 1932-45.* Lincoln: University of Nebraska Press, 1983. Assesses America's transition during the Roosevelt years from traditional isolationism to full-scale engagement abroad.

Doenecke, Justus D. *Not to the Swift: The Old Isolationists in the Cold War Era.* Cranbury, N.J.: Bucknell University Press, 1979. Takes a balanced view of modern isolationist doctrine, particularly that developed during the early Cold War period. Focuses on the Truman Doctrine, NATO, the rise of communism in China, Korea, McCarthyism, and Eisenhower's firm commitment to interventionism.

Hufbauer, Gary Clyde. *The Free Trade Debate: Reports of the Twentieth Century Fund Task Force on the Future of American Trade Policy.* New York: Priority Press, 1989. Attempts to clarify the debate between free trade and protectionism (or managed trade), by presenting articles on both sides of the debate.

Lawrence, Robert Z., and Charles L. Schultze, eds. *An American Trade Strategy: Options for the 1990's.* Washington, D.C.: Brookings Institution, 1990. Papers presented at a conference focused on alternative trade strategies for the United States, including free trade, "aggressive bilateralism," and "managed trade" (protectionism). Includes thorough evaluation and summary of the issue of free trade versus protectionism in general.

Ray, Edward John. *U.S. Protectionism and the World Debt Crisis.* New York: Quorum Books, 1989. General discussion of protectionism in the United States and its contribution to the world debt problem.

Steve D. Boilard

Cross-References

JOHN OF SALISBURY'S POLITICAL PHILOSOPHY

Field of study: Political philosophy

John of Salisbury's Policraticus *(1159 C.E.) is the first major work written in the Middle Ages on political philosophy and government. John's prescriptions for governing and being governed are a mirror of his age and provide an alternative and thought-provoking view of some perennial issues of governance.*

Principal terms

COMMONWEALTH: the state, understood not in the modern sense, but as a vague term that John applied to such radically different places as England and Brittany

HUMANIST: in the twelfth century, one steeped in such classical thought and literature as was then available

MIDDLE AGES: a period in European history, often dated from the deposition of the last western Roman Emperor in 476 C.E. to the conquest of Constantinople in 1453 C.E.

TYRANT: ruler who does not govern in accord with the universal law that John considered to govern all peoples

Overview

John of Salisbury's *Policraticus* (written between 1156 and 1159 C.E.) captures the spirit of its age and is an important document for understanding later developments. It presents views on the nature of the commonwealth (or state); the responsibilities of the ruler; the proper relations between those in the commonwealth; the rule of law; tyranny and corruption; and tyrannicide and other remedies for abuse of power. It is a work of political theory, a moral commentary on royal aides and administrators, a how-to book on governing, a hodgepodge of sermonizing, and an amazing feat of philosophy and learning.

John of Salisbury (c. 1115-1180) was a medieval churchman and a member of the community of scholars that flourished in Western Europe at that time. Born between 1115 and 1120 in Old Sarum (Salisbury) in southern England, John studied in Paris and Chartres under the leading scholars of the time. Deeply involved in the practical affairs of church and state, he was confidential secretary to Archbishop Theobald of Canterbury, and made many journeys to France and Italy. John wrote that he trifled away twelve years in administrative affairs. John was well acquainted with Cardinal Nicholas Brakespear, who became Pope Adrian IV. He also was an intimate counselor and the secretary to Thomas Beckett, an archbishop and the primate of England, who was murdered in 1170 on the steps of Canterbury Cathedral by four knights at the instigation of King Henry II. John dedicated *Policraticus* and other books to then-chancellor Beckett; it is likely that John influenced Beckett's switch, against the king's interests, to the policy of defending ecclesiastical liberties and privileges, and probable that John dined with Thomas on the evening before the latter's martyrdom. John was largely instrumental in advancing the cause for Thomas Beckett's canonization as a saint. John died in 1180 while serving as Bishop of Chartres.

The spirit of *Policraticus* is medieval, in that John and his audience take it as a given of their reasoning that temporal matters are purely preliminary; this world is an anteroom. Political activity for a medieval churchman had the goal of facilitating the search for eternal bliss in the next life. Political and moral commentary could not be divorced, and the primary relationship was that between the person and the divine will. Recognizing these assumptions is essential to understanding the political prescriptions of *Policraticus*.

At the center of John's political philosophy is his view that the higher law, the precepts of rational nature, and the will of God are the same. This equivalence is convenient, because it meets the problem of how to interpret the equity that makes up the higher law. In John's view, all people and all relationships are governed by a higher law that exists independently of any human laws. The higher law goes further than later international law in that it is directly binding, not merely on sovereign powers, but on all persons. John equates this higher law largely with scriptural commandments and prohibitions. The substance of the Golden Rule (although neither John nor anyone else before the modern era used this name) in both its negative and positive forms is described as binding on all peoples: "What thou wouldst not should be done unto thee, do thou not unto another" and "what thou wouldst should be done unto thee, do that unto others." The *Policraticus* also makes liberal use of Deuteronomy. John valued Roman law because he saw that as representing the divine law and as rational.

John offers an organic analogy for the commonwealth or state, comparing it to the living human body. This idea was used by others in John's time and was a natural idea for churchmen imbued with the notion of Christians constituting the Body of Christ. It should not be confused with an evolutionary view of the body politic; it was static. The state was not a politically organized community; that concept did not exist in the twelfth century. It also is doubtful that John intended to present a completely organic theory. The *Policraticus* explains that the prince is the head; the priests are the soul; judges and provincial governors are the eyes, ears, and tongue; officials and soldiers are the hands; financial officers are the stomach and intestines; and the husbandmen are the feet. Several principles have been recognized as following from this. The commonwealth is naturally hierarchical, and there is nothing voluntary in its makeup. Each member is mutually interdependent. Because this body is governed by the higher law, members or constituent parts should recognize their respective appropriate places. The organic analogy can be read as acknowledging the worth of the lowest element, the husbandmen who constitute the feet. John, however, was not speaking of an organic society of individuals so much as of ranks and elements that were, he thought, divinely established.

The prince is a given in the *Policraticus*. John lived at a time when both king and pope wished to expand their powers, and there was a managerial revolution in government. The medieval prince needed a larger governmental machinery to discharge the increasingly activist role that circumstances imposed on him. John preferred the biblical arrangement of governance through prophets and believed that kingship resulted from the activities of what he and others considered the fallen nature of human beings. That was not a real issue in *Policraticus*, however, and John did not discuss the relative advantages of the alternative forms of government. John was a practical person, even though *Policraticus* exhibits a detached quality. As the martyrdom of his archbishop, Thomas Beckett, at the prompting, intentional or not, of King Henry II would later attest, it was appropriate to be careful. Thus, John offers his organic analogy not as his own, but claims that he is paraphrasing Plutarch's "The Instruction of Trajan." This was a document that probably never existed, but it provided him with a cover. Even so, the king was annoyed, and John later was exiled.

John asserted that the prince was the image of God; like other offices in the commonwealth, the prince's was a religious office. *Policraticus* also contains such notions as the king as representative of the commonwealth and as servant of the people. The prince is not responsible to the commonwealth; the relationship between prince and commonwealth is like that between guardian and ward. This patriarchal-ecclesiastical conception of monarchy lasted through the sixteenth century.

Although the powers of the prince come from God, they are not absolute. The prince is obligated to follow the higher law. In a sense, he is to shepherd, but not rule; the commonwealth is ruled, where ruling is understood in a strong sense, by God. The prince must protect and ensure that every office is performed appropriately. The prince also is obligated to acknowledge the authority of the priestly element, treating it as the head should regard the soul. The church and the state are agents for the administration of the same higher law, and the spiritual should not be judged by the temporal component. Also limiting the power of the prince is the conception of freedom of speech that John advocates. Further, heredity gives no more than a presumption of succession to the prince's heir; good stewardship is also required.

Applications

The main objective of *Policraticus* was to find ways by which those in authority could be persuaded to promote the public welfare. The best way was to persuade princes and others in authority to respect the higher law. The prince is, according to John, responsible for ascertaining and applying the higher law; thus, he should be a reader or willing to listen to those who know about the higher law. The prince should respect the primacy of the priestly authority, which could assist him in ascertaining higher law. The *Policraticus* is the work of a preacher, using Christian and classical examples intended to persuade the prince to reign appropriately. The majority of the text consists of illustrative and exhortative examples of people and events that supported John's aim of encouraging good government; the examples were moral tales.

Tyrannicide is presented as a method for correcting corrupt and inappropriate behavior in rulers and as an option open to individual community members rather than being limited to collective action. The prince who does not follow the higher law is, in John's view, not a prince at all; he is a tyrant. John intended that this description of a tyrant should not be limited to the monarch, but to anyone in a power position, whether in the state, church, or even in the family. It is appropriate for tyrants to be killed subject to specified exceptions: Tyrannicide is not to be undertaken if the slayer is bound by fealty to the tyrant or if the slaying would sacrifice honor and justice. Also, poisoning is not allowed.

This view of tyrannicide is open to various interpretations. Some point to supposed contradictions in John's account; certainly it is problematic for those with an organic view to encourage opposition to the head. John pointed out that tyranny may be God's method of dealing with poor human behavior. Thus, prayer is a recommended response from abused members of the commonwealth. God might choose either to change the tyrant's mind or to strike the tyrant down. The encouragement to both the direct action of tyrannicide and the indirect action of prayer can be seen as contraries. To explain such apparent contradictions, some critics have noted that John's thinking developed over time.

The medieval view raises issues for contemporary thinking. On the negative side, much in *Policraticus* is irrelevant in the twentieth century. For example, *Policraticus* raises the issue of the importance of emphasizing the virtues of personal morality, but John did not recognize and understand the complementary importance of designing systems for curbing the abuses of power. On the positive side, there is John's notion of not limiting our understanding of tyranny to the political sphere. In modern times, those concerned with democracy in the political sphere are often insensitive to tyranny in the private or economic sphere. As another example, John saw an intimate relationship existing among the metaphysical, the moral, and the political spheres. Separating the issues of politics and ethics would have seemed wrongheaded to John. He would have rejected the atomization of living, where the moral can be seen as separated from the economic, for example. He would have rejected value-free social science and resisted the accelerating specialization of disciplines. He believed that human beings live their lives holistically.

Context

John's views reflected the thinking of the medieval world and of John's particular time. His views on the nature of law, the commonwealth, and the source of princely authority followed well-established and general medieval thinking. For example, John's view of the law was typical for his times. Other contemporaneous thinkers, such as Gratian, a canon lawyer who wrote the *Decretum* circa 1148, identified the natural law with scriptural injunctions. John and his contemporaries saw law largely as a matter of discovery, rather than invention; making laws was seen as a function of judges rather than legislators. His view of the higher law can be traced from earlier natural law thinkers, such as the stoic Cicero (106-43 B.C.E.), and was a widely accepted view among churchmen. John of Salisbury was substantively original only at the margins, for example, in his view on tyrannicide, a doctrine that thinkers such as Thomas Aquinas later rejected. His originality lies primarily in the comprehensive character and the style of his presentation. Unlike most medievals, John was alive in his writings: *Policraticus*, while rambling, projects the verve of life.

John lived at a time before the reintroduction of Aristotle, but during which humanism flourished. John's *Policraticus* was the only book of its type written before the reintroduction of Aristotle upgraded Western medieval scholarship. Aristotle's major works were unknown in Western Europe until well after John's death, when they entered from the Islamic world through Spain, and from the Eastern Empire. Aristotle's *Politics* was translated from the Greek in 1260, approximately a century after the completion of *Policraticus*. If John had known this work, he might have included a discussion of the relative advantages of various forms of government.

The Middle Ages was not a long prairie of sameness. There were radical differences between subepochs, such as the differences between the Dark Ages and the High Middle Ages. The twelfth century is often described as a time of renaissance, a precursor to the later and more celebrated Renaissance that started in Italy. John was a leading example of a twelfth century humanist, finding his source of intellectual and other energy in classical thinking and scholarship. John's chatty writing abounds with examples not only from the biblical and Christian tradition, but also from the Romans and the Greeks. In the *Metalogicon*, John describes the debt of his contemporaries to the classical thinkers, the former being like dwarfs seeing far because they rest on the shoulders of giants.

In later years, the views John advanced were further refined. For example, the articulation of the natural law and the relationship of the various types of law was given more precision by later thinkers such as Thomas Aquinas, the thirteenth century Dominican philosopher and theologian. John did not have access to many of the concepts that became available to later thinkers. For example, he held that the community could act only through the prince. In a sense, the understanding that the prince alone should control the governmental machinery was an advance over feudal thinking; it was one that can be found even more clearly in Henry de Bracton, a judge and compiler of English law (d. 1268). The organic analogy was developed further in writers such as Nicholas of Cusa (1401-1464). Some of John's ideas may be seen unfairly as leading to unfortunate developments. For example, the patriarchal theory of monarchy has been connected to seventeenth century personal absolutism, and the idea of the ruler's authority emanating from God has been characterized as foreshadowing the divine right of kings. John's views also had a direct impact on later politics; for example, his views on the commonwealth and on tyrannicide influenced the thirteenth century English barons in their opposition to King Henry III.

Bibliography

Dickinson, John, trans. *The Statesman's Book of John of Salisbury*. New York: Russell and Russell, 1963. This contains a translation of the most important parts of John of Salisbury's *Policraticus*, and these parts are the fourth, fifth, and sixth books and parts of the seventh and eighth books. Dickinson's introduction is very useful and readable. A full Latin version was edited by Clemens C. I. Webb (New York: Arno Press, 1979).

Liebeschutz, Hans. *Medieval Humanism in the Life and Writings of John of Salisbury.* Nendeln, The Netherlands: Kraus-Thomson Organization, 1980. This book, while not especially well written, is very informative.

McGarry, Daniel D., trans. *The Metalogicon of John of Salisbury.* Berkeley: University of California Press, 1955. This later work, containing references to the *Policraticus,* provides a good picture of the life, of the circumstances, and of more of the ideas of John of Salisbury. The edition contains an excellent bibliography.

Millor, W. J., H. E. Butler, and C. N. L. Brooke. *The Early Letters (1153-1161).* Vol. 1 in *The Letters of John of Salisbury.* London: Thomas Nelson and Sons, 1955. The letters give a valuable portrait of John of Salisbury up to shortly after completion of *Policraticus.*

Nederman, Cary J., trans. *Policraticus: Of the Frivolities of Courtiers and the Footprints of Philosophers.* New York: Cambridge University Press, 1990. A recent translation of parts of *Policraticus.* Nederman's introduction is helpful.

Wilks, Michael, ed. *The World of John of Salisbury.* Oxford: Basil Blackwell, 1984. This is an excellent collection of twenty-five scholarly articles on John of Salisbury. An extensive bibliography is included.

David John Farmer

Cross-References

Augustine's Political Philosophy, p. 121; Church and Government in History, p. 230; Dante's Political Philosophy, p. 483; Feudalism, p. 688; History of Government, p. 829; Hooker's Political Philosophy, p. 842; Individual Versus State Rights, p. 910; Monarchy in History, p. 1221; Political Ethics, p. 1461; Political Philosophy, p. 1505; Religion and Politics, p. 1685; Statesmanship, p. 1898; Stoic Political Philosophy, p. 1904; Succession, p. 1909; Thomas Aquinas' Political Philosophy, p. 1974.

JUDICIAL REVIEW

Field of study: Law and jurisprudence

Judicial review is the power of a court to determine whether actions of government officials are in accord with the U.S. Constitution, when the matter is before the court in a proper case. Changing interpretations of the Constitution have enabled the eighteenth century document to respond to modern problems.

Principal terms
AMENDING PROCESS: process for making changes in the Constitution, as set forth in Article 5
COMMERCE CLAUSE: clause in Article 7, section 8, of the Constitution authorizing Congress to regulate interstate and foreign commerce
JURISDICTION: areas in which a court has authority to act
LEGITIMIZE: to make acceptable by formally recognizing an action as being within the scope of lawful authority
OVERRULE: to decide that a previous decision was incorrect and will no longer be followed
STATUTE: law enacted by a legislature

Overview

Under the Articles of Confederation, the first governing document of the United States, there was no national court system. When that document was replaced by the Constitution of the United States in 1789, Article 3 of the Constitution provided that the new government would have a court system. It stated that the judicial power of the United States would be lodged in one Supreme Court and whatever lower courts Congress would create. Much of Article 3 is devoted to defining the jurisdiction of the Supreme Court. There is no statement in the judicial article that the Supreme Court was being given the power to review the constitutionality of the actions of Congress or the president.

Had U.S. political and legal development faithfully followed British tradition, U.S. courts would not have had the power of judicial review. Many other legal practices in the United States have their roots in the nation's British heritage, but not judicial review. In the largely unwritten British constitution, the legislative branch of government is supreme.

The United States, however, has a written Constitution that explicitly states that "This Constitution" is the "supreme Law of the Land." This is known as the supremacy clause. It further states that laws passed by Congress are the supreme law of the land, but only if they are pursuant to the Constitution. It does not say that all laws passed by Congress are supreme. If all laws are not supreme, then there must be a decision maker to decide which laws of the Congress are the supreme law of the land and which laws are unconstitutional. That decision maker might also be called upon by persons who claimed that the president had exceeded the authority conferred on that office by the Constitution. Although the language of the Constitution appeared to have abandoned the British tradition of legislative supremacy, it did not identify any particular decision maker in the government as having the power to decide which laws were constitutional and which were not. The Supreme Court was not expressly given that power.

The Supreme Court assumed the power of judicial review in 1803, in the case of *Marbury v. Madison*. In that case, steeped in the partisan politics of the period, the Supreme Court for the first time held congressional legislation unconstitutional. Since the Constitution did not explicitly confer on the Court the authority to do this, the task fell to Chief Justice John Marshall to write a judicial opinion justifying the Court's decision. Marshall observed that the Constitution is law and that it is the function of the justices to interpret and apply the law. When a law enacted by Congress conflicts with the law of the Constitution, the Supreme Court is obliged to apply the law of the Constitution rather than the law of Congress, because the Constitution is the supreme law of the land, and the justices of the Supreme Court swore to uphold the Constitution when they took their oaths of office. Thus, Chief Justice Marshall justified the Supreme Court's exercise of judicial review.

Although his opinion was well reasoned, it did not win universal acceptance. Critics of Marshall's opinion accurately observed that all public officials, not just Supreme Court justices, take an oath to support the Constitution. The doctrine of judicial review was opposed because it was believed that it would make the Supreme Court, whose members were appointed to office, superior to the president and Congress, both of which were elected to office. Marshall denied that judicial review meant judicial supremacy, contending that it merely implied the supremacy of the Constitution over all three branches of government. He contended that without judicial review, a written constitution would be meaningless.

During the remainder of Marshall's years as Chief Justice, the Supreme Court did not again hold congressional legislation unconstitutional. That does not mean, however, that the court did not exercise judicial review. In 1819, in the case of *McCulloch v. Maryland*, it used judicial review to uphold a congressional statute that created the Bank of the United States, when the constitutionality of that legislation was challenged by the state of Maryland. Although the creation of a bank was not among the enumerated powers of Congress, the Supreme Court found ample constitutional authority for the legislation in the necessary and proper clause of Article 1, section 8. Over the years, the Court has used its power of judicial review far more often to legitimize the actions of the elected branches of government than to hold them unconstitutional.

Even the legitimizing use of judicial review could result in controversy and rejection of the judiciary's special role as constitutional interpreter. Although Congress had seen fit to create a national bank, and the Supreme Court had exercised judicial review to uphold the power of Congress to do so, President Andrew Jackson vetoed similar legislation in 1832, when Congress rechartered the bank. Jackson contended that the legislation was unconstitutional and that he was not bound by the Court's contrary interpretation of congressional power. He too had taken an oath to support the Constitution and so had the right and the responsibility to interpret the document himself in the exercise of the powers of his office. Judicial review had not yet won universal acceptance. That would not come until the post-Civil War period, when the Court aligned itself with the dominant political and economic forces of industrialization.

Whatever doubts remained concerning the Supreme Court's power in relation to Congress and the president, the two elected branches that were considered co-equal with the Court, there were few real doubts about the authority of the Supreme Court to review the constitutionality of state actions, when they were brought before the Court in a proper case. After the Constitution went into effect, the first Congress passed the Judiciary Act of 1789, the statute that set forth the structure of the national judicial system. Section 25 of the Judiciary Act gave the Supreme Court the power to review state legislation challenged as being inconsistent with the Constitution. Even though the Court was clearly given the power of judicial review over state legislation at various times throughout American history, individual states have defied, or attempted to defy, the Court's authority when it held their legislation unconstitutional. Defiant states were rarely able to win the support of a significant number of states not directly involved in the controversy. Those not directly involved have tended to recognize the Supreme Court's power of judicial review over state legislation. They have recognized that such power is necessary, if the federal union is to be maintained.

Whether called upon to exercise judicial review of congressional actions, executive actions, or state actions, the constitutional decisions of the Supreme Court are relatively permanent. They may be reversed by constitutional amendment, but the amending process is difficult; it requires extraordinary majorities in Congress and the states. If a constitutional decision is to be changed, it is far more likely to be done by the Court itself. After the passage of time, the Court may overrule an earlier decision. An overruling decision is generally the result of new justices having been appointed to the Court who interpret the Constitution differently than earlier justices did. In a few instances, however, decisions reached by a closely divided Court have been overruled when one or more members of the Court's majority changed their minds about how the Constitution should be interpreted. Since the Court's constitutional decisions are infrequently overturned by constitutional amendments or overruling decisions, the power of judicial review is an important power.

Applications

Among the Supreme Court's more controversial exercises of judicial review have been those in the area of civil rights. At various times, the Court has reviewed actions of Congress and actions of state governments, sometimes legitimizing those actions and sometimes holding them unconstitutional.

In the aftermath of the Civil War, the Fourteenth Amendment was adopted to overturn the pre-Civil War Supreme Court decision *Dred Scott v. Sandford* (1857). In the *Dred Scott* decision, the Supreme Court said that slaves were not citizens of the United States, could not be citizens, and had no rights under the Constitution. The Fourteenth Amendment overturned the *Dred Scott* decision by extending citizenship to all persons born or naturalized in the United States and under its authority.

The Fourteenth Amendment, however, did more than extend citizenship to the recently freed slaves; it prohibited the states from denying them "the equal protection of the laws." The amendment concluded with an authorization to Congress to enforce the amendment by appropriate legislation.

Relying upon that authorization, Congress passed the Civil Rights Act of 1875. The law prohibited persons who operated various kinds of businesses, such as hotels, restaurants, theaters, and coaches, from discriminating against potential customers on the basis of their race. Challenges to the constitutionality of the law came from business operators in various parts of the nation who denied service to blacks. They argued that in enacting this law, Congress had exceeded its constitutional authority.

The Supreme Court agreed. In the *Civil Rights Cases* of 1883, the Supreme Court exercised its power of judicial review to hold the Civil Rights Act of 1875 unconstitutional. The Court concluded that the Civil Rights Act was not appropriate legislation for enforcing the terms of the amendment because it was directed at the operators of private businesses, but the Fourteenth Amendment did not restrict the activity of private businesses, only that of states. In a dissenting opinion, Justice John Marshall Harlan criticized the Court's majority for its interpretation of the language of the Fourteenth Amendment, which he believed violated the spirit of the amendment.

Title II of the Civil Rights Act of 1964 represented a twentieth century attempt to accomplish what the Supreme Court had held unconstitutional in the *Civil Rights Cases* of 1883. It prohibited racial discrimination in public accommodations. In passing the 1964 statute, however, Congress did not rely upon the Fourteenth Amendment alone as the source of its authority to enact the legislation. Congress also asserted its authority under the commerce clause, which has been a major source of congressional power in the twentieth century.

Like the Civil Rights Act of 1875, the Civil Rights Act of 1964 was challenged as unconstitutional. In *Heart of Atlanta Motel v. United States* (1964), however, the Supreme Court handed down a decision that legitimized the use of the commerce power to prohibit racial discrimination in public accommodations. The Court examined the legislative history of the 1964 Civil Rights Act and found that there was considerable testimony at congressional hearings that discrimination continued to exist in all parts of the country and that this discrimination in public accommodations had a detrimental effect on interstate travel by African Americans. The Court held that Congress had acted within its legitimate commerce power when it passed the Civil Rights Act. Since the commerce clause provided ample support for this legislation, the Court did not find it necessary to reexamine the extent of congressional authority under the Fourteenth Amendment; thus, it did not overrule the *Civil Rights Cases* of 1883.

Judicial review of state legislation requiring segregation of the races followed a path somewhat similar to that of congressional legislation banning discrimination in public accommodations, in that the Court initially legitimized state segregation statutes but years later adopted a different interpretation of the Constitution. In *Plessy v. Ferguson* (1898), the Supreme Court upheld a Louisiana law requiring that black passengers and white passengers ride in separate railroad cars. Homer Adolph Plessy, legally considered black although racially mixed, had challenged the constitutionality of the state law, arguing that it denied him the equal protection of the laws which the Fourteenth Amendment guaranteed. He argued that this state-imposed segregation placed a badge of inferiority on black people.

The Supreme Court rejected Plessy's argument and legitimized state-imposed segregation of the races. The Court considered the Louisiana law to be a reasonable regulation that took into consideration the customs and traditions of the people. Out of this came the "separate but equal" doctrine, which came to be applied not just to railroad transportation but to virtually all areas of life in the southern states.

By 1954, the Supreme Court was using its power of judicial review to begin dismantling the segregated society that it had previously legitimized. In that year, it rendered a decision that state-imposed racial segregation violated the Equal Protection Clause of the Fourteenth Amendment. In the landmark case of *Brown v. Board of Education*, the Supreme Court overruled *Plessy v. Ferguson*, insofar as it applied to public education. Writing for a unanimous Supreme Court, Chief Justice Earl Warren stated that it was impossible to determine how those who proposed and ratified the Fourteenth Amendment intended for its Equal Protection Clause to apply to public education, for the simple reason that public education was virtually nonexistent then. By the mid-twentieth century, however, public education was among the most important functions of state and local governments, as their own compulsory school attendance laws recognized. The Court concluded that in this modern context, legally imposed racial segregation could never provide equal education, even if all tangible elements were equal, because of the psychological damage done to black children. In the view of the Court, such segregation generated feelings of inferiority in black children, which had a detrimental effect on their motivation to learn. Thus, the Court rejected "separate but equal" in public education.

Context

Judicial review is not a power that belongs solely to the Supreme Court of the United States. It may also be exercised by federal district courts and federal courts of appeals. The decisions of those courts, however, may be appealed to the Supreme Court. State courts may also exercise judicial review and determine whether challenged actions of their own state officials are in accord with the United States Constitution. The decisions of the highest court of a state on such matters may be appealed to the Supreme Court of the United States. Thus, the Supreme Court provides uniformity in constitutional interpretation.

The decisions of the Court have involved a multitude of constitutional issues, not just civil rights. The Supreme Court has defined the constitutional authority of the states and of the three branches of the national government. In the late twentieth century, for example, the Court held that the legislative veto—that is, the power of one house of Congress to pass a resolution negating a decision of administrative officials—was unconstitutional. Another decision legitimized congressional legislation creating the position of independent counsel.

Because the justices of the Supreme Court are politically appointed, the Court's exercise of judicial review has generally reflected the dominant values of U.S. society. As those values change over time, the Court's interpretation of the Constitution changes. The flexible language of the Constitution and the infusion of new ideas and values as new justices join the Court have enabled the United States Constitution, adopted by a young nation in the eighteenth century, to remain the basic governing document of the United States for over two hundred years. Judicial review has become as much a part of the constitutional system in the United States as those powers specifically written in the Constitution.

Bibliography

Clinton, Robert Lowry. *Marbury v. Madison and Judicial Review*. Lawrence: University Press of Kansas, 1989. Argues that *Marbury v. Madison*, as currently understood, is a myth that gives the Supreme Court more power than John Marshall ever did. Contains extensive notes and bibliography.

Corwin, Edward S. "The Steel Seizure Case: A Judicial Brick Without Straw." In *Essays in Constitutional Law*, edited by Robert G. McCloskey. New York: Alfred A. Knopf, 1957. Originally published as a law review article, an outstanding legal analysis of the Supreme Court's review of a presidential action. Within the grasp of the general reader.

Cox, Archibald. *The Court and the Constitution*. Boston: Houghton Mifflin, 1987. Excellent discussion of the Supreme Court and judicial review intended for the nonspecialist by the Watergate special prosecutor fired during the famous "Saturday Night Massacre." Well documented but no bibliography.

Garraty, John A., ed. *Quarrels That Have Shaped the Constitution*. Rev. ed. New York: Perennial Library, 1987. Each chapter is a case study of an important constitutional decision of the Supreme Court, written for the nonspecialist by a recognized scholar. No bibliography.

Warren, Charles. *The Making of the Constitution*. New York: Barnes & Noble, 1967. Day-by-day summary of the Constitutional Convention intended for the general reader. Thorough index permits easy location of references to the judiciary.

Patricia A. Behlar

Cross-References

p. 439; Courts: U.S. Federal, p. 471; Legal Systems in Anglo-American Governments, p. 1085; Policy Development and Implementation, p. 1414; Separation of Powers: Presidential Government, p. 1815; The Supreme Court: Organization and Purpose, p. 1929; The Supreme Court: Role in Government and Law, p. 1935.

JURISPRUDENCE

Field of study: Law and jurisprudence

Jurisprudence is the science of law that deals with ascertaining the principles on which legal rules should be based.

Principal terms

COMMON LAW: body of unwritten principles originally based on the usages and customs of the community that were recognized and enforced by the courts

EQUITABLE: that which is generally recognized as just and fair

METAPHYSICS: system of principles underlying a particular study or subject, such as the law

PRECEDENT: previously adjudicated case or court decision that furnishes an example or authority for rulings in similar cases

SOCIAL CONTRACT: implied agreement whereby government bases its authority on the consent of the governed

SOVEREIGN: person, body, or state in which independent and supreme authority is vested

Overview

Jurisprudence is the science of law whose function is to discover the theories on which legal rules are based. It not only classifies such rules in their proper order and shows their interrelationships, it also settles the manner in which new or doubtful cases should be decided. Jurisprudence can also be described as an attempt to explain the theory behind all law, whether it be the law of the United States or the law of Iran. It uses existing law for its support and as raw material for the exercise of reasoning.

Twentieth century legal specialists, or jurisprudents, have drawn on the ideas of philosophers who go as far back as Aristotle and Plato in order to classify differing jurisprudential schools of thought. It is difficult, however, to classify such schools on anything more than an arbitrary basis.

Saint Thomas Aquinas is credited with being the first to define natural law. The earliest jurisprudential school, natural law as a practical force in law may be traced as far back as Marcus Tillius Cicero; as a theory of law, it goes as far back as Aristotle. Natural-law thinkers hold that men and women are created by God and impressed with certain qualities or makeups. Human law is binding only within the limited auspices of temporal authority, but natural law is binding on everyone and everything. To the question of whether there is such a thing as objective right or wrong, natural law replies that human beings can ascertain what is objectively right or wrong for themselves within their human nature. Natural law is thus an informed intuition of what is just and equitable. As applied by scholastic philosophers, such as Aquinas, it contains principles that are discoverable by reason—taking into account human nature—that are universally valid. Modern political theorists see natural law as transmuted into the foundation of a scheme of basic rights that people retain as they enter the social compact that delegates limited powers to government.

Natural law was intended to denote a system of rules and principles for the guidance of human conduct which—independently of enacted human law—might be discovered by the rational intelligence of humans, and which would grow out of, and conform to, human nature. Within ethics, natural law consists of the practical universal judgments that the individual elects. These express fundamental rules of human conduct the are essential to the divine purposes in the universe. According to the scholastics, these rules have been promulgated by God solely through human reason. The attraction of natural law to nonscholastics is that it provides a method of evaluation. It considers not only what law is, but what it should be.

During the second quarter of the nineteenth century, a new school of jurisprudence arose that reflected a full-scale rebellion against the metaphysics that underlay natural law. Advocates of this new school, who are called positivists, were dissatisfied with past attempts to derive fixed rules for human action and behavior. The positivists wanted to restrict jurisprudence to the study of the content of existing law. Positive law is thus law that is actually adopted by the government authority of an organized society. In this view, law exists only when it is capable of enforcement. Positivists thus rejected Justice Oliver Wendell Holmes, Jr.'s conception of natural law as "a brooding omnipresence in the sky." To positivists, law was the command of a sovereign power. To be effective, this command had to be enforced by penalties for noncompliance. Abstract concepts of ethics, morals, customs, and public opinion were therefore outside the classification of law.

In the last half of the nineteenth century, a renewed interest in the history of law took hold and gave rise to another school of jurisprudence that stressed historical continuity. This school, aptly called historical jurisprudence, stressed investigation of the historical origins and development of legal systems, and of their institutions, doctrines, and precepts—looking to the past to glean the principles of the law today. It also attempted to organize authoritative materials of judicial action on the basis of historically developed materials. In essence, the historical school postulated a continuity of development culminating in the official legal matters of time and place.

The historical school was most popular in Germany, when the German people were in the process of achieving national unity. In the resulting atmosphere of an emerging national spirit, German jurists hoped to abandon the pervasive Roman law and create a legal order based on the indigenous *volkgeist*, or the spirit of the people. Many believed that the character of any people's law was fixed at the earliest stage in its history and that law, like language and customs, arose out of habits, characteristics and general history.

Although this mystical accent on the spirit of the people (*volkgeist*) as a basic source of law found little place in the Anglo-American world, emphasizing history was attractive to a legal system that had long relied on ancient precedents. In fact, the study of legal history then took hold both in Great Britain and in the United States. Students studied the past and viewed the present as a culmination of historical developments. This approach is used as a means of determining the background and sources of legal principles and rules in order to assess them better.

During the middle of the twentieth century the dominant strain in legal thought was the sociological school of jurisprudence. This school has two branches; its dominant branch is the social-philosophical school; the other is the group called the realists. To some extent, the social-philosophical school is an outgrowth of the natural law school of jurisprudence. Instead of predicating rules on the concept of a divine lawgiver, however, it substitutes branches of knowledge outside the law, such as economics, sociology, psychology, politics, and history. Ideally, law should be declared with a view to the needs not only of today, but of tomorrow as well. The knowledge necessary to anticipate the needs of the future must be gleaned from disciplines outside the law.

Problems exist in applying this forward-looking idea to the adjudicative processes of the courts that are not present in the legislative arena. Legislatures, by definition, pass laws that will operate in the future. They have investigative facilities far superior to those of the courts, such as hearings and committees. By contrast, courts seem almost compelled to maintain a sort of historical continuity that can be seen in the tendency of judges to act on what they may have learned decades earlier. Thus, changes in tradition and in thinking come very slowly.

Arising spontaneously in the 1920's, the realist group cannot be classified as a true school of jurisprudence because it has no definite doctrine or creed. The primary concern of the legal realists was to call attention to the divergence between law as written in the books and law as it appears in fact. Their approaches are as diverse as their individual personalities. Lawyers, judges, professors, cynics, idealists, intellectuals, and pragmatists are all represented in this group. There is thus no body of principles common to the realists, beyond a serious and overwhelming concern to view law as it is, with all its pretensions removed, and to have law reflect reality, using all the resources of knowledge available. The effort of the realists, like that of the social-philosophical school, is to move law from the domain of pure speculation into the light of practical application.

As a "science" jurisprudence is more formal than material. None of its schools is directly concerned with questions of moral or political policy. In its broadest sense, the function of jurisprudence is to consider the ultimate effect that would be produced if a particular rule were applied to an indefinite number of like cases, and then choose that rule that would produce the greatest advantage for the greatest number.

Applications

Although one cannot say that jurisprudence has been without effect on the course of law, its actual impact is difficult to assess. It is impossible accurately to assess the effect of books, articles, speeches, and lectures of legal philosophers on a century and a half of lawyers and judges. Such influences might subtly and unconsciously affect listeners and readers, but their tangible influence can neither be traced nor proved.

Other factors making difficult any assessment of the effect of jurisprudence are the traditions and methods of common law that do not approve of judges referring to particular jurisprudential theories in their opinions. Legal training, as well as traditions of the bench, require that a legal opinion be woven into the fabric of the law, and that each case be decided with reference only to case precedent or statute. Consequently, even if a judge were to analyze a problem along jurisprudential lines, the judge's legal opinion is normally written in the language of the law, rather than the language of legal philosophy.

The vague and general nature of jurisprudential principles is a central reason that they are not used in writing judicial decisions. Nevertheless, one principle of jurisprudence did gain some standing in judicial opinions. This was the principle of natural, or inalienable, rights—those that are incapable of being surrendered, such as liberty. For instance, it has been held that the right of any citizen to pursue any lawful business venture is inalienable. Likewise, a person's right to privacy is also inalienable. Property, including employment, has been declared to be another important inalienable right, and for a time legislative attempts to restrict the hours that employees may work was considered an invasion of the inalienable right of employees to contract for employment. Increased attention to the role of government as the protector of the public interest led to a change in this attitude during the 1930's. The courts approved legislation that controlled wages and hours of employees, thus recognizing the weak bargaining power of employees and the specious nature of the prior argument that in restricting hours a legislature was inhibiting the freedom of employees to sell their labor.

In the area of legislation, the influence of jurisprudence, especially that of natural law, is more apparent, but can by no means be viewed as dominant. The U.S. Constitution, for example, reflects the thinking of such political philosophers as Thomas Hobbes and John Locke, not only in the republican form of government that it describes, but in the areas of so-called natural rights that it protects. The Founders created a vibrant federal system that grants enumerated powers to the national government while reserving the people's natural rights. Nevertheless, the quintessential expression of natural law for American constitutional interpretation appears in the Declaration of Independence, which explicitly states that all men are created with certain inalienable rights.

A narrow illustration of how the theories of jurisprudence can be applied is in the area of Sunday closing laws, sometimes called "blue sky laws," that are enforced in some states. These are ordinances forbidding the conduct of certain businesses on the Christian sabbath day. The standard legal positivist position on such laws is fairly simple: as valid positive laws, they should be enforced and obeyed. Natural law thinkers would generally agree that unjust laws are not law and should therefore not be enforced or obeyed. Since Sunday closing laws restrict economic freedom, a natural law person of strong laissez-faire opinions would regard the laws as unjust. A natural law person who is also a Christian traditionalist would take the opposite view. American legal realists would note that the typical failure of governments to enforce such laws vindicates the realist distinction between law in action and law in the books.

Historical and sociological jurisprudents would identify the historical and social factors that originally led to the enactment of these laws, such as religious sentiment and the political power of religious groups. The sociological-philosophical group would note the political influence of businesses on states that do not enforce these laws. They could further suggest that a balancing of interests between consumer values, business interests, and religious influence explains why Sunday closing laws have not been repealed outright. Finally, some sociological thinkers might argue that law should follow the times; because people want to shop on Sundays, the laws should either not be enforced or should be repealed.

Context

Once one considers the different schools of jurisprudence together, it becomes apparent that a synthesis, not a choice between the schools, is needed. Such a synthesis should build on what is valid in all the schools. The legal aspect of social order must be approached in terms of the moral principles which it embodies, partly in terms of the political authorities that shape it, and partly in terms of historical experience, as well as in the values that it expresses.

Law is a social institution that integrates processes of behavior and ideas to restore, maintain, and create social order. Jurisprudence provides insight into every aspect of law, thereby forcing judges to view the law in a broad perspective. It provides a method of placing law in its proper context within the broader culture, along with religion, economics, politics, and sociology.

Law is one of the great civilizing forces in human society. The growth of civilization has been linked with the gradual development of systems of legal rules, together with the necessary machinery for regular and effective enforcement. The role of the judiciary and the legislature in the legal system is of special significance. Law is in a constant process of flux and development. Although much of its development is the result of the enactments of legislatures, the judiciary has an essential role to play in developing the law and adapting it to the needs of society.

Law plays a crucial role in shaping development. Conditioned by social forces, it is the principal instrument through which society exercises control over itself and directs social change. It reflects the intellectual, social, economic, and political climate as well as ideas, ideals, and ideologies that are part of a distinct legal culture. Ideas about the legal order and the general theories about law have been, and continue to be, most influential on the law, which is the central subject in the study of jurisprudence. Such ideas and theories have effects in the legal profession, and more broadly, on social order.

Bibliography

Abraham, Henry. *The Judicial Process.* 2d ed. New York: Oxford University Press, 1968. Introductory analysis of the courts of the United States, Great Britain, and France. Clearly distinguishes how the different schools of jurisprudence define the law and how the different cultures interpret the law.

Cicero, Marcus. "The Laws." In *Readings in Political Philosophy*, edited by Frances William Coker. Rev. ed. New York: Macmillan, 1954. Discusses the origin of natural law, as well as Cicero's definition and use of natural law.

Cotterrell, Roger. *The Politics of Jurisprudence: A Critical Introduction to Legal Philosophy*. Philadelphia: University of Pennsylvania Press, 1992. Critical introduction to legal philosophy that defines the law in terms of the schools of jurisprudence.

Gray, John Chipman. *The Nature and Sources of the Law*. New York: Columbia University Press, 1916. Examination of the different types of positive law. Provides a particularly good illustration of the individual's legal rights in terms of the power to command.

Hart, H. L. A. *Law, Liberty, and Morality*. London: Oxford University Press, 1963. Defines positive law in terms of a separation of law and morality and sums up the legal positivist tradition that laws must be obeyed, just or unjust, so long as promulgated by a political authority.

Murphy, Cornelius. *Modern Legal Philosophy: The Tension Between Experiential and Abstract Thought*. Pittsburgh: Duquesne University Press, 1978. Outlines the tension between experiential and abstract thought; also discusses positive law, natural law, and sociological jurisprudence, and how these schools affect the definition of law.

Murphy, Jeffrie, and Jules Coleman. *The Philosophy of Law: An Introduction to Jurisprudence*. Totowa, N.J.: Rowman & Allanheld, 1984. Good introduction to legal philosophy and to legal philosophers which defines jurisprudence in general terms, while analyzing the differing schools of thought.

Pound, Roscoe. *The Spirit of the Common Law*. Boston: Marshall Jones, 1921. Discusses common law as judge-made law. Shows the need for sociological jurisprudence as a response to popular disrespect for law and a need to keep legal processes in tune with popular aspirations.

Susan M. Taylor

Cross-References

Aristotle's Political Philosophy, p. 83; Courts: U.S. Federal, p. 471; Hobbes's Political Philosophy, p. 836; Hooker's Political Philosophy, p. 842; International Law, p. 956; Legal Systems in Anglo-American Governments, p. 1085; Locke's Political Philosophy, p. 1142; Mill's Political Philosophy, p. 1204; Montesquieu's Political Philosophy, p. 1228; Plato's Political Philosophy, p. 1396; Political Ethics, p. 1461; Thomas Aquinas' Political Philosophy, p. 1974.

KANT'S POLITICAL PHILOSOPHY

Field of study: Political philosophy

Kant's political philosophy is the application of his theory of knowledge and morality to law, the state, and international relations.

Principal terms
AUTONOMY: condition of not being determined by causal forces, existing in the realm of pure reason within the mind. Contrasted with heteronomy
CATEGORICAL IMPERATIVE: Kant's formula for determining which course of action is morally right. In one formulation, this formula states: Act as if the maxim by which you act could by your will become a universal law. Another formulation of the imperative states: Treat everyone as an end and not only as a means
CRITICAL PHILOSOPHY: Kant's theory of knowledge contained in his critique of pure reason
HETERONOMY: state of being determined by causality in the world of phenomena. Contrasted with autonomy

Overview

Immanuel Kant (1724-1804) is generally reputed to be one of a handful of the most brilliant and influential philosophers in history. He lived in the East Prussian city of Königsberg, where he taught in the local university. Königsberg now lies in Russia, its name changed to Kaliningrad. Although Kant spoke often of cosmopolitanism, he was hardly a man of the world. A lifelong bachelor (like many other great philosophers, such as Plato, Hobbes, Locke, and Nietzsche), Kant passed his entire life without venturing more than a few hours by coach from the walls of his city, never sleeping outside them.

Kant's epistemology (theory of knowledge) represents the climax and the demise of the Enlightenment's celebration of reason, because in Kant's view, while there is a realm of pure reason, it is limited in the knowledge it can attain. Without attempting to describe Kant's epistemology in any detail, the following comments describe how Kant put an end to a century of often uncritical adulation of reason.

Kant argues that because of the character of the mind there are definite limits on the knowledge that reason can provide. When people perceive the external world they experience it as having characteristics such as causality and substance. Kant argues, however, that these categories of experience are built into the human mind. People are unable to experience the world except in terms of causality, substance, and the like. People feel certain that they experience the world as it really is, but this certainty is unwarranted.

Rather, because the characteristics of the human mind compel people to see the external world in terms of categories, people can know the world only insofar as it conforms to categories. People are unable to experience things as they really are. Kant calls things as they are *dinge-an-sich* or *noumena*, "things-in-themselves." On account of the limits to reason that Kant's analysis implies, the Enlightenment's uncritical celebration of human rationality must come to an end. Instead, Kant's critical philosophy places definite limits on what people can know and therefore limits the seemingly limitless possibilities of reason.

Kant's moral philosophy is connected with his political philosophy, and one should therefore have a general view of his moral philosophy before reading of his political philosophy. Reality is divided into two realms. One is the external realm of nature, which is ruled by causality and therefore determinism. The other is the internal reality of human consciousness. The rational faculty of the human mind is not subject to causality and is therefore free of determinism.

The rational faculty of the mind and the will that can guide behavior is the source of a person's moral life. Kant said that two things fill him with "ever renewed wonder: the starry skies above me, and the moral law within me." The moral law that tells one what to do is discovered by reason, without regard to the effects of one's behavior on the world. People should not, Kant says, calculate whether their actions will cause pleasure or pain in the world. This idea is the doctrine of utilitarianism, led by the English philosopher Jeremy Bentham. The external world is a world of causal determinism, or heteronomy, not of freedom. Only the realm of reason, insofar as it is not led by appetites and emotions, is capable of moral freedom, or autonomy. If people allow the external world's determinism to dictate what they do, then they act according to mere inclination and are not full, free human beings. Therefore, moral action does not calculate its possible effects in the deterministic external world. People must discover the moral law within, not without, and then act in the world in accordance to the moral law's dictates.

Moral law must be universal, applicable to everyone, and it must not be self-contradictory. The source of the moral law is the autonomy of a rational being, of which a person is an example. Moreover, "it is impossible to conceive anything in the world, or indeed out of it, which can be called good without qualification save only a good will."

To discover what the contents of the will should be, Kant put forward his doctrine of the categorical imperative. This imperative states: Act as if the maxim by which you act were to become through your will a universal law. Another version of the categorical imperative states: Treat everyone as an end and not only as a means. This formula places the human personality at the center of Kant's moral philosophy. One may wonder how this philosophy can be followed, since there are many occasions in which one person must treat another as a means. What Kant says, however, is that one must not treat others only as a means. Thus, Kant himself had a housekeeper who was a means for the performance of domestic tasks. He did not treat her, however, as just an instrument of convenience. By treating her with respect and dignity as a rational being, Kant could comply with the categorical imperative.

Kant's moral philosophy is connected with his political philosophy in that only a certain kind of political regime is consistent with the full expression of the moral freedom of the human personality. This regime is a republic, a state with a government whose policies aim for the good of the whole, not of some self-interested portion.

A part of Kant's philosophy as applied to morality and politics was influenced by Jean-Jacques Rousseau. Some interpreters believe that the central place Kant gives to the idea of a good will in his moral philosophy reflect's Rousseau's influence. Rousseau's view of the human personality distinguished between a higher self and a lower self. The morality of the higher self is embodied in the constitutional principles to which citizens agree in establishing the state. The establishment of the constitutional state is an act of the general will of the citizenry as a whole. Rousseau conceived the general will as good by definition. The will of the lower self, however, is a selfish will. Even if a sovereign people are agreed on some issue, if their agreement is based upon selfish will, it is merely the lower will of all. Thus, what is right cannot be established empirically, by what people actually do. Instead, whether an act or decision is right depends upon its adherence to rational principles of justice.

In the higher self Kant puts the realm of pure intellect and the laws it devises without reference to their empirical operation in the world. The phenomenal world is the realm of causation and therefore of heteronomy, the opposite of the autonomy of the rational mind. As in Platonism and in Christianity, the external world (the realm of desire and determinism) is inferior to an interior world that is intelligible by reason. For Kant, the moral law of the free operation of reason transcends humanity's lower nature.

In his application of moral philosophy to political philosophy, the fact that Kant lived in Prussia is not irrelevant. Prussia was ruled by a monarchy, during much of Kant's life by the benevolent despot Frederick the Great. When the French Revolution began in 1789, the crowned heads of Europe were frightened and eventually gathered their forces to resist it. During this period, if Kant openly championed violent revolution as a popular right, he did so in great danger. That he did not champion such a right may or may not be the result of the political circumstances in which he worked, but one may surmise that his view of revolution was not entirely uninfluenced by them.

Although he condemned the Reign of Terror, Kant was, nevertheless, a supporter of the principles of the French Revolution. One reason Kant could support its principles, in particular its republicanism and its message of the universality of the fundamental rights of man, was that Kant's philosophy led to no elitist conclusions. There is no class of persons who possess the special knowledge required for rule. The moral law within Kant that awed him was within everyone. Larger numbers of ordinary men and women knew the moral law.

The character of Kant's moral philosophy and its nonelitist implications for politics led him to embrace the republicanism more ardently advocated by Rousseau. Moreover, Kant argued that peace among nations could only be attained if states adopted republican constitutions. Such constitutions have three features. First, they have the principle of freedom for all members of society as human beings. Second, all members depend on a common legislature. Third, all citizens are equal. Kant added that the republican constitution is the only one "derived from the idea of an original contract upon which all rightful legislation of a nation must be based." The supposition of an original contract comes from Rousseau.

Republican government did not, for Kant, mean democracy. Democracy is a form of rule in which all possess the power to rule. Rather than a form of rule, republicanism is a form of government, referring to how the state sets up its governing power. Kant argues that the key difference between republics and other forms of government, all of which are despotic, is that the executive power be separated from the legislative. If this separation is absent, the state arbitrarily executes the laws it makes, "in other words where the public will is treated by the prince as if it were his private will."

In saying this Kant is flirting with the arguments of Madisonian constitutional analysis, but without either James Madison's deep learning in the subject or much experience. Kant sees that all power must not lie in the same hands but does not see that the key to political liberty, far more than the separation of executive from legislative power, is the independence of the judiciary.

In opting for republicanism, Kant does not support universal suffrage and equal civil rights for all adults. Women and poorer classes are to be denied full political participation on the ground that they hold essentially dependent positions in society, while full citizens must be independent. In this attitude, Kant echoes the opinion of his age on both sides of the Atlantic.

Kant's philosophy of law brought him to the high point of liberal theory. The final state of human development for Kant is life in a republic that adheres to the ideas and institutions of freedom under law, an idea first put forward by John Locke and developed by Rousseau. For Kant, the arena in which right action is performed includes the conditions under which the voluntary actions of one person can be harmonized with those of all other persons, in accordance with a universal law of freedom. Thus, freedom for one must be compatible with freedom for all. This is implicit in the categorical imperative.

Applications

Kant applied his philosophy to international relations in his essay *Perpetual Peace* (1795). His application is still relevant and continues to inform the views of a segment of those who study or work within the context of international politics. In *Perpetual Peace*, Kant discusses politics among nations and allows himself to dream "that sweet dream of peace." What could the philosopher, who, after all, had no divisions at his command, do to further the cause of world peace? Kant's answer was to turn the gaze of his critical intelligence to the conditions that further peace, and, in the end, bring a peaceful world into being.

These conditions require that the nations of the world must conclude a mutual treaty of peace. This message is the philosopher's first contribution. Second, it is the task of philosophy to set forth the terms of this treaty. Kant argued that peace would be perpetual only when a world federation came into being. (His idea of "federation" is actually a "confederation," in which members are states, not individuals.) Were it conceivable, Kant would prefer a united humankind within a single world state. He recognized the utopian character of this desire. Others after him, such as Hannah Arendt, have concluded that a world state, far from being a "sweet dream," would lead to despotism, a moral nightmare.

The terms for a treaty of perpetual peace among nations contain six preliminary articles, followed by three definite articles that spell out the conditions for peace. As in his moral philosophy generally, Kant is careful in his essay to tell his readers that his principles are not derived from experience (the phenomenal world of physical causation and heteronomy) but from the inner world of reason (of moral autonomy and undetermined freedom).

The preliminary articles of perpetual peace made certain demands: that no peace treaty be concluded with a secret reservation of the material for future war, that states not be bought and sold or given to rulers (as if they were private property), that standing armies gradually disappear, that no debts be contracted for the foreign affairs of states (so that monarchs could not carry on war as a sort of private game), that no state interfere by force in the constitution and government of another state, and that a state's acts during war (such as use of assassins and violation of articles of surrender) not make future peace impossible by destroying mutual confidence.

The definite articles of the treaty were that the civic constitution of each state be republican, that the law of nations be based upon a federalism of free states, and that the cosmopolitan or world law be limited to conditions of universal hospitality.

With regard to the first article, one reason why republican constitutions are conducive to peace is that the consent of citizens is required if the state goes to war. (Here Kant assumes that the constitution is followed, though this does not always occur.) Nonrepublican states, whose heads feel they own the state as personal property, wage war with ease, needing no one's consent.

The second article is required because states without common rules to govern them are like individuals in a state of nature (a condition of anarchy). To secure peace, each state must enter into an international constitution similar to its own civil one. This international constitution establishes a union of nations, not a world state. In creating this union, states leave a condition of lawless liberty and enter one of reasonable liberty, or freedom under law.

The third article spells out an important limit to the kind of union that states enter. It says that people have the right to visit other states and to be received in them without hostility. It does not give members of one state the right to emigrate permanently to other states. Such a right would imply a world state, which Kant rejected.

Context

The political aspects of Kant's philosophy place him solidly within the growing tradition of European liberalism in the late eighteenth century. In the previous century, Thomas Hobbes had advocated authoritarian government, but based his conclusions on the liberal premises of universal human freedom and equality. Later in the same century, Locke took Hobbes's premises and fashioned a liberal philosophy that demanded strict boundaries on the power of government, limiting it to protecting the life, liberty, and property of the governed, who must consent to become obliged to obey and who retain a right to revolution. In the middle decades of the eighteenth century, Rousseau, twelve years Kant's senior, added previously unexplored moral and psychological dimensions to liberalism. In 1776, Thomas Jefferson's noble pen expressed Lockean liberalism in the language of universality—"All men are created equal." Thirteen years later, the French Revolution's Declaration of the Rights of Man and Citizen reframed the universality of human rights. Kant's climactic contribution to the growth of liberalism lay, in part, in his finely tuned philosophical defense of the idea of "freedom under law" within the framework of republican government to which its members freely consent.

Kant also went further than anyone before him in applying philosophical method to international politics. In 1651, Hobbes saw the international scene as an anarchic state of nature, in which nations have no obligations beyond self-interest. In the same century, the Dutch jurist Hugo Grotius had already taken a giant step toward fostering a law-governed international environment in his *Concerning the Law of War and Peace* (1625).

Kant, who called Grotius and other international lawyers "miserable consolers" (for they merely "consoled" humanity for the presence of war), presented a third view of international politics. Hobbes declared it anarchy and Grotius showed its potential for community. Kant spoke with authority of the possibility of a complete international society governed as republics are governed by law to which all members freely consent. Kant, the critic of reason, was the acme of the Age of Reason. His political philosophy is a reflection of this position.

Bibliography

Cassier, Ernst. *Rousseau, Kant, Goethe: Two Essays*. Translated by James Gutmann et al. Princeton, N.J.: Princeton University Press, 1945. Penetrating discussions of Rousseau and Kant by a brilliant German interpreter of the Enlightenment.

Copleston, Frederick Charles. *A History of Philosophy*. Westminster, Md.: Newman Press, 1960. Contains a clear exposition of Kant's philosophy. Lucidly written and readily accessible to philosophical laypersons.

Kant, Immanuel. *The Metaphysical Elements of Justice*. Part 1 of *The Metaphysics of Morals*. Translated by John Ladd. Indianapolis: Bobbs-Merrill, 1965. Essential for understanding Kant's moral and legal philosophy, this work includes discussions of justice and of private and public law. Ladd's introduction is particularly helpful.

_____. *The Philosophy of Kant: Kant's Moral and Political Writings*. Edited by Carl Joachim Friedrich. New York: Modern Library, 1977. Compiled, edited, and partly translated by a renowned German-born Harvard professor, whose introductory essay is of considerable help to students and general readers.

Kemp, John. *The Philosophy of Kant*. New York: Oxford University Press, 1968. Concise and clearly written exposition of Kant's philosophy.

Charles F. Bahmueller

Cross-References

Hobbes's Political Philosophy, p. 836; Idealism, p. 855; Liberalism, p. 1118; Locke's Political Philosophy, p. 1142; Political Philosophy, p. 1505; Republicanism, p. 1706; Rousseau's Political Philosophy, p. 1756; The Social Contract, p. 1827; Utilitarianism, p. 2077.

KEYNESIANISM, MONETARISM, AND SUPPLY-SIDE ECONOMICS

Field of study: Economic issues

Keynesianism implies discretionary governmental intervention in the economy. Monetarism substitutes rules for discretion and focuses on the money supply and on interest rates. Supply-side economics emphasizes private individual incentives to production.

Principal terms

BUSINESS CYCLE: tendency of capitalist economies to follow a pattern of boom and depression

CROWDING OUT: idea that increased government expenditures will necessitate higher interest rates and reduced private investment. Rather than promoting and complementing private initiative, the government, by this view, forces out capital

FEDERAL BUDGET: total government revenues and all government transfers or expenditures; the deficit equals the national debt

INVISIBLE HAND: Adam Smith's idea that competitive market forces driven by self-interest lead to the socially desirable objective of an efficient economy

MONETARISM: belief that the central bank, by regulating the money supply and interest rates, should be the principal tool for maintaining economic stability

PHILLIPS CURVE: economic paradigm behind the idea that inflation and unemployment are alternative policy options that must be traded off

STAGFLATION: simultaneous occurrence of increasing prices (inflation) and increasing unemployment (stagnation)

SUPPLY-SIDE ECONOMICS: economic theory behind the view that less government and fewer taxes will provide greater opportunities and incentives, thus promoting economic growth

Overview

The Great Depression, which began in the 1929 crash of the stock market, brought to the forefront the question of the appropriate role of the government in regulating the economy. The prevailing view, often referred to as classical economics, was that the laws of supply and demand, driven by private initiative, would ensure that the entire economy would move toward full employment. Adam Smith, in *The Wealth of Nations* (1776), referred to this as the "invisible hand" of private initiative that worked toward public good. The French economist J. B. Say assumed that supply creates its own demand, ensuring that surpluses and unintended inventory accumulations would not persist. In the same way that people were expected to live within their means and balance their budgets, so also was the government expected to balance its budget by collective taxes to meet its expenditures, except in times of national emergency. While the economy experienced business cycles before, the magnitude and the persistence of the downturn in economic activity in the early 1930's led many to feel that market forces, as explained by classical economics, were not sufficient to get the economy restarted.

John Maynard Keynes (1883-1946) asked whether governments elected by the people did not have a responsibility to adopt policies to protect society from economic instability. His critics argued that in the long run the problem would solve itself through the workings of the market (the invisible hand); that in time the depression would end. Keynes's reply was that "in the long run we are all dead" and the government has a responsibility to take remedial action. Keynes theorized that the most effective course for the government to take was control of aggregate expenditures by manipulating government spending and taxing. Discretionary control of spending and taxes is fiscal policy. Keynes and his disciples, known as Keynesians, have argued that by changing taxes and expenditures, dramatic effects can be realized in the economy. Net taxes are monies collected by the government less any welfare payments. The latter are referred to as government transfers. Government expenditures are monies spent by the government on roads, bridges, national defense, and other goods and services. The essence of Keynes's theory was that a government-provided dollar to build a bridge would be received as private income by someone who would in turn use the dollar to buy something now (consumption) or later (savings). The amount spent now would be received by someone else, who would spend part of that dollar. The original dollar would be respent, exerting a multiple, beneficial impact on the economy. The magnitude by which the initial dollar spent by the government would change income is the multiplier. Conversely, reductions in government spending or increases in taxes would have a multiple contractionary effect on the economy.

The size of the multiplier has been hotly debated among economists, but it will increase the more people spend and the less they save. The fraction of any additional dollar in income that is consumed is called the marginal propensity to consume. The greater this propensity, the larger the secondary consumption respending of the initial amount that the government spent. In the 1940's and 1950's there was less concern with estimating the size of the multiplier than there was with what the implications were for government policy. If the government could control the economy, then it could prevent business cycles from causing disruptions in economic activities. In recessions or downturns, the government could reduce taxes, increase expenditures, or both, to stimulate the economy. In periods of boom, the government could increase taxes and decrease government spending to reduce expenditures and therefore prices. In Keynesian economics, inflation and unemployment are seen as alternatives. Policy-makers must weigh the two and make trade-offs. The alternative levels of inflation and unemployment may be displayed on a graph in what is known as the Phillips curve.

In the Keynesian theory of the budget, the government can regulate the economy. In recessions, deficits (expenditures greater than taxes) would stimulate economic activity, while in inflationary times surpluses (net taxes greater than expenditures) would dampen the economy. The assumption is that while over the course of the business cycle one might observe surpluses and deficits, the two would tend to balance out. The impact of fiscal policy may be measured by the "full employment" budget rather than the current budget. If measured relative to full employment, the budget is in surplus, and fiscal policy is contractionary. If the full employment budget is in deficit, expenditures exceed revenue, more money is being put into the economy than is taken out, and fiscal policy is expansionary.

The implication of Keynesianism is greater government involvement in the economy premised on the belief that the laws of supply and demand are not sufficient to achieve a stable prosperity. Monetarists, on the other hand, have kept faith in the market system and in individual incentives. The leading exponent of monetarism, Milton Friedman, was awarded the Nobel Prize in Economics in part for his work in monetary theory. Friedman's view is that government policy, rather than stabilizing the economy, had actually contributed to economic instability. The economy is too complicated and complex, in Friedman's analysis, to be fine-tuned by fiscal policy. Equally important, the increased role of government compromises something essential to a democracy, namely, individual rights and freedom. Monetarists argue that discretionary fiscal policy is ineffective and that government money simply displaces private initiative. The government, if it acts in a Keynesian manner, is crowding out the private sector. Government policy should be directed toward giving individuals greater opportunities, and this is best served, according to monetarists, by regulating the money supply, not by altering fiscal policy. Regulating the money supply will influence the price of money. The price of money is the interest rate. Decreases in the interest rate will stimulate private investment and economic activity, while decreases in the money supply will increase the interest rate and retard economic activity. Unlike fiscal policy, which generally requires legislative approval and the inherent delays, monetary policy can be carried out by the central bank of the United States, known as the Federal Reserve, with less delay. Many monetarists believe that even discretionary monetary policy is ill-advised because of the inability of policymakers to know what policy is best at any particular time. These monetarists advocate a fixed annual rate of increase in the money supply. This, they contend, will facilitate the workings of the market and provide people with greater economic certainty.

The monetarist view is sometimes described in the classical equation of exchange. The amount of money times the velocity with which it turns over in the purchase of currently produced goods and services is a money measure of national income. Classical economists assumed that the velocity was relatively stable and that national income would be at its full employment level, so that there was a direct relationship between the price level and the money supply.

The Keynesian response to the monetarists is that changes in money and interest rates in a recession simply make conditions more favorable for a recovery, but they do not ensure recovery. A more direct stimulus is needed through increased government spending. In a recession people are unwilling to take risks and are more inclined to hoard, so making more money available at a lower cost will not be enough to stimulate the economy. The government must step in to directly increase expenditures, even to the point of creating jobs.

The debate between Keynesians and monetarists raged during the 1960's, but the combination of both increasing prices (inflation) and unemployment (recession) in the 1970's led many to doubt whether the traditional models of the economy were in fact valid any longer. Supply-side economics asked some fundamental questions about the prevailing views of economics. While Keynesians thought that taxes could be increased to finance government spending, the supply-side view was that higher taxes had negative effects on people's incentives to work and be productive. Arthur Laffer, one of the leading exponents of this new theory, argued that to stimulate the economy it may be better to reduce taxes. To do so gives incentives to increase efficiency, which will ultimately lead to more income and higher tax revenues. Higher tax rates did not necessarily imply greater tax revenue if the higher rates discouraged initiative and reduced income. In many respects supply-side economics was a return to the philosophy underlying classical economics. Government policy should be focused on providing people with incentives to work and excel, which would ultimately lead to the greatest good for society as a whole. This was the policy that Ronald Reagan espoused in his campaign for president in 1980. Supply-side economics reaffirmed the importance of competition and market forces in regulating business and, at the same time, providing incentives. It was the philosophy behind the cuts in federal taxes during the 1980's, and many argue it was the reason for the high growth rates in the U.S. economy in the 1980's. Taxes were reduced, but government expenditures and income support programs were not, so that a consequence of Reagan's policy was a dramatic increase in the federal deficit. The ballooning deficit had serious implications for the global competitiveness of the United States and for future generations of Americans who must bear the burden.

Applications

From the 1930's through most of the 1960's economic policy in the United States and other developed democracies was premised on the Keynesian model. The focus of government was on taxing and spending. The New Deal of Franklin Delano Roosevelt and the Great Society of the Kennedy-Johnson presidential administrations involved the government in affecting the economy. Keynesian economists thought that the government could bring about the elimination of poverty and the realization of full employment. The election of president Richard M. Nixon in 1968 led to a change in focus from fiscal policy to monetarism. Greater emphasis was given to the role of the monetary authorities in setting the money supply and influencing interest rates. At the same time, it was becoming obvious that trying to use government to solve domestic problems and at the same time fight a war in Vietnam was very expensive and of questionable impact. While President Nixon found merit in the monetarist approach, he was not totally convinced of the efficacy of the market and he harbored some skepticism of the effectiveness of market forces to regulate the economy. In fact he was the last president to attempt to legislate controls over wages and prices. The conflict of paradigms reached a climax during Jimmy Carter's presidency. The economy went through a period of stagflation—rising unemployment and inflation at the same time. Keynesianism had predicted that the economy would experience either inflation or unemployment but not both at the same time. The inability of the Keynesian model to explain the economic events of the late 1970's led many to question it. The change in focus was from a model that stressed expenditures and the demand side of the market to one that stressed the supply side and the factors that affected productivity and initiative. Big government had not lived up to the expectations people had for it. Taxes rose and the government became ever bigger but social problems did not appreciably lessen in many people's minds. The election of President Ronald Reagan in 1980 marked a change in the philosophy of the role of the government, a distrust of the effects of government on individual freedoms and initiative, and a return to faith in the markets.

Although economists differ on the relative importance they give Keynesianism, monetarism, and supply-side economics, most agree that it is very difficult to grasp the total complexity of the economy. The interdependencies among sectors within the United States and among other nations make the appropriate policy difficult to ascertain and make the effects of policy close to impossible to predict or measure. The implication is that the government must be very cautious in attempts to regulate the economy.

Context

What separates the three economic models from one another is the efficacy given to market forces and competition in bringing the economy to full steam. It is generally agreed that the more effective the market system and individual initiative are in achieving this objective, the less the need for government intervention. What the three models do not agree on is how effective the market system is, and how or if government should intervene. The relation between economic theory and political philosophy is often complex. Conservative views regarding the importance of the individual and the limited role of government find their economic complement in classical economics, monetarism, and supply-side economics. While the specifics of these economic paradigms differ, they are alike in their belief in the ability of a competitive market system to achieve an efficient economy and high employment. These economic theories have been widely adopted by Republican administrations. Keynesians justify the interventionist programs of Democratic administrations in the latter part of the twentieth century by arguing that market forces have limited effectiveness. Modern versions of Keynesian economics acknowledge the failures of a myopic tax-and-spend policy, while still believing that government can and should meet important social needs that would not be satisfied otherwise. While Republicans stress the efficiency of the private market system, Democrats stress the importance of equity in dividing society's wealth. A fair distribution can only be achieved by having the government play an activist role. All economic theories must address the issues of efficiency and equity. Governments must foster policies that produce goods and services using the fewest resources possible and that distribute goods in the fairest way possible. All three theories share these objectives, but they embody very different policies for their realization.

Bibliography

Friedman, Milton, and Walter Heller. *Monetary vs. Fiscal Policy*. New York: W. W. Norton, 1969. Readable summary of the monetarist and Keynesian views.

Friedman, Milton, and Anna Jacobson Schwartz. *A Monetary History of the United States, 1867-1960*. Princeton, N.J.: Princeton University Press, 1963. Systematic effort to interpret macroeconomic activity in the United States in terms of changes in the money supply.

Hall, Robert, and John Taylor. *Macroeconomics*. 4th ed. New York: W. W. Norton, 1993. One of many texts that attempt to systematically and analytically develop each of the models.

Keynes, John Maynard. *The General Theory of Employment, Interest, and Money*. New York: Harcourt, Brace & World, 1965. Originally published in 1935, this is arguably the most important economic treatise in the twentieth century. The case for government intervention in the economy is eloquently and convincingly made.

Leijonhufvud, Axel. *On Keynesian Economics and the Economics of Keynes*. New York: Oxford University Press, 1968. Interprets Keynesianism in the context of classical economics, avoiding technical complexity.

Lipsey, Richard G., et al. *Economics*. 10th ed. New York: HarperCollins, 1993. Popular introductory text clearly and succinctly traces the various theories.

Rock, James, ed. *Debt and the Twin Deficits Debate*. Mountain View, Calif.: Mayfield Publishing, 1991. Much of the controversy among theories is centered on the role of the deficit. This collection of brief papers views the deficit from different ideological perspectives.

Smith, Adam. *The Wealth of Nations*. New York: Alfred A. Knopf, 1991. Originally published in 1776. Makes the case for a laissez-faire economy with minimal government intervention.

John F. O'Connell

Cross-References

Budgets of National Governments, p. 158; Business and Government, p. 177; Capitalism, p. 197; Debts and Deficits in the U.S. Federal Budget, p. 489; Funding of Government, p. 724; Government Roles, p. 778; Liberalism, p. 1118; National Economies, p. 1248; The New Right, p. 1293; Political Economy, p. 1455; Social Democratic Parties, p. 1846; Taxation and Appropriation, p. 1941; Treasury Systems in the United States, p. 2013.

LABOR RELATIONS

Field of study: Functions of government

Labor relations are the negotiations and agreements between management and employees regarding employee wages, benefits, and working conditions. In the United States, labor relations are conducted under detailed collective bargaining guidelines established by law and regulated by independent government agencies.

Principal terms

ARBITRATION: method of resolving a disagreement between two parties, in which a third party makes a decision after hearing both sides of the dispute

BARGAINING UNIT: group of employees who choose a single bargaining agent, such as a union, to represent them

CERTIFICATION: designation by the National Labor Relations Board or state labor board of a labor organization, entitling it to bargain as the representative of a bargaining unit

COLLECTIVE BARGAINING: negotiations between an organization of employees and their employer for the purpose of reaching an agreement or contract describing wages and working conditions

GOOD FAITH BARGAINING: requirement of law that both parties make a sincere effort to negotiate and reach agreement

GRIEVANCE: employee complaint about an employer whose actions violate the collective bargaining contract

RIGHT-TO-WORK LAWS: laws making it illegal to require a job applicant or employee to be a member of a union in order to obtain or keep a job

UNFAIR LABOR PRACTICE: action by either the union or employer which is prohibited by law

Overview

Government involves itself in labor relations in order to promote public safety, social equity, improved economic conditions, and national security. Government itself is also an employer and engages in labor relations with its own employees. In the early days of the Industrial Revolution, companies sometimes engaged large numbers of employees, even young children, at very low wages and in often unsafe working conditions. In many cases, railroads, canals, coal mines, textile and steel mills, and other industrial plants were built and operated with something akin to slave labor. In Pennsylvania's anthracite coal mines, for example, about four hundred deaths occurred each year in the late nineteenth century. One year, after the turn of the century, more than 7,000 people were killed in U.S. mine and railroad accidents. In 1911, 146 young women died in a textile mill fire due to unsafe working conditions. Labor organized to fight against unsafe conditions, but large businesses controlled the economy, law enforcement, and the courts. Strikes were broken by hired guards and court injunctions. The unsafe working conditions persisted until state and federal governments began passing legislation limiting child labor and reducing the number of hours in a working day.

In the early years of the labor movement, unions attempted to gain a bargaining position through strikes and boycotts. During the Long Strike of 1875, coal miners were unsuccessful in changing working conditions. They were forced to accept a 20 percent wage reduction, and twenty-four miners were charged with criminal offenses. Ten were executed. The railway strike of 1877 left hundreds of workers dead and property damage exceeding ten million dollars. Famous strikes such as the one in 1892 against Carnegie Steel, in which the company employed Pinkerton guards, and the Pullman Strike of 1894 by rail workers ended in violent confrontation with dozens dead. Court injunctions ended the strikes, with workers often losing ground on pay and working conditions. In 1934, the United Textile Workers were able to bring one million workers into a nationwide strike, but this, like other union efforts, usually ended in failure. After three weeks, the union ended the strike with no gains and eighty thousand workers losing their jobs. Unions were overwhelmed by the legal power behind the companies. If there were an economic depression, conditions for unions became impossible. As a result of surplus labor, the bargaining leverage of unions would weaken and organized unions often fell apart. Eventually, laws were passed by Congress protecting unions from prosecution, court injunctions without a hearing, and unfair labor practices by employers.

In the midst of the Great Depression during the 1930's, hundreds of thousands of workers were left unemployed and unable to provide the consumer spending needed to get the economy moving again. In addition, the number and severity of labor-related conflicts increased. Companies lost valuable production time as workers left their jobs to demand better pay and working conditions. The federal government intervened following the election of President Franklin D. Roosevelt and enacted several measures to stimulate the depressed economy. The National Industrial Recovery Act (1933) and the National Labor Relations Act (1935), for example, gave workers protection by guaranteeing a minimum wage, reasonable hours of work, and the right to bargain collectively. With these protections, union membership skyrocketed, rising from around three million during the early 1930's to over eighteen million in the 1950's.

Some industries, like railroads and steel, were seen by the government as essential to national security. To protect such industries from labor unrest, especially during times of national crisis, the federal government acted to ensure the continued operation of strategic industries. During World War II, the president established the War Labor Board to settle labor disputes in key industries. In 1943, government agents seized mines on strike in order to sustain war production of coal. That same year, Congress passed legislation allowing the government to take over any industrial plant if workers threatened production of materials essential to the conduct of war. After the war, railroads and steel mills were seized under the pretense of national security.

Although government came to recognize labor as an important part of the economy, it was slow to acknowledge its importance within government. The first federal government workers to organize were the postal workers in 1863. Later, custom agents formed a national union and three general unions of government workers were formed permitting workers from all government occupations to join. These labor movements were not well received by government executives and not enthusiastically embraced by most government workers because of a generally antiunion atmosphere in government. By the 1960's, the growth in government employment and experience with unions in the private sector caused a change in attitude toward government unions. In 1962, President John F. Kennedy signed an executive order guaranteeing government workers the right to union representation and the right to bargain collectively on a limited number of issues. The change in the legal environment spurred a tremendous growth in union membership, growing to nearly half the civilian government workforce by 1968.

Since the beginning of the Industrial Revolution, the federal government interceded in labor relations to pursue its view of public policy at the time. At times, government has come down on the side of management by enacting laws to deter union organizing. At other times, the government has come to the aid of workers, guaranteeing them the right to bargain collectively and organize into unions. The government's role in labor relations has traditionally been to promote its own public policy, not necessarily as a means of supporting or harming either management or labor. Government has intervened in labor relations as a means to reduce conflict, preserve economic prosperity, protect citizens from exploitation and dangerous conditions, and ensure national security.

Applications

Two examples of the federal government's role in labor relations illustrate its pursuit of public policy. During the Korean War, President Harry S Truman's administration established several government agencies to control wages and inflation. At the end of 1951, the collective bargaining contract between the United Steel Workers and major steel companies expired without reaching agreement for a future contract. Truman persuaded the union to continue working while the case was submitted to the Wage Stabilization Board, an agency established to settle labor disputes and control wages during the war. The board was composed of equal numbers of representatives for labor, management, and the general public. The board did not reach a decision until March 20, when board members from labor and the public agreed. While the case was being considered by the board, the president convinced the union not to strike, but a date of April 9 was set for a strike if the board did not reach a decision by then. When steel company executives heard the board's decision, they immediately rejected it as too costly. Labor leaders used the decision as a bargaining tool, saying it was their lowest acceptable position.

A third factor in this case was the war. A strike halting steel production seemed inevitable, but military leaders warned the president that Chinese and North Korean advances made continued steel production absolutely necessary. The president appealed to the steel companies and unions and convinced them to return to negotiations before the threatened strike. The federal government was called in to mediate, but no settlement could be reached between the two parties. Two hours before the strike deadline, President Truman seized the steel industry, ordered the mills run by a government agency, and made all steelworkers government employees.

The question of whether a president could seize private industry was taken to district court, and the president lost. When the union heard the news, it immediately went on strike, but in a few days the decision was appealed to the U.S. Supreme Court. Workers returned to their jobs while everyone awaited the decision. On June 2, the Supreme Court decided against the president; private industry could not be seized—even in times of war. The union went on strike, closing the steel mills for seven more weeks. Finally, after the government agreed to pay the steel industry considerably more for the steel that it bought for government purposes, an agreement between the United Steel Workers and the steel industry was concluded.

President Truman's handling of the 1952 steel strike shows how government can become involved in labor relations because of its interest in promoting public policy. The government was interested in the situation between the steel industry and workers because of implications for national security. From the beginning, the president offered the government's services for mediation or arbitration. When a strike was imminent, the president acted to ensure a continuous supply of steel to the military effort in Korea. Although declared illegal, the president's action illustrates the government's ability to become directly involved in labor relations.

The second example of government's role in labor relations deals with government employees. The Professional Air Traffic Controller's Organization (PATCO) was originally established as a professional organization of air traffic controllers, who are employees of the federal government. Relations between PATCO and the Federal Aviation Administration (FAA) were not good from the beginning, as PATCO endorsed a number of job actions (numerous grievances, sickouts, and work slowdowns) and the FAA attempted to cut union privileges. After the contract between PATCO and the FAA expired in 1981, negotiations continued for two months, but the two parties were still very far apart in their demands. On August 3, 1981, PATCO members went on strike.

PATCO leaders expected President Ronald Reagan to support their cause because he was a former president of the Screen Actors' Guild, and thus a fellow union leader who should be sympathetic to their cause. PATCO seriously misjudged President Reagan, who took immediate and forceful action. He called for the imprisonment of strike leaders and fired all strikers who would not return to work. Reagan went to court to fine the union for their disruption of air traffic and won with a penalty to the union of one million dollars per day.

In this case, public employees were clearly in violation of federal law prohibiting strikes by federal employees as well as an earlier promise by the union not to strike. President Reagan declared an end to the strike and began hiring new air traffic controllers. He commissioned military air controllers to assist their civilian counterparts, and air traffic was only minimally disrupted. The union was something other than minimally disrupted. Having misjudged the president as well as public reaction, PATCO lost its labor dispute with the FAA. It lost certification as exclusive representative of the air traffic controllers' bargaining unit, and eventually lost its appeals in court.

The government had two roles during the PATCO strike: employer and regulator of labor relations. The government held negotiations with PATCO as the exclusive bargaining agent for air traffic controllers until collective bargaining broke down without agreement. As a result of the illegal strike, Reagan fired those who would not return, and hired replacements. He used his authority as commander in chief to call the military in to help train new controllers until their numbers were sufficiently large to do the job themselves. The president went to the courts to seek penalties against the union, and appealed to the Federal Labor Relations Authority to decertify the union as the exclusive representative of the bargaining unit.

Context

The government has not always taken as dominant a role in the conduct of labor relations as it does today. Public policy toward organized labor has evolved as the interests of government have changed from a probusiness attitude to a greater concern for social equity. The stages of government's change in policy can be measured by the court decisions, legislation, and presidential executive orders.

The earliest approach was indicative of the laissez-faire disposition of the federal government during the nineteenth century. During this time, government viewed labor organizing as attempts to interfere with management's legitimate right to control its business. Labor organizers were arrested as criminal conspirators who were attempting to harm businesses. State laws enacted to prevent the exploitation of children and to make the workplace safer were struck down by federal courts as an infringement on the rights of business.

The next governmental approach could be termed the "business law" phase, in which government enacted laws to actively support business efforts. This period began with the passage of the Sherman Antitrust Act in 1890. Although the act prohibited business monopolies, it also became a forceful tool used to limit unions. Using this law, businesses could argue in court that many union activities were an illegal restraint on interstate trade. Court injunctions were used to jail union leaders and force unionized workers back to their jobs.

In the environment of economic depression and the threat of war shortages, the government began taking a new, more permissive approach to labor relations. In 1932, the Norris-LaGuardia Act limited the ability of the courts to issue injunctions unless unions had the opportunity to fully explain their case to the court. The 1935 National Labor Relations Act provided unions with the right to organize, outlined unfair labor practices by employers, and established the National Labor Relations Board to oversee labor relations. This oversight authority allows the board to certify exclusive bargaining agents, hear appeals on unfair labor practices, and make determinations on enforcement of the act. Feeling it had gone too far in support of unions in 1935, Congress passed the Labor Management Act in 1947 to list unfair labor practices for unions and establish the Federal Mediation and Conciliation Service to aid in the resolution of disputes. In 1962, President Kennedy issued Executive Order 10988, giving federal employees the right to organize and bargain collectively on nonwage issues but maintaining the prohibition against strikes by federal workers.

Bibliography

Hunt, James W. *The Law of the Workplace: Rights of Employers and Employees.* 2d ed. Washington, D.C.: Bureau of National Affairs, 1988. Describes federal laws relating to labor relations in clearly understandable terms. Not only are laws related to collective bargaining covered, but also laws relating to wages and working conditions, the minimum wage, privacy rights, job safety, unemployment, disability, equal employment opportunity, and discrimination are described in a clear manner.

Kearney, Richard C. *Labor Relations in the Public Sector.* 2d ed. New York: Marcel Dekker, 1992. Good summary of labor relations as they apply to public sector employees. Sections on the legal environment, collective bargaining, and impasse resolution are particularly helpful in understanding the differences between public- and private-sector bargaining.

Kenny, John J. *Primer of Labor Relations.* 23d ed. Washington, D.C.: Bureau of National Affairs, 1986. Takes the union perspective and guides the reader through the practice of labor relations, including organizing, selecting a bargaining representative, bargaining, strikes and other actions, dispute resolution, and federal regulations.

Labor Relations Reference Manual (LRRM) and *Government Employee Relations Report* (GERR). These two periodicals are published by the Bureau of National Affairs, Washington, D.C., and they describe the law of labor relations at the federal and state levels, court opinions relating to labor relations, and National Labor Relations Board decisions. The GERR is designed to address labor relations in the public sector.

Morris, Charles J., ed. *American Labor Policy: A Critical Appraisal of the National Labor Relations Act.* Washington, D.C.: Bureau of National Affairs, 1987. Discusses U.S. policy toward labor and especially the policy as defined by the National Labor Relations Act of 1935.

Paradis, Adrian A., and Grace D. Paradis. *The Labor Almanac.* Littleton, Colo.: Libraries Unlimited, 1983. Lists labor history highlights, prominent labor leaders, principal federal laws and executive orders affecting labor, federal government agencies concerned with labor relations, state agencies concerned with labor relations, sources of labor information and statistics, and a glossary of labor terms.

Tomlins, Christopher L. *The State and the Unions: Labor Relations, Law, and the*

Organized Labor Movement in America, 1880-1960. New York: Cambridge University Press, 1985. Description of government's role in labor relations in the United States. Emphasis is placed on the phases of public policy toward unions listed as corporate policy, New Deal policies, and responsible unionism.

W. David Patton

Cross-References

Business and Government, p. 177; Capitalism, p. 197; The Civil Service in the United States, p. 310; Commerce Regulation, p. 357; Government Powers, p. 772; Industrialization, p. 916; Policy Development and Implementation, p. 1414; The Social Contract, p. 1827.

LAND MANAGEMENT IN THE UNITED STATES

Field of study: Functions of government

Land management in the United States involves the control and regulation of the nation's public and private property by each level of government—federal, state, and local. Zoning is the prime land-use method, which strikes a balance between concern for the natural environment and economic growth.

Principal terms

BUREAU OF LAND MANAGEMENT: federal agency that regulates large tracts of sparsely populated federal land in western states

COMPREHENSIVE PLAN: official planning guide, adopted by local governments, that recommends future desirable land-use patterns and areas for growth

EMINENT DOMAIN: government's power to take private land for public purposes, while owners receive monetary compensation

GROWTH MANAGEMENT: state policies that may limit or balance growth, and usually require local governments to develop plans

POLICE POWER: right of government to regulate the public health, safety, and welfare, which gives zoning its legitimacy

SUBDIVISION REGULATIONS: local government ordinances to regulate single-family housing concentrations

ZONING: major land-use regulation method in the United States, which divides a city or town into different sectors or zones, each having different uses and requirements

Overview

Land management as a function of government in the United States distributes power and responsibility among the three levels of government: national, state, and local. There are also significant divisions between private and public property, which have evolved over time. Most land-use management in the United States has been authorized or developed by the states and implemented at the local level.

The power to pass and enforce laws to protect the welfare of all people is the exercise by government of its police power. In the United States, police power was retained by the sovereign states when the federal government was formed. States delegate police power to local governments through specific legislative acts or their state constitutions. The authority to create laws and extensive regulations that impact the citizenry in their communities and regulate their use of their property lies at the heart of U.S. land-use management.

Another important land management concept is the power of eminent domain, by which government has the right to take private property to use for a public purpose. When government exercises its power of eminent domain, for example, taking property to build a school, it must compensate the owner. If an agreement on price cannot be reached, it is decided in court. Eminent domain is a selectively used device, because the government's authority is limited by the constitutional protection of individual rights. Taking property for a trivial reason or for an unfair price would not be allowed by the courts.

During the twentieth century, zoning gradually became the prime legal method for the application of police power to regulate the use of land. Zoning divides a community or county into different sectors or zones, in which different activities or land uses are permitted. Property in each zone must conform to specific standards of bulk, area, and population density. Typical zones include agricultural, residential, commercial, and industrial areas. More specialized zones may be created to address the unique concerns of a particular community. For example, it is not uncommon to construct different residential zones to achieve different population densities. Mixed zones, which were initially discouraged as a violation of zoning's separation-of-uses philosophy, became more popular in the 1980's and 1990's. A planned residential and limited commercial mixture in one zone—for example, small shops and apartments—has been shown to provide a desired lifestyle setting for some urban professionals, while reducing their reliance on personal vehicles for transportation.

Most planning authorities have come to believe that the zoning ordinance and its accompanying zoning map, which delineates the boundaries of each zone within each political subunit, should be based on a comprehensive plan. The comprehensive plan is a general policy statement about future land use, developmental priorities, and alternatives. As a public policy guide, it states the community's goals and develops a strategy for implementation. Most comprehensive plans review the area's historical growth and develop a series of maps that reveal current and future housing patterns, commercial and industrial development, public buildings, roads, sewer and water systems, open space and recreation, and public transportation.

The plan covers the entire geographic area and ideally attempts to be compatible with adjacent communities. While it is not as specific as the zoning ordinance, the comprehensive plan is a policy guide that has been approved by the community's legislative body. Thus, the plan attempts to convert long-range goals into public policy. It focuses on the physical development and offers a vision of the future within the context of social and economic trends, such as population, employment, and land-use patterns. While the comprehensive plan is the general policy guide, the zoning ordinance and its map have been viewed as the plan's most significant implementation devices. Other examples of implementation devices are building codes, subdivision regulations for new residential housing developments, and capital budgets, which assure the financial backing for public infrastructure investment.

Many early plans were done at the request of courts, who insisted that a comprehensive land-use plan form the foundation of the zoning ordinance. Space needed to be allocated for homes, various types of buildings for businesses, light and heavy industry, recreation, and traffic flow. Thus, a system of land-use classification was developed in most cities, as well as some smaller communities, using the plan as a guide for orderly growth. This document would attempt to organize and coordinate the complex relationships between urban and rural land uses and reflect the various policy alternatives where the plan's goals could best be reached. Some authorities assert that the plan is a process more than a conclusive statement about what the community must look like in twenty years. Since these are public plans about the direction of both public and private ventures, it is important to develop a credible process that all parties respect. A stumbling block to an otherwise seemingly rational planning process is the political dimension. Tensions usually exist among the various players who have stakes in the outcomes of the plan—state and local legislative officials, interest groups, developers, and professional planners.

While zoning became the prime land-use control mechanism in the United States in the twentieth century, it has been challenged on a number of grounds. For example, the courts have struck down numerous attempts by suburban municipalities to use their zoning power to keep out minority and low-income groups. While overt racism or classism in the ordinance would be easy to detect, subtle restrictions, such as requiring large resident lots, produce a mosaic of planned subdivisions that sometimes result in economic or racial segregation. Other planning and design critics assert that zoning has produced orthodox surburban communities by dividing vacant land into ineffi- cient, cookie cutter-like patterns and separating workplaces from living places. These neoclassical planners urge a return to a denser village core, with more integration among the various uses.

Zoning ordinances have created more rules governing development, which in most instances have slowed the overall process of formal proposal approval. When viewed in concert with numerous state regulations from departments of environmental pro- tection, as well as local building codes and the subdivision review process, zoning applications and other regulations can present a maze for many developers. Zoning in the late twentieth century does not appear to be protecting the public interest in land-management issues as it was designed to do. Since traditional zoning has not effectively controlled urbanization or encouraged meaningful economic development, other options such as growth management and economic development have flour- ished.

The growth management movement developed from a variety of citizen groups that demanded more control over the forces of growth than were available in most communities. Typically, suburban sprawl—extreme growth outside of a central city— became a catalyst for different types of land-use regulation. Some people were no-growth advocates, hoping to stop growth completely, which was found to be difficult and often illegal. Slow-growth and balanced-growth proponents responded with a more moderate stance of limiting growth to a certain rate and amount.

Greater citizen participation encouraged the development of and experimentation with additional land-use techniques. By the 1990's, many communities had made zoning more flexible by introducing cluster zoning, performance zoning, inclusionary zoning, and bonus or incentive zoning. In some places, exactions were charged to offset the costs that development was presumed to impose on the community.

Several states directed statewide planning efforts at their communities as a response to growth phobia. Previously, many states had allowed communities to decide how active they would be in planning and land-use activities. In general, the larger cities and suburban areas had been more active than the smaller towns and rural areas.

Advocates of a strong economic base at the community and regional levels were also frustrated with traditional land-use practices. By the 1990's many suburban communities and small towns had joined larger cities in proactive planning for economic growth. Many city managers believed that the economic development function had become an important element of their job description. Economic theory to encourage growth at the local level began to take on a more selective and strategic approach. An inventory of unique community needs produced different approaches, such as retention and expansion of existing basic industries, downtown development, and new business creation and development. Regardless of the direction selected by the citizens, economic development was as much an exercise in organizational change and group dynamics as an application of economic theory. Communities that had depended on one major industry began to chart their future by diversifying their economic base.

Applications

During the 1980's, Maine was one of a relatively few states attempting to implement a balanced, growth-management policy. Maine was an ideal environment to test growth-management theory, because its sluggish, regional economy had been based on declining industries such as pulp and paper, fishing, potato farming, and shoe manufacturing, all of which were impacted by global competition. Suburbanization had come late to this small, rural state, but southern Maine and select coastal communities had experienced extensive residential growth. For many observers, growth seemed to be out of control when the economy peaked during the 1980's.

A political coalition of environmentalists, municipal officials, Republicans, and Democrats urged that state laws be enacted that would push communities to comply with a rigorous planning and land-use process. After such a bill became law in 1988, municipal comprehensive plans and zoning ordinances, which previously had been optional, became difficult to avoid. A process of bottom-up citizen participation, local resource protection, development zones, and long-range financing devices such as capital improvement programs for infrastructure, was monitored and supported by a state agency. Most of the larger towns and cities previously had been involved in planning and land management, but smaller towns typically had resisted local planning initiatives. Moreover, a state land-use regulation commission was responsible for the huge tract of the state's unorganized, northwestern territory. Despite a progressive state response to the issues of growth, by the mid-1990's, the legislation had been weakened because of financial problems within the state government and the downswing of the regional economy.

A case that illustrates the application of economic development measures to a changing downtown area is that of Longmont, Colorado. During the late 1970's and early 1980's, this plains community of almost fifty thousand had lost shoppers to suburban malls, while its central business district's vacancy rate reached 20 percent. Its drainage system was deteriorating, its streets and sidewalks were in disarray, and there was a growing perception that the central business district was unsafe for shopping. The city council approved a development authority with the power to acquire property and make necessary site improvements in the 240-acre downtown district. The council also approved the concept of tax increment financing (TIF), which allowed the city to issue bonds for development purposes. Rather than relying on federal or state funding, TIF provided money for needed repairs and beautification projects.

Longmont reversed the decline of its central business district through the collaborative efforts of merchants, residents, and elected officials. Vacancy rates had declined to 7 percent by the end of the 1980's. Most of the infrastructure work was done quickly and at a reasonable cost. As the momentum for change built, additional grants from public and private sources were secured to enhance the quality of life.

Context

Although most land-use planning and management in the United States has been at the state and local levels, national planning and land management activities have a long history. Usually this was not seen as national planning, because no person or agency drew up a master plan that dealt with the same physical aspects that are found in most community comprehensive plans.

An ordinance passed by the Continental Congress laid out the six-square-mile township boundaries for the western territories. It also influenced the rapid settlement and division of the Northwest Territory into farm-sized plots. This established low density and relatively small farms, instead of the patterned European village with its surrounding fields.

In 1862, the Morrill Land Grant Act allotted states thirty thousand acres of federally owned land for each of its Congressional delegates. The states could use the monies from the sale of this land to create colleges to teach agriculture and the mechanical arts, which was the birth of the nation's land-grant college system. The Homestead Act was another illustration of the federal government's role in land management. Settlers were permitted to take 160-acre blocks of public land at virtually no cost, if they would live on the land for five consecutive years. Eighty million acres of land were homesteaded, but much of it was west of the Mississippi River and lacked the rainfall to sustain crops. Eventually the federal government began developing major water enhancement and irrigation policies, which spurred agricultural and community development.

Federal transportation policies have greatly influenced land management decisions. The Railway Land Grant Act of 1850 guided a national rail network and had significant impact on the pattern of settlement throughout the West. Liberal grants of public lands continued until 1873, when 160 million acres had been given to the railroads. Eventual sales of adjacent property to settlers and speculators proved to be quite lucrative.

The interstate highway system was another federal transportation-oriented stimulus to growth. Each major city was linked to a highway network of three million square miles in a cooperative arrangement between the states and the federal government. The Federal Aid Highway Act of 1956 established uniform standards of highway design and construction. It also created the Highway Trust Fund, which would provide public money from excise taxes on new vehicles and sales taxes on gasoline to support the massive building project. More than 42,500 miles had been completed by 1994 at an estimated cost of $130 billion. The relation of transportation infrastructure to land development was an important catalyst of growth.

Other examples of federal planning policies include electric power generation, experiments such as the Tennessee Valley Authority, flood control, management of the 119,000-square-mile national park system, and Native American reservations. More than a million square miles of the United States, the bulk of which is in the Western states, are national public land. The Bureau of Land Management of the Department of Interior manages hundreds of millions of acres, much of which is inaccessible, arid, and valued very low.

Numerous unrelated federal policies have contributed to the national government's planning activities that relate to land management. In 1943, Congress ended the National Resources Planning Board, which had served briefly as a national planning agency, but prohibited any other federal agency from assuming this role in the future.

Bibliography

Babcock, Richard F. *The Zoning Game: Municipal Practices and Policies.* Madison: University of Wisconsin Press, 1966. Lively account by an experienced legal practitioner, including roles of developers, planners, attorneys, judges, and government.

Baldwin, A. Dwight, Judith DeLuce, and Carl Pletsch, eds. *Beyond Preservation: Restoring and Inventing Landscapes.* Minneapolis: University of Minnesota Press, 1994. Multidisciplinary collection of academic readings on ecology and the reconstruction of landscapes through archaeological, historical, and geological analysis.

Blakely, Edward J. *Planning Local Economic Development: Theory and Practice.* 2d ed. Thousand Oaks, Calif.: Sage Publications, 1994. Revised edition of a leading work in the field by a professor of planning, written in a clear style for a practitioner audience.

Clawson, Marion. *The Bureau of Land Management.* New York: Praeger, 1971. Detailed inside view of the BLM. Dated, but still useful for historical background.

DeGrove, John M., ed. *Balanced Growth: A Planning Guide for Local Government.* Washington, D.C.: International City Management Association, 1991. Traces the development of the growth management movement. Excellent examples of many experimental laws and strategies at the state and local levels.

Frieden, Bernard J., and Lynne B. Sagalyn. *Downtown, Inc.: How America Rebuilds Cities.* Cambridge, Mass.: MIT Press, 1989. Cases of both innovative and problematic development of land in core cities. Emphasis on experimentation in commercial development, especially shopping malls.

Makielski, Stanislaw J., Jr. *The Politics of Zoning: The New York Experience*. New York: Columbia University Press, 1966. Excellent case study of adoption and implementation of nation's first comprehensive land-use law (1916).

Nelson, Robert H. *Zoning and Property Rights: An Analysis of the American System of Land-Use Regulation*. Cambridge, Mass.: MIT Press, 1980. Economic analysis that disputes the commonly held legal view that the purpose of zoning is to protect the public interest and argues instead that it is to enhance property value.

Soil Resources, Management and Conservation Service. *Guidelines for Land-Use Planning*. Rome: Food and Agriculture Organization of the United Nations, 1993. Guide to assist with planning the development, management, and conservation of rural land. Provides overview for countries who adopt land-use plans.

Stein, Jay M., ed. *Growth Management: The Planning Challenge of the 1990's*. Newbury Park, Calif.: Sage Publications, 1993. Excellent academic study that focuses on states that have adopted rigorous growth-control legislation.

G. Thomas Taylor

Cross-References

Agriculture Management, p. 41; Environmental Protection, p. 617; Public Works, p. 1647; Resource Management, p. 1718; State and Local Government, p. 1885; Transportation Management in the United States, p. 2006; Urban Policy, p. 2057.

LATINO POLITICS

Field of study: Politics

The interests of Hispanic people of Mexican, Puerto Rican, Cuban, and Central and South American origin in the United States constitute Latino politics.

Principal terms
> ASSIMILATION AND ACCULTURATION: process of becoming like another group in language and culture
> BARRIO: neighborhood with a high proportion of Latino residents
> NATURALIZATION: process by which a foreign-born person acquires citizenship
> URBAN PARTY MACHINE: tightly knit political party operation, often supported by ethnic groups, that organizes voters to vote for party members

Overview

Latino Americans have long been an important component of the population of the United States. Until the late twentieth century, however, their numbers were so small that they were politically weak. Throughout most of American history their political impact has been limited except in some Southwest locales. Substantial changes started in the 1970's, when a great increase in the Latino population, with increasing numbers eligible for citizenship, educational improvement, and a developing political consciousness, occurred. In New York, Miami, Chicago, and all the major cities of the Southwest, to understand local politics is to understand Latino politics.

Some serious problems in studying the Latino population limit the accuracy of statistical generalizations. It is not known exactly how many Latinos there are in the United States because many are in the United States illegally and avoid contact with government. Before 1980, the census did not systematically investigate Hispanic identity. Only infrequently do studies differentiate the various Latino groups, who, although they may have a language in common, can be very different culturally and ethnically.

Despite these uncertainties, some facts remain clear. The most important change has been the dramatic increase in the number of Latinos. By the 1980's, they comprised more than 54 percent of new immigrants. Between 1970 and 1990, the Latino population in the United States increased from 9.1 million (4.5 percent of the total) to 22.4 million (9.0 percent). With high immigration and birth rates, the Latino American population is projected to surpass the African American population by about 2012.

It is a serious mistake to think of Latinos as a homogeneous, unified group, and as distinct from other racial and ethnic groups. Regrettably, this mistake has often been made in the pursuit of votes or simpler statistics. Biologically, Hispanics do not constitute a racial group. They are composed primarily of three racial groups, though almost all identify themselves as white. Differences among various Latino groups often far outweigh cultural similarities. For example, in a 1992 survey, 64 percent of Cuban Americans preferred the Republicans, while only 14 percent of the Puerto Ricans did.

A few traits, however, are generally found across all Hispanic groups. A very high proportion, about 90 percent, are urbanized. Most are recent immigrants or are second generation. As a result, they have generally low socioeconomic status. The overwhelming majority are Roman Catholic, although many Latinos have weaker ties to the church than was typical of other Catholic immigrant groups. The Roman Catholic church has not played an important role in assimilating Latinos into Anglo-American society nor in protecting their political interests.

According to the 1990 U.S. census, the largest number of Latinos are Mexicans (64 percent), followed by Puerto Ricans (11 percent) and Cubans (5 percent). The most recently arrived and the fastest-growing groups are from Central and South America (13 percent), but information about their politics is quite limited. To understand better the political outlook of Latino groups, one needs to look at where each group came from, what it came with, and what its experience has been in the United States.

The earliest group is also the largest. Most of the Mexican American population is from post-World War II immigration, although Mexicans moved into the Southwest before the European settlers. By the end of the Mexican-American War of 1848, the United States had acquired Texas, New Mexico, Arizona and California, and Mexican influence waned. It should be kept in mind, however, when examining the politics of the southwestern United States, that much of the land once belonged to Mexico.

Originally, Mexicans played a role in the state conventions, particularly in New Mexico and California. They fought to protect not only their property, but also their cultural rights. In 1910, New Mexico officially became a bilingual state. In California, initially, all laws had to be translated into Spanish. Even after California became an American state in 1850, the first mayors and city councils of Los Angeles were Mexican. Over time, however, the Anglo-Americans (and later Asians and African Americans) grew in number and politically displaced the Mexican Americans. Later, particularly in Texas, a number of schemes were used to deprive many Mexican Americans of the vote.

Mexican immigration increased after World War I. During the 1930's, when jobs were scarce, four hundred thousand Mexicans were repatriated back to Mexico. When need for cheap labor grew in the 1950's, immigration picked up and then mushroomed starting in the 1970's. Mexicans increasingly came north because of the pull of jobs in the economically expanding Southwest, and the push from growing overpopulation in Mexico. Although the economy of Mexico was improved, it was unlikely to grow sufficiently to prevent continued emigration.

The Puerto Ricans have a different history. Following the island's conquest in the Spanish-American War (1898), the Jones Act (1917) implemented full American citizenship to Puerto Ricans, with free rights of access to the mainland and nonvoting representation in Congress.

Large-scale Puerto Rican migration did not begin until the late 1940's. Unfortunately, these people, who were, to a large extent, Spanish-speaking, rural, and with low levels of education, came primarily to metropolitan New York at a time when the region started to lose semiskilled jobs in manufacturing. As a result, the New York job market, though far better than Puerto Rico's, did not offer the same gateway to economic success that had been available for earlier immigrants.

Proximity to Puerto Rico and commercial flights made for easy travel to and from the island. The cultural shock of big-city life in New York, with its freezing winters, shortage of good permanent jobs, and absence of extended family, led many to return periodically to Puerto Rico, only to return again to the mainland for lack of economic opportunity. In addition to the problems of job instability, this nomadic life created special educational problems for children, who faced obstacles in language, overcrowded schools, and home environments not supportive of higher education.

One consequence of these difficulties is that Puerto Ricans remained poor. They did not develop a strong interest in or facility with national and local politics. Puerto Ricans did not put down roots in the community. Indicators of political influence such as home ownership and higher education remained relatively low.

In addition, interest in American politics was deflected by the big political issue in Puerto Rico—whether to seek either independence or statehood, or to retain the commonwealth status. Much of the energy and organization that might have been spent in mainland politics was preempted by politics back on the island.

The last of the major groups with a long political history in the United States is the Cubans. They came to the United States in the shortest, most concentrated span, primarily right before and after Fidel Castro's takeover in 1959. There was also a smaller wave of immigration in 1980. Unlike most immigrants, many of the first immigrants were middle class; their economic interests would have been persecuted under Castro's communism.

Initially, much of the Cuban political interest was devoted to island politics. Cuban expatriates were among those who plotted and engaged in the disastrous Bay of Pigs invasion. Over time, however, with Castro's success in maintaining power, the Cubans largely gave up hope of militarily recapturing Cuba and instead devoted their energy to economic and political issues in the United States.

The distinguishing traits about the Cubans are their heavy concentration in south Florida and their relative economic success, much higher than for the other Hispanic groups although still a little lower than the American average. Among the three groups discussed in this article, Cubans have the highest percentage of immigrants and members of the second generation. Among the three groups, the Cubans are demographically the oldest, and the most Spanish-speaking. Their educational and economic success reflects their relatively quick acculturation to the United States. At the same time, they have maintained strong ethnic bonds.

Applications

As a result of differing backgrounds, Latino groups have different levels of interest in and orientation to U.S. politics. Many recent Mexican immigrants in the Southwest live in highly ghettoized areas and feel uncomfortable with English. The proximity to Mexico facilitates periodic trips to visit families. Many Mexican immigrants are illegal aliens, so they avoid contact with the government. As a result, although most intend to stay in the United States, they comprise the group with the lowest rates of naturalization. One study found that only 15 percent of Mexican-born adults in the United States were naturalized.

In addition, the Mexicans tend to be young, poorly educated, unskilled, and from rural backgrounds. The large majority has very little political involvement in Mexico, whose political structure is corrupt and alienating. Among Mexican Americans who are citizens, voter registration rates are low. Among those who register, voting rates are distinctly lower than they are for other Americans. Only a small number become naturalized, it should also be remembered, and thus many remain ineligible to vote.

Mexicans are primarily Democratic in their party affiliation. Although they support relatively liberal economic positions, they also hold moderately conservative social positions on capital punishment and on family issues such as abortion.

Until the 1980's relatively few Mexican Americans had been elected or appointed to government positions. Even after considerable gains in Texas, which has the largest number of elected Hispanic officials, Latinos constitute only 8 percent of the officials, although Hispanics (overwhelmingly Mexican) comprise 26 percent of the Texas population. Only in New Mexico are Mexican Americans almost proportionately elected.

Nevertheless, there is demonstrable progress. Nationally, the total number of Hispanic elected officials—primarily Mexican—increased about 60 percent from 1983 to 1993. Between 1987 and 1993, Mexicans served in four Cabinet positions—three appointed by Republicans. In 1951 only two members of Congress were Hispanic. That increased to nine in 1984 and up to seventeen in 1992. Eleven were Mexican, all but one a Democrat. Hispanic caucuses exist in the national as well as several state legislatures.

On the local level, especially in the Southwest states, the Mexican American presence is expanding. It is clear that as more Mexican Americans become naturalized, register to vote, and vote, there will be greater presence of Mexican American candidates and support from interest groups.

Puerto Ricans, who, like Mexican Americans, have been largely inactive, and for similar reasons (except citizenship), will likely increase their influence. The second and particularly the third generations of Puerto Ricans are considerably more educated than their parents. With higher education comes more interest and participation in politics. With the growing involvement of a third generation of Puerto Ricans, more politicians in both New York City and Chicago will likely be of Puerto Rican heritage. In 1992, New York elected, for the first time, a Puerto Rican woman to Congress. In Chicago, starting in the early 1990's, over three hundred Puerto Ricans served as elected members of local school boards. The growing importance of New York's Puerto Rican Day Parade, which attracts many regional political leaders, symbolizes the growing political consciousness and importance of Puerto Ricans.

Their very low socioeconomic status and their concentration in New York and Chicago—two very strongly Democratic cities—is reflected in the fact that Puerto Ricans have high rates of Democratic Party affiliation. They are solidly liberal on economic issues and somewhat moderate on social issues. Their agenda is much better represented by the Democratic Party: jobs for the poor, cheap housing, expanded medical coverage, and money for public education.

The Cuban political experience is notably different. As escapees from Castro, Cuban Americans have been strongly anticommunist. Many are entrepreneurs; they are not sympathetic to government regulation of business and higher taxes. Combined with a generally conservative position on family matters and abortion, they are often counted on for a strong Republican vote. Cuban Americans are by far the most educated Hispanic group, and are much more likely to be naturalized than the Mexican Americans. More Cuban Americans are able to register and to vote. Their numbers in Dade County, Florida, have enabled them to exert considerable influence over Miami politics, evidenced by Miami's, Cuban-born mayor, Xavier Suarez. The community also elected two Cuban-born Congressmen (both Republicans) in the early 1990's.

Of all three groups, the political differences across the generations are strongest for the Cuban Americans—and in direction, opposite from the others. Young Mexican Americans and Puerto Ricans are less likely to be Democratic partisans than their elders. Second- and third-generation Cuban Americans, more educated and American-ized than their parents, tend to be less anticommunist and more moderate on social issues, and so less strongly Republican, although still more conservative than other Hispanics generally.

Context

American politics has always reflected America's ethnic makeup. The national leadership and the electorate have largely been of West European origin, although in the twentieth century, the population growth of other ethnic groups in the large cities provided strength for the ethnic urban party machine.

The urban machines, once a major political factor, have been seriously weakened, partly because the economic success of ethnic groups with an established history of machine politics led to their move outside the inner city. Although African Americans have remained largely liberal and Democratic, even as their income levels rise, for third- and fourth-generation members of other ethnic groups, socioeconomic class has become more important than ethnic heritage in determining party affiliation.

Relative latecomers on the American political scene, Latinos have been late in organizing and slow in seizing power. The Mexican Americans, in particular, have been adept at creating political organizations but have been largely unsuccessful at grassroots organizing. A notable exception is Cesar Chavez's union, the United Farm Workers.

The Mexican Americans have been held back by several demographic factors, such as continuous immigration of newcomers and lack of success at developing pan-

Hispanic political group consciousness and organization. Among Latinos, there is a lack of common culture and historical ties. Until the 1990's, each group tended to be geographically distinct from the others (except in Chicago). That began to change, with increased Central American immigration.

As a result, there are few specific Hispanic issues. For example, citizenship and immigration laws are simply not a concern of the Puerto Ricans, but to Mexicans and Mexican Americans, they are. Unlike the others, the Cubans do not see themselves as a poor community and they oppose government regulation of the economy, although they do lobby for government help for their community. Even within a group, for example, the Mexicans, those whose families have been in the United States for generations have interests that differ from those of the newcomers. The more established citizens often want protection against the immigration of poor laborers.

The increase in the population of Hispanic citizens offers the possibility of the renewal of urban ethnic politics. In fact, political change has already been occurring, mostly in the legal system. The successes include outgrowths from the Civil Rights movement: outlawing the all-Anglo American primary, extending the Voting Rights Act to the Southwest, eliminating the poll tax, eliminating the English literacy requirement for voters, and transforming electoral districts from city-wide districts— where Latinos are a minority—to local districts, where many Latinos may win office. With more Hispanic officials in office will come greater political awareness, more organization, and more political power.

What meaningful changes might occur as a result of the electoral success of the Hispanics? Most of the significant change might be at the local level as Latino-owned businesses might benefit from more government business contracts. More Hispanics might be hired as government workers and more might serve on local commissions. Government services in Hispanic neighborhoods might be improved as well as more incentives given to private business to expand jobs and services in the barrio.

One area of potential change is immigration policy, which has been hard for any one political group to control effectively. Ultimately, immigration responds to the larger issue of economic opportunity. Immigration is not a high priority for most Latino American citizens, whose views on immigration are surprisingly like those of other Americans. Hispanics may influence specific policies such as amnesty and family reunification.

As Latino political power in the United States continues to develop, there will be more elected Latino leaders, more Hispanic interest groups, and more government responsiveness to the needs of the Latino community.

Bibliography

Boswell, Thomas D., and James R. Curtis. *The Cuban-American Experience: Culture, Images and Perspectives.* Totowa, N.J.: Rowman & Allanheld, 1984. Overall review of the development of Cuban American culture.

Fitzpatrick, Joseph P. *Puerto Rican Americans: The Meaning of Migration to the Mainland.* 2d ed. Englewood Cliffs, N.J.: Prentice-Hall, 1987. Detailed sociological portrait of Puerto Ricans—their cultural attributes, religious and racial attitudes, and their assimilation problems.

Garcia, F. Chris, ed. *Latinos and the Political System.* Notre Dame, Ind.: University of Notre Dame Press, 1988. Compilation of twenty-seven important articles on political demography, participation, representation, and policies.

Garza, Rodolfo de la, et al. *Latino Voices: Mexican, Puerto Rican, and Cuban Perspectives on American Politics.* Boulder, Colo.: Westview Press, 1992. Demographic findings of the Latino National Political Survey (1989-1990).

Alan M. Fisher

Cross-References

African American Politics, p. 28; Asian American Politics, p. 115; Civil Rights Protection, p. 304; Immigrants and Politics, p. 861; Immigration and Emigration, p. 868; Immigration Regulation, p. 875; Mexico: Politics and Government, p. 1179; Political Machines and Bosses, p. 1468; Political Participation, p. 1479; Race and Ethnicity, p. 1654; Voting Behavior in the United States, p. 2109.

LAW ENFORCEMENT

Field of study: Functions of government

Law enforcement refers to the power, authority, and ability of a government to enforce the expectations and norms that a community has for its members' behavior. If a citizen violates the criminal laws of a community, he or she may receive governmentally sanctioned punishment, including imprisonment, or even execution.

Principal terms

COMMERCE CLAUSE: portion of the Constitution that authorizes the federal government to pass criminal laws to ensure an efficient and fair system of commerce

DEFENDANT: person that is formally charged with a crime

DUE PROCESS: criminal law rights to which every defendant is entitled under the Fifth and Fourteenth amendments to the United States Constitution

EXCLUSIONARY RULE: rule that prevents evidence from being used against a defendant at trial if the police violated constitutional protections in obtaining the evidence

FEDERALISM: government at two levels: the state level and the federal (national) level

LAW ENFORCEMENT AGENCIES: national, state, and local entities engaged in crime prevention, law enforcement, and apprehension of criminals

POLICE POWER: constitutional authority of each state to pass criminal laws to ensure public safety, health, and morals

Overview

Law enforcement is a means by which governments control the behavior of their citizens. Usually, the stated goal of law enforcement is to allow citizens as much freedom as possible while still maintaining public order, safety, health, and morals. Most justice professionals believe that law enforcement agencies exist to ensure that the social values of a majority of society are maintained. Others would argue, however, as did Karl Marx in the 1800's, that governments are controlled by dominant social and economic groups, who use laws to benefit their own interests. Indeed, in the former Soviet Union, based on Marxist ideology, criminologists thought that crime could be controlled if capitalism could be eliminated.

Virtually all societies have adopted formal governmental structures to enforce social norms. Most countries allowed social norms to be enforced through tribal laws, religious doctrines, and social customs. When strong centralized governments were absent, local groups, religious leaders, and aristocrats created their own laws, which they often applied in an arbitrary and unpredictable manner. At different times in

England, for example, a murderer could be sentenced to death or merely ordered to pay a minimal fine.

Probably the earliest governmentally sanctioned and codified law existed in what is now Iraq and Saudi Arabia. The Sumerians (c. 3100 B.C.E.) almost certainly had written laws; the ruler Hammurabi, who about 1750 B.C.E. developed the Code of Hammurabi, left evidence of the first written law, which codified social norms on stone. The Code of Hammurabi lists, for example, specific acts as crimes and prescribes punishments.

Later, about 600 to 500 B.C.E., Greek rulers such as Draco, Solon, and Cleisthenes, published written laws, abolished imprisonment for debts, created appellate courts, and permitted jury trials. Under King Henry II in the late twelfth century, C.E., England developed a common law that allowed deviant actions to be prosecuted by a community leader. The early American colonists believed that crime was caused by the devil. The Quaker persecutions of the 1650's and the witchcraft hysteria of 1692 reflect that belief.

Governmentally sanctioned law enforcement developed more formally in the twelfth and thirteenth centuries. In England, the frankpledge system required groups of families to pursue and apprehend lawbreakers. When any male over the age of twelve discovered that a crime had occurred, he was required to raise a "hue and cry," which notified other families to pursue the alleged criminal. The government fined the families, groups of ten called "tithings," for failing to exercise their duties.

Also in England, in 1285, law enforcement became more structured with the passage of the Statute of Westminster. The statute authorized a parish system in which a local constable organized citizens to pursue criminals. The constable was a man from the local parish who served without pay for one year. Although the constable system served satisfactorily for centuries, the Industrial Revolution in the late 1700's brought social disorder. Confronted with widespread riots in England in 1780, the people still so feared government tyranny that they were reluctant to form more organized police forces.

In 1829, however, Parliament created the Metropolitan Constabulary for London, which became the model for police forces in England and the United States. Centrally controlled and supervised by Home Secretary Sir Robert Peel (from whom the English "bobbies" take their name), the force was charged with preventing crime and fostering public order without resorting to violence and repression. In the United States, although utilizing the English model of law enforcement, police forces have confronted unique problems that have necessitated alternative models. Racial divisions have created tensions, the tradition of independence and the right of gun possession have fostered violence, and the federal-and-state system of government (federalism) has created territorial disputes about the authority of different governmental entities.

Ultimately, in the United States, law enforcement was organized nationally, regionally by states, and locally. The vast majority of police functions are conducted by personnel working for local police forces. This structure contrasts significantly with that in other countries, where law enforcement is often centralized under a national police force. In France, for example, the criminal code and justice procedures, along with most political power, emanate from central bureaucracies in Paris. The two main police forces in France are organized under the national ministries of Defense and Interior, respectively.

American ideas about law enforcement have evolved significantly. Placing great value on independence and civil liberty, Americans have regarded even local police forces with skepticism but with ultimate acceptance. The growth of a new country and civil disorder in American cities during the 1800's similar to that in England required the creation of constabularies. The era of constabularies in U.S. law enforcement extended from 1840 to 1920 and was known as the political era. Then, politicians appointed only their most loyal supporters to police forces; these police often took bribes. During this era, police officers reacted to crime and social disorder only as politically troubling problems arose. Then during the professional era (1920-1980) in law enforcement, reformers argued that police forces should be neutral and nonpartisan. They believed that officers should be well-trained members of a disciplined force and that all laws should be enforced without favor or prejudice.

Since 1970, much of American law enforcement has been organized around the community policing model. Advocates of this model believe that the police can deter crime by attending not only to crime fighting, but also to maintaining general order. Communities that have adopted this model might place officers on foot patrols so that officers can better understand local citizens and problems. Like Japanese officers, who almost always patrol on foot, such officers focus on developing personal interactions with community members and groups. Local control and community policing may require officers to accept innumerable responsibilities. Beyond apprehending criminals, these responsibilities may include mediating family disputes, providing care for homeless and mentally ill persons, and directing traffic.

In the United States, the Constitution's Commerce Clause, contained in Article 1, permits the federal government, as the police powers inherent in the Tenth Amendment permit the states, to pass criminal laws. Having the legal authority to prevent and prosecute crime, law enforcement agencies must also ensure that criminal defendants receive every constitutional right to which they are entitled. If an agency violates a constitutional right, then any evidence that the agency obtains as a result of the violation cannot be used at trial to prove the defendant's guilt. The exclusion of such evidence is known as the "exclusionary rule."

If the judge finds, for example, that the police entered a house without a warrant or probable cause (a violation of the Fourth Amendment), then the judge will not allow the prosecution to show the jury any incriminating evidence, such as guns or drugs, that the police found inside the house. If the judge excludes such incriminating evidence, it is less likely that the jury will find the defendant guilty. Judges exclude such evidence so that the police will be deterred from violating citizens' constitutional rights.

Law enforcement functions extend throughout American society. When making an arrest, police officers take the defendant to court, where the judge determines whether to set bail. The prosecutor then assumes control of the case and presents the evidence to a grand jury (composed of up to twenty-three citizen jurors), or to a judge at a preliminary examination. The grand jury or the judge determines the charges that will be finally lodged against the defendant. At any point in the proceeding, the government and the defendant may agree on a disposition of the case, which is called a "plea bargain."

If no plea bargain is offered by the prosecution, or if the defendant refuses an offer of a plea bargain, a trial begins. If the defendant is found guilty, the trial judge sentences the defendant. Generally, sentences range from probation (supervised release) to a term of imprisonment. During a term of probation, the defendant will not be imprisoned, but the defendant's civil liberties will be restricted and the government can monitor his or her behavior. In some states, if the defendant is convicted of murder, the state may execute the defendant, but the death penalty may not be administered for any crime but murder. If the jury finds the defendant not guilty, the defendant is released from any obligation to the government.

Applications

Although some countries, such as China, use laws mainly to further political ideology, most countries use criminal laws to regulate individual behavior. In these countries, the goals of law enforcement and the rights of citizens often come into conflict. Law enforcement officials wish to apprehend and prosecute a defendant in the most efficient manner. Defendants wish to assert every possible right so that they may avoid prison. At some point, the courts must determine how to balance law enforcement objectives and individual rights.

The balancing focuses on what individual liberties may be curtailed so that law enforcement may engage in more efficient crime prevention and prosecution. In the United States, for example, in one case, *Terry v. Ohio* (1968), the Supreme Court concluded that police officers, for their own safety, should be free to stop and "pat down" a citizen, if the officers have reasonable suspicion that the citizen has a weapon. Thus, in a relatively few instances, the police may curtail a citizen's freedom without believing that the citizen committed a crime.

In another case, the Supreme Court attempted to balance the differing interests of society and its citizens when, in 1966, it rendered one of its most controversial decisions ever, *Miranda v. Arizona*. In that case, the defendant, Ernesto Miranda, had orally and in a written statement confessed to the crimes of kidnapping and rape, for which he was convicted and sentenced to prison. At Miranda's trial, the police officers who had questioned Miranda and obtained his confession admitted that they had not notified him of his right to an attorney. Before the *Miranda* decision, the Supreme Court, in another case, *Gideon v. Wainwright* (1963), had concluded that every criminal defendant had the Sixth Amendment right to an attorney, but the Court had not required the police to notify a defendant of this right.

In the *Miranda* case, then, the question before the Court was whether the police also had to notify the defendant of his right to an attorney. The Supreme Court held that the police did have to inform every defendant of this right, because if a defendant is not aware of the right to an attorney, then he or she cannot really exercise the right. In *Miranda*, the Supreme Court concluded that a defendant could not knowingly and voluntarily make a statement to police without being informed of the right to an attorney. The Supreme Court reversed Miranda's conviction and sent the case back for a new trial.

The *Miranda* decision had a significant effect on law enforcement. The states lost some of their historical authority over criminal matters. They saw the Court's decision (a federal court's decision based on the federal Constitution) as one that reversed notions of federalism, that is, the right of states to exercise control over state and local matters. Conversely, many civil libertarians hailed the decision as a check against police officers' misconduct in their questioning of suspects.

Also, by reversing the defendant's conviction in *Miranda*, the Supreme Court utilized a classic application of the exclusionary rule. The Court found that the police had violated the defendant's constitutional rights by not telling him of his right to an attorney. Therefore, Miranda's confessions should not have been introduced as evidence at his trial. Given that the confession might have led the jury to convict the defendant, the Court ruled that the conviction should be reversed and that the defendant should receive a new trial.

Finally, the costs and benefits to law enforcement and government of a decision such as *Miranda* are significant. Law enforcement officials have fewer opportunities to coerce or trick a defendant into confessing. Most important, it will be less likely that an innocent person will be coerced into confessing to a crime that he or she did not commit. On the other hand, although Ernesto Miranda may have been absolutely guilty of kidnapping and rape, and his confession may have been perfectly true, his original conviction was overturned. The *Miranda* decision remains one of the most significant and controversial decisions that the Court has made regarding the balance between individual rights and police powers.

Context

The regulatory functions of law enforcement officers and agencies will continually conflict with individual liberty. While the United States Constitution has guaranteed many procedural protections for criminal defendants, it has not prevented the federal and state governments from using the commerce clause and their police powers to regulate behavior at virtually every level of society, from the packing of meat to the prosecution of murder. The proponents of regulation argue that the government needs to foster strict controls in a technological world. Violent crime must be stopped, food must be safe, and citizens' desires to advance their selfish interests must be controlled. Law enforcement is the means by which government must exercise control. The opponents of stricter regulation lean on the Constitution's Bill of Rights to protect society from expansive and authoritarian law enforcement activity. They would argue that the exclusion of reliable evidence from a criminal case is justified to maintain civil liberties.

It is possible that the Supreme Court will henceforth entertain few criminal cases of great significance. In the 1960's, the Court heard many cases, as a result of which it advanced the due process rights of criminal defendants. In the 1970's and early 1980's, the Court refused to expand the rights of criminal defendants. In the 1990's, the Court considered a relatively few criminal cases. The Court concluded that law enforcement could be conducted more efficiently and properly by the states. Law enforcement officials can fairly reliably determine what police actions will conform to the U.S. Constitution.

Defendants can be expected to resort to state constitutions to achieve greater protections. Under the principle of federalism, the states are free to provide their criminal defendants with more protections than what defendants might obtain under the United States Constitution, so long as no federal rights are diminished. Thus, having determined what is proper police behavior under the U.S. Constitution, law enforcement officials must determine what is proper under their state constitutions as well. By contrast, in Great Britain, where there is no federalist system, law enforcement agencies have only to examine the laws that Parliament passes to determine what is legal.

A government that has national, state, and local laws will need a variety of law enforcement agencies to implement and enforce the laws. To operate efficiently at all these levels, law enforcement agencies need resources, expertise, and structure. To prevent and prosecute crime, these agencies must limit certain freedoms. On the other hand, to foster citizens' growth, potential, and productivity, these agencies want to ensure as much liberty as possible. The balance of these two goals that law enforcement achieves within a formal governmental structure is the measure of its success.

Bibliography

Allen, Ronald J., and Richard B. Kuhns. *Constitutional Criminal Procedure: An Examination of the Fourth, Fifth, and Sixth Amendments and Related Areas.* Boston: Little, Brown, 1985. Clearly outlines the legal responsibilities of U.S. law enforcement. Suitable for detailed research.

Cole, George F. *The American System of Criminal Justice.* 6th ed. Monterey, Calif.: Brooks/Cole, 1992. Readable and comprehensive book on the justice system, from investigation and arrest to sentencing and correctional processes.

Farber, Daniel A., and Suzanna Sherry. *A History of the American Constitution.* St. Paul, Minn.: West, 1990. Contains the rationale behind the adoption of various constitutional provisions. Most helpful in its discussion of the Fourteenth Amendment.

Israel, Jerold H., Yale Kamisar, and Wayne LaFave. *Criminal Procedure and the Constitution: Leading Supreme Court Cases and Introductory Text.* St. Paul, Minn.: West, 1993. Detailed discussion of the Supreme Court cases that shaped the limits of law enforcement.

Lowi, Theodore J., and Benjamin Ginsberg. *American Government: Freedom and Power.* New York: W. W. Norton, 1994. Guide on the functions, structure, and interrelationships of governmental institutions.

Samaha, Joel. *Criminal Justice*. 3d ed. St. Paul, Minn.: West, 1994. Excellent focus on the practical problems of law enforcement.

Timothy Bakken

Cross-References

The Bill of Rights, p. 134; Civil Liberties Protection, p. 291; The Constitution of the United States, p. 425; Government Roles, p. 778; Judicial Review, p. 1012; Jurisprudence, p. 1019; Legal Systems in Anglo-American Governments, p. 1085; Legislative Functions of Government, p. 1098; Organized Crime and Political Corruption, p. 1355; The Supreme Court: Role in Government and Law, p. 1935; Urban Governments, p. 2052.

LEADERSHIP

Field of study: Politics

Leadership is associated with the ability of office holders to have their positions accepted and adopted as the proper course of action by a group or society. In politics, strong leadership is most frequently required and evident during periods of acute crisis.

Principal terms

IDEOLOGICAL LEADER: person who pursues political goals and bases policy choices on personal beliefs about what should be done

NEW DEAL: policies of President Franklin Roosevelt designed to lift the U.S. economy out of the Great Depression of the 1930's

PERESTROIKA: reforms of Soviet president Mikhail Gorbachev designed to revitalize the Soviet Union, which he led from 1985 until 1991

PRAGMATIC LEADER: person who lacks clearly defined goals and makes case-specific policy decisions based on practicality and expediency

RATIONAL LEADER: person who pursues political goals and bases policy choices on reasoned analysis of information

Overview

The study of leadership emphasizes individual units of analysis. It is argued that individual human beings—not inanimate institutions, systems, or forces—lead. If leadership is individualistic by nature, then what personal qualities characterize leaders? Do leaders think and act in certain and predictable ways?

The historical record is replete with examples of leaders. In reviewing history it is clear that no one set of personal traits can characterize or predict who will or will not become a leader. The world has seen introverted and extroverted leaders, rich and poor leaders, male and female leaders, physically capable and physically challenged leaders, homosexual and heterosexual leaders, formally educated and informally educated leaders, leaders from different races, leaders that practice different religions, leaders that speak different languages, and leaders from different regions of the world. There is no one model or set of characteristics that leaders possess. While the personal characteristics of leaders vary greatly, they share the ability to persuade people to adopt and accept courses of action that they advocate, particularly in response to crises.

Three broad styles can be identified as to how leaders develop policies that will be accepted and adopted by others. Some leaders make decisions on the basis of pragmatism, some are goal oriented and rational in their approach to decision making, and some are ideologically motivated and base policy decisions on their own belief systems.

Pragmatic leaders have no clear goals or comprehensive agenda in mind, but make policy choices on a case-by-case basis with the practicality, feasibility, and expediency of policy options being paramount. Pragmatic decision makers are not interested in realizing any particular philosophies or ends. They are thus not bound to particular patterns of decisions. A political pragmatist might adopt a policy solution from one particular school of thought, then turn around and adopt another policy solution from a rival school of thought.

While pragmatists are not goal oriented by nature, other leaders are, and their policy decisions are geared toward pursuit of their goals. Rational decision makers exhibit a leadership style that is goal oriented. They define goals that they want to achieve and advocate policies that will best meet these goals. Rational leaders select policies on the basis of a reasoned analysis of what will best help them achieve their goals. The reasoned analysis of policy options involves a careful and meticulous review of all available information to make sure the policy selected is the correct one.

Like rational decision makers, ideological decision makers are goal oriented by nature. Unlike rational decision makers, however, ideological decision makers have preconceived notions of which policies will achieve their goals. They choose policies on the basis of their own beliefs, rather than on fresh objective and reasoned review of pertinent information.

Though the study of leadership puts an overwhelming emphasis on the traits of individuals as leaders, it should be understood that individuals must be in the right positions at the right times in order to have opportunities to lead. This situational aspect of leadership cannot be overlooked, as no one knows how many potential leaders never had chances to lead because of circumstances beyond their control. For individuals to be able to lead, their personal skills and talents must mesh with situational opportunities.

Applications

Case studies of three political leaders in the twentieth century will help elucidate the problems of leadership in Western democracies, Eastern bloc countries, and the Third World.

Franklin Delano Roosevelt was born in Hyde Park, New York, in 1882. In 1932, he defeated Herbert Hoover in the U.S. presidential election and he was reelected president in 1936, 1940, and 1944. The only U.S. president elected four times, he died shortly after beginning his fourth term of office on April 12, 1945. During his service as president, Roosevelt faced two crises, the likes of which no other American president has ever faced: the Great Depression and World War II.

By 1933, both the U.S. and the global economies were mired in depression as a consequence of the global turn toward protectionist economic policies following World War I, the inability of European states to overcome the physical and psychological scars of World War I, and the collapse of the U.S. stock market in October, 1929. The American people were in serious economic trouble after seeing their banks fail and many of their jobs lost. As president, Roosevelt accepted the challenge of trying to lift the U.S. economy out of depression. His overall program for solving the problems associated with the Great Depression was the New Deal, which greatly enlarged the role government played within the United States. It directed expenditure of government funds to relieve human misery and suffering caused by the Depression; it led to the hiring of many workers by the government to build roads, dams, and other public works projects; and it launched unprecedented regulation of the market economy through the creation and empowerment of numerous boards, agencies, and commissions.

On September 1, 1939, Germany invaded Poland. Shortly thereafter, Great Britain and France declared war on Germany. Roosevelt now had to deal not only with the lingering economic problems of the Depression, but also with the outbreak of war in Europe. By the end of 1940, France had fallen to Germany, and Britain was being subjected to German aerial bombardment. The predominant mood in the United States was one of isolationism, which severely limited Roosevelt's ability to assist his West European friends. Through the passage of his Lend-Lease program by the U.S. Congress in 1941, Roosevelt found a way to supply the allies with war material and financial assistance without the United States having to directly enter the war.

Debates over the Lend-Lease program became moot after Japan's surprise attack on the U.S. naval forces based at Pearl Harbor, Hawaii, on December 7, 1941, and Germany's subsequent declaration of war on the United States. Roosevelt suddenly found himself the commander in chief of a military force that was at war against powerful Asian and European enemies. By the time of Roosevelt's death in April, 1945, the United States and its allies were on the verge of defeating both Germany and Japan. The Great Depression was soon to fade to a memory as the post-World War II economic boom took the U.S. economy and society to unprecedented levels of prosperity.

Mikhail Sergeyevich Gorbachev was born on March 2, 1931, in Privolnoye, Russia. He joined the Communist Party of the Soviet Union in 1952. In 1980, he was elevated to the Party's politburo, the highest policy-making body in the country. In March, 1985, he succeeded Konstantin Chernenko as general secretary of the party and thereby became the political leader of the Soviet Union. At this moment, the Soviet Union was a troubled superpower. The Soviet people had become disenchanted with Communist rule and its repression. All incentives to work hard were tempered by the drudgery of everyday life in a centrally planned economy. Food, clothing, and other basics for living could be acquired only after considerable time in lines or on lists; consumer goods were scarce and shoddy, and alcoholism was rampant. The Soviet Union was falling ever further behind the capitalist and democratic Western countries in terms of technological capability and both quantity and quality of output.

Shortly after assuming power, Gorbachev introduced policies designed to halt the Soviet slide. Initially, his reforms called for increased diligence and discipline within the existing Soviet political and economic system. When it became apparent that his policies of "intensification" and "acceleration" were not working, Gorbachev moved to overhaul the existing Soviet system through his perestroika reform program, which rested on four pillars: restructuring of the economy, increased democratization of the political system, greater openness in the society (glasnost), and new thinking in foreign policy.

From its initiation in 1987-1988, Gorbachev's perestroika process grew more radical as the reforms failed to produce desired results. By 1991, perestroika had led to unprecedented Soviet disarmament, the dismantling of the Soviet empire in Eastern Europe, the transfer of political power from the Communist Party to a new governmental structure at the national and regional level, legalization of rival political parties, election of noncommunists and nationalists to political office, and an uninhibited press.

Somewhere along the line, Gorbachev lost the ability to control the reform process that he initiated. Many in the Soviet Union lost faith in his vision of "democratic socialism" and wanted to move where he did not want to go, either further toward liberal democracy and the market or back to authoritarian Communist rule. In August, 1991, a cabal of orthodox Communists attempted a coup against Gorbachev. The coup failed largely as a result of resistance by democratic and nationalist groups. While Gorbachev survived, the torch of political power had been passed from the central Soviet government to the regional governments of the fifteen Soviet republics. Gorbachev acknowledged this fact when on Christmas Day in 1991 he resigned as leader of the Soviet Union and the country ceased to exist.

Mohandas Gandhi was born on October 2, 1869, in Porbandar, India. He was reared in a deeply religious family that shunned materialism and believed in respecting all living things. As a consequence of its beliefs, Gandhi's family practiced pacifism, vegetarianism, and fasting when he was young. He learned to be tolerant of those different from him and not to let the pursuit of possessions and wealth dictate his actions. The type of upbringing Gandhi received profoundly affected him throughout his life and served to mold his political values, beliefs, and policies.

After having studied law in London, England, Gandhi accepted a position as a clerk in Natal, South Africa, in 1893. Gandhi was shocked by the amount of bigotry and discrimination directed toward him in South Africa simply because he was an Indian and not a European. In 1894, he led the opposition to a proposal by the Natal Legislative Assembly to deny Indians the right to vote. While unsuccessful in blocking the measure, the notoriety and publicity that Gandhi received for his efforts led him to found the Natal Indian Congress later that year.

By 1906, Gandhi's activity on behalf of Natal Indian people had resulted in a new strategy of response to the hostile policies of the new South African national government. The strategy was one of nonviolent noncooperation. That is, Gandhi and his supporters began to disobey the laws and measures that they opposed. They did so passively and peacefully. When the authorities came to arrest them they did not actively resist, fight, or engage in violence. The purpose of the exercise was to show that unjust laws and punishment would not have any effect on them. They would not sacrifice their dignity by submitting to political power that was neither just nor fair.

Gandhi's policy of nonviolence required incredible discipline and strength on the part of its practitioners as they faced persecution for their actions by the authorities.

Yet, the policy was successful in bringing to light the plight of Indians living in South Africa as the movement's activities were reported by media from around the world.

By 1919, Gandhi had become involved in a campaign of nonviolence in opposition to British imperial rule in his native homeland. In 1920, he assumed leadership of the Indian National Congress and turned the organization into the leading voice for Indian nationalism in the country. As a result of his calls for civil disobedience, Gandhi was imprisoned on several occasions by the British authorities. He remained faithful to his beliefs, however, engaging in protest fasts when he was incarcerated and even resigning as leader of the Congress Party in 1934 when he questioned its true commitment to the principles of nonviolence.

In 1947, after years of turmoil, the British granted the Indian subcontinent independence. Instead of one unified state being created, however, two were: India and Pakistan. The two new states reflected the deep divisions between the two predominant religious groups in the region, the Hindus and the Muslims. Gandhi was disheartened by the partition of his homeland. He engaged in a new campaign of nonviolence to bring the two sides closer together. In 1948, Gandhi, the prophet of nonviolence, was assassinated by a Hindu fanatic opposed to his peacemaking efforts.

Context

Not all scholars and theorists believe that the actions and policies of a country are a consequence of effective leadership supplied by significant individuals. Rather than placing focus on the individual unit of analysis as leadership studies do, these analysts place greater emphasis on such phenomena as the relative position of power a country occupies within the international system, the structure and organization of the institutions of government, and the political culture of a society.

An international system theorist would argue that a landlocked, resource-poor country is most likely to remain in an impoverished, underdeveloped state for the long term, whether it has great leadership or not. Because of its position within the international system, such a country has its fate dictated to it, and there is nothing that one leader can do about it.

A statist or institutionalist also downplays the significance of individual leaders. For these theorists, it is the structure of the government that is of paramount importance because it is that structure that determines the process by which public policy is formulated. For example, in a liberal democracy such as the United States, the U.S. Constitution establishes a system of fragmented political power in which different branches and levels of government share power. Statists would argue that no matter how great or powerful a particular president is, U.S. policy will still be the product of consensus and compromise, and incremental in nature, because that is what the system is designed to produce.

Finally, social theorists look at individual leaders as products of the dominant political culture in the societies that they rule. They do not have the independent capability to adopt policies that go against the dominant attitudes, beliefs, and values endemic to their people. For example, a leader that tries to adopt secular policies in a theocracy is doomed to failure because the society is used to religious rule. Such a leader is behaving in a manner inconsistent with society's expectations and is likely to lose power unless he conforms to those expectations.

Bibliography

Bass, Bernard M. *Stodgill's Handbook of Leadership: A Survey of Theory and Research.* Rev. ed. New York: Free Press, 1981. This comprehensive handbook abstracts the most important scholarly articles on the study of leadership and organizes them under thematic categories. An excellent source of information for anyone interested in the evolution of academic research on leadership.

Dogan, Mattei, ed. *Pathways to Power: Selecting Rulers in Pluralist Democracies.* Boulder, Colo.: Westview Press, 1989. Comparative analyses of how individuals rise to positions of leadership in the democratic political systems of France, the United States, Norway, Italy, Britain, Japan, India, and Ireland.

The International Year Book and Statesmen's Who's Who. East Grinstead, England: Reed Information Services, 1953-. Useful annual reference work that contains more than eight thousand biographies of world political leaders. The yearbook also provides descriptive information about the different countries of the world and leading international and national organizations.

Kellerman, Barbara, ed. *Political Leadership: A Source Book.* Pittsburgh, Pa.: University of Pittsburgh Press, 1986. A compilation of essays on political leadership by an eclectic group of authors, this book attempts to present the thoughts and ideas on political leadership of some of the most famous and infamous people who have ever lived.

Sheffer, Gabriel, ed. *Innovative Leaders in International Politics.* Albany: State University of New York Press, 1993. Chapters in the first of three parts address theoretical questions associated with the study of leadership and provide a literature review. The second and third parts offer case studies of significant leaders in democratic and authoritarian political systems.

Samuel E. Watson III

Cross-References

Charismatic Leadership, p. 209; Heads of State, p. 804; Machiavelli's Political Philosophy, p. 1148; Modern Monarchy, p. 1209; Nietzsche's Political Philosophy, p. 1300; Political Pragmatism, p. 1519; Populism, p. 1551; The Presidency in the United States, p. 1590; Statesmanship, p. 1898; Term Limits, p. 1956.

LEAGUES

Field of study: Types of government

A league is a formal association, confederation, or alliance of independent city- or nation-states, established to ensure their mutual cooperation, promote their mutual interests, and enhance their security.

Principal terms

ARAB LEAGUE: league of twenty-two Arab states and organizations formed in 1945

CONFEDERATION: compact, or league, among political states to serve mutual interests and provide mutual support

DELIAN LEAGUE: formal association of Greek city-states; led by Athens during the fifth and fourth centuries B.C.E.

EMPIRE: assemblage of diverse peoples and extensive territories under the rule of one political authority

HELLENIC LEAGUE: alliance of independent Greek city-states led by Sparta, organized in the early fifth century B.C.E. to resist the Persians

LEAGUE OF NATIONS: formal international association of nations to ensure world peace; established in 1919, lasted until 1946

POLIS: independent Greek city of antiquity

POLITICAL SOVEREIGNTY: form of political autonomy, common to nation-states, that recognizes no ultimate authority beyond its own

UNITED NATIONS: formal supranational association of nations created in 1945 to succeed the League of Nations as a peacekeeping body

Overview

Leagues, which are formal associations or alliances of independent states, have proven to be an effective and enduring mode of political organization since the sixth century before the common era (B.C.E.). Usually leagues have had their authority and structure specified by treaties, charters, or constitutions, which also have provided for congresses, councils, diets, or directorates to oversee operations. Additional liaison among league members generally has been maintained through exchanges of ambassadors, delegates, or other plenipotentiaries representing the participating polities.

Leagues often have appeared to offer their participants distinct political advantages. Independent city-states and sovereign nation-states alike have been able to organize leagues to achieve mutually beneficial goals without sacrificing their independence or their sovereignty. These goals have included a wide range of cooperative ventures, some commercial and monetary, others legal and institutional, and still others intended to ensure greater measures of military, diplomatic, racial, religious, or national security.

In many historical instances, the pursuit of these goals reflected the relatively short-term interests of those who organized or participated in leagues. Unlike attempts to found an enduring city-state or to establish a nation that was expected to survive long passages of time, the organization of leagues carried the added advantage of impermanence. League members, all of whom were autonomous states, were not committed to lengthy and cloying obligations that outlasted the satisfaction of their immediate interests. Members of the Hellenic League (fifth century B.C.E.), led by Sparta, for example, were generally allowed to secede from the League when they wished to do so, and in theory the same was true for members of the Delian, or Athenian, League. The Delian League, formed in 478 B.C.E., was originally designed almost solely to enhance Athens' strength in the face of impending Persian invasions. Certainly its founders never foresaw that with time and force the League would be transformed into the Athenian Empire.

An effective type of interstate cooperation, leagues succeeded one another in Greece between the sixth and the third centuries B.C.E. The prerequisite for what classical scholars refer to as "the century of hegemonic leagues" was the prior sophistication of hundreds of autonomous Greek city-states, such as Sparta, Athens, Argos, Corinth, and Megara, that allowed one or another of them to create and then dominate a league. The pattern for this process was begun during the second half of the sixth century B.C.E., with formation of the Peloponnesian League, and league followed league for the next three centuries, without resulting, it should be noted, in Greek unification.

Impressive leagues continued to be formed in Europe many centuries after the leagues of ancient Greece had disappeared. By 1294, for example, a number of north German city-states, prominent among them Lubeck, Hamburg, Bremen, Rostock, Visby, Riga, and Dorpat, had created the Hanseatic League. Drawn together by their common interests in dominating several types of long-distance trade, the Hansa towns subsequently established mercantile branches throughout western Europe, notably in London, the Low Countries, southern Germany, and Russia. Leadership of the league initially was held by the seaport of Visby on the Baltic island of Gotland, but it shifted to the German city of Lubeck in 1294 and remained there until the seventeenth century. Through most of its existence, the league was governed by a diet, an assembly of representative cities, estates, and princes, that oversaw the commercial activities of the 100 to 160 cities that variously composed the league. The last meeting of the Hansa Diet occurred in 1669.

Between the fourteenth and the seventeenth centuries, other European leagues emerged, most of them called into existence in response to the diplomatic, military, and religious perils faced by fledgling polities. The Swabian League, some twenty-six cities, princes, and prelates supported by the Holy Roman emperor and designed as an instrument of imperial power, was created in 1488 and lasted for the next half century. The Schmalkaldic League of 1531, the Rhenish League of 1658, the League of the Hague founded in 1683, and the League of Augsburg established in 1686, all represented the frequent collective attempts by smaller political authorities to survive amid the breakdown of feudalism, the consolidation of new nation-states, and the eruption of religious warfare associated with the Protestant Reformation and Catholic reactions against it.

Even in an age of powerful nation-states, the efficacy of leagues, particularly supranational ones, was demonstrated again in the twentieth century. There were numerous reasons for their establishment: Two world wars of unprecedented devastation, half a century of Cold War between the United States and its allies and the Soviet Union and Communist bloc countries, the collapse of the world's major empires, the emergence of scores of new states, and a revival of racial and religious identities among Middle Eastern, Asian, and African peoples, all were potent sources of disorder and threatened continuous global conflict. This persisting specter of wars stimulated popular and governmental efforts to create forums in which they might defuse tensions and advance peaceful international cooperation, without sacrificing national sovereignty.

Both the League of Nations, established in 1919 by the major European powers with the initial backing of the United States, and the United Nations, which formally succeeded the League in 1946, represent governmental responses to these widespread fears and sentiments. Despite the notable refusal of the United States to join the League of Nations after helping draft its founding covenant, most countries of the world have been participants in both the League and the United Nations—the latter having been founded chiefly by the efforts of the United States, which influenced it heavily for many years.

Both supranational organizations tended to be dominated by the major powers—in the case of the League by Great Britain, France, and Russia, and in the case of the United Nations by the United States and its former World War II allies, Great Britain, France, the Soviet Union, and China. The League of Nations failed chiefly because its leading members were unwilling to subordinate their national interests to the interests of world peace during crises provoked by clear acts of armed aggression in the 1920's and 1930's. Chiefly because of the salient influences of the United States and major western European powers, the United Nations has been less reticent about challenging aggression with force, perhaps the ultimate test of the organization's effectiveness.

Other leagues with more specific agendas than those identified with the United Nations have come into existence since 1945. The most prominent of these has been the Arab League, founded in 1945 and headquartered in Cairo, Egypt. By the 1970's, twenty-two Arab states or organizations had become members. The links that have tied members of the Arab League together have been shared cultural traits; common history, language, and religion; and, perhaps above all, common enemies, foremost Israel and its allies. By the mid-1990's, however, there was scant evidence that the Arab League would result in the establishment of a comprehensive, unified Arab state.

Applications

The most famous and enduring of the early leagues was the League of Delos, also known as the Delian League or Confederacy, founded and led by Athens, itself the classic polis and city-state of antiquity. The League took its name from the politically neutral Aegean island of Delos, which served as an early meeting place for the

League's governing council. Despite its name, the League was dominated by Athens during the two principal phases of its existence: from 478 to 404 B.C.E., and from 378 to 338 B.C.E. The governing council abandoned Delos to conduct its meetings in Athens; the league's treasury was eventually sited there too. The original purpose of the league, when Athens first called upon other Greek cities to join it in 478 B.C.E., was to resist Persian attempts to conquer Greece. Although the Persian menace did not disappear, Athens later turned the League's attention toward checking its rival city-state, Sparta.

Fifty years after its founding, the Delian League incorporated all the islands of the Aegean Sea except Melos and Thera; the cities of Euboea; and most of the Cyclades—about 220 islands in the southern Aegean, including Samos, Rhodes, Lesbos, and Chios. Most Greek cities along the coasts of Thrace and the Chaldician Peninsula were also league members, as were a majority of the Greek cities of Asia Minor and those located along the Dardanelles.

Athenian leadership of the league was assured by the city's preeminence as a seapower. Other city-states such as Sparta wielded more formidable power over much of mainland Greece and its peninsulas than did Athens, but at critical times Athenian ships proved the key to checking Persian invasions of Greek territories.

For the security provided to league members, in large measure by the Athenian fleet, there was a price. Athens levied a tribute assessment upon all who joined the league. Those who chose not to offer Athens money were obliged to furnish ships and men in its place. There were, nevertheless, compensations. Athenian management of the league was, for many years, both honest and efficient. In the absence of international law, there were advantages in having trade disputes between members settled in Athenian courts, which were objective and impartial even in disagreements to which Athenians were party. In theory, League members were free to quit the League when they so desired.

As Athens grew wealthy and powerful, in substantial measure because of its management of the League, its leaders forcefully rejected the refusals of some cities to join the League and used force to crush them and to attack those that tried to secede. From official Athenian perspectives, it seemed unfair that communities of the Greek world could enjoy the security that Athens provided without making reasonable contributions to it. By the end of the fifth century, Athens treated the league as a barely disguised empire.

Scholars frequently have asked why, with its imperial control of the Delian League, Athens did not attempt the creation of an Aegean state. A partial answer often suggested is that Athenians so closely identified the quality of their lives and freedom with their own independent polis—advantages that distinguished them from barbarians—that they were incapable of conceiving life under other political circumstances. In trying to strike a balance between survival in the face of aggression and a retention of its independence, Athens found the league-empire the best of a tragic bargain.

Not all Greek leagues were hegemonic, that is, dominated by single powers such as Athens or Sparta. Some functioned on a consensual basis among members who dealt with one another as equals in their decision making. Such was the character of the Boeotian League (447-387 B.C.E.), and it was also the mode in which the defeated and then revitalized Athens behaved within the Second Sea League, which it founded in 378 B.C.E. There were, in short, leagues where active authority was balanced in true Greek fashion.

Context

Historically, leagues have been established to serve common causes, such as the security of states, trade, or other special interests of overriding importance to potential members. Although some Leagues—the Hanseatic League, for example—cohered for centuries, most have been shorter-lived, representing the temporary cooperation of city-states or nations whose long-term interests did not usually coincide. Indeed, the intended impermanence of leagues constituted one of their advantages. Unlike binding alliances, they allowed their members greater flexibility in determining when a compelling interest in association had ended. Thus, as was sometimes true of the leagues of ancient Greece, cities and city-states often could secede at will. Similarly, as was later true of both the League of Nations and the United Nations, member states could withdraw, as Germany and Italy did from the League in the 1930's, without penalty.

Broadly speaking, leagues have given evidence of the need for closer interstate or international cooperation in the pursuit of important goals. To that extent, some scholars have interpreted the formation of leagues through the centuries as tentative groupings toward genuine regional or worldwide supranational government. Viewed from another perspective, however, leagues may be seen simply as reaffirmations of the refusal of peoples or their governments to sacrifice any measure of their independence or of their sovereignty.

As cooperative political devices, leagues frequently have been extremely effective in attaining limited ends. Only through the formation of the Delian League, for example, was it likely that Athens, foremost among scores of other Greek cities, could have withstood Persian invasions aimed at the subjugation of Greece. Nor is it likely that Athens could have sustained the lengthy Peloponnesian War (431-404 B.C.E.) against Sparta and its allies without the strength the League afforded it.

It was equally unlikely that more than a millennium later the commercial cities and towns of northern Germany and the Baltic shores could have defeated the heavy pressures brought against their struggles for independence by kings, princes, and prelates without the mutual protection they devised by means of the Hanseatic League. Under the auspices of the League they were able successfully to introduce their products, merchants, factors, and financial instruments into nearly every major city in Europe from London to Novgorod.

While the critical weakness of modern leagues such as the League of Nations, the United Nations, and the Arab League have been identified with their members' failure to modify or abandon their sovereignty, their achievements, if often undramatic, have been appreciable. Both the failed League of Nations and the United Nations compiled impressive records in settling minor disputes, conducting health surveys, overseeing international labor relations and assembling labor statistics, aiding refugees, helping end traffic in opium and white slaves, establishing international postal standards, and extending relief and financial aid to economically troubled nations.

More restricted in the scope of its operations than the League of Nations or the United Nations, the Arab League has represented the most comprehensive effort to unite the Arab world since the fall of the Ottoman Empire in 1919. While its members were drawn together until the mid-1990's largely by hostility toward Israel and its allies, the league's less dramatic activities brought greater interstate and interorganizational cohesion to the Arab peoples and nations by establishing postal and telecommunications links, as well as by forming the Arab Bank, an extensive Arab Financial Organization, and the Arab Common Market.

Over the past fifteen hundred years, most leagues have failed to achieve or sustain pursuit of their major objectives—the defeat of enemies, military security, or trade advantages. Nevertheless, in the absence of powerful supranational government or any signs that city-states and nations would surrender a measure of their sovereignty, they have demonstrated considerable effectiveness in extending interstate and regional cooperation.

Bibliography

Dollinger, Philippe. *The German Hansa*. Translated and edited by D. S. Ault and S. H. Steinberg. Stanford, Calif.: Stanford University Press, 1970. Outstanding, clearly written study that details the development of an elaborate trade network that lasted more than five hundred years. Illustrations, notes, bibliography, and index. Authoritative, but meant for serious readers.

Hourani, Albert. *A History of the Arab Peoples*. Cambridge, Mass.: Belknap Press of Harvard University Press, 1991. Divides Arab history into five phases. Authoritatively treats politics, philosophy, religion, the arts, literature, and nationalism. Part five deals with pan-Arab efforts and the evolution of the Arab League. Scholarly work written for laypeople. Maps, illustrations, notes, fine bibliography, and useful index.

Jones, Arnold H. M. *Athenian Democracy*. Baltimore: The Johns Hopkins University Press, 1986. Scholarly work for nonexperts. Chapter 3 discusses the Delian League economic, political, and social effects upon Athens, and also deals with the Peloponnesian League. Annotated page notes, index of passages cited, and index. Not exhaustive, but informative.

Kitto, H. D. F. *The Greeks*. Rev. ed. Harmondsworth, Middlesex, England: Penguin Books, 1977. Written for nonexperts by a leading classical historian, this study treats the Delian League in the context of overall Greek development during the fifth century B.C.E. Brief but informative discussion of Greek leagues in their broader settings.

Rorig, Fritz. *The Medieval Town*. Berkeley: University of California Press, 1967. Brilliant scholarly survey of the subject for nonexperts. The Hansa towns and the

League are discussed throughout. Illustrations, photos, bibliography, and index.
Sealey, Raphael. *A History of the Greek City States, ca. 700-338 B.C.* Berkeley: University of California Press, 1976. Scholarly and richly detailed. Part two treats hegemonic leagues. Part three discusses leagues of a more equal type. Essential for serious readers. Useful maps, glossary of technical terms, and valuable index.

Clifton K. Yearley

Cross-References

Alliances, p. 47; Confederations, p. 391; Empires and Empire Building, p. 597; Federations, p. 675; Hegemony, p. 817; International Agreements, p. 949; Islam and Government, p. 994; The Nation-State, p. 1241; Supranational Government Institutions, p. 1922; Treaties, p. 2020.

THE LEFT AND THE RIGHT

Field of study: Politics

The concepts of Left and Right are elastic but provide a rough guide to the political orientation of a person or group. The term "Left" refers to a more liberal orientation, and "Right" to a more conservative position.

Principal terms

CAPITALISM: system of private ownership of the means of production for profit, usually through well-developed financial institutions

COMMUNISM: in theory, a classless society managed by the dictatorship of the working class, and with most property owned by the state

NEW LEFT: advocates of equality in economic and class concerns and compensatory adjustment of equality in matters of race and gender

NEW RIGHT: advocates of freedom in economic matters and a social order with strong emphasis on traditional moral values

SOCIALISM: government ownership and management of the distribution of goods and services

Overview

The birth of the terms "Left" and "Right" as political concepts took place on May 5, 1789. Beset by financial stringencies, King Louis XVI of France convened the Estates General of the kingdom for the first time since 1614. The king and his ministers were seated at center stage facing the Estates. The place of honor, on the king's right, was given to the First Estate (the clergy) with the Second Estate (the nobility) next to them. The remaining seats were taken by the commoners, the Third Estate. After the Third Estate seceded and proclaimed themselves a National Assembly, they invited the other estates to join them; most of the clergy and many of the nobility did so. They were given the places of honor, on the right, with the Third Estate on the left. Eventually the seating arrangements placed the royalists on the right and those seeking rapid change on the left; since then Left and Right have been loosely used to indicate political or ideological orientation.

These terms disappeared during the nineteenth century (Karl Marx, the patron saint of much of the twentieth century Left, never used them) but returned during the twentieth century. They have been used sometimes with pride: There was a Left Book Club in England, and the columnist William F. Buckley, Jr. labeled his column "On the Right." These terms have also been used as invective, especially when coupled with adjectives such as "far," "radical," or "extreme." In reality, Left and Right have been justifiably used in a variety of meanings.

In one sense, Left and Right can mean the ends of a continuum along which individuals or positions on a given issue can be placed. For example, in 1993, *Time* magazine placed the newly appointed members of President Bill Clinton's cabinet along a left-right axis, with Secretary of Health and Human Services Donna Shalala at the extreme left and Secretary of the Treasury Lloyd Bentsen at the far right. Bentsen's position, however, would have been toward the left in the cabinet of Clinton's predecessor, George Bush. The use of this continuum also implies a center. Boundaries between the three groups are hard to draw, and in describing multiparty coalition governments, as in Italy between 1948 and 1990, writers often spoke of center-left (Christian Democrats and Socialists) or center-right (Christian Democrats plus Republicans and Liberals) coalitions. Excluded were the extremes at either end of the spectrum, the Communists and smaller radical parties on the Left and the "National Right," a coalition of monarchists and neo-Fascists, on the Right.

Left and Right are also used as an identification of extremes: Left as "beyond liberal" and Right as "beyond conservative," whether as a general orientation or as a position on a particular issue. Left and Right have been used so much as invective, and their extremes so often identified with radicalism and violence, that most persons in the 1990's identify themselves as centrists, perhaps with qualifications such as left or right of center. Liberalism, for example, has been placed between socialism and communism on the Left and conservatism on the Right. Conservatives, in turn, often have used "liberal" and "Left" as synonyms, and deny any connection with fascist, racist, or paramilitary survivalist groups.

Finally, Left and Right have been used to describe orientations in the political sense, rather than concrete positions on given issues. The French Catholic philosopher Jacques Maritain, writing in the middle years of the twentieth century, identified the pure man of the Left as preferring "what is not to what is," whereas the person purely of the Right prefers "injustice to disorder." As examples, he cited the German philosopher Friedrich Nietzsche as a man of the Right and the Russian author Leo Tolstoy as a man of the Left. As a warning, he stated that, "There are no more dreadful revolutions than revolutions of the left carried out by men of rightist temperament," citing Vladimir Lenin's Bolshevik revolution that created the Soviet Union as an example, and "no weaker governments than governments of the right run by leftist temperaments" (an allusion to Louis XVI). His prescription was for persons to bring their temperaments into an equilibrium approaching a point where the tendencies of Left and Right converge. In any case, positions of Left and Right are more ideological than practical, and less amenable to compromise.

Often there are more heated and violent disputes between factions on each side than between the extremes, which often converge in attitudes and behavior. Nazis and communists united in Germany in the early 1930's to bring down a centrist government through violent street brawls. One example of the fierce battles that have been fought between different factions of Leftist or Rightist groups is the Spanish Civil War (1936-1939). Although it has been viewed as a Left-Right conflict, with the insurgents of the Right under Francisco Franco seeking to overthrow an elected Leftist government, the Leftists were rent by factions, with the communists eventually destroying the anarchist and trade union factions on their Left and Right. In other cases, people occupy a position on the Right on economic issues and on the Left on social matters, or vice versa. For example, near the end of the twentieth century, abortion was a highly divisive issue on the Right. The religious and traditionalist Right strongly opposed it, but many economic conservatives wanted the issue eliminated because it drove away prospective supporters who were liberal on social issues but conservative on economic ones or who even welcomed abortion for eugenic purposes.

Applications

In the closing decades of the twentieth century, there are Left and Right positions on many social and economic issues, usually with a convergence of attitudes on both but sometimes with striking differences. Examining a social and an economic issue will illustrate these concepts.

Abortion has been one of the most divisive concerns in the United States, perhaps second only to the abolition of slavery in the nineteenth century as a polarizing issue. Its legality was the result of a Supreme Court decision (*Roe v. Wade*, 1973) rather than legislation passed by elected officials, and those with strong feelings on the issue often have abandoned their traditional party affiliations to vote for the candidate whose views on abortion most closely resemble theirs. Yet it is possible to discern Right and Left positions and attempts at a centrist compromise.

On the Right, there is the view that abortion is absolutely wrong, a violation of the biblical commandment "Thou shalt not kill," and there are no circumstances that justify it. The Left believes that abortion is an absolute right, and that the government should ensure its availability to poor women by including it as part of any government provided health care program. Some gradations along the continuum are possible: on the Right, the acceptance of abortion in cases of rape, incest, or to protect the life of the mother; on the Left, the acceptance of some controls so that abortion is not used for frivolous purposes such as sex selection, is entered into only after deliberation and informed consent, and is not forced on poor women to avoid granting them welfare payments. Centrist positions include strict regulation of abortion clinics to provide the backup safeguards that hospitals have, waiting periods, consent of one or both parents of a minor, and assuring that abortion is not only safe and legal but also rare. Some lawmakers, usually but not exclusively Roman Catholic, are liberal on economic issues but opposed to abortion.

Health care is an issue with both economic and social overtones. On the Right, the extreme position is that individuals should provide for their own health care and that the government should step in only when lives are threatened, humanitarian standards are outraged, or controls over defective drugs or incompetent physicians are needed. The extreme Left position is that everyone is entitled to health care of the highest quality, which should be provided by the government.

The prevailing economic issue regarding health care is how it should be paid for. The Right maintains that health care in the United States is the best in the world because of the operation of free market forces and the combination of private (pharmaceutical companies) and public (research grants) support of medical research. They contend that reforms should be limited to eliminating the grosser inequities, such as permitting people who change jobs to continue their health insurance despite preexisting medical conditions and permitting the establishment of tax-exempt individual retirement accounts for medical expenses. The Left argues that employers should be required to pay a substantial part of their employees' health insurance premiums, and patients should be placed in managed-care alliances; the most extreme factions on the Left would have the government provide all health care, with hospitals and drug companies owned and managed by the state, and doctors paid by the government.

Both the Left and the Right believe their position more appropriately addresses the question of equality. The Left views government-provided health care as a means of leveling up, making a modicum of health care available to everyone, as has been done in Cuba and China under communist regimes; the Right views government-provided health care as leveling down, often achieved by rationing health care, usually by denying certain procedures on the grounds of age or life expectancy. In Great Britain, for example, only those under fifty-five years of age can receive kidney dialysis; in communist East Germany, low-birth-weight babies were drowned and listed in the statistics as abortions.

Context

Left and Right are flexible terms more than absolute descriptions. Vladimir Lenin's tract "Left-Wing Communism: An Infantile Disorder" (1920) accused those in the West who refused on principle to cooperate with trade unions, such as the Industrial Workers of the World or "Wobblies," or to participate in parliaments because they were tainted with compromise, as being childish. On the other hand, he referred to the socialists as social chauvinists, because most of them supported their native countries during World War I. Thus the communists recognized positions that were adjacent, but too far to the Left or the Right of their own stands on issues.

Some issues of Left and Right are bound to particular times or countries. In France, the Right was strongly connected with the Roman Catholic church, because the church had been persecuted during the French Revolution and the Paris Commune of 1871. In Italy, many conservatives were also anticlerical because the Roman Catholic church opposed the unification of Italy, which deprived the popes of the Papal States, centered in Rome, which they had governed for several centuries.

Some scholars contend that the inclination toward a Left and Right position on issues comes from a person's view of the human condition. People who believe humanity is naturally good and perfectible, with defects the result of error, superstition, or social pressures beyond one's control, are more likely to be part of the Left. Their main watchword is equality, not only of opportunity but also of results, with a benevolent government to oversee the achievement of an earthly paradise. Those who believe humanity is naturally flawed, and that people have choices through freedom of the will, and are ultimately responsible for outcomes are more likely to identify with the Right. Their main watchword is liberty, defined as freedom from interference by the government.

Certain descriptive words have been associated with Left and Right. Such terms as socialism, welfare, workers, poor, change, revolution, future, idealism, equality, entitlement, feminism, open-mindedness, peace, and environment awaken connections with an aspect of the Left. For the Right, capitalism, free enterprise, bourgeoisie, rich, opportunity (and opportunistic), status quo, tradition, military, law enforcement, businessmen, authority, discipline, economy, and low taxation are among the more frequent associations.

The United States has never had home-grown movements of either the extreme Left or Right. In contrast to unions in Europe, the U.S. labor movement has worked within the democratic system to achieve greater gains for its members. The nearest thing to a homegrown Right, the Ku Klux Klan of the 1920's, contained strong elements of populism and was soon undermined by the financial and moral corruption of many of its leaders.

The Left has been reproached for its belief that the state is the source of all good; that individuals are not responsible for their actions; and that equality should be not only of opportunity but also of outcome, with special arrangements and compensations for those who have been deprived in the past. Among the worst extremes of the Left have been the government of Cambodia in the 1970's, when anyone with education was suspected of being a class enemy and executed; and the Shining Path guerrillas of Peru who enforced their program of extreme egalitarianism with a particularly violent form of terrorism during the 1980's and early 1990's.

The Right's besetting sins have been identified as complacency, callousness, and particularism. These include the willingness to accept environmental pollution in order to create jobs and profits, ignoring the problems of the poor and homeless with too great a penchant for blame rather than attempts at understanding, expecting private charity rather than governmental aid to alleviate misfortune, and tolerating or even fostering forms of racism or ethnic discrimination. On the other hand, overt racism declined in the United States during the last three decades of the twentieth century; anti-Semitism has been more a European than a United States phenomenon and a feature of the Soviet Left as well as of the prewar German, French, and Rumanian Right; and the worst environmental degradation occurred in the former Communist bloc countries.

Bibliography

Barash, David P. *The L Word*. New York: William Morrow, 1992. Explanation of liberalism, containing a positive manifesto for revived liberalism as well as indictments of conservative positions on various issues.

Dershowitz, Alan. *Contrary to Popular Opinion*. New York: Pharos, 1992. Essays that include exploring intolerance on both Left and Right, by a law professor who describes himself as a civil libertarian whose views lean to the left.

Laponce, J. A. *Left and Right: The Topography of Political Perceptions*. Toronto: University of Toronto Press, 1981. Systematic study of how concepts of Left and Right are perceived by a variety of groups in the United States, Canada, and France.

Lenin, Vladimir Ilich. *Left-Wing Communism: An Infantile Disorder.* New York: International Publishers, 1940. Official English translation of Lenin's exposition of positions to the Left and Right of Soviet Communism in 1920, as well as Marxist strategy and tactics in democratically gaining power.

Limbaugh, Rush. *The Way Things Ought to Be.* New York: Pocket Books, 1992. Essays from the standpoint of the Right, some humorous and some outrageous, by the popular radio talk-show host. They provide almost a polar opposite to Barash's evocation of liberalism.

Maritain, Jacques. Translated by Michael Cuddihey and Elizabeth Hughes. *The Peasant of the Garonne.* New York: Holt, Rinehart and Winston, 1968. The clearest statement in English of the description of Left and Right as an orientation.

Orwell, George. *Homage to Catalonia.* Boston: Beacon Press, 1952. First published in 1939, this is a vivid description of the battles on the Left during the Spanish Civil War by a participant, one of Great Britain's finest writers.

Rogger, Hans, and Eugen Weber, eds. *The European Right: A Historical Profile.* Berkeley: University of California Press, 1965. Series of essays by specialists on the Rightist movements in various European countries, emphasizing the nineteenth and early twentieth centuries.

Seidel, Gill, ed. *The Nature of the Right.* Amsterdam: John Benjamins, 1988. Examination of right-wing discourse and language from a feminist viewpoint, with emphasis on Great Britain and France.

R. M. Longyear

Cross-References

Burke's Political Philosophy, p. 171; Communist Parties, p. 377; Conservatism, p. 419; Dialecticism, p. 540; Equality and Egalitarianism, p. 630; Fascism and Nazism, p. 656; Neo-Conservatism, p. 1281; The New Right, p. 1293; Political Correctness, p. 1441; Radicalism, p. 1661; Scientific Humanism, p. 1784; Social Democratic Parties, p. 1846; Socialism, p. 1865; Totalitarianism, p. 1987; The Welfare State, p. 2135.

LEGAL SYSTEMS IN ANGLO-AMERICAN GOVERNMENTS

Field of study: Law and jurisprudence

Both the United States and Canada use a legal system based on principles derived from colonial experience under Britain. The three legal systems have diverged over the years, but the general outline of Anglo-American legal principles has remained recognizable and distinguishable from other legal systems.

Principal terms

COMMON LAW: legal system in use in the United Kingdom and many of its former colonies; called "common" because it is expected to be uniform across an entire nation, it is distinguished by great reliance on "judge-made" rather than legislatively enacted law

JUDICIAL REVIEW: critical part of American jurisprudence in which the U.S. Supreme Court has the power to declare acts of the other national government branches to be out of conformity with the Constitution

ROMAN LAW: system of law (also called Continental or civil or statutory) most widely used in the European continental states, typified by relatively greater reliance on statutes enacted by legislatures rather than on decisions made by judges

RULE OF LAW: general principle that society should be governed by laws, not persons, with laws prospective, predictable, as clear as possible, formally written, relatively few in number, and enacted through orderly procedures

STARE DECISIS: Latin phrase that means "let the decision stand" (or more generally "a decision should be followed in all like cases") and is the basis of the rule of precedent

Overview in

In the popular mind, the Anglo-American legal system depends on statutes passed by a legislature, whether Parliament or Congress. The U.S. system is a common law rather than a statutory law system typical of continental Europe; it is derived from the Anglo-Saxon common law tradition rather than a rival Roman law tradition. Although the two systems have some distinct differences, the common law and Roman law traditions both can be compatible with a broader concept known as the rule of law. A basic distinction has to do with the source of the law, that is, whether the law comes principally from judges or from legislatures. Although both traditions are mixed in practice, the common law legal tradition follows the notion that judges "discover" what the law is that "naturally" ought to be accepted by all citizens. In theory, judges are not lawmakers, but as a practical matter much of this "discovery" is actually the making of new law.

The fact that realistically judges do make law should not detract from the common law's ideal notion that judges should be merely "discoverers" of what the law is. To depart from this ideal of the judge as a neutral, impartial discoverer of the law is to open the legal system to politicization. If judges openly become lawmakers, then they increasingly face pressure to be treated as legislators who must be directly controlled by an electorate. Making judges becoming more dependent on the electorate threatens the independent judiciary, one principle of the rule of law.

The common law arose out of the desire of English kings following William the Conqueror to create a common system of courts and thereby a common law throughout the country. The word "common" in this case does not mean "ordinary," but rather that the law is "common" or uniform throughout the country. Uniformity evolved over at least a few hundred years. To further this goal, courts of appeal were created so that an individual judgment in a local court could be reviewed by a higher court with a broader perspective.

Uniformity was important not only across the country but also over time, leading to the important practice of courts following the precedents set in earlier cases. This rule of precedent is also known as the concept of *stare decisis*, a Latin phrase that means generally that a decision should be followed in all like cases. The practice of establishing precedents continues in American, British, and Canadian courts. The notion that a judge discovers the law by finding precedents in similar cases is important if the system is to maintain its uniformity.

The concept of stare decisis is strongly related to predictability, valued in the rule of law. Predictability applied to legislatures as sources of law requires that legislatures enact clear statutes. The same principle applies to judge-discovered (or judge-made) law, in that judges should discover the uniform principles behind current and previous decisions. Ordinary citizens can then be educated as to what the law requires because they can know the precedents.

These important principles of the common law are not followed in the Roman law tradition. In the Roman legal tradition, the critical source of law is the body of statutes passed by the legislature or provided by a lawgiver. In earlier times, this tradition included the notion that legislatures also "discovered" natural laws, but that idea was less important to the Roman tradition and gradually declined. The common law tradition has judges discovering "natural" laws that may be in a sense higher than ordinary law passed by a legislature. The Roman law tradition has no such notion. Legislatures became paramount sources of law, and judges tended to restrict themselves to deciding facts rather than acting as referees in an adversarial proceeding in which juries decided facts.

Judges still interpreted the law to a degree, but unlike common law judges, they were bound more by context than by precedent. Roman law judges took over this fact-deciding role because they had a much more limited role in interpreting what the law was. In contrast, the common law system has jurors or panels of ordinary citizens (called peers) to act as the neutral deciders of fact. The judge in the common law system is to act as a referee between two sides in an adversarial legal system. The adversarial tradition expects that the truth will emerge from the conflict between two sides presenting their positions before a neutral jury, with the judge acting as a referee to make sure neither side misleads the jury with false information. This role as referee means that the common law judge must be extremely well informed as to previous decisions on the law. The common law judge also has a large role in deciding what the law is or should be.

Judges in the Roman law tradition decide facts rather than discover the law; the law has already been provided in detailed codes. Accordingly, in the Roman law tradition the judge always applies a statute to the facts of the case rather than relying on a prior decision. The judge's role is to decide the facts, select an appropriate statute, and apply it.

Because the Roman law system has the judge so involved in deciding the facts, there is far less need for an adversarial system to discover facts. The Roman law system does not depend on juries relying on an investigative arm of the government to assist the judge in the search for truth. The defense attorney's role is much more limited and tends to be reduced to pleading for mercy for the accused. There is a greater presumption of guilt: The police and procurator (government investigator) presumably are committed to never convicting an innocent person. The accused then would not be brought to trial in the Roman law system unless the police have determined the accused to be the perpetrator of some crime recognized by statute.

The common law and Roman law traditions coexist in Western thought. Neither can be said to be superior in principle. Both systems have advantages and disadvantages from the point of view of the rule of law. The common law system has a disadvantage from the rule of law perspective in that it may tend to create uncertainty when new cases arise and judges must discover what the law should be after a particular event has occurred. The judge-made or judge-determined law then becomes somewhat retroactive in its effects. On the other hand, Roman law can have a disadvantage from the point of view of the rule of law in that the need for detailed codes may lead to a legal fabric so complex that it cannot easily be understood by citizens. Thus, it may work against the goal of predictability.

The common law system obviously cannot solve all problems. Common law systems need a corresponding, alternative form of law known as equity law, or a law based on fairness. Fairness becomes particularly important when a citizen is faced with the threat of future damage. Equity legal systems usually include the possibility of an injunction to prevent an action. Both equity law and injunctions are infrequently used in the Roman law tradition because presumably statutes have taken account of all possible situations, so that an illegal future action would prompt certain punishment. Under common law, injunctions delay actions while judges decide if they are legal.

The common law tradition has never prohibited the passage of statutes. In a common law system, statutory law replaces common law as decisions are codified into laws. Common law systems have converged with Roman law systems as statutes increasingly replaced the common law as a source of prevailing law. In twentieth century

Canada, Britain, and the United States, statutory law has become increasingly important. The notion of the courts as interpreters of statutes, however, continues to follow
the common law tradition, and precedent remains important.

Applications

One indication of the importance of precedent in the Anglo-American legal systems
is the nature of law schools and legal libraries. American, Canadian, and British law
libraries use codes, but a more prominent place is given to various "reporters" of
decisions in cases. These reporters are important sources of the prior decisions or
precedents that have such value under the concept of *stare decisis*. Law libraries in
the Roman law tradition focus on the detailed codes of law.

Both these legal traditions may produce constitutions as a form of higher statutory
law. The constitution as statute in the Roman law tradition does not necessarily include
the concept of judicial review, which rests somewhat uncomfortably with the Roman
law tradition. In those Roman law countries allowing judicial review, the notion of
precedent has become more important; this has tended to move Roman law closer to
the common law. In the common law tradition, a constitution is a discovery of the most
important higher (or natural) law principle that exists. Constitutions then can include
the notion of judicial review, as in the United States.

Although the United States, Canada, and Britain all follow the same basic legal
principles, there are some clear differences. The United States has used a written
constitution since 1789, and Canada has done so since its independence in 1867, but
Britain has never done so. The British have no single document from which one can
date the British legal or "constitutional" regime. It is frequently said that British
parliamentary practice has been reasonably uniform at least since the Reform Act of
1867. After that act, mass political parties developed, as American political parties
had. From the mid-1800's on, both the United States and Britain had democratic
systems with mass political parties and reasonably modern governments. Both generally accept basic principles of the common law.

Within that common law tradition, Britain and the United States diverged after the
American Revolution and the ratification of the U.S. Constitution. The United States
came to rely more on statutory law than on common law. The most obvious example
is the Constitution, which set a standard against which statutes could be measured.
Statutory textualism was also implied by the concept of judicial review, which allows
courts to strike down laws as being unconstitutional. The U.S. Constitution stands
above all three branches of the government, but the branches are equal to each other.
The British maintain that Parliament is supreme, so no constitution is higher and no
institution exists to declare laws unconstitutional.

To say that British courts cannot declare a law unconstitutional is not to say that
courts are powerless, for they have the common law power to interpret parliamentary
statutes. Although they cannot declare parliamentary enactments unconstitutional,
their interpretation is broad enough to include limits on Parliament they derive from
the "traditional" constitution included in the common law. Judicial review is growing

now that British courts have an obligation to interpret the European Community Charter as it bears on acts of Parliament.

At the top of the U.S. court system is the nine-member Supreme Court. The British "court of last resort" consists of eleven Law Lords. The Law Lords are distinguished judges appointed by the prime minister to be "life peers" in the House of Lords. These specifically designated Law Lords sit on cases in panels of three to five judges. Although appointed by the prime minister, they are not narrow partisans. Customary practice requires them to be distinguished in the law. Less distinguished judges have probably been appointed to the U.S. Supreme Court than as Law Lords in Britain.

The rights of the accused are not as carefully protected in Britain as they are in the United States. For example, the U.S. Constitution provides the guarantee of a writ of habeas corpus; no such overriding guarantee exists in Britain. The accused are not normally incarcerated for long periods without trial, but occasionally people have been held for long periods without being charged.

Context

All legal systems can be evaluated as to how closely they correspond to the rule of law. Within that concept, there are two grand traditions: the common law and Roman law. The common law is more dependent on judge-made or determined law, and the Roman legal tradition is more dependent on statutes. Both traditions use both statutes and judge-made law to various degrees. The common law developed in England after the Norman Conquest of 1066 and was used in all British colonies, including the United States and Canada. Although the United States and Canada are still recognizable as common law countries, both diverged from the British experience. Most notably, Canada and the United States have written constitutions, but Britain does not.

Common law countries rely on juries to determine facts as those emerge from an adversarial proceeding. A judge acts as a referee between the contending parties. The judge acts as an authority on the law bearing on the case, finding the law by consulting precedents, or prior cases of similar nature. To provide uniformity, an appeals process allows for higher courts to unify judgments. The United States uses juries to a far greater degree than do either Canada or Britain.

Roman law countries rely on judges to determine facts and apply relevant law. Roman law judges are expected to rely on the words of the statutes and are less dependent on precedents. Roman law countries use a procurator system in which the state is expected to determine that an accused is in fact guilty before a trial is held. The defense attorney has a much more limited role in the Roman law system. Over time, the common law and Roman law systems have tended to converge, although real differences still exist.

Bibliography

Dragnich, Alex N., Jorgen S. Rasmussen, and Joel C. Moses. *Major European Governments.* 8th ed. Pacific Grove, Calif.: Brooks/Cole, 1991. Excellent examination of the governments of Britain, France, Germany, and the Soviet Union.

Finnis, John. *Natural Law and Natural Rights*. Oxford, England: Clarendon Press, 1992. Discusses Anglo-American legal principles from the perspective of trying to reinvigorate the notion of "natural law" from a nonreligious perspective. Argues against legal positivism but ends up near the position of legal positivist Joseph Raz.

Glendon, Mary Ann, Michael Wallace Gordon, and Christopher Osakwe. *Comparative Legal Traditions in a Nutshell*. St. Paul, Minn.: West, 1982. Typical of law books in the "nutshell" series, this book provides a succinct summary of the major legal traditions in the world from a comparative legal perspective.

Raz, Joseph. *The Authority of Law*. Oxford, England: Clarendon Press, 1979. Analyzes Anglo-American principles from a legal positivistic perspective but ironically arrives at principles not far removed from those of Finnis. Raz defines the rule of law succinctly on pages 210-229.

Walker, Geoffrey De Q. *The Rule of Law*. Carlton, Victoria, Australia: Melbourne University Press, 1988. This excellent book describes the degree to which the rule of law and other Anglo-American legal principles can be used as objective standards to evaluate governmental and legal systems.

Richard L. Wilson

Cross-References

The British Parliamentary System, p. 146; Comparative Government, p. 384; Congress, p. 412; The Constitution of the United States, p. 425; Constitutional Law in the United States, p. 439; Courts: State and Local, p. 465; Courts: U.S. Federal, p. 471; Judicial Review, p. 1012; Jurisprudence, p. 1019; Law Enforcement, p. 1059; Parliamentary Government, p. 1377; The Supreme Court: Role in Government and Law, p. 1935.

LEGISLATIVE BODY TYPES

Field of study: Functions of government

Legislative bodies are among the most fundamental of all democratic institutions. Legislatures are deliberative, governing units whose members are usually elected by the people they represent. They may vary in size, composition, rules, powers, and length of terms, but all legislative bodies share the common role of being the institutions responsible for the "making of laws."

Principal terms

BICAMERAL LEGISLATURE: legislature with two separate and distinct lawmaking bodies, such as a senate and a house of representatives

CABINET: collective heads of the bureaucratic agencies of a government

CONSTITUENT: person residing within the legislative district of a particular member of a legislative body

DIRECT DEMOCRACY: system of governance in which all citizens are directly involved in making laws

MAJORITY PRINCIPLE: notion that the will of the majority of citizens must prevail in public matters

PARLIAMENTARY SYSTEMS: governments in which executive powers are merged with legislative powers of making laws

PRESIDENTIAL SYSTEMS: governments in which the executive powers of administering laws are distinct from the legislative powers of making laws

REPRESENTATIVE DEMOCRACY: system of governance in which the citizens elect representatives to an assembly or legislative body charged with the task of making laws

SEAT: right to membership in a legislative body

UNICAMERAL LEGISLATURE: legislature with only one lawmaking house or branch

Overview

From prehistoric tribal councils of elders, the Athenian assembly, and the Roman senate to the United States Congress, legislative bodies are deliberative assemblies whose purpose is to make rules governing membership in a given society or group. Considered indispensable to democratic forms of government, legislatures give voice to the collective will of the people who have chosen their members. Even nondemocratic systems, in which the people do not actually choose members of the legislature, often utilize legislative bodies to help legitimize the regimes in power.

Legislative bodies vary greatly in structure, size, membership eligibility, power, and length of terms of their members. The main distinction between types of legislatures in various polities is whether executive power, that is the enforcement and administration of the laws, is separate from the legislative functions. In the United States and other presidential systems, the legislature is distinct from the executive branch. In Great Britain and other parliamentary systems the legislative body is merged with the executive office. In the modern world, most democratic polities employ either parliamentary legislative systems, presidential systems, or hybrid combinations of the two.

Legislative bodies are considered the backbone of democracy because they are the institutions most responsive to ordinary citizens. Representative democracy, manifested by some type of legislative body, has been the common characteristic of every democratic system that has ever existed beyond the smallest of scale. The concept of the majority principal and representative democracy permeate all aspects of how citizens living in democracies govern themselves. The number and variations of legislative bodies that impact American lives is staggering. Congress, state legislatures, county legislatures, city and town councils, village boards, school boards, library boards of trustees, and student councils, are all legislative bodies. The legitimacy and existence of legislative bodies are never questioned by citizens of democracies, though the honesty, competence, and usefulness of their individual members often is. In public opinion polls, members of legislatures are often ranked somewhere below used-car salesmen.

Applications

Parliamentary democracy evolved in England over several centuries out of the struggle between the monarchy and the people. It was not until the eighteenth century that the English Parliament achieved the status of general equity with the monarchy. Democratic reform movements during the late eighteenth and early nineteenth centuries eventually rendered the monarch a mere figurehead and Parliament the supreme governing body of the land. The British parliamentary model was subsequently duplicated in many of the world's democracies, particularly former colonies and members of the British Commonwealth of Nations. Examples of parliamentary systems include Great Britain, Canada, Israel, Italy, Japan, Australia, New Zealand, and India.

Parliamentary legislative bodies may be unicameral, with one house, or bicameral, with two houses. In most cases the real power and authority is reserved for the so-called lower house, while the upper branch provides advice or performs ceremonial functions. In democratic regimes, members of parliament are elected as members or nominees of political parties, using a single-member district system in which one representative is elected from each defined geographical district, or a proportional representation system that awards seats to parties in proportion to the percentage of the votes they receive overall. If three parties split the popular vote in a district, each receives one-third of the seats from that district.

In two-party electoral systems, the party that receives a majority of the seats in parliament forms the "government." The party that receives the next highest number of votes forms the "opposition," sometimes termed the "loyal opposition." In multi-party systems, the party that wins the most seats (a plurality) usually forms the government. In many instances plurality parties are required to form "coalition" governments by including in the cabinet members from other parties. Coalition governments are often necessary because a majority of votes in the entire parliament is required to form a government.

The executive branch in a parliamentary system comprises the prime minister, the cabinet, and the civil service. The chief executive officer in such a system is a member of parliament who is designated the leader of the party that forms the majority. Prime ministers are therefore not chosen in national elections; they face electorates that are no larger than those of other members of parliament. The other ministers who compose the cabinet, or government, are also members of parliament selected by the members of their party—often upon the recommendation of the prime minister. The civil service, or national bureaucracy, in a parliamentary system usually contains more professional and nonpolitical officials than do presidential systems.

The "opposition" in parliamentary bodies designate a leader who would become prime minster should their party form a majority. They also name a "shadow government," which has a designated member to fill each cabinet ministry in the event the opposition gains a majority after an election. It is their responsibility, in theory, to offer citizens alternatives to policies advanced by the majority party.

Parliamentary government is not characterized by a struggle between the executive and the legislature over policies and programs. Prime minsters generally do not have to worry about passage of their programs since a legislative majority is prerequisite for their obtaining office. "Divided government," a system in which the executive is of one party and the majority in the legislature of another, now common in the United States, is not possible in parliamentary government. There is, by definition, a unified system. Policy-making is therefore considered more coherent and more streamlined than in presidential systems; however, if prime ministers and their governments do not maintain the confidence of their rank-and-file party members—who are termed "back-benchers"—they risk inciting intraparty revolts that can result in votes of no confidence and the collapse of the government. Unpopular prime ministers, moreover, may be voted out as party leaders by other members of their own party, regardless of the standing of the party with the public at large.

In parliamentary legislatures, committees of subject jurisdictions do not play as important a role as they do in presidential systems. Since the executive branch and the legislature are merged, the majority party does not scrutinize and debate the legislative program submitted by the executive, as happens in non-parliamentary systems.

The primary task of individual members of the parliamentary bodies is deliberation and debate within the framework of lawmaking. Nevertheless, in most legislatures, members spend considerable time trying to solve problems of their own constituents and serving as links between their constituents and bureaucratic agencies.

In presidential-style legislative systems the executive and the legislature are separate institutions. The term "separation of powers" is actually an inaccurate depiction of presidential systems, since both institutions function within the areas belonging to the others. A more accurate description is that of noted presidential scholar Richard

Neustadt, who calls the system one of "separate institutions sharing powers." The term "presidential" may also be misleading since that is only one form of executive officer; governors, chancellors, and executives, for example, all refer to the executive branch. Examples of presidential systems include the United States (the federal government and all fifty states), Mexico, and the Republic of South Africa.

The liberal theorists of the Enlightenment Period, including John Locke, Charles Montesquieu, and Thomas Jefferson, believed that separating the legislature from the executive would help control the excesses of government. The idea was to place limits on each branch. The sharing of powers and "checks and balances" were regarded as safeguards to ensure individual liberty from tyrannical executives or despotic legislatures (what was termed "tyranny of the majority"). The U.S. Constitution embodies these beliefs, following a century-old tradition of separate legislative bodies in the American colonial legislatures.

Legislatures in presidential systems may be unicameral or bicameral. Within the United States, the federal Congress and forty-nine states are bicameral; only Nebraska has a one-house state legislature. Members of legislatures are typically elected from single-member districts that send the largest vote getters to office; however, some systems use proportional representation. Although executives are generally members of one of the main political parties in the legislature, their election is not directly linked to that of members of the legislature. Voters cast separate ballots for the executive and members of the legislature. Other high offices in the executive branch, such as cabinet members, are typically appointed by the chief executive—with some type of legislative consent.

Legislative leadership positions go to the parties that win a majority of the seats, as do committee posts and other tangible benefits. Yet, parties in presidential systems are far less cohesive than in parliamentary systems. Members often vote against the positions of party leadership. In the U.S. Congress, Democratic legislators from the South often vote with the Republicans, and "liberal" Republicans, often from the Northeast, occasionally vote with the Democrats.

In presidential systems the president typically sets the legislative agenda—the issues to be discussed, debated, and voted upon. The legislature may dispose of this program as they see fit, but the tone and framework for their action begins with the executive. In the United States, the president annually delivers a State of the Union Address to a joint session of Congress for this purpose.

Committees play central roles in most presidential-style legislative systems. All legislation, including the program of the executive, originates, is debated, and is voted on by committees before the legislature as a whole deliberates upon it. Accordingly, much proposed legislation never comes before the full body because it does not pass successfully through the committee process. Conversely, legislation that does make it through the committee process generally has a good chance of final approval. Unlike parliamentary systems, in which legislative adoption of laws is final, action by chief executives in presidential systems is required. The chief executives may approve an act, thereby making it law, or disapprove ("veto") an act, thereby sending it back to the legislative body. The legislature may then override the executive's disapproval, but this is often a difficult process. In the U.S. Congress, a two-thirds vote of both houses is required to override a presidential veto.

With all this said, presidential systems are designed to slow the wheels of government in order to safeguard the people from overly aggressive legislatures. Policy-making processes in presidential systems are thus more sluggish and more laborious than in parliamentary systems. The three-step process—committee action, full-house votes, and executive approval—is often criticized for being overly arduous and "stalemate" and "gridlock" are terms often applied to it. Yet, others argue that it is the most appropriate way to enlarge and refine the public will and curb the excesses of runaway government.

While the main responsibility of legislators in presidential systems is to deliberate and make laws, they also exercise administrative oversight, that is, keeping tabs on the executive branch. Not unlike parliamentary systems, the majority of their time and effort, however, is spent on constituent problems—particularly those of financially or politically powerful constituents. Termed "case work," this area of responsibility is viewed as particularly important in systems—such as the United States—in which there is extensive government activity in public affairs. It is common for members in these systems to run reelection campaigns exclusively on their case-work record.

Prior to World War II, there were few genuinely democratic governments in the world. As defeated nations rebuilt their political systems in the postwar period, and European colonies in Asia and Africa gained independence, scores of democratic governments were born. Another period of rapid democratization and state building occurred in Eastern Europe and the former Soviet Union, after the collapse of the Soviet Empire in the early 1990's. Some states adopted parliamentary forms of government based on the British model, others adopted presidential systems, and many adopted what might be classified as mixed systems. These have both parliamentary legislatures and independent executive authority. Examples of mixed legislative systems include France, Russia, Poland, and the Czech Republic.

Mixed systems are typically characterized by the existence of a chief executive officer who is independent from the legislature—some are only figureheads, but others have genuine executive authority—and a legislature based on the parliamentary model, particularly in its structures, rules, and nomenclature. Such systems typically have both a president and a prime minister. Presidential duties generally involve foreign affairs and defense policy and the administration of the government bureaucracy, while the prime minister and the "government" are responsible for the legislative program.

Context

Legislatures have come under increasing attack for their inability to affect the numerous problems facing modern societies. The most fundamental question about them is whether they should function as deliberative bodies concerned with the national or common good—if such a thing exists—or function as ombudsmen and agents for the localized interests within individual constituencies. The former view has been dubbed the "trustee model," and the latter the "delegate model." In other words, should legislators serve only the needs of their constituents, or should they also look to a larger public good? If they ignore their constituents, the public will become distrustful and resentful; however, if they look out only for their immediate constituents, difficult long-range problems facing the entire polity will be left unsolved. In the United States, many would argue that Congress's inability to tackle the massive budget deficit is a manifestation of such a dynamic.

A second and perhaps related concern is the extent to which groups of citizens, or "special interests," guide legislative policy agendas. Few would argue that interest groups and powerful business interests do not exercise inordinate influence on most legislatures. One might argue that the very responsiveness of legislatures to the people is what allows special interests to exert such influence. It is, from this perspective, the way that representative bodies should act. But others might ask if a minority of citizens should be able to guide public policy simply because they are better organized, more affluent, and more vocal. In the United States, interests such as the National Rifle Association and the American Association of Retired Persons wield significant power in Congress though they comprise small minorities of the public. Many are forced to ask who will represent the unorganized and poor in such a system.

A final concern is what has been termed the "incumbency advantage." Members of nearly all legislative bodies running for reelection are overwhelmingly returned to office. In the United States, roughly 90 percent of incumbent members of Congress who run for reelection win. At the same time most citizens believe their legislatures are unresponsive to their needs. An explanation of this paradox are the advantages afforded incumbent candidates. Simply put, many believe that members of legislatures have a host of advantages over challengers during campaigns. Examples include greater campaign finances, better media coverage, the use of government-paid mailings, and higher name recognition because of their case work. In this light, elections are seen as lopsided and generally undemocratic. Campaign finance reform and term limits have been suggested as means to minimize, if not eliminate, this problem. Yet because the legislatures themselves may be called upon to change the process, many people are pessimistic about the chances of significant reform.

Bibliography

Dodd, Lawrence, and Bruce Oppenheimer, eds. *Congress Reconsidered.* 5th ed. Washington, D.C.: Congressional Quarterly Press, 1993. Collection of articles about the U.S. Congress by leading congressional scholars.

Fenno, Richard F. *Home Style: House Members in Their Districts.* New York: HarperCollins, 1978. A telling work on how congressmen and congresswomen perform their "representation" function.

Fiorina, Morris P. *Congress: Keystone of the Washington Establishment.* New Haven, Conn.: Yale University Press, 1989. Deals with the inner workings of Congress and the incumbency advantage.

Hamilton, Alexander, James Madison, and John Jay. *The Federalist Papers.* Edited by Clinton Rossiter. New York: New American Library, 1961. The best source for the original understanding of the nature and role of the Congress.

Jacobson, Gary. *The Politics of Congressional Elections.* 2d ed. Boston: Little, Brown, 1987. Leading work on congressional elections and the incumbency advantage.

Lijphart, Arend, ed. *Parliamentary Versus Presidential Government.* New York: Oxford University Press, 1992. Collection of essays providing comparisons between the two types of systems.

Suleiman, Ezra, ed. *Parliaments and Parliamentarians in Democratic Politics.* New York: Holmes & Meier, 1986. Analysis of parliamentary legislatures in several countries.

Daniel M. Shea

Cross-References

The British Parliamentary System, p. 146; Cabinet Government, p. 184; The Canadian Parliamentary System, p. 190; Checks and Balances in U.S. Government, p. 216; Congress, p. 412; Democracy, p. 513; Filibuster, p. 694; Government Types, p. 785; Legislative Functions of Government, p. 1098; Lobbying and Lobbyists, p. 1130; Local Governments, p. 1136; Parliamentary Government, p. 1377; Separation of Powers: Political Philosophy, p. 1809; Term Limits, p. 1956; Town Meetings, p. 1993; Tribal Government, p. 2027; Veto Power, p. 2097.

LEGISLATIVE FUNCTIONS OF GOVERNMENT

Field of study: Functions of government

Elected legislatures are the cornerstone of modern democracies. People periodically elect representatives who make the laws which govern society. In the United States, lawmaking is divided at the national level between Congress—which has primary responsibility—and the president. American citizens also elect legislators at the state, county, and city levels.

Principal terms
> ADMINISTRATIVE LEGISLATION: regulations issued by bureaucracies which are delegated powers by Congress
> DELEGATE: representative who discharges his or her role in accordance with constituency desires
> INCUMBENCY ADVANTAGE: the financial and visibility edge lawmakers have over potential challengers by serving in office
> INITIATIVE: procedure by which citizens, instead of legislators, propose policies (through petition) that become law if passed by a majority of state voters
> PARLIAMENTARY SYSTEM: government in which all lawmaking authority is vested in a legislature
> PRESIDENTIAL SYSTEM: government in which lawmaking authority is divided between legislative and executive branches
> REPUBLICAN GOVERNMENT: system in which people indirectly rule through an elected legislature
> TRUSTEE: representative who discharges his or her role in accordance with what they feel is in the best interests of their constituents and nation

Overview

A legislature's primary function is to create a body of laws or rules within which its society functions. All democratic nations of the world are republican governments in which legislatures elected by a national citizenry wield most, if not all, of the legitimate lawmaking authority. In presidential systems, such as the United States, legislative power is divided among more than one branch of government with the legislature having primary authority and the chief executive usually possessing a role in approving or rejecting bills. The judiciary also may play a part in interpreting or reviewing such bills. In contrast, parliamentary systems, such as Great Britain, vest all power to make laws in their legislatures. Also, many federal nations, such as the United States, divide sovereignty between a national government and various states or provinces. In the United States, therefore, the legislative function is discharged by a wide set of governments: the nation, states, counties, cities, and special districts. The common element to all types is that the citizens select officials and hold them accountable through periodic elections.

In contrast to republican governments, citizens in the first democracies of ancient Greece gathered together, debated, and voted on laws directly. These pure democracies did not persevere, with later political philosophers criticizing them for degenerating into mobs where the passions of the moment, rather than careful deliberation, seemed to carry the day. Elected legislatures are less than four hundred years old, dating to the British Parliament of the 1600's. Early legislatures, including the U.S. Congress of the 1789 Constitution, acted in the name of the people and perhaps, at times, in the interests of the community, but they did not allow the majority of adult citizens to vote. It was not until the ratification of the Fifteenth Amendment to the Constitution in 1870, which explicitly ensured that African Americans had the right to vote, and the Nineteenth Amendment in 1920, which gave women the right to vote in national elections, that any of the world's legislatures accurately could be said to represent a majority of citizens.

Some American states allow citizens to vote on their laws directly. In the early 1900's, the Progressive Movement won majority control of several state legislatures. In states such as California, the progressives campaigned against elected legislatures, claiming they had been taken over by corrupting forces such as big business or political party bosses. In response, the Progressives gave the people tools of direct democracy to bypass the legislature, including the initiative. It allows state citizens to draft and approve laws themselves if they can get a certain percentage of people to sign a petition to put an issue on a statewide ballot, and then obtain majority approval for it to become law. California, for example, requires 5 percent of the total who voted in the last election for governor. A majority of modern state legislatures share the lawmaking power with citizens. There is no such device available to American citizens in national elections.

Under the U.S. Constitution, all legislative powers are vested in the Congress. Article 1 describes the means (how lawmaking works) and the ends (the areas in which Congress can properly legislate). For a proposal to become a law, House and Senate majorities must first pass a bill, agreeing exactly on its contents. Concerned that elected legislators could abuse power and trample on the authority of the president's power, the Philadelphia convention made lawmaking a shared enterprise. The president may either veto a bill and return it to the chamber which first passed it, together with any objections he or she may include, or sign it, in which case it becomes law. If the president chooses neither to veto nor to sign the bill, it becomes law after ten days, except at the end of a two-year congressional session, when the bill dies (referred to as a "pocket" veto). A veto may be overridden by the Congress and become law if two-thirds of the members present in each chamber so vote.

The veto is an important source of presidential power. Without it, Congress could ignore presidential preferences. With it, because less than one in ten vetoes are overridden, Congress typically must accommodate at least some of the president's positions. The veto, combined with constitutional stipulations that presidents provide "information on the state of the union" and recommend measures to Congress "necessary and expedient," permits presidents to play a role in leading the legislature. Since the presidency of Franklin D. Roosevelt (1933-1945), presidents have indeed worked closely with Congress in order to get their legislative agendas enacted into law.

The ends of government have changed significantly since the congresses of the eighteenth century. Many men involved in the process of drafting and ratifying the Constitution, such as James Madison, believed that congressional authority was limited to those matters specifically enumerated in Article 1. These include the powers to tax, declare war, and regulate interstate commerce. Others, such as Alexander Hamilton, held that the elastic clause which states that Congress has the power "to make all laws which shall be necessary and proper for carrying into execution the foregoing powers" gave Congress other powers not specifically mentioned. In interpreting the Constitution, the Supreme Court has favored the broader interpretation of legislative power. During its first century and a half, Congress did not legislate in areas much beyond regulating and promoting interstate commerce and taking care of national security. Most other functions were left to the states.

Even as Congress extended its reach, it also gave some of its legislative power away. In response to the Great Depression of the 1930's, President Roosevelt, together with Democratic congresses, moved the national government into new areas of policy-making. Since that time, Congress has legislated in every facet of society, ranging from agriculture subsidies to worker safety. In response to the question of how the legislative branch may intervene in so many different areas of society, Congress has delegated some of its power for legislating to other government agencies. For example, it might establish an agency with purview over a part of economic activity and then give it the power to formulate rules in that area. In one example, Congress created the Occupational Safety and Health Administration (OSHA) to set, monitor, and enforce health and safety standards in the workplace. The rules that OSHA sets have the force of law and, in fact, are referred to as "administrative legislation."

Despite the fact that Congress has vested unelected administrators with some control over lawmaking, popular control over the making of legislation remains a key assumption of republican governments. While the public may contact members of Congress directly and have their views heard through interest groups and political parties which they join, the principal mechanism for controlling legislators comes through elections. Members of the House of Representatives are elected from local districts, the boundaries of which are drawn by state legislatures, and they serve two-year terms. Members of the Senate, in contrast, represent entire states and serve six-year terms. Without periodic elections, there would be little incentive for officials to pay attention to public desires and interests. With elections, members of Congress try to strike a balance between two alternative conceptions of representation, acting as a delegate or a trustee.

When members act as delegates, they solicit and follow constituency opinion. Members of Congress receive heavy input on issues that generate public interest.

These include, for example, tax proposals, decisions to use armed forces, and bills either enhancing or restricting access to firearms. Delegates generally side with the majority of their constituents. The role of trustees, according to eighteenth century British parliamentarian Edmund Burke, is not to follow constituency opinion slavishly, but to exercise their judgment on what is best for their constituencies. Burke believed that a legislature should be deliberative and consider all opinions and sides to a question before deciding. Fortunately for the electoral fortunes of members of Congress, representing constituents does not usually require a stark choice between constituency views and personal conscience. House members cast between up to a thousand recorded votes during every two-year term. Because members are from the districts that they represent, their views typically parallel constituency opinions. Only on a small percentage of votes is there significant public attention, leaving members free to follow their personal views on other votes.

In legislatures other than the Congress, members often follow their parties' views. They do this regardless of whether they believe that their party's view is best for the nation or is consistent with constituency opinion. The public is assumed to have its input at election time when voters choose among competing party platforms and philosophies. Consequently, once in office, a party holding a majority would have almost certain support from its members and universal opposition from the minority. In many nations, renegade party members might be denied places on the ballot if they were to depart from the party line. Because American parties do not control access to the ballot, members of Congress make more independent judgments concerning policy proposals.

Applications

Throughout the 1980's, there was a great paradox in American politics. Voters seemed to believe that the performance of their political institutions was poor yet, at the same time, they continued to reelect many members of Congress who were at the center of the political system. During the 1980's, for example, more than 95 percent of House incumbents who sought reelection were successful. In 1992, however, the picture changed. Incumbents retired in near-record numbers and, in the November election, voters elected a new Democratic president, 110 new House members, and fourteen new senators. This was the largest turnover in Congress since the 1948 election. These changes illustrate that the legislative function of government is ultimately responsive to the public, if voters use the political tools available to them.

Several trends during the 1980's explain the low opinions that voters held for elected officials. Voters reacted negatively to ethical scandals—forcing the resignation of the Speaker of the House of Representatives, Jim Wright; they resented seeing members of Congress raising their own pay by 40 percent in 1989; and they became impatient with the apparent inability of government to deal with such vexing policy problems as annual budget deficits—which soared above $200 billion. Nevertheless, although Congress as an institution was extraordinarily unpopular, few members seeking reelection were rejected by their constituents. Congressional scholars offered several reasons for this lack of collective turnover on Capitol Hill. One was the advantage held by incumbents who raised large amounts of money for their campaigns and used the resources of their office to increase their visibility. Another was the paucity of credible challengers willing to devote the time, raise the money, and subject themselves to intense public scrutiny in heated campaigns. Finally, many members of Congress managed to stay in office by assuring the public that they were fighting against the corruption and gridlock that paralyzed the very institution in which they served.

A combination of factors explains the large group of new members in the Congress in 1992. Many senior members, frustrated with their inability to change the institution or public policy, either retired or ran for other offices, opening many seats to new members. Also, with the economy in recession in 1991 and 1992, and with public disapproval of Congress so strong, a credible group of challengers ran against incumbents and won. Finally, after the 1990 census, congressional district lines were redrawn by state legislatures, reshaping the constituencies of many members who no longer enjoyed the advantages of incumbency. Running for many of those seats were women and minority group members who, because of the low numbers of non-whites and women in Congress, could credibly claim the mantle of outsider and gain the public confidence that they would change things. The new House of Representatives seated record numbers of thirty-eight blacks, seventeen Hispanics, and forty-seven women.

Context

The events of the late 1980's in Eastern Europe, where many repressive regimes were replaced by freely elected governments, suggest that the institutions of democracy, including elected legislatures, enjoy nearly universal appeal. Despite this, the public opinion of legislators in individual nations is typically quite low. In some ways, this is natural because legislatures handle public policy problems which, like economic downturns, often defy easy solutions.

When the Framers of the U.S. Constitution made lawmaking a shared enterprise in 1787, they intended to strike a balance between limited government, which protects the liberty of individuals, and an energetic government which can respond to public problems. Institutional obstructions, combined with the social, ethnic, religious, and regional diversity in the United States and the weak party system that encourages members to heed constituency desires, make majority coalitions difficult to assemble in the Congress. This difficulty was what James Madison expressed in the Federalist Papers in suggesting that a large, diverse republic would itself be a protector of liberty. Therefore, individual or collective frustration that legislative action is slow or non-existent is a natural byproduct of representative legislatures and serves to protect individual liberty.

Nevertheless inaction cannot always prevail if a democracy is to work; differences at some point must be set aside and the majority must be allowed to rule. Whether it is the state of the economy, health care, unemployment, or the U.S. role in the world community, there are always problems that the public expects government to address. No better example exists than the federal budget deficit, a perennial issue on which the public demands action, but one in which the public and attentive lawmakers are at odds about the solutions of cutting public programs or raising taxes. Ultimately, however, the absence of action, coupled with extreme public hostility toward lawmakers at all levels, may cause the public to call into question the authority of the law itself potentially leading to societal chaos. In the long run, there must be a general acceptance of the legislative process's legitimacy—whether it be a local, state, or national legislature—for democracy to work.

Bibliography

Congressional Digest. 1922-. Bimonthly publication that presents recent important debates and issues before the Congress. Includes testimony offered by members of Congress.

Federal Regulatory Directory. 6th ed. Washington, D.C.: Congressional Quarterly Press, 1990. Comprehensive guide to the administrative agencies in the U.S. government, with descriptions of agency missions and personnel. Describes how to find agency regulations and lists recent executive orders, regulations, and acts passed by Congress.

Governing. Washington, D.C.: Congressional Quarterly Press, 1987-. Monthly publication that analyzes and summarizes state and local politics in the United States.

Green, Alan. *Gavel to Gavel: A Guide to the Televised Proceedings of Congress.* Washington, D.C.: C-SPAN, 1992. Concise description of the legislative process accompanied by tips on viewing C-SPAN's wide-ranging programming on national, state, and international politics.

Hamilton, Alexander, James Madison, and John Jay. *The Federalist Papers.* Edited by Clinton Rossiter. New York: New American Library, 1961. Collection of essays arguing the Constitution should be ratified. The best source for explaining the motivations of those who drafted the Constitution.

Light, Paul C. *Forging Legislation.* New York: W. W. Norton, 1992. Highly readable and interesting case study that explains how one policy proposal eventually became law, describing the figures involved and the structure of the Congress.

Ripley, Randall B. *Congress: Process and Policy.* 4th ed. New York: W. W. Norton, 1988. Excellent interpretation and description of the role of Congress in the policy-making process. Analyzes the president's legislative role and contains an outstanding bibliography on Congress.

Stephen D. Van Beek

Cross-References

Accountability in U.S. Government, p. 1; Administrative Procedures in U.S. Government, p. 14; The City-State, p. 272; Congress, p. 412; Government Agencies, p. 765; Government Roles, p. 778; Initiatives and Referendums, p. 923; Legislative

Body Types, p. 1091; Local Governments, p. 1136; Montesquieu's Political Philosophy, p. 1228; Parliamentary Government, p. 1377; Policy Development and Implementation, p. 1414; Political Representation in the United States, p. 1525; Progressivism, p. 1609; Republicanism, p. 1706; Veto Power, p. 2097.

LEGITIMACY

Field of study: Political philosophy

Legitimacy is what signifies acceptance of a political system. It is belief in the legitimacy of a government that causes most people to follow voluntarily the decisions of the government, rather than having to be coerced, even if they disagree with particular policies.

Principal terms

AUTHORITARIAN STATE OR REGIME: government that controls individuals and organizations so that all activity is in line with the policies and goals of the government

COMMUNISM: economic and political ideology that advocates state ownership of all resources and a one-party government, with an eventual goal of total equality for all people

DEMOCRACY: ideology based on individual freedom and government responsiveness to the desires of the people; often seen in conjunction with the capitalist economic system

GOVERNMENT: institution through which state sovereignty is expressed, the ultimate rule-making authority in the state

IDEOLOGY: basic economic, political, and social ideals that serve as the foundation for a social system

POLITICAL SYSTEM: institutions a society uses to run the government

STATE: social group that occupies territory and is organized within a political system that has sovereign government

Overview

The political concept of legitimacy deals with why people accept the power of government, even though it limits personal freedom. Normally, legitimacy is based on a mixture of structure and expectation. Structure is the political system, or mechanism, in any society, such as its institutions, its members of the government, its ways of making the laws, and its traditions. Expectation is how the members of the society view the nature of the political system, within the larger social system. Expectation includes their conception of the government and state, the role of the individual, the nature of the social system, and the objectives of the society. All of these blend together in such a way that an individual or a group pronounces something to be legitimate or illegitimate. In addition to the complexity of how to measure legitimacy the issue is further clouded by the fact that there are two basic approaches. One is to accept those systems which measure up to some normative standard, while the other is to accept as legitimate any system which is supported by a vast majority of people in the system. There is no set standard for determining legitimacy, so different people can come to different conclusions based on the same evidence.

There are so many factors in the concept of legitimacy, it is often said to be a soft concept, difficult to measure directly. If a government, or a system, is seen to be legitimate the people will accept the actions of the government and most will voluntarily be obedient to its policies. It is generally easier to identify what is not legitimate than to define completely what constitutes legitimacy. Force can be used to gain public acceptance of certain governmental policies; however, long-term governmental efficiency and stability require that a sizeable majority of people accept the government. Continued use of coercion to force the acceptance of governmental decisions leads to increased resistance to the government, and, when the force is weakened, to the dissolution of that government. The acceptance of the governmental system, and to a lesser extent its policies and leaders, as legitimate is necessary for stability. Even if various people choose not to follow the decisions of the government or not to support those who are in positions of power, if most people believe that a government is legitimate, it has a strong foundation within the society. In this situation, the government can focus upon the issues confronting the society, rather than upon how to convince its citizens to abide by governmental policy.

With some exceptions, prior to the modern period, monarchy was the normal system of government. The primary question of legitimacy in this system was whether the proper person was the ruler. At times of dynastic change, or the assumption of power by a military leader, the new ruler would often go to great lengths to show that by either divine choice or family history the right person was now ruling the nation. In Western culture the transition into the modern period was also a time of transition from monarchy to the beginning of the movement toward democracy. As the period opened, the defense mounted for monarchs was the divine right of kings. Essentially, this stated that within the world a divine order had been established, giving some the privilege and responsibility for governing society. Legitimacy was not based upon performance, rather it was based upon a natural order well beyond the purview of the day-to-day operation of government. Religion blended with politics to provide a foundation for government. Legitimacy was not something the people decided; it came from above. Government was a part of the natural order.

The political concept of legitimacy changed with the beginning of the modern era. One element of change that came with this period was a broader range of choice, which challenged strict adherence to tradition. A major movement that dealt with some of the underlying assumptions of democracy was based on the idea of the "social contract." According to this idea, social institutions, such as government, are the result of an agreement by those in the society. There is no divine system of government that is ordained from above. This being the case, a legitimate system of government is that system which expresses the ideals of the society. Legitimacy is determined by the people. Those examining the state as resulting from a social contract question not only the role of those involved in governmental leadership, but the system itself. Historically, this second question of legitimacy—the legitimacy of the system—has been answered upon ideological or moral grounds.

As political thought continued to develop in the modern era, some advocated that legitimacy includes more than just the construction of the basic system or determining if the individuals ruling a country have obtained their positions through the proper means. A third question pertaining to legitimacy arose, having to do with the relationship between political and economic systems. For some, a governmental system is legitimate only if it is able to meet the needs of its citizens in the areas of social and economic welfare. Others go even further and claim that a system is legitimate only if it is the best one possible to serve the needs of its citizens. During the competition of the Cold War, this approach to legitimacy was often used by proponents of the Communist system as well as by proponents of the capitalist-democratic system. Each group sought to show how the other was inferior in assisting its citizens and thus illegitimate.

As can be seen, the concept of legitimacy has become more complex over time. Not everyone, however, is as demanding as those who judge legitimacy by the effectiveness of the governmental system in providing welfare and justice. Different people use different criteria to make their judgments, resulting in even more discrepancies in trying to answer whether a particular government is legitimate. For those who are not familiar with the definition being used by a writer, statements concerning the legitimacy or illegitimacy of a government might actually obscure the writer's true intent. It is important to understand what criteria are being used when a statement is made concerning the legitimacy of a political system.

Applications

During the early 1990's, the world community was greatly changed as many governmental systems, and even states, collapsed because of the lack of legitimacy. Those that had depended upon force to sustain the government had the greatest amount of change. The most visible changes were the states in Eastern Europe, as the former Communist Bloc nations not only changed political and economic systems, but also their underlying ideology. During the course of a few years, Albania, Bulgaria, Hungary, Poland, and Romania turned away from the Communist system and moved at different speeds toward democracy and capitalism. At the same time, the Democratic Republic of Germany was unable to sustain the Communist system, and was incorporated into the Federal Republic of Germany. In all these cases, the former governments had never totally been accepted as legitimate, since the military power of the Soviet Union had been used to sustain the economic and political systems since their establishment after World War II.

Czechoslovakia, the Soviet Union, and Yugoslavia not only saw the end of Communist domination in the political system, but the disintegration of their states as well. Czechoslovakia peacefully agreed to split the predominately Czech territory from the predominately Slovak area. Within the territory of the former Yugoslavia, it was not a peaceful transition; five states, and three warring ethnic groups, destroyed the Yugoslavia that had previously existed. Although the splintering of the Soviet Union had already started when its last leader, Mikhail Gorbachev, resigned, a total of fifteen states finally emerged from the territory that had been the Soviet Union. His personal perception that military force was not a legitimate tool to hold together the Eastern

Bloc, or even the Soviet Union, allowed the dramatic events of the early 1990's to unfold. The people in all three regions did not see the multinational state as the legitimate servant of their ideals. Without the coercive power of the military and whatever unity that Communist ideology had given to the multinational state, each nationality was free to construct its own government system.

In all the countries of the former Eastern Bloc, Communism had been imposed from the outside. This was a major factor in the perception by many people that the Communist system was not a legitimate expression of the people of these countries. It could be argued that Communism was not legitimate by any conception of the term. Many would say that the Communist system was not the result of the social contract by the citizens of those countries, that the system of government was not the result of any widespread acceptance of the basic constitutional principles, and that the Communist system was not efficient in providing a variety of services for the people.

Another example of the question of legitimacy comes from the Republic of South Africa in the early 1990's. The transformation in South Africa was also the result of a widespread rejection of the system underlying the government and ultimately the unwillingness of the government to continue to use force to maintain itself. The foundation of the governing system was white minority rule based on apartheid, or the separation of the races. This had been challenged for decades by people inside and outside the state. The system of apartheid was outlawed, a new electoral system was put into place which for the first time allowed citizens of all races to participate, and the first multiracial national government was elected. While the impact of the transformation was as great as any that occurred in the former Communist countries, the change within the political system was actually much less. The major change was that the new electoral system allowed universal suffrage. The multiparty electoral system, the form of government, and the state remained intact, even though the underlying ideology changed from racial separation to inclusiveness. That part of the government considered illegitimate was abandoned; what was considered legitimate was kept.

These cases exemplify the cataclysmic events which can occur when a political system, government, or state is seen as illegitimate. Events in the future will prove to be no less monumental. While it is not possible to predict which systems, governments, or states will lose the support of their citizens, those that have depended upon the threat of force face prospects similar to those listed above.

Much smaller changes occur when the question of legitimacy is raised in situations in which force has not been generally used to control the population. The resignation of U.S. president Richard Nixon was a case in point. While he was legally reelected in 1972, the scandal that emerged from his campaign and the way in which the investigation was treated by the White House staff called into question his capacity to lead the American people. He lost the aura of legitimacy that normally goes with the office of the president. Although he had the legal right to remain president (at least until he received the impeachment he was facing), Nixon's decision to regain was based upon the judgment by the majority of Americans that he no longer had the legitimate right to be the leader of the United States. This judgment, however, was directed toward the person, not the system or government. Thus even though President Nixon resigned, the government continued under President Gerald Ford; the system operated as before, and there was no major threat to the stability of the state.

Context

Legitimacy is a basic concept in political science. In the reciprocal relationship between the state and the citizen, legitimacy is the key to many questions. What gives the state the right to limit the freedom of its citizens, and from the other point of view, what is the basis for the obligation a citizen has to obey the state? In addition to these questions, political science must deal with the question of what mechanisms can be used for conferring legitimacy. How does legality relate to legitimacy? Are there absolute limits on what can be considered a legitimate governmental activity, or are limits only relative, based on public acceptance of governmental activity? These are all questions that have been and will be major issues in political science on the theoretical as well as the practical level.

The stability of any government, even of the state itself, depends upon the people's acceptance of it as a legitimate expression of the social order. Except for authoritarian regimes built on a foundation of domination by the forceful repression of their citizens, all states and governments are greatly concerned with the issue of legitimacy. As was shown by the collapse of the Soviet Union, however, even the leader of an authoritarian state can be concerned with the legitimacy of the use of force and cause major upheaval through changing the governmental policy. The ability of a government to change policy and law radically can be limited if most citizens believe this is not an appropriate area for governmental action. The ability of leaders to perform the tasks of political leadership can be greatly limited if the people do not believe them to be the legitimate leaders of the nation. Even the existence of the system, or state, itself can be called into question. Thus legitimacy is one of the most important issues facing any political leader.

Historically, the question of legitimacy developed in a series of steps concerning the individual ruler, the system, and the state's effectiveness in meeting needs beyond the strictly political realm. There is no reason to doubt that questions in each of these areas concerning legitimacy will continue to be important in the future, and in fact it is possible that new areas could be added as new demands are placed upon the state. While examples of political leaders, governments, systems, or states losing power because of the loss of legitimacy can be seen in any era, the events of the early 1990's have strongly reinforced the importance of legitimacy. The fact that much of the pressure for change in Eastern Europe was attributable to the Communist governments' not being perceived as meeting the needs of their citizens will strengthen the examination of government policy. Those who strive to limit the question of legitimacy to basic principles of government have been in the minority. Whatever the scholarly trends might be in the future, the basic relationship between a citizen and the state will always be a valuable area of study, as well as a practical concern of people around the world.

Bibliography

Barker, Ernest, ed. *Social Contract: Essays by Locke, Hume, and Rousseau.* New York: Oxford University Press, 1962. Essays by each of the political philosophers illustrate the transition in political thought to the idea of the social contract.

Barnard, F. M. *Pluralism, Socialism, and Political Legitimacy: Reflections on Opening Up Communism.* Cambridge, England: Cambridge University Press, 1991. Focuses on the problems the former Communist countries face in moving to democracy.

Brilmayer, Lea. *Justifying International Acts.* Ithaca, N.Y.: Cornell University Press, 1989. Examines the role legitimacy plays in the international arena.

Dogan, Mattei, ed. *Comparing Pluralist Democracies: Strains on Legitimacy.* Boulder, Colo.: Westview Press, 1988. Examines the question of legitimacy from a broad perspective, using quantitative data.

Habermas, Jurgen. *Legitimation Crisis.* Translated by Thomas McCarthy. Boston: Beacon Press, 1975. This landmark book has provided the framework for the debate on legitimacy since it was published.

Rigby, T. H., and Ferenc Feher. *Political Legitimation in Communist States.* New York: St. Martin's Press, 1982. Comprehensive examination of the methods used by leaders in European Communism to gain legitimacy for their policies and governments.

Donald A. Watt

Cross-References

Accountability in U.S. Government, p. 1; Charismatic Leadership, p. 209; Church and Government in History, p. 230; Citizen Movements, p. 248; Civic Education, p. 278; Civil Unrest and Rioting, p. 317; Civil Wars, p. 325; General Will, p. 745; Hobbes's Political Philosophy, p. 836; Individual Versus State Rights, p. 910; Islam and Government, p. 994; Locke's Political Philosophy, p. 1142; Mexico: Politics and Government, p. 1179; Political Philosophy, p. 1505; Protest Movements, p. 1621; Rousseau's Political Philosophy, p. 1756; The Social Contract, p. 1827.

LIBERAL NATIONALISM

Field of study: Political philosophy

Modern nationalism is largely a product of the French Revolution and the Napoleonic Wars, an era which also gave birth to liberalism as a political, social, and economic movement. Giuseppe Mazzini was a paradigm of the liberal nationalist in his attempt to unite his homeland, Italy.

Principal terms

ASSOCIATION: uniting with others for a common good; antidote to egoistic individualism

INDIVIDUALISM: product of natural rights philosophies

LIBERALISM: early nineteenth century movement committed to liberty, equality, and individual freedom

NATIONALISM: promotion of one's culture, language, and tradition; major movement of the nineteenth century

REPUBLICANISM: system wherein citizens elect governing representatives

SOCIALISM: economic and political theories advocating public ownership of the means of production

Overview

Giuseppe Mazzini, the revolutionary apostle and agitator of liberal nationalism, was born in Genoa, Italy, in 1805. Nationalism, which grew out of the American and French revolutions and the Napoleonic Wars, was one of the major movements of the nineteenth century. Mazzini was influenced by numerous nationalistic currents, particularly in philosophical and literary circles, that were occurring in Italy and elsewhere in Europe in the early part of the century. For Mazzini, nationality was sacred. The nation was the linchpin of society, as the individual was too weak and all of humanity too vast. Mazzini also was inspired by the ideas of liberalism, another influential movement of the century, and was committed to equality, freedom, and liberty from arbitrary authority, whether divine right monarchy, aristocratic domination, or institutional religion. Combining liberalism and nationalism, Mazzini sponsored numerous revolutionary uprisings from his early twenties until his death in 1872. So much of his life was spent in exile in Switzerland, France, and especially England that his knowledge of Italy was primarily historic and literary. He never had any significant contact with the Italian masses. His returns to his homeland were usually of short duration, and it was generally from abroad that he planned and plotted the Italian *Risorgimento* (resurrection) in order to achieve a united and republican Italy.

As a writer, Mazzini the revolutionary was primarily an essayist. A propagandist rather than an original thinker, his most famous political writings are collected in *The Duties of Man*, a series of essays linked together by his liberal and national beliefs that first appeared in the mid-1840's. A passionate writer, Mazzini combined his own interpretations of liberalism and nationalism in the hopes of creating a liberal Italy out of the several conservative and reactionary states then governing the peninsula, and from the backward, illiterate masses who doubtless neither knew him nor understood his message. His critics, in Italy and elsewhere, portrayed him as a violent and destructive revolutionary, but he was very much a product and a prophet of two of the major movements of his time.

Nineteenth century liberalism was greatly indebted to the natural rights philoso-phies associated with England's John Locke, the American Declaration of Inde-pendence, and the French Revolution's Declaration of the Rights of Man. Mazzini recognized the value of individual rights but argued that the fervent devotion to rights found in contemporary England and France—liberty for the sake of liberty—was too limiting and ultimately destructive. An exclusive commitment to rights resulted in individualistic egoism and materialism, tendencies that Mazzini found in the utilitarian ideas of Jeremy Bentham and the laissez-faire beliefs of Adam Smith.

While liberalism in Britain gave ideological support to maximizing individual freedom for the newly evolving middle class associated with the Industrial Revolution, Mazzini's *The Duties of Man* was directed to the Italian working class. In an Italy divided among various states, including the Austro-Hungarian Empire, the Kingdom of Piedmont-Sardinia, and the Papal States, and without a significant industrial base to support a middle class, Mazzini's vision was necessarily different. His idealistic and philosophical commitment to duties or responsibilities is beyond question, but there was also a practical aspect to this emphasis. He had to create a sense of what the peoples of the Italian peninsula had in common. In an already unified Great Britain, British nationalism was assumed and seemingly assured, and British writers and politicians could logically emphasize individual freedom. Mazzini could not. If the focus was upon individual rights rather than communal obligations, Italian unification might never occur. Thus duties to family, nation, and humanity were paramount, not rights, and he encouraged the development of what he referred to as association, union with others who held a common vision and had a common goal.

Along with a shared culture and language, this connection could come from the past. History, real or legendary, was crucial to advocates of nationalism among those peoples who had yet to achieve a nation as a validation of their dreams and ambitions. As the Greeks looked to the glories of ancient Athens, and Germans to their Teutonic tribes, Mazzini turned to the Italian past—to the Roman Republic, the early Catholic church, and Dante, one of his great heroes. For Mazzini, history did not merely sanction a unified Italy, it made it inevitable.

Liberty could not exist without equality. Concentration on individual rights had rewarded some, but the majority were still illiterate and lodged in poverty. Mazzini, along with several other liberals, argued that neither socialism nor communism was an acceptable alternative to reactionary conservatism. Socialism or communism could also divide society, not unite it, leading to envy, stagnation, or even violence, so that progress would be impossible. For Mazzini, private property was a natural right, an aspect of liberty, but unrestrained individual rights could lead to inequality, even to a capitalist tyranny. Mazzini envisioned a system whereby all were producers and consumers, wherein capital and labor were in the same hands. Cooperative production and ownership through associations was the solution. Government had a positive role to play, a larger role than British liberals were willing to grant. Government could encourage associations, improve the means of communication and distribution, create a more equitable tax system, and, most controversial, appropriate the wealth of the Catholic church in Italy.

Faith in education as a transforming element in society was a hallmark of nineteenth century liberals; conservatives and reactionaries often feared the consequences of educating the lower classes. In a largely illiterate Italy, education had a high priority for Mazzini; however, he differentiated between education, which was moral in scope, and instruction, which he defined as intellectual. Education would lead to a recognition of one's duties, and instruction would give one the means to fulfill them. Education and instruction must be national, compulsory, free, and common to all, or unity would never result.

Mazzini also fervently accepted the liberal belief in the inevitability of progress, not only change but also improvement and betterment. Some associated progress with material advancement, but Mazzini claimed that progress was primarily moral and spiritual, not merely material. The Industrial Revolution's capacity to produce more and more goods for more and more people placed an emphasis upon materialism as almost an end in itself. This, to Mazzini, was fallacious and dangerous and again was the result of an emphasis upon rights rather than duties.

A unique element to be found in Mazzini's liberal nationalism was his religious beliefs. Like his hero Dante, Mazzini was a Catholic who was harshly critical of the institutional papacy of his time, with its censorship and reactionary policies. He was confident, however, that there were individual clerics who supported his liberal nationalism. Completely rejecting atheism, his writings are imbued with spiritual sentiments and religious allusions: He asserted that people's duties originated from God and were defined by God's laws and that humanity's task was to discover and apply those laws. He believed that God demanded action, not merely contemplation, and that a united Italy was part of God's evolving and progressive plan. Individual conscience and the collective wisdom of humanity could discover and implement God's law. Religious toleration should be guaranteed by the state, but nations indifferent to religion would be at the mercy of divisive self-interest. A common religious faith gave a nation unity and permanence.

More controversially, Mazzini's commitment to liberal nationalism included the use of force and violence. Most liberals of his era eschewed violent revolution as a means to nationhood. The bloodshed of the French Revolution and Napoleon's wars were still recent memories. British liberals had already captured the government and German liberals hoped to do so by peaceful means, but Mazzini saw no alternative to armed revolution because of the brutal nature of the opponents of Italian unity. Mazzini spent his entire adult life planning violent uprisings that were to lead to a republican Italy.

Mazzini's liberal nationalism stressed the obligation of duties over rights, of association over individual egoism, which for him culminated in the nation state: "Without country you have neither name, token, voice, nor rights, no admission as brothers into the fellowship of the peoples. You are the bastards of humanity." On the other hand, he discussed duties to family, including women, who Mazzini claimed should have equal civil and political rights with men. Beyond the nation was humanity. Mazzini's crusade for Italian unity was not xenophobic. He viewed the nation as part of a greater whole, with Italy's mission the moral unity of Europe, and then the rest of humanity.

Applications

Mazzini was a republican, and his challenge was not only to create a unified Italy out of the existing collection of mainly monarchical states but also to usher in a republican form of government. Traces and claims of divine right monarchy had lasted longer in southern Europe than in the north, where Great Britain's monarchy had long had its powers clipped by Parliament. The major external impediment to Italian unity was the Austro-Hungarian Empire, which ruled much of northern Italy, but within Italy the existing states of Piedmont-Sardinia, the Kingdom of Naples, and the Papal States showed little support for unity and none for a republic. Some nationalists hoped that Italian unification might result from the leadership of Piedmont-Sardinia, and although Mazzini often indicated that the national question was more important than the constitutional question, he remained suspicious of any breed of royalist.

In 1831, Mazzini organized Young Italy and in 1834, Young Europe, in order to further his nationalistic and humanistic ideals, but almost two decades of plotting came to little. In 1848, monarchical and reactionary governments throughout Europe were shaken by revolutionary movements, giving Mazzini hope that his dream might become reality. The archetypal conservative, the Austrian chancellor Klemens von Metternich, was driven from power in Vienna. The monarchy of Louis-Philippe of France was replaced by the democratic Second Republic; there were marches and speeches in the German states, and Karl Marx and Friedrich Engels published *The Communist Manifesto*. Demonstrations and riots in Milan against the Austrians led the cautious and conservative King Charles Albert of Piedmont-Sardinia to move against Austria in hopes of extending his own borders. Some Milanese objected, demanding an independent Lombard republic, but Mazzini, returning to Italy after an exile of seventeen years, supported Charles Albert. Fearing French intervention, Mazzini argued that unity had a higher priority than a particular form of government, and that Italians alone should unify Italy. Nevertheless, the Austrians eventually triumphed and Charles Albert abdicated.

Another opportunity presented itself in 1849. In the course of the upheavals, Pope Pius IX had fled Rome, taking refuge in the Kingdom of Naples. In February, an elected assembly ended the temporal powers of the papacy and declared Rome a republic. Mazzini had escaped to Switzerland, but he journeyed to Rome in March hoping to continue to fight for Italian unity. For a hundred days Mazzini was the governor of

Rome, establishing a liberal government. Religious toleration was mandated, censorship and the death penalty were ended, protective tariffs and duties were abolished, and taxes on the poor were lowered. Giuseppe Garibaldi and others joined Mazzini in resisting the pope, Austria, Spain, Naples, and ultimately France, whose army forced a surrender in July. Pope Pius IX returned and the French remained as an occupation force, but the defeated Mazzini and the fallen Roman republic entered into the patriotic annals of Italian history.

Italy was finally unified under Victor Emanuel II, Charles Albert's successor, and his prime minister, Count Camillo Cavour, a brilliant diplomat who distrusted Mazzini's revolutionary ardor. Cavour wished to rely upon French assistance in driving Austria from Italy while unifying Italy under the leadership of Piedmont-Sardinia. In 1860, Garibaldi captured Sicily and then Naples, which was incorporated with Victor Emanuel's territories in the north. As the result of a diplomatic agreement with Prussian chief minister Otto von Bismarck, Venice joined Italy in 1866 after Austria's defeat in the Austro-Prussian War. Mazzini, always distrustful of diplomats and foreign assistance, returned to Italy in August, 1870, hoping for a republican revolution in Rome. He was arrested, and while he was jailed near Naples, the forces of Victor Emanuel captured Rome in September. Italy had been unified, but under a conservative monarchy. Released under an amnesty, Mazzini left for England but returned to Italy secretly in 1871. His crusade only partially completed, he spend the last year of his life writing articles to educate his fellow Italians about the virtues of republicanism, social duties, and association, and warning against both Marxism and laissez-faire capitalism. He died in Pisa in February, 1872, holding his liberal national principles to the end.

Context

The Italian republic came into being only after World War II, after the defeat of Benito Mussolini and abolishment of the Italian monarchy. At the time of Mazzini's death, liberal nationalism had waned considerably from its heyday in the early part of the century. To many in the 1870's and after, Mazzini appeared as a figure of an irrelevant history. It was Cavour, the Machiavellian diplomat, and Garibaldi, the military man of action, who were credited with creating modern Italy.

Liberal nationalism, with its idealistic humanitarianism, reflected the hopes and values of the early nineteenth century, reaching its apogee in 1848. The Second French Republic was soon transformed through a bloody coup d'état into Napoleon III's Second Empire. The liberal nationalists in the German states were swept away by Otto von Bismarck, the conservative Prussian aristocrat; he pursued a policy of "blood and iron" in creating the North German Confederation at the expense of Austria in 1866, and, using his diplomatic wiles against Napoleon, the German Empire in 1870. The new German Empire, proclaimed in France's Palace of Versailles in 1871, planted the seeds for the wars of the twentieth century. Marx was also foreshadowing the twentieth century by pitting class against class; he postulated a revolutionary outbreak against the bourgeoisie, or middle classes, who in many ways exemplified nineteenth century liberalism, if not necessarily in Mazzini's terms. Charles Darwin was transforming the intellectual milieu with his ideas of natural selection and the survival of the fittest, which seemingly allowed little space for a discussion of duties, voluntary associations, beneficent progress, a common humanity, or God.

Nationalism survived 1848, but with a greater emphasis upon power, war, imperial rivalry over Asia and Africa, and jingoism. Liberalism also survived, but more in the classical, British mode of individual rights. In the twentieth century, communism and fascism flourished for a time, threatening both liberal values and the concept of a family of humanity made up of free nations. Mazzini's liberal nationalism did not entirely vanish, however. The League of Nations and the United Nations gave some recognition to the idealistic values of liberalism within the context of independent nation states, and the development of the European Community in the latter part of the twentieth century probably would have met with Mazzini's approval.

Bibliography

De Ruggiero, Guido. *The History of European Liberalism*. Translated by R. G. Collingwood. Boston: Beacon Press, 1959. Classic study of various aspects of European liberalism, first published in 1927. The author finds Mazzini more important as a revolutionary agitator and organizer than as an intellectual prophet.

Kedourie, Elie. *Nationalism*. London: Hutchinson University Library, 1960. In this wide-ranging interpretation of nationalism, the author argues that Mazzini and many nationalists of his generation suffered from a spiritual restlessness and subsequent quest for a new order of things, occasioned by the failure of the old order because of the impact of the French Revolution.

Kohn, Hans. *Prophets and Peoples*. New York: Macmillan, 1946. Kohn, one of the great historians of nationalism, insightfully interprets several major figures of nineteenth century nationalism, including Mazzini, England's John Stuart Mill, France's Jules Michelet, and Germany's Heinrich von Treitschke.

Langer, William L. *Political and Social Upheaval, 1832-1852*. New York: Harper & Row, 1969. A volume in *The Rise of Modern Europe* series, this standard work covers the European scene from the period of Mazzini's early revolutionary activities through the failure of the Roman Republic in 1849 and beyond.

Mack Smith, Denis. *Mazzini*. New Haven, Conn.: Yale University Press, 1994. This brilliant and necessary work is the first scholarly biography of Mazzini in English by one of the major historians of modern Italian history. Discusses Mazzini's ideas within the context of his life and times.

Mazzini, Giuseppe. *The Duties of Man and Other Essays*. New York: E. P. Dutton, 1929. Collection of Mazzini's seminal essays, first published in 1907. Includes a perceptive introduction by Thomas Jones.

Eugene Larson

Cross-References

Citizenship Rights and Responsibilities, p. 260; Dante's Political Philosophy, p. 483; Liberalism, p. 1118; The Nation-State, p. 1241; National Liberation Movements, p. 1255; Nationalism, p. 1268; Patriotism, p. 1384; Religion and Politics, p. 1685; Republicanism, p. 1706; Revolutions, p. 1738; Self-Determination, p. 1796; The Vatican, p. 2091

LIBERALISM

Field of study: Political philosophy

Liberalism means different things to different people. At root, it is about support for personal freedom. As a political movement, it began as business and trading interests struggled against the power and privilege of the landed aristocracy. It is associated, contradictorily perhaps, with open-market economics and with government intervention to correct social ills.

Principal terms

CLASSICAL LIBERALISM: one variety of liberalism associated with the concern to limit state power, especially over economic behavior

LAISSEZ-FAIRE: doctrine opposing governmental interference in economic affairs except to protect property rights and to enforce contracts

MARKETPLACE OF IDEAS: the hypothetical place where ideas are allowed a hearing in an open setting, and where the value or truth of an idea will be demonstrated by the number of people who "buy" the idea

NATURAL RIGHTS: theory embraced by early liberal philosophers that people naturally or innately have freedoms that the state has to respect

NIGHTWATCHMAN STATE: nineteenth century liberal view that the state should stay in the background and limit itself to protecting the life and property of citizens against domestic and foreign enemies

REFORM LIBERALISM: variety of liberalism developed in the twentieth century characterized by an acceptance of greater state involvement in economic affairs and of the state's providing welfare provisions for citizens in need

Overview

"Liberalism" is derived from the Latin word *liber*, meaning free. As liberalism developed in the Western world from the seventeenth century on, its central tenet was individual freedom in the areas of religion, politics, economics, and intellectual life. A liberal society allows its members as much freedom as possible to pursue their own goals and ideas. Unless a strong case can be made for a limitation of individual freedoms, a liberal stands opposed to constraints placed on individual freedom.

Liberalism can be viewed as a collection of personal freedoms, including the freedom from religious conformity, the freedom from autocratic rule, the freedom of expression, and economic freedom. Ideally, liberalism tries to assure the privacy in which all are at liberty to act and to think for themselves. The great nineteenth century liberal thinker John Stuart Mill phrased the issue thusly: "Under what conditions can society justly restrict the freedom of any individual?" He answered: "The only purpose for which power can be exercised over any member of a civilized community, against his will, is to prevent harm to others." Freedom is a positive good for the individual as well as for society except in those cases where such freedom does direct harm to another person.

As the European medieval order waned in the sixteenth and seventeenth centuries, liberalism replaced many formerly unassailable assumptions. In particular, liberalism opposed religious conformity, political absolutism, social status by birth, and the restrictions placed on economic activities.

The medieval world tried to maintain and uphold a theological system of one correct belief. To tolerate unorthodox beliefs was viewed as a threat to the teachings of Christianity and a setback in the Church's efforts to save souls; however, the Church's power to enforce uniformity started to unravel with the start of the Reformation in the early sixteenth century. The Reformation unleashed great political and religious turmoil throughout Europe; various protestant sects sprang up to defy Rome over how to interpret the Bible and how Christianity should be practiced. Gradually and grudgingly, more and more people saw that the only way to escape religious wars was to embrace toleration and the separation of church and state.

Liberalism also challenged medieval political institutions, which placed political authority in the hands of an absolute monarch. The natural rights tradition, spear-headed by the writings of seventeenth century English political philosophers Thomas Hobbes and John Locke, held that human beings possessed a set of natural rights (to life, liberty, and property) with which the state should not interfere, and which it was also obligated to protect. Both Hobbes and Locke argued that political authority came from a social contract entered into by people in order better to protect their rights. Prior to this concept of the social contract, few real restrictions were placed on the power of the state. By liberal thinking, however, state authority is not absolute but limited by a set of rules—the terms of the contract—clearly defining what rights the citizens possessed, and what powers the state legitimately held. Consequently, it was logical that if the terms of the contract were violated by the political authorities, the authorities could be justly removed from power. Since the people created their government, and set the conditions of state rule, they also had the right to withdraw their consent.

Another tenet of liberalism that arose from the English social contract tradition was the rejection of the practice of ascribed status. Ascribed status is the belief that one's place in society is fixed or predetermined by nature. For example, liberals held that it was not true that peasants could only give birth to peasants and that the nobility sired only nobles. With the breakdown of the social hierarchy of medieval societies, people were no longer locked into a fixed place on the social ladder. Instead, people were freer to determine their place in society based not simply on their birthright, but also on their talents, skills, and motivations. Over the next two centuries the medieval belief in natural social inequality gave way to the liberal position that everyone starts life as equals and has equal opportunities to make what they can of themselves.

The rise of Western liberalism between the sixteenth and eighteenth centuries was also the beginning of the scientific age, the artistic revival associated with the Renaissance, and the intellectual ideas linked to the Enlightenment. The common denominator in all three was the importance attached to the power of human reason and creative thought. Freedom in art, literature, philosophy, and the natural sciences, and the belief in human progress, necessitated what liberals call the marketplace of ideas. According to liberal thinking, no authority had the right to limit the debate. All ideas, even unpopular and sacrilegious ideas, have the right to be heard and contested in the public domain. It was John Stuart Mill who argued for the greatest possible toleration of all ideas because, first, they might turn out to be true or at least partially true, and second, even if the ideas are false, progress in human knowledge is more likely to move forward when there is a vigorous competition among ideas.

Finally, in the area of economics, liberal thought in the eighteenth and nineteenth centuries supported the economic interests of the middle class and the economic system known as capitalism. It was the Scottish economist Adam Smith, writing at the end of the eighteenth century, who gave the most convincing arguments for free markets and for why the obstacles against individual economic freedom should be removed. Smith observed that state-supported monopolies, regulations, and controls over economic behavior acted as a brake on the creation of wealth. Smith held that self-interest and the profit motive should not be viewed as terrible vices, but as natural human traits that may be channeled in ways that promote greater levels of efficiency and productivity. J. G. Merquior summarizes this classical liberal economic idea:

> Social well-being [is] not so much the result of any virtue, private or civic, as the unintended consequences of many selfish acts. The very pursuit of self-interest [can] lead to general prosperity and ultimately to social harmony.

In making the case for capitalism, liberal thinkers argued for a laissez-faire policy. Under laissez-faire, the government keeps its hands off the economy and allows for individual choice in buying, selling, manufacturing, and choosing a profession. In a laissez-faire economy the state has limited duties or responsibilities, namely, to provide for national defense, to establish and administer a system of justice, and to erect and maintain public works (such as roads, canals, and bridges) that would not be undertaken by private citizens. Instead of controlling the economy and restricting the freedom of individual citizens, liberalism worked to unleash their energies.

Applications

A number of historical examples can be cited to illustrate the impact of liberal ideas. Clearly the American Revolution in the late eighteenth century is an example of liberalism in action. The Declaration of Independence was undoubtedly influenced by John Locke's ideas. Thomas Jefferson followed Locke's basic ideas in constructing an argument for the American rebellion against English rule. The second paragraph of the Declaration of Independence is a classic summation of liberal ideas about natural rights and the social contract. It says, in part:

All men are created equal, that they are endowed by their Creator with certain unalienable rights, that among these are life, liberty, and the pursuit of happiness—That to secure these rights, governments are instituted among men, deriving their just powers from the consent of the governed, that whenever any form of government becomes destructive to these ends, it is the right of the people to alter or to abolish it, and to institute new government.

The colonists were not revolting because of a few minor disputes with the English king; they were reacting reluctantly after a long train of abuses. The Americans were simply acting in self-defense against the king's violations of their natural rights.

Immediately after the new American nation emerged it faced a major problem: namely, how to reconcile the liberal principle that "all men are created equal" with the institution of human slavery and later, after the Civil War, with a legalized system of discrimination. This major inconsistency was aptly labeled "the American dilemma" by the Swedish social scientist Gunnar Mrydal. The dilemma, obviously, was the glaring discrepancy between the liberal belief in equality and equal opportunities, and the actual practices in many parts of the United States where African Americans were denied equal and fair treatment. In short, Americans were not practicing what they claimed to be one of their highest values. It took an additional one hundred years after the abolition of slavery for the nation to begin to deal with this embarrassing dilemma. Only with the U.S. Supreme Court's decision in 1954 declaring segregated public schools unconstitutional, and with the passage of the Civil Rights Act and the Voting Rights Act in the 1960's, did America start to bring its practices more in line with its liberal principles.

A 1989 Supreme Court case dealing with free speech also illustrates how liberal principles operate to protect individual rights even when opposed by the majority. In 1984 in Dallas, Texas, during the Republican National Convention to renominate Ronald Reagan as a presidential candidate, a small group of political protesters held a demonstration attacking various government policies. During the demonstration, Gregory Lee Johnson was given an American flag taken from a nearby federal building. He set the flag on fire. The Dallas police arrested Johnson, charging him not with theft or with disrupting public safety, but with a Texas statute against the "desecration of a sacred object," the American flag in his case. Johnson's defense was based on his claim that his action was a form of expressive speech and, therefore, was protected under the First Amendment to the U.S. Constitution. His lawyers argued before the Supreme Court that the Texas law was unconstitutional because it put the protection of the flag ahead of a more important goal of guaranteeing Johnson's right of free speech. The state of Texas, on the other hand, argued that the American flag could be put into a special category and the state could act to protect this venerable symbol from being destroyed or mutilated. Furthermore, Texas argued, Johnson was only denied one form of expression (flag burning); he could still march, carry signs, or chant, if he wished to make a political statement.

In a five-to-four decision (*Texas v. Johnson*), the majority sided with Johnson.

Although the majority found Johnson's action to be disrespectful and in poor taste, they supported his right to express his political views by burning the flag. The Court's decision provoked much criticism across the country, but the Court held that the First Amendment was meant to invite disputes and to protect individuals expressing unpopular ideas. Even if the vast majority of Americans found Johnson's political ideas repugnant, under normal conditions the majority does not have the right to stop the expression of those ideas. In this case the Court clearly embraced Mill's position that all ideas should be heard, even obnoxious ones. The remedy that the Court endorsed for those outraged by Johnson's burning of the flag was not to take away his right to express himself, but to wave their own flags. If one thinks the flag symbolizes important American values, one does not show one's commitment to those values by suppressing political speech.

Context

The United States is, broadly speaking, a liberal society. In fact, the dominance of liberal principles is what sets the United States apart from many other nations. There are two basic reasons for this: First, when the American political system was being formed in the late eighteenth and early nineteenth centuries, liberal principles were reaching their full stride; second, since the American political world was new and lacked the weight of history of other ideologies (such as medieval feudalism), liberalism had the field to itself in America.

Throughout the nineteenth century, with the notable exception of slavery, America embraced and practiced what is commonly called classical liberalism—a political arrangement characterized by limited government power, a free market economy, and individualism. With the rise of the modern industrial system by the end of the 1800's, however, more and more people were calling for greater, not less, state intervention to help ease the savage inequalities connected with laissez-faire capitalism. Finally, during the Great Depression of the 1930's, the national government took steps to manage and regulate the economy and moved to establish basic welfare programs.

What transpired was a fundamental split in American liberalism into two wings. Alongside the traditional brand of classical liberalism, a variation known as reform liberalism was born. While both were largely committed to the core values of liberalism, reform liberals accepted a much larger role for the government, indicating less fear of state power than their classical liberal cousins. Consequently, reform liberals see the state playing a positive and constructive role in helping individuals realize their full potential.

In the second half of the twentieth century, political life in the United States turned into a contest between these two wings of liberalism. In late twentieth century usage, reform liberals are "liberals," and classical liberals are "conservatives." Although conservative television and radio pundits may have hated to admit it, their defenses of free market capitalism and smaller government were liberal, not conservative. American conservatives have not been conservatives in the classical sense. They can best be depicted as having tried to "conserve" nineteenth century liberalism. Although major political battles have taken place between liberals and conservatives in American political life, both groups generally have shared, or have said that they share, a commitment to the liberal principles found in the Declaration of Independence and in the U.S. Constitution.

Bibliography

Arblaster, Anthony. *The Rise and Decline of Western Liberalism.* Oxford, England: Basil Blackwell, 1984. Readable analysis of liberalism, covering not only its political views but also its influences on the arts, literature, and economic theory.

Girvetz, Harry K. *The Evolution of Liberalism.* Rev. ed. New York: Collier Books, 1963. Traces the development of liberal thought, arguing the case for a mixed economy and a liberal welfare state.

Manning, D. J. *Liberalism.* New York: St. Martin's Press, 1976. Philosophical and historical overview of the liberal tradition.

Medcalf, Linda J., and Kenneth M. Dolbeare. "Liberalism: The 'Collapse' of an Ever-Resilient Center." In *Neopolitics: American Political Ideas in the 1980's.* New York: Random House, 1985. Analyzes the course of liberalism in the United States after World War II. Argues that liberalism's strength and longevity is connected to its flexibility and adaptability.

Merquior, J. G. *Liberalism, Old and New.* Boston: Twayne, 1991. Discussion of the main ideas of liberal thought, starting with its earliest developments to the New Deal liberalism of Roosevelt.

Lawrence J. Connin

Cross-References

Civil Liberties Protection, p. 291; Conservatism, p. 419; Existentialism, p. 642; Hobbes's Political Philosophy, p. 836; Human Rights and International Politics, p. 848; Individual Versus State Rights, p. 910; Kant's Political Philosophy, p. 1025; Keynesianism, Monetarism, and Supply-Side Economics, p. 1032; Liberal Nationalism, p. 1111; Locke's Political Philosophy, p. 1142; Mill's Political Philosophy, p. 1204; Montesquieu's Political Philosophy, p. 1228; Right of Revolution, p. 1744; Scientific Humanism, p. 1784; Separation of Powers: Political Philosophy, p. 1809; The Social Contract, p. 1827; Social Democratic Parties, p. 1846; Spinoza's Political Philosophy, p. 1872.

LIBERATION THEOLOGY

Field of study: Political philosophy

Liberation theology is a new and controversial theology that originated in the 1960's as a response to poverty and injustice in Latin America. Utilizing a Marxist analysis of society, its proponents emphasize the mission of the Christian church to the oppressed and downtrodden, of whom Christ is proclaimed as liberator.

Principal terms

CEB: Christian base community, or small group of Latin American Christians who assemble to engage in Bible study, "conscientization," and communal action

CELAM II: popular name for the Second Assembly of the Latin American (Roman Catholic) Episcopate held in Medellín, Colombia, in 1968

CONSCIENTIZATION: consciousness-raising process by which the impoverished come to understand the causes of poverty and their capability to improve society

MARXISM: social, economic, and political theories associated with the nineteenth century philosopher Karl Marx

PRAXIS: interaction of thinking and doing; world-transforming practices

VATICAN II: popular name for the Second Vatican Council (1962-1965) convened by Pope John XXIII

Overview

Liberation theology has taken a variety of forms, but in all cases it addresses the oppression of classes of people. In the United States it has found expression among blacks, feminists, and Native Americans. Its most important and articulate expression, however, has taken place in Latin America. Theological motifs formulated in the context of Latin American Roman Catholicism have served as models for liberation theologians elsewhere. Among the prominent Latin American liberationists are Leonardo Boff, Gustavo Gutierrez, José Porfirio Miranda, and Juan Luis Segundo.

For classical, or traditional, Christian theology the starting point has been divine revelation, or "the view from above." Liberation theology, however, begins with the experiences of oppressed peoples, or "the view from below." Its supporters interpret the Christian faith from the point of view of the downtrodden. Whereas classical theology has struggled to sustain faith in the God of truth in an age of science and technology, liberation theology labors to sustain faith in the God of justice in a world that crushes and dehumanizes the poor.

Classical theology has relied upon philosophy for its structure; liberation theology gravitates toward the social sciences. It contends that theology is able to contribute to the resolution of humanity's problems only as much as it allows its thinking to be guided by relevant sociological and economic sciences. Of these disciplines Marxist analysis is believed to be the most relevant. Marxism is particularly attractive because it purports not only to explain the causes of inequality and exploitation but also to prescribe the proper measures to overcome them. The reliance of most liberationists upon Marxist social theory has led many critics to charge that liberation theology is nothing more than Marxism wearing a Christian mask, a charge that theologians of liberation vigorously deny. Although Marxism may be indispensable as a tool for social analysis, liberation theologians insist that it has no value as a philosophical worldview.

According to liberation theologians, theology is not simply a system of religious beliefs. Rather, it is basically critical reflection on historical praxis. Praxis, a term borrowed from Marx, is the unending dialectical process in which action compels one to reflection and reflection drives one to action again. By means of praxis, Christians strive not merely to understand the world but to transform it. According to liberation theologians, the validity of a theological position is not determined by correct opinions about doctrine (orthodoxy) but by participation in the process of liberation (orthopraxis). Authentic theology is an action-oriented undertaking that works unceasingly for the liberation of the oppressed.

One may ask from what oppression humanity needs liberation. The usual Christian response is that humanity is in bondage to sin, which it perceives primarily as a personal act that is contrary to the divine will, that disrupts the individual's relationship to God, and that affects the individual's eternal destiny. The orthodox view stresses the vertical dimension of sin: It is basically an offense against God. Liberation theologians, however, understand sin differently; they emphasize the social, or horizontal, dimension of sin. In liberation theology, sin is defined primarily in terms of man's inhumanity to man; it is essentially an offense against one's neighbor. Many liberation theologians describe sin as the refusal to love one's neighbor. This refusal is the fundamental cause of human misery.

Salvation, like sin, is understood by liberation theology more in social than in individual terms. Liberation from dehumanizing misery is an essential component of salvation. Although recognizing the primacy of the spiritual dimension of salvation, liberationists insist that salvation also includes the realization of a just social order in this world. Genuine salvation transforms the whole person—body as well as soul. The physical and temporal aspect of salvation cannot be separated from the spiritual and eternal aspect.

Liberation theologians view salvation as a cooperative enterprise: God and people work together to transform the world. Exponents of liberation theology declare that the most appropriate means available to Christians to attain that end is not religious activities, such as the evangelization and conversion of sinners, but political action. Christians must become politically active. They should engage not only in legally acceptable but also in morally legitimate political activities, including such extralegal behavior as passive resistance, boycotts, nonviolent strikes, and even guerrilla warfare and violent revolution. Although liberation theologians favor nonviolent tactics, many do condone violence in the service of a just cause.

Most Latin American liberationists contend that liberation requires the destruction of capitalism, which, they maintain, exalts greed and impoverishes the masses. Like the Marxists, liberation theologians argue that the primary motive of capitalism is to make a profit and not to serve the needy; thus it is an immoral system. They opt for a form of socialism that will be free of the defects of other types of collectivism.

Liberation theologians have also criticized the classical doctrine of God. They claim that orthodoxy has been dependent upon ancient Greek notions that perceive the deity as a static, immutable being who is aloof and remote from human history. Distortions of God's transcendence and grandeur have produced a worldview that thinks of God as "up there." One unfortunate consequence of the classical doctrine of God is that it has tended to sanction the existing social order. Furthermore, liberationists lament that distorted conceptions of God have made the majority of Latin Americans passive in the face of injustice. Liberation theology attempts to counter traditional conceptions of the deity by stressing the immanence of God and his involvement in the struggle for human liberation. Liberation theologians declare that God is on the side of the poor and the exploited and that he is involved in their struggles. As evidence of God's involvement in human history, they point to the incarnation, or the coming of God to earth in the person of Jesus Christ.

The Bible is seen in liberation theology primarily as a book of history, not as a book of timeless truths and rules. The history in the Bible is not simply a narrative of past events; it is also a disclosure of the divine determination to deliver humanity from every form of bondage. Liberation theologians give special attention to ancient Israel's liberation from Egyptian bondage in the Exodus and Jesus' life and death, since these biblical events stand out as models for contemporary liberation movements.

The importance of Jesus for liberation theology resides in his identification with marginal people. Although the creator of the cosmos, he was born in a stable. A humble carpenter himself, he associated with the dispossessed and denounced the rich and the powerful of his day. Feared by the authorities as a subversive, Jesus was executed as a common criminal. He died not to appease the wrath of an offended deity but in order to emancipate ordinary people from enslavement to oppressive powers. Always the liberator, Jesus continues to challenge contemporary oppressors.

The church in liberation theology is viewed as the people of God. Its primary mission is not to guarantee people access to Heaven but to denounce social injustice and to participate in the crusade to create a free and just society. In order to fulfill its mission, the church must enter the political arena. The fear of mixing religion and politics must not paralyze the community of believers. Liberation theologians attack the notion that the church ought to be content to operate on the spiritual plane and leave the temporal plane to others. Many proclaim that the church should be at the very center of revolutionary struggle.

Applications

The political impact of liberation theology has been felt throughout Latin America. From Mexico to Argentina, it has been effective in uniting traditional religious values with a commitment to political action on behalf of the impoverished. It has been able to influence the course of social change as well as policy-making in various parts of Central and South America.

The major vehicle for the popularization of liberation themes has been Christian base communities (or CEBs, following the Spanish initials), which were originally established as part of the educational program of the Roman Catholic church. CEBs are small groups of fifteen to twenty families that meet once or twice a week. Although priests occasionally visit the groups and exercise a measure of control over them, most of the time CEBs remain under the supervision of lay assistants. Since 1968, when their formation was encouraged by CELAM II (acronym for the Second Assembly of the Latin American Episcopate), the number of CEBs has proliferated. According to some estimates, by the early 1980's the number of people participating in the groups was nearly three million, with perhaps two-thirds of the members in Brazil.

The most important CEB activities are Bible study, conscientization, and communal action. Bible study involves discussions of the relevance of Scripture in everyday life. In discussions that last an hour or so, members reflect upon the meaning of biblical teaching in view of their personal experiences. Bible study sessions may be followed by extemporaneous prayer and a communal meal.

Conscientization is the attempt to bring the poor and the powerless to esteem themselves as worthy members of society. The indigent must also be brought to an awareness that they are the victims of exploitation and that this exploitation is a scandal that must not be tolerated. Conscientization aims to accomplish a revolutionary transformation in self-understanding.

CEB members engage in communal action in order to improve local social and economic conditions. For example, villagers frequently pool their resources to purchase a community tractor, or to clear a field, or to dig wells. They often cooperate to deal with recalcitrant merchants or landlords. Slum dwellers organize to pressure magistrates to improve educational and health services or other living conditions. Usually communal activities do not extend to overtly political action until other approaches have been attempted. CEB participants characteristically eschew violence in favor of mass demonstrations and passive resistance.

During the 1970's and 1980's the CEBs were among the most dynamic and politically active groups in Latin America. Their emphasis on open discussion, coupled with compromise and consensus, has made them a school for democratic politics in regions long dominated by authoritarian political systems. As such, they have contributed to whatever gains democracy may have made in Latin America since 1970. For example, many observers have attributed to the more than one hundred thousand CEBs in Brazil a significant role in that nation's transition from military rule to civilian rule and democratic politics in the mid-1980's.

Liberation theology also played a major role in the 1979 Nicaraguan revolution and later helped to provide legitimacy for the Sandinista regime. Many of the leaders of the Sandinista National Liberation Front had previously been active in the CEB movement and consequently had received conscientization concerning the problems of oppression and injustice associated with the corrupt dictatorship of the Somoza family. Many liberation theologians, as well as numerous CEBs, continued to support revolutionary change in Nicaragua after the Sandinistas came to power. Several liberationist clergymen held prominent positions in the collectivist government headed by Daniel Ortega. For example, Ernesto Cardenal served as minister of culture, Edgar Parrales as minister of social welfare, and Fernando Cardenal as director of the national literacy program.

Context

Liberation theology originated in Latin America in the late 1960's. Conditions in the region had a significant bearing upon the emergence of the new theology. Latin America was characterized politically by repressive and undemocratic governmental systems, economically by underdevelopment and dependency upon the United States and other capitalistic nations, socially by injustice and extremes of wealth and poverty, and religiously by the dominance of the Roman Catholic church. Roman Catholicism had long been a major force in shaping the culture and worldview of Latin Americans. For many decades the hierarchy of the church in Central and South America had generally maintained an antiprogressive stance on social justice issues, thus lending legitimacy to the political and social status quo. By the early 1960's, however, some Latin American clergymen had begun to recognize the need for a novel and more radical theological response to the problems of poverty and injustice.

Two events of the 1960's were particularly instrumental in the creation of Latin American liberation theology: Vatican II and CELAM II. Vatican II was a great catalyst for change within Roman Catholicism worldwide and especially in Latin America. It engendered a new freedom and creativity as the church reassessed its role in the modern world. The documents issued by the council highlighted the obligations of Christians toward the poor and the afflicted.

Although emerging from a matrix of Latin American Roman Catholicism, liberation theology borrowed from German theologians, especially Jurgen Moltmann and Johann Baptist Metz. Metz emphasized the political ramifications of religious faith and the church as an agency of social criticism. According to Moltmann, the church should participate in the liberating mission of Jesus by working to change society.

Latin American liberation theology lacked identity or systematic expression until the publication of Gustavo Gutierrez's *A Theology of Liberation: History, Politics, and Salvation* (1973). After 1973, liberation theology became one of the most significant theologies to emerge in the twentieth century. From Latin America, it has spread to other parts of the world, including North America, Africa, and Asia. The appeal of liberation theology stems from its compassion for poor people and the conviction that Christians must not remain apathetic to wrongs suffered in this world.

Bibliography

Ferm, Deane William. *Profiles in Liberation: Thirty-six Portraits of Third World Theologians*. Mystic, Conn.: Twenty-Third Publications, 1988. Vignettes of practitioners of liberation theology—twelve from Africa, eight from Asia, and sixteen from Latin America—illustrating the diversity and vitality of the movement.

Gutierrez, Gustavo. *A Theology of Liberation: History, Politics, and Salvation.* Translated and edited by Sister Caridad Inda and John Eagleson. Maryknoll, N.Y.: Orbis Books, 1973. The Peruvian priest delineates three major components of liberation: political, historical, and spiritual.

Mainwaring, Scott, and Alexander Wilde, eds. *The Progressive Church in Latin America.* Notre Dame, Ind.: University of Notre Dame Press, 1989. Relevant essays discuss the influence of the CEBs upon Brazilian politics and the connection between radical theology and radical politics in Nicaragua.

Nash, Ronald H., ed. *Liberation Theology.* Milford, Mich.: Mott Media, 1984. Essays by several critics of liberation theology, who castigate the movement for its departure from theological orthodoxy, its uncritical acceptance of socialism, and its hostility toward the values and institutions of democratic capitalism.

Nunez C., Emilio Antonio. *Liberation Theology.* Translated by Paul E. Sywulka. Chicago: Moody Press, 1985. Moderately critical account written from the perspective of a Latin American evangelical theologian. Contains an extended analysis of liberation theology's historical roots, methodology, employment of Marxist social theory, and distinctive themes.

Planas, Ricardo. *Liberation Theology: The Political Expression of Religion.* New York: Sheed & Ward, 1986. Discussion of the origins of liberation theology, its association with Marxism, its views on social change, and the controversies it has generated within the Roman Catholic church.

Pottenger, John R. *The Political Theory of Liberation Theology.* Albany: State University of New York Press, 1989. Focuses on liberation theology as a political movement rather than as a theology. Especially valuable for its discussion of the political significance of the CEBs and the relationship between liberation theology and Nicaragua's Sandinistas.

Roelofs, H. Mark. "Liberation Theology: The Recovery of Biblical Radicalism." *American Political Science Review* 82 (June, 1988): 549-566. Roelofs' thesis is that liberation theology is not Marxism masquerading as Christianity but rather a genuinely Christian radicalism.

Smith, David L. *A Handbook of Contemporary Theology.* Wheaton, Ill.: Victor Books, 1992. Survey of the origins, major emphases, and leading proponents of four theologies of liberation: Latin American, black American, African, and Korean.

Ronald W. Long

Cross-References

Church and Government in History, p. 230; Class Conflict, p. 331; Dialecticism, p. 540; Marxism-Leninism, p. 1155; Religion and Politics, p. 1685; Socialism, p. 1865; Thomas Aquinas' Political Philosophy, p. 1974; Underdeveloped Nations, p. 2039; The Vatican, p. 2091.

LOBBYING AND LOBBYISTS

Field of study: Politics

Lobbyists represent interest groups, unions, associations, or private corporations. Their job is to persuade government officials of their groups' positions on political issues. They are one way that citizens can communicate their policy needs to government officials.

Principal terms

HONORARIA: financial reimbursement for speaking, travel, hotel, or other expenses paid by an interest group or other organization

INDEPENDENT EXPENDITURES: expenditures made by an individual or group that are not directly connected with the candidates or issues that they are designed to support

INTEREST GROUP: organized group of individuals that seeks to influence public policy

POLITICAL ACTION COMMITTEE (PAC): special committee set up to collect and spend money for political campaigns

Overview

Members of Congress, the White House, state legislatures, bureaucratic agencies, and the courts continually make decisions on public policies. These decisions may profoundly impact organizations such as interest groups, corporations, and trade associations. The affected organizations want their opinions to be heard by decision makers and often rely on lobbyists to communicate their interests.

Many organizations employ former members of Congress to lobby the federal government. The first requirement in lobbying the Congress is to get the attention of congresspeople, and former members have several built-in advantages. Not only were they formerly colleagues of the people they are lobbying, but also they are granted special privileges: They are allowed in the congressional gyms, the members' dining rooms, and the floor cloakrooms where many deals on legislation are decided. Their former service in Congress also gives them extensive knowledge of the political process, such as the complicated rules and procedures that are followed, and which members can be trusted, or pressured, on certain bills. Lobbying by former members of Congress has raised substantial ethical questions. Many have questioned whether they should be allowed to lobby other members right after they leave Congress, because of their special advantages. Former members of Congress have another advantage: Frequently they are lawyers. Legal expertise is often needed on complicated public policy issues.

There are several types of lobbyists. Many bureaucracies have their own liaison lobbyists. They are paid with taxpayer money to lobby specific issues for bureaucratic agencies such as the Defense Department and the State Department. Even the White

House has its own liaison staff who are hired solely to lobby Congress on behalf of the administration. These liaison lobbyists do not include the hundreds of former officials who once worked for presidential administrations. Many former top officials in the Carter, Reagan, and Bush administrations became well-paid lobbyists. There are also in-house lobbyists. These lobbyists are members of specific interest groups who lobby on behalf of their group. Since they are members of the organizations they represent, in-house lobbyists are usually more committed to the organization than a hired lobbyist would be. Their membership also gives them greater knowledge of the organization. Groups with extensive financial resources may hire full-service lobbying firms. These firms have experts on staff, including lawyers, accountants, and public relations consultants. They are very expensive, but are suited to corporations or organizations that do not have in-house lobbyists, but have the money to ensure that lobbying is professionally done.

Once lobbyists have been hired, the organization and its lobbyists must decide whether they will lobby government officials directly or indirectly. With direct lobbying, lobbyists personally contact public officials and try to persuade them of their point of view. An important but often unrecognized part of a lobbyist's job is to provide information. The need for information is critical because it is difficult and time-consuming for government officials to understand every policy issue perfectly. Thus, lobbyists try to establish a working relationship by attending hearings and visiting their offices frequently.

Money can also be used in direct lobbying. Interest groups and corporations frequently donate money to government officials, particularly members of Congress, hoping that government officials will pay more attention to their issues. Many questions have been raised about whether donating money to a member's campaign allows an interest group to buy that member's votes on legislation. On one side of this debate are public interest groups such as Common Cause, who claim that members of Congress cannot ignore a hefty donation from an interest group when voting. On the other side, many political scientists believe that money does not buy votes, although it might buy access to government officials. Access may be as important as buying the vote, because it allows interest groups the chance for their views to be heard. Lobbyists also use honoraria. Interest groups have traditionally given speaking fees to government officials and reimbursed their expenses when traveling to events hosted by interest groups. These donations have raised many questions, and in the 1990's, Congress put many restrictions on them.

Indirect lobbying is more subtle. Rather than contacting government officials directly, lobbyists use the media, stage letter-writing campaigns, help officials get elected to office, or use more active measures to try to influence officials. With the growth of television and mass communications systems, indirect lobbying changed significantly in the 1960's. Instead of using letter-writing campaigns, lobbyists began to rely on the media to send their messages to the public. The media can be used in three primary ways. First, interest groups and corporations can use a media campaign as a gesture of goodwill to help enhance their images. Thus, the League of Women

Voters sponsors debates, and oil companies advertise their record in saving the environment. Sometimes the image needs a more aggressive campaign, usually because the organization has done something that has created negative publicity. Hence, after the oil company Exxon had an oil tanker accident, spilling thousands of gallons of oil off the Alaskan coast in 1989, it launched numerous commercials showing its aggressive cleanup efforts. Finally, media campaigns may be offensive when the organization is seeking a policy change from government officials.

Traditional letter-writing campaigns have also changed. Sophisticated communication technology can make a letter-writing campaign appear to have been done by hand, even if it was mass-produced. Interest groups have established massive phone banks where callers interested about a particular issue can be automatically connected to their members of Congress to register their opinions. Interest groups have also produced form letters and pamphlets to make it easier for their members to write personalized campaigns. These lobbying campaigns appear to be taking place at the grassroots level, when in fact they are engineered by an interest group, probably located in Washington, D.C.

Interest groups seeking to lobby government officials indirectly can also use electioneering or some more active measures. Electioneering is when groups try to elect their friends and supporters to public office, either through using the media or by making financial contributions to their campaigns. Electioneering also can be negative, with an interest group working against a particular candidate. To do this, lobbyists often rely on independent expenditures, that is, expenditures made by an interest group, campaign, or individual on behalf of a candidate or issue that is not directly connected with that candidate or issue. Independent expenditures can pay for television advertising, either for or against a particular opponent. For example, the Willie Horton advertisement used against Democratic candidate Michael Dukakis in the 1988 presidential campaign was sponsored not by Republican candidate George Bush, but by a conservative interest group. Finally, lobbyists can take a more active approach, using direct-action techniques similar to those of activist interest groups.

Applications

The National Rifle Association (NRA) is an interest group that is particularly successful with both direct and indirect lobbying. The NRA, like many effective interests, has a unified goal—the elimination of restrictions on owning or using guns. Thus, the NRA lobbied for a 1986 bill that would have lifted restrictions on the interstate sale of rifles, and against the 1968 Gun Control Act, the Brady Bill, and other attempts at gun-control legislation. The Brady Bill was named for President Ronald Reagan's presidential aide, James Brady, who was wounded in an assassination attempt on Reagan in 1981. Brady argued that he would not have been shot if Reagan's assailant, John Hinckley, Jr., had been forced to wait before purchasing his gun. The Brady Bill thus required a waiting period and a records check for those who wish to purchase guns.

The NRA, with only three million members, is not the largest interest group, but it has been effective in keeping gun control off the public agenda. Much of this success stems from the loyalty of its members. The NRA gives its members numerous benefits, including *American Rifleman* magazine, discounts on weapons purchases, a hunter's information service with advice on trips and hunting equipment, awards for big-game trophies, and low-cost firearms and hospital insurance. NRA members are active in helping their organization with indirect lobbying. One of their most effective lobbying techniques is the letter-writing campaign. NRA officials once claimed that they could generate a half million letters within three days, and that was before it upgraded its computer capacity to target members of Congress by congressional district. These grassroots efforts have helped the NRA to convince members of Congress that it has potential voting power in their districts. The NRA also uses electioneering tactics to demonstrate its influence. Electioneering tactics are most successful when an interest group can convince elected officials that its membership can reward or punish a candidate on election day. The NRA has had such success. In 1970, it was credited with the defeat of four senators who had voted for gun-control legislation.

To reinforce its message, the NRA often uses another indirect lobbying technique—a media campaign. The NRA has fought the image that it contributes to crime by using a media campaign based on goodwill advertisements. These ads have featured attractive people who said that they were proud to be members of the NRA, including football star John Riggins, test pilot Chuck Yeager, and a police chief. To counteract this lobbying, one of the NRA's opponents, the Handgun Control Association, launched offensive ads claiming that the NRA promotes legislation that endangers public safety.

Finally, the NRA has used direct lobbying techniques. The loyal membership of the NRA has contributed millions of dollars to political candidates through the NRA's PAC, the National Rifle Association Political Victory Fund. The NRA also has an extensive lobbying team, including in-house lobbyists and hired lobbyists that visit congressional offices and attend both congressional and state-level hearings on gun control legislation.

Context

Lobbying serves many important purposes. Hiring lobbyists allows interest groups the chance to get their voices heard in government, whether at the White House, the Congress, or the state governments. Lobbying thus gives citizens a greater chance to participate in politics. Lobbying increases the number of political actors on every issue. The greater number of voices means that it is not merely members of Congress or a presidential administration representing citizens' interests and creating policy. People can hire lobbyists to represent their views.

It is also clear that lobbying is not always a positive force in politics. Many of the positives can be turned into negatives. The greater number of players can be a detriment, making it more difficult to implement any type of policy. Because of lobbying, government officials may never hear the voices of private citizens at all, only the paid voices of lobbyists. For example, citizens in the United States have generally supported restrictions on gun ownership, but the NRA has traditionally blocked legislation that would impose such restrictions.

The most damaging criticisms of lobbying, however, emphasize the potential for corruption. According to this view, lobbying is harmful to politics because it gives organizations with more resources a greater chance to be heard than those with fewer resources. This may distort public opinion on any given issue. The potential for bribery and bought votes, and the backroom deals associated with lobbying, have led many citizens to distrust lobbyists and the officials they lobby.

Despite these problems, relatively few limits have been placed on lobbyists when compared with most other institutions. The most significant lobbying legislation, the Federal Regulation of Lobbying Act, was passed in 1946. This bill is only four pages long and was the subject of little debate. It requires that any person who is hired by someone else for the purpose of lobbying Congress register and file quarterly reports of the activity. This legislation has substantial loopholes. Interest groups have claimed that lobbying is not their official purpose, that congressional testimony and grassroots lobbying are excluded, and that using one's own resources negates the need for registration. One of the largest interest groups in the early 1900's, the National Association of Manufacturers, claimed that lobbying was not its official purpose and thus avoided registering for twenty-nine years, until 1975.

Since 1946, Congress has passed only three other types of legislation restricting lobbyists. In 1974, the Federal Election Campaign Act (FECA) placed limits on the amount of money federally elected officials could receive from individual contributors and political action committees. Although this reform ensured that most donations would be disclosed for the first time, the bill had several loopholes. First, it encouraged the growth of political action committees, who give most of their money to incumbents. This has made it difficult for challengers to compete with congressional incumbents. Moreover, the bill did not cover either independent expenditures or "soft money." Soft money is money raised outside the restrictions of FECA with the intention of influencing the outcome of an election. For example, interest groups may raise funds for voter registration drives in certain districts, thereby helping particular candidates.

The Ethics in Government Act of 1978 placed restrictions on federal officials' ability to lobby after leaving office. It is significant, however, that Congress exempted itself from this act, thus allowing former members of Congress to lobby with fewer restrictions. In the 1980's and 1990's, members of Congress limited the amount of gifts they could receive from interest groups, including honoraria.

Although these reforms may appear to be substantial, much of the everyday business of lobbyists has been left unregulated. The 1946 act has never been amended, and many reformers believe that the fundamental weaknesses of the act would still remain, even if amendments could be passed. Lobbying reform has been difficult to accomplish for two reasons. First, lobbying regulation may be an unconstitutional violation of the First Amendment right to free speech. Second, members of Congress are not motivated to regulate lobbying if it would harm their reelection chances.

Although lobbying is loosely regulated, it is likely to remain a fixture of U.S. politics. Lobbying helps citizens to communicate with their government, interest groups to get their voices heard, and government officials to stay in office.

Bibliography

Birnbaum, Jeffrey H. *The Lobbyists—How Influence Peddlers Work Their Way in Washington*. New York: Times Books, 1993. Behind-the-scenes look at corporate lobbying in Washington, D.C., during the 101st Congress.

Cigler, Allan J., and Burdett A. Loomis. *Interest Group Politics*. 4th ed. Washington, D.C.: Congressional Quarterly Press, 1994. Edited volume of articles examining several types of interest groups.

Hertzke, Allen D. *Representing God in Washington: The Role of Religious Lobbies in the American Polity*. Knoxville: University of Tennessee Press, 1988. In-depth study of religious groups and how lobbying by these groups might be different from other types of lobbying.

Hrebenar, Ronald J., and Ruth K. Scott. *Interest Group Politics in America*. 2d ed. Englewood Cliffs, N.J.: Prentice-Hall, 1990. One of the best overall books on interest groups and their lobbying techniques. Examines numerous different lobbying techniques, while surveying the literature in the field.

Petracca, Mark P. *The Politics of Interests: Interest Groups Transformed*. Boulder, Colo: Westview Press, 1992. Theoretical book with excellent updated bibliography on interest groups and lobbying.

Wolpe, Bruce C. *Lobbying Congress: How the System Works*. Washington, D.C.: Congressional Quarterly Press, 1990. Short book that provides tips on how to lobby, then looks at a series of case studies on lobbying.

Jan Carol Hardt

Cross-References

African American Politics, p. 28; Aging and Politics in the United States, p. 35; Congress, p. 412; Consumer Politics, p. 445; Grassroots Politics, p. 797; Interest Groups, p. 936; Iron Triangles, p. 981; Legislative Body Types, p. 1091; Legislative Functions of Government, p. 1098; The New Right, p. 1293; Pluralism, p. 1402; Policy Development and Implementation, p. 1414; Political Action Committees, p. 1420; Political Ethics, p. 1461; Public Policy, p. 1633; Right to Bear Arms and the Second Amendment, p. 1750.

LOCAL GOVERNMENTS

Field of study: Local and regional government

The oldest and most widespread of all forms of government, local governments are now usually found incorporated in larger governmental units, under which they provide many basic government services to citizens.

> *Principal terms*
> CONFEDERATION: form of government in which local or subunit governments retain sovereignty and usually may secede if the central government fails to serve local interests
> DILLON'S RULE: legal notion that because American local governments are "creatures of the state," they may exercise only such powers as are granted to them by the state constitutions or legislatures
> FEDERALISM: system of government in which a central government and local or subunit governments have separate bases of authority defined by written constitutions
> HOME RULE: provision in most U.S. state constitutions that partly erodes Dillon's Rule to give some true autonomy to various local governments
> MUNICIPALITY: the most general term for a unit of local government, such as a city, town, village, or township
> TOTALITARIAN GOVERNMENT: system of government that recognizes no limits in law or politics to interfere in the lives of citizens; such governments are usually—but not always—unitary in practice
> UNITARY GOVERNMENT: form of government in which a central authority has final power over all local or subunit governments, which it may alter or abolish at will

Overview

Local governments have a long and distinguished history. Indeed, all the governments that originally governed humankind were local governments evolving out of families, extended families, clans, and tribes. Such arrangements provided the most efficient opportunity for people to govern themselves as they saw fit. Naturally not all citizens voted, for some governments must have been dominated by a strongman, chief or father. Still with all this freedom of local governments to govern their own people, the question arises as to why larger governments emerged. One answer is that small local governments can be threatened by larger neighbors. The inability of small governments to protect themselves forced them to combine into larger units, either voluntarily through leagues of independent autonomous city-states, or involuntarily through the conquest by more powerful neighbors.

The fate of the ancient Greek city-state is instructive. The Greeks initially lived in small city-states, such as Athens, Corinth, and Sparta. Because of outside threats,

Sparta formed a confederation with neighboring city-states, which were similarly governed by military aristocracies. The Athenian democracy, on the other hand, created a small empire in which they subjugated several neighboring Greek city-states. The Peloponnesian War of the early fifth century B.C.E., so weakened both the Spartan confederation and the Athenian empire that both were ultimately conquered by Phillip of Macedon, who created the empire that his son Alexander transformed into a far-flung empire. This type of transition from local governments to massive empires must surely have been duplicated in nearly every empire in the world.

The question of how much authority remains in local hands as larger states develop turns on how much freedom or autonomy the local government must give up while providing adequately for its defense. The degree of freedom allowed to subunits in various countries has led scholars to categorize the amount of autonomy according to whether the systems were unitary, federal, or confederal. In a unitary government, the central government has ultimate power and the local governments have only as much power as the central government allows. At the other extreme, a confederation offers maximum political power to the local governments and the central government has only as much authority as it is granted by the local units. Between these two extremes are federal systems in which the central government and local governments, have separate bases of authority described in some kind of written document. These documents only describe the relationship between central governments and subunits; they do not describe how democratic or dictatorial the different levels of government are.

Despite the historical tendency of local governments to combine together, there is a nearly universal tendency for local governments to continue to exist. While some national governments may have no regional subunits—such as states, provinces, or regions—no such government, except small city-states, lacks some form of local government. Local governments are essential to deliver services that fill some of the most basic needs people have. Local governments have, for example, always provided basic law enforcement within their local areas. As population density increases, the primitive law enforcement function typically expands from the simple presence of a few officials (such as sheriffs or constables) into full police protection. Similarly, other functions are added as new needs arise. The education of children expands from home schooling to primitive local schools to the kind of extensive education offered by modern urban societies. Fire protection is another function that is added eventually. Other safety and health functions are also added as population density increases.

All these functions require local control to meet diverse local conditions. This is why federal and confederal arrangements are attractive for promoting services that meet conditions that might not be anticipated by even the most omniscient of remote national authorities. Even unitary regimes find it necessary to provide local representatives through large bureaucratic mechanisms. These arrangements typically forgo the advantages of local input to perform their functions, but this is a price that national regimes are willing to pay in return for the advantages of uniformity provided by tight central control. Whether the people living in the local areas agree is a different question.

The authority left to local governments ranges from totalitarian regimes at one end of the spectrum to nearly independent city-states within loose confederal arrangements. At the one extreme, local governments appear to be mere administrative subunits of large bureaucracies, such as the communes in communist China. At the other extreme, certain city-states (such as Andorra or the Vatican in Europe and Singapore in the Far East) have been able to carve out virtually complete independence. In between are national governments that provide widely varying amounts of local government autonomy.

Local governments within extreme totalitarian regimes seem to be dominated by the center and to have very little autonomy. In principle, local government authorities are appointed by the next higher level and are totally responsible to the national leadership. Such local governments are truly "creatures of the state." There have been reports of local governments being used as buffers against central control even in repressive regimes. The fact that some local governments may serve as buffers against large external neighbors or overweening central governments does not mean that all local government relationships are equally effective. Clearly, the amount of autonomy allowed for local governments as subunits in a large national bureaucratic apparatus in unitary systems has not been great. Conversely, if local governments are virtually autonomous, a central government's authority may be weak or nonexistent.

It might be argued that the most effective arrangements for creating sufficient national strength to protect the whole country while providing for meaningful local autonomy can be found within federal systems. In federal systems, the rules assigning powers to the national and local governments are clearly spelled out in some kind of widely recognized legitimate document such as a charter, constitution, or treaty. The U.S. Constitution is a prime example of an attempt to spell out the powers of the national and state governments in considerable detail. Within the United States, it is worth noting that while all fifty states have a specially recognized constitutional status under the federal Constitution, there is no similar federal provision for local governments. From the point of view of the U.S. Constitution, there are only states and individual citizens with which the national government must deal. Local governments may enjoy freedom and autonomy, but only if provided by their state governments.

In the United States, a general legal precept known as Dillon's Rule regards all counties, cities, towns, villages, and special districts essentially creatures of the state. In the late twentieth century, many states sought to recognize legitimate autonomy for their local government by making provisions for home-rule charters under the aegis of their state governments. So far as the U.S. Constitution is concerned, however, local governments remain strictly creatures of the state. The relationship between the national government and the states may be federal, but the relationship between each of the fifty states and their local governments is unitary.

In other parts of the world, local governments may define their own special relationships to their national governments and their states, and provinces or regional governments may be comparatively weak. The local governments in most European countries have relatively more authority within their counterpart intermediate units than they do in the United States.

In both Britain and France, the national government is a supreme unitary government in which all sovereign authority resides. In both countries, the intermediate provinces or counties are tightly controlled by the national governments, but certain traditional arrangements have allowed local governments to retain certain measures of authority. The relative balance between large subunit regional governments and the local governments is thus shifted in favor of local governments in both countries. By contrast, within the Federal Republic of Germany, and the Swiss confederation, the balance tends to favor the larger subunits over the localities.

Applications

What difference do local government arrangements make? Some examples from around the globe may be useful. Under the national government of China and other communist regimes, local autonomy is distinctly limited and the only thing that local people can do is develop cooperative arrangements that essentially hide their opposition to national policies. If there is a sufficient amount of internal local unity, such local governments can work out informal autonomy even though they lack legal authority by sabotaging or disregarding national directives.

Even at the peak of communist power in China, there were many examples of local authorities sabotaging national rules in order to follow local desires. The communist-led central government sought to extend its authority to the lowest possible level in Chinese communities. Using their revolutionary army—which itself had made broad grants of autonomy to each guerrilla unit—the communists sought to spread their authority throughout the country after their initial revolutionary success in 1949. By 1955, the communists had consolidated their control over much of the country and were tightening the central authority by transforming local villages into communal farms. While there was enthusiasm for this communization in some areas, many families and clans resisted the policy in other areas. If they did so openly, they were frequently beaten down; but, if they pretended to comply with the national leadership, they were often able to continue family ownership and operation of small plots of land as their ancestors had for generations. Even the most tightly organized totalitarian government failed to eradicate local government resistance to central power. While obviously less effective in totalitarian regimes, local governments may empower local people to resist the total domination of themselves by large central governments.

On the other hand, in a country such as the United States in which the rule of law (or the notion that law is above both the people and the government) and written constitutions are pervasive, local governments play a special role. Local governments act as a buffer against overweening national power and they have been known to be quite effective in their resistance to either state or national authority. To see how this works, one might take a hypothetical example.

In a certain town, there is a large factory with smelly smokestacks emitting large quantities of noxious gases. The local home owners protest to their local government by attempting to organize their neighbors. If many home owners are affected, the neighborhood may organize easily. When they marshal their forces on city hall, however, they may discover that the offending business is so well entrenched politically that the city government will not comply with the wishes of residents.

Under the federal system, the neighborhood group then goes to the next higher level of government by taking its case to the state. If the local neighborhood group is unable to prevail in the state legislature, it may combine with other similarly situated groups across the nation to attack the problem on the federal level. While this is difficult, the practical experience the group has had on the local or state level will still prove valuable. Naturally, the offending business may also choose to move the conflict to another arena, local, state, or national depending on their prospects for success. The federal system allows either group several levels to which an appeal can be made and should empower all of its citizens.

By contrast, citizens in unitary governments, such as China may have to transform an entire national government in order to make local changes. In 1989, Chinese students faced the enormous task of trying to overthrow the government of one billion people in order to make changes in their local area and were defeated in what is known as the Tiananmen Square massacre. The existence of autonomous political subdivisions in the United States makes the task of changing local government much easier, and the system even permits the use of subunit governments to resist, delay, or frustrate national policies. Above all, the citizens have a place to initiate change.

Context

Local governments are the oldest, most ubiquitous of all forms of government in the world, for they must have existed from the earliest times. Close to the people, they might be the only form of government necessary were it not for the dangers that any small government faces from hostile larger units. Because of the wide variations in size of local governments, they either have formed alliances with others or have simply been absorbed by more powerful neighbors. The status of local governments is often improved if there are specific legal arrangements included in a treaty, charter, or constitution governing the relationship of the subunits to one another and to any higher level. Such laws in any society in which the rule of law is important are very helpful.

Even under the most tightly organized unitary government, local governments still exist to perform needed police, fire, education, and welfare functions. Some local autonomy can normally be scratched out by determined local groups who use the existence of any kind of local unit to try to prevent the imposition of rules they do not like. Sometimes the forms of government are false. When Russia was governed by a communist government, they described themselves as a "federal" state although the reality was that Russia had a totalitarian regime in which all officials were required to follow the commands of the hierarchically arranged Communist Party. All local governments were in effect a part of a larger bureaucratic apparatus, an appearance to the contrary notwithstanding. In them were local groups who resisted the national policies through sabotage or passive resistance.

Among the nations, variations in local governments are great. Citizens are generally most empowered to act on their own in small countries with decentralized confederal systems, such as Switzerland. Among large nations, the U.S. federal system provides a balance. In the French and British unitary systems, citizens look to local representatives of the national government, but must always be conscious of their need to form coalitions with others elsewhere in the nation in order to affect any national policies that govern local conditions. Conflict in any society may well be inevitable, but conflict may be more manageable in a federal system.

Bibliography

Curtis, Michael, et al., eds. *Introduction to Comparative Government*. 2d ed. New York: HarperCollins, 1990. Essays by distinguished scholars who examine governments around the world. The book covers the industrial democracies of Britain, France, Germany, and Japan; the major communist states of the Soviet Union and China; and the Third World countries of India, Mexico, and Nigeria.

Dragnich, Alex N., Jorgen S. Rasmussen, and Joel C. Moses. *Major European Governments*. 8th ed. Pacific Grove, Calif.: Brooks/Cole, 1991. Excellent examination of the governments of Britain, France, Germany, and Russia from a traditional institutional perspective.

Glendon, Mary Ann, Michael Wallace Gordon, and Christopher Osakwe. *Comparative Legal Traditions in a Nutshell*. St. Paul, Minn.: West, 1982. Typical of law books in the "nutshell" series, this book provides a succinct summary of the major legal traditions in the world from a comparative legal perspective.

Kesselman, Mark, et al. *European Politics in Transition*. 2d ed. Lexington, Mass.: D. C. Heath, 1992. Sophisticated treatment of the governments of Britain, France, Germany, Italy, Sweden, and Russia, with discussions of some of the smaller European governments.

Mahler, Gregory S. *Comparative Politics: An Institutional and Cross-National Approach*. 2d ed. Englewood Cliffs, N.J.: Prentice Hall, 1995. A new approach to comparative government distinguished by separate discussions of the relationships between the central and subunit governments in Britain, France, Germany, Japan, Canada, Russia, Mexico, and Nigeria.

Richard L. Wilson

Cross-References

City Government in the United States, p. 266; The Civil Service in the United States, p. 310; County Government, p. 458; Courts: State and Local, p. 465; Disaster Relief in the United States, p. 558; Federal Mandates, p. 662; Political Machines and Bosses, p. 1468; Regional Governments, p. 1672; Rural Community Government, p. 1763; State and Local Government, p. 1885; Town Meetings, p. 1993; Urban Governments, p. 2052; Urban Policy, p. 2057; Urbanization, p. 2071.

LOCKE'S POLITICAL PHILOSOPHY

Field of study: Political philosophy

The political philosophy of John Locke (1632-1704) serves as the foundation for many contemporary political organizations—including the United States government. Modern ideas about individual rights of free speech, the freedom of religious worship, and the right to privacy owe much to Locke's work.

Principal terms

CIVIL SOCIETY: state of governed society freely entered by rational people who choose to leave the state of nature and seek stability by establishing a sovereign

DIVINE RIGHT: belief that rulers derive their right to rule from God and so cannot be questioned or rebelled against

FEUDALISM: political and economic system in which nobility hold land and power

LAISSEZ-FAIRE: hands-off approach to government—the doctrine that minimal government is the best government

LIBERALISM: belief that each individual is entitled to as much freedom as does not interfere with the freedom of others

NATURAL LAW: idea that the universe is governed by an observable principle of reason which should guide judgment about just and unjust laws

RATIONALISM: belief that there is a rational principle at work in the universe that is discernible by human reason; reason, not experience, helps one understand reality

SOCIAL CONTRACT: political theory explaining how free individuals can be bound to a ruler and to law; it supposes people give up freedom for protection

SOVEREIGN: supreme ruler of a state

STATE OF NATURE: prehistoric state in which humans exist without society

Overview

John Locke's *Two Treatises on Government* (1690) has long been influential in both political theory and political practice. In the first treatise Locke argues against the divine right of kings. He maintains that there is no biblical support for any special relationship between a particular sovereign and God, much less for a hereditary line of divinely chosen rulers. If rulers are not chosen by God, Locke believes, they should be chosen by the people whom they are to govern—rule by the consent of the ruled. This is a radical challenge to the political order of the time, and so Locke, in the second treatise, explains both how such a system of government is natural and how it should operate.

In the second treatise, Locke argues that people, equal and free in the state of nature, enter the state of civil or political society by way of a contract. This contract limits each individual's freedom and alters some aspects of equality. Locke writes that the primary reason for abandoning the state of nature for civil society is the preservation of property. In fact, Locke's political theory is based on the concept, extension, and protection of one's right to property. The state was created to protect the right to property, a right that exists even in the absence of civil society.

Locke believed that people enter civil society and accept a common judge in order to gain the protection of their property; the people form a contract to create a government. This agreement entails rights and obligations on both sides. The people surrender certain freedoms and rights to the government, which in turn is responsible for the protection of these freedoms and rights. The government, for example, may not violate one's right of self-preservation, for this is contrary to its purpose.

Locke augments the belief that the world was given to humankind in common for everyone's individual use, with the belief that God gave people reason to use the gift of the world well. The right to use those things necessary for one's preservation is the foundation for the concept of property. The use of anything, according to Locke, first requires its appropriation. The appropriation of goods is accomplished by an individual's labor. Locke assumes people appropriate property through their labor because they first possess themselves. It is people's right to themselves that establishes their right to that upon which they expend their labor.

Each person being equal and free in the state of nature has an equal right to appropriate and to enjoy property. In this state people are guided by the dictates of reason and limited by the spoilage of goods. Locke presumes that people have a right to those things necessary for their preservation, in the amount they deem necessary, as long as there is enough left for use by others and as long as nothing that they have taken will go to waste. Property is thus a natural phenomenon that occurs among people even without the existence of government or civil law.

Property came to be seen as an unlimited right when money came into use. Locke contends that money, as well as property, preceded the advent of civil society. There is an assumption in Locke's reasoning that people naturally desire to accumulate things to themselves but were prevented from doing so by the temporary nature of natural goods. Money, a lasting commodity, freed people of the limitations of spoilage, and humankind naturally began to hoard.

This state of an unbounded right to property would be chaotic except that each person possesses reason. The state of nature is not necessarily synonymous with the state of war because of the use of reason. Reason, which is the natural law of humankind, dictates a state in which people seek peace. Reason dictates a state in which the natural rights of life, liberty, and property are honored.

All people whose first duty is to preserve themselves see by reason that they should promote and protect the life, liberty, and property of others in order to secure their own. This duty also requires that people be able to protect themselves. As all people must have this right, so they must make judgments concerning what threatens their lives or those of others. The danger is one of people misjudging what is necessary for their own safety and becoming so preoccupied with their own security that they may become a threat to peace themselves.

It is the absence of a common judge that causes uncertainty and potential disharmony and makes the state of nature intolerable. The law of nature—reason—proves an inadequate limitation because not everyone possesses it in sufficient quantity. People not well versed in the law of nature may also act in ways contrary to their own self-interest. To protect against such misjudgment, Locke believes people form a contract. This contract is to form a government that holds the power of the people who created it in trust. The government acts as a judge, and it must act to preserve its citizens. People surrender certain freedoms and alter their equality to gain the benefit of government, which is protection of their property against the freedom of others.

The purpose of civil society is to allow a people the security to appreciate their lives. It must provide the means for each person to enjoy the right to life, liberty, and the means to self-preservation. It must act as a control to ensure that liberty is both promoted and restrained so that it is equivalent to a well-ordered state of nature.

The law of civil society balances each person's liberty against the liberty of others. People are not free to do as they please, but they do have the right to be free from the possibility of others doing as they please. The government is not exempt from this balance; it is not free to do as it pleases, but it may act in the interests of society.

Locke sees that it is legitimate for the people to resist a government that acts contrary to its contracted role, just as they would any person who threatened their existence. The human inclination to a secure life motivates one to leave the state of nature while this same inclination protects one once in the civil society created. Locke contends that the danger to a secure life is in fact increased in civil society because the power given to those who govern is greater than that which any single person in the state of nature might have. The right of rebellion is necessary if people are truly to be free.

People form government by giving to it the power which they themselves possess. What cannot be given—the right to self-preservation—cannot be taken by the government, while the entity of property, for which people surrender their equality and liberty, must always be protected. All rights of a government must come from the consent of the people.

If a government is to preserve itself, it must look to its own security. The government's legitimacy is affected if it fails to act according to the law of nature—reason— which requires one to act in such a way as to preserve one's own life and the lives of those one is responsible for. If the government, formed by consent, threatens the existence of an individual or group of people, it is violating its purpose of preservation and is so not legitimate.

For Locke, the only legitimate sovereign is a limited sovereign. People are to be left to govern their own consciences and the government should not interfere with the beliefs and actions of a person or group unless such beliefs and actions threaten to harm another or to destabilize the social order and so threaten everyone's security. In his *Letter Concerning Toleration* (1689) Locke discusses the separate and distinct roles of the sovereign and the church. In his view, the separation of church and state must be absolute. The sovereign is to be concerned with civil affairs only: life, liberty, health, and property. The sovereign is to use impartial and equal laws to ensure that these rights are protected for everyone. The sovereign, however, may neither prescribe nor proscribe any religious belief. This would violate the private space of individual conscience and so undermine the free choice that serves as the very legitimizing foundation of government.

Locke also makes it clear, however, that the sovereign cannot tolerate individuals or groups who hold opinions that run contrary to the peaceful preservation of society. All who wish to remain in civil society must agree not to harm others or to interfere with the property of others. They must also agree not to set religious leaders before the sovereign in civil affairs. Locke notes that while the sovereign cannot prescribe religion, civil society cannot tolerate atheists. Without faith, he believes, their promises are void. Beyond this, though, tolerance must be extended if people are to be free to govern themselves.

Applications

Locke's political theory is at work in some way everywhere there is a move toward democracy. His influence is clearly seen in both the American and French revolutions. The U.S. Constitution is based on Locke's theory, and the American legal system still reflects his views. Some concrete examples of Locke's influence in the United States include: the separation of government into three branches (executive, legislative, and judicial), the separation of church and state, freedom of religious worship, freedom of assembly, freedom of speech, and the right to privacy. Locke's notion that people possess property in their own person and so are free to use it as they wish, as long as they do not harm others, serves as the foundation for limited government.

The idea that government's role should be limited to protecting the people from harm and should not extend to legislating positive social behavior is ambiguous at best and is something with which any democracy must constantly struggle. Laws that prohibit smoking or drinking may be seen as protecting the public from harm or they may be seen as crossing the line and promoting certain behaviors. People continue to debate whether the right to bear arms secures or endangers public safety. People continue to debate whether laws censoring erotic or pornographic materials protect the public or interfere with privacy. These issues are understood by the legal system as conflicts between private and public interests. Locke's theory sets this conflict as the only proper function of government jurisdiction: protection of as wide a private sphere of freedom as possible without threatening public security.

The idea that a clear distinction between private and public interests can be discerned and maintained is criticized by many. Communitarians, socialists, some feminists, and pragmatists are among those who maintain that private and public interests are intricately interconnected because as individuals people are embedded in social relations with connected interests. While Locke's theory served to liberate people from the tyranny of absolute sovereigns, people are not left with a clear way to determine whose interests should prevail when there is a social conflict.

Context

Locke developed his political theory during a time of change. The feudal system, in which some are born to rule and others born to serve, had fallen into decline. The right of each person to choose the course of one's life for oneself was emerging, but there was still the belief in the divine and absolute right of the sovereign. This absolute form of government, often combined with religious intolerance, kept people from being free. Locke's theory challenged this remaining hindrance to freedom and laid the foundation for the establishment of liberal democracies.

Locke's time was also one of advances in science. The Industrial Revolution was about to disrupt old patterns of life. People were being uprooted from communities and occupations and coming face to face with people who had different worldviews. The concept of the liberal individual served to allow for this change and challenge and to allow for the avoidance of conflict and oppression. The liberal individual promoted freedom and tolerance simultaneously and so helped people adapt to a changing world.

It is also useful to note that classical liberalism not only serves as a philosophical foundation for contemporary democracies, but also is often attached to the rise of capitalism as well. The concept of a free market running without government interference is based on the notion that free and rational individuals, doing what maximizes their self-interest, tend to act in the interest of society as a whole. In political terms, such agents freely join together under a social contract; in economic terms, such individuals freely compete in a common and free market.

It is important to realize that while liberal theory has served as the foundation for much of the contemporary political and economic order, it has never been applied in its most radical form. In the same way that no economic market has ever really been free (in all markets there are protections and special privileges), no political order has ever found a way to operate without legislating morality and so interfering with personal conscience. Locke allows for civil disobedience, as well as rebellion, if in the face of injustice. Locke must have realized the difficulty of achieving a society based on freedom and tolerance.

Bibliography

Anderson, Charles W. *Pragmatic Liberalism*. Chicago: University of Chicago Press, 1990. Defends pragmatic liberalism as a viable political and economic theory.

Grant, Ruth W. *John Locke's Liberalism*. Chicago: University of Chicago Press, 1987. Good introduction to Locke's moral and political theory. Focuses on differentiating between legitimate and illegitimate power.

Hirschmann, Nancy J. *Rethinking Obligation: A Feminist Method for Political Theory*. Ithaca, N.Y.: Cornell University Press, 1992. Offers a critique of the source of political obligation from a feminist perspective.

Levine, Andrew. *Liberal Democracy: A Critique of Its Theory*. New York: Columbia University Press, 1981. Good basic discussion of liberal theory and an examination of its usefulness in politics. Discusses freedom, rights, representation, and rational agency.

Locke, John. *Two Treatises on Government: A Critical Edition*. Rev. ed. Introduction and notes by Peter Laslett. New York: New American Library, 1965. Critical edition, with notes. Provides an introduction that discusses Locke's life and his place in the history of political theory.

Macpherson, C. B. *Democratic Theory: Essays in Retrieval*. Oxford, England: Clarendon Press, 1973. Critically examines the historical roots of liberalism. Discusses the strong link between liberalism as political theory and its role in economic theory.

_____. *The Political Theory of Possessive Individualism: Hobbes to Locke*. Oxford, England: Clarendon Press, 1962. Provides a critical stance on the political theory of Locke.

Nicholson, Linda J. *Gender and History: The Limits of Social Theory in the Age of the Family*. New York: Columbia University Press, 1986. Critiques Locke's distinction between the public and the private, especially Locke's view that the family and state are separate.

Schochet, Gordon J., ed. *Life, Liberty, and Property: Essays on Locke's Political Ideas*. Belmont, Calif: Wadsworth, 1971. Introductory essays concerning many aspects of Locke's political theory.

Wolff, Robert Paul. *The Poverty of Liberalism*. Boston: Beacon Press, 1968. Critiques the assumptions and applications of liberalism. Challenges the idea that free individuals can subject themselves to the rule of another.

Erin McKenna

Cross-References

The Bill of Rights, p. 134; Burke's Political Philosophy, p. 171; Civil Disobedience, p. 285; Deism, p. 495; General Will, p. 745; Hobbes's Political Philosophy, p. 836; Hooker's Political Philosophy, p. 842; Individual Versus State Rights, p. 910; Kant's Political Philosophy, p. 1025; Legitimacy, p. 1105; Liberalism, p. 1118; Mill's Political Philosophy, p. 1204; Montesquieu's Political Philosophy, p. 1228; Political Philosophy, p. 1505; Right of Revolution, p. 1744; Rousseau's Political Philosophy, p. 1756; Separation of Powers: Political Philosophy, p. 1809; The Social Contract, p. 1827; Spinoza's Political Philosophy, p. 1872; Thomas Aquinas' Political Philosophy, p. 1974.

MACHIAVELLI'S POLITICAL PHILOSOPHY

Field of study: Political philosophy

Machiavelli, a sixteenth century Italian political philosopher, is best known for his political writings in which he expressed disdain for conventional morality in politics. He also wrote extensively on the formation and preservation of republics and authored many literary works.

Principal terms

FORTUNA: Italian word for fortune or luck; the object of *virtù* is to forestall the consequences of inevitable ill-fortune

NECESSITA: word used by Machiavelli to describe changing political circumstances that must be confronted realistically and with *virtù*

REALISM (OR REALPOLITIK): approach to politics that takes human nature and the nature of politics as they are—morally flawed—rather than as one would wish them to be

UNARMED PROPHETS: reformers who reject the use of force and other realistic measures, with disastrous results

VIRTÙ: word that Machiavelli used to describe political resourcefulness or ingenuity and public-spiritedness

Overview

The name of Niccolò Machiavelli (1469-1527) has become synonymous with the use of deception, double-dealing, and brute force to pursue political, and sometimes nonpolitical, ends. Machiavelli did, in fact, argue that moral scruples could be a political disadvantage. As a result, he thought that good people must sometimes do bad things in order to wield power effectively. The alternative would be to leave a monopoly over the sphere of politics to those individuals who are naturally unscrupulous. Likewise, the maintenance of popular government requires the occasional use of morally questionable measures, lest freedom be jeopardized in the name of ethical or moral purity. In this sense, Machiavelli's thought may accurately be considered an example of political realism. It is realistic, as opposed to idealistic, about human nature and the nature of political power.

Machiavelli's best-known work, *The Prince*, details the most effective ways to obtain, maintain, and expand princely power. Using numerous contemporary and historical examples, Machiavelli advocates several morally questionable tactics. First, princes must, at times, ruthlessly exterminate political opponents who cannot be won over to their side, even young heirs to hereditary power. Necessary cruelties should be entrusted to henchmen, who can then be disposed of so that the prince can maintain moral distance from harsh measures. He further asserts that princes must operate on the assumption that it is better to be feared than loved. Therefore, princely power is based on intimidation at some basic level. Although it is good to have a reputation for honesty, princes should only keep their word when it is in their best interest to do so.

Finally, princes must be expert in the use of military force. The willingness and ability to wage war effectively are crucial to the maintenance of princely power.

The effective prince must know when to be a lion and when to be a fox. At times, brute force is necessary; at other times, deception and trickery will be more effective. Neither of these metaphoric identities includes Christian charity or benevolence. Such traits are acceptable when they are manifestly affordable. The prince is advised to maintain the appearance of good-heartedness, as long as it does not dramatically raise expectations, thus fomenting discontent or even sedition.

In Machiavelli's lengthiest, but less well known, work, *The Discourses*, additional evidence may be gathered as to his disdain for conventional morality when it comes to politics. Citing the bloody myth of Romulus and Remus, Machiavelli notes that the founding of a political order requires an initial act of violence to ensure the monopoly of power needed for long-term stability. He also cites circumstances in which the common people must be manipulated into supporting the republic, either through civil religion or false prophecy, as in the case when it is necessary to go to war. As this last point suggests, the conduct of war is a primary political resource.

All this adds up to what has become known as Machiavellianism: the elevation in importance of personal or collective political ends over conventional moral scruples such as the biblical prohibitions against lying, stealing, and killing. Stereotypical Machiavellians pursue their own ends, or the ends of the nation or some other collectivity, by any means necessary to achieve success.

This conjures up a number of unsavory visions. On a minor level, one might think of slippery-tongued politicians, conniving corporate climbers, and any number of cover-ups. On a more serious level, one with stunning resonance in the twentieth century, the images of Adolf Hitler, with his theory of the "big lie" and international trickery, and Joseph Stalin, with his bloody purges, emerge as monstrous examples of Machiavellianism carried to an extreme.

Topping off this negative view of Machiavellianism is the belief of some observers that the man himself was a self-serving sycophant. They base this judgment on Machiavelli's note to Lorenzo Medici at the outset of *The Prince*, in which he offers the work as a gift meant to win the Medicis' favor.

This sinister image of Machiavelli and his thought is misleading. Machiavelli was a committed supporter of the Florentine republic that Lorenzo Medici helped to supplant. Indeed, a close reading of Machiavelli's introduction reveals hints of irony. Nowhere in the book does he suggest that selection of a clever adviser is the key to political success. In addition, *The Prince* constitutes a very small portion of Machiavelli's political writing. He wrote far more extensive works on the maintenance of free republics, the art of war, and the history of Florence. Nor should Machiavelli be understood solely as a political writer. He also wrote plays and short stories of lasting literary merit. A truer image of Machiavelli would be that of a Florentine patriot with numerous interests and talents.

It is also misleading to view Machiavelli's thought as entirely sinister. Machiavelli did not invent ruthlessness or trickery; they already were manifest in politics at the time he wrote. Even the Roman Catholic church had become a prominent political actor, dealing quite expediently with the unpleasant realities of political power. What Machiavelli asserted was that, given the ways of the world, those who refused to use morally questionable tactics when they were necessary would be politically ineffective. This would, in turn, leave power to the worst individuals and regimes.

Machiavelli decried the futility of "unarmed prophets." He had a particular prophet in mind: fifteenth century Christian reformer Girolamo Savonarola, who called for a return to the original principles of Jesus Christ. Savonarola, for whom Machiavelli had much sympathy, was admirably idealistic and pure of heart. He also ended up being tortured, hanged, and burned at the stake. To Machiavelli, the lesson of Savonarola was clear. It was not enough to be a good man with worthy ideals and purity of heart. In order to have an effect, one must deal with political necessities, including the ability to defend one's self militarily.

On the other hand, there is more to Machiavelli's thought than a mere call to surrender one's scruples. A prince must display *virtù* in the face of *fortuna*, that is, luck, which is distinctly variable. The word "*virtù*" is used in *The Prince* to mean a sort of political and military ingenuity, as one translator puts it. It includes the ability to foresee and deal effectively with all sorts of political necessities (*necessita*) produced by *fortuna*. *Virtù* is identified with the boldness or impetuousness that is needed to make the best of *fortuna*. There are, however, no guarantees. One can have considerable *virtù* and still be defeated by *fortuna*. *Virtù* increases the odds in one's favor, while its absence leads to ruin as soon as the tides of *fortuna* change.

While *virtù* does not equate to the conventional moral virtues, it does contain a moral component. At one point in *The Prince*, when discussing a particularly ruthless but effective ruler, Machiavelli says that such cruelty cannot properly be called *virtù*. This and other passages suggest that the effective ruler exercises what has been called an "economy of violence." Political effectiveness requires harsh measures, but this unpleasant reality leaves room for moral distinctions. In this regard, twentieth century despots such as Hitler and Stalin can easily be criticized according to Machiavelli's standards, because they went beyond realism to obsessive, irrational violence. Thus, while Machiavelli rejected idealism, he did not sink to nihilism or complete amorality. He advocated taking a realistic stance toward the occasional need for violent and deceptive measures but believed such measures are to be minimized.

Machiavelli clearly embraced the republic as the best form of government. The republic, as Machiavelli envisioned it, was a mixed form of government with a substantial measure of popular control. In *The Discourses*, he examines the formation and maintenance of republics. Based primarily on the example of the Roman Republic, Machiavelli accepts as a starting point the natural life cycle of polities according to the Greek philosopher Aristotle. According to Aristotle's biological analogy, political orders are born, come to maturity, thrive, ultimately age, and die. For Machiavelli, the task of the *The Discourses* was to show how, by human design, the natural decay of republics could be forestalled, and their lives extended indefinitely. The terms *virtù* and *fortuna* take on somewhat different meanings in this work. *Fortuna* is associated with time, which ages and threatens to dissolve the republic. This occurs when *virtù*, understood here as active civic-spiritedness, is replaced with self-interest, passivity (which Machiavelli identified with Christianity), or some combination of the two. To forestall this natural occurrence, republics must occasionally be returned to their original principles and reinvigorated, a process that can be bloody.

While Machiavelli was indeed a political realist, he was also a major cultural figure of the Italian Renaissance. His advice to princes goes well beyond the mere advocacy of unscrupulousness, and he was most preoccupied with the formation and preservation of republics.

Applications

Machiavelli's writing on politics was meant to be applied. He was attempting to draw lessons from historical examples that could then be used to emulate effective behavior while avoiding costly mistakes. Machiavelli offered no guarantees, but he did think that one could learn from the past. In fact, Machiavelli's ideas have been applied, although perhaps not in the manner in which he hoped. Generally ignored by the rulers of his own time, most of whom were already thoroughly unscrupulous, Machiavelli has had significant influence into the twentieth century.

Machiavelli's most noted influence on statecraft has been in the field of diplomacy and foreign affairs, where he is often credited with being the originator of realpolitik and the doctrine of *raison d'état*. Realpolitik connotes the elevation of national interests, primarily national security, over more idealistic moral, religious, and ideological imperatives. *Raison d'état* is a related concept, which expresses the belief that the needs of the state legitimize the means by which goals are attained, even if they are morally reprehensible. These two concepts have been important focal points of nineteenth and twentieth century diplomacy and foreign relations.

Both concepts can also be applied to domestic statecraft. Recognizing the limitations of their constituents, political leaders sometimes lie or use heavy-handed measures to ensure domestic tranquillity.

A less well-known application of Machiavellian principles pertains to the founding of the United States. While Machiavelli must share credit with other political philosophers, such as John Locke, Thomas Hobbes, and Montesquieu, his presence at the founding was felt both directly and through seventeenth century English authors who had inherited and elaborated on the basic premises of *The Discourses*. The U.S. Constitution can be seen as thoroughly Machiavellian. As the Federalist Papers, written by the Constitution's most avid supporters, make clear, the Founders' Enterprise was to design a republican form of government that could withstand the ravages of time (or *fortuna*) despite the inevitable failings of human nature. Like Machiavelli, the Founders did not think that civic virtue was made obsolete by their "new science" of government.

Machiavelli's thought has been applied in two other ways that are not directly political. Although it is not quantitatively oriented, Machiavelli's methodological attempt to use the lessons of history in a systematic way has often been imitated and is sometimes seen as a pioneering effort in the field of social science. Second, a number of late twentieth century authors have applied Machiavellian principles to the field of business and management.

Context

Despite his great originality, Machiavelli was a creature of his times. He was a representative figure of great importance in the Italian Renaissance. His thought can also be understood as a response to the chaotic politics and institutional corruption of his times. The Renaissance signaled the rediscovery and legitimization of pagan art and literature, including the classics of Greek and Roman civilization. Implicit in this was rejection of the primacy of religion that had developed during the Middle Ages. Machiavelli's thought certainly fits in with this trend. His theory of politics is secularized and owes much to Aristotle and other classical writers. *The Prince* counters the idealized image of statecraft in the "mirror of princes" tracts produced by churchmen. These tracts were especially ironic at a time when the Roman Catholic church was both manifestly involved in political intrigue and conspicuously corrupt. Machiavelli attempted to unveil the realities of political power so that good people would not be handicapped by their innocence while unscrupulous rulers and pretenders monopolized power.

While the Reformation and rise of Protestantism provided religious alternatives to Catholic hegemony, Renaissance thinkers looked to sources predating the rise of Christianity and redefined the world from a humanist perspective. The politics of the period, however, was anything but humane, or even orderly. In this context, Machiavelli's writing, even at its most cynical, can be seen as an attempt to lay the groundwork for a more humane politics. Machiavelli offered advice to princes that, if followed, would have led to greater stability, improved laws, and perhaps the opportunity to pursue popular or free government.

Machiavelli must also be seen as part of a line of political philosophers, ranging back to Socrates and Plato and forward at least to Karl Marx and John Stuart Mill. While he probably is most indebted to Aristotle, Machiavelli shares certain characteristics with all the thinkers in this tradition. He attempted to blend substantial elements of realism with those of idealism. This distinguishes political philosophy from amoral quests for power, and also from utopian or purely idealistic thought. Machiavelli shared with thinkers as diverse as Plato, Rousseau, and Hobbes the desire to formulate theory that was grounded in reality but that at the same time transcended the apparent limitations of politics.

Bibliography

Bondanella, Peter, and Mark Musa, eds. and trans. *The Portable Machiavelli*. New York: Penguin Books, 1979. A broad cross section of Machiavelli's work, including *The Prince*, extensive selections from the *Discourses*, *Mandragola*, excerpts from *The Art of War* and *The History of Florence*, and selected letters.
Buskirk, Richard H. *Modern Management and Machiavelli*. Boston: Cahners Books,

1974. Quoting liberally from *The Prince* and *Discourses*, Buskirk applies Machiavellian lessons to problems facing modern business executives. Buskirk rejects the view that Machiavelli's teachings consist solely of deception, force, and treachery.

Gilbert, Felix. *Machiavelli and Guicciardini, Politics and History in Sixteenth-Century Florence.* Princeton, N.J.: Princeton University Press, 1965. Helpful analysis of Machiavelli's political thought in tandem with that of his contemporary and fellow Florentine, Francesco Guicciardini.

Jay, Antony. *Management and Machiavelli: An Inquiry into the Politics of Corporate Life.* New York: Holt, Rinehart & Winston, 1968. Another application of Machiavelli's ideas beyond the sphere of politics. Cited as a practitioner of the book's theories, Jay himself was profiled in *Forbes Magazine* in 1992.

Machiavelli, Niccolò. *The Discourses.* Edited by Bernard Crick. Baltimore: Penguin Books, 1974. This edition of Machiavelli's lengthy treatise on the effective maintenance of republics is distinguished by Bernard Crick's careful editing, based on a translation by Leslie J. Walker as revised by Brian Richardson, and by a lengthy introductory essay.

Meinecke, Friedrich. *Machiavellism: The Doctrine of Raison d'État and Its Place in Modern History.* Edited by W. Stark. Translated by Douglas Scott. London: Routledge & Kegan Paul, 1957. This book was originally published in Germany in 1924. Meinecke traces Machiavellism, understood as the broad license granted to heads of state in the interests of the state, from the early stages of European nationalism to World War I.

Pocock, J. G. A. *The Machiavellian Moment: Florentine Political Thought and the Atlantic Republican Tradition.* Princeton, N.J.: Princeton University Press, 1975. Traces the rekindling of republican ideals from Machiavelli and like-minded contemporaries, through seventeenth-century English thinkers such as James Harrington, to some of the most influential founders of the United States. The U.S. Constitution is treated as a direct product of Machiavelli's focus on the defense of free institutions against the ravages of time brought on by the imperfections of human nature.

Ridolfi, Roberto. *The Life of Niccolò Machiavelli.* Translated by Cecil Grayson. London: Routledge & Kegan Paul, 1963. A scholarly yet readable biography of Machiavelli.

Skinner, Quentin. *Machiavelli.* New York: Hill & Wang, 1981. Brief but penetrating contextual analysis of Machiavelli's work. His career as a diplomat, his awareness of Roman political and moral ideas, and the influence of Renaissance humanism are examined to expose his intellectual debts as well as his stunning originality.

Wolin, Sheldon S. *Politics and Vision: Continuity and Innovation in Western Political Thought.* Boston: Little, Brown, 1960. This book fits Machiavelli's thought into the larger context of Western political thought. Wolin argues that Machiavelli advocates a strict "economy of violence," the aim of which is to minimize the amount of bloodshed needed to pursue political ends.

Ira Smolensky

Cross-References

Charismatic Leadership, p. 209; Constitutional Governments, p. 432; Despotism and Tyranny, p. 527; Elitism, p. 591; Fascism and Nazism, p. 656; Force, p. 712; Geopolitics, p. 759; Leadership, p. 1066; The Nation-State, p. 1241; Political Ethics, p. 1461; Political Myths and the Philosophies of Mosca and Pareto, p. 1474; Political Philosophy, p. 1505; Realpolitik, p. 1668; Spinoza's Political Philosophy, p. 1872; War, p. 2129.

MARXISM-LENINISM

Field of study: Political philosophy

Marxism-Leninism is the political philosophy underlying communism. Its major tenets were laid down by Karl Marx, who stated the theory, and Vladimir Lenin, who applied it in practice. The goal of Marxism-Leninism is to transform capitalist societies into socialist ones.

Principal terms
BOURGEOISIE: capitalist economic class that owns and controls business firms and industries and derives its income from profit
CAPITALISM: economic mode of production using wage labor for the production of commodities with the ultimate aim of generating profit
DIALECTICAL MATERIALISM: Marxist social theory holding that economics and technological development account for the nature of society and social change
DICTATORSHIP OF THE PROLETARIAT: theory originated by Marx and elaborated by Lenin describing government run by the working class during the transition from capitalism to socialism
SOCIALISM: theory of social organization based on social ownership of the means of production
SPONTANEITY OF THE MASSES: doctrine held by Rosa Luxemburg and opposed by Lenin that argues that the masses may engage in revolutionary activity and mass collective action without centralized leadership
VANGUARD: elite leadership of professional revolutionaries

Overview
Karl Marx (1818-1883) and Vladimir Lenin (1870-1924) are the source of Marxism-Leninism. Marx set forth the general theoretical principles of socialism and Lenin applied them concretely in revolutionary practice. Marx was the architect and Lenin the builder. A key to Marx's social theory is dialectical materialism. According to this theory, modern society, is divided into two great economic classes—those who control money, or capital, and those who sell their labor—that are locked in a world historical struggle. Ruling society is the capitalist class and rules by virtue of being the class that owns productive property. Under its rule is the proletariat, oppressed by virtue of being without capital and therefore obliged to sell their labor. Following Marx's line of thinking, the proletariat's mission is to organize, mobilize, seize political power from the capitalists (also known as the bourgeoisie), abolish private property, and create a socialist society.
It was Friedrich Engels (1820-1895), Marx's friend and collaborator who popularized the theories of Marx. Engels expounded on the materialist concept of history, in

which the economic conditions of a given epoch are believed to determine the form and changes of society, its politics, and culture. According to Engels, history and society are driven by laws similar to the laws of nature. The object of scientific socialism, as opposed to utopian socialism, is to understand these social laws in order to regulate society more efficiently.

In effect, Marxist socialism stands for economic planning and social regulation of production, as opposed to the social anarchy of the capitalist free market. The latter is characterized by periodic crises because of overproduction resulting from the absence of centralized planning. Socialized production, Engels argues, is necessary to avoid such crises. For this to happen, however, the proletariat must first seize political power. In a capitalist society, the government, Marx argued, is nothing but a bureaucracy administering the affairs of the bourgeoisie. From a Marxist point of view, then, the state is a repressive apparatus.

Lenin, the Bolshevik leader of the 1917 Russian Revolution, set forth an instrumentalist theory of the state. According to this view, the state is an instrument in the hands of the ruling class. It serves to maintain class rule. It becomes imperative, therefore, for the proletariat to seize the state and use it as a weapon to eliminate the capitalist class and to construct socialism. Because of the class-based nature of the state, it will wither away with the elimination of classes. In the transition from capitalism to communism, there will be two distinct stages. In the first stage, the lower stage of socialism, there will be a dictatorship of the proletariat—the working class will control government. In the higher stage of communism, with the elimination of classes, the class-based state will wither away. Lenin called for party leadership by professional revolutionaries. He believed that if workers are left to their own understanding they will only develop trade-union consciousness and not a revolutionary consciousness. Therefore, they need to be led by a vanguard of professional revolutionaries who possess class consciousness and are ready to make any sacrifice for the revolution. Spontaneity of the masses, unplanned mass uprisings, and trade unionism amounted, in Lenin's view, to submission to capitalism. In order to ensure the success of the revolution, Marxism-Leninism requires an elite leadership, hierarchical organization, centralized authority, and secrecy.

Lenin explained why the proletariat should join forces with the bourgeoisie in a liberal revolution to overthrow the czar. Given the feudal social structure of early twentieth century Russia, a bourgeois revolution for democratic freedoms and for civil rights is a necessary first step for the proletariat. Thus, Lenin recognized the need for a political alliance between the proletariat, peasantry, and bourgeoisie. Nevertheless, a strategic problem arises as a result because the bourgeoisie and the proletariat ultimately have different aims. The solution, as Lenin understood it, is to forge unity in the first phase of the struggle and overthrow the czarist feudal regime. After the revolution, the proletariat will wage class struggle against the bourgeoisie to obtain state power and create a workers' state. Lenin advocated two struggles—first, a revolution for democracy, and, second, a revolution for socialism.

Lenin also pointed out how imperialism sets the stage for socialism. Imperialism represents the monopoly stage of capitalism. Monopolies become more powerful as capitalism advances. When industrial capital merges with finance capital, capital is exported along with commodities. For example, a capitalist empire buys up things of value in a small country, then sells manufactured goods to that country. The small country borrows money from the capitalist empire to buy the goods (cars, for example, or guns or computers). In debt, the small country is obliged to sell what it can (iron ore, coffee) to the capitalist empire. The small country is in effect conquered by the capitalist empire. Ironically, the globalization of capital lays down the foundation for the emergence of socialism.

Applications

A socialist revolution, according to Engels, is inevitable because the fundamental contradictions of capitalist society create the conditions for it. First, production is social—commodities result from the collective labor of many workers. Yet, the commodities are privately owned by the capitalists who derive profit from selling the commodities at prices above costs of production. Second, the difference between the workers' lack of money and the property ownership of the capitalists leads to a social antagonism between the two classes. Third, a contradiction also exists because individual firms engage in social organization, planning, and regulation, but in the market anarchy reigns. Fourth, another contradiction arises because technological development increases productivity, leading to greater output, unemployment, and recession. Machines replace workers, who, unemployed, cannot afford to buy what the machines make. Finally, a contradiction occurs between a capitalist fantasy that defends competition and a free market and a capitalist reality of mergers, cartels, and monopolies. For a solution Engels proposes the socialization of production, centralized planning, and the abolition of private property.

How can one get the workers to agree to the proposed solution? For Lenin, the answer is to create class consciousness and organize a vanguard of revolutionary leaders who possess this consciousness. Lenin cites several reasons for justifying a vanguard of professional revolutionaries. One is that a stable organization of leaders will maintain the momentum of the revolution. A second is that as membership of the revolutionary movement grows, greater need arises for stable organization. Also, organizational leadership in a revolutionary movement requires full-time professional revolutionaries. Finally, for the sake of protection and security, secrecy is required. The more professional the leadership the more secrecy can be maintained.

Leon Trotsky (1879-1940) was, along with Lenin, a major force behind the Russian Revolution. One of his key ideas is "permanent revolution." Trotsky argued that undeveloped countries do not have to take the historical steps from feudalism to capitalism to socialism as described by Marx. The idea of a permanent revolution argues that in an underdeveloped state, a proletariat could develop without a correspondingly important bourgeois class and without a bourgeois revolution. He also disagreed with Joseph Stalin's theory of developing socialism first in one country. Trotsky believed in encouraging socialism in other countries—an international revolution. He bemoaned the fact that the Russian Revolution, under Stalin, had degenerated to an expansive parasitic bureaucracy. He was forced out of Russia by Stalin and assassinated in Mexico City on Stalin's orders.

Joseph Stalin (1879-1953), who joined the Bolsheviks in 1904, eventually succeeded Lenin in 1924. Stalin stressed the importance of Marxist-Leninist theory. To brush aside Marxist-Leninist theory, Stalin warned, was to go against Lenin's spirit. Like Lenin, he spurned the idea of the spontaneity of the masses and emphasized the leading role of the vanguard. He also reinforced Lenin's ideas on the dictatorship of the proletariat. In Stalin's view, the proletariat is the instrument of the revolution, and its dictatorship means the dominion of the proletariat over the bourgeoisie. The Soviets, political units made up of workers, peasants, and soldiers, form the dictatorship of the proletariat. Stalin, like Lenin, was concerned only with the socialization of the Soviet Union.

György Lukács (1885-1971) was a leading Hungarian communist and an ardent Leninist. He profoundly influenced Marxist thinking in Western Europe. Following Lenin, he placed a strong emphasis on class consciousness in theory and practice. His book, however, was condemned by the Stalinist regime in 1924. Lukács argued that the revolution will not come about as a result of capitalism's inherent contradictions. Certainly, a breakdown of capitalism will result from a crisis of capitalism's economic contradictions, he argued, and certainly economic crisis prepares the conditions needed for the proletariat to prepare for revolutionary action. Lukács was dubious, however, about the revolutionary potential of the masses and emphasized the need for revolutionaries to organize and lead the masses.

Context

Theoretical alternatives to Marxism-Leninism came from Eduard Bernstein, Karl Kautsky, and Rosa Luxemburg. According to Bernstein (1850-1932), socialism is a gradual process, eventually mitigating the destructive features of capitalism and improving the lot of the working class. Bernstein argued against the theory advocated by revolutionary Marxists that socialism should be induced by a forceful takeover of state power. Bernstein argued for an evolutionary concept of socialism.

Instead of revolutionary activity, Bernstein believed that socialists should concentrate their energies on two fronts. First, they should concentrate on trade unionization. Second, they should work for the democratization of government. Like his revolutionary counterparts, Bernstein believed that workers should gain control of government, but he differed on how that should be done. Bernstein believed that the best way to achieve a socialist revolution is by the democratic struggle for political rights and by the industrial organization of workers into trade unions.

Trade union activity extends democracy to the workplace. Its effect is to destroy the absolute power of capitalism. It also procures a place for worker influence in management. Political participation by the working class could lead to democracy, which Bernstein redefined. He rejected the idea of democracy as rule of the majority. Rather, he defined democracy as the absence of class government.

Karl Kautsky (1854-1938) advocated democratic socialism and worker rule but opposed Lenin's centralism. Kautsky took issue with Lenin and Trotsky on party politics. He insisted on universal suffrage and parliamentary democracy against Lenin's absolute rule of party dictatorship. He demanded freedom of press, assembly, and other rights. He saw the numerical strength of the proletariat as a safeguard for democracy. Kautsky found it important to distinguish between "class" and "party." Class is an economic category. Party is a political category. What is true for the one may not be true for the other. Extension of universal rights is necessary to promote mass organization and mass action. Socialism requires the support of the majority.

Kautsky, moreover, was not so pessimistic about capitalism. He claimed that the destruction of capitalism is not the ultimate goal of socialism. Rather, capitalism is the necessary precondition for the success of socialism. Capitalism stimulates industry, provides for social wealth, and provides for the organization of labor. These conditions need to exist before the proletariat may obtain political power. For Kautsky, the dictatorship of the proletariat is a political condition, not a form of government.

Rosa Luxemburg (1871-1919) pointed out that the factors so valued by Bernstein— trade union activity and parliamentary work—could not by themselves remove capitalism without the aid of economic conditions. Luxemburg agreed that trade union activity and parliamentary practice raise proletariat awareness, but she did not believe that such things alone can socialize the economy. Rather, trade union activity and parliamentary practice alone lead to reformism. Reformism leads to compromise and diplomacy, but not to taking power. Socialism, she argues, will result from a combination of objective factors—the contradictions of capitalism—and subjective ones— the political awareness and activity of the working class. Luxemburg agreed that the fate of democracy is bound up with the fate of the labor movement.

For Luxemburg, the choice for revolution is not absolute. According to Luxemburg, the choice between legislative reform or revolution depends on class struggle and circumstance. Along with Lenin, she believed that legislative reform instead of taking power leads not to socialism but to the mere reform of capitalism and the mitigation of the abuses of capitalism. Capitalist domination cannot be transformed by legislation, because capitalist domination is based on economic relations that did not come about through legislation. Those economic relations must be reorganized along socialist lines.

According to Luxemburg, democracy is necessary, however, because it creates the tools the working class will use to transform society. Democracy does not take the place of conquest of power, it makes conquest of power possible. The transformation from a capitalist society to a socialist one, therefore, supposes a long struggle. As a result, there will be a tendency for premature attacks. She criticized Lenin's concept of a centralized vanguard, which she believed would prevent workers from reaching their full political potential. She also criticized Lenin and Trotsky for substituting dictatorship for democracy.

After the Bolshevik Revolution of 1917, Marxist-Leninist governments were established in the U.S.S.R., the People's Republic of China, North Korea, Vietnam, the

People's Republic of Mongolia, Albania, Bulgaria, Czechoslovakia, East Germany, Poland, Romania, Yugoslavia, Cuba, and, briefly, Nicaragua. Communist activity, both legal and subversive, occurred throughout the globe, principally in Third World countries. In the late 1980's and early 1990's, communist governments were overthrown in the U.S.S.R. and East-Central Europe. The countries moved toward multiparty elections and free-market economies.

Bibliography

Lenin, V. I. *Collected Works*. 45 vols. Moscow: Progress Publishers, 1970-1975. Complete and accessible collection of the works of Lenin.

Lichtheim, George. *Marxism: An Historical and Critical Study*. 2d rev. ed. London: Routledge & Kegan Paul, 1964. Focuses on the historical development of the critical ideas of Marxism.

Lukács, György. *History and Class Consciousness*. Cambridge, Massachusetts: MIT Press, 1971. Essays written by Lukács before 1922. It was condemned by the Stalinists in 1924 and influenced much Marxist thinking in the West.

McLellan, David, ed. *Marxism: Essential Writings*. Oxford, England: Oxford University Press, 1988. Readings from many of the great Marxist thinkers, beginning with Marx and including Marcuse.

Tucker, Robert C., ed. *The Marx-Engels Reader*. 2d ed. New York: W. W. Norton, 1978. Best English reader on the market. Very comprehensive and contains selections from different areas.

Michael R. Candelaria

Cross-References

Anarchism in Marxist Thought, p. 72; Capitalism, p. 197; Chinese Communism, p. 223; Communist Parties, p. 377; Dialecticism, p. 540; Empires and Empire Building, p. 597; Existentialism, p. 642; General Will, p. 745; Idealism, p. 855; Irrationalism in Politics, p. 987; Liberation Theology, p. 1124; National Economies, p. 1248; Oligarchy, p. 1344; One-Party Systems, p. 1350; Political Myths and the Philosophies of Mosca and Pareto, p. 1474; Revolutionary Governments, p. 1725; Revolutionary Parties, p. 1731; Revolutions, p. 1738; Right of Revolution, p. 1744; Russian Political History, p. 1770; Scientific Humanism, p. 1784; Socialism, p. 1865.IBolshevism

THE MEDIA AND ELECTIONS

Field of study: Politics

In political elections, the media act as major intermediaries between voters and political candidates. This is a potential problem, because the press is a business and neither a political organization nor an impartial messenger. Political scientists are concerned that the press, especially the electronic broadcast media, may not be providing appropriate information about political candidates.

Principal terms

ATTACK JOURNALISM: intensive and repetitive media focus on a politician's real or perceived failing

HORSE RACE COVERAGE: news coverage of elections that focuses on the standings of the candidates in the polls instead of issues

INFORMATION SUPERHIGHWAY: technological improvements that may allow citizens to vote at home using an interactive television or personal computer

MAGIC BULLET THEORY: notion that news information passes directly from the television to the viewer without distortion

MASS MEDIA: organizations such as newspapers, radio stations, or television companies that reach the mass public

PRIMARY ELECTION: election that determines a political party's nominee to compete in the general election

REPRESENTATIVE DEMOCRACY: system of government in which voters elect candidates to political office by means of competitive elections

Overview

In a democracy, a crucial link between voters and political candidates is information. Ideally, voters may expect to have fairly presented information about each candidate before an election. In modern elections, however, most voters depend on brief television news reports for their information about candidates for statewide or national office. Not all candidates are given the same amount of press coverage. Television news tends to cover candidates as if the election were a horse race. Many times news reports concentrate simply on the standings of the candidates in the polls. Candidates who are ahead receive more attention than candidates who lag behind.

Television news also devotes considerable time to stories involving personal scandals or character flaws of candidates. Once such a flaw is discovered, the press sometimes converges into an attack and floods the airwaves with information about the scandal. These stories tend to increase news ratings. A likely conclusion to be drawn is that news organizations make business decisions to seek out scandals about political candidates in order to increase their corporate profits. Likewise, reporters have been accused of slanting the news in terms of an ideological bias. Some scholars are concerned that reporters have a liberal bias and that liberal candidates or issues are covered more favorably and more extensively than conservative candidates or issues.

Political scientists have expressed concern that the growing influence of the mass media may somehow upset the democratic process. If representative democracy depends upon an informed citizenry, then it is important to examine the quality of information that the news media present to the voters. Some have argued that the media's effects, and therefore responsibilities, are limited because of the "magic bullet effect." The idea of the magic bullet effect is that news from television might transmit directly to a viewer, without distortion. Research indicates, however, that the magic bullet effect does not occur in most instances, because viewers do not always pay attention to what they watch and many times viewers misremember the information. Other studies show that some aspects of attack journalism may increase audience attention, providing results similar to those anticipated by the magic bullet theory. Just as there is no bullet, however, that will always find its target, it seems unlikely that information directed at a person both reaches that person and affects that person in exactly the manner intended, even if the manner intended is fair and honest.

Concern about the quality of election news information presented by the electronic broadcast media continues to increase as more and more voters use television news as a primary source for campaign information. For example, if the electronic broadcast media do not provide fair coverage of the candidates, then voters are deprived of the essential information needed to make an intelligent choice on election day. Potential candidates may decline to seek public office because of fears of intensive media investigation into their personal lives. Journalism sometimes also causes active candidates to drop out of campaigns before a single vote is cast. Each of these concerns raises serious questions about the nature of representative democracy in the modern communications age.

Social scientists are also considering the impact of new media technologies on the electoral process. The development of the information superhighway and of interactive television may significantly change elections and possibly our system of government. On the positive side, these technological improvements may provide more diverse sources for news information and more effective educational opportunities. On the negative side, many people may not be able to afford the equipment, such as computers or interactive television sets, needed for a ride on the new information superhighway. People without the hardware or the knowledge to use it may be shut out of the process. Those who have access to the information superhighway may become overwhelmed with information.

With the possibility of voting at home by means of one's television or computer, the country may end up with instant democracy—public policy referenda made without careful study and complete deliberation. If such systems take root, there are also problems of voting privacy to consider. Voting at home by means of computers and television opens up an opportunity for private or government monitoring of one's voting behavior. With prudent implementation, however, such fears may never come to pass.

There is no doubt that the mass media have had a significant effect on the American electoral process. New media technologies may have even greater effects on the conduct of elections in the United States. The American system of government, however, is extremely adaptable. Members of the academic community continue to provide helpful research and critiques of the electronic broadcast media's role in political elections. News organizations themselves often evaluate their coverage of elections and many times make positive adjustments in order to provide better election news information. Political parties, candidates, and elected officials continue to plan and adjust for the requirements of the information age. Whatever the future holds, it is clear that new media technologies will continue to affect elections.

Applications

In February, 1992, the presidential campaign of Arkansas governor Bill Clinton was nearly derailed by a media attack three weeks before the first Democratic presidential primary in New Hampshire. It is important to examine the facts and circumstances of these news stories that handicapped Clinton's campaign during the New Hampshire primary, because some of the charges continued to haunt him later. It is also vital to explore how Clinton was able to survive charges of marital infidelity and draft evasion during the Vietnam War, because similar news stories about other candidates in past elections had ended their presidential aspirations. It should also be noted that both the charges of womanizing and draft-dodging had been recycled from Clinton's past campaigns for governor of Arkansas.

Before Clinton's entry into the 1992 presidential contest, Democratic officials and several national news outlets investigated charges that he had several adulterous affairs while he was governor of Arkansas. Their investigations stemmed from a lawsuit filed by a Larry Nichols, a disgruntled former employee of the Arkansas Development Finance Agency. Legal documents from the suit alleged that the termination of Nichols for making personal long-distance telephone calls on the job was part of a cover-up of a government slush fund used to finance Clinton's extramarital liaisons. Nichols claimed to have tape recordings of the women, and he attempted legally to expose five of them including a Clinton staffer named Gennifer Flowers.

Clinton denied the allegations, and the legal action against him was unsuccessful. Many of the women identified in the legal action presented by Nichols also refuted the stories. The issue seemed settled until a national tabloid newspaper, *The Star*, published the details of the legal action by Nichols after Clinton announced himself as a presidential candidate. Then on January 23, 1992, *The Star* printed a front-page interview with Flowers, who asserted that she had had a twelve-year affair with Governor Clinton and that she had taped telephone conversations to prove it. Perhaps sensing a drama similar to the demise of the campaign of Democratic presidential candidate Gary Hart in 1988, the national press began to cover the story about Flowers, forcing Clinton and his wife, Hillary, to rebut the charges on a special segment of the CBS news show *60 Minutes* that aired right after the Super Bowl. Clinton's aggressive gambit on America's top investigative news program, somewhat like vice presidential candidate Richard Nixon's 1952 televised "Checkers" speech, seemed to satisfy reporters and quiet the controversy.

Unfortunately, the quiet for Clinton did not last long. News articles about potential draft-dodging during the Vietnam War immediately followed the Flowers scandal. These charges had roots from a past Arkansas gubernatorial campaign. On October 27, 1978, a retired Air Force officer accused Clinton of evading the Vietnam draft by securing a Reserve Officer Training Corps deferment and then failing to enroll in the ROTC program. After the 1978 campaign for governor, the draft issue remained dormant until three weeks before the New Hampshire primary, when the *Wall Street Journal* published an article about the matter that included interviews with former ROTC officials. The Clinton campaign, in answer to the allegations, released the text of a letter Clinton had written in 1969 to Colonel Eugene Holmes regarding the draft deferment. Once again, Clinton appeared on a special news broadcast, this time *Nightline* with Ted Koppel, in order to counter potentially career-ending charges.

How did Clinton survive these media feeding frenzies and win the 1992 presidential election? Public opinion polls taken during the campaign and postelection analyses indicate that voters were more concerned with the poor condition of the U.S. economy and the performance of the incumbent president, George Bush. Many voters were able to grant less importance to media reports concerning Clinton's alleged marital infidelity and charges of draft dodging. Many voters thought Clinton represented a change in the federal government and thought that he could help fix the U.S. economy. Events that took place during Clinton's college days and the issues of his private life were not as important to these voters as current political problems.

The other positive aspect to the 1992 campaign which might have benefited the Clinton campaign is the overall improvement in election coverage provided by the mass media. The press was roundly criticized for its performance in 1988 and news organizations made an effort to improve the quality of election news in 1992. For example, the media provided analysis of the political advertisements aired by the candidates in terms of truthfulness and accuracy. The media provided new forums for presidential candidates such as television talk shows, voter forums, and different debate formats. The presence of H. Ross Perot as a strong third-party candidate also helped to keep the campaign dialogue on the issues.

Context

The electronic broadcast media hold a powerful role in political elections mainly because the role that American political parties play in the selection of nominees during primary elections has diminished. While it can be argued that the mass media first showed growing influence at the national level in presidential elections, the power of the electronic broadcast media in elections quickly spread to the state and even the local level. A discussion of how the media became influential in national elections may provide a historical context.

At the national level the power of the mass media can be attributed to the American presidential selection process. The lack of stability in the presidential election process can be traced to the failure of the Framers of the U.S. Constitution to anticipate and plan for the role of political parties in presidential selection. From 1787 to 1796 the election of the American chief executive was run by members of the electoral college. State legislators determined how members of the electoral college were chosen and each state was assigned a number of electors equal to the total number of senators and representatives. The candidate who received a majority of these electoral college votes became president and the second place finisher became vice president. The House of Representatives determined the winner in case of a tie vote of the electoral college.

From 1800 to 1816, the process changed. Political parties began to organize, requiring some form of nomination process to select a party's candidate. During this time, a "King" caucus of congressional leaders chose the party competitors for the general election. The electoral college still was (and is) the body that elects the president, but the newly passed Twelfth Amendment to the U.S. Constitution required separate votes of the electoral college for president and vice president. Moreover, political party involvement broadened the base of the political constituency needed to obtain office. From 1832 to 1908, political parties began to use large meetings, called "conventions," in order to choose their nominees. From 1924 to 1968, progressive reformers demanded that delegates to party conventions be elected by the people instead of selected by political party bosses. Slowly, the presidential primary process became a mix of primaries and conventions similar to the system now in place.

Political party king-makers gradually lost strength over time after the majority of delegates to political party conventions became popularly elected by means of the primary process. Presidential candidates discovered that they could achieve success by creating their own campaign organizations outside the traditional party organization. These campaign organizations allowed candidates to be relatively independent from the party leadership. Party bosses no longer had the power to screen and select nominees. From the beginning, then, the selection process for the U.S. president has demonstrated a tendency toward horse race campaigning, in which candidates are selected as much for their perceived chances of winning as for their qualities as leaders, and a tendency toward ever-increasing numbers of people involved in the process, which is more democratic but favors those with the established means of obtaining the votes of large numbers of people. By 1952, political candidates were exploring the use of television as a means to reach a wide audience of voters.

Candidates now struggle to raise huge sums of money in order to produce and air paid political advertisements, which have the potential to influence thousands, if not millions, of voters. Candidates also attempt to appear on as many television news programs, talk shows, and televised debates as possible in order to get media exposure. Over time, the mass media has begun to replace the major political parties as the primary link between candidates and voters. This raises serious questions about the democratic process in the United States, as the mass media are for-profit businesses with their own exigencies. One may argue that the U.S. election process now depends on unelected, corporate entities, who screen out candidates and provide political information to voters. Some scholars suggest that problems in political elections can only be corrected by strengthening the role of political parties in political campaigns. Simply improving the way the electronic broadcast media cover political campaigns may not be enough to repair the link between candidates and voters.

Bibliography

Abramson, Jeffrey B., F. Christopher Arterton, and Gary R. Orren. *The Electronic Commonwealth: The Impact of New Media Technologies on Democratic Politics.* New York: Basic Books, 1988. Resource for those researching the effects of the mass media on democratic theory.

Bennett, W. Lance. *The Governing Crisis: Media, Money, and Marketing in American Elections.* New York: St. Martin's Press, 1992. Provides a historical overview of past election practices and examines modern mass-media elections, with special attention to the role of fund-raising and political advertisements.

Dye, Thomas, Harmon Zeigler, and S. Robert Lichter. *American Politics in the Media Age.* 4th ed. Monterey, Calif.: Brooks/Cole, 1992. Excellent college-level textbook that explores the role of the media on American elections, institutions, and public policy.

Entman, Robert M. *Democracy Without Citizens: Media and the Decay of American Politics.* New York: Oxford University Press, 1989. Explores the impact of the mass media on the democratic process with special attention given to how the media affect what people think.

Neuman, W. Russell. *The Future of the Mass Audience.* New York: Cambridge University Press, 1991. Extensive look at the potential impact of the information superhighway on society.

Patterson, Thomas E. *Out of Order.* New York: Alfred A. Knopf, 1993. Describes how the mass media has displaced political party organizations in the presidential selection process.

Sabato, Larry J. *Feeding Frenzy: How Attack Journalism Has Transformed American Politics.* New York: Free Press, 1991. One of the most important works on modern journalism and political campaigns. This book established the concept of attack journalism and provides several case studies.

John W. Cavanaugh

Cross-References

Citizenship Rights and Responsibilities, p. 260; Communications Management, p. 370; Democracy, p. 513; Elections, p. 578; The Media and the Conduct of Government, p. 1167; Nomination Processes, p. 1312; Political Campaigns in U.S. History, p. 1434; Political Participation, p. 1479; Political Representation in the United States, p. 1525; Presidential Elections in the United States, p. 1596; Primary Elections, p. 1603; Propaganda, p. 1615; Public Opinion Polling, p. 1627; Voting Behavior in the United States, p. 2109; Voting in History, p. 2116; Voting Processes, p. 2123.

THE MEDIA AND THE CONDUCT OF GOVERNMENT

Field of study: Political philosophy

The media provide continual reports and commentary on politics and the conduct of government. This coverage of public affairs influences what government officials do and how they carry out their responsibilities.

Principal terms
AGENDA SETTING: determining the most important issues or problems that government needs to address
CONDUCT OF GOVERNMENT: by which government officials carry out their responsibilities
DECENTRALIZATION OF CONGRESS: dispersal of power, allowing more members to be involved in the policy-making process and reducing the power of committee chairpersons and senior members to dictate policy
MEDIA: agencies of mass communication, particularly television and newspapers
MEDIA CONTENT: news stories and editorials
POLITICAL CONSULTANTS: professionals hired by politicians to devise, coordinate, and advise on communications strategies

Overview

By reporting and discussing politics and government activities, the media influence the conduct of government in three major areas. Media coverage helps to determine who has governmental authority and political power, and it shapes political strategies. Its attentions or lack thereof affect government's ability to make policy and solve problems. People in government and outside government who seek to influence public policies are aware of the media's power and consequently try to influence media content.

Focusing on individuals rather than government institutions, the media have altered the pathway of political power. Traditionally, people who wanted to run for public office had to be affiliated with a political party and rise through the ranks of the party hierarchy, moving gradually from local government offices to positions at the state and national level. With the growth of the media, particularly television, individuals have an alternative way of reaching potential supporters. If a person can gain media attention—by creating conflict or by introducing controversial or unusual ideas, for example—he or she does not have to rely on the party to generate support. Party affiliation is still beneficial, even essential, perhaps, but political candidates' and government officials' access to the media allows them more autonomy in their decision making. They are less beholden to the party for their success, leaving parties with little way to discipline officials who oppose the party position.

Similarly, media coverage of individuals has contributed to the decentralization of power in Congress. Young members of Congress have discovered that they can take their opinions and policy ideas to the media rather than waiting until they gain seniority or chair committees to obtain power and be heard. Their willingness to talk to reporters, combined with congressional reforms, has spread power in Congress among many members.

Aside from transforming government power structures, the media have made agenda setting a central concern in both campaigning and governing. By emphasizing some issues and ignoring others, the media help determine what the public thinks is important and therefore what issues the government is expected to deal with. These priorities are referred to as an agenda. Not every issue or problem can be addressed, so competition for the public agenda is fierce. Public leaders try to direct media attention toward issues they consider important and that coincide with their capabilities, while others in government and groups or individuals outside government seek media attention to highlight different concerns. Whoever wins the battle for control of the agenda can to a large extent determine to what the government will devote its time and resources.

The media's reporting on public opinion polls has made politicians hypersensitive to gaining public support for their positions. Leaders want to maintain public approval not only to ensure their reelection, but also to improve their bargaining position. Having public opinion behind them gives public officials leeway to compromise and more power to persuade others to support their positions. Presidents have increasingly found that they can go around opposition in Congress by appealing directly to the public to back their policies. Likewise, when members of Congress know the president does not have popular support, they are more likely to reject the president's plans in favor of their own. Therefore, public officials try to present themselves and their policies to the media in ways that will generate favorable coverage. They focus on benefits while avoiding discussion of a plan's costs. This desire for public approval often leads politicians to make public promises that will be favored by the public but may in reality be unfeasible.

This direct communication with the public encouraged and facilitated by the mass media also provides an alternative to face-to-face communication among those inside government. As political power has become less concentrated, more individuals must be consulted to pass legislation and make policy. The media give members of Congress or the executive branch of government a way to reach many politicians at once. The president and members of Congress can test support for alternatives by leaking them to the media—known as floating trial balloons. Along with their coverage of trial balloons, the media will frequently seek the reactions of key politicians to these proposals. In this way, policymakers can learn where others stand on an issue or plan without actually meeting with them.

The increased use of the media in campaigning and policy-making has led to the rise of political consultants—professionals employed by politicians to devise and coordinate media and communications strategies. The president has a communications director in addition to press secretaries and other media relations personnel, and almost all members of Congress have at least one press secretary. Although they are not elected and many have little policy expertise, political consultants often have an important effect on policy because they advise presidents and members of Congress on what policies the public will support and how proposals should be communicated.

The media have opened up many government processes to the public. Television cameras and reporters have been permitted in congressional committee hearings since the 1970's. C-SPAN and C-SPANII enable the public to see some parts of both chambers of Congress in action. Presidential press conferences are often televised live. Court television reveals aspects of the legal system at work. Even meetings that take place away from the glare of television cameras may be accessible to the media through information leaked by the participants.

This coverage has allowed interested citizens and groups to become more informed about government. They can see how political processes work and the points at which they can influence policy. Only those who are interested in politics, however, are likely to pay attention to and benefit from the opening up of political processes. There is no evidence that coverage will motivate those who are indifferent to or disillusioned with government. Furthermore, the media choose what to report on, leaving many issues, problems, and activities uncovered, or only partly covered. What is more, much coverage is at best incomplete, representing only one side of the story. In sum, the media's coverage of government is a mixed blessing. It informs some and ignores others. It brings issues to public attention but encourages attempts at solutions that are more suited to the media's limitations than to the issues at hand. Such limitations include the brevity and simplicity of television debate.

Greater media access to political processes has been accompanied by some unintended consequences for debate and government's ability to solve complex problems. Publicity can make compromise more difficult. Because political actors are encouraged by the media to take firm positions on issues, they are portrayed in the press as weak willed if they back away from these stances in negotiating policy. Thus, officials do not always have the flexibility necessary for bargaining. At the same time, if they refuse to compromise, they may be depicted as rigid and inflexible.

The possibility that policy debates may become public also limits the policy options available to officials as they try to avoid alternatives that would evoke an unfavorable public response. With more people involved in the policy-making process because of the dispersal of political power, bargaining is essential to reach solutions. As compromise becomes more difficult, it can become more difficult for government to solve society's problems.

Given these obstacles to the process of negotiation in the public spotlight, political officials may opt for more informal, off-the-record discussions. While this secrecy may enable politicians to make policy, it also makes it harder for the public to hold elected leaders accountable for their actions.

Applications

In 1980, Ronald Reagan, with no experience in national government, after defeating several primary opponents who were Washington insiders, then bested the incumbent, President Jimmy Carter, to become president of the United States. His administration's strategies, particularly in getting his economic proposals through Congress quickly, demonstrate the dramatic influence of the media on the conduct of government. Two of his closest advisers—Michael Deaver and David Gergen—were primarily concerned with communications and media relations tactics.

In an effort to control the public agenda, they instituted the line-of-the-day strategy. Each day, the president's appearances and speeches were coordinated around one theme, allowing both visual and verbal reinforcement. The topic was also disseminated to all the departments in the executive branch. Thus, all executive officials could emphasize one major issue or idea, leaving the media little choice but to cover the president's theme, which, at that time, was generally some aspect of economic recovery. This helped to keep Congress and the public focused on the president's agenda.

Borrowing heavily from Reagan's campaign strategies, his advisers utilized Reagan's personality and high personal approval rating to sell his policies. They focused on Reagan's image as a strong leader rather than on the substance and details of his policies, which would have been more difficult and less appealing for the media to convey. Reagan did not hesitate to make direct public appeals. When he appeared to be losing momentum on his first economic package in Congress, Reagan scheduled a prime-time televised speech to Congress that refocused attention and boosted his public support. Within two months the plan was passed.

While the Reagan Administration illustrated how government officials can employ strategies that use media coverage to their advantage, the first year of Bill Clinton's presidency revealed the obstacles that the media can build against compromise and the decisive handling of complex problems. Clinton's effective use of the media through television talk shows, plus his ability to focus media attention on the economy, facilitated his 1992 election as president in spite of his lack of experience in national office. Once he became president, however, the media caused numerous problems for Clinton.

Even though Clinton had a Democratic majority in both houses of Congress, he quickly discovered that many members would not vote the party line. The result was a series of battles in Congress over Clinton's proposals, with perhaps the most dramatic being the budget vote. Media coverage of the budget began unfavorably as Clinton was forced by new estimates of the federal deficit to renege on his campaign promise of a middle-class tax cut; in fact, he admitted that some new taxes would be necessary.

To test support for various options, Clinton sent up trial balloons, disclosing that he was considering an energy tax designed to help the environment by taxing the least efficient fuels the most. Anticipating public anger about new taxes, Clinton gave a televised prime-time address from the White House, explaining the environmental benefits of the energy tax and insisting that only the wealthiest citizens would bear the brunt of other tax increases. This direct public appeal might have worked, but members of Congress responded with their own televised public appeals, in the form of press conferences, in which they opposed the budget in general and the energy tax specifically. With opposition mounting, Clinton gave up the energy tax for a small gas tax, and consideration of any major tax hikes that would obviously affect the middle class was no longer an option.

As the vote approached in the Senate, it became clear that Republicans would vote against the Clinton budget. The president then began to try to negotiate with undecided Democrats. Most of these members were not in particularly powerful positions in Congress. Some were only in their first term. Many of them called press conferences to discuss their doubts about the budget plan, indirectly (or in some cases, directly) communicating to the president what it would take to win their vote. Clinton made deals with many of them, and the budget passed the Senate by one vote, with the vice president casting the decisive vote. The media, during this affair, portrayed Clinton as too willing to compromise and very weak on principles. The image made an impression on members of Congress, who held out their votes on other legislation, such as the North American Free Trade Agreement, in hopes of receiving favors from the president.

Context

The media have become the primary means of communication between elected officials and citizens, leading to the raising of a number of concerns. Many have criticized the media for not providing the kind of information necessary for citizens to participate effectively in a democracy and to hold to their elected officials accountable. Content analysis of news coverage of government shows that the media rely heavily on government and official sources for their stories. Noting the increase in the use of campaign tactics for governing, some scholars have worried that government leaders have become so adept at strategic communication—using the media to accomplish their goals—that journalists can no longer fill their traditional role as watchdogs over government. Consequently, the public is likely to learn only what government wants it to know, allowing politicians to avoid responsibility for their actions.

While some have argued that the media do not provide the right kind of information for citizens to participate in government, others have suggested that the media have encouraged more citizen participation. Television has allowed citizens to see how Congress works and how they can influence the policy process. C-SPAN allows viewers to learn about more issues facing Congress than merely the ones the news media deem important. Talk shows on radio and public access television give audiences a chance to call in and participate in public debate. In addition, the media's extensive use and reporting of public opinion polls gives the impression that public preferences matter to those in government. In these ways, the media encourage people to voice their opinions.

This raises the question of how responsive government should be to citizens' preferences. There is a consensus that government should fall in line with the general values and preferences of its constituents. Unfortunately, the opinions expressed in polls and call-in shows are more likely to be gut reactions to the events of the moment rather than well-reasoned positions that consider broader contexts and long-term implications. By focusing on these snapshot views, the media may place pressure on politicians to cater to short-term demands to the detriment of the public's long-term interest.

In light of these issues and concerns, the media's effects on the conduct of government may force citizens to rethink their ideas of what effective participation in democracy is and what representative government means.

Bibliography

Ansolabehere, Stephen, Roy Behr, and Shanto Iyengar. *The Media Game: American Politics in the Television Age.* New York: Macmillan, 1993. Tells how television influences various aspects of politics.

Bennett, W. Lance, and David L. Paletz, eds. *Taken by Storm: The Media, Public Opinion, and U.S. Foreign Policy in the Gulf War.* Chicago: University of Chicago Press, 1994. Illuminating essays on the relationships among the media, public opinion, and U.S. foreign policy before, during, and after the Gulf War.

Cook, Timothy E. *Making Laws and Making News: Media Strategies in the U.S. House of Representatives.* Washington, D.C.: Brookings Institution, 1989. One of the few books that examines the relationship between the media and members of Congress in detail.

Grossman, Michael B., and Martha J. Kumar. *Portraying the President.* Baltimore: The Johns Hopkins University Press, 1981. Describes the president's relationship with the press, with a detailed discussion of the president's communications organization.

Iyengar, Shanto, and Donald Kinder. *News That Matters: Television and American Opinion.* Chicago: University of Chicago Press, 1987. Presents evidence from a series of experiments that show the effects of television news on agenda setting and priming.

Manheim, Jarol. *All of the People, All the Time.* Armonk, N.Y.: M. E. Sharpe, 1991. Looks at politicians' and other elites' improved ability to use the media in strategic communication and the problems associated with this development.

C. Danielle Vinson
David L. Paletz

Cross-References

MERCANTILISM

Field of study: Political philosophy

Mercantilism is an economic philosophy wherein a nation accumulates money and precious metals through the export of high-quality and cost-competitive manufactured goods and services. By restricting foreign investment and instituting import barriers and punitive taxes against foreign goods, it attempts to develop a favorable balance-of-trade regime in order to increase the state's material wealth and national power at the expense of other nations.

Principal terms
> FAVORABLE BALANCE OF TRADE: situation in which a nation sells more goods and services to other nations than it buys
> NATIONAL ECONOMIC POWER: cumulative total of a state's generation of wealth based upon both successful exports trading and imports restriction policies with other nations
> PROTECTIONISM: policy of protecting domestic manufacturing and other sectors of the domestic economy through administrative rules, restrictive tax policies, and other discriminatory laws
> WEALTH: generation of gold and other forms of bullion for the state's treasury through the selling of more high-valued and cost-competitive manufacturing goods and services to other states than those goods and services sold to it

Overview

The historical and philosophical origins of mercantilism both as an economic system and a discourse on economic thought arose from a unique European approach to statecraft and policy. Beginning in the early fifteenth century, leading economic thinkers of Europe (especially the British) suggested that newly emerging nation-states could increase their national wealth and economic power significantly by orientating their economies toward maximization of international trade. They addressed such strategic economic issues as how nation-states could grow rich; what is meant by a nation's riches; whether a nation's money or bullion should be sent to foreign countries; how much should a nation protect its domestic manufacturing industry; whether a nation should buy foreign goods; and whether a nation's raw materials should be sent to foreign states. Most early European economic thinkers who addressed these issues were both self-interested merchants and hard-headed empiricists. They were leading members of emerging national commercial societies intent on shedding the moral and religious influences of the archaic late medieval European precapitalist economic system, which was more concerned with the moral distribution of wealth than with the purely economic issues and questions of how to produce material wealth that would add to national power and statecraft.

In response to the political problems and economic questions that emerged with the rise of the nation-state and the market system, economists developed the balance-of-trade theory, which became the empirical basis of the European mercantilist system. This theory argued that nation-states could increase their wealth and power by exchanging goods and services with other states, with the aim of earning gold, silver, and other forms of money or bullion in exchange. Simply put, it was argued that a nation-state that exported more manufactured goods than it imported could produce wealth and power to meet its security and welfare needs. Despite their general agreement on this point, early European thinkers viewed mercantilism not as a coherent economic system, but as a discourse, a language, a process, and a theory of ideas addressing a wide range of political, economic, and societal problems and international trade issues associated with the rise of the nation-state and its search for security and welfare.

From the early sixteenth until the late eighteenth century, mercantilism, or its variants, developed from a vibrant ongoing continental-wide European discourse. This discourse produced brilliant and original thinkers who approached the mercantilist discourse with deep nationalist attitudes while trying to develop a "general science of trade" in order to maximize the wealth and power of their own countries. These thinkers included Spain's Luiz Ortiz and Geroinmo de Uztaritz; Italy's Antonio Giovanni Botero, Galiani, and Cesare Beccarri; France's Jean Bodin, Antoine de Monchretien, and Jean Baptiste Cobert; Germany and Austria's Johann Joachim Becher, Wilheim von Schroder, and Joseph von Sonnenfels; Great Britain's Thomas Mun, William Petty, John Locke, and Adam Smith; and many others.

These thinkers concerned themselves with a variety of economic, industrial, and trade policy issues. These included how to develop profitable domestic manufacturing and semimanufacturing export industries; how to accumulate and keep gold, silver, and other bullion and raw materials for the benefit of one's own country; how to export high-valued manufactures to other states to attract gold, silver, and other forms of bullion as payment for raw materials imported; and how to translate these trading, monetary, and economic gains toward strengthening the nation-state and financing their wars with other European states. The favorable balance of trade became an important political and economic paradigm. It represented a central means by which to measure whether a nation-state was meeting its strategic goals.

Because of the variance in political, economic, social, cultural, and legal institutions that existed among European countries, it would be incorrect to conclude that "mercantilism" as a economic ideology or as a trading system was accepted as a new science of economics, trade, and wealth promotion; or that there was a unified consensus on what mercantilism actually meant. The historical reality is that there was never full agreement among European thinkers on the correct means to create and maintain wealth and power in a mercantilist system. There was, however, total agreement that the pursuit of wealth to acquire national power was worth pursuing as a matter of statecraft and policy.

Applications

A modern example of mercantilist or neomercantilist behavior by a nation-state in the international economy is Japan, which exhibits most of the classical elements of a mercantilist state. It exports high-quality and cost-competitive manufacturing and technological goods to capture foreign market share and control. It also protects its domestic manufacturing, technological, and other strategic national industries from foreign investment and goods penetration with protectionist, administrative, and tax measures in order to maintain a favorable balance of trade with all its trading partners, and it accumulates large quantities of gold, silver, and other forms of bullion and national wealth from other trading states.

Japan's experimentation with mercantilist principles began in the late nineteenth century with its reluctant opening to the United States and the West, and the sending of its brightest students to the United States and Western Europe to study Western capitalism. Then keenly aware of its structural inability to compete with the West economically, industrially, financially, and militarily, Japan began the internal governmental, administrative, and ideological processes of changing from an agrarian-based economy to that of a major industrial capitalist economy with broad mercantilist dimensions. It intended to end its national deficiencies and become a global economic, industrial, financial, and military power.

During the Meiji Reformation (1860-1934), leading Japanese reformers in and out of government followed the slogan "enrich the nation, strengthen the army" with the purpose of competing effectively and quickly with the West. As Christopher Layne, an international economic historian on Japan, points out, Japan in 1874 developed a mercantilist orientation with the national government participating fully in developing the productive labor capacity of the population through education, and providing administrative support and economic subsidies for the expansion of manufacturing, trade, and shipping export opportunities to increase its wealth accumulation and national power. From 1934 to the beginning of World War II, Japan continued its rapid neo-mercantilist development, as it began to ship semi-manufactured and manufactured products to foreign markets, enabling it to import the raw materials it needed for further economic and industrial development and to maintain a favorable balance of trade with other nations.

After the economic devastation of World War II, Japan returned to its mercantilist policies. It decided that the only way that it could again compete with the United States and the West was to regain its economic and financial strength. To achieve this, its leaders decided to protect its strategic industries (steel, manufacturing, energy, agriculture, and others) by developing high-quality and cost-competitive semimanufactured and manufactured goods which it could sell on the international market, and to begin the process of accumulating wealth and bullion and thereby develop its national power to global economic, industrial, and financial levels. To these ends, Japan erected administrative and economic barriers to the entry for foreign goods and services, put in place discriminatory tax structures on imported foreign goods and services, and instituted protectionist policies to protect strategic domestic industries from foreign competition. At the same time, Japan developed mercantilist-oriented export strategies for its manufactured and other high-valued goods in order to acquire both market penetration and market share, and to command critical market niches in other nations' manufacturing and high-technology sectors, with the goal of accelerating the acquisition of wealth and power which comes from a mercantilist economic strategy.

In hindsight, Japan has reaped the full benefits of a highly productive and wealth-producing mercantilist economy, which ranks second in total wealth in the world behind the United States. By protecting its manufacturing, high-technology, auto, and other high-valued strategic industrial sectors from significant foreign penetration while simultaneously exporting such high-valued goods to other states, it built strong account surpluses with other nations and amassed a huge financial reserve. The drawback to Japan's mercantilist economy, however, is that by closing its domestic markets to foreign investment and goods and by maintaining its strong export orientation, the value of its currency, the yen, rose so high that it threatened to undermine Japan's most efficient industries, while also threatening to reward its most inefficient sectors, such as agriculture. As a result, Japan's mercantilist orientation developed into a major irritant to nations which transfer their national wealth to Japan, with little chance of selling their own goods and services to reduce either their mounting trade deficit or their continuing wealth transfer. This political economy situation is the downside of mercantilist strategies in the post-Cold War global economy.

Context

The system of feudalism in continental Europe from the twelfth to the late fifteenth century was the primary form of economic development and material progress. This system, steeped in religious and moral conceptions of humanity's role in the economic universe, took the view that wealth had to be distributed based on religious values and principles, and not on market-based or empirical laws. Economic thinkers in the Middle Ages wanted an economy that favored the "moral" distribution of wealth over the production of material wealth. At the same time, however, it was a period of independent lords and private landowners who effectively worked against the economic interests of their lands by taxing the use of highways and rivers in their immediate territories and generally impeding trade and commerce. Another primary economic activity of these individuals was to use cheap labor to engage in agricultural and semi-industrial pursuits for their own benefit, and often at the economic expense of their sovereigns.

This medieval form of territorial capitalism with a moral face gave way to a new mode of economic thought and policy. With the rise of the nation-state, there emerged forms of society and organization never seen before in continental Europe, as well as the birth of a rational and empirical view of the economic universe. In line with this revolutionary transition from religion to empiricism in the early sixteenth century, a new form of economic thinking was born in Europe called "mercantilism." Philosophically, it represented a fundamental shift away from the moral-distribution-of-wealth theology which had dominated the late medieval period, and issued in a revolutionary movement toward an empirical and scientific perspective on market forces and material factors associated with people, the society, and the nation-state in the emerging system of global capitalism.

With its theoretical origins in Great Britain, early mercantilist thought suggested that "economic wealth was a function of trade and manufacture," and that the negative balance of payments problem, so much a part of trade policy, was not attributable to evil speculation and usury, but to the problem of the balance of exports and imports. In other words, with the rise of a scientific approach to understanding economic behavior, the line had been crossed from religion to empirical analysis of what the market was composed of, how it operated and why, and who was going to benefit, among other economic dynamics, all within the context of the nation-state and its institutions.

At the statecraft level, however, mercantilism was a political, economic, and cultural response to an increasingly dangerous world of military rivalry and techno-logical change occurring throughout continental Europe, and a new economic and trading methodology and approach by which to manage and control these novel developments. In this regard, the late sixteenth century was a period of conflict between the states of Europe, all of which felt vulnerable to the others' economic potential and military strength. They concluded that wealth generated the power needed to ensure their security and economic well-being in a world of dangerous nation-state competition. Jacob Viner, an early twentieth century economic historian and observer of the mercantilist period in Europe, argued that four propositions defined European mercantilist thought: that wealth is essential to power; that power is essential to wealth; that wealth and power are both proper ends of national policy; and that there is a long-run harmony to these ends.

During the seventeenth century, European states viewed the mercantilist economy as a system, lawlike, rigorous, and subject to market forces, wherein prices, wages, interest rates, monetary values, and other market factors interacted to produce out-comes critical to the nation-state's security and welfare. As a result, European states were concerned with the most efficient means of generating wealth—either through the export of manufactures or the hoarding of gold and bullion—in order to finance wars, to engage their populations in meaningful work, and to strengthen the economic bases of their national power. In summary, economic expansion through foreign trade, producing gold and bullion through such trade, internal control over raw materials, and strong administrative structures to strengthen the nation-state became the rule and not the exception throughout Europe from the late fifteenth until the eighteenth century.

Bibliography

Buck, Philip W. *The Politics of Mercantilism.* New York: Henry Holt & Co., 1942. A fine book on the politics of English mercantilism as a subdiscipline of national trade and economic policy.

Coleman, Donald C., ed. *Revisions in Mercantilism.* London: Methuen, 1969. Excellent and well-written compilation of articles by major mercantilist thinkers accessible to high school and college students.

Heckscher, Eli F. *Mercantilism*. Translated by Mendel Shapiro. 2 vols. London: Allen & Unwin, 1935. Classic analysis and treatment of mercantilism written by an acknowledged expert.

McFarland, Floyd B. *Economic Philosophy and American Problems*. Savage, Md.: Rowman & Littlefield, 1991. Excellent treatment of the philosophy of economics, particularly useful for high school and college students wishing to understand the evolution and development of mercantilism and economic history from an American perspective.

Magnusson, Lars. *Mercantilism: The Shaping of an Economic Language*. New York: Routledge, 1994. Well-written work that takes the view that mercantilism is a literature, a discourse, on trade and economics.

Minchinton, Walter E., ed. *Mercantilism: System or Expediency?* Lexington, Mass.: D. C. Heath, 1969. Well-edited collection of essays on mercantilism by some of the leading economic theorists of Western capitalism.

Smith, Adam. *An Inquiry into the Nature and Causes of the Wealth of Nations*. Edited by Roy H. Campbell, Andrew S. Skinner, and W. B. Todd. Oxford, England: Clarendon Press, 1976. This modern edition of Smith's classic work contains an excellent analysis of his perspectives on English mercantilism thought and practice. Also has a useful index and bibliography.

Michael J. Siler

Cross-References

Commerce Regulation, p. 357; Force, p. 712; Foreign Relations, p. 718; Government Roles, p. 778; History of Government, p. 829; Industrialization, p. 916; Isolationism and Protectionism, p. 1000; National Economies, p. 1248; National Security, p. 1261; Political Economy, p. 1455; Power Divisions in Governments, p. 1578; Power in Politics, p. 1584; Realpolitik, p. 1668; The State, p. 1878; Trade with Foreign Nations, p. 2000.

MEXICO: POLITICS AND GOVERNMENT

Field of study: Comparative government

The Mexican political system has been characterized by single-party rule since 1929. The rise of opposition parties and the development of a closer relationship with the United States, however, have introduced new challenges for the national government and the dominant party.

> *Principal terms*
> CHIEF EXECUTIVE: leader of the administrative branch of government
> LEGITIMACY: general public's respect for and support of a government
> NAFTA (NORTH AMERICAN FREE TRADE AGREEMENT): 1993 treaty that provides for Mexico, the United States, and Canada to reduce tariffs and other barriers to trade
> PAN (NATIONAL ACTION PARTY): Mexico's main opposition party since 1939, generally conservative in orientation
> PRD (DEMOCRATIC REVOLUTIONARY PARTY): leftist party that became important in national politics in the 1980's
> PRI (PARTY OF THE INSTITUTIONAL REVOLUTION): Mexico's dominant political party since 1929 (known as the PNR, for National Revolutionary Party, from 1929 to 1938 and the PRM, for Party of the Mexican Revolution, from 1938 to 1946)
> SECRETARIAT: large government agency or department

Overview

Mexico's long history has been characterized by two closely related tendencies: a centralized system of government and power concentrated in the hands of the chief executive. For most of the centuries of Spanish colonial rule (1519-1821), the viceroy in Mexico City controlled the enforcement of Spanish law, commanded the imperial army, and exercised authority in economic and religious affairs. Mexico's achievement of independence from Spain in 1821 was followed by a half century of political turmoil that ended with the rise of another powerful chief executive in the person of Porfirio Díaz, who dominated the nation from 1876 to 1910. Díaz extended the strengths of the presidency to become a dictator who, much like the viceroys had before him, used executive authority to enlarge the role of the central government.

The revolution that overthrew Díaz in 1911 ushered in a decade of civil conflict as rival factions fought for control of the central government. A step toward stability came with the adoption of the constitution of 1917, which gave the national government a more active role in dealing with economic and social problems. Political calm returned in the 1920's only to be threatened in 1928 when president-elect Alvaro Obregón, a hero of the revolution and president from 1920 to 1924, fell victim to assassination. In 1929, as conditions seemed to worsen, another former president, Plutarco Elías Calles, wielded his extraordinary influence to form the National Revolutionary Party

(PNR, later known as PRI), a highly structured party that concentrated power at the national level.

In the decades since its revolutionary experience, Mexico's national government has been led by a powerful president who controls a cabinet made up of approximately twenty major government agencies, including the secretariats of defense and foreign relations. As a result of the demands for public education during the revolutionary years, Mexico has a national secretariat of education. The government also emphasizes the promotion of economic growth, which makes the secretary of the treasury an important position. The president and the cabinet officials have broad discretion in the formulation and enforcement of national policies. Although federalism (the reservation of rights and responsibilities by state and local governments) is incorporated into some aspects of Mexico's political system, the focus of political power is Mexico City and not the provincial capitals. The limited state budgets and the even more restricted resources of municipalities mean that these lower levels of government can provide few services. In public education, for example, the national secretariat of education has the dominant role in funding schools and training teachers.

Although the executive is the most powerful branch of the government, the legislature does have important functions. Mexico's legislature is bicameral, with a chamber of deputies and a senate. The chamber of deputies is the larger and more influential of the two, having approximately five hundred members; the senate has sixty-four members. In theory, the chamber of deputies acts on proposals submitted by the president. In practice, the president is almost certain to see his or her initiatives passed because the chief executive has great influence within the ruling Party of the Institutional Revolution (PRI). The president, therefore, has a major role in the selection of the slate of candidates for election to the chamber. One of the main duties of the senate is to consider appointments to high positions in the executive branch. Although senate review is largely a formality, the president's choices for appointments can stimulate controversy and media coverage in cases in which irregularities appear.

The third branch of government is the judiciary. Compared to the independent-minded Supreme Court of the United States (and its practice of evaluating legislation), the Mexican Supreme Court is rather restricted in its scope. In general, the Mexican courts do not rule on whether laws initiated by the chief executive and passed by the legislature are in accord with the constitution. Instead, the Mexican judiciary, from the Supreme Court to the state and local courts, confines itself to the application of the law to individual cases. Appointments to the Supreme Court are not for life and tend to involve politics; judges have little insulation from outside influences.

One of the most distinctive aspects of the Mexican political system has been the domination of a single party, the PRI, since 1929. According to the constitution, Mexico is a representative democracy, with regular elections for the presidency, the chamber of deputies, and the senate. The key to understanding the structure of Mexican political power, however, is that for more than half a century the PRI has won most of the important elections, especially the presidential elections. All twelve men elected to the presidency between 1930 and 1994 were members of the PRI. Their control of the party machinery enabled them to influence the outcome of local and state elections as well as the contests for the chamber of deputies and the senate. That the chief of the executive branch is also the commanding figure in the nation's major political party helps to explain Mexico's record of relative stability since 1929 and suggests that the historical traditions of the Spanish viceroy and Porfirio Díaz continue to have relevance in Mexican politics.

Although the PRI holds extraordinary power, it does not have complete control of the political system. Since 1939, the PAN has been Mexico's main opposition party. The PAN gained more than 10 percent of the popular vote in the 1964 election and has usually received at least that amount in subsequent elections. A second opposition party, the PRD, emerged in the presidential election of 1988. It consists of a loose coalition of leftist parties led by Cuauhtémoc Cárdenas, the son of Mexico's popular president from 1934 to 1940, Lázaro Cárdenas. The PRD and the PAN serve as channels for the expression of discontent with the PRI. In the dramatic presidential election of 1988, with public frustration at a peak, the PRD received 31 percent of the vote, the PAN had 17 percent, and the PRI candidate, Carlos Salinas de Gortari, won with a slim majority of 51 percent. In 1994, the PRI candidate, Ernesto Zedillo, won by a narrow margin. He received approximately 50 percent of the vote. The PAN increased its vote to 29 percent, and the PRD fell to 16 percent. In spite of the PRI's record of consecutive victories, the PAN and the PRD have become important factors in Mexican politics.

Applications

A major challenge to the Mexican political system is the establishment of its legitimacy with the Mexican people. The public's demands for social justice during the long revolutionary period of 1910 to 1940 left a lasting impression on the nation's political leaders. One of the crucial events in the quest for social justice occurred in the presidency of Lázaro Cárdenas. Elected in 1934 as the PNR candidate, Cárdenas took the leftist goals of the party's platform seriously. When a dispute between Mexican oil workers and large multinational oil corporations erupted, the nation's supreme court ruled in favor of the workers. The oil companies defied both the workers and the supreme court, only to discover that Cárdenas was not intimidated. On March 18, 1938, he ordered the expropriation of the corporation's properties; the Mexican government took possession of them. In the international uproar that followed, Mexico faced the threat of military intervention. Eventually, Mexico and the United States negotiated a peaceful settlement to the dispute, including financial compensation for the oil companies. Cárdenas, whose expropriation order had established him as an immensely popular president, had also enhanced the legitimacy of the national government as a defender of the workers of Mexico.

For a generation after the Cárdenas presidency, the nation's political leaders seemed to be guiding Mexico along the path to greater economic prosperity and increased levels of participation in politics. The government, the PRI, and the nation suffered a shock, however, in 1968. Gustavo Díaz Ordaz, who was president from 1964 to 1970, committed the resources of his administration to hosting the summer Olympics in Mexico City. He and his cabinet saw the international attention generated by the Olympics as an opportunity to display Mexico's impressive economic growth to the world. The Mexican people, supportive to some extent, also expressed doubts about the expenditure of large amounts of government money for Olympic construction projects and other preparations while many social and educational programs lacked funding. Student protests began to grow, especially in Mexico City. On August 27, an estimated half million people jammed into the large public square in front of the presidential offices to demonstrate their opposition to the Díaz Ordaz government. The government responded with armored cars and tanks. After several injuries and one death, the protesters dispersed, but tensions continued to build. Several weeks later, a crowd assembled in a large open area in a section of the city known as Tlatelolco. The exact sequence of events that transpired there on October 2, 1968, remains unclear, but the outcome had major implications for the national government and its relationship with the Mexican people. The army and police used military vehicles and automatic weapons against the demonstrators, some of whom may have been armed. The confrontation was one-sided. Officials admitted that about fifty demonstrators died, but most informed observers place the number who perished much higher—as many as four hundred more. The Olympics took place as scheduled but at a very high cost to the legitimacy of the government.

Aware of the growth of opposition to the government and to the PRI in the 1970's and 1980's, Carlos Salinas de Gortari, president from 1988 to 1994, initiated basic changes in the political and economic life of the nation. Inaugurated half a century after Lázaro Cárdenas' expropriation of the foreign-owned oil properties, Salinas turned Mexico in an entirely different direction: the privatization of government-operated businesses in order to attract foreign investors. Salinas ordered the sale of the telephone system to a private corporation, Teléfonos de México, and turned over other government agencies to private ownership. At the same time, the Salinas Administration negotiated, signed, and implemented the North American Free Trade Agreement (NAFTA). The agreement opened Mexico to integration into the North American economy. Salinas was adept at the promotion of NAFTA as the crowning achievement of his administration, but uncertainties loomed large in his last year in office as a result of the assassination of the PRI presidential candidate Donaldo Colosio during the summer campaign of 1994. The PRI's second choice, Ernesto Zedillo, won a narrow victory and then faced an economic crisis early in his tenure with a sharp drop in the value of the peso in 1995. As the Mexican people absorbed the first waves of higher prices for imports from the United States as a result of the peso's sudden decline, foreign investors pulled their money out of Mexico, causing a sudden drop in the Mexican stock market. Despite Salinas' public relations campaign for NAFTA, Zedillo and the Mexican political system faced a restive and heavily burdened public.

Context

Mexico has had a unique role in world affairs because of its shared border with the

United States. There are few cases in which a developing nation shares a border with an industrialized global power. Since the late nineteenth century the United States has been an international leader in economic expansion and technological innovation while Mexico has struggled to rise above the problems typical of developing nations, including limited capital for investment, a small domestic market for manufactured goods, and widespread poverty. The two-thousand-mile border that runs from the Gulf of Mexico to the Pacific Ocean has often been crossed by American investors looking for profitable enterprises in mining, petroleum, cattle ranching, and low-cost manufacturing. The border has also been crossed by Mexican workers moving north to find employment in agriculture and industry. The Mexican government must deal with these flows of investments and people. To an extent that is unusual, if not unique, in world affairs, the Mexican political system faces immense pressures not only from the demands of its own people, but also from its rich and powerful neighbor. The United States has the material wealth, technological capacity, and political strength to buttress or to undercut policies that originate in Mexico City. NAFTA brings the two nations closer together, with formal treaty obligations that require more extensive cooperation between the governments of Mexico and the United States.

These closer ties with the United States mean that the ability of the Mexican government to earn the respect and support of its people is even more essential to the political well-being of the nation. In the 1980's and early 1990's, opinion polls revealed that the general public has less confidence in the national government than it did in other institutions such as the Roman Catholic church and public schools. Widespread distrust of politicians and cynicism toward politics have established barriers to the legitimization of the government and also have created complications in the democratization of the political process. The late twentieth century trend toward democracy in Latin America makes the continued hold of the PRI on the government increasingly controversial. In a sense, democratization is at work in the surge in popularity of the PAN and the PRD since the 1970's. They have become serious rivals to the PRI in many parts of Mexico. The PRI's leaders, a resilient and resourceful group for more than half a century, continue to face broad challenges in popular demands for a more open political system and in uneasy mixtures of popular hope and doubt about the effects of NAFTA.

Bibliography

Camp, Roderic. *Politics in Mexico*. New York: Oxford University Press, 1993. Succinct study of the cultural, social, and economic factors in Mexican politics.

Jenkins, Barbara. *The Paradox of Continental Production: National Investment Policies in North America*. Ithaca, N.Y.: Cornell University Press, 1992. Has much to say about the economic and political context behind NAFTA. Argues that governments will continue to play major roles in the process of international economic integration, particularly through currency exchange rates, taxes on corporations, and investment incentives.

Langley, Lester. *MexAmerica: Two Countries, One Future*. New York: Crown, 1988.

Entertaining survey of the coming together of Mexico and the United States at a variety of levels from complex issues involving politics and economics to the day-to-day matters involving cultural and personal interactions.

Mabry, Donald J. *Mexico's Acción Nacional: A Catholic Alternative to Revolution.* Syracuse, N.Y.: Syracuse University Press, 1973. Pioneering examination of the PAN. Concentrates on the crucial period from 1939 to the early 1970's, when the PAN struggled to become a factor in national politics.

Meyer, Michael, and William Sherman. *The Course of Mexican History.* 4th ed. New York: Oxford University Press, 1991. Traces Mexican history from the Maya and Aztec eras to the late twentieth century. The last sixteen chapters cover the revolution and the period of PRI domination.

Pastor, Robert, and Jorge Castañeda. *Limits to Friendship: The United States and Mexico.* New York: Alfred A. Knopf, 1988. Features contrapuntal chapters by the two authors analyzing the perspectives of their two countries on issues such as attitudes and stereotypes, political leadership, economic integration, foreign policy, the drug trade, and the border region.

Riding, Alan. *Distant Neighbors: A Portrait of the Mexicans.* New York: Alfred A. Knopf, 1985. Mexico was reeling from the aftershocks of a severe financial crisis when Riding wrote this survey of political, economic, and social conditions. Focuses on the faulty policy decisions and corruption that contributed to the economic problems and the loss of public confidence in the government.

Story, Dale. *The Mexican Ruling Party: Stability and Authority.* New York: Praeger, 1986. Explores the internal workings of the PRI. Discusses the PRI's decline relative to opposition parties but insists that it has continued significance as a source of moderation and coherence.

Vazquez, Josefina, and Lorenzo Meyer. *The United States and Mexico.* Chicago: University of Chicago Press, 1985. A survey of Mexican-United States relations over two centuries.

John A. Britton

Cross-References

Comparative Government, p. 384; Developed and Developing Nations, p. 533; Immigration and Emigration, p. 868; Latino Politics, p. 1052; Legitimacy, p. 1105; One-Party Systems, p. 1350; Political Parties, p. 1485; Political Party Roles, p. 1499; Separation of Powers: Presidential Government, p. 1815.

MILITARY CONSCRIPTION AND
CONSCIENTIOUS OBJECTION

Field of study: Military

Conscription is government-mandated service in the military whose burden may fall evenly or selectively on the population. Citizens who choose to avoid military service for ethical or moral reasons are known as conscientious objectors.

Principal terms
    CONSCIENTIOUS OBJECTION: refusal to serve in the military on grounds of religious beliefs or conscience
    DRAFT: selection of people for compulsory military service
    RELIGIOUS OBJECTOR: one who holds pacifism as part of his or her religious beliefs and thereby refuses to serve in the military
    SECULAR OBJECTOR: one who refuses to perform required military service because of a personal nonreligious philosophy
    SELECTIVE SERVICE ACT: legal and procedural mechanism for the U.S. military draft

Overview

The antecedents of conscription date back to the Egyptian Old Kingdom of the twenty-seventh century B.C.E. Then, as in modern times, conscription was a means of achieving the state's goals of defense or territorial acquisition. Over time, the need to require miliary service from a citizenry has been a function of political, economic, and social forces. As societies evolved from the small units of feudalism to larger nation-states, the role of a large, professional military became more critical. By the end of the eighteenth century, no nation was deemed a power without military might and the commercial wealth needed to sustain it.

Governments came to monopolize the production and employment of military force as a way to ensure their power. Accordingly, manpower levies progressed from occasional impressment of peasants by the nobles, to a citizen militia raised by the central government, to a professional standing army employed by the government. Centralization of military power was, at the last step, complete, but standing armies were at first small and insufficient to conduct large wars. This limitation was the result of the great cost of maintaining a standing army. Large wars require mass armies and, ultimately, conscription of the masses.

Ancient Greece and Rome offer early examples of conscription under democracy. In Greece, the military forces of the city-states of Athens, Marathon, and Salamis were assembled by drafts of their respective citizenries. These drafted soldiers and sailors received no pay, were required to supply their own weapons, and served for an extended period of time. Compulsory service, with all its attendant hardship, was viewed, however, as superior to living in a state under foreign domination. Eighty percent of the qualified male citizenry served in the Athenian militia during the Periclean Age (490-429 B.C.E.).

In Rome, during the fourth and third centuries B.C.E., the entire freeborn body of male citizens was subject to conscription. The Roman draftee also received no pay and provided his own weapons. As a result, the wealthiest citizens tended to enter the cavalry, while less well-to-do citizens became infantry. The poorest, who were without property, were left home.

The Middle Ages offer but one notable example of conscription—the Swiss model, which has continued to operate, in modified form, to modern times. In 1291, three Swiss states (cantons) united in a program of universal conscription as a means of self-defense against stronger neighbors. All Swiss males aged sixteen and upward were subject to military training and service in war. Those physically unable to serve paid a compensatory tax, while draft avoiders became social and economic outcasts. Through shared sacrifice, the Swiss were able to knit a tight social fabric that has remained intact for centuries.

In 1793, Napoleonic France instituted the mass conscription, a trend that would spread across Europe, and be retained, in different forms, throughout the twentieth century. The French government enacted a draft on all men aged eighteen to twenty-five to aid in the war against Prussia and Austria. Within several months, more than a million conscripts were added to the military rolls. Exemptions were limited to the physically incapable, while the guillotine awaited draft protestors.

In the United States, the public perception of conscription and of military service in general followed the nation's evolution from a loose federation of states to a national entity. Fear of centralized government power gradually gave way to endorsement of a common purpose against foreign aggression.

The United States has historically been of two minds with respect to national defense. One opinion has been that the U.S. military be a force of military profession-als, the other that it should it be a body of citizen soldiers responding to a call to duty. The U.S. response to internal and external security threats has reflected this dichotomy.

The obligation of every able-bodied male to bear arms in times of national peril is a cornerstone of Anglo-American history. The British tradition of the citizen militia was adopted by the colonies, with one notable difference. Each American colony maintained its own militia, manned by its own citizens. This militia was a separate and distinct force from any national army. The American Revolution was fought by a small Continental (national) Army augmented by a larger force of militias from the various states. Many of the soldiers in the militias were draftees. In 1783, George Washington described the dangers that a professional army posed for nationhood, while extolling the Swiss model of universal service by citizen soldiers.

As ratified by the states in 1789, the U.S. Constitution grants legal authority to Congress to raise an army, but does not explicitly allow for drafting citizens into a standing army. Through its provisions for "calling forth the militia," however, the Constitution implicitly grants Congress authority to conscript. The constitutionality of Congress' authority to conscript citizens has survived a number of tests before the U.S. Supreme Court.

The first serious call for mass conscription in the United States was issued by President James Monroe during the War of 1812. Monroe's proposal was hotly debated in Congress but not enacted. It remained for the Civil War to provide the testing ground for conscription in the United States. Initially fought with relatively small armies of volunteers, the conflict expanded as the North and the South resorted to conscription to build their forces. Both sides were liberal in their exemption policies and allowed draftees to pay a fee, which became a bounty for the substitute soldier, in lieu of service. Resistance to the draft was vocal and violent in both camps, the bloody New York City draft riots of July, 1863, being an example.

Proponents of compulsory military training began a campaign for conscription at the beginning of the twentieth century. Their arguments were based on the inadequacies of the volunteer armed forces most recently evidenced in the Spanish-American War of 1898.

Advocates of universal military training believed that such a program would enable the nation to react quickly to foreign aggression, foster mental and physical fitness, be in keeping with the spirit of democracy by imposing a more equal burden, and guide men's natural aggression constructively.

The arguments for universal military training gained support with America's entry in World War I. The Selective Service Act of 1917 was enacted to raise armies through a draft and to establish a system of draft exemptions that would maximize the efficiency of human resources in both military and civilian employments. The military quickly grew to more than two million members. After World War I ended, the draft was quickly dismantled and the standing army was reduced to a force of less than two hundred thousand. By 1939, the U.S. armed forces had shrunk to the seventeenth largest in the world.

The onset of World War II in Europe led to the Draft Act of 1940, which established the first U.S. peacetime system of conscription. American entry into the war in 1941 allowed for automatic extensions of the draft legislation. By 1942, voluntary enlistment was shelved in favor of the draft as the more efficient allocator of human resources.

After World War II, the draft was allowed to expire in 1947. In 1948, however, following the Soviet Union's success in expanding its influence into Europe and the onset of the Cold War, Congress reinstituted draft legislation. During the Korean War (1950-1953) a bill came before Congress that proposed, on the principle of an even burden of military service, universal military service. The bill failed by a narrow margin.

The Vietnam War was the impetus for abandonment of conscription and the transformation of the armed services into an all-volunteer force. By the late 1960's, the draft was viewed an inequitable, inefficient, and arbitrary. The Gates Commission was convened by President Richard Nixon to consider the draft's demise. In 1973, the conscription system was dismantled after a quarter century of continuous operation.

With conscription came the conscientious objector. A conscientious objector opposes war as a matter of conscience and refuses to participate in military training or service. Conscientious objection can be traced to the Protestant Reformation in Europe, and particularly, to the Anabaptist movement. Sects within the movement (Hutterites, Mennonites) stressed pacifism and withdrawal from the greater society.

The first conscientious objectors in the United States belonged to religious groups opposed to the concept and practice of war. The Quakers arrived in 1657, followed shortly by the Mennonites, Brethren, Shakers, Christadelphians, and Rogerenes. These groups refused to take part in the militia duty required of all male citizens and, as a result, were vilified by other settlers. Eventually, however, their adamant stance against militia service was balanced by their otherwise good citizenship, hard work, and strong moral character. The sects won acceptance within their home colonies.

Problems arose when conscientious objectors were conscripted to national service, as in the Civil War. Their objections to service won no sympathy before military tribunals, composed in large part of draftees. As a result, the physical abuse of conscientious objectors was not uncommon.

Over time, the ranks of conscientious objectors became more diverse. By 1917, Jehovah's Witnesses claimed draft exemption as ministers, and were joined by the Molokans and the Dukhobors, who had emigrated from Russia to escape military service under the czar. Conscientious objectors were offered alternative, noncombatant service to fulfill their service obligation. Those who refused to participate, or who were not judged to have an adequate claim to conscientious objector status, were jailed in federal penal institutions, including Alcatraz Island in California and Fort Leavenworth in Kansas.

By the time of the Korean War, the face of conscientious objection had begun to change, becoming less religious and more secular in nature. Political and philosophical objections to war, or even some wars, shared equal stage with religious, pacifist beliefs. This evolution continued throughout the cauldron of the Vietnam War, during which, toward its end, as many young men were being exempted from service on the basis of principle, as were inducted.

Conscientious objectors (COs) can be broadly segregated as religious (pacifist religious beliefs) or secular (personal or philosophical objection to war). COs can further be classified as universal (opposed to all wars), discretionary (allowing certain weapons and disallowing others, such as nuclear bombs), or selective (considering some wars just, others not). Henry David Thoreau provides a premier example of a selective CO. Thoreau regarded, not without reason, the Mexican-American War as a means of expanding slavery in the United States. He refused to pay a tax in support of the war and, as a result, spent a night in jail. On the other hand, when John Brown led his abortive raid on Harpers Ferry as a means of provisioning a slave revolt, Thoreau praised the act. He likened the subsequent execution of Brown to the crucifixion of Christ.

Also distinguishing the degrees of conscientious objection is the willingness of the CO to comply with the will of the state. Noncombatant COs are willing to serve in the military in an unarmed, lifesaving function; typically in the medical corps. Alternativist COs agree to serve in public, nonmilitary projects such as health, education, and conservation. This form of alternative service is particularly popular under draft regimes in Europe. Absolutist COs refuse to participate in any aspect of a conscriptive system and therefore are the most likely to be prosecuted.

Applications

The Vietnam War put conscription in the United States to the ultimate test. During the 1950's, 70 to 80 percent of eligible males were needed to meet the military's quotas. There was little resistance to the draft because serving in the military had come to be regarded as part of citizenship. By the mid-1960's, the leading edge of the huge baby boom (1947-1963) generation came of age and the percentage of eligible males required by the military fell to 30 to 35 percent. Given the excess supply of eligible males, the Selective Service system widened the scope of deferments. Channeling human resources away from the military toward other occupations weakened the consensus behind conscription. Increasingly, the burden of the draft fell on the less educated, the less skilled, and minorities, while the more advantaged obtained deferments.

As the Vietnam War grew worse in the 1960's, American support for the war declined. In an effort to make the burden of the draft fairer, deferments were reduced, subjecting many college students to draft eligibility for the first time. Protests against the war and the draft became more numerous as casualty and draft rates rose. For the first time, major politicians and public figures spoke out against the futility of the Vietnam War.

Draft evasion and draft avoidance increased. During the Vietnam conflict, draftees failing to report for duty numbered approximately 500,000. An additional 50,000 are estimated to have avoided the draft by moving to Canada, Britain, and Sweden. Concurrently, the Supreme Court redefined conscientious objector status in a more inclusive manner, allowing exemptions for "beliefs that are purely ethical or moral in source." In 1971, for every 100 inductees, 42 received conscientious objector exemptions. In 1972, there were 130 conscientious objector exemptions granted for every 100 inductees. Between 1965 and 1970 more than 170,000 draft registrants were successful in applying for conscientious objector status.

In 1967, presidential candidate Nixon became a proponent of an all-volunteer military service. Upon election in 1968 he appointed a commission (the Gates Commission, chaired by former Secretary of Defense Thomas Gates) to study the abandonment of the draft and enactment of the all-volunteer service. The findings of the commission were unequivocal. From a perspective of economic efficiency, the costs of a draft (in terms of unfairness, disrupted careers, and evasion) exceeded its benefits. Viewed as a tax on both draftees and the greater society, conscription was perceived as excessively inefficient.

Consequently, the draft was abandoned in 1973, and the all-volunteer service was born. Since 1980, young men aged eighteen have been required to register for a draft, but the potential of its occurring is slim. Many questions remain about the all-volunteer service concerning its lack of representativeness, disproportionate minority composition, and ability to expand quickly in the event of national emergency.

Context

The need to provide for the national defense and the right of individuals to refuse to participate in that defense provides one of the inherent conflicts of a democracy. As part of the social contract of representative democracy, the people grant to an elected government necessary powers that a centralized polity can provide more effectively. Such powers include coinage, national defense, and other public services. When some refuse to honor a contract agreed upon by the majority, the social contract weakens. On the other hand, in a democracy, individual rights (so long as they do not impinge on the rights of others) are held in the highest accord. The right to conscientious objection is not directly addressed by the U.S. Constitution, so conscientious objection is a subject of continuing debate.

Conscription involves the power of government to require people to serve in the military. When the burden of conscription is spread evenly over the population (universal conscription or military training) a draft is usually regarded as fair. As a draft becomes more selective and fewer people are conscripted, the draft becomes unfair.

Conscription may become necessary in the event of war or the need to maintain a large standing army. The alternative to a conscripted army is a professional army. In times of national peril it may be difficult to raise military pay to levels at which sufficient personnel are enticed to enlist. Military service has been viewed by many national leaders as a duty of citizenship, much like voting or jury duty.

Public attitude and court decisions have become less restraining on the right to conscientious objection in the United States. Founded originally in religious liberty and later in civil liberty, CO status has become more encompassing and more accessible to dissenters.

Bibliography

Burkema, Herman. "The Social and Political Aspects of Conscription: Europe's Experience." In *The Military Draft*, edited by Martin Anderson. Stanford, Calif.: Hoover Institution Press, 1982. Burkema finds that conscription under democracy strengthens a democratic society in the aftermath of war.

Chambers, John W. *To Raise an Army*. New York: Free Press, 1987. Chambers details U.S. military conscription and enlistment from colonial days onward. Excellent coverage of conscription during World War I and the legacy of conscription in America.

Gillam, Richard. "The Peacetime Draft: Voluntarism to Coercion." In *The Military Draft*, edited by Martin Anderson. Stanford, Calif.: Hoover Institution Press, 1982. Gillam considers the evolution of conscription in the United States, from wartime necessity to peacetime insurance policy during the Cold War.

Moskos, Charles, and John W. Chambers. "The Secularization of Conscience." In *The New Conscientious Objection*. New York: Oxford University Press, 1993. Solid overview of conscientious objection in the United States and worldwide.

Schlissel, Lillian, comp. *Conscience in America*. New York: E. P. Dutton, 1968. History of conscientious objection in America.

John A. Sondey

Cross-References

Armed Forces, p. 89; The City-State, p. 272; Civil Disobedience, p. 285; Civil Wars, p. 325; Government Powers, p. 772; Military Structure, p. 1198; The Nation-State, p. 1241; Patriotism, p. 1384; The Social Contract, p. 1827; War, p. 2129.

MILITARY GOVERNMENTS

Field of study: Military

Military governments do not respect civil liberties and constitutional rights; the judiciary is not free to protect individual rights and the police may terrorize opponents of the military rulers. Military dictatorships frequently usurp political power from democratically elected governments.

Principal terms

CONSTITUTIONAL RIGHTS: rights guaranteed to citizens but denied by some military governments

INDEPENDENT LEGISLATURE: lawmaking body free to make decisions even when those conflict with the desires of the executive branch

JUDICIAL AUTHORITY: power of judges to limit abuses of civil liberties by the government

ONE-PARTY RULE: system in which a single political party runs the government and often suppresses competing parties

POLICE STATE: a political system in which the police enforce the will of the government's leaders

RULE BY ARBITRARY DECREE: a government's declared right to impose any laws of its choosing

Overview

A military government is clearly incompatible with a democratic form of government. In a true democracy, all political power comes from the people, who express their will in free and open elections; power is divided among legislative, judicial, and executive branches. In contrast, military governments take power by force. All three branches of a democratic government have the authority to examine decisions rendered by the other two. This serves to protect individual constitutional rights, which may include religious freedom, freedom of speech, the right to vote, and the right to a fair trial by a jury in open court. In democracies, the chief of state must obey all laws and cannot rule by decree. The members of the legislature receive their authority from the citizens, who choose these representatives in regularly scheduled elections in which several competing parties present candidates. The chief of state and the members of the legislature serve for specified periods of time and are not permitted to annul or to postpone elections, even during war. In democracies, judges are independent and have constitutional authority to examine decisions made by the other two branches of government. In democracies, all government officials are subject to removal from office because of gross malfeasance of duty or the commission of high crimes. A democratically approved constitution specifies the procedures to be followed before a government official can be removed from office. Only temporarily, under a state of martial law declared in a crisis, are these rights and functions changed.

Under a military government, few or none of these political rights may exist in reality, although such governments frequently permit the preparation of a meaningless written constitution. They reserve the power to abrogate arbitrarily any provision of those constitutions. Military governments often approve, for example, preventive detention laws that permit the government to arrest and imprison political opponents for unlimited periods of time without having to bring specific charges before a court of law, and with no recourse to courts for those detained. The use of preventive detention laws in dictatorships such as Tito's Yugoslavia, Kwame Nkrumah's Ghana, Joseph Stalin's Soviet Union, and Nicolae Ceausescu's Romania gave dictators a legal means to eliminate political dissidents. Many military dictators hypocritically pretend that they wish to protect individual rights but also affirm that the general interests of the government must take precedence over individual rights.

Throughout the twentieth century, millions of people around the world were terrorized and killed under military governments. Although some analysts have tried to establish a distinction between military governments, in which the head of state wears a military uniform, and totalitarian governments, in which the military maintains the dictator in power by harassing, threatening, and killing political dissidents, such a distinction is artificial. The effective loss or destruction of freedom and civil rights is the same for citizens whether the chief of state wears a military uniform, as General Augusto Pinochet did in Chile or General Leopoldo Galtieri did in Argentina, or wears a business suit, such as Erich Honecker did in East Germany or François and Jean-Claude Duvalier did in Haiti.

Military governments can usurp power in a variety of ways. In some cases, military forces violently overthrow a democratically elected government in fear that it will eliminate the wealth and the political and social influence of corrupt military officers. Such was clearly the case in Haiti in 1991, when army officers drove into exile the democratically elected president, Jean-Bertrand Aristide. Military leaders understood that Aristide was serious in his efforts to place the various branches of the Haitian armed forces under civilian control. In other cases, such as in the early 1960's in Ghana, a politician wins executive power in a freely conducted election but then abrogates the constitution and names himself "president for life." The Haitian colonels and Kwame Nkrumah of Ghana believed that they were acting with complete impunity, but they were badly mistaken. A revolt in 1966 drove Nkrumah into exile, and the threat of an American invasion gave the Haitian colonels no choice but to go into exile. In both cases, military force or the threat of military force was necessary to restore a democratic government. A dictator may also inherit or seize power from a preceding tyrant. This was the general pattern in the former Soviet Union. Joseph Stalin attained power after the death of Vladimir Ilich Lenin and remained in power for almost four decades largely because he ordered the execution of almost all potential political opponents. Citizens understood that opposition to Stalin's totalitarianism might result in a death sentence or many years in a gulag. State-approved terror and violence against citizens have remained a reality in military governments around the world.

The effects of unrestrained military governments on the daily lives of citizens can be and have been devastating. Military governments do not tolerate any behavior or practice considered unacceptable to the government. Freedom of religion has been consistently violated in totalitarian governments, in part because leaders desire whole-hearted allegiance safe from moralistic scrutiny and in part to force membership in a purportedly superior religion. The Holocaust, in which Nazis murdered millions of Jews and others in state-run concentration camps, is the most infamous violation of religious freedom and basic human rights. Other egregious violations of religious freedom occurred in Russia, when Stalin ordered the execution of people who practiced the Russian Orthodox faith; in the People's Republic of China, when hundreds of thousands of Chinese and Tibetan Buddhists were ordered killed by Mao Tse-tung; and in Iran, where many Bahai's were martyred by the followers of Ayatollah Khomeini.

Gross violations of the personal right of privacy are also common in totalitarian regimes. Although the magnitude of the Nazi crimes against humanity has never been equaled, genocide has taken place in other countries. Pol Pot led a campaign of terror against the Cambodian people in the 1970's. In the former communist states of East Germany and Romania, the secret police were omnipresent and kept voluminous files on all those who had contact with foreigners and those whose absolute fidelity to the communist regime had been questioned by informants. After the unification of East Germany and West Germany, the files of the Stasi (the East German secret police) were opened to public inspection. It became clear that the Stasi knew much about the public and private lives of large numbers of East Germans. It has been estimated that perhaps 25 percent of East Germans were informants for the Stasi. The situation was similar in Romania under Ceausescu.

Restrictions on the right to travel have also been common in totalitarian regimes. East Germans who tried to escape over the Berlin Wall were shot on sight, and unsuccessful escape attempts were punished with long prison terms. Violations of reproductive rights have also occurred frequently in totalitarian regimes, in contradictory ways. Romanian dictator Ceausescu punished women who chose to have abortions or not to have large families, whereas in China women lost government housing benefits if they had more than one child. In neither case did the dictators consider the rights of individual women to decide whether to have children and how many children to have. Such denial of choice is a hallmark of military governments, which maintain control through force rather than through meeting the desires of citizens.

Applications

It is understandably difficult for people who respect human life and liberties to understand the genocide deliberately undertaken by the Nazis against the Jews, by the Khmer Rouge under Pol Pot against the Cambodian people, and by the Chinese communists in Tibet during the 1950's. The situation in Argentina between 1976 and 1983 illustrates how innocent civilians can suffer as a result of dictatorial rule. The first half of the 1970's was a period of political, economic, and social instability in Argentina. A small Trotskyite group called the Revolutionary Army of the People began harassing army officers, and trade unions called numerous strikes to protest salary reductions that the government of Isabel Perón wished to impose in order to fight inflation. The heads of the Argentine army, navy, and air force decided in 1976 to overthrow Perón's government in order to restore order in Argentina. Their tactics were brutal. Thousands of citizens were tortured or killed, and many others simply disappeared. It has been widely assumed that they were secretly murdered by death squads controlled by the junta. Regular protests in Buenos Aires by mothers and grandmothers of the disappeared were, at first, violently broken up by the police, but these courageous women gradually convinced their fellow citizens that something terribly wrong was happening. In 1979, the Organization of American States condemned the gross violations of human rights by the junta, and soon thereafter the World Bank refused to approve any more loans to Argentina.

Like many earlier tyrants, the junta members, then led by General Leopoldo Galtieri, tried to divert attention from their own failures and misdeeds by starting a war. In 1982, Galtieri decided to invade the Falkland (or Malvinas) Islands, which Great Britain had occupied since 1833 but Argentina still claimed. Galtieri believed that Great Britain would not defend the Falklands, and he hoped that a military victory by his forces would eliminate political opposition at home. His plans failed miserably. The British successfully defended the Falklands, and members of the junta were humiliated in the eyes of the citizens of Argentina. Soon after the defeat, the junta was forced to relinquish power. In the freely conducted presidential elections of 1983, Raúl Alfonsín, who favored the full restoration of democracy, easily defeated the candidate supported by the discredited members of the junta. During his presidency, Alfonsín made public proof of the numerous crimes committed against innocent civilians during the seven years of military dictatorship.

Context

Military dictatorships were common throughout the twentieth century, but the situation began to change in the 1980's and 1990's, when totalitarian regimes in Eastern Europe, Africa, South America, and Central America were replaced with governments committed to preserving democracy and individual rights. Many military dictatorships collapsed from within as citizens simply refused to tolerate further violations of their basic human rights. Large demonstrations in Bucharest, for example, convinced Romanian military leaders that they no longer needed to fear Nicolae Ceausescu. Similarly, large protests demonstrated that East Germans would not put up with manipulation of their lives by the Stasi and the East German military dictatorship of Erich Honecker. Shortly after the dismantling of the Berlin Wall, East Germans voted to join West Germany, and more than forty years of dictatorship ended. Changes toward democratic governments occurred in other former communist countries in Eastern Europe.

The transition from totalitarianism to democracy has not been easy. It often takes many years for a newly independent country to change from a state-controlled government and economy to a truly free economic and political system. In South and

Central America, entrenched dictatorial regimes that had shown contempt for basic human rights were replaced with freely elected governments, which accepted the reality and even the necessity of multiparty elections, in such diverse countries as Panama, Nicaragua, Brazil, Bolivia, Chile, and Paraguay. The new leaders of these democracies strived to convince their citizens that, although imperfect, democracy is the best form of government because it allows gradual and natural political evolution in accord with the desires of the people, who in turn will work to support the government.

Perhaps even more extraordinary is the change that occurred in the Republic of South Africa. For generations, white South Africans had imposed their will on the black majority through enforcement of racial apartheid laws. Black citizens received an inferior education in their separate public schools, and they were denied access to good-paying jobs. Those who protested against this racist system were killed or imprisoned. Strong opposition from within the country and the refusal of foreign companies and governments to continue investing in South Africa caused a major decline in the South African economy. These changes convinced the white South African government that it was in its self-interest to create a new democracy in which all South Africans would have equal civil and political rights. No violent revolution was necessary, and Nelson Mandela in 1994 became the first president of a truly democratic South Africa.

In military dictatorships, people feel powerless and are profoundly alienated from their government. Democracies, on the other hand, give citizens an incentive to improve the quality of life for themselves and for their entire country because each citizen in a democracy has an equal say in controlling the political direction in his or her country. Military governments rule by force; their denials of the rights of citizens are often accompanied by repression, fueling dissent and further repression. Abuse begets further abuses until the government is replaced.

Bibliography

Chapman, Brian. *Police State*. New York: Praeger, 1970. Contains an accurate description of the manipulation techniques used by totalitarian governments. Chapter 5 explains clearly how the Nazis systematically created a judiciary and police force subservient to the wishes of the Nazis.

Chirot, Daniel. *Modern Tyrants: The Power and Prevalence of Evil in Our Age*. New York: Free Press, 1994. Insightful analysis of the destructive nature of military dictatorships in such diverse countries as China, Haiti, Cuba, Libya, the Soviet Union, Iran, and Iraq. Includes an excellent bibliography.

Halperín Donghi, Tulio. *The Contemporary History of Latin America*. Edited and translated by John Charles Chasteen. Durham, N.C.: Duke University Press, 1993. Excellent historical overview of the political changes in Latin America between the end of the colonial period and the late 1980's. Clearly describes the difficult transition from dictatorship in many Latin American countries.

Mitchell, Otis C. *Hitler over Germany: The Establishment of the Nazi Dictatorship*

(1918-1934). Philadelphia: Institute for the Study of Human Issues, 1983. Solidly researched historical study of the techniques the Nazis used to transform Germany from a democracy into a police state. An insightful epilogue explores why Germans allowed Hitler to destroy their country.

Omari, T. Peter. *Kwame Nkrumah: The Anatomy of an African Dictatorship.* New York: Africana, 1970. Describes Nkrumah's efforts to transform Ghana from a free democracy into a totalitarian regime in which he was to serve as president for life. Contains a foreword by Judge Ollennu of the court of appeals of Ghana explaining how Nkrumah attempted to destroy judicial independence.

Rubin, Barry. *Modern Dictators: Third World Coup Makers, Strongmen, and Populist Tyrants.* New York: McGraw-Hill, 1987. A study of dictators in less-developed countries, with particular attention to Idi Amin of Uganda, Ferdinand Marcos of the Philippines, and Anastasio Somoza of Nicaragua.

Edmund J. Campion

Cross-References

Armed Forces, p. 89; Comparative Government, p. 384; Dictatorships, p. 546; Executive Functions in U.S. Government, p. 636; Force, p. 712; Insurgencies and Coups d'État, p. 930; Leadership, p. 1066; National Security, p. 1261; Political Violence, p. 1539; Totalitarianism, p. 1987; Underdeveloped Nations, p. 2039.

MILITARY STRUCTURE

Field of study: Military

In order to satisfy the requirements of its special mission, the structure of a military organization may differ greatly from that of civilian governments.

Principal terms

ARTICLES OF WAR: body of law for the military forces of a nation

CHAIN OF COMMAND: vertical structure of responsibility from lowest to highest authority

COMMANDER IN CHIEF: ultimate governor of a military entity, usually a highly placed civilian executive officer

CONSENT OF THE GOVERNED: agreement of those being governed to accept the leadership of the ruling class

CONSISTENCY: regularity of structure

INTERCHANGEABILITY: uniformity among military entities, allowing one unit to replace another

MUTINY: rebellion against military rules or authority by members of the military entity

OLIGARCHY: government by an elite minority

UNIT: discrete body of military personnel, holding a formalized complement of people and equipment

Overview

As in any large organization, a military body needs to have a formal system of government. The systems developed by the world's military forces differ from the governing practices of the civilian population.

In all except totalitarian rule there is a contract between those ruled and those who rule. This contract ostensibly gives consent of the governed to the rulers. In constitutional governments this consent is formalized in a document or series of documents that are ratified by the population or their representative agents at the time of its adoption. Such consent, however, is amendable; the culture of a democratic republic allows peaceable dissent and affords means for popular change of the laws.

Obviously, the military cannot be ruled in the same way. While it adheres to a body of law created by the legislative branch of the civilian government of the country it serves, this body of law is not accessible to the members of a military organization for challenge or change. In every military society the crime of mutiny is a serious one in peacetime, and a capital one in wartime. This rule is a pivotal part of military law.

One of the least popular duties falling upon military personnel is that of facing certain danger, severe injury, or risk of death. Since only the suicidal welcome such a situation, it is incumbent upon a military structure to cause the nonsuicidal to accept such challenges. Traditionally this was accomplished by threatening punishment if the personnel shirked or shrank from the task. In modern military forces this is replaced with a structure of obedience based on tradition and pride as well as the threat of punishment. The threat, however, must be present also, even if veiled.

This sounds harsh to the nonmilitary person. It seems less harsh, however, when one is part of such an entity. One soon learns by training and example that timely obedience is indispensable when one depends for survival upon others who may be tempted to shirk a hazardous duty but do not. The government of a military entity must provide a sense of the necessity of cooperation and of loyalty if it is to have useful personnel.

In addition, there is a need for consistency. Each military unit must resemble its counterparts in organization, level of authority, equipment, and training. It is vital that, for example, the 96th Heavy Mortar Company of the 192d Battalion be exactly like the 120th Heavy Mortar Company of the 211th Battalion. A military commander cannot afford to treat groups as a politician would a neighborhood. Just as a mechanic needs to have the assurance that a nine-sixteenths-inch wrench is always going to fit a nine-sixteenths-inch bolt head, a military commander needs to know that one unit is interchangeable with another.

This concept of interchangeability of human beings runs counter to modern ideas of individuality, but one cannot carry out military missions with unsized wrenches or uncertain unit potentials. To accomplish the end of having truly interchangeable unit capabilities, the military places great emphasis on uniformity. This is a difficult task, given that the raw materials of the system—humans of diverse backgrounds and cultures—are so nonuniform. In the military, however, the concept of uniformity is inviolate. If this requires that some work below their capabilities in order to resemble their counterparts, the resulting inefficiency is accepted.

This concept of interchangeability must extend to the very highest ranks. It is as vital that a general behave appropriately and in accordance with determined guidelines and mission strategies as it is that a private do so. Severe punishment has befallen even the highest for ignoring the chain of command and doing what was not asked. General Douglas MacArthur was removed from his command during the Korean War by President Harry S Truman for taking action that was not approved by his commander in chief.

Each unit is under the command of a single person, assisted in the advisory and intelligence roles by the leaders of the subdivisions immediately below and by a set of auxiliary departments that are divided into intelligence, administration, personnel, training, and supply functions. Selection of leaders is by merit, each candidate for promotion being judged by his or her superiors. Usually this information is made a permanent record in a dossier that accompanies the individual throughout his or her career.

Some promotion is also earned as a consequence of special leadership training, such as through an officer's candidate school. Finally, exemplary and valorous performance in battle may earn a soldier a "mustang" promotion, that is, from enlisted man to officer.

The military governmental system is based on the chain of command, a linear command ladder extending from each soldier up to the highest level. Each person is required to know his or her place in the chain and the route of his or her access to justice. Mutiny against authority is a severe offense, but each person does have the right to claim redress for unfair or unusually harsh treatment. Like the courts-martial that hear accusations against people for their alleged offenses, a court may also be requested to hear and adjudicate a person's complaints. It is incumbent upon the person, however, to take whatever action he or she is assigned by competent orders. Only afterward, the mission satisfied, may the person bring complaint. This is necessary to avoid having a mission jeopardized by one who wishes to protest the order.

Applications

In modern military government, of which the army of the United States is an example, ultimate control resides in the president as commander in chief. The commander in chief is advised by the cabinet. Primary responsibility in the cabinet resides in the secretary of defense and staff, who coordinate the several military branches such as the army and navy. At the uppermost uniformed level are the highest-ranking officers of the branches who, acting separately and as the joint chiefs of staff, coordinate the tactical efforts of the branches.

For each branch there is a juridical arm, which in the army is headed by the judge advocate general. There is an arm headed by the inspector general to oversee the level of training and living conditions. There is an adjutant to maintain records and transmit orders from the executive branch of the government to the units concerned. In addition, there are departments specifically concerned with housing, food services, ordnance, transportation, medical services, and finance. Others coordinate special services, such as chemical, biological, and radiological weapons. To provide religious functions there is a chaplaincy. There are departments to coordinate the functions of the army reserves and the state national guard units.

At these departmental levels there are close interactions with civilian entities to secure goods and services. These are overseen by several federal agencies in order to ensure good fiscal practices and adherence to the military budgets. Considerable autonomy is allowed for specific specialty items, however. As a result, a large staff function is concerned with creating specifications for goods, particularly highly technical modern weapons and equipment.

For each branch there is a chain of command that extends from the cabinet ministers through their staffs and the chiefs of staff down a formal ladder of responsibility; each unit leader has a unique chain to the top. This avoids the confusion often found in civilian organizations resulting from conflicting orders given to one person by different officers representing more than one managerial entity.

Military government is an oligarchy; the members are selected from within on the basis of merit. Except in issues which qualify for legal complaint and redress, the individual has no right to refuse orders within the scope of his or her ability and training given by duly authorized leaders.

If an individual believes he or she has been wrongly treated, he or she may request a formal legal procedure in which the judge advocate general's (JAG) staff serves in the role of judge and will arrange for counsel for the plaintiff if necessary. Military courts are separate from civilian ones, and they have precedence over civilian disposition of cases. Their law is codified by the articles of war, which provide regulations and punitive provisions for every facet of military life.

In crimes, the role of the JAG's staff is similar, except that in crimes that are civilian in character the accused may be relinquished to civilian courts. At the least serious level the perpetrator may be judged and sentenced to minor punishment by his or her immediate unit commander.

One pivotal attribute of a military force is transparency. An army is most effective when it translates the aims of the civilian government of the nation into action not substantially affected by the structure of the military. This transparency is strange to people accustomed to free self-expression. It is necessary, however, in order to attain the highest efficacy. For this reason it is necessary that the military, while governing itself, must maintain an elasticity that assures that each duty is performed accurately and uniformly without the necessity of that duty being overseen by anyone but the individual's immediate supervisor.

While any high-ranking leader may give an order to an individual in an emergency, even at those times the orders of the individual's immediate leader take precedence. Normally, orders to the individual are given by the unit commander. The smallest units, the squads, are often grouped for command into the next level, the platoon, or the company of 150 to 200 persons. The difficulty of communicating directly with hundreds of people necessitates that orders affecting larger entities are usually relayed through the smaller unit commanders. Entire armies may be directed by a single communication to unit commanders in accordance with a previously determined set of strategic actions.

As the number of levels of command between the commander requesting the action and the unit or individual carrying out the mission becomes larger, fineness of control decreases. Each unit's response is scaled to the level of command. Squad leaders issue detailed commands to individuals within the framework of their mutual experience and training. Platoon leaders direct squads in only as much detail as is found in the standard squad actions, leaving the deployment and direction of the individual to his or her squad leader. From there the specificity diminishes until the general on the field is necessarily ignorant of the specific orders a battalion commander may have given to his or her company commanders.

Context

Government of modern military institutions has evolved to oligarchy guided by principles of social conscience. In order not to be a burden or threat to the populace, military government is placed under civilian rule and has within it provisions for redress of grievance. It has a stable structure that allows the individual to understand his or her role in relation to others. Promotion is by merit. Lapses are not permitted to doom a career; all of a person's performance and character are maintained to permit balancing the poor with the good.

Consistent with tactical necessity, military justice, while necessarily contained within the structure of the service itself, contains the same safeguards as are afforded to a civilian. The accused may have even the least significant offense judged by a court rather than having punishment be decided arbitrarily by a commander. A common requirement placed on the military by its civilian government is that documents describing the basic law governing the military are read to every person in the entire military establishment at frequent intervals.

As emergent nations develop, their military structure often is at odds with the liberal governments they adopt. It is incumbent upon their mentor countries to assist them in restructuring their military entities to include human rights safeguards, since the unfamiliar concept of a civilian government controlling the military hierarchy is not always easily accepted by military leaders.

Consideration must also be given to the progress toward a consensus on the power that should reside in organizations such as the United Nations. Just as units with identical functions in a nation's military structure must have similar levels of training, equipment, and tactical experience, it is important that there be this same sort of uniformity among units of allied function offered by the several contributing nations. As the various states of the United States have brought their militias to the same level of training under identical rules of format and command, so multinational forces need to enjoy the same sort of uniformity. The success of the state militias serves as an example of the degree of regularity that can be achieved without losing the regional and cultural attributes of the contributing regions.

Finally, there is a need to strive for humane and law-based rule for emergent nations that have lacked it for generations. The traditional enforcer of tyrannical regimes has been military force under the direct control of a dictator. This political system not only discourages popular dissent but places the military itself in an untouchable status; excesses by its members go unpunished. For modern representative government to thrive in a country with such a history, the people must be made to believe that it is they, through popular democratic processes, who control the military, viewing it as their servant rather than their master. If this security is not achieved, the people will have little trust of a supposedly representative government.

Bibliography

Huntington, Samuel. *The Soldier and the State*. Cambridge, Mass.: Harvard University Press, 1967. Describes military-civilian relationships from the colonial days of the United States until the period after the Korean War.

Karsten, Peter. *The Military in America*. New York: Macmillan, 1986. Describing nine historic periods, this book treats the social as well as political development of the military in the United States, describing the development of civilian control of the military, the emergence of human rights movements in the military, and the history of war protests.

Millis, Walter. *Arms and Men*. New York: Capricorn, 1967. The history of the military establishments in the United States, with emphasis on the development of the armed forces and the politics of their use in domestic and global arenas.

Weigley, Russell. *History of the United States Army*. Bloomington: Indiana University Press, 1984. Comprehensive work on the history of the American military establishment from colonial times to 1983. Focuses on campaigns as well as the political evolution of the Army.

Yarmolinsky, Adam. *The Military Establishment*. New York: Harper & Row, 1971. An attack on every phase of the operation of the United States armed forces. The military-industrial conspiracy, the Pentagon's lying to the people, the injustice of U.S. military operations throughout the world, and the arbitrary nature of military justice are described in detail.

Loring D. Emery

Cross-References

Armed Forces, p. 89; Arms Control, p. 95; The Civil Service in the United States, p. 310; Jurisprudence, p. 1019; Military Conscription and Conscientious Objection, p. 1185; National Security, p. 1261; North Atlantic Treaty Organization, p. 1332; Protest Movements, p. 1621; Superpowers and World Politics, p. 1916.

MILL'S POLITICAL PHILOSOPHY

Field of study: Political philosophy

John Stuart Mill, the most prominent English philosopher of the nineteenth century, is widely recognized as the preeminent advocate of utilitarianism as a normative ethical theory and as the most influential champion of the social and political freedom of the individual.

Principal terms

LIBERALISM: political doctrine or movement that affirms and seeks social progress and the promotion of the social and political liberties of the individual

NORMATIVE ETHICAL THEORY: any theory of morality, in conjunction with a rational justification of it, that actually prescribes how human beings should behave

PATERNALISM: the prevention of one from acting as one chooses or the compulsion of one to act otherwise than one would choose, for one's own good

PROPORTIONAL REPRESENTATION: electoral system designed to represent each political party in a legislature in approximately the same percentage as it is represented in the electorate

UTILITARIANISM: normative ethical theory that designates human actions to be morally correct to the extent that they produce a greater balance of good over bad consequences than alternative courses of action

Overview

John Stuart Mill (1806-1873), the most prominent English philosopher of the nineteenth century, is widely recognized as the preeminent advocate of utilitarianism as a normative ethical theory and as the most influential champion of the social and political freedom of the individual. Mill's political philosophy is closely related to his ethical theory insofar as he believed that the well-being of one's society is not only consistent with, but necessary for, the successful promotion of one's own well-being. What cements this relationship between Mill's political philosophy and his ethical theory is his unwavering commitment to the belief that the self-development of a person's character is of paramount importance.

As a proponent of utilitarianism, Mill believed that a human action is morally correct to the extent that it produces a greater balance of good over bad consequences than any alternative course of action. For example, if one were to find oneself in a moral decision-making situation in which one is the only witness to a ten-dollar bill falling from the pocket of another who, by all appearances, is financially impoverished, one might face, at least fundamentally, two options: whether to retrieve and keep or retrieve and return to its owner the ten-dollar bill. The principle of utility, as articulated above, would prescribe the action morally likely to produce more good or fewer bad consequences than the other. It is this prescriptive nature of such a theory that renders it a normative ethical theory.

In *Utilitarianism* (1863), Mill argues that the principle of utility is preferable to other types of normative ethical theory. He analyzes both the idea and sentiment of justice and tries to dispel what he regards as the myth that justice is more noble, more objective, or otherwise superior to the idea of utility. He argues that once the ideas of justice and utility are properly understood, it becomes evident that the two are consistent and that justice is ultimately subordinate to utility. He demonstrates this by showing how applying the principle of utility is the best way to resolve disagreements over matters such as the most just methods of distributing goods.

In *On Liberty* (1859), Mill presents a defense of both the social freedom and the political liberty of the individual. In this treatise, he asks the classic liberalistic question about social and political philosophy: What is the proper balance between the power of authority over society's members and of the government over its citizens and the freedom of individual choice? As this question implies, individual freedom and societal authority are correlative. They stand in an inverse relationship; the more there is of one, the less there must be of the other. Mill's concern is twofold: first, the potential for moral coercion of the individual's freedom by others in the society, and second, the potential for legal constraints on the individual's liberty by one's government. Mill sees only one legitimate reason for a civilized society or its government to interfere with the liberty of one of its members—self-protection. In other words, the only justification for coercing or constraining a person is to prevent harm to others.

With this liberty principle, Mill draws a clear distinction between actions that concern only oneself and those that concern others—especially that do so in a hurtful manner. For example, a single man who chooses to smoke cigarettes at home alone should presumably be allowed to do so. However, since medical research indicates that inhalers of second-hand smoke and that fetuses of expectant mothers who smoke, are at risk, it would be a legitimate use of coercion or constraint to interfere with the liberty of both a father of young children to smoke in their presence and the expectant mother to smoke. In both cases, the rights of others are detrimentally affected, and there is a definite risk to the health of others. It must be acknowledged, however, that Mill is willing to trade the preservation of the individual's freedom for the risk of harm to oneself. The single man in the example above clearly places his own health at risk, but, to the extent that no one else's health is placed in jeopardy, he should be allowed to exercise his freedom to do so.

Why is the liberty of the individual so important? The answer is that to protect individual freedom and liberty is to satisfy as completely as possible the principle of utility. For Mill, the ideal utilitarian society is one in which all members of society accurately recognize the compatibility of their own interests with those of the society as a whole. To the extent that individual freedom and liberty are preserved, both the interests of the individual and those of the society are promoted. The interests of the individual are fostered to the degree to which individuals may develop their own character in order to realize their own natural capacities as rational and social human beings. That is, one's freedom and liberty are important as the prerequisites for the self-development of one's full potential for human nature. Conversely, a society that allows for such individual freedom and liberty benefits to the extent that more, rather than fewer of its members, may take advantage of their citizenship through greater participation in the society. This is important because social apathy breeds both incompetence and corruption in government. Consequently, not only is the principle of utility as applied to individuals satisfied, it is also satisfied as it applies to the society as a whole, through social progress.

In *Considerations on Representative Government* (1861), Mill acknowledges that democracy is the best form of government to accommodate the mutual needs of the individual and the society. Not only does a democratic form of government nurture an active character by requiring individuals actively to participate in the process of government, it also encourages the development of a genuine concern for the society's well-being. A democracy in which every citizen actually participates in governmental decision making would be ideal, but, because this is impractical on any but a small scale, a representative democracy is the next best type of government. In such a democracy, every citizen would have the opportunity to exercise some control over the government through elected representatives.

It should be noted that Mill is fully aware of the fact that not every society can institute a democracy successfully. Only societies with people who are intellectually capable and morally willing to accept the responsibilities imposed on them by democratic forms of government can successfully sustain them. Governmental restrictions for the purposes of social order and social progress vary in degree and in number depending on the stage of development of the particular democracy in question and of its people. Furthermore, the mark of a good government is the extent to which it promotes the character development and virtue of its citizens.

Mill follows Alexis de Tocqueville in calling the major potential problem in any democracy is the "tyranny of the majority." By this he means the possibility that the majority will impose its will on, and thereby oppress, a minority. For example, laws might reflect the interests of a racial or a religious majority to the detriment of racial or religious minorities. Among the various political mechanisms that Mill advocates to mitigate this threat is proportional representation. Ultimately, however, such artificial means can never be as effective as the education of the electorate to the importance of individual liberty and to a truly democratic process.

Applications

Mill's views concerning the importance of individual political liberty surface in legislative halls and public forums throughout the Western world, whenever legislative bodies consider legislation that would restrict or otherwise impede an individual liberty in order to protect citizens from harm. Such legislation is paternalistic in that it intends to safeguard individuals from the consequences of their own actions. For example, any type of modern seat-belt legislation that requires operators of motor vehicles to wear seat belts would be a paternalistic law. The intention of such a law directly conflicts with Mill's liberty principle—that the only legitimate purpose for coercing or constraining individuals is to prevent harm to others—because the intention of such laws is to protect persons from harming themselves.

Mill was willing to risk the potential harm to oneself resulting from one's own actions in order to preserve individual liberty. He saw the preservation of individual liberty as far too important to both individual members of society and society as a whole to relinquish merely in order to safeguard individuals from themselves. In the absence of a paternalistic law, such as a mandatory seat-belt law, each individual is free to choose whether to protect himself. Mill would be the first one to say—as he does in *On Liberty*—that, in such situations, one may legitimately try to persuade people to protect themselves. However, it is never legitimate either to compel or abuse competent adults for not doing so.

Context

Historically, liberalism and its concern for the protection of individual civil and political liberties is a modern phenomenon. The idea of character development on the part of individuals in order to realize their potential in human nature is a purely Aristotelian moral concept. Mill's political philosophy is noteworthy if only for his ability to conjoin these two notions in a relatively coherent fashion. The cornerstone of his political philosophy is to allow all members of society a chance to develop their character. Society should, through its social and political institutions, facilitate such development. The result is mutually beneficial.

Mill is also important for proposing a solution to what he regarded as democracy's most debilitating threat, namely, the tyranny of the majority. He recognized that democracy can take away rights as easily as it confers them. Since democratic forms of government place political power in the will of the majority, the majority may use its power to oppress minorities. Mill recognized that since majorities are likely to comprise the working middle class, they might be disposed to wield their political power out of ignorance, selfishness, malevolence, or intolerance. A solution to this danger is the aspect of Mill's liberty principle that tries to distinguish between legitimate and illegitimate uses of authority over individual liberty.

Throughout his life, Mill took strong public and often unpopular stands on several controversial issues. For example, he supported the abolition of slavery in the United States and he took an active role in promoting civil and political rights for women. With his wife, Harriet Taylor, Mill was a strong advocate of gender equality in virtually every aspect of life.

Mill's eloquent and commonsense arguments in *On Liberty* for the individual's freedom of speech and expression have, almost certainly, won for him an acclaim that he has maintained from liberals in the United States for generations. By contrast, his defense of the individual's freedom to pursue whatever manner of living she or he might choose has been met with mixed reviews, even in the United States. The fact that some people champion Mill's efforts in the former case yet are wary of them in the latter might reveal an intellectual inconsistency on their part, given that the fundamental reason that justifies each of these kinds of freedom is, literally, a genuine pursuit of truth.

Bibliography

August, Eugene. *John Stuart Mill: A Mind at Large*. New York: Charles Scribner's Sons, 1975. The eighth chapter concisely places Mill's *On Liberty* in its biographical and historical contexts. Other chapters cover other works relevant to Mill's political philosophy.

Berger, Fred R. *Happiness, Justice, and Freedom: The Moral and Political Philosophy of John Stuart Mill*. Berkeley: University of California Press, 1984. Persuasive argument relating Mill's moral and political philosophies. Specifically, the second part of this two-part work attempts to demonstrate how the conception of happiness and the function of rules in practical morality illuminate and influence Mill's theories of justice and freedom.

Britton, Karl. *John Stuart Mill*. 2d ed. New York: Dover, 1969. The third chapter, "Politics," provides an illuminating discussion of the main issues and themes of Mill's political philosophy.

McCloskey, H. J. *John Stuart Mill: A Critical Study*. London: Macmillan, 1971. The fourth chapter, "Political Theory: Liberty and Equality," provides a good exposition and examination of most of the major themes of Mill's political philosophy, framed within a context that illustrates both influences on Mill and his influence on later political philosophers.

Radcliff, Peter, ed. *Limits of Liberty: Studies of Mill's "On Liberty."* Belmont, Calif.: Wadsworth, 1966. A good collection of critical studies of Mill's *On Liberty* intended for undergraduates. Some selections focus on particular issues and difficulties raised by Mill's essay; others analyze the essay's concepts and principles.

Stephen C. Taylor

Cross-References

Citizenship Rights and Responsibilities, p. 260; Civic Education, p. 278; Democracy, p. 513; Epicurean Political Philosophy, p. 624; Government Roles, p. 778; Government Types, p. 785; Liberalism, p. 1118; Locke's Political Philosophy, p. 1142; Political Participation, p. 1479; Political Philosophy, p. 1505; Political Representation in the United States, p. 1525; Positivism, p. 1557; Self-Interest in Politics, p. 1802; Spinoza's Political Philosophy, p. 1872; Tocqueville's Political Philosophy, p. 1981; Utilitarianism, p. 2077.

MODERN MONARCHY

Field of study: Politics

Monarchy is a form of government in which one person is the head of the state, usually by hereditary right. Modern monarchs in developed countries have little or no political powers; however, some monarchs in developing countries have much greater powers in governmental affairs.

Principal terms

ABSOLUTE MONARCH: monarch who has complete control of government; people and property within the nation are subject to his or her will

CONSTITUTIONAL MONARCH: monarch who, bound by the provisions by which the country is governed, usually has little real power

HEAD OF STATE: one who provides ceremonial leadership, continuity in times of governmental transition, and, within limits, ensures a government is formed

LINE OF SUCCESSION: order of individuals to succeed the monarch, established prior to the monarch's death to ensure a smooth transition

SALIC LAW: legal convention that prevents females from inheriting the throne under any circumstances

Overview

Monarchy is a form of government in which one person, due to his or her ancestry, is the ruler of the state. The term "monarchy" is derived from Aristotle's classification for political systems. The Greek words *mon* (one) and *archy* (rule) describe the system of government. However, in Aristotle's system only those individuals who rule for the benefit of the people are monarchs. Individuals who rule basing their decisions only on self-interest are tyrants.

Modern monarchy takes two forms. The first is an absolute monarchy, in which a ruler has control of all government actions and, directly or indirectly, controls all people and property in the state. Few absolute monarchies remain today, with most being on or near the Arabian peninsula. The second form is a constitutional monarchy, in which powers are granted to the ruler by the constitution of the country governed. In Western Europe, the constitutional monarch is most often a figurehead, with little real power in the daily operation of the government. Outside Europe, many constitutional monarchs have more extensive powers. Within either system, one of the central roles of the monarch is to be a unifying factor in the country.

Adapting modern economic development to the traditional social order is a major part of the governing process for the remaining absolute monarchs. Generally, the monarchs are opposed to the total modernization or Westernization of their countries, which might lead to republican governments. Thus the monarchs tend to be conservative (all follow the Salic law) and seek to keep the military and other strong social forces, such as religious groups, placated. Balancing the necessity to be a part of the global economic system against the desire to retain traditional social values is the major challenge facing all absolute monarchs.

Constitutional monarchy includes a much wider range of systems and powers. This is especially true among the less developed countries of the world. In these countries, the constitutions were usually established by colonial powers, as part of the emerging country's independence. The monarch reflects the precolonial system of government, in which the monarch generally had extensive, if not absolute powers. Thus in a kingdom such as Lesotho the official pronouncements state that the system of government is patterned after the British system, in which the monarch has only ceremonial powers and any political statements reflect the position of the elected parliament. Nevertheless, since independence in 1966, Lesotho's king has played a very active role in the government. From January, 1970, until January, 1986, the king and his council of ministers ruled the country. In January, 1986, a military coup removed the king's powers. The king represented a threat to the coup leaders, so in November, 1990, he was dethroned, exiled, and his son Letsie III made king. In March, 1993, the military returned the government to civilian rule after an election. As a result of political instability, however, King Letsie III dissolved parliament and dismissed the prime minister in August, 1994. This would be impossible if the constitutional system in Lesotho were identical to that of the United Kingdom. The fact that many people will follow the traditional ruler, the king, rather than constitutionally elected officials, however, allows the king to go well beyond any formal powers granted at the time of independence.

Monarchs in modern developed nations are all constitutional monarchs. These nations include about half the countries of Western Europe. The extent of the monarch's influence in the political system varies from country to country and from time to time. In the twentieth century, however, the role of the monarch has always remained within the bounds established by the various constitutional systems. In countries with many political parties and a parliamentary system of government, such as Belgium or The Netherlands, the monarch can often affect politics by deciding which political leader is to be prime minister from among the many politicians contending for the post. Each country has its own constitution, which defines the powers of the monarch, and these powers can be interpreted differently at different times and by different monarchs. The reputation of the royal family, the mood of the country, and the personalities of both members of the royal family and members of the government all have an influence on how much and in what ways the monarch can affect the country, its foreign and domestic policies, and the daily lives of its citizens.

The European monarchy in which the monarch has the least power is probably Sweden. The present royal family of Sweden, the Bernadottes, has led Sweden since the Napoleonic era. While the legislature has always had substantial power throughout this period, the constitution adopted in 1975 took away the monarch's remaining political power. Contrary to historical precedent, a major statement on the equality of the sexes was made as the constitution designates the eldest child of the monarch as heir, regardless of gender. Although the monarch remains as the head of state, all duties are purely ceremonial. The general atmosphere of equality is so strong in Sweden that when the king applied to a local council for a parking permit for the delivery of groceries, it was denied on the grounds that it might create a precedent.

In Spain, by contrast, the constitutional monarch has political powers. The Bourbon family ruled Spain from 1700 until 1931, when King Alfonso XIII went into voluntary exile in the hope that this would prevent a civil war. The war occurred anyway, the fascists won, and the country came under the rule of Francisco Franco. Being a conservative, Franco did not wish to do away with the traditional Spanish form of government. He therefore chose the grandson of Alfonso XIII, Juan Carlos, as his successor, and had him trained in military and governmental matters. At the time of Franco's illness, Juan Carlos assumed power in October, 1975, and became king upon Franco's death the following month. King Juan Carlos I has proven to be much more liberal than Franco might have desired, but he has been an able ruler in a time of transition. Juan Carlos is the supreme representative of the Spanish nation, commander of the armed forces, and holds its national sovereignty in his person. The king exercises political as well as administrative power. He also has a voice in the formation of the cabinet, and thereby the political direction of the government. Paradoxical though it might seem, Juan Carlos has played a pivotal role in moving Spain to the mainstream of Western liberal democratic politics.

Applications

The development of the modern monarchy in Europe was a gradual process in which the legislative branch of government, ultimately representing the citizens, gradually gained power over the monarchs. In the British system, this was the result of a series of steps. Over time the British parliament used financial coercion to gain further control over the monarch. In the seventeenth century the conflict escalated, leading to a civil war, the execution of the monarch, and the declaration of a republic. The monarchy was restored when the republic failed. In 1689, William of Orange and Mary accepted the invitation to rule jointly, but this involved accepting the Bill of Rights, which stated that all laws passed by Parliament would take precedence over any other governmental act. The issue of supremacy was decided in Britain somewhat earlier than in most of the European nations. Parliament's victory ensured its supremacy, but it did not make the monarch a total figurehead. Many activities must be done by the monarch, or in the name of the monarch, for them to be legal. Convening the Parliament, approving international treaties, appointing various officials are all prerogatives of the monarch. With a very few exceptions, all of these are done in response to the desires of the politicians in the government, as the British monarch is considered above politics.

The Kingdom of Swaziland is an example of a constitutional monarch who has been granted extensive powers under the constitution, at the same time the average citizen has been given a larger role in selecting the government. The constitution adopted in 1992 gave the average citizen a vote for members of the lower house of Parliament. Fifty-five seats are selected in this manner, with members of the royal family being ineligible for these seats. The king, however, appoints an additional ten members to the lower house, and these may include members of the royal household. The upper house of Parliament (the senate) is composed of ten people elected from the lower house, by members of the lower house, and twenty individuals appointed by the king. As legislation must pass both houses, it is obvious that these items will represent the values of the king, since the majority of the members of the senate are appointed by the king. The king also appoints the prime minister, and in the first government established under the 1992 constitution this was a member of the royal household who had been appointed to Parliament. Technically the king is only the head of state, while the prime minister is the head of the government, who oversees the day-to-day operations of the government. The extensive powers given to the king, however, to appoint members of the legislature, to choose the prime minister and cabinet without regard to party affiliation or support of the lower house of Parliament, and to participate in the governing process, allow the king to direct the governing process.

The modern state of Saudi Arabia is an example of an absolute monarchy created in the twentieth century. While monarchs have ruled various areas of the Arabian peninsula for centuries, it was not until 1932 that Ibn Saud, first king of Saudi Arabia, unified many of the small emirates and principalities into the kingdom of Saudi Arabia. An Islamic kingdom, the only restrictions that are placed upon the monarch are those that are mandated by Islamic law. The king is also the prime minister, with his heir deputy prime minister. While all authority is vested in the king, in practice the king tries to develop a consensus on major policies. Those who might be consulted are the two hundred most important members of the royal family and the council of ministers. All nonreligious regulations are made either by royal decree or by action of the council, over which the king presides and whose acts he must sanction before they become law. In 1970, the government, in a step that consolidated its power, added a judicial system, taking power from the religious legal system, which is administered by Islamic clerics. Under this new system, the king is the final court of appeals and can change any judicial ruling at his discretion. Although a token constitution was issued by the king in 1992, he still remains the focal point of government. Executive, legislative, and judicial powers ultimately reside in the person of the king.

In order for one to fully understand the powers of a monarch, there are times one must look beyond the designations. Jordan and Thailand are generally listed as constitutional monarchies, but there is a great difference in the role of the monarch. For more than twenty years, beginning in the late 1960's, King Hussein ruled Jordan as an absolute monarch. He rarely allowed the legislature to meet, and when he did it was not to deal with any substantive issues. On the other hand, since 1932 in Thailand, the monarch has had powers similar to those a European monarch might possess, and the Thai monarch lived within these constitutional constraints. Politicians have sought the Thai king's consent on issues, however, in order to gain legitimacy for their positions. The role of the monarch varies widely and cannot always be predicted based on the powers listed in a country's constitution.

Context

Monarchy is a form of government which goes back into prehistory. There has never been a period in recorded human history when it has not existed. Many argue that the institution is an anachronism. If one looks at the dozens of states given their independence in the decades following World War II, one finds that relatively few new monarchies were established. Even with the rapid growth of democracy and the republican form of government in the post-World War II era, however, monarchies of various types are still viable.

The influence exerted by the approximately twenty-seven monarchs in the world depends largely on whether they are constitutional monarchs with limited powers or monarchs with more extensive powers. In constitutional monarchies, the monarch serves mainly as a symbol of national unity, although virtually all of them also serve other functions. Monarchs who serve as head of the government in addition to being head of state represent the monarchical tradition of the premodern period. The unity that these individuals offer goes beyond symbolism to a unity of power. The value of a monarch to unify a nation undergoing a period of crisis is great. This can be seen by the number of proposals that surfaced in Eastern Europe, during the tumultuous first few years after the fall of communism, to revive various monarchies. Prior to the modern period, crises caused by monarchs might have led to choosing a new monarch. In this period these crises can quickly lead to the end of the government. Recent examples are the social and economic turmoil caused by a self-declared king such as Bokasa I of the Central African Empire (now the Central African Republic) and the military and social upheaval caused by Ethiopian emperor Haile Selassie's attempt to annex Eritrea.

The twentieth century has seen a decrease in the number of monarchies and an even greater decrease in the scope of most monarchs' power. The democratic ideal, which has spread so widely, stresses the inherent equality of all people. This stands in opposition to the monarchical tradition of asserting that certain individuals or families are best able to fill the position of head of state. This democratic trend in political thought has been against the continuation of monarchies as anything more than figureheads or tourist attractions. Votes taken in Italy in 1946 and Greece in 1974 not to restore their monarchies underscore the tendency.

To the extent that monarchy can play a role in the governing process or in building national unity, however, the institution should remain viable. Globally, if the liberal democratic tradition increases its influence, one would expect a trend toward fewer monarchs, and a great decrease in their power. In the last decades of the twentieth century, however, this tradition based on liberal Western political thought was challenged by those who reject the worldview that Western thought represents. For example, the monarchies in Islamic culture have worked to limit the influence of modern Western thought on the citizens of their nations, thus allowing traditional

Islamic society to go on. If this situation continues, one would expect the monarchy to play an important governmental role in these states well into the twenty-first century.

Bibliography

Cannon, John and Ralph Griffiths. *The Oxford Illustrated History of the British Monarchy*. New York: Oxford University Press, 1988. This history of the British monarchy is lavishly illustrated and describes the changing powers and role of the monarch.

Gurney, Gene. *Kingdoms of Europe*. New York: Crown, 1982. Histories of the ruling monarchs and their influence from antiquity to the present, with maps, illustrations, and charts.

Holden, David and Richard Johns. *The House of Saud: The Rise and Rule of the Most Powerful Dynasty in the Arab World*. New York: Holt, Rinehart and Winston, 1981. History of the Saud family, including an in-depth study of their involvement in domestic and international politics.

Lacey, Robert. *Majesty*. New York: Harcourt Brace Jovanovich, 1977. Biography of Elizabeth II and the House of Windsor (George V, Edward VIII, and George VI).

Montgomery-Massingberd, Hugh. *Burke's Royal Families of the World*. 2 vols. London: Burke's Peerage, 1977. Volume I is a genealogical study, starting from the nineteenth century, of the royal families of Europe and Latin America. Volume II covers royal families in the rest of the world.

Packard, Jerod M. *Sons of Heaven: A Portrait of the Japanese Monarchy*. New York: Charles Scribner's Sons, 1987. History of the Japanese imperial family, with ample attention to the changes in power after World War II.

Zahlan, Rosemarie Said. *The Making of the Modern Gulf States*. Winchester, Mass.: Unwin Hyman, 1989. Describes the political systems in the monarchies of Bahrain, Kuwait, Oman, Qatar, and the United Arab Emirates.

Donald A. Watt
Priscilla A. Watt

Cross-References

Asia: Politics and Governments, p. 108; The British Parliamentary System, p. 146; Government Types, p. 785; History of Government, p. 829; Islam and Government, p. 994; Leadership, p. 1066; Monarchy in Constitutional Governments, p. 1215; Monarchy in History, p. 1221; Pacific Islander Governments, p. 1362; Republicanism, p. 1706; Succession, p. 1909.

MONARCHY IN CONSTITUTIONAL GOVERNMENTS

Field of study: Types of government

Many countries, especially in Europe, combine democratic political institutions with hereditary monarchs, persons who have limited formal powers but who may still play roles in making their systems work. Such monarchies are the pale survivors in the modern age of once-powerful kings and emperors.

Principal terms

COMMONWEALTH: loose, non-binding association of former British colonies, many of which continue to accept the British monarch as their head of state

CONSTITUTIONAL: in accordance with the fundamental principles of government, usually but not always set out in a written document accepted by citizens and controlling the actions of public officials

HEREDITARY PRINCIPLE: choice of a monarch based on family blood lines rather than election or force

MONARCHY: government with a hereditary head of state

PARLIAMENT: body of people's representatives centrally involved in the making of laws and policy

REPUBLIC: form of government in which a monarch is not the formal sovereign

Overview

Constitutional monarchy is a form of government in which the role of head of state is inherited, but the monarch has severely limited power over the conduct of govern-ment. In countries where they are found today, constitutional monarchs are a far cry from earlier monarchs, who either exercised unlimited power over their people or were partners with nobles or parliaments in ruling their countries. This newer form of monarchy is associated with the rise of democratic institutions in the nineteenth and twentieth centuries. In the 1990's, only a few countries used this form of government. Constitutional monarchies were found more frequently in smaller, less populous democracies, such as in Scandinavia and the Low Countries, although they also existed in larger ones, such as Great Britain, Spain, and Japan.

Monarchy as a type of rule is often contrasted with the republican form of government, in which the head of state, often a president, is an elected rather than a hereditary official. Because constitutional monarchies in the late twentieth century are now only shadows of the monarchies of earlier centuries, they blend in fairly easily with democratic values and institutions. Conversely, the fact that a country has a republican form of government does not guarantee that it is a democracy in practice.

A key feature of constitutional monarchies is the insulation of the monarch from real power or political controversy. Such monarchs are usually busily engaged in the dignified, patriotic, and symbolic activities of the states, but take no significant part in making policy, choosing government leaders, or influencing elections. In many countries, among them Sweden and Japan, the monarch's limited role is set forth in law and the constitution; in others, such as Great Britain, the monarchy has become sidelined from politics not so much by formal rules as by the growth of the decisive authority of the parliament, the prime minister, the cabinet, and the major political parties. After World War I, constitutional monarchs accepted the reality of having to give up most of the powers of their ancestors as the price of political survival.

Although in the ancient and medieval worlds monarchs sometimes were elected, such as the Holy Roman emperors in the Middle Ages, or seized the crown by physical or military force, such as William the Conqueror in Britain in the eleventh century, in recent centuries constitutional monarchs usually reached the throne through heredity. They are descendants of a royal bloodline, usually the sons or daughters of a deceased monarch. The fact that they were not democratically elected is another reason that constitutional monarchs dare not assert much political power, even where, on paper, such power is theirs to wield. For a modern monarch to take sides in controversies involving political parties and their elected representatives is to put the monarchy itself into the political fray, where it might lose instead of win, which would jeopardize the fragile unwritten agreement that guarantees its continuation.

The French Revolution of 1789 accelerated the movement away from hereditary rulers and toward more popular sovereignty in many European nations. Two centuries later, there were only a handful of powerful monarchs left in the world, those being found in traditional societies such as Morocco, Saudi Arabia, Thailand, and Swaziland. Most of the surviving monarchies that have been included in their country's constitutional order are located in Western European nations: Belgium, Denmark, Great Britain, Liechtenstein, Luxembourg, Monaco, The Netherlands, Norway, Spain, and Sweden. Voters in two other European nations, Greece and Italy, replaced their monarchies with republics just after World War II.

Applications

Four late-twentieth century examples show both the common elements in the concept of constitutional monarchy and how it can vary in practice. Three are from the heartland of constitutional monarchy—Western Europe—and the fourth is from the Far East.

Great Britain has the oldest and most famous constitutional monarchy. The decline in real power of British monarchs in the period from Henry VIII in the early fifteenth century to Queen Elizabeth II in the late twentieth century has been great, even though theoretically the queen continued to have most of the formal powers possessed by earlier monarchs. In particular, two events of the seventeenth century spelled the end to absolute monarchy and gave rise to the idea of severely limited regal powers. The English Civil War (1640-1649) between the forces of King Charles I and the Parliament culminated in the beheading of the king; the Glorious Revolution of 1688 brought forth the English Bill of Rights that further clipped the wings of the restored monarchy and elevated the power of Parliament. Despite their prominence as symbols of national unity, their titular leadership of the Church of England, and their occasional involvement in formal international diplomacy, British monarchs in the twentieth century had no important political powers. Their most evident connection with the day-to-day political process came in weekly meetings with prime ministers, when the latter could use the monarchs' traditional right to consult, to advise, and to warn. The monarchs left to the political parties the selection of the prime minister and the cabinet, and have not withheld their signature from bills passed by Parliament for more than a century. Although acts of Parliament have been promulgated, and appointments and government decisions have been made in the name of the monarchs, the prime ministers and their cabinets have actually made the selections, dominated the process by which bills have been passed by the Parliament, and controled how laws are administered. British monarchs have taken considerable pains not to identify themselves with particular ideological or political groups. For example, the speeches delivered by the monarchs to open each session of Parliament by outlining the government's legislative plans have actually been written by the prime ministers and have not contained the monarchs' own views. These limits on royal power are not embodied in a fully written constitution but are deeply embedded in tradition and in the expectations of the British people. These facts help to explain how even the age of the democratic franchise, and in the face of highly publicized problems of other members of the royal family, the British monarchy has continued to be accepted by a majority of the British people.

Another more weakened, but still active, European monarch is the Swedish king. Swedish monarchs once wielded enormous personal and political powers, but they have been thoroughly tamed in the age of constitutionalism. Unlike that of their British counterparts, the Swedish monarchs' hereditary position is granted and limited by a written constitution. The powers of the royal office are almost entirely symbolic, and the duties limited to such activities as making state visits, greeting dignitaries, and cutting ribbons. In 1974, a constitutional amendment removed the last real political powers of the Swedish king: He no longer opens parliamentary sessions, or even nominally appoints the prime minister. Unlike the British monarch, but like their counterparts in The Netherlands and elsewhere, the Swedish royal family follows a middle-class lifestyle, short on majesty and pageant. Like their Dutch counterparts, they are famous for being "monarchs on bicycles." Swedish monarchs must heed public opinion. For example, King Carl Gustaf's request to the Stockholm city council in 1988 for a special parking permit to speed the collection of his dry cleaning was turned down on the grounds that it would set an unfortunate precedent.

In contrast to the modern British and Swedish monarchs, the king of Spain possesses, and at critical times has used, a number of the historic powers of monarchy. Spanish monarchs sat on the throne from the late 1400's, the time of Columbus and Ferdinand and Isabella, until a republic was declared in 1931. That republic lasted only until 1939, a casualty of the Spanish Civil War and the dictatorship set up by its victor, General Francisco Franco (1892-1975). Although Franco established a military dictatorship, he did keep a figurehead king in the background, and as an old man declared that his successor as head of state would be Prince Juan Carlos, a young, untested member of the old royal family. On Franco's death in 1975, King Juan Carlos inherited many of the dictator's strong executive powers but soon showed himself willing to support a new constitutional system and share power with an elective parliamentary government. Juan Carlos's democratic commitment was tested dramatically in 1981, when a group of Franco loyalists in the military took the Spanish parliament captive and called on the king to scrap the new constitutional order and reinstate the military dictatorship through his remaining powers as commander in chief. In rejecting military rebels' demands, Juan Carlos set Spain firmly against a return to dictatorship. Here a constitutional monarch with substantial powers used them in the cause of democracy—one reason why Spain is now referred to as a "parliamentary monarchy."

No monarchy has gone from having enormous power to virtually none in so brief a time as that of Japan, whose emperors trace their royal lineage back to the sixth century. Until Japan's defeat in 1945, the emperor was treated by his people as a semigod. The contrast between the emperor's powers in the 1890's and the 1990's is stark. Under the so-called Meiji Constitution of 1889, the emperor was declared to be "sacred and inviolable," the head of the empire, combining in himself ultimate military, political, and religious powers. Not all emperors in the Meiji period (through the end of World War II) chose to exercise all these powers; however, when they did, they could claim to be acting constitutionally. All of this ended under the so-called MacArthur Constitution of 1947, which was imposed on the defeated Japanese by the commander of the victorious U.S. military occupation forces in an effort to establish democratic institutions in Japan without making a total break with the country's conservative traditions.

Under the MacArthur Constitution, the emperor was retained, but lost all except symbolic and ceremonial powers. The constitution states that the people are the source of legitimate power in Japan, and that the emperor will have no powers whatsoever related to government. Unlike the British monarch, the emperor is not consulted, kept informed, or asked for advice by the government in power. On a few rare occasions, the emperor becomes embroiled in political controversy, as when Emperor Akihito undertook an "apology tour" to China and the United States in 1994 to make amends for Japan's actions in the time of his father, Emperor Hirohito. For doing this he was sharply criticized by the right-wing political parties. Still, of the four constitutional monarchs discussed, the Japanese emperor is the most distantly removed from the working of his nation's political system and has moved most quickly from the highest to the lowest rung of genuine power.

Context

Compared to the controversies over the appropriate choice of basic government forms—for example, democracy or authoritarianism, presidential or parliamentary systems, centralization or federalism—the question of the virtues and drawbacks of constitutional monarchy has not been a burning one in the late twentieth century.

Nevertheless, the history of the development of constitutional monarchy shows that it has served as an important option for societies concerned with finding institutions to combine traditional symbols with modern forms of governing.

The twentieth century has been hard on traditionally strong monarchies. World War I swept away the German, Austro-Hungarian and Russian emperors, and World War II and its aftermath saw the end of monarchies in nations such as Romania, Yugoslavia, Albania, Greece, Italy, and Japan. A number of nations in the British Commonwealth chose not to accept the British monarch as their own head of state, although others, such as Canada, Australia, and New Zealand, did. Generally, when monarchy has survived in the democratic world it has done so in the constitutional rather than the traditional version. Observers have suggested that the relatively small number of monarchs who survived the coming of democracy were those who accepted the loss of most of their political power in return for continuing in office with severely diminished roles.

These roles are several. Unlike politically divided parliaments and the usually partisan prime ministers and cabinet members, constitutional monarchs are expected to remain above the politics of the day. They must do so in order to serve as a tangible focus of the unity of the country, a human link with past glories and patriotic symbols. Whatever their historic antagonisms, the English, Scots, Welsh, and Northern Irish can come together in the person of Queen Elizabeth II of the United Kingdom. Antagonistic regions of Spain, such as Castile, Catalonia, and the Basque country, can unite in their acceptance of King Juan Carlos. Constitutional monarchs call attention to the continuity of tradition and the force of nationalism in societies with deep regional, religious, or class divisions. Constitutional monarchs may also be symbols of national unity because of their close connection with their country's established religion, as in Britain and Sweden. They may offer a highly visible model of stable and traditional family life. Indeed, when they fail as role models, royal families may jeopardize their emotional hold on their populations and bring the institution of monarchy into political debate. Media attention can both bolster and weaken popular acceptance of the monarchy in democratic societies.

Constitutional monarchs can also serve the process of governing indirectly. Like so-called figurehead presidents in countries such as Germany and Italy, they may spare the democratically selected heads of governments the necessary but often boring ceremonial tasks of state, thus permitting the political leaders to concentrate their energies on policy and administration. Writing during the Victorian era, the English essayist Walter Bagehot stressed the distinction between what he termed the "dignified" and the "efficient" tasks of government. Both are essential for a government to work, he believed, but by relegating the colorful, innocuous, time-consuming, "dignified" jobs to the monarchy, the "efficient" elements of government—the prime minister and members of the cabinet—are free to do their work in a more concentrated and efficient manner. Whether or not the American president gains or loses by having both roles combined in a single person has long been a source of argument; but it is clear that in countries having constitutional monarchs, much of the monarchs' efforts are given over to "dignified" roles, well-publicized examples of which tend to confirm in the public mind how hard-working and essential their monarchy really is.

The future of constitutional monarchy would seem to be secure in the countries where it now exists. There is little serious challenge to its continuation, although unforeseen events might threaten that stability. At the same time, few republics have been tempted to replace their preferred system with a constitutional monarchy. It is unlikely that constitutional monarchy as a form of government will occupy more than its present limited stages in the near future.

Bibliography

Cannon, John, and Ralph Griffiths. *The Oxford Illustrated History of the British Monarchy*. New York: Oxford University Press, 1988. Historically sound chronicle of the evolution of the British institution, illustrated in color.

Friedrich, Carl J. *Constitutional Government and Democracy: Theory and Practice in Europe and America*. 4th ed. Waltham, Mass.: Blaisdell, 1968. Places constitutional monarchy in perspective of democratic theory.

Nicolson, Harold G. *Kings, Courts, and Monarchy*. New York: Simon & Schuster, 1962. Good overview of modern monarchies and their courts by a former British diplomat and biographer of King George V.

Packard, Jerrold M. *Sons of Heaven: A Portrait of the Japanese Monarchy*. New York: Charles Scribner's Sons, 1987. Traces path from autocratic early mikados to Emperor Hirohito's acceptance of human identity and constitutional limitation after World War II.

Petrie, Charles. *Monarchy in the Twentieth Century*. London: Andrew Dakers, 1952. Historical treatment of European monarchies in the first half of the twentieth century.

Wilson, A. N. *The Rise and Fall of the House of Windsor*. New York: W. W. Norton, 1993. Lively, controversial discussion of the British monarchy in the 1990's, with suggestions for reforming it to forestall its abolition.

James B. Christoph

Cross-References

Church Government, p. 241; Constitutional Governments, p. 432; Heads of State, p. 804; History of Government, p. 829; Leadership, p. 1066; Modern Monarchy, p. 1209; Monarchy in History, p. 1221; Parliamentary Government, p. 1377.

MONARCHY IN HISTORY

Field of study: Types of government

Monarchy is a form of government in which supreme power or sovereignty rests in one person whose right to rule is often hereditary and lasts for life. The power of a monarch may vary from absolute to severely limited by custom or constitution.

Principal terms

ABSOLUTE MONARCH: European ruler of the seventeenth and eighteenth centuries who claimed unlimited powers over his or her subjects

CONSTITUTIONAL MONARCH: royal ruler who accepts legal limits on his or her authority and shares power with parliamentary and other institutions

DIVINE RIGHT OF MONARCHS: doctrine asserting that royal authority to rule comes from God alone and that rulers are not accountable to their subjects

ENLIGHTENED DESPOTISM: form of absolutism during the eighteenth century in which rulers claimed to govern in the interests of the people

SOVEREIGNTY: supreme and independent political authority exercised by governments and absolute monarchs

Overview

Monarchy is one of the oldest forms of government, for it can be found among technologically primitive peoples as well as among modern states. The term is derived from the Greek word *monarchia*, which means the rule of one. In traditional monarchical governments supreme or sovereign power is centered in a single person, who functions as head of state and supreme commander of armed forces. Such an individual often inherits the position and holds it for life. In the late twentieth century few states remain with sovereign kings or emperors, since monarchical governments have evolved into limited or constitutional monarchies in which crowned heads have largely a symbolic and ceremonial role.

Among tribal communities the monarchical principle is most clearly found in chieftainships. Before the seventh century B.C.E. the ancient Greeks had kings, but then turned to oligarchies (rule of the few) or, as in the case of the city-state of Athens, to democracy. Only the military city-state of Sparta retained elective kings, who were under the supervision of officials.

After the mid-fourth century B.C.E., however, Greek individuality and commitment to republican city-state government could not withstand the expansion of the Macedonian monarchy under King Philip II and his illustrious son, Alexander the Great. Though Greek self-government was maintained under Alexander and some of his successors, the prevailing mode of rulership was now dynasties and empires. In many ways, Alexander's empire became the model for the later Roman Empire. It merged Hellenic (Greek) and Oriental despotic practices, including the deification of rulers.

Not unlike the Greek city-states, Rome began as a monarchy and, after 509 B.C.E., evolved into a republic. At the end of the first century B.C.E., under the pressures of civil strife, breakdown of public order, and severe threat to the expanding frontiers far beyond Italy, the Roman Republic gave way to the Empire under a centralized, professional, military, and bureaucratic monarchical rulership. Before long Roman emperors were deified and worshipped as an act of civil loyalty. Imperial succession was frequently accompanied by troubles and violence, for the principle of hereditary succession following blood lines was never overtly established in the Roman Empire. An element of lasting consequence was added to imperial rule when Emperor Constantine legalized Christianity in 313 C.E. . By actively participating in church councils and determining their outcome, he started the tradition of subordinating the church to the state, which became the practice of Byzantine emperors, Russian czars, and some of the monarchs in the West.

The Western Roman Empire collapsed in 476 C.E., but East Rome with its capital Constantinople lasted as the Byzantine Empire for another thousand years. Whereas the East Roman emperors continued the traditional monarchical system, the Latin West modified its concept of monarchy. For several centuries the pope in Rome asserted monarchical prerogatives over all Christians in secular and spiritual affairs, thereby keeping alive the ideal of universal empire as represented by the unity of Christendom. The rulers of the Germanic kingdom that carried on government in the various regions of the former West Roman empire adopted monarchical ideas of antiquity, while also retaining characteristics of tribal chieftains that based power on personal loyalty rather than impersonal authority. A blending of Roman, Germanic, and Christian principles was achieved with the coronation of Charlemagne, king of the Franks, as emperor of the Romans by the pope on Christmas Day 800. This effort at revival of the Roman Empire was followed by another, the coronation of the German king Otto the Great in 962. From it followed the formation of the Holy Roman Empire, which lasted until 1806 when the French emperor Napoleon dissolved it.

In practice, neither Holy Roman emperors nor medieval kings came to exercise traditional monarchical powers akin to Roman emperors. Holy Roman emperors were engaged in controversies over authority with popes in the eleventh and twelfth centuries. Later they faced German princes and free cities who jealously guarded their liberties and, after the seventeenth century, their independence within the empire. Kings in medieval England and France generally had to share their power with the nobility and were bound by feudal contracts as well as limitations imposed by representative assemblies or parliaments. Monarchs during this time were regarded as being under the law rather than above it. What provided stability and ensured more orderly succession when thrones became vacant was the custom of making them hereditary in certain families.

Starting in the fourteenth century and continuing during the Renaissance, the decentralizing tendencies of feudal regimes were reversed under the "new monarchs" who appeared in France, England, Spain. With the help of growing revenues drawn from expanding trade and new sources of taxation, the kings of France and England maintained stronger military forces, successfully challenged the powers of the nobility, and centralized the functions of the state. Their governments relied on the services of able and often well-educated members of the urban middle class, the bourgeoisie, who willingly served their royal masters as long as they enhanced public order, security of persons and property, and commercial opportunities.

In the seventeenth century, monarchical rule developed into full absolutism, especially on the European continent. This trend was significantly propelled by bitter religious and political conflicts, which necessitated the concentration of power in monarchical hands to ensure the survival of states. Philosophers such as England's Thomas Hobbes and France's Jean Bodin espoused absolute government as a way to protect society from the selfish nature of individual members. Royal lawyers appealed to Roman law to defend the exercise of "plenitude of power," which kept subjects from lawfully resisting the king's will. The Stuart king James I of England insisted that kings ruled by divine right. Though none of the crowned European heads could totally disregard custom and the limitations imposed by strong bureaucracies, several monarchs of France, Spain, Prussia, and Russia in the seventeenth and eighteenth centuries wielded power so freely as to mark this era as the age of absolutism. In the second half of the eighteenth century, King Frederick the Great of Prussia, Empress Catherine the Great of Russia, and Emperor Joseph II of Austria accommodated themselves to the ideas of the Enlightenment. As enlightened despots they showed no inclination to share power with their subjects. However, they pursued reformist policies to promote efficiency in government, and writers of the Enlightenment praised their fostering of the welfare of their subjects.

While England paralleled some of the continental developments that culminated in royal absolutism, it was also the first modern state to break with it and establish limited monarchy in the late seventeenth century. Since the Middle Ages English government had comprised two basic institutions: monarchy and Parliament. The Tudor kings Henry VII and Henry VIII practiced near absolutism by ruthlessly controlling Parliament. One of their Stuart successors, Charles I, provoked parliament into rebellion and civil war, during which he lost his head in 1649. A bloodless revolution in 1688 chased the last Stuart king, James II, off the English throne and firmly established the principle that the king ruled only with and by consent of Parliament. However, it took another century to give constitutional monarchy its full institutional form. In France and elsewhere in western Europe, the French Revolution of 1789 set an end to royal absolutism and ushered in a century of constitutional changes during which monarchs found their powers increasingly limited by representative institutions.

Applications

A closer examination of absolute monarchy in France under King Louis XIV and constitutional monarchy in Great Britain under Queen Elizabeth II illuminates these two systems of government in practice. They provide a contrast between a traditional dynastic monarchy of the past and a contemporary parliamentary monarchy. After King Louis XIV inherited the French throne as a minor in 1643, he reigned for seventy-two years until his death in 1715. Throughout his adult life, he was the working head of the French government, taking absolutism to its greatest height and transforming France into the strongest country in Europe. As sovereign ruler he claimed to have sole control over lawmaking and supreme command over all armed forces in his kingdom. Only he could declare war and make peace, conclude alliances, levy taxes, administer justice, and appoint officials. These functions were epitomized in his reputed boast, "L'etat c'est moi" ("I am the state").

By taking control of the army and making certain that all armed persons in France fought only for him, Louis ensured peace and order in his realm while strengthening France's ability to war against other states. Armed forces had previously been almost private armies, usually in the hands of the nobility. Another method used by Louis to discipline the French nobility was to engage them in elaborate ritual and ceremony at his court. He built a magnificent palace at Versailles to display worldly splendor but also as a place where he made noblemen reside in order to keep them out of mischief. If they wanted to procure a post or a pension from the king's favor, they had to be in his presence. Having a high post in the king's household or in the royal family was the proudest honor to which a great nobleman could aspire.

Two institutions in which the nobility had a strong foothold were the Estates General, a representative assembly, and the parlements, which were law courts that registered royal edicts before they were formally enacted. Louis did not abolish either, but refused to call the Estates General. In fact, they were not called again until 1789. The parlements continued to register royal edicts but were restricted in their freedom to raise objections. Effective administration was centered in a number of councils of state and in an elaborate system of intendants, who represented these councils throughout France. The king made it a point personally to attend the councils of state. Since councilors and intendants were drawn from the middle class or the newly ennobled, they owed allegiance solely to the crown. Each intendant in his district exercised the functions of royal government by supervising the flow of taxes and the recruitment of soldiers; by controlling office holders as well as keeping an eye on the local nobility; by performing police and judicial duties; and by relieving famines. This centralized system of royal functionaries came to be regarded as the best organized of the large monarchies on the Continent. Intendancies were the forerunners of the prefectures of modern France.

While France was creating the most elaborate form of royal absolutism in Europe, England inaugurated a model parliamentary monarchy, which began to dominate European constitutional politics after the French Revolution had run its course. The concept of parliamentary supremacy in Britain was fleshed out with the adoption of the prime ministership and cabinet in the eighteenth century, the emergence of an effective party system in the nineteenth century, and the full democratization of the British monarchical government through universal suffrage in the twentieth century. All these changes impacted upon the role of the crown extricating itself from the political decision-making function, so that since the nineteenth century it can be said the monarch "reigns" but does not "govern."

In theory, Queen Elizabeth II, Britain's reigning monarch since 1952, proclaims laws, selects the prime minister and cabinet ministers, negotiates treaties, and issues pardons. In actuality, the British monarch has few political prerogatives and cannot publicly take a partisan stand. In general, all the acts the monarch performs are under the direction of the prime minister and the cabinet, whose tenure in office is determined by periodic elections. The monarch does, however, have the right to be informed on all actions of government and to be consulted. When an election is held and one party wins a clear majority, the monarch asks the winning party's leader to become prime minister. If there is no obvious leader of the majority party, it is important to receive advice from party leaders before an appointment is made. The monarch might have some flexibility when elections do not produce a clear majority, as happened in February, 1974. At that time, the conservatives won 38.2 percent of the vote and 297 seats, whereas the Labour Party carried 37.2 percent of the vote and 301 seats. At least 318 seats out of 635 were necessary to have a majority in the House of Commons. Queen Elizabeth asked the outgoing conservative prime minister, Edward Heath, to form a government. When he proved unable to do so, the queen approached the Labour leader Harold Wilson, who established a minority government.

Among the most useful contributions that Britain's monarch has made is the performance of many of the ceremonial duties of a head of state: making public appearances, paying state visits to foreign countries, receiving ambassadors, honoring artistic and scientific achievements. Above all, the British monarchy has been a popular symbol of unity. The monarch personifies the state through pomp and pageantry, linking the present with a glorious past. On a larger scale, the crown is the symbol that unites the former dependencies of the British Empire in the Common-wealth of Nations. Queen Elizabeth is the Queen of Canada, Australia, New Zealand, and several other former colonies. Earlier British dependencies that have become republics with their own heads of state—such as India, Pakistan, Nigeria, and Zambia—acknowledge the queen as head of the Commonwealth.

Context

Monarchy was the preferred form of government before the twentieth century. Traditional absolutism ended in much of Europe during or after the French Revolution. Most monarchies survived into the early twentieth century by incorporating a mini-mum of constitutional features and parliamentary institutions. A few of them entered this century as full parliamentary monarchies. However, the political, social, and economic changes caused by or exacerbated by the two world wars were unkind to many crowned heads in Europe and the world. Though only a few monarchs lost their lives, many were removed from or abandoned their thrones. At the end of World War I the empires of Russia, Germany, and Austria-Hungary came to inglorious ends. Their rulers were among those who had retained considerable personal power and could not escape blame for defeat and disaster in war. Republican forces overthrew the Manchu

Dynasty in China in 1912. Ottoman Turkey was declared a republic in 1923 and the monarchy in Spain was overthrown in 1931; however, Spain became the notable European country which under the dictator Francisco Franco called itself "a kingdom" beginning in 1947 and where a parliamentary monarch was formally reinstated in 1975 following Franco's death.

The outcome of the World War II settlement sounded the death knell for monarchies in south and southeastern Europe. The Italian king's association with the Fascist dictatorship brought the abolition of the monarchy by plebiscite in 1946. Yugoslavia ended its monarchy in 1945 after the communist leader Tito prevailed in a popular election. In Bulgaria and Romania the kings lasted until 1947, though greatly restricted by communist regimes. The Greek monarchy survived the war and a communist insurgency but not a military coup in 1967. Next to Britain, only the Scandinavian and Benelux countries remain among the noted monarchies of Europe. Elsewhere in the world Japan's emperor survived World War II but renounced his divinity and became "the symbol of the state and of the people." Coups deposed monarchs in Egypt (1952), Iraq (1958), Libya (1969), Ethiopia (1974), and Iran (1979).

In the last decade of the twentieth century, among a handful of small traditional monarchies, the Kingdom of Saudi Arabia survived as the striking example of an absolute monarchy and a singular anachronism of its age.

Bibliography

DeBeer, E. S. "The English Revolution." In _The Rise of Great Britain and Russia, 1688-1715/25._ Vol. 6 in _The New Cambridge Modern History_, edited by J. S. Bromley. Cambridge, England: Cambridge University Press, 1970. Concise but detailed overview of the era that established England's constitutional monarchy under William and Mary.

Dragnich, Alex N., J. S. Rasmussen, and J. C. Moses. _Major European Governments._ 8th ed. Pacific Grove, Calif.: Brooks/Cole, 1991. Textbook on comparative European government that comments succinctly on the role of monarchy in the history of British, French, German, and Russian governments.

Koebner, Richard. _Empire._ Cambridge, England: Cambridge University Press, 1961. Erudite study of the changing concept of empire from Roman times to the nineteenth century.

Krieger, Leonard. _Kings and Philosophers, 1689-1789._ New York: W. W. Norton, 1970. Perceptive general synthesis that gives considerable attention to the nature of kingship in the eighteenth century.

Lough, J. "France Under Louis XIV." In _The Ascendancy of France, 1648-88._ Vol. 5 in _The New Cambridge Modern History_, edited by F. L. Carsten. Cambridge, England: Cambridge University Press, 1961. Excellent survey of seventeenth-century French government.

Nicolson, Harold. _Kings, Courts, and Monarchy._ New York: Simon & Schuster, 1962. Readable and well-illustrated history of monarchy from its primitive beginnings to its modern constitutional forms.

Petrie, Charles. *Monarchy in the Twentieth Century*. London: Andrew Dakers, 1952. Somewhat dated but still significant study of the Spanish, Italian, Greek, British and central European monarchies.

George P. Blum

Cross-References

Commonwealths, p. 364; Despotism and Tyranny, p. 527; Empires and Empire Building, p. 597; Feudalism, p. 688; Government Types, p. 785; Hobbes's Political Philosophy, p. 836; Islam and Government, p. 994; John of Salisbury's Political Philosophy, p. 1006; Leadership, p. 1066; Modern Monarchy, p. 1209; Monarchy in Constitutional Governments, p. 1215; Montesquieu's Political Philosophy, p. 1228; Vico's Political Philosophy, p. 2103.

MONTESQUIEU'S POLITICAL PHILOSOPHY

Field of study: Political philosophy

An eighteenth century French jurist, historian, and political philosopher, Montes-quieu is best known for The Spirit of the Laws, *in which he enunciated the doctrine of the separation of powers as a counter to despotism.*

Principal terms
FEDERALISTS: those Americans who supported the new Constitution, designed to create a strong central government
PARLEMENT: high court of law prior to the French Revolution, which had the power of judicial review and the ability to block royal decrees
PARLIAMENT: legislative branch of the British government; composed of two chambers, the House of Lords and the House of Commons
PARLIAMENTARY GOVERNMENT: form of government in which the legislative branch is supreme, with the ruling executive body being chosen by the legislators
PHILOSOPHES: enlightened thinkers of the eighteenth century who expounded upon politics, economics, science, philosophy, and society in general

Overview

Charles de Secondat, Baron de Montesquieu (1689-1755) belonged to that remark-able group of intellectuals known as the philosophes, who dominated the political thought and critical thinking of the eighteenth century. Born at La Brede in southwest-ern France, he was trained in law and eventually inherited a title of nobility. He was president of the Bordeaux parlement, an active member of the Academy of Science in Bordeaux, and was eventually elected to the French Academy. He traveled widely in his youth, was an inveterate reader and collector of information, developed a profound respect for the scientific method, and acquired a number of influential contacts in France and abroad. By temperament he was cautious, thoughtful, scholarly, and skeptical, but at the same time, he was immensely popular in social circles, noted for his amusing, witty, and entertaining conversation. After returning from England in 1731, he spent most of his time either at his chateau at La Brede with its magnificent library, or in Paris, participating in that city's rich and stimulating social and intellec-tual life.

Montesquieu's political ideas are found principally in his three most famous works, *Persian Letters (1721), Considerations Upon the Causes of the Greatness of the Romans and Their Decline* (1734), and *The Spirit of the Laws* (1748). In these works, he demonstrated an impressive familiarity with a wide range of topics, including history, sociology, anthropology, geography, and political science. His knowledge of history, especially ancient history, allowed him to make many penetrating observations about the nature of society and the principles governing the world of politics. *The Spirit of the Laws* took almost two decades to write, and it caused a sensation when it was published, quickly going through twenty-two editions. To the modern reader, the book can be frustrating. It is ponderous, running close to seven hundred pages. The title is misleading, since Montesquieu had more to say about politics than the law. The book seems to be lacking in organization; some segments are difficult to interpret while others obviously need elaboration; and there are times when Montesquieu simply got his facts wrong. Yet it contained some of the most imaginative, daring, and liberating ideas of the age. With ruthless logic and appeals to decency, Montesquieu attacked despotism, corruption, slavery, genocide, judicial torture, religious intolerance, and wars of expansionism.

Montesquieu believed that there were three major types of government: republican, which was government by the people; monarchical, which was the rule of one person constrained by fixed and established laws; and despotism, which was the unbridled and capricious rule of a single person. To each of these forms, he ascribed a motivating force: For a republic, it was virtue; for monarchy, honor; and for despotism, fear. While he admired the early republics of the ancient world, most of the book deals with monarchy, hardly surprising since this was the most common form of government in Montesquieu's age. The key to understanding Montesquieu's political philosophy lies in his deep antipathy to despotism; indeed, one of the reasons for writing this book was to criticize the reign of Louis XIV, who had died in 1715. Montesquieu despised this regime because Louis XIV had attempted to establish an absolute monarchy, thereby violating the ancient unwritten constitution of France, and because the expansionist wars of that period brought nothing but bankruptcy and human misery.

Montesquieu made his great contribution with his theories on preventing the rise of despots. He believed that only power could check power. Intermediary powers were needed to protect the people from monarchs with despotic tendencies. In France, Montesquieu believed the nobility, the parlements, and the church could exert restraining influences upon the monarchy. While Montesquieu had no illusions as to the level of corruption found in all three, he believed that the parlements would be the most effective. An independent judiciary, composed of judges who were free, impartial, and consistent, could protect the liberties of the people.

Montesquieu's ideas eventually evolved into his famous doctrine of the separation of powers, whereby power and authority would be split among three main branches of government: executive, legislative, and judicial. He did not define these three branches in exactly the same fashion that they are described today, but the principle behind this formula was recognized and appreciated. His admiration for England helped him arrive at these conclusions. Between 1729 and 1731, he lived in that country, observing its institutions, and came to the conclusion that it was a land where the rule of law, impartial courts, and free speech held sway. He believed that this was largely attributable to the separation of powers, held jointly by the monarch, the houses of Parliament, and an independent judiciary. Critics claim that Montesquieu misjudged the situation and that England actually was well on the way to developing a parliamentary system of government in which the houses of Parliament would gain mastery over the executive branch.

An essential component of Montesquieu's political theory was the relationship he saw between a country's institutions and a host of other factors, including climate, topography, population, wealth, customs and mores, and territorial size. He believed that the republican form of government was best suited to small countries, monarchy to countries of moderate size, and despotism to huge empires. While he personally favored monarchy, he was too much the skeptic to believe in human perfection and political utopias. Montesquieu was a pioneer in political relativism, believing that the best form of government was that which suited a people, given their unique historical, geographical, and cultural circumstances.

His views on the law are generally regarded as an integral part of his political philosophy. He believed liberty consisted not in doing what one pleased, but rather in doing what one ought to do and in not being forced to do what one ought not to do. He held that the number of laws should be kept to a minimum and that a sharp distinction should be made between what one thought and what one actually did. For this reason, he suggested that states be very careful when framing laws on treason. The most serious punishments should be reserved for crimes of violence against either persons or property, since these crimes generated the most fear in society. He firmly believed in the right to a jury trial by one's peers; was against the use of torture in extracting evidence; and believed that when a person was being tried, the law should proceed slowly and carefully to ensure a fair trial. Given these legal precepts, it is not surprising that Montesquieu has been regarded not only as a political theorist of the first rank, but a key figure in the development of modern liberalism as well.

Applications

Montesquieu's ideas and writings left a rich and practical legacy to future generations. With other philosophes, he helped to create an intellectual environment that made the French Revolution not necessarily inevitable, but certainly possible. Although he was not a radical and did not postulate some visionary society that could inspire revolutionaries, he did help to discredit the Old Regime, exposing its corruption, despotic tendencies, and needless wars. During the early months of the Revolution, he was a favorite of the nobility, which was scarcely surprising, since he believed that a powerful nobility, especially when acting through the parlements that they dominated, could serve as an effective check against the monarchy. Once the French Revolution entered a more radical stage, references to him diminished substantially.

It was in America that Montesquieu had his greatest influence. Even before the American Revolution, his books were found in the libraries of towns, universities, and the political elites. John Witherspoon, one of the great presidents of Princeton University and an admirer of Montesquieu, used *The Spirit of the Laws* as a text in one course. Montesquieu was frequently cited in the newspapers and gazettes of the period, as well as in political pamphlets and the debates of colonial legislatures. His greatest impact occurred after the American Revolution, when the fledgling country debated, in 1787 and 1788, whether to adopt the new federal constitution drafted in Philadelphia. James Madison was perhaps Montesquieu's greatest admirer, but George Washington, Thomas Jefferson, Samuel Adams, John Dickerson, James Otis, John Adams, and others also had read his work. Not all agreed with everything he wrote, but they took him seriously. He was referred to in newspapers, private letters, the Federalist Papers, and in the debates of the Constitutional Convention and the various state ratifying conventions.

Montesquieu's influence is easy to understand. The central feature of the debate was whether the new federal U.S. government would prove to be a tyranny, eventually diminishing the powers of the several states and eroding the liberties of the American people. Montesquieu had spoken favorably of a tripartite division of power, and the most obvious aspect of the new constitution was a system of checks and balances, combined with a rigid separation of powers. The new government would be composed of a strong executive, a powerful legislature, and an independent judiciary. Within this framework, there were additional checks and balances. Only the House of Representatives could initiate money bills, but the Senate's concurrence was necessary for these bills to become law. It was assumed the House would represent the interests of populous states, while the Senate would represent small states with sparse populations. The executive could conduct foreign policy, but only the Senate could approve treaties. The legislature could pass bills, but the executive could veto them. The legislature and the executive could combine to pass laws, but the courts could negate this legislation if it was deemed unconstitutional. The executive was popularly elected, but a potential tyrant could be impeached by the House and removed by the Senate. Throughout the U.S. Constitution runs a common theme of which Montesquieu would have approved: Only power can check power, and only a separation of power can prevent despotism. Within two years after the new Constitution took effect, ten amendments were adopted, appropriately labeled a Bill of Rights. These legal guarantees, which established freedom of speech, press, and assembly, defended the individual against the arbitrary power of government, gave citizens the right to a fair trial by jury, and protected even the guilty from cruel and unusual punishment, incorporated many of the enlightened legal precepts that Montesquieu had so eloquently advocated. It is with good reason that James Madison wrote in Federalist No. 47 that Montesquieu was "the oracle" who was always consulted and cited.

One must beware of exaggerating Montesquieu's influence. He certainly was an inspiration in a general way, but Americans also relied upon English law, and, even more important, upon their colonial experiences. They quoted Montesquieu when he validated what they already believed or wished to accomplish. A good example of this regards his views on the relationship between forms of government and size of territory. Here, both the Federalists and Antifederalists quoted him. Antifederalists argued that if a new national government was created, it would be large and powerful by European standards, and, according to Montesquieu, most likely to devolve into despotism because republicanism was best suited to small countries. Federalists countered by pointing out that in another section of his work, Montesquieu had stated that small republics could federate, and the resulting government would have all the virtues of a republic domestically but would have the impact of a powerful monarchy on the foreign scene.

Context

Montesquieu is part of several honorable traditions in Western civilization. First, he was one of the best known of the philosophes. He used his intellectual authority to expose the lies and calumnies of the past and offered sensible advice to the future. What perhaps separated Montesquieu from many philosophes was his caution and skepticism. In some respects, he was fundamentally conservative. He was no democrat in the modern sense of the word, believed that monarchy was probably the best form of government, and never embraced any utopian theory of progress. A few critics have gone so far as to label Montesquieu a reactionary, a wealthy landowner who defended aristocratic privilege against monarchical encroachments. It should be remembered that the philosophes were not defined by their politics, but by the sum total of their enlightened thought.

Second, Montesquieu is part of that remarkable line of political theorists that dominated much of Western thought after the Middle Ages, and includes such names as Niccolò Machiavelli, Thomas Hobbes, James Harrington, and John Locke. Some scholars claim that Montesquieu never formulated a disciplined and comprehensive political philosophy, that his political system is a haphazard collection of valuable ideas and thoughts, and that therefore he does not deserve to be ranked with theorists such as Hobbes and Locke. Nevertheless, a number of political thinkers and activists have acknowledged their debt to Montesquieu, one of the most famous being Alexis de Tocqueville, who wrote a masterful analysis of the political society of the United States in the nineteenth century. Anyone wishing to be familiar with Western political thought should read Montesquieu.

He also made a substantial contribution to humanizing the law. Government under law may be a tired cliché to those who possess it, but it was achieved only after much struggle and sacrifice. For centuries, the application of law was characterized by bribery, arbitrariness, perjury, torture, and cruelty. Montesquieu recognized that the essence of decent government was law. His dictum that law should relate to the other institutions of society and the character of the people, as well as the cultural and geographical environment, was sensible and useful. He wrote eloquently on the nature of law and gave sound advice on how to frame just laws and equitable punishments. Montesquieu deserves an honored position in the pantheon of those individuals who labored to establish the rule of law, an esteemed tradition that resulted in the Magna Carta, the Petition of Right, and other noble documents.

Finally, Montesquieu played a vital role in the scholarly traditions of the West. He contributed to the development of several academic disciplines, particularly sociology, history, and anthropology. No less an authority than Émile Durkheim, a giant in the field of sociology, asserted that Montesquieu had established the fundamental principles of modern social science. Historians see Montesquieu as a seminal figure in the philosophy of history, and some have labeled him as the founder of modern historical methodology. Perhaps his most unheralded achievement was being one of the first to embrace cultural relativism. He rejected absolutes and universalist panaceas; he claimed no special superiority for European civilization but believed that other cultures and previous epochs had equally valid solutions to their unique problems.

Montesquieu's reputation still remains anchored in the field of political philosophy. Some of the more sinister events of the twentieth century appear to validate Montesquieu's warnings and the wisdom of his solutions. Terrible dictatorships were established in a number of countries, including Nazi Germany, Fascist Italy, and Communist Russia. These regimes are examples of what happens when power is not divided: Despots concentrated all executive, legislative, and judicial power in the hands of their political party and systematically destroyed all countervailing power, including that of the courts, churches, universities, legislatures, and the press. Those seeking to fight tyranny and create an open society will find a valuable ally in Montesquieu's political philosophy. The power of his ideas has retained its potency, and history suggests that despots fear truth and ideas more than anything else.

Bibliography

Conroy, Peter V. *Montesquieu Revisited.* New York: Twayne, 1992. Excellent introduction for the mature student. While accepting the traditional view that he was a seminal political thinker, Conroy also seeks to establish Montesquieu's reputation as a major literary figure. Superb annotated bibliography.

Montesquieu, Charles de Secondat, Baron de. *The Spirit of the Laws.* New York: Hafner Press, 1949. Translated by Thomas Nugent. For decades this was the most easily available edition, but the translation has been faulted for its awkward English and tendency to misinterpret some of Montesquieu's words or their meaning.

Shackleton, Robert. *Montesquieu: A Critical Biography.* London: Oxford University Press, 1961. Though dated, this book still remains the standard biography. Shows how Montesquieu's works grew out of his reading, travels, and friendships, but is poorly indexed and crucial quotations remain in the original French.

Shklar, Judith. *Montesquieu.* Oxford, England: Oxford University Press, 1987. Outstanding, brief introduction to Montesquieu, focusing primarily on his political writings. Easy to read, yet the scholarship is impressive. Excellent bibliographical essay.

Spurlin, Paul Merrill. *Montesquieu in America, 1760-1801.* University: Louisiana State University Press, 1940. In this readable and scholarly study, the author expertly examines the dissemination of Montesquieu's writings in the United States and the use that Americans made of him during forty critical years in their history.

David C. Lukowitz

Cross-References

Checks and Balances in U.S. Government, p. 216; Deism, p. 495; Despotism and Tyranny, p. 527; Executive Functions in U.S. Government, p. 636; Hobbes's Political Philosophy, p. 836; Legislative Functions of Government, p. 1098; Liberalism, p. 1118; Locke's Political Philosophy, p. 1142; Monarchy in History, p. 1221; Parliamentary Government, p. 1377; Political Philosophy, p. 1505; Power Divisions in Governments, p. 1578; Republicanism, p. 1706; Rousseau's Political Philosophy, p. 1756; Separation of Powers: Political Philosophy, p. 1809; Tocqueville's Political Philosophy, p. 1981.

MULTIPARTY SYSTEMS

Field of study: Politics

Political systems in which three or more parties are regularly represented in the national legislature qualify as multiparty systems. There are usually one to three large parties, plus small parties that are intensely devoted to certain issues and ideas.

Principal terms
> COALITION GOVERNMENT: government in which cabinet positions are shared among two or more parties that together command a majority in parliament
> IDEOLOGY: consistent philosophy or system of beliefs that guides the actions of those who adopt it
> PARLIAMENTARY SYSTEM: system of fused executive and legislative power, where the executive emerges from a legislative majority
> PROPORTIONAL REPRESENTATION: electoral system that uses multimember districts to allocate legislative seats to political parties in proportion to the size of the vote that they receive
> SINGLE-MEMBER PLURALITY ELECTORAL SYSTEM: electoral system based on single-member districts, which allocates a single seat to the candidate that receives the most votes in each district

Overview

Multiparty systems occur in countries where three or more political parties consistently gain representation in national legislatures. Neither the electoral participation of large numbers of parties nor the occasional electoral successes of third parties that do not essentially alter a two-party system produces a true multiparty system. In spite of the apparent strictness of this definition, multiparty systems are the most common political systems in competitive democracies.

The origins of multiparty systems lie in the structure of their societies and the electoral laws that shape them. Unlike the United States, most countries had experienced sharp divisions, or cleavages, in their societies prior to the implementation of democracy. Almost universally, the class divisions produced by industrialization, as well as preindustrial divisions, such as those imposed by feudalism, were well entrenched before democracy emerged. In addition, the separation of church and state was virtually nonexistent, religious minorities were often subjected to official persecution. Finally, the process of defining national boundaries, primarily through war and diplomacy, left concentrated ethnic and linguistic minorities within most countries. The move to electoral democracy in the nineteenth and twentieth centuries promoted the political organization of these various segments of society.

The divisiveness of politics in these societies also caused fears of majority tyranny and efforts to ensure that the various groups had a voice in government. As a result, electoral laws were crafted to provide for the representation of numerous distinct groups. The most common choice was proportional representation under a parliamentary system of government. Unlike the single-member plurality electoral systems of the United States and Great Britain, proportional representation uses multimember districts to allocate seats in the national legislature in proportion to the votes received by the party. Thus, the percentage of seats is roughly proportional to the percentage of the vote received by the party. This system greatly increases the likelihood that small parties will consistently gain representation. If the single-member plurality system were used, a party would have to get the most votes (a plurality) in a district in order to receive that district's seat.

While the resulting multiparty systems are typically dominated by one to three large parties, they are often highly fragmented, with relatively narrow political parties forming around highly specific social groups and ideological positions. This is the result of the degree of social division in society, the intensity of ideological conflict, and proportional representation's relatively direct translation of these features into political parties. Indeed, many of the parties in multiparty systems focus on only a handful of related issues, and their survival depends on small electorates who are intensely attached to these issues. For example, many countries have Green parties, whose platforms center on environmental issues and environmental consciousness. Denmark's Progress Party, on the other hand, emphasizes tax reform. Multiparty systems are fragmented further by their accommodation of extremist political movements. In Italy, for example, the Communist Party has been the second largest party throughout most of the post-World War II era, although with the 1994 election their name changed to the Democratic Party of the Left and their ideological stance softened considerably. The Italian elections of 1994 also resulted in representation for the neofascist National Alliance.

The sensitivity of multiparty systems to the prevailing electoral conditions makes them relatively changeable. Unlike two-party systems, where shifts in social support and the emergence of new issues are addressed by changes in the platforms of the parties, shifts in the electorate are likely to result in the emergence of new political parties and the decline or disappearance of older parties. This is the case for a number of reasons. First, parties within multiparty systems are based on fairly narrow appeals to clearly defined electorates. This makes large changes in their platforms difficult, although they do occur. Voters, who have become accustomed to these systems of representation, also expect a close fit between their interests and the positions of their parties. Finally, potential political leaders who are interested in forming new parties are aware that the threshold for representation is low, thus giving them additional incentive.

Multiparty systems have significant effects on the behavior of their governments. In multiparty systems, it is unlikely that any single party will receive an absolute majority in the legislature. Thus, lawmaking requires that coalitions be built among several parties. In parliamentary systems, where the executive branch emerges from a legislative majority, coalition building becomes even more important. In this situation, a number of parties must agree on both a basic policy agenda and the division of ministerial responsibilities to ensure that the prime minister and cabinet have the support of a majority in parliament. The more fragmented the party system, the greater the number of partisan positions that must be accommodated and the more delicate the bargaining process becomes. Recent research on coalition formation in multiparty systems indicates that these coalitions tend to be built around either socialist or social democratic parties on the left of the political spectrum, or conservative or Christian democratic parties on the right of the spectrum, as these parties tend to receive the largest amount of electoral support, and, therefore, the greatest number of seats in parliament. In spite of a certain degree of dominance by these parties, the process of coalition formation gives smaller parties leverage disproportionate to the electoral and legislative strength, if their support is needed in order to form a government (parliamentary executive).

The process of coalition building is often extended to electoral politics itself. Potential coalition partnerships among the parties may be announced prior to elections, or permanent arrangements for coordinated action may exist among some political parties. Electoral politics in some countries may also revolve around two or three blocs of parties whose informal, but well-known, affiliations provide the basis for alternative governing coalitions, though each bloc may require additional support from other parties in order to achieve a parliamentary majority. This is typically the case in the Scandinavian countries, where politics centers on competition between the capitalist and socialist blocs of parties, with a number of small parties drifting between them.

Applications

The West German party system after World War II and the party system of united Germany illustrate most of the themes discussed above. The German party system reflects the themes of social and cultural fragmentation and conflict, although the lessons of Germany's failed efforts at maintaining democracy under the Weimar Republic (1919-1933) and reorganization of the parties and electoral laws following the Nazi period have diluted the effects of these conflicts somewhat. These efforts have reinforced the dominance of two parties: the Christian Democratic Union (CDU) and the Social Democratic Party of Germany (SPD). As in most multiparty systems, politics revolves around moderate left- and right-wing parties. Indeed, this tendency is stronger in Germany than in other countries with similar party systems. In spite of efforts to ensure moderation and consolidation through institutional change, various dimensions of social conflict have been evident in the German party system. Radical right-wing nationalist parties have appeared in the German party system on several occasions. Their presence was greatest in the early 1950's, although a resurgence seemed to be under way in the 1990's, led by the Republican Party, which had run nationally but had not gained seats in the German Bundestag (parliament) as of 1990. Radical left-wing parties also have made appearances in the German party system.

The German Communist Party (KPD) received seats in the Bundestag in 1949, and the Party of Democratic Socialism (PDS), formerly called the East German Communist Party, was elected to the first united German Bundestag in 1990. Differences in regional cultures also have had an impact, particularly during the Federal Republic's formative years; however, the Bavarian Christian Social Union (CSU) has added a strong regional flavor to every German parliament from 1949 to the mid-1990's.

The German party system illustrates the impact of changes in political interests and issues on the emergence and decline of specific political parties. After 1949, the German Bundestag contained as many as twelve political parties and as few as four. Increases and decreases in the number of parties are linked to changes in the attitudes of the German electorate, and, to a lesser extent, changes in the Electoral Law that were designed to hinder small parties. The first two Bundestags, in 1949 and 1953, contained a number of parties that had strong connections to Germany's imperial and authoritarian past. The party system was at its peak in terms of fragmentation at this time; however, as German citizens became more comfortable with their new democracy, the number of parties fell rapidly to four. This process was aided by the Electoral Law of 1956, which included a requirement that parties receive at least 5 percent of the vote in order to be represented in the Bundestag. This period of stability and consolidation was disrupted by the protest movements of the 1960's and 1970's. The political agenda of this era ultimately resulted in the formation of the Green Party, which conducted its first national campaign in 1980 and entered the Bundestag for the first time in 1983. The reunification of East and West Germany resulted in the further expansion of the German party system, with the inclusion of the Party of Democratic Socialism and Alliance 90 in 1990.

The importance of coalitions is illustrated by the formal alliance between the CDU and the CSU at both the electoral and parliamentary levels. Although their policy positions are somewhat different, the two parties mount coordinated campaigns and essentially behave as a single party in the Bundestag. Their alliance is best illustrated by the fact that the CDU does not run in Bavaria, and the CSU does not run in the other German states. The relationship between multiparty systems and coalition building is also evident in the nature of German parliamentary executive. Only once in the history of the Federal Republic has an election resulted in a majority for a single party, and, therefore, a chancellor and cabinet composed entirely of a single party, the CDU-CSU. Even this case constituted a coalition government, because, in spite of their formal alliance, the CDU and CSU are separate organizations. German coalition governments also demonstrate the disproportionate leverage that is often granted to small parties in multiparty systems. Ten of the twelve German cabinets that were formed between 1949 and 1994 included the Free Democratic Party (FDP). Although the FDP has never received more than 13 percent of the vote, and typically receives less than 10 percent, it holds the balance of power between the CDU-CSU and the SPD. Thus, the FDP is in a position to decide which of the larger parties will be allowed to form a government, and often receives significant policy concessions and ministerial positions in return for its support.

Context

The impact of multiparty systems on the performance of democratic governments is often debated. On the positive side, multiparty systems are often praised for their ability to represent effectively the interests of the electorate. Because two-party systems emphasize moderate policies, they fail to capture the full spectrum of opinion in the electorate; therefore, the governments that they produce often fail to consider the full range of policy alternatives. Multiparty systems provide at least a partial remedy to this problem. Voters whose views are not within the mainstream have a clear expression of their interests and values, rather than existing as a permanent minority within a broad centrist party that is unlikely to act on their interests, leading to alienation and dissatisfaction. The coalition governments produced by multiparty systems must by definition come to grips with considerable diversity, and, through bargaining, produce a consensus.

While multiparty systems are highly representative of the electorate, the fragmentation that they produce makes the connection between election results and the composition and policies of the government less clear. This is the case because the process of coalition formation rests on bargains struck by the parties, rather than a mandate from the voters. Even when potential coalitions are announced prior to an election, the precise policy balance is not known, and voters are generally unaware of the trade-offs that their party has made. Coalition governments are far less stable than their single-party counterparts, because the multiparty majorities that produce them are prone to disagreements and defections. This leads to frequent dissolutions of parliament and an unsettling frequency of elections. This problem becomes more acute as the number of parties increases.

Multiparty systems are also criticized for accommodating extremist parties and movements that are opposed to democracy itself. They are more prone to totalitarian takeovers, because the participation of these parties provides their leaders with legitimacy, while the instability of coalition governments helps to undermine the legitimacy of democracy. The multiparty system of the German Weimar Republic allowed the Nazi Party to come to power through democratic procedures, and the instability of its coalitions provided support for Hitler's claim that Germany needed authoritarian leadership.

In spite of their fragility in comparison to two-party systems, multiparty systems have been the most common political system among democracies. They emerge in highly divided societies with significant numbers of cohesive social groups, which is the typical situation in countries where democracy followed, rather than preceded, the Industrial Revolution. Their ability to provide adequate representation and to keep conflict within accepted institutional channels is likely to ensure their continued prevalence among competitive party systems.

Bibliography

Lijphart, Arend. *Democracies: Patterns of Majoritarian and Consensus Government in Twenty-One Countries*. New Haven, Conn.: Yale University Press, 1984. Discusses party systems, the electoral laws underlying them, and the coalition governments that result from them. Lijphart's treatment is accessible, unlike most books devoted specifically to multiparty systems.

Mackie, Thomas, and Richard Rose, eds. *The International Almanac of Electoral History.* 3d ed. London: Macmillan, 1991. Covers election results in twenty-five major democracies, most of which are multiparty systems, from the nineteenth century through 1990. Each country's chapter begins with a summary of major political issues and a description of the electoral system and the parties. Almanac includes a useful appendix on electoral mechanics.

Mair, Peter, ed. *The West European Party System.* New York: Oxford University Press, 1990. Excellent collection of essays that covers existing scholarship on most important topics related to multiparty systems. Some essays are a bit sophisticated, but many are accessible to the general reader. Bibliography with partial annotation.

Sartori, Giovanni. *Parties and Party Systems: A Framework for Analysis.* New York: Cambridge University Press, 1976. Arguably the most important book on multiparty systems; however, it is written for scholars. Covers various types and subtypes of party systems and their implications. A diligent reader might make good use of this book after gaining some background from Lijphart, Mair, or Wolinetz.

Wolinetz, Steven B., ed. *Parties and Party Systems in Liberal Democracies.* New York: Routledge, 1988. Collection of essays focusing on how party systems change. The book's strength is the number of thorough, well-written case studies that it contains. The average reader can grasp the history of multiparty systems in eleven countries through this book.

W. David Patterson

Cross-References

Cabinet Government, p. 184; Elections, p. 578; Executive Functions in U.S. Government, p. 636; Legislative Functions of Government, p. 1098; Parliamentary Government, p. 1377; Political Participation, p. 1479; Political Parties, p. 1485; Political Party Roles, p. 1499; Political Representation in the United States, p. 1525; Two-Party Systems, p. 2033; Voting in History, p. 2116; Voting Processes, p. 2123.

THE NATION-STATE

Field of study: Types of government

The nation-state is the fundamental building block of international relations, the locus of sovereignty, and the principal political unit in which peoples pursue common goals and ends within a multinational setting. Unifying features of a nation-state include common history, language, ethnicity or race, culture, religion, or shared values.

Principal terms

FEDERALISM: national system of government where constituent elements are under the sovereign authority of a central government, but have a degree of local autonomy

IRREDENTISM: claim by one country to territory lying under the sovereign jurisdiction of a neighboring country, based on the nationality or ethnic ties of the local population to the claimant nation

MULTINATIONAL STATE: state comprising many different, sometimes conflicting, ethnic or racial groupings

NATIONALISM: ideology based on the belief in the unity of a people based on their cultural, linguistic, historical, religious, and ethnic characteristics

SELF-DETERMINATION: right of a people to achieve sovereignty and independence

SEPARATISM: desire of a portion of a country's population to achieve sovereign independence from an existing country, often because of ethnic divisions

UNITARY STATES: national system of government in which constituent elements have no autonomy, but serve as administrative units for the enforcement of national policy

Overview

The nation-state is the focal point for both domestic politics and international relations in the modern world. Nation-states are the highest sovereign authorities for governance of peoples. People within the nation-state look to it as the formulator, enforcer, and interpreter of law. Nation-states are the culminating political units and legal entities empowered to protect and defend their populations and territories. As such, nation-states are the principal building blocks of international relations. Governments of nation-states sit at the intersection between domestic politics and foreign relations. They unite peoples under the domestic banner of national sovereignty, but divide peoples in the international arena.

Forerunners to the nation-state are found in the city-state systems of ancient Greece, India, and China, as well as in Renaissance Italy. The modern nation-state, however, resulted from the gradual collapse of Christendom during the Reformation and the religious wars it precipitated. The Reformation fed on local and national jealousies against the influence of Rome and the Roman Catholic church in secular affairs, and the corruption this was perceived to have caused in the spiritual realm. Local princes allied with religious reformers staked out claims against church domination. Distinctly national churches emerged: Lutheranism in Germany, Calvinism in Geneva, Anglicanism in England. Religion and national fervor were joined as princes proclaimed their sovereign independence from Rome. Religious wars ensued as Roman Catholic kings interceded on behalf of Catholics suffering under Protestant rule, and as Protestant princes interceded on behalf of fellow Protestants under Catholic dominion. These bloody wars, which culminated in the Thirty Years War, came to an end in 1648 with the promulgation of the Peace of Westphalia, which, among other things, declared princes to be sovereign within their own territorial boundaries, and thus the sole determiners of the religion of their state. A principle of nonintervention emerged, even as princes and kings consolidated their hold on the administrative machinery of the state.

The genie of nationalism had been set afoot, and people began to identify themselves as part of groups sharing common religions, languages, historical traditions, and ethnic backgrounds. This common sense of national traditions galvanized the national spirit and was channeled by monarchs to support their symbolic role as the unity of the nation. This strengthened monarchy for a time, but later, popular demands for participation were unleashed, leading to revolution and eventually to the seemingly inexorable progress of democratic forms of government.

The consolidation of national sentiments in Europe coincided with Europe's gradual colonial expansion so that by the late 1800's virtually the entire globe was brought under the control of the Westphalian state system, and eventually the nonselfgoverning areas sought their own national self-determination and independence. The state system in Europe economically benefited from this colonial expansion; this was accompanied by increased national sentiments, both in Europe, where by now many stable nation-states existed, and in the colonized portions of the globe, where colonialism itself stoked the fires of local nationalist sentiment.

In Europe, as in the nation-states that emerged in North and South America, two essential varieties of states emerged, federal and unitary. The classic example of a federal state was Switzerland, where local cantons reflecting French, German, and Italian influences were granted significant autonomy but shared basic foreign, defense, trade, and monetary policies shaped by the central government. The United States also reflected the decentralized features of the federal model.

Unitary systems, however, were far more prevalent. In these systems, the local, state, or provincial governments have no autonomy but serve instead as the administrative apparatus through which the central government enforces and applies the law. In France, for example, the regional departments serve as arms of the national government.

At least in theory, one of the advantages of the federal system is that it lends itself more flexibly to countries whose populations are more ethnically, culturally, or regionally fragmented. The unitary model, on the other hand, tends to be more rigid and better adapted to homogeneous states. In most, but not all, European countries, the unitary model fit nicely with the establishment of stable homogeneous nations with distinct unifying cultures. In the case of the Austro-Hungarian and Soviet empires, however, the states created were multiethnic in character. When these empires broke up, Austro-Hungary after World War I and the Soviet empire at the end of the Cold War in the early 1990's, it became clear that underlying nationalist sentiments were a major factor in each collapse. Although the Soviet Union was nominally a federal system, it was so thoroughly controlled by the Communist Party that it was, in fact, unitary. Underlying ethno-nationalistic impulses that continued to seethe in non-Russian republics eventually served as the engine for the eventual collapse of the Soviet Union. In Eastern Europe, especially in Czechoslovakia and Yugoslavia, nationalistic impulses led to the disintegration of the state, Czechoslovakia peacefully through the so-called Velvet Revolution, and Yugoslavia through violent wars of secession and independence.

Apart from these exceptions, state-building in Europe corresponded fairly neatly with nation-building, and the problem of the multiethnic state was atypical. The colonized portions of the globe faced more difficult situations, especially in Africa, but also in Asia and the Middle East. Most of the former colonial areas that gained independence after World War II could claim to have established states but not unified nations. In many instances, such as in Nigeria or Sudan, the state encompassed many different and conflicting nationalities or tribes. Hence the tendencies toward separatism were considerable, and the political life of many new nations was aggravated by continual ethnic strife.

Even as the stable nations of Europe began to explore wider integration and regional unity after World War II, nationalism, which had cooled in Western Europe, emerged as a volatile force for change in both Eastern and Central Europe and in the newly independent states of the Third World. In those areas where genuine nationalist sentiments long had been repressed or were finding their first coherent expression, great instability was experienced as older, established states yielded to newly emerging claims to national self-determination.

The ideal, stable nation-state is one in which the state governs a stable population that shares a common national sentiment. The sense of nationhood—of shared history and values and a common vision for the future—lends great stability to a country. Other factors besides cultural similarity are needed, however, for the stability of a nation-state. Countries must be large enough to protect and defend their interests and to be economically viable. These practical considerations also play a role in defining national stability, and they may be at odds with cultural and national claims to divide existing states. When claims for self-determination are vigorously advanced by peoples within a state who no longer, or perhaps never did, share in a common sense of nationhood with the rest of that state's population, serious problems arise for the stability of that state. Wars of independence, separatist movements, and irredentist claims reflect the fact that there is often a great discontinuity between the territorial jurisdiction of a state and the national loyalties of its citizens or subjects.

Applications

Nation-states perform many roles. Three of the more important ones are to guard the national culture, to promote national economic prosperity, and to protect and defend the physical integrity of the nation.

In its role as guardian of national culture, a nation-state promotes civic education to transmit the political culture, history, and traditions of the society to its youth. It promotes the arts and music, encourages the celebration of national holidays, and displays various symbols of the nation in an effort to preserve national unity. Apart from its educational and propaganda efforts, the government also may seek to curb foreign immigration and other influences on the language or culture. In multiethnic states, the government's capacity to build a sense of unity is substantially circumscribed, and in such states cries for separate education, multiculturalism, and diversity are often heard. These tend to run against the goal of assimilation into a common culture and present problems for the attainment of national unity. Where such subnational sentiments exist in a nation-state, especially when these sentiments are tied to specific geographical regions, and when the cleavages are not only ethnic, but also reinforced by religious and linguistic differences and economic grievances, the prospects for civil conflict and secession increases.

Nation-states, as the ultimate sovereign entities in modern politics, are responsible for promoting economic viability, growth, and prosperity for their peoples. Most states attempt to protect their economic interests through controlling trade, encouraging domestic industrial growth, preserving employment, and controlling fiscal and monetary policy. Even the largest, most naturally well-endowed, resource-rich, and climatically diverse country, however, is not economically self-sufficient. Thus, countries must trade, invest abroad, and seek foreign investment, to encourage the diffusion and transfer of technology, and often to allow migration across borders to ensure the availability of a labor supply. During times of economic exigency and severe unemployment, states often employ protectionist trade measures and restrictive immigration policies. In times of plenty, they may be less restrictive regarding immigration and more open to free trade.

Another principal function of nation-states is to maintain the security and physical protection of the population. This responsibility ranges from promoting health and controlling disease to providing for a common national defense. Almost all nations maintain armed forces to protect against foreign attack, and virtually all of them have police forces to ensure domestic order, protection of property, tranquillity, and social stability. This goal of physical security, both domestic and foreign, may preoccupy a nation to such a degree that it can no longer sustain its economic viability. On the other hand, where states are stable and free of multiethnic disputes, they can more easily promote both economic prosperity and physical security.

The various functions of the nation-state are, in practice, interrelated. Where domestic instability owing to ethnic disputes exists, promotion of economic growth and protection from foreign incursion are problematic. Where national unity exists, whether because of an underlying ethnic homogeneity or because of a consensus of shared values across ethnic communities, economic growth and common defense are more easily attained.

All nation-states seek the ultimate ends of political independence, territorial preservation and security, economic prosperity, and social stability. These ends are most easily achieved in the context of a common national sentiment; where they are not, questions arise about whether the particular nation-state is viable or whether it might best be divided into more stable subunits. Although peaceful efforts in achieving the latter are not unheard of, the tendency is for such issues to be resolved by conflict.

Context

The stubbornness and the growth of the nationalist sentiment since the seventeenth century is one of the distinctive features of the modern world. The nation-state, though often declared by experts to be anachronistic and moribund, continues to be the central feature of political organization around the globe, for conducting both domestic policy and foreign affairs. Old nations have disintegrated, but new and more numerous ones have risen to take their place. Czechoslovakia split into two independent republics. The Soviet Union disintegrated into fifteen sovereign national entities. Even among these, further calls for self-determination by various ethnic minorities were raised. Yugoslavia underwent violent civil conflict as new states in Slovenia and Croatia, reflecting ancient national aspirations, emerged. Serbs asserted irredentist claims against Bosnia-Herzegovina, as Somalia did against neighboring Ethiopia, based on the fact that these areas under the nominal control of the neighboring state are populated by people of the claimant state's ethnic or historical affiliation. This often leads to conflicts over territory. In Sri Lanka, Tamils sought independence from the Sinhalese majority. Eritreans successfully seceded from Ethiopia. Southern Sudanese peoples struggled for independence from the Arab-dominated northern Sudanese government. Hutus and Tutsis slaughtered one another in Rwanda. French-speaking Quebecois have sought independence from the English-speaking provinces of Canada.

In each case, as particular nation-states face disintegration, new, if smaller, nations rise up, seeking self-determination and a seat among the councils of independent nations. The nation-state system, then, seems highly resilient even if certain nation-states pass away.

It is often claimed that the nation-state, fueled by nationalism, is one of the principal causes of war. Certainly many wars of the nineteenth and twentieth centuries were begun in nationalistic fervor. In the late twentieth century, however, nationalism seemed less a cause of international than civil conflict. A major irony of this may be that advanced nation-states could, in the course of cooperating to resolve manifold civil conflict around the world, at last find viable measures for reducing nationalistic wars among themselves. In the meantime, it is likely that the world will see a downsizing of multiethnic states and an increase in the number of smaller homogeneous, but also less economically viable, nation-states. Once the ethnonationalistic puzzle has been broken down to its smaller constituent elements, the process of cooperating to meet economic necessities will reemerge and growing interdependence may lead the disparate nations once again back to the logic of larger economic confederacies.

Bibliography

Akzin, Benjamin. *State and Nation*. London: Hutchinson University Library, 1964. Brief, readable introduction to the terminological distinctions, literature, and theory of nations, states, and nationalism. Examines the varieties of nations, single and multiple ethnic states, integrationist and pluralist states, secessionist questions, and the problem of nationalism in developing countries.

Armstrong, John. *Nations Before Nationalism*. Chapel Hill: University of North Carolina Press, 1982. Scholarly historical treatment of the emergence of nations from earliest times to the nineteenth century. Examines the religious, ethnic, linguistic, and social origins of the nation.

Cobban, Alfred. *The Nation-State and National Self-Determination*. New York: Thomas Y. Crowell, 1969. Classic history and analysis of the rise of nationalism in Europe and the role of the great powers in the affairs of smaller states.

Horowitz, Donald. *Ethnic Groups in Conflict*. Berkeley: University of California Press, 1985. This scholarly book provides useful insights into workings of ethnic conflict, irredentist and separatist claims, and assimilationist and pluralist strategies for overcoming tensions produced by ethnic diversity.

Kohn, Hans. *Nationalism, Its Meaning and History*. Rev. ed. Princeton, N.J.: D. Van Nostrand, 1965. Classic, beautifully written work that traces the history of nationalism. Provides a representative sample of readings from primary sources that illustrate both the meaning and potency of nationalism as a source of identity and affection for peoples in different times and places.

Ronen, Dov. *The Quest for Self-Determination*. New Haven, Conn.: Yale University Press, 1979. Tracing the right of self-determination to the American and French revolutions, this book examines the history of the development of this right, the various forms it has taken, and several contexts in which the right has been asserted.

Suhrke, Astri, and Lela Garner Noble. *Ethnic Conflict in International Relations*. New York: Praeger, 1977. Useful anthology of case studies in ethnic conflict and its national and international implications. Comparative case studies include Cyprus, Northern Ireland, Lebanon, Eritrea, the Kurds in Iraq, Kazakhs in China, and Muslims in Southeast Asia.

Tivey, Leonard, ed. *The Nation-State: The Formation of Modern Politics*. New York: St. Martin's Press, 1981. Essays devoted to such questions as the origin of the nation-state; the varieties of nationalism; the relationship between socialism and nationalism; the experience of nation-states in Asia, Africa, and Europe; and the future of the nation-state.

Tucker, Robert. *The Inequality of Nations*. New York: Basic Books, 1977. Examines the discontinuity of power among and between nation-states, making a case for the responsible use of power by those states capable of maintaining global order and stability.

Robert F. Gorman

Cross-References

The City-State, p. 272; Confederations, p. 391; Federations, p. 675; Government Types, p. 785; Hobbes's Political Philosophy, p. 836; Indigenous Peoples' Governments, p. 903; International Law, p. 956; International Relations, p. 969; Leagues, p. 1072; Liberal Nationalism, p. 1111; Nationalism, p. 1268; Secessionism, p. 1790; The State, p. 1878.

NATIONAL ECONOMIES

Field of study: Economic issues

A *national economy consists of the process by which scarce economic resources—human resources, capital goods, and natural resources—are used to produce the goods and services that are the basis for people's standard of living. Government policies strongly affect the national economy.*

Principal terms
AGGREGATE DEMAND: total spending on goods and services by households, business firms, government, and other countries
CAPITAL GOODS: items that have been produced and are used for further production
FACTORS OF PRODUCTION: inputs that contribute to production: human resources, natural resources, and capital goods
FISCAL POLICIES: government policies relating to taxation, expenditures, and management of the national debt
GROSS DOMESTIC PRODUCT (GDP): market value of the final goods and services produced within a nation in one year
INFRASTRUCTURE: government-provided facilities that make an economy more productive, such as highways and schools
MONETARY POLICIES: government measures that determine the amount of money (currency and deposits) in the economy
REAL GROSS DOMESTIC PRODUCT: GDP adjusted to measure only changes in the quantity of output produced
TRANSFER PAYMENTS: income payments by government for which the government does not receive goods or services of comparable value in exchange

Overview
Any people's economic well-being is an important determinant of their political behavior. Twentieth century governments must concern themselves with the economic well-being of their citizens to achieve electoral support, minimize social unrest, and secure the resources necessary for their own operations.

The national economy contains resources that can be used to produce goods and services. The most important are the human resources—the skills, motivation, energy, and creativity of the people. Productive people utilize capital goods, such as buildings and equipment, and natural resources, such as farmland, mineral resources, and climate, to become more productive in turning out goods and services that people want. Most national economies are organized around buying and selling. Households supply services of labor and property and receive money incomes in exchange. They use these money incomes to buy the goods and services they choose. For an individual household, economic well-being appears to be defined by the money income available to spend. For the entire economic system, however, economic well-being depends on the total quantity and quality of goods and services produced. Business firms that need to pay for the inputs they use have an incentive to use efficient methods of production in order to keep costs down. Using resources efficiently helps to get more output for the system as a whole. Business firms also have an incentive to produce those goods and services that yield the most profit, since those will be the ones that are most strongly desired by households.

During the twentieth century, many governments experimented with socialist and communist methods of economic organization, which substituted government decision making for private buying and selling. These experiments generally were not successful, and the trend in the 1980's and 1990's was back to market systems, in which individuals own the factors of production and decide how to use them.

Two measures commonly used to analyze national economies are Gross National Product (GNP) and Gross Domestic Product (GDP). Both GNP and GDP measure the market value of all final goods and services produced within a national economy in one year. GDP, which has become more widely used, includes the income earned by foreigners in a nation and subtracts income earned abroad by the nation's citizens. For the United States, the two measures are very close together. In measuring GDP, only final products are counted. For example, if the market value of a loaf of bread is included, the value of the flour used in making it would not be added in also. In general, only goods and services sold for money are counted. Bias can result from the exclusion of important unpaid services, such as those of homemakers.

There are many ways of subdividing GDP. One is to see who purchases the goods and services produced and what the major types of production consist of. From this perspective, there are four major components of national output. First is the consumption of goods and services, measured by households. In the United States, this category accounts for about two-thirds of the total. The second is investment in currently produced capital goods, such as machinery, structures, and increased business inventories of goods in process or awaiting sale. The third category, government purchases of goods and services, includes both wages and salaries paid to government employees, and government purchases of material goods, from airplanes and computers to paper and pencils. This category does not include government transfer payments for which no current products or services are received by government. The final factor, net exports, represents the difference between the value of exports and the value of imports. Combining these factors yields the aggregate demand for goods and services.

GDP can also be looked at as a measure of the value added by each production sector in the economy. To measure the value added by the automobile industry, for example, one would measure the value of the industry's sales and deduct the industry's purchases of inputs from other business firms. Adding the value-added figures for all sectors of the economy will give the GDP. The value-added figure for each industry would correspond to the industry's payments for wages and salaries, interest, rent, and business taxes, its allowance for capital depreciation, and its profits. For all industries combined, GNP corresponds to the total of these various incomes paid by productive business. Equality between output value and total incomes reflects the identity between the dollar value of sales and the dollar value of receipts. Value-added data are a good indicator of the relative importance of individual industries.

It is often useful to know how GDP has changed over time. Changes in GDP occur because either the quantity of output or the price level has changed. Increased quantity of output generally means an improvement in people's economic well-being, but an increase in prices does not. Therefore, governments present data on GDP measured both in current prices and in constant prices, or real GDP. Goods produced, for example, in 1994, can be valued at what they would have cost in 1990. Comparison of real GDP for different years indicates changes in economic well-being more accurately than examining GDP in current prices for different years.

Since part of output growth over time is matched by population growth, it is common to examine changes in real GDP per capita. When discussing per capita income, certain related factors should be considered. One is the distribution of income—how much goes to the top income brackets, and how much to the lowest income brackets. Another is the quality of life, which includes such things as environmental conditions and the extent of crime and violence.

Economic growth involving increases in real GDP over time comes either from increases in the quantity of resources or from improvement in productivity because of technological change or improved organization of the economy.

Another measure of economic concern is the rate of unemployment: the number of people willing and able to work but unable to find suitable jobs. If the labor force grows by 1 percent per year, and worker productivity also increases by another 1 percent, real GDP must increase at least 2 percent per year to keep unemployment from rising. Year-to-year changes in unemployment are strongly affected by aggregate demand.

The interactive nature of a modern economy can be represented by an input-output table. For each major economic sector, this shows the amount of goods and services received from each other sector and the amount this sector supplied to each other sector.

Applications

The national economy affects government in many ways. Government officials have an incentive to try to improve people's economic well-being. If the economy's condition worsens, incumbent politicians may be defeated for reelection. Recession and unemployment helped explain George Bush's defeat by Bill Clinton in November, 1992. Economic distress can even lead to the overthrow of a governmental system. Germany's crisis of mass unemployment in the early 1930's destroyed the shaky democratic system created by the Weimar Constitution of 1919 and brought Adolf Hitler to power. Economic failures also led to the disintegration of communist regimes in the Soviet Union and its former satellites beginning in the late 1980's.

The impact of government on the national economy can be analyzed in a few major categories. At the most basic level, government sets the legal framework. Public and private law, supported by police, courts, and other public institutions, define and protect property rights, identify and assist in enforcement of contracts, and reward or penalize many types of behavior.

Government also is a major purchaser of goods and services, as well as a major employer. In modern industrialized countries, government purchases typically absorb 15 to 25 percent of GDP. Industries such as defense contractors and construction firms depend heavily on government. Reductions in United States defense spending in the early 1990's caused economic hardship to defense-dependent communities, especially in California and Washington.

Many people other than government employees depend on government for some or all of their income. Millions of Americans receive social security checks for retirement, disability, or dependent benefits or temporary unemployment compensation. These are forms of transfer payments, as are many types of welfare targeted to low-income families.

Government supplies goods and services that help the economy to be more productive. Many of these are constructed facilities, termed infrastructure, such as highways, airports, and river and harbor improvements. Public education facilities contribute to a more productive labor force. Controversy can arise, however, when government provides goods and services that could also be provided by private business. Generating and distributing electricity is one example; the post office is another. The cost-effectiveness of government programs may be impaired by concern for the welfare of suppliers.

Government can powerfully affect aggregate demand for goods and services through monetary and fiscal policies. Reduction in tax rates or increase in government expenditure are likely to stimulate increase in aggregate demand, although the degree of such stimulation is the subject of debate among economists. Government can also stimulate aggregate demand by measures to speed the growth of the money supply, involving the Federal Reserve system in the United States.

Stimulating aggregate demand tends to raise real GDP when the economy has substantial unemployment and when productive facilities are not working to capacity. Some degree of unemployment is normal in a changing economy, but when the unemployment rate exceeds 6 or 7 percent, the political pressure for demand stimulation tends to increase. Demand stimulation, however, can aggravate inflation, worsen deficit financing, and open the way for wasteful or harmful spending programs.

Finally, government regulates the private sectors of the economy. During much of the twentieth century, federal agencies in the United States have monitored and regulated pricing practices of such sectors as railroads, interstate motor truck lines, airlines, long-distance telephone services, and natural gas, through such agencies as the Interstate Commerce Commission, the Federal Power Commission, and the Federal Communications Commission. Such price regulation ostensibly was designed to protect consumers but often contributed to monopoly practices in the regulated sector. A movement toward deregulation, which began in the late 1970's during the presidency of Jimmy Carter, opened most of these sectors to greater competition and reduced government involvement in pricing decisions. A contrary move was the imposition of rate regulation on cable television in 1993, a move followed by rate increases in many areas. Agriculture in the United States is subject to federal intervention affecting output and prices for many products. These programs were instituted during the Depression of the 1930's and have been retained in efforts to keep farm incomes higher than they would be otherwise.

Other federal regulatory programs include the regulation of food and drugs, dating from 1906, and efforts of the Federal Trade Commission, created in 1914, to prevent unfair competition and false and misleading advertising. Banking and finance are regulated by several federal and state agencies. Regulation of labor conditions includes laws prohibiting wages below the statutory minimum and excess hours of work, and laws regulating the formation and activities of labor unions. After the 1960's, programs to prohibit discrimination against ethnic groups, women, the aged, and the disabled were added.

During the presidency of Richard Nixon (1969-1973), significant new types of federal regulation were undertaken, creating two federal agencies that later grew in importance: the Environmental Protection Agency (EPA) and the Occupational Safety and Health Administration (OSHA).

In the United States, state and local governments also have extensive regulatory programs. Entry into many businesses and professions—driving a cab, practicing law or medicine, operating a barber shop—requires a license. Food stores and restaurants must meet sanitary standards. These regulations protect the public, but they also protect existing firms against entry of new competitors.

Context

There has been constant controversy concerning the appropriate role for government in the economy. In his classic *The Wealth of Nations* (1776), Adam Smith argued in favor of restraining the economic role of the government for two main reasons. First, private markets oriented around buying, selling, and the pursuit of profits would work in a socially beneficial way if there was vigorous competition and property and contract rights were properly defined and protected by government. Second, government was by its nature unsuited to an extensive economic role, for it would always be swayed by powerful special interests eager to use government power to enrich themselves at the expense of the general public. Such arguments have been updated and extended by Nobel Prize-winning economists Friedrich Hayek and James Buchanan.

In the United States, extensions in the economic role of government often have occurred in response to wartime emergencies. Political pressure from the business community had led to tariffs, subsidies for transport development, and similar services and favors from government to business.

The Depression of the 1930's led to a great expansion in the economic role of the federal government. New programs included extensive regulation of agriculture, promotion of labor unions, setting minimum wages and maximum hours, and social security. Many intellectuals believed the private economy was unfair, inefficient, and unstable. Relatively successful programs of regulation during World War II and fear of a postwar depression strengthened the case for interventionist government. A common image was that of a welfare state, relying on private enterprise for most production but with extensive programs to ensure a minimum standard of living for all and with demand management by monetary and fiscal policies to achieve full employment without inflation. Social security was extended by the creation of Medicare and Medicaid (1965), and the administration of President Lyndon Johnson undertook a War on Poverty.

Disillusionment with the apparently unlimited agenda of the welfare state arose in many parts of the world in the 1970's and 1980's. This was a period in which most of the industrialized countries experienced economic distress, both short-run (inflation and unemployment associated with disruptions of the world petroleum market in the 1970's) and long-run (slowdown in economic growth). The War on Poverty was not being won; instead, the proportion identified as poor seemed immune to improvement. Backlash against government intervention was manifested in the deregulation campaign during the Carter Administration, the election of Ronald Reagan in 1980, and the support for H. Ross Perot in 1992.

Bibliography

Dahl, Robert A., and Charles E. Lindblom. *Politics, Economics, and Welfare.* Chicago: University of Chicago Press, 1976. A political scientist and an economist collaborated on this comprehensive analysis, which stresses such issues as control, organization behavior, and bargaining. Relatively advanced.

Economic Report of the President. Washington, D.C.: Government Printing Office, 1993. Annual survey of economic developments and proposals for policy changes, written for the general public. Appendix is a mine of statistical information about all aspects of the American economy.

Friedman, Milton. *Capitalism and Freedom.* Chicago: University of Chicago Press, 1982. Nobel Prize-winning economist gives a vigorous defense of free markets and a strong critique of extensive government involvement in the economy. Very readable position paper.

Galbraith, John Kenneth. *The Affluent Society.* 4th ed. Boston: Houghton Mifflin, 1984. Now a classic; discusses many elements of the modern U.S. economy. Argues there is too much stress on further increases in private consumption and advocates greater government spending on public goods and income redistribution.

Gregory, Paul, and Robert Stuart. *Comparative Economic Systems.* 4th ed. Boston: Houghton Mifflin, 1992. The national economy is a system, and this college-level text puts the United States economy in perspective by comparing it with other major national economies.

Gwartney, James D., et al. *Economics: Private and Public Choice.* 6th ed. Fort Worth: Dryden Press, 1992. This college textbook for the introductory economics course gives a shrewd and comprehensive overview of the major aspects of the national economy.

Lee, Susan P., and Peter Passell. *A New Economic View of American History*. New York: W. W. Norton, 1979. The national economy can usefully be studied from a historical perspective, and this college text provides an interesting basis for such an approach.

Paul B. Trescott

Cross-References

Budgets of National Governments, p. 158; Business and Government, p. 177; Capitalism, p. 197; Commerce Regulation, p. 357; Debts and Deficits in the U.S. Federal Budget, p. 489; Funding of Government, p. 724; Government Roles, p. 778; Industrialization, p. 916; Isolationism and Protectionism, p. 1000; Keynesianism, Monetarism, and Supply-Side Economics, p. 1032; Liberalism, p. 1118; Marxism-Leninism, p. 1155; Mercantilism, p. 1173; Political Economy, p. 1455; The Social Security System, p. 1852; Treasury Systems in the United States, p. 2013; The World Bank, p. 2153.

NATIONAL LIBERATION MOVEMENTS

Field of study: Civil rights and liberties

For as long as there has been colonialism, there have been various forms of local opposition to it. In many cases national liberation movements (the form that much of the resistance has taken) have had goals and effects beyond that of freeing lands and peoples from foreign domination.

Principal terms
> ANTICOLONIALISM: opposition to a foreign government's maintenance of a government and other dominant institutions on native land
> COLONIALISM: system of government applied to dependencies of a more powerful and advanced country
> COLONY: population and occupied land with official links to the parent state
> COUNTERINSURGENCY: actions of an established authority to quell armed resistance
> IMPERIALISM: policy, practice, or advocacy of one nation's seeking to control, colonize, or extend other forms of dominion over another
> INSURGENCY: guerrilla warfare by the disinherited against an established authority
> NATIONAL LIBERATION MOVEMENT: rebellions, often armed, of national or minority groups against colonial governments or native governments under foreign control
> NEOCOLONIALISM: colonialism without the name; political, economic, cultural, or other dominance exercised by strong nations over weaker ones, often by means of multinational corporations, counter-insurgency, foreign aid money, military bases, and other means

Overview

Colonization is the act of a government's placing settlers in new territories, when the settlers maintain ties to the parent state. The profit motive is usually central to colonization. If there are people displaced by the settlers, those displaced may make war against the settlers and the parent state. The settlers may grow dissatisfied with the parent state and strive to form a new nation, as happened with the United States. The parent state, in turn, by means of military superiority, development of the colony, and able administration, may maintain control of the colony. A colony is a colony when the parent state calls it such. Colonization is not a neutral term; it has developed negative connotations. For this reason, nations may claim that they are subject to colonial exploitation when they are not officially colonies; hence the word "neocolonialism," which describes the practices of colonialism (especially as they relate to economic exploitation, rather than as they relate to settlement) without the official acknowledgment of colonization.

Modern colonialism started with the Spanish and Portuguese voyages of discovery to America and India in the late fifteenth century. The Dutch, British, French, and other European powers followed soon after. This period of colonization continued until the twentieth century. After World War II many colonies of the European powers gained independence.

This period of colonization did not, however, follow a linear progression from the fifteenth to the twentieth centuries. By the mid-nineteenth century, European enthusiasm for colonialism was waning. For example, some European leaders, such as Benjamin Disraeli, prime minister of Great Britain, were having second thoughts about the costs and benefits of colonialism. Great Britain had long since lost the colonies that became the United States, and the British espousal of free trade seemed to make colonialism less attractive than it was under earlier systems of managed trade. The creation of a unified Italy and Germany, with their own colonial aspirations, in the mid- to late nineteenth century and more intensive rivalry among European nations, which was fueled by nationalism, considerations of prestige, an arms race, and the perceived need to acquire coaling stations and bases, rekindled the scramble for colonies in the latter part of the nineteenth century and the beginning of the next. The movement peaked shortly before the outbreak of World War I, to which it contributed.

World War I set into motion the events that heralded the end of colonialism, which the Western powers began to forswear. For example, President Woodrow Wilson of the United States proposed the Fourteen Points as terms for the end of World War I in 1918. The Fourteen Points promoted self-determination. World War II, which for the allies was a war fought for the sake of freedom, self-determination, and independence against foreign invaders, made the continuation of colonialism increasingly untenable. Intensification of anticolonial public opinion accelerated the momentum of change.

National liberation movements may be said to have started in earnest in 1945 with the Fifth Pan-African Congress in Manchester, England, which demanded an end to all forms of political and economic imperialism and advocated the use of force, if necessary, to achieve independence. As a result of independence movements and other factors (including diminishing rewards for the maintenance of colonies), Great Britain withdrew from India in 1947, and from Burma, Ceylon, and Palestine in 1948. Additional blows to colonialism came with the Bandung Nonaligned Conference in 1955, with its resolution insisting on national sovereignty, and with the United Nations Declaration on the Granting of Independence to Colonial Countries and Peoples in 1960. This declaration, passed by an overwhelming majority of the general assembly, may be considered the historical marker of the end of modern colonialism.

The road to self-determination was not always smooth. For example, four years of bloody fighting preceded Indonesia's independence from Dutch rule in 1949. The French recognized Algeria's sovereignty in 1962 only after an eight-year struggle engaging over half a million troops and a large number of French settlers. Vietnam gained independence from France in 1954 after years of war. Immediately thereafter, it became involved in a struggle—which soon became a war—to expel the United States, which it did in 1975. To do so, it collaborated with the Soviet Union, which itself maintained foreign territories and governments under its dominion by force of arms.

Accelerating the process of national liberation movements was the fact that the Soviet Union—as well as the People's Republic of China and Fidel Castro's Cuba—supported national liberation movements in Latin America, Africa, and Asia. The United States, in turn, supported democratic independence movements.

The Soviet Union's motives, one should note, were no more altruistic in supporting the resistance of, for example, Cuba, to neocolonial exploitation than were those of the United States in supporting the resistance movement against the Soviets in Afghanistan in the 1980's. The United States proclaimed its support of democracy and contributed to the overthrow of the democratically elected government of Chile in 1973; the Soviet Union decried Western economic imperialism and kept Eastern Europe under its control until 1989. Having become unseemly by the beginning of the twentieth century, colonialism became something to denounce, even if still practiced.

The wave of post-World War II decolonization movements had causes that were both external and internal to the colonies. Externally, the traditional colonial powers in Europe had been weakened greatly militarily and financially by the conflict and were replaced by the new hegemonies—the United States and the Soviet Union. Internally, a number of nationalist leaders, such as Mohandas Gandhi in India, Kwame Nkrumah in Ghana, Fidel Castro in Cuba, and Daniel Ortega in Nicaragua, were preaching the gospel of liberation to peoples who were politically better informed than their forebears had been.

Paradoxically, the wave of decolonization brought about the perceived condition of neocolonialism still subordinating less-developed countries to more advanced ones. A number of newly liberated countries felt obliged to continue their financial, technical, educational, and even military ties with their former parent country, thereby perpetuating the latter's influence. Multinational corporations play an important role; they serve as the means of export of raw materials from, and import of manufactured goods, capital, and technology to, the former colonies.

Applications

Few countries provide better examples of a national liberation movement than Egypt, which has a long history of foreign domination and resistance to foreign domination. It was ruled (after having been an empire itself) for approximately 2,000 years by Greeks, Romans, Persians, Arabs, the Ottoman Turks, the British, and by Egyptians with foreign backgrounds or orientations. Predictably, Egypt generated revolutionary leaders who fought foreign and native surrogate rulers.

In 1882, British troops defeated a native Egyptian force that was in revolt against the foreign-affiliated Egyptian elite. The British occupied the country but did not formally establish a dominion over Egypt, which therefore remained under the rule of the Ottoman overlord in Istanbul and the local governor, an Egyptian descendant of the Albanian-born Muhammad ʿAli. The Ottoman Empire allied itself with Germany, an enemy of Great Britain, in World War I. In response, Great Britain made Egypt a protectorate in 1914. Great Britain granted Egypt its independence in 1922, but maintained a convincing military presence in Egypt's cities and especially in the Suez canal zone. The Suez Canal, which opened in 1869, was Great Britain's shipping lifeline to India and the Far East. Without it, ships in the Indian Ocean would have to sail around Africa to reach England. The canal had been the major reason for Great Britain's acquisition of majority stock in the Universal Suez Canal Company in 1875 and for the invasion seven years later.

Especially after the signing of the Anglo-Egyptian Treaty of 1936, under which Britain agreed eventually to withdraw militarily from all strategic points except the Suez Canal Zone, the Egyptians began to agitate for real independence and against the privileged position that Britain still enjoyed. World War II intervened; Egypt became a major allied base for fighting against German and Italian forces in neighboring Libya. As soon as the war was over, Egypt resumed its agitation for independence from Great Britain. The British withdrew their troops from Cairo and elsewhere in 1946, but they would not relent on the issue of leaving the Suez Canal zone or the Sudan, which Egypt claimed as its own.

Another war intervened, this one between Israel and its Arab neighbors, in 1948. Again, the liberation movement resumed in Egypt at the war's end. In 1950, the Egyptian government unilaterally renounced its 1936 treaty with Great Britain and declared King Farouk—the last monarch of Muhammad ʿAli's dynasty—to be the sovereign of Egypt and the Sudan. Britain rejected both measures and Egyptian guerrillas began to harass British units along the Suez Canal.

The liberation struggle had a domestic dimension as well. In 1952, a group of officers of lower-middle-class Egyptian origin carried out a plot to end the corrupt "alien" rule of King Farouk. The monarch was exiled. Expropriation of land from the royal family and other members of the landed aristocracy was soon to follow. A young officer, Gamal Abdel Nasser, emerged as a leader among the group of revolutionaries.

Nasser, who had since his high school days campaigned against Great Britain's presence in Egypt, successfully negotiated Great Britain's evacuation from the Suez Canal Zone in 1954. The evacuation was to occur in 1956. In July, 1956, he nationalized the Universal Suez Canal Company, allegedly because of a reversal of a promise by Great Britain, the United States, and the World Bank to help finance the building of the Aswan High Dam, a major hydroelectric project. The crisis escalated into conflict when Great Britain, together with the French and the Israelis, returned in force to the Suez Canal area in October, handing Egypt a military defeat. The United States, the Soviet Union, and the United Nations opposed Great Britain's actions. A major war threatened until the tripartite armies withdrew from Egyptian territory between December, 1956, and March, 1957. Playing major powers against one another, Nasser won Egypt's full independence.

The Egyptianization of the country's economy, which to a large extent had been under foreign control, was also under way. The title to the French-administered Suez

Canal Authority was transferred to the Egyptian Suez Canal Authority and many foreign enterprises were nationalized. Egypt's military defeat of 1956 was represented as a major political triumph of which Nasser was the hero. This event spearheaded nationalist movements elsewhere in the Arab world.

Context

National liberation movements have had the effect of redrawing the political map of the world in the post-World War II era. They have led to a large increase in the number of the world's countries and to the formation of a Third World bloc, which often acts in unison on issues that affect its interests. This bloc may act within the United Nations or outside it, at conferences and through organizations. The former satellites of the Soviet Union, facing problems similar to those of the Third World bloc, have strived to make a successful transition from Russian control to development, democracy, and capitalism.

In much of the world, national liberation movements face the problem, upon achieving political independence, of developing and maintaining economic independence. National liberation movements often quickly evolve into struggles against poverty, disease, and hunger. These struggles merge with the challenge of developing freedom, equity, and democratic participation.

Since the inequality of resources and power distribution seems to be inherent in the human condition, national liberation movements seem destined to continue. They will take place in individual countries and will also involve people from different countries with similar economic interests. From the American War of Independence against Britain in the eighteenth century to the overthrow of foreign-backed governments in Eastern Europe and Central America in the late twentieth century, the striving for freedom, equality, and a better life has shown itself to be universal; it is certain to continue.

Bibliography

Harrison, Paul. *Inside the Third World: The Anatomy of Poverty.* 3d ed. New York: Penguin Books, 1993. Strongly anticolonialist tract that blames the poverty, inequity, and tyranny in the non-Western world mostly on the rule of the former colonial powers through native Westernized elites.

Henry, Paget, and Carl Stone, eds. *The Newer Caribbean: Decolonization, Democracy, and Development.* Philadelphia: Institute for the Study of Human Issues, 1983. Profiles preindependence problems, such as opposition to colonial rule, and post-independence ones, such as development issues, in different countries.

Houser, George M. *No One Can Stop the Rain: Glimpses of Africa's Liberation Struggle.* New York: Pilgrim Press, 1989. Personal account of the movement from the 1950's to the 1970's. The author's first-person anecdotes about a few African leaders of the anticolonialist movement are insightful.

Kempton, Daniel, R. *Soviet Strategy Toward Southern Africa: The National Liberation Movement Connection.* New York: Praeger, 1989. Comprehensive study, relying on sources within the Soviet Union, of the ties since 1920 between Moscow and different national liberation movements.

Miller, Norman, and Roderick Aya, eds. *National Liberation: Revolution in the Third World.* New York: Free Press, 1971. Eight essays on rebellion, revolution, colonialism, national liberation, counterinsurgency, and cultural revolution in the non-Western world.

Peteet, Julie M. *Gender in Crisis: Women and the Palestinian Resistance Movement.* New York: Columbia University Press, 1991. An anthropologist's account of the little-known role of women in the Palestinian national movement from its beginnings in 1948 to the 1990's.

Selassie, Bereket Habte. *Conflict and Intervention in the Horn of Africa.* New York: Monthly Review Press, 1980. History of the liberation struggle in Ethiopia, Somalia, Eritrea, and Djibouti against their colonial and national rulers by an Eritrean scholar previously active in his country's national liberation movement.

Ungar, Sanford J. *Africa: The People and Politics of an Emerging Continent.* 3d ed. New York: Simon & Schuster, 1989. Profiles national liberation movements in several African countries.

Peter B. Heller

Cross-References

Civil Wars, p. 325; Colonial Government, p. 344; Colonialism and Anticolonialism, p. 351; Developed and Developing Nations, p. 533; Empires and Empire Building, p. 597; Imperialism, p. 889; Independence Movements and Transitions, p. 896; Insurgencies and Coups d'État, p. 930; Nationalism, p. 1268; Revolutionary Governments, p. 1725; Revolutions, p. 1738; Right of Revolution, p. 1744; United Nations, p. 2045; World Political Organization, p. 2186.

NATIONAL SECURITY

Field of study: Functions of government

National security is a widely used conceptual approach for analyzing how to provide safety for a government and its society. Although this approach, based on realpolitik, is used by the United States and the majority of other government leaders, a growing number of analysts question its validity.

Principal terms

COLD WAR: global conflict between the United States and the Soviet Union from about 1947 to 1990, characterized by high levels of tension but no direct combat

GOVERNMENT: individuals and institutions responsible for making binding rules for a state

INTERDEPENDENCE: situation of mutual dependence, including both mutual sensitivity and mutual vulnerability

NATIONAL SECURITY ACT OF 1947: legislation passed by the U.S. Congress that changed the structure and process by which foreign policy advice was given to the president

REALPOLITIK: traditional perspective for analyzing how states interact, emphasizing self-help and the pursuit of power

SECURITY: being or feeling free from danger, harm, or threat

SOVEREIGNTY: legal characteristic of a state that enables its leaders to make rules independent of any higher political authority

Overview

Government is composed of the people and institutions that make and carry out rules for society. To govern a society means to direct and manage its affairs. Government leaders in the twentieth century derive their power to rule from the fact that the world is geographically divided into a number of sovereign states. Western European states were legally recognized as the main global actors in 1648, and their number has continued to grow ever since. Each state possesses sovereignty, a legal principle embodying the supreme power to make rules for the territory over which the government of the state has jurisdiction. How leaders of the government are chosen and the procedures by which the rules are made are determined by the people who live within the state.

Government may take place informally or be quite complex and specialized, depending on the range of activities thought appropriate within particular societies. At one extreme are societies in which governments seek to maintain domestic political order and provide protection from other states with the minimum of involvement. At the other extreme are governments that add a broader agenda of social and economic activities, which might include owning major industries or regulating the media. Most governments fall somewhere in between, providing a mix of activities that can vary over time as determined by the interests and values of the leaders and citizens of the community.

Perhaps the most basic of all governmental goals is to provide security for its citizens, to protect their lives and enable them to live free from danger, harm, or threat. Such security is the prerequisite for accomplishing whatever other goals government adopts. How a government pursues its security depends on what kind of goals it has and what kind of harm or threats its leaders fear. Security has two dimensions: a physical condition of being free from actual danger and harm, and a psychological condition of being free from threat. Both what is being protected and the nature of the threats can vary.

Although the term "national security" was not widely used until after World War II, this concept encompasses the traditional view of security that emphasized the physical condition and was rooted in the idea of being free from attack by outsiders. National security suggests that the leaders have a special responsibility to protect the community of people who live within their state. In this traditional view, each of the world's governments has a similar responsibility to maximize protection of its own citizens against others. In a world of sovereign states with no central government at the global level, whatever enhances the security of the state and its people is beneficial, even though such a view pits states against one another.

National security usually has been pursued in military terms, because each state ultimately must rely on its own resources for self-protection. This approach to national security is known as realpolitik. It is based on the assumption that humankind is at base evil and greedy, and therefore people organized collectively as states must constantly struggle for power to deter potential enemies and prevent domination by other states. In such a world, national security and military force are largely synonymous.

The result of the realpolitik basis for national security is the security dilemma. As each state pursues its own security through building larger armies and acquiring more arms, its neighbors find themselves feeling less secure. They enlarge their own armies and provide more weapons, requiring others to continue the process or accept insecurity. Because not all states can be more secure at the same time, some become better off at the expense of others, and spiraling arms races can ultimately leave all worse off.

Applications

The realpolitik view dominated the thinking of the United States government as it emerged from World War II and found itself forced to redefine how best to pursue its security. Under George Washington, the first U.S. president, the nation, which consisted of scattered farming settlements, needed only to preserve its borders and the newly formed union. With the Monroe Doctrine of 1823, President James Monroe began to enlarge the scope of U.S. safety to include other states within the Western Hemisphere. By the 1940's, President Franklin Roosevelt believed U.S. security was intertwined with the fate of democratic states throughout the world. With Roosevelt's death in 1945, his successor, President Harry S Truman, carried this enlarged definition of national security into the postwar world, as the threat shifted from the defeated Axis powers to the increasingly worrisome Soviet Union. Truman believed that the United States had been ill-prepared for World War II, as evidenced by the enormity of the disaster inflicted by the Japanese at Pearl Harbor. He concluded that a major executive branch reorganization was necessary so that the United States would not be caught off guard again nor find itself unable to carry out the growing responsibilities it was assuming as the leader of the Western democracies.

To realize this expanded version of national security, Truman felt that the president needed ongoing foreign policy advice that included an integrated diplomatic and military perspective as well as the most current intelligence information, not only during war but in peacetime as well. Before 1940, U.S. foreign relations were a relatively minor part of the executive agenda, managed largely by the State Department through diplomatic means. Truman proposed, and in 1947 the U.S. Congress enacted, the National Security Act as the Cold War conflict with the Soviet Union intensified. The act created the National Security Council as the chief adviser to the president. Its permanent members were the president, vice president, secretary of state, and secretary of defense, a new position that was created to oversee the old departments of the Army and Navy and the newly separate Air Force. The Central Intelligence Agency, the first peacetime U.S. civilian intelligence organization, also was created. The actors in this core group have been the president's key advisers in the foreign policy area. While the group has been used somewhat differently by each president, the presence of such a body reflected the growing importance of foreign policy and the realpolitik view after 1945, when the United States saw itself as the bastion of democracy in the struggle against communism.

For the next four decades, the United States pursued national security in predominantly military terms, fearing global nuclear or conventional war with the Soviet Union. Although war with the Soviet Union was avoided, U.S. Department of Defense figures show defense spending as a percentage of gross domestic product remained greater than 4 percent from 1950 to the early 1990's, reaching 11.9 percent in the early 1950's during the Korean War, 9.1 percent in the late 1960's during the Vietnam War, and 6.3 percent in the mid-1980's during the military buildup under President Ronald Reagan. U.S. analysts could not accurately calculate Soviet defense spending; however, the combination of the first Soviet atomic test in 1949, the launching of the first Soviet intercontinental ballistic missile in 1957, and the strong Soviet military and expanding global naval presence pushed by General Secretary Leonid Brezhnev (1964-1982) was seen as a national security threat by the United States and many other nations. At the same time, U.S. defense efforts represented a continuing national security threat to the Soviet Union. As a result, both the United States and Soviet Union built thousands of long-range, intermediate-range, and tactical nuclear weapons that could be launched against each other from land, sea, or air, built large supplies of conventional and chemical weaponry, and engaged in ongoing research and development on new weapons and launching systems.

The costs of such programs were staggering, and the negative effects were felt first in the Soviet Union. In 1985, Mikhail Gorbachev became the head of the Communist Party, proposing and gradually implementing a number of domestic economic and political reforms, among them a redefinition of how to achieve Soviet security. Gorbachev accepted Western proposals for arms reductions, first on intermediate-range nuclear forces, in an agreement signed with President Ronald Reagan in 1987, and then on strategic nuclear arms, in an agreement signed with President George Bush in 1991. Gorbachev had underestimated the growing opposition to communism, however, and, at the end of 1991, the Soviet Union broke apart into fifteen sovereign states. Russia, led by President Boris Yeltsin, was designated as the legal successor to the Soviet Union, but was unable and unwilling to carry on the large military programs of its predecessor. Yeltsin instead dedicated his government to achieving a democracy and a free-market economy modeled on those in the West, cutting the former Soviet Union's 3.5 million active duty military forces to 1.2 million under Russian leadership in the mid-1990's.

These dramatic changes led to the end of the Cold War and called for a rethinking of U.S. national security and the nature of threats in the world. As high levels of defense spending became harder to justify, government leaders and opponents advocated sizable force reductions and cuts in weapons development and acquisitions programs, with the major point of difference being exactly how big a cut could be sustained while still maintaining security. During the 1992 election campaign, candidate Bill Clinton emphasized the need for change and, although he did not directly challenge the previously accepted view of national security, stressed that reinvigorating the U.S. economy was crucial for a successful foreign policy. He also talked of creating an Economic Security Council modeled on the National Security Council. Once elected, President Clinton proposed decreasing defense spending to less than 3 percent of gross domestic product, and planned to cut the U.S. armed forces from 2.2 million to 1.4 million by the end of the 1990's.

Context

In the late twentieth century, there has been a growing movement to rethink the idea of security and to shift the perspective from the national to the global level. In 1980, an international commission headed by former German chancellor Willy Brandt stressed that global security demanded greater attention to the economic needs of the developing countries. Threats to security are not limited to those of a military nature, but include economic and environmental threats, population pressures, ethnic conflict, immigration, and human rights violations. In 1987, global environmental concern was spotlighted by Norwegian prime minister Gro Bruntland's emphasis on a common environmental future, laying the groundwork for the 1992 Earth Summit, where representatives of almost every state gathered to deal with environmental and development problems from a global perspective.

The tendency of countries to consider security from a national perspective has been blamed for leading states to act unilaterally to increase their security, thereby threatening others. The new thinking calls for a global perspective, in which states work together to pursue common interests on a wide range of issues and promote increased security for all those involved. Just as arms control enabled the United States and Soviet Union to slow their arms buildup and finally reduce weapons levels significantly, other states can find mutually accommodative solutions that will provide greater security for all.

Modern security thinking is rooted in growing interdependence, in which states are increasingly interconnected through international trade and financial links as well as through the growing impact people have on one another. Rapid global population growth makes it harder to deal with environmental problems such as the declining ozone layer and global warming, puts pressure on limited supplies of natural resources such as fossil fuels, and compounds the difficulties of dealing with global health issues. Recognizing such problems has led to increasing calls for strengthening cooperative efforts such as international law and United Nations programs such as the Population Fund.

Global cooperation, however, is not the only process at work in the international arena that is in the midst of a transition in the aftermath of the Cold War and the breakup of the Soviet Union. While cooperative efforts are clearly at work and especially evident among the states of the Northern Hemisphere, military concerns and aspects of realpolitik remain an important part of their activities. Even as the United States, Europe, and Japan have come to recognize the growing cost of maintaining large militaries, they continue to disagree on economic competitiveness, environmental issues, and nuclear and conventional arms proliferation. These states have been reluctant to surrender sovereignty to global organizations and often disagree among themselves on appropriate policies. Some even resist cooperation on new agenda issues such as the environment; for example, President George Bush refused to sign the Biodiversity Convention at the Earth Summit in 1992 out of fear that it might put U.S. companies at a competitive disadvantage. Great Britain, France, and Germany disagree about how best to pursue cooperation within the European Union.

Although the more powerful developed states of the Northern Hemisphere considered approaching security from a global perspective in the late twentieth century, the developing states of the Southern Hemisphere continued to favor the predominantly national viewpoint. Saddam Hussein's invasion of Kuwait is typical of a number of developing countries, such as China, India, Pakistan, and North Korea, which remained intent on reaffirming sovereignty and acquiring military power, including nuclear capabilities, to advance national interests. For the developing countries, economic development was the key goal and the basis for security. The majority were convinced that their colonial legacy left them behind and that the developed countries were trying to keep them weak. Thus they concluded that self-help was their only alternative.

Global trends suggest that security remained a basic goal for sovereign states in the 1990's. Just as the international system underwent transition with the demise of the

Cold War, so too did thinking about how best to pursue security. Some leaders of developed states began to push a global perspective that advocates common interests and enhanced security for all on some issues, but they retained the national security approach in a number of areas and especially in dealing with developing countries. The developing countries seemed to be largely wedded to the more traditional realpolitik perspective on national security; they were concerned about ongoing economic dangers, and many felt threatened by military dangers. Given the conflicting trends within the global arena, it seemed unlikely that either the national security or the global security perspective would be adopted exclusively. They were both likely to coexist and provide competing viewpoints for government leaders trying to determine how best to pursue security in an increasingly complex world.

Bibliography

Allison, Graham, and Gregor F. Treverton, eds. *Rethinking America's Security: Beyond Cold War to New World Order*. New York: W. W. Norton, 1992. Presents varied conceptions of the changing international system and the problems the United States faces in redefining security at the end of the twentieth century.

Inderfurth, Karl F., and Loch K. Johnson, eds. *Decisions of the Highest Order: Perspectives on the National Security Council*. Pacific Grove, Calif.: Brooks/Cole, 1988. Survey of the origins, evolution, and activities of the National Security Council, including case studies of NSC directors and proposals for reform.

Klare, Michael T., and Daniel C. Thomas. *World Security: Challenges for a New Century*. 2d ed. New York: St. Martin's Press, 1994. Reconceptualization of security from the global perspective with status reports on the evolution of key issues such as nuclear and conventional weapons, regional and ethnic conflict, women, the environment, human rights, and global debt.

Kruzel, Joseph, ed. *American Defense Annual: 1993*. New York: Lexington Books, 1993. Annual review published by the Mershon Center at Ohio State University surveys defense issues relevant to national security.

Mathews, Jessica Tuchman. "Redefining Security." *Foreign Affairs* 68 (Spring, 1989): 162-177. Recognizes the broadening of the definition of national security in the 1970's to include international economics; recommends that resource, environmental, and demographic issues be added as well.

Morgenthau, Hans J. *Politics Among Nations: The Struggle for Power and Peace*. 2d ed. Rev. and enl. ed. New York: Alfred A. Knopf, 1958. Classic statement of the realpolitik view which first appeared in 1948 and continues to be read by students of international politics.

Snow, Donald M. *National Security: Enduring Problems in a Changing Defense Environment*. 2d ed. New York: St. Martin's Press, 1991. Survey of how U.S. national security policy is made, and the conventional and strategic threats faced by the United States.

Judy Bell Krutky

Cross-References

Alliances, p. 47; Armed Forces, p. 89; Conflict Resolution, p. 397; Developed and Developing Nations, p. 533; Foreign Relations, p. 718; Geopolitics, p. 759; Government Roles, p. 778; International Relations, p. 969; North Atlantic Treaty Organization, p. 1332; Realpolitik, p. 1668; Superpowers and World Politics, p. 1916; War, p. 2129; World Government and Environmental Protection, p. 2167.

NATIONALISM

Field of study: History of government and politics

A difficult concept to define satisfactorily, nationalism is essentially the belief among residents of a country or region that they collectively constitute a single community with shared culture, history, and goals. Though nationalism is essentially emotional, it can become a powerful political force, particularly in a country's foreign relations.

Principal terms
AUTONOMY: self-government, usually of a minority group within a state
ETHNIC: describing a people who share distinctive cultural and historical traditions
IRREDENTISM: policy of seeking to incorporate subjects of one country into another country to which they may be historically or ethnically connected
MINORITY: national group different from the rest of a community in ethnic origin, religion, language, or culture
NATION: self-defined ethnic group, usually independent or at least autonomous; also a synonym for a modern country
SEPARATISM: independence or autonomy for a particular ethnic or cultural group
TRIBE: group of families or clans who share a common language, religion, territory, and political leadership

Overview

The scenario for the development of a nation is usually reconstructed in the following manner: A few extended Stone Age families formed themselves into a band for purposes of hunting or defense. Intermarriages within the band eventually produced the idea of a common ancestor. With increased numbers, the band became a clan. The clan eventually associated its common ancestor with mythic symbols, engaged in agriculture or war under a patriarchal chief, claimed territory, and often had rules that forbade marriage within the clan. Such prohibitions led to blood relationships among several clans, which joined into a tribe under a common leader. The twelve tribes of Israel in the Old Testament, for example, each claimed descent from a son of Jacob.

From Roman times to the end of the Middle Ages, the various tribes of Western Europe—such as the Ostrogoths, Visigoths, Vandals, and Celts—combined into nations. Nations often took their name from one of the dominant tribes; for example, France was named after the tribe of the Franks. Often one group became dominant by subjugating other ethnic groups, as the invading Normans subdued and absorbed the British, Welsh, Irish, and Scots, which had been separate groups with their own cultures and languages.

Shakespeare's play Henry V dramatically shows the end stage of this nation-building process. England was united in its war against France in 1415. Shakespeare portrayed members of the army that Henry V led against the French by using broad national stereotypes: the talkative Welshman, Fluellen; the taciturn Scot, Jamy; and the hot-tempered Irishman, MacMorris, who takes offense when Fluellen speaks of the latter's "nation." In encouraging his soldiers, Henry refers to their common English ancestry and ends with "Cry 'God for Harry! England and Saint George!'" The French king's daughter Katherine, who eventually marries Henry, has an English lesson, during which she voices distaste at the sound of the words. In this play, Shakespeare revealed a central problem of the modern state: creating one nation from disparate ethnic groups.

The founding of the nation-state has been viewed as an integral part of the development of Europe. Political states that include only one national group within their borders are rare; often they are islands, such as Iceland and Japan, or are at the end of a peninsula, such as Portugal and Norway. Traditional nation-states are often compounds of various groups. France was forced to shed much of its regionalism during the French Revolution, when its provinces were abolished and replaced by *départements* usually named after natural features. Research has shown, however, that most of France's peasants did not regard themselves as "Frenchmen" until World War I. Spain includes two fractious national minorities: Basques, whose language is related to no other known speech, and Catalans. Great differences exist between north and south in Germany and Italy. These are among the most stable political entities called "nation-states."

Whereas Western Europe was characterized by the so-called nation-state, Central and Eastern Europe saw the creation of multinational empires such as the Austro-Hungarian, Prussian (German after 1871), and Russian, achieved through marriage, succession, and conquest. The large, formerly independent kingdom of Poland was partitioned in the eighteenth century, Austro-Hungary acquired Florence in central Italy through dynastic succession, and Russia moved steadily westward after wars with Poland and Sweden that ended in 1721. The expansion of these states meant acquiring numerous other nationalities, great and small, at various stages of cultural development. In 1914, the mobilization orders for Austro-Hungary were sent out in fifteen different languages.

Some of these acquired nationalities had histories as independent countries, such as the Czechs, who came under Hapsburg domination after the end of the Thirty Years' War in 1648. Others, such as the Slovaks and Ruthenians, at first had no national consciousness but knew, or were made to feel, that they were neither Germans, Hungarians, or Poles. Russia's wars of conquest were not limited to the West, where Estonians, Latvians, Lithuanians, Ukrainians, and Poles were added; Russia also made many non-European conquests, acquiring Tatars, Georgians, Armenians, and Azeris to the south, and Uzbeks, Tadjiks, Kyrghyz, and other Asian groups to the east. Although these peoples were the source of exotic materials for composers and poets, they did not develop national consciousness until the twentieth century.

Because of its many contradictory elements, nationalism, like its contemporary movement, Romanticism, is difficult to define. One must seek to isolate and identify its most common characteristics. Foremost among them is language, either as spoken or as developed into a literary language. Folk poetry, tales, and music have been among the main sources for cultural nationalism, whether German folk poetry, the tales collected by the Brothers Grimm, or the Russian folk songs. Nationalities also had a common history, even if some of it was mythical, such as the reign of King Arthur for the English, or of the distant past, such as the Middle Ages when the Czech Charles IV was Holy Roman Emperor. Of great importance were territory, a fatherland or motherland; hopes for an autonomous or independent government, if one did not already exist; and a feeling of separation from other linguistic or ethnic groups, whether expressed through ethnic jokes and slurs, social prohibitions against inter-marriage, or outbreaks of violence. Jews were the particular objects of separation and its consequences, and even those who sought to assimilate as much as possible into the dominant culture, such as composers Felix Mendelssohn and Gustav Mahler, were subjected to vicious anti- Semitic remarks. Although each nationalism is different, all carry strong emotional overtones that often make objective discussion difficult.

Not all these elements produced unity among peoples. The Roman Catholic faith, for example, provided a cohesive element through which the Irish and Lithuanians could maintain their common identities in the face of oppression, but it has not unified the Belgians, who remain divided between speakers of French and Flemish. English is the common language of Northern Ireland, yet its inhabitants are bitterly and violently divided between "Papists" and "Prods." Historical memory plays an impor-tant role; in Northern Ireland, incidents such as the persecutions by the English queens Mary I and Elizabeth I, the invasion by Oliver Cromwell, the defeat of James II by William III, and the crushing of the Irish Easter Rebellion in 1916, have contributed to the continuing conflict.

Attempts by the rulers of the multinational European empires to inculcate national feeling among their many subject populations were often unsuccessful. Using the language of the dominant country as the language of administration and military command made government more efficient but was viewed as oppression by the other linguistic groups. Few bureaucrats of the dominant country were willing to learn the language of the peoples living where they had temporarily been posted. Attempts by subject populations to achieve greater equality brought forth fierce resentments and a particularly virulent nationalism among the dominant group.

A side effect of nationalism is irredentism, a term taken from the slogan *Italia irredenta* or "unredeemed Italy." After the wars with Austria in 1859 and 1866, several pockets of Italians remained under Austrian rule, and the slogan *Italia irredenta* was used by politicians who sought to claim Trieste, the Austro-Hungarian empire's seaport, and the south Tyrol for Italy. Attempts to reunite people subject to one country with a country to which they are ethnically or historically related continued throughout the twentieth century.

Austria practiced a policy of divide and rule in controlling its multinational empire, using soldiers from other ethnic groups who did not speak the language of the peoples they were guarding and thus were less likely to fraternize and more likely to follow orders to suppress them. For example, Croat soldiers were used to put down the revolt of the Viennese populace in 1848. Colonial powers often used minorities among the subject peoples as "native" police, as the British used the Sikhs in colonial India, Burma, and Malaya. These minorities, in turn, often were subjected to reprisals after the colonies gained their independence.

Applications

Probably the worst applications of nationalism, leaving behind a bitter legacy, were those effected in the peace treaties that concluded World War I. The self-determination of nations that had been a proclaimed war aim of the Allies was, in practice, used to justify the breakup of the defeated multinational empires, Austro-Hungary, Germany, Russia, and Turkey's Ottoman Empire. The successor states assumed various forms; some, such as the Baltic states of Estonia, Latvia, and Lithuania, were relatively ethnically homogeneous; others were federations, such as Czechoslovakia, which consisted of Czechs, Moravians, Slovaks, and Ruthenians. Serbia was known as the Kingdom of the Serbs, Croats, and Slovenes (later Yugoslavia). Everywhere that boundaries were adjusted, some of the formerly dominant group had become minorities and were subjected to real or perceived oppression. Austria and Hungary were drastically reduced in size to provide territory for the successor states. As rewards for fighting on the Allied side, Italy was given the southern Alpine provinces of Austria, and Romania was awarded Transylvania, in which many Hungarians and Germans lived.

Although some national aspirations were satisfied, others were delayed. The Arab provinces of the former Ottoman Empire were not given independence, but were assigned to Britain and France as mandates under the supervision of the League of Nations. When the Nazis attained power in Germany in 1933 and increasingly sought territorial gains, the plight of the German minorities, such as the Sudeten Germans in Czechoslovakia, was used as a pretext for invasion. During World War II, the Germans exploited national resentments in Eastern Europe, creating the client states of Slovakia and Croatia and recruiting soldiers and camp guards among Ukrainians, Latvians, Bosnians, and other anticommunist ethnic groups.

After World War II, the boundaries in Eastern Europe were redrawn. The Polish boundaries were moved west, with the Ukrainian and Lithuanian minorities placed within the Soviet Union, while Germans were left as refugees or were expelled. In the Baltic states, many natives emigrated or were deported, to be replaced by ethnic Russians. Massive population transfers were regarded as the solution to the ethnic minority problem.

After World War II, the focus of nationalism shifted to Asia and Africa, in which millions of people sought to cast off European colonial rule. In the forefront were Western-educated intellectuals who transformed their struggles for independence into mass nationalist movements. By the late 1960's, all the European colonial powers had voluntarily left or been driven from Asia; a decade later, the same was true in Africa. Struggles for liberation united the native populations, but ethnic nationalism divided them soon after independence.

Liberal nationalism on the European model largely failed. Whereas colonialism tended to foster tribal structures as a means of indirect rule and policing, Africa's newly independent states considered the concept of the nation-state to be an idea transplanted within boundaries that had been drawn by colonial powers at the Congress of Berlin in 1885. Members of the Ovambo tribe, for example, were ruled by Portugal in Angola and by Germany in Southwest Africa (later a mandate under South Africa before attaining independence as Namibia in 1990). Colonial languages continued to be used as the language of government since most countries could not easily choose from among their many competing languages, except in East Africa, where Swahili had become the lingua franca of commerce. The Cold War between the Atlantic powers and the Soviet bloc—which lasted from 1946 to 1989—was fought by proxy in Asia and Africa, with nationalism as one of the weapons, especially since the colonial powers were allied with the West. The oppressive Marxist government of Ethiopia provoked a separatist movement in Eritrea, a former Italian colony, with the struggle including one of the worst famines in modern history. Yet the attempt of Eastern Nigeria to secede as Biafra in 1967 failed, partially because the European powers would not accept revision of the old colonial boundaries.

Context

Ethnonationalism is the name often given to nationalist movements. In view of the great ethnic diversity that exists within most states, the consensus is that ethnonationalism is fundamentally political and emotional rather than economic and is a mass movement. The overriding question is how to accommodate these various ethnic groups within one country so that their members regard themselves as citizens of the country first and as members of their ethnic groups second. This process took several centuries in Western Europe. Several practical solutions have been proposed, such as a youth service corps whose members do their service in ethnic homelands other than their own; the support of trade unions with a class or craft rather than ethnic base; strong central governments; constituencies of a given ethnic group being represented by members of other such groups but subject to recall; and retention of colonial languages, because they are politically and ethnically neutral as well as necessary for dealing with an international economy. Education needs to be stressed, especially technical and agricultural. Music, art, and theater are excellent ways of building a national consciousness and providing appreciation for the heritage of all of its constituent peoples.

Modernization does not necessarily mean Westernization. Supernational religions such as Christianity or Islam can play important roles but have also served as points of division, such as in the Sudan, divided between a Muslim north and a Christian south. Quotas for coveted situations, such as university admissions or government jobs for minorities, often have aroused sharp resentment among the majority ethnic groups.

There are no easy solutions to be envisaged in those countries formerly called the Third World.

In Western Europe and North America, nationalism has had strong anti-immigrant overtones. The influx of peoples from the Third World, especially to countries that were once their colonial overlords, or the importation of residents of poorer countries to perform unpleasant or low-paying jobs that the native inhabitants declined, often has resulted in substantial numbers of persons of different cultures taking up permanent residence. Resentment of these new inhabitants has been a means of political manipulation, especially among working-class members of the dominant ethnic groups.

In 1991, the Soviet Union separated into fifteen independent republics, all of which contained populations of ethnic Russians. Ethnic conflicts soon erupted, such as the separatism of Abkhasians and Ossetians in Georgia, and the armed conflict over enclaves of Armenians and Azeris in each others' territory. The fate of Russia, by far the largest of these successor states, was of great concern in the mid-1990's. Options for the future ranged from Russia's fragmenting even further into smaller national groups, to an aggressively nationalistic "Greater Russia" using its ethnic minorities abroad as pretexts for pressuring or even reconquering some or all the successor states.

When Yugoslavia broke up in 1992, the world was horrified at the ensuing ethnic violence. The Serb minorities in Croatia and Bosnia coined the term "ethnic cleansing" to describe their campaign of terror to expel non-Serb residents in order to create a Greater Serbia eventually. Although the United Nations imposed sanctions, they were only loosely enforced and peacekeeping forces were powerless to stop the mutual reprisals. Proposals were made to send armies to enforce a peace, but memories of the Axis powers' Balkan campaign during World War II, with its high casualties, discouraged the Atlantic powers from sending their soldiers to perform a thankless task such as the British had been performing in Northern Ireland for decades. The civil war fought in the Balkans during World War II had merely broken out again fifty years later. The peace enforced after World War II by Marshal Tito and his successors had collapsed, showing the intractability of ethnic conflict and how easily a new generation of hatreds can be created.

Bibliography

Bugajski, Janusz. *Nations in Turmoil*. Boulder, Colo.: Westview Press, 1993. One of the many studies of the European successor states to the Soviet breakup, it includes studies of national enmities and disputes.

Connor, Walker. *Ethnonationalism: The Quest for Understanding*. Princeton, N.J.: Princeton University Press, 1994. Excellent international survey of the concept of ethnonationalism, emphasizing its psychological content and cautioning against misuse of terminologies that inaccurately describe nationalist sentiments.

Gellner, Ernest. *Nations and Nationalism*. Ithaca, N.Y.: Cornell University Press, 1983. A philosophical rather than historical survey of nationalism with emphasis on the European variety, it provokes questions rather than provides easy answers.

Longyear, Rey. *Nineteenth-Century Romanticism in Music*. Englewood Cliffs, N.J.: Prentice-Hall, 1988. Includes discussion of nationalism in art and music during the nineteenth century.

McNeill, William. *Polyethnicity and National Unity in World History*. Toronto: University of Toronto Press, 1986. Brief survey of multiethnic societies from ancient times to the present, with the thesis that nationalism and the ethnically unitary state are brief aberrations from the normal multiethnicity.

Mazrui, Ali, and Michael Tidy. *Nationalism and New States in Africa from About 1935 to the Present*. Nairobi: Heinemann Educational Books, 1984. Country-by-country survey of African nationalism and ethnic conflicts, especially valuable because it is written from a non-European perspective.

Moynihan, Daniel Patrick. *Pandaemonium*. New York: Oxford University Press, 1993. Reflections on ethnicity and nationalism in international politics and how the idea of national self-determination can result in almost limitless conflicts. The author, a senior United States senator, points out several of the pitfalls for the multiethnic society.

Tibi, Bassam. *Arab Nationalism*. Edited and translated by Marion Farouk-Sluglett and Peter Sluglett. New York: St. Martin's Press, 1990. A history of Arab nationalism to 1967, it is most valuable in contrasting European and Third World nationalisms and in pointing out the conflicts between European and Islamic concepts of ethnicity.

R. M. Longyear

Cross-References

Africa: Politics and Governments, p. 21; Asia: Politics and Governments, p. 108; Dante's Political Philosophy, p. 483; Demagoguery, p. 507; Empires and Empire Building, p. 597; Geopolitics, p. 759; Hegemony, p. 817; History of Government, p. 829; Hooker's Political Philosophy, p. 842; Immigrants and Politics, p. 861; Independence Movements and Transitions, p. 896; Irrationalism in Politics, p. 987; The Nation-State, p. 1241; Pan-Africanism, p. 1369; Race and Ethnicity, p. 1654; Secessionism, p. 1790; Self-Determination, p. 1796; Zionism, p. 2192.

NATURALIZATION

Field of study: International government and politics

Naturalization is the process by which noncitizens of a particular country gain citizenship in that country.

Principal terms
ALIEN: resident of a country in which the person is not a citizen
CITIZEN: member of a state or nation by birth or naturalization
DENIZEN: person whose legal status within a nation is greater than that of an alien but less than that of a citizen
IMMIGRATION: act of entering a region or country of which one is not a native for the purpose of establishing permanent residence
NATURALIZATION: conferring of citizenship on one who did not have that citizenship before

Overview

Naturalization is the legal process of conferring citizenship on people who are not citizens. Citizenship through naturalization may be sought by alien residents as a means of acquiring legal rights and privileges not otherwise available. In extending citizenship to those who do not have citizenship, the nation may be motivated by a number of factors. For example, the offer of citizenship may attract immigrants with desired skills, it may attract people with financial resources, or it may be an attempt to create a sense of belonging to the society that strengthens allegiance to the state.

In the Roman Empire, citizenship was often conferred on people who were not Roman by birth. Emancipated slaves and those who would desert enemy armies were frequently naturalized and occasionally even given property. Roman citizenship accorded the individual an advantageous legal standing, particularly in dealing with provincial authorities. Granting citizenship in this manner was an efficient and effective device of gaining aliens' support.

Development of modern doctrines of nationality and naturalization can be traced to fourteenth century England. Medieval English law did not make a distinction between subjects and aliens, but did stress the personal allegiance of the individual to the monarch while also placing people on a continuum of social status that decided rank and privilege. For example, persons born in France were not denied the right to own land in England because they were aliens but because they owed allegiance to foreign monarchs. The fortunes of war or the allegiance of the individual could be reversed, however, and what would come to be known as naturalized citizenship later acquired. Laws and customs on naturalization evolved over centuries. Early English courts were clearer in their statements of the legal barriers posed by not being a citizen than on the positive rights and privileges of citizenship. For example, in the fifteenth century the taxes owed by aliens were as much as double those owed by subjects.

The legal opinion of English jurist Sir Edward Coke in *Calvin's Case* (1608) was perhaps the earliest legal treatise on citizenship in Western societies. Coke provided a theory of allegiance, subjectship (citizenship), and by inference a perspective on naturalization, although that term was not used until the late sixteenth century. The theory developed the idea that the relationship between monarch and subject was founded on the assumption that within the community there exists a permanent social and political hierarchy. The natural law principle of hierarchy assumes that once a person becomes a subject (by birth or by naturalization), allegiance and obedience are owed henceforth. In return, the monarch owes the subject protection.

By the early seventeenth century fairly clear distinctions were made among natural-born subjects, naturalized subjects, denizens, and aliens. Natural-born subjects had rights that were not in question. Naturalized subjects had full rights, but naturalization could come only as a result of parliamentary action. Denizens, whose status was created through royal patents granted by the grace of the monarch, had some rights although not the full range of those held by a natural-born or naturalized subject. Aliens had none of the rights or privileges available to subjects or denizens. In the seventeenth century, the most important of the rights concerned ownership and control of real property. Beyond the purely economic benefits of property ownership and control, one gained greater access to legal process. Aliens could purchase but not control property outright, presumably because the allegiance of aliens was always in question. Denizens could purchase and own land, but not inherit property. Only citizens had full property rights.

Today, while virtually all nations have a naturalization process, a disproportionately high number of applications for citizenship are made in the more prosperous regions of the world, particularly in North America, Northern and Western Europe, and Australia. Sovereign nations establish the criteria for citizenship within their political boundaries, and there are considerable differences in those criteria among different countries. In general, the differences reflect different philosophies of how best to integrate and assimilate permanent residents and how to build allegiance to the nation.

The become a naturalized citizen of the United States, an applicant generally must be at least eighteen years old, have lived in the United States as a legal resident for at least five years, be of good moral character, be loyal to the United States, be able to read, write, speak, and understand English, have a basic knowledge of the United States Constitution, history, and governmental structure, and be willing to take an oath of allegiance to the United States.

Australia, in contrast, has one of the most liberal naturalization policies in the world. Only two years residency are required for naturalization and there are no restrictive rules or expensive fees to process citizenship applications. Australia, like Canada and Sweden, has declared itself a multicultural society and has taken steps to encourage and facilitate immigrant naturalization. Some countries, such as the United States, include an oath of allegiance and require an exclusive loyalty to the nation. Others, such as Germany, have concluded that offering dual citizenship actually promotes integration.

The significance of a person's status within the state continues to evolve. In Europe, following World War II, there existed a labor shortage and many countries adopted guest worker programs. These programs ended in the early 1970's, but large foreign populations remained. Some countries, including France and Germany, offered monetary incentives to the foreign workers to leave. While many workers did leave, hundreds of thousands did not. In an effort to integrate more fully those who remained, France and Germany adopted liberal naturalization policies. Austria's policy was more rigid, requiring, among other things, ten years of continuous residency to be considered for naturalization.

Population pressures and integration of alien populations into the community are among the most important factors a country must consider when defining its naturalization policy. Switzerland, which had no residency requirement before 1876, later adopted a two-year residency requirement, then a six-year requirement, and in 1952, a twelve-year residency requirement and proof of assimilation, that is, language ability.

The European Union has virtually eliminated internal borders. There are few restrictions on the movement of people, money, goods, and services across the national boundaries between member states. As a consequence, the immigration and naturalization policies of each country in the union potentially affect all, since entry into one country is tantamount to entry into all. The trend in Europe, as elsewhere among the more prosperous nations, is toward increasing the restrictions on naturalization and limiting the numbers.

Applications

The process of becoming a naturalized citizen varies greatly from country to country. In most instances the first step is to gain legal residency. Generally, this is the most difficult step as the number of immigrants admitted legally, particularly in Europe, has declined sharply since the 1980's. In Germany, virtually the only people considered for citizenship of those who do not possess it *jus soli* are those who meet the *jus sanguinis* rule; in Germany's case, that means that at least one parent must possess Germany citizenship. In principle, citizenship through naturalization is excluded. France's immigration policy is quite restrictive, but naturalized citizenship is granted almost automatically to offspring of immigrants born in France. French concern with cultural assimilation of foreigners and concern with the French language are major issues. Naturalization became more difficult in Italy as the number of immigrants entering the country exceeded the number of emigrants leaving. In 1990, immigration law was changed to establish stricter rules for legal residency while also increasing the residency requirement for naturalization from five to ten years. The process of becoming a naturalized citizen within member states of the European Union is more difficult now than in the past, and there is pressure within the Union to develop a "harmonization" of immigration policies, although criteria and processes of naturalization remain the prerogative of each sovereign state.

In the United States, one must first be admitted as a permanent resident. This means that individuals admitted as visitors or students are not eligible for naturalization.

These individuals may seek permanent residency, but their presence is not itself an advantage in applying for permanent residency, nor does the time in the United States as a visitor or student count towards the residency requirement. To apply for naturalization, one must also be at least eighteen years of age. The applicant admitted as a permanent resident must live in the United States continuously for at least five years before applying for naturalization. This does not mean that the applicants must not have left the country during the five-year period, but that they may not have been outside the country for one year or more continuously or a total of thirty months during the five-year period. At least the last six months of the five-year residency must be in the state where the petition for naturalization is filed. In general, if these restrictions are violated, a new period of residency must be completed. Exceptions to these stipulations can be made if an applicant is employed by American organizations, the United States government, or religious organizations.

Further, an applicant for naturalized citizenship must be of good moral character and be loyal to the United States. Applicants involved in prostitution or narcotics dealing, alcoholics, professional gamblers, polygamists, and criminals or convicts who have been jailed for six months or more, or who have been convicted of murder, would be disqualified on moral grounds. Applicants who lie under oath to benefit from immigration laws, those who refuse to serve in the United States armed services, those who have deserted, those who have been a member of the Communist Party, those who favor a dictatorship in the United States, and those who advocate violence in the United States are also disqualified from citizenship.

Applicants must also pass examinations on the history and system of government of the United States as well as English reading, writing, and speaking. A short dictation is given in English to test this. Any person fifty years of age who has been living in the United States at least twenty years is exempt from the English test. A person exempt from the English language examination may take the history and government tests in a language other than English. In some instances individuals do not have to meet all these requirements to become naturalized citizens. For example, some of these requirements can be waived for spouses of U.S. citizens, children, former U.S. citizens, aliens who have served in the armed services of the United States, and employees of organizations promoting the interests of the United States in other countries.

Persons meeting the requirements must file applications, take the examinations, and appear for a final court hearing. The application includes a biographical information sheet, photographs, and a fingerprint chart. All forms are filled out under oath. After reviewing the materials, immigration officials may require additional documentation to corroborate the biographic information. Following the application review, an interview is scheduled. The examiner may ask questions about the application and assist the applicant in filling out the petition for naturalization, the document that is filed with the naturalization court. If the examination is passed, the applicant must pay a fee to file the petition.

The final court hearing is the last stage in the naturalization process. The examiner will appear and recommend the applicant be granted or denied citizenship. The applicant is entitled to an attorney at the hearing. If the examiner recommends against citizenship, the applicant or applicant's attorney may offer arguments for naturalization. If the judge grants citizenship, the applicant is then administered an oath of allegiance to the United States at which time loyalty to all other countries is renounced. The applicant is then a naturalized citizen of the United States.

Context

Citizenship distinguishes between members of the community and outsiders. Those who are citizens by birth or by descent are entitled to certain rights and privileges (legal protection, political participation as prescribed by the constitution and statute, social services, employment opportunities) which are not necessarily made available to aliens. Naturalized citizenship imparts community membership and the rights and privileges that this bestows, thus making it desirable to many resident aliens. For the state, the benefits of naturalized citizenship are allegiance to the state and a greater likelihood of integration into the society.

The decision to seek naturalized citizenship depends in large part on the nature of the migration. For example, "chain migration," whereby individuals make arrangements to receive assistance from friends or family residing in the place of destination, is more likely to generate requests for naturalized citizenship than "circular migration," in which the movement is not viewed as permanent, as for example in seasonal agricultural employment. "Colonizing migration," such as the type found in Australia or the United States, virtually always leads to requests for naturalized citizenship. Additionally, many countries throughout the world are anxious to grant naturalized citizenship to immigrants possessing desired skills or who are willing to make a significant capital investment in the country. Some countries in Eastern Europe and Latin America actively encourage immigration and naturalization of retired citizens from North America and Western Europe as a means of gaining hard currency.

A changing political climate affects requests for naturalized citizenship. "Coerced migration," is caused by persecution, the fear of persecution, or warfare, and the more time that passes before the refugee is able to return safely home, the more likely it is that he or she will become an immigrant and seek naturalized citizenship.

Following the demise of European colonial systems in the 1950's and 1960's and the end of guest worker programs in most industrialized countries in the 1970's, there was a dramatic increase in applications for naturalized citizenship from citizens of the former colonies and from guest workers. In the aftermath of the Cold War there was also a significant increase in applications for naturalized citizenship in many countries from citizens of Eastern European countries. Additionally, the end of apartheid in South Africa increased applications for residency and naturalized citizenship in that nation.

Naturalized citizenship is a status defined by national governments, so the conditions under which it is granted will vary from country to country and will depend heavily on domestic and international political conditions.

Bibliography

Brubaker, William Rogers, ed. *Immigration and the Politics of Citizenship in Europe and North America.* Lanham, Md.: University Press of America, 1989. Conference papers comparing immigration and naturalization policies in North America and Europe.

Coenen, Harry, and Peter Leisink, eds. *Work and Citizenship in the New Europe.* Brookfield, Vt.: E. Elgar, 1993. Papers presented at an international conference on the quality of citizenship in post-guest worker, post-Cold War Europe.

Hammar, Tomas. *Democracy and the Nation State: Aliens, Denizens, and Citizens in a World of International Migration.* Brookfield, Vt.: Gower, 1990. Well-known Swedish immigration scholar examines the rights and obligations of individuals of differing residency statuses in the modern state.

Meehan, Elizabeth. *Citizenship and the European Community.* Newbury Park, Calif.: Sage Publications, 1993. Examines the state citizenship versus European Community membership as a philosophical and practical matter.

North, David S. *Alien Legalization and Naturalization: What the United States Can Learn from Down Under.* Washington, D.C.: New TransCentury Foundation, 1984. Examines the legalization and naturalization policies in New Zealand and Australia and how they might apply to the United States.

Patel, P. J. *Patel's Immigration Law Digest: Digest of Opinions in Immigration and Naturalization Cases.* Rochester, N.Y.: Lawyers' Co-operative Publication, 1982. Reference source for rulings in administrative courts in the United States on immigration and naturalization issues.

U.S. Department of Justice. Immigration and Naturalization Service. *An Immigrant Nation: United States Regulation of Immigration, 1798-1991.* Washington, D.C.: Author, 1991. Overview of the history of immigration to the United States and summary of current law.

Miles W. Williams

Cross-References

NEO-CONSERVATISM

Field of study: Political philosophy

Neo-conservatism developed as a coherent set of political ideas in the United States in the 1970's. It was largely a reaction to political events of the 1960's: the activist Great Society programs, the disruptive events surrounding the Vietnam War, and social reform movements.

Principal terms
ADVERSARY CULTURE: term used to define the radical attack on U.S. values unleashed by the 1960's counterculture movement
AFFIRMATIVE ACTION: policies designed to achieve employment and educational equity by eliminating discrimination and increasing opportunities for groups historically denied such access
CRISIS OF GOVERNABILITY: condition in which the demands placed on the state become too overwhelming for the state to effectively solve them, resulting in a loss of faith in the state's authority to lead
LAW OF UNINTENDED CONSEQUENCES: situation in which steps taken by the state to solve a problem either make things worse or cause new, unforeseen problems
NEW CLASS: term used negatively by neoconservatives to identify highly educated professionals who favor an active role for the state in solving society's problems
NEW LEFT: term used to define the radical youth movement of the 1960's

Overview

Neo-conservatism first became a recognized set of political ideas in the United States in the early to mid-1970's. The term was coined by U.S. socialist Michael Harrington to identify a group of formerly liberal intellectuals who had moved to the political right in reaction to the political upheavals of the 1960's. Harrington described the neo-conservatives as "those who came to their position from a liberal or socialist background, after being disillusioned of their Great Society dreams." They saw many of the government reform efforts of the 1960's as excessive, misguided, and ultimately unworkable when put into practice. While typically supportive of many of the goals held by liberals in the 1960's, such as ending racial discrimination, abolishing poverty, and promoting equal opportunities for all Americans, neo-conservatives concluded that the federal government's efforts in these areas had largely backfired. They argued that the Great Society policies tried to do too much, resulting not in positive, progressive changes, but in too many unintended consequences that made matters worse. The high-minded idealism that drove the many reform efforts of the 1960's proved that good intentions do not always produce workable policies. Faced with the many failures of the Great Society's programs, neo-conservatives argued for a more realistic or pragmatic approach on how the state should tackle many of the country's pressing problems.

The major themes of neo-conservative thought include an acceptance of a minimal welfare state; support for capitalistic or free market economics; concern over the loss of traditional American values; the crisis of governability; and a militant anticommunist position in foreign policy.

Unlike many traditional twentieth century conservatives who wish to keep the scope of government activity as limited as possible, neo-conservatives are not philosophically opposed to government. They may wish to trim the size of the state and to lower taxes, but they recognize that some government programs, such as social security for the elderly and unemployment insurance for workers, are valuable state-operated programs. They support a conservative welfare state where government programs can work effectively to protect the public against, in the words of conservative commentator George Will, "the vicissitudes and hazards of a dynamic and hierarchical industrial economy." The state should take an interest in promoting domestic stability and in easing the hardships individuals and families face, so long as the aid is temporary. Most neo-conservatives support the welfare provisions of Franklin D. Roosevelt's New Deal, but found many of the welfare reforms of Lyndon Johnson's Great Society to be too intrusive, too bureaucratic, too costly, and largely ineffective. For example, welfare rules that tend to discourage work, break up families, and encourage young single women to have children are strongly criticized by neo-conservatives. They believe that government welfare programs should provide security for those in need but not create a paternalistic state caring for a sizable class of dependent welfare recipients.

On the issue of economic policy, neo-conservatives generally support the free market system as opposed to direct government involvement in planning or guiding the economy. Neo-conservative spokesman Irving Kristol has explained their position on economic policy in his book *Two Cheers for Capitalism* (1978). Kristol argues that capitalism can claim two important victories. First, when compared to socialism or state-directed economic controls, capitalism has proven to be efficient, supportive of economic growth, and conducive to higher levels of material well-being. Second, the relatively high level of economic freedom associated with a market economy supports other forms of individual liberties and freedoms. Simply put, a high level of economic freedom to buy, sell, and trade is a necessary condition for greater levels of individual freedoms in other areas of life. History has demonstrated that when the state controls economic life, the level of freedom in noneconomic areas also becomes subject to state control.

Although Kristol gives capitalism two cheers for these two results, he does not give the traditional "third cheer." In the area of cultural values and the goal of creating a just or virtuous society, he believes that twentieth century U.S. capitalism comes up short. Capitalism's stress on material well-being, self-interest, and the pursuit of profit to the exclusion of important "moral" values, works to undermine many of the virtues required to maintain a well-ordered and healthy society. From Kristol's perspective, efficiency is not a moral virtue, and freedom by itself cannot guarantee a virtuous society. Capitalism, according to neo-conservative critics, can work to subvert the moral fiber of a society when, for example, a businessman sells pornographic materials because a profitable return can be made. When every product or service is evaluated solely in terms of profitability, the moral impact of the capitalistic system often is overlooked.

This leads to the next main theme of neo-conservative thought, namely, the decline of traditional American values. Neo-conservatives maintain that the high level of material affluence and individual freedom in the United States has been built upon an important set of cultural values, which have seriously eroded since World War II. The Puritan or Protestant values of frugality, industry, sobriety, reliability, and piety are often mentioned as the key to the American success story. Beginning in the 1960's, however, an adversary culture or counterculture emerged, connected to the radical youth movement of that period. This generation has been described by neo-conservatives not as high-minded idealists, but as self-absorbed, hedonistic utopians. When a serious attack was launched in the 1960's against traditional core values, American society began to drift dangerously off course. While neo-conservatives have paid much attention to this decline, they have been less certain about corrective measures required to restore those important cultural values, beyond advising the restoration of the virtues associated with the Judeo-Christian ethic.

When analyzing the workings of the U.S. political system, neo-conservatives have identified two serious problems. The first they call an excess of democracy, whereby the public sector becomes overloaded with an extreme number of demands to solve a wide array of social and economic problems. The second problem is the resulting crisis of governability, when citizens begin to lose confidence in the state's ability to deliver on these promises. Whenever politicians promise too much, and citizens come to expect quick and easy solutions, the prospects of failure and disappointment become a near certainty. Neo-conservatives worry about this loss of confidence and have argued for a greater awareness of the limitations of social policy.

Unfortunately, those holding positions of power in the United States have not been guided by an awareness of these limitations. The excess of democracy has been created by a new ruling elite, labeled the "new class" by their neo-conservative critics. This new class represents a cadre of political operatives who began to surface during the 1960's, motivated primarily by gaining access to power to help deliver on the promises of the Great Society programs. Members of this new class are highly educated middle-class professionals, who view state power and state budgets as positive forces in solving problems from economic inequality and poverty to civil rights and public education. Since their power comes from an expanding role for the state, they are primarily responsible for creating the overload and the resulting crisis in governability.

On foreign policy issues, neo-conservatives are noted for their strong antipathy toward the communist world and their strong support for Israel. For many of the key figures in the neo-conservative movement, the rise of totalitarianism in the Soviet Union and in Germany during the 1930's were defining moments. Stalin's brand of socialism and Hitler's genocide against the Jews of Europe led to their active support of the Cold War policy of containment and the unconditional backing of democratic Israel. Even during the era of détente, the relaxation of tensions with the Communist world initiated by President Richard Nixon in the early 1970's, many neo-conservatives preferred to remain staunch Cold Warriors.

Applications

Most neo-conservatives have a keen interest in public policy issues, and are comfortable using the latest social scientific techniques in analyzing the effectiveness of particular government programs. They support programs that demonstrate their effectiveness, but if a program falls short of its goals or creates negative side effects, the pragmatic neo-conservative steps forward.

Neo-conservatives have paid special attention to government efforts to promote greater opportunities for groups that traditionally have faced discrimination in the United States. They support efforts to create an equal opportunity society in the United States and recognize that for many minorities and women the doors to upward social mobility have been tightly closed in education, employment, and housing. They criticize not the end goal, but the means used by the state to reach the desired objectives. In *Affirmative Discrimination: Ethnic Inequality and Public Policy* (1975), Nathan Glazer analyzed the impact these programs have had in areas of education, housing, employment, and racial segregation. He asserted that most of the affirmative action plans used to assist previously excluded groups had largely failed. Glazer and other neo-conservatives have attacked the idea that jobs, promotions, or admission to colleges or professional schools should be based on reaching statistical parity, that is, 50 percent male, 50 percent female; 80 percent white, 12 percent African American, 8 percent Hispanic. When racial, religious, or gender quotas take priority, unacceptable developments can result. First, instead of using measurable skills or qualifications to determine who will be hired, promoted, or selected, arbitrary factors such as race, gender, or ethnicity are used. Neo-conservatives worry that these limited social goods are given to less qualified or unqualified people, instead of people who have earned them by their talents, skills, and achievements. Second, instead of creating greater harmony among the races or between the sexes, one of the results of affirmative action programs has been to generate a white or male backlash against minorities or women, who, they believe, have unfairly benefited from these programs. Third, those who have been assisted by affirmative action may come to feel that their selection was based not on their skills or talents, but on their race or gender. They may become defensive, rightly or wrongly, because they believe others see them as undeserving. The results of these programs illustrate the neo-conservative concern that many well-intended social programs create unforeseen, negative consequences.

Another example concerns government efforts to integrate public schools in the United States after decades of unequal educational opportunities. Neo-conservatives support the principle of integration but raise many questions about busing students to reach a particular racial balance in public schools. Many neo-conservatives claim that, despite the arguments of probusing advocates, there is no clear evidence that educational achievement has been enhanced by using busing to integrate the public schools. Second, instead of creating greater levels of understanding and cooperation among racial groupings, in many cases busing has resulted in greater racial problems. There was great public resistance to court-ordered busing, including outbreaks of violence between the racial groups affected by the busing plan. In some school districts, the level of racial integration did not improve but, in fact, got much worse. Once busing plans were introduced, many white families moved out of affected school districts or sent their children to private schools. In both cases, "white flight" left many public school systems more racially segregated than they were before busing was introduced. Again, the result was not foreseen and, at least in the short-term, the effect of busing was the exact opposite of the intended policy objective.

The insight that neo-conservatives have brought to public policy initiatives is that policies must be carefully considered before being implemented and constantly reviewed to assure that they are working to achieve their stated goals. Ineffective policies must be redesigned or abandoned.

Context

The neo-conservative movement developed in the early 1970's, led by a small but extremely influential cadre of intellectuals associated with a number of serious journals, private think tanks, and prominent U.S. universities. The first generation of neo-conservatives were born between 1920 and 1930; many were second-generation Americans; many were Jews; and most lived and attended schools in and around New York City. They came of political age in the 1930's and 1940's, when socialism had a strong pull in U.S. intellectual circles, and many of them briefly flirted with moderate socialism before the horrors of the Soviet totalitarian state became widely known. They began their intellectual passage from the liberal-left to the moderate conservative position soon after the political upheavals of the 1960's and the excesses they saw in the liberal policies of the late 1960's and the early 1970's. As they interpreted the political agenda of the New Left, they believed that important American principles were being destroyed. Instead of promoting equal opportunities for all Americans, the New Left was promoting equality of results; instead of rewarding merit, rewards were being distributed according to a political agenda to make the United States a more egalitarian society. Disillusioned by the Great Society programs and the nihilistic thrust of the militant counterculture of the 1960's, the neo-conservative movement claimed that it was acting to save the United States from the radical agenda of the new class. After much work during the 1970's to establish neo-conservative think tanks and journals to publish their writings, neo-conservatives' ideas began to have a direct impact on governmental policies. Their policy recommendations in such areas as criminal justice, welfare reform, taxation, and government regulation dominated the debates on these issues in the 1980's. With a second generation of neo-conservative thinkers waiting in the wings, this intellectual movement continued to play a major role in public policy debates.

Bibliography

Coser, Lewis A., and Irving Howe, eds. *The New Conservatives: A Critique from the Left*. New York: Quadrangle/New York Times, 1974. Early discussion of the neo-conservative movement by opponents on the political left.

Glazer, Nathan. *Affirmative Discrimination: Ethnic Inequality and Public Policy*. New York: Basic Books, 1975. Analysis of how affirmative action programs have worked to undermine public commitment to individual rights by replacing them with group rights.

Gottfried, Paul, and Thomas Fleming. *The Conservative Movement*. Boston: Twayne, 1988. Characterizes the neo-conservatives as a revolt of intellectuals against the liberal-left political developments of the 1960's.

Kristol, Irving. *Reflections of a Neoconservative: Looking Back, Looking Ahead*. New York: Basic Books, 1983. Intellectual autobiography of the most prominent figure in the neo-conservative movement. Kristol traces his early flirtation with socialism and the story of his gradual move to the political right starting in the 1950's.

_____. *Two Cheers for Capitalism*. New York: Basic Books, 1978. Essays by the intellectual godfather of neo-conservative thought.

Steinfels, Peter. *The Neoconservatives: The Men Who Are Changing America's Politics*. New York: Simon and Schuster, 1979. Critical, but fair, analysis of the major themes embodied in the movement. Special attention is given to neo-conservative thinkers Irving Kristol, Daniel Bell, and Daniel P. Moynihan.

Lawrence J. Connin

Cross-References

Burke's Political Philosophy, p. 171; Capitalism, p. 197; Conservatism, p. 419; Equality and Egalitarianism, p. 630; The Left and the Right, p. 1079; The New Right, p. 1293; The Welfare State, p. 2135.

NEO-IDEALISM

Field of study: Political philosophy

In its ethical form, neo-idealism is a philosophy that seeks to rescue humanity's moral consciousness from the attempts that have been made to reduce it to mere utilitarian self-interest. Politically, neo-idealism is a reaction to the extreme individualism that denies the reality of humans as social beings.

Principal terms

GENERAL WILL: force that drives the state to attain the objective for which it was created, namely the common good

LIBERALISM: key doctrine in post-idealism that stresses the importance of the freedom of individuals to express themselves in their own ways

NOUMENALISM: Immanuel Kant's concept of ultimate reality, which is contrasted with "phenomenon," or appearance

PLURALISM: idea that political power is diffused within a society, in which no group has a monopoly

RIGHT: Georg W. F. Hegel's term for the complex of ideas and practices noted by such concepts as individual freedom, morality, duty, justice, and the rule of law

UTILITARIANISM: philosophical doctrine advanced by Jeremy Bentham and John Stuart Mill that all moral, social, or political action should be directed toward achieving the greatest good for the greatest number of people

Overview

The neo- or post-idealist school of philosophy was led by a group of English philosophers known as the Oxford Idealists. Dominated by the philosopher Thomas Hill Green (1836-1882), neo-idealism has been seen as a reaction to the extreme individual liberalism of Jeremy Bentham and John Stuart Mill, who led a philosophical school of thought called utilitarianism. The idealism of the Oxford school is often interpreted as a series of attempts to correct the defects of the heavy emphasis that the utilitarians placed on individualism. The contributions of the Oxford group were to pave the way for the democratic thought of L. T. Hobhouse, A. D. Lindsay, and Ernest Barker, as well as Woodrow Wilson and John Dewey.

Ernest Barker, a leading Oxford Idealist, argued that some redistribution of rights between the social classes might be necessary if the greatest number of people were to enjoy the greatest possible development of their capacities of personality. However, he argued that utilitarians failed to see that at the same time that social thought about redistributing social and economic justice grew, so also did democratic insistence on liberty and equality for all. Similarly, R. M. MacIver, another leading exponent within the neo-idealist tradition, defined democratic societies as those in which the general will encompasses the community as a whole, or at least the greater portion of the community, and that the general will is the conscience and support of a genuinely democratic form of government. He specifically distinguished democratic states from class-controlled states and found that in modern civilizations a wide range of interest groups and associations make up a social universe that is characterized by turmoil and struggle. The political party system, however, would serve as the effective way of reducing the tremendous differences of opinion to relatively simple alternatives. The central task of a democratic state is to express and enforce the general will by representing people as citizens rather than as holders of particular interests.

In his general philosophy, Thomas H. Green, more than any of his colleagues, was influenced both by Immanuel Kant and G. W. F. Hegel—particularly the former. For Green even as "reason" and "will" exist in people, they are one in the sense that they are similar expressions in humankind's quest for self-realization. By practical "reason" he meant a consciousness of the possibility of perfection by the individual. By "will" he meant the effort of a self-conscious subject to satisfy the individual's desire for self-enrichment. The only good thing, Green argued, is a good will. Freedom, then, consists not simply in the absence of restraint but in the pursuit of those objects which "good will" presents. It consists in obeying the law of one's own moral being. Hence, freedom is not a negative thing, but something positive. It is through seeking self-perfection or self-improvement that true freedom is to be found. Freedom for Green was in some sense the goal of all moral endeavor; the will toward freedom resides not in a person's voluntary action but in person's pursuit for a higher self in accordance with Kant's view of selfhood. To Kant, selfhood consists of two wills, or selves, in human beings: the "pure" will, or ego, and the "empirical" will. Independent of a person's actual desires, the pure will is directed toward fulfilling a universal law, of which it is itself the giver. However, self-perfection, Green says, can never be realized apart from other individuals. Social institutions are necessary in order that individuals may achieve this self-perfection, and there can be no individual well-being apart from social well-being. Individuals must therefore derive their conception of perfection from social morality, from a conception of a common good that is embodied in that morality. That conception of common good changes as civilization itself progresses and changes. What binds individuals in society is never simply fear, much less physical compulsion, but the will to do that which they conceive to be in their own and in the common interest.

Green reduced all so-called natural and unalienable rights to "one" right, namely, the right to pursue one's own good so long as that good is recognized by the whole society. All individual claims against the state and society must always be compatible with the common good. At one point Green called the state a "society of societies"; however, it is not the simple conventional and historical sovereign state, but a moral entity—somehow identical with the "true selves" of all its members. It secures and extends political powers to the common good—a condition in which all members in society feel capable of producing. Green saw democratic rights as but one aspect of the necessity for all moral acts to be directed toward the common good. Rights, thus, inhere in individuals only insofar as those individuals are members of a society that recognizes such rights. Society, or the state, is the determiner of the good, not the individual. Conceivably, individuals could challenge the state in the name of certain ideal rights; however, presumption is always against such resistance to the will of the state. Since resistance is liable to result in general anarchy and since such a destruction of the state would mean a general loss of freedom, it is necessary carefully to weigh the possibility of anarchy against the ideal freedom desired. The burden is placed on the individual citizen to point to some public interest, generally recognized as such, which is involved in the exercise of the power claimed by him as a right.

The state, in Green's thought, ascends to the role of a natural force encompassing the social whole from which its individual members cannot escape, and to which humankind owes everything. The state emerges as a harmonizer of social relations and conflicts. The major social conflicts that loomed in Green's thought were the problems of education, temperance, landed property, and justice. In these matters he favored considerable state intervention and regulation. It is the function of the state to remove all obstacles to these public functions and responsibilities. To Green, classical liberalism went wrong in regarding freedom simply in negative terms; freedom is positive. Thus he laid the intellectual foundations for the modern social welfare state, which provides old age pensions, unemployment insurance, health insurance, and other schemes designed to promote social security and justice. Liberal governments ought to legislate in any cases wherein the law can remove obstacles to the moral development of their citizens. In place of laissez-faire and freedom of contract it opened the way—in the name of positive freedom—for any degree of social legislation that might be justified as effective in improving standards of living. What Green added to liberal theory was the conception of collective well-being as a precondition of individual freedom and responsibility.

A more Hegelian conception of the state finds expression in the writing of two other British idealists, F. H. Bradley (1846-1924) and Bernard Bosanquet (1848-1923). According to Bradley, the state is a moral organism that actually lives; it is the objective mind which is subjective and self-conscious in its citizens. The state feels and knows itself in the heart of each of its citizens. It speaks the word of command and gives the field of accomplishment. And in the activity of obedience it has bestowed individual life and satisfaction and happiness. The individual has no real existence apart from the state, which is the means of realizing the true idea of humankind. Whatever an individual person is, that person is only by virtue of the community in which the person exists.

Bosanquet carried Green's philosophy to its Hegelian limits. For him, the state includes the entire hierarchy of institutions that determine life: from the family to the trades, and from the trades to the church and university. The state is above all things, not a number of persons, but a working conception of life. In submitting to the general will of the community, one submits to one's own real and rational will, and thus, to oneself. Hence, one is more free when one submits to the dictates of the general will than when one yields to one's own momentary impulses or desires. The general will is embodied in the state and in the laws laid down by the state; hence true freedom is to be found in loyalty to the state and in submission to its laws.

Applications

In the work of the American philosophy professor John Rawls, idealism is raised to a high level of abstraction, especially when Rawls elaborates on his controversial 1971 work, *A Theory of Justice*. The conception of equality that Rawls presents in his principles of justice begins with a firm foundation in the work of Immanuel Kant. Kant's distinction between positive and negative freedom serves to situate what Rawls means by a concept he calls the "original position." Rawls asks what rules free and rational persons concerned with furthering their own interests would accept in an initial position of equality. He then creates a hypothetical situation in which all individuals are treated fairly with respect to human and civil rights. What, he asks, is the logical order of basic goal values and procedural rules that underlie a political system of rational freedom? And following upon that, he tries to show what public policy programs derive logically from the initial commitment to ground rules. The two together define the just society.

Starting with what he feels to be a Kantian position, Rawls adopts a concept of negative freedom that builds on a conception of "right" rather than individual or group interests or satisfaction. In this original position, Rawls argues, persons would choose equality in the assignment of basic rights and duties, while agreeing that social and economic inequalities are just only if they result in compensating benefits for everyone, and in particular for the least advantaged members of society. However, there is no injustice in the greater benefits and advantages in the greater rewards earned by a few, provided that the situation of less fortunate persons is thereby improved.

In order to provide for positive freedom, it is imperative that the parties are conceived as free and equal moral persons who play a decisive part in framing the conception of justice. The assumption that the parties are free and equal moral persons emphasizes basic liberties; it also regards individuals as free and responsible masters of their own desires and assumes that all are to share equally in the means for the attainment of ends—unless the situation of everyone can be improved, taking fair and equal division as the starting point. Any society that realizes these principles, Rawls argues, would attain positive freedom.

It is upon the Kantian conception of the equality of moral persons and the moral imperative that all individuals are to be regarded as ends in themselves, and not simply as means to an end, that Rawls builds his prescription for relative political, social, and economic equality that is the substance of the liberal welfare state. Rawls argues that human beings should be treated as ends in themselves because of their capacity for moral choice, which gives them a dignity not enjoyed by nonhuman objects. A moral person is a subject with self-chosen ends and a fundamental preference for conditions that enable the individual to lead a life that expresses his or her nature as a free and rational being.

In Daniel Bell's *The End of Ideology* (rev., 1988), and Francis Fukuyama's essay "The End of History" (1989), the authors claim that Hegel is the origin of their basic ideas. Bell advances the proposition that following World War II, politics in the West was characterized by broad agreement amongst major political parties and the absence of ideological division or debate. Fascism and communism had both lost their appeal, while the remaining parties disagreed only about who could be relied upon to deliver economic growth and material prosperity. In effect, economics had triumphed over politics. Reduced to technical questions about "how" to deliver affluence, politics ceased to address moral or philosophical questions about the nature of the "Good Society." In effect ideology had become irrelevant.

A broader Hegelian perspective has been adopted by Francis Fukuyama in "The End of History." Unlike Bell, Fukuyama does not suggest that political ideas have become irrelevant, but that one particular set of ideas, Western liberalism, has triumphed over all its rivals. History as a continuing series of unpredictable events will continue, but history as the human quest for the fully satisfying social order has reached an end because most of the people in the world today agree in principle that liberal democracy is the only fully satisfying social order. In practice, of course, the ideals of liberal democracy—liberty and equality for all—have not been completely attained. Nevertheless, even if people disagree about how best to achieve these ideals, most people now agree on the ideals themselves. Fukuyama views this consensus as a unique development, for never before has there been so nearly universal agreement about what the ideal society would be like.

According to Fukuyama, there are two reasons for the triumph of liberal ideals. First, liberalism satisfies the human desire for material security and comfort through economic productivity and the scientific conquest of nature. Second, liberalism satisfies the human desire for recognition through an egalitarian cultural and political order that recognizes all human beings as equal in dignity. Thus, the history of human striving for satisfaction comes to an end when human beings discover that liberal democracy is the only social order that satisfies their deepest longing—the longing for material prosperity and the longing for non-materialist recognition.

Context

By the end of the nineteenth century many people had come to regard human welfare as the ultimate criterion of political and social justice, and to recognize wide-ranging experiment and compromise as proper means of achieving their objectives. Many liberals, such as the Englishman, T. H. Green, without abandoning their preference for free enterprise, went so far as to argue for wages-and-hours laws, social insurance, and other forms of government intervention to correct certain undesirable consequences of free competition.

Neo-idealistic pluralism became a strong intellectual current in early twentieth century liberal-democratic thought. Democratic party systems seemed the best way to overcome the dangers of class government. Neo-idealist thinkers wrote favorably about how the democratic process, led by a rational, well-intentioned citizenry with a variety of different interests, could adjust their differences in the peaceful, rational, give-and-take of party politics, pressure groups, and the free press.

Bibliography

Barker, Ernest. *Reflections on Government.* New York: Oxford University Press, 1958. Highly readable history of liberalism that praises the virtues of government by discussion and decisions arrived at democratically.

Barry, Brian. *The Liberal Theory of Justice.* Oxford, England: Clarendon Press, 1973. Clear exposition of John Rawls's theory of justice.

Green, T. H. *Lectures on the Principles of Political Obligation.* London: Oxford University Press, 1941. Excellent overview of the idealist tradition by its leading modern exponent. Green sets universal brotherhood as a political goal and vigorously attacks war as a solution to international tensions.

Lidsay, A. D. *Kant.* London: Oxford University Press, 1934. Surprisingly readable account from one of the leading authorities on Immanuel Kant, focusing on Kant's most significant political thoughts.

Ruggiero, Guido de. *History of European Liberalism.* London: George Allen and Unwin, 1927. Readable history of European liberalism in both its theoretical and political influence. Particularly fine treatment of John Stuart Mill and the utilitarian liberals.

Andrew Raposa

Cross-References

Conservatism, p. 419; General Will, p. 745; Idealism, p. 855; Kant's Political Philosophy, p. 1025; Liberalism, p. 1118; Political Philosophy, p. 1505; Rousseau's Political Philosophy, p. 1756; Utilitarianism, p. 2077.

THE NEW RIGHT

Field of study: Politics

The New Right is a conservative movement that achieved prominence in the United States in the 1970's and 1980's. It consists of political leaders, business leaders, conservative political action committees, conservative institutes, think tanks, and grassroots evangelical Christian organizations.

Principal terms

CHRISTIAN COALITION: religious organization created by evangelist Pat Robertson that became the dominant right-wing religious group in the 1990's

MORAL MAJORITY: religious right organization created by evangelist Jerry Falwell in 1979. This group was the dominant right-wing religious organization in the 1980's

NEW RELIGIOUS RIGHT: group of religious organizations that emerged in the 1970's, including the Moral Majority, the Religious Roundtable, and Christian Voice

STATUS POLITICS: theory that political movements in the United States have been related to a sense of power and status

YOUNG AMERICANS FOR FREEDOM: organization created in 1960 for the purpose of mobilizing American youth to promote a conservative agenda and conservative candidates

Overview

In the early 1960's, sociologist Daniel Bell asserted that an age of ideology had ended and that the old ideologies of both the Left and the Right were no longer applicable. The Right no longer saw laissez-faire policies as essential and the Left no longer emphasized the need for a socialist state. Instead there was a type of consensus favoring a welfare state, a mixed economy, decentralized power, and political pluralism. Bell and Seymour Martin Lipset viewed the American right wing of the 1950's and 1960's as a transitory movement resulting from the upward social mobility occurring in American society. Status politics provided the most common explanation for this phenomenon. Groups whose political, social, and economic status were threatened were attracted to various right-wing movements. Once the status of these groups, was settled, however, their activism was expected to decline. While some of these organizations did decline, others continued to grow in the 1960's and gave rise to a new era of ideology in the form of the New Right in the 1970's.

The leaders of the New Right had ties to conservative causes and movements from the earlier decades. Three publications, *National Review*, *Human Events*, and *Modern Age* provided an outlet for conservative thought prior to the 1970's. Two conservative organizations, The Intercollegiate Society of Individualists and the Young Americans for Freedom, attracted young conservatives to their ranks in the same era. In 1964, conservatives rallied around the presidential candidacy of Republican Barry Goldwater. While Goldwater won his party's nomination, he was soundly defeated in the election, carrying only his home state of Arizona and five Deep South states. The conservative movement continued to grow, however, and while conservatives were unable to secure the Republican Party's nomination for Ronald Reagan in 1968, they were recognized by party nominee Richard Nixon as a group whose support was necessary to win the party's nomination.

The expansion of the conservative movement beyond its Republican base in the 1970's was a result of the breakdown of the American consensus in the 1960's. The student movement, black activism, the counterculture, and protest against the Vietnam War created a backlash that benefited the conservative movement and the Republican Party. White Southerners, blue-collar workers, and Catholics were potential recruits. Many supported George Wallace's presidential campaign in 1968 and contributed to Nixon's landslide victory in 1972. Watergate, however, was a major setback for both the Republican Party and the conservative movement. The New Right began to organize during the administration of President Gerald Ford. It was not a result of the challenge of the Democratic Party's liberalism but rather of a perception of Ford as being too moderate. Ford policies that especially alarmed rightist leaders included his offer of limited amnesty for Vietnam era draft resisters and his selection of moderate Republican Nelson Rockefeller as vice president.

A series of crises in the 1970's and the election of Democratic President Jimmy Carter in 1976 resulted in the growth of the New Right. The crises included a stagnant economy, a world order less amenable to American influence, growing domestic conflict over the family, gender roles, and basic values, radical social movements that questioned basic features of American society, and a government that lacked the resources to meet the demands placed on it. This crisis culminated in the election of Ronald Reagan as president and a Republican majority in the Senate in 1980.

Applications

The actual development of the New Right may be seen as having occurred in three areas. First, there were groups of activists who defended the traditional family against a variety of challenges including the women's movement, the gay movement, and education innovation. The second area involved networking of the activists, of their financial contributors, of research institutes, of the organizers, and of the political candidates. Finally, the third area involved organizations created to mobilize the evangelical and fundamentalist Protestants. By 1980, the New Right was fully developed, with an eclectic network of political action committees, research arms, and grassroots organizations.

The New Right began its development of a network of leaders and organizations in 1973 and 1974. One key figure was Richard Viguerie. The first executive director of the Young Americans for Freedom, Viguerie was a direct-mail fundraiser. He started his direct mail operation in 1965 with lists initially obtained from contacts in the Young

Americans for Freedom and the Barry Goldwater presidential campaign. His operational success was attributed to a decline in partisan voting and changes in federal campaign contribution laws which placed an emphasis on small contributors. The former led to more single-issue voting and to the desirability of using the mail to contact voters, while the latter placed an emphasis on using the mail to solicit small contributions. By the early 1970's he had a computer data bank of approximately fifteen million names of contributors to conservative causes. With these lists his company became the major fundraising organization for the New Right.

Another major figure was Paul Weyrich. Weyrich, a conservative Catholic, had worked as a journalist and as a staff member for a senator. An admirer of "Mr. Conservative," Senator Robert Taft, Weyrich gained valuable experience from his years in Washington, D.C., but developed a dislike for the Republican Party leadership. In 1975, he created the Committee for the Survival of a Free Congress, which was largely financed by conservative brewer Coors. Weyrich also organized three different coalitions. These were discussion groups which met to discuss strategy and to propose legislation concerning economic issues, family issues, national security issues, and political strategy. Finally, Weyrich was instrumental in persuading Joseph Coors to contribute to the Heritage Foundation, a conservative think tank.

John Terry Dolan was a third major actor. A conservative Catholic and a former member of the Young Americans for Freedom, Dolan headed the National Conservative Political Action Committee, which was created in 1975. This group became one of the largest political action committees and was an important force in Senate elections in 1978, which resulted in the election of Republicans to seats previously held by Democrats in Colorado, Iowa, and New Hampshire. Another major figure was Howard Phillips. The Harvard-educated Phillips had also been active in the Young Americans for Freedom. He organized the Conservative Caucus, which was designed both to coordinate locally based single issue groups and to lobby Congress. His efforts helped the New Right develop a grassroots contact with organizations promoting traditional family values. The Conservative Caucus was also a vehicle through which New Right leaders could recruit candidates and train activists. Other figures who were seen as significant contributors to the New Right include Phyllis Schlafly, Morton Blackwell, Jesse Helms, Patrick Buchanan, Phillip Crane, Jack Kemp, and Larry McDonald.

Corporate groups and business interests were also part of the New Right. Their involvement was a result of the perceived decline of business dominance in the country and the world. Business leaders felt threatened by taxes, government deficits, and expansion of government entitlement programs. This resulted in the mobilization of businessmen in the 1970's. One organization created was the Business Roundtable, which represented large corporations and lobbied on their behalf. By the early 1980's more than two hundred corporations were associated with the Business Roundtable. It also created task forces to develop position papers on specific issues. Corporate executives also engaged in lobbying.

Corporations contributed to conservative think tanks and policy centers. The

American Enterprise Institute had its budget increase more than tenfold to more than $10,000,000 in a thirteen-year period. More than six hundred corporations contributed to it. The Heritage Foundation's budget went from a few hundred thousand dollars to over $10,000,000 in ten years while the Hoover Institute's budget increased fourfold over thirteen years. In 1983, its budget was $8,300,000. Finally, a new organization, the Institute for Education Affairs, was created to provide financial support for conservative campus newspapers. It also provided internships for conservative student journalists.

The use of the religious right was the final piece of the New Right's puzzle. The religious right's growth was a result of discontent with social issues as well as its enhanced ability to mobilize evangelical Christians. Religious rightists were unhappy with a perceived American weakness in the international arena as well as a decline of the free enterprise system. Their greatest concern, however, was a perception of secular humanists controlling government, education, and the media. In their minds, this had resulted in the moral decay of society. Using an infrastructure of Christian schools, churches, and electronic ministries, they were able to mobilize support.

The first New Right religious group was Christian Voice, which was formed by Robert Grant and Richard Zone, two fundamentalist ministers from California. This organization was a merger of several antigay, antipornography, and pro-family organizations. The group's board of directors included several well-known figures, such as singer Pat Boone, author Hal Lindsey, and fifteen members of Congress. The leaders of Christian Voice described their organization as a national political lobby, representing the Christian community in Washington. They appointed Gary Jarmin, a one-time member of Sun Myung Moon's Unification Church, as their legislative director. Jarmin issued report cards on congressmen and senators, rating them as "moral" or "immoral" based on their votes on selected bills.

The most important organization was the Moral Majority, which was formed by the Reverend Jerry Falwell of Lynchburg, Virginia, where Falwell was minister of the 17,000-member Thomas Road Baptist Church. He also operated a children's academy, a Bible institute, a correspondence school, a seminary, and Liberty Baptist College (now Liberty University). He used a three-pronged strategy to promote the Moral Majority. First, the group engaged in direct mail fund-raising. Second, he issued moral report cards for members of Congress. Finally, he emphasized grassroots activism in which local chapters focused on everything from school curricula to public libraries to topless bars to anatomically correct, or even exaggerated, gingerbread men.

Falwell maintained contact with his 5,000,000 contributing members through a newspaper, the *Moral Majority Report*, and in 1984 the group raised $11,000,000. In January, 1986, Falwell, complaining that the press had "bloodied and beaten" the name "Moral Majority," merged the group into a new organization, the Liberty Federation. The group continued dealing with moral issues but also focused on communism, national defense, the federal budget, and other conservative issues. In 1989, Falwell dissolved the Moral Majority but claimed that he would continue with the Liberty Federation. He said that during a ten-year life span, the Moral Majority had raised

$69,000,000 for the political causes of conservative Christians.

The demise of the Moral Majority was quickly followed by the rise of a new religious group, the Christian Coalition. The Christian Coalition was started in October, 1989 by Pat Robertson. Robertson claimed he started the group because he saw a need for a large, national, grassroots citizen-action organization. Robertson quietly organized the Christian Coalition at the grassroots level but with strong centralized control. The first stage was to focus on creating viable local grassroots organizations that would have ties to local Republican party organizations. The stated goal was to have a working majority in control of the Republican Party by 1996 and to run candidates favorable to the Christian Coalition from school board to president.

While there was a grassroots emphasis, the Christian Coalition was a top-down, tightly controlled political unit. For example, the coalition's action plan stated that starting a chapter would not necessarily be done through a democratic process. Rather, the state office would assign a president, who would then appoint an executive committee. The coalition's activities were eclectic. It sponsored Citizen Action Training Schools, operated a governmental affairs office in Washington, D.C., distributed voting guides, and published newspapers and newsletters.

The coalition used a sophisticated network of computers, phone banks, direct mail, and fax machines to communicate with members and supporters. In 1994, it claimed it had 350,000 grassroots activists on its national mailing list, 1,600,000 households on its voter database, a membership of more than 1,400,000 in about nine hundred chapters in all fifty states, and an annual budget of $20,000,000.

The election of Ronald Reagan in 1980 and the Republican Party's capture of the Senate were seen as the triumph of the New Right. It was a result of the efforts of skillful leaders and their mobilization of business and the religious right. Through their efforts the Republican Party was revived. Once in power, the New Right experienced only limited success. Ronald Reagan cut taxes, decreased government regulation, increased military spending, and appointed conservatives to the federal judiciary. Many social programs survived, however, and the moral agenda had limited success. Scandals and crises during Reagan's second term limited the implementation of the New Right's agenda. Democrats also rebounded in congressional elections and regained control of the U.S. Senate in 1986. The election of George Bush in 1988 did little for the New Right since he was not seen as one their supporters.

Jerome Himmelstein attributed many of the failures of the New Right to the fact that they were used to being outsiders. The traits that made for effective opposition did not result in effective governing. With the election of Democrat Bill Clinton in 1992, the New Right was able to direct their efforts once again as the outsiders. As they had done before, conservatives portrayed government as the problem. Many of the difficulties of the Clinton presidency can be attributed to the ability of the New Right to convince Americans that government is the problem; whether it be economic or moral. The New Right remains a force in American politics. The question is whether it can consistently convince the American public that it has answers to society's problems.

Context

The roots of the New Right are in conservative movements that existed in America prior to the 1970's. What distinguished it from its predecessors was its political triumphs in the late 1970's and early 1980's. The supporters of the New Right are predominantly white Protestants promoting traditional economic and social values. The New Right appeals to a segment of the population that believes that American society can exist without extensive government intervention and that conservative family values and strict morality are compatible with contemporary capitalism and technological change. In addition, these people view the world as being justly swayed to American purposes. New Rightists view those opposed to this view as collectivists and secularists. Its visibility and periodic success in the last quarter of the twentieth century is evidence that the era of ideology is not over in American politics. Ideology remains an important component of American political culture and the New Right illustrates its continued appeal.

Bibliography

Bell, Daniel, ed. *The Radical Right*. Garden City, N.Y.: Doubleday, 1963. Analyzes the right-wing movements in the United States during the 1950's and the early 1960's.

Crawford, Alan. *Thunder on the Right: The "New Right" and the Politics of Resentment*. New York: Pantheon Books, 1980. Conservative journalist argues that the New Right has abandoned traditional conservatism for backlash politics and single-issue causes.

Himmelstein, Jerome L. *To the Right: The Transformation of American Conservatism*. Berkeley: University of California Press, 1990. Analysis of American conservatism and of the emergence of the New Right.

Hixson, William B., Jr. *Search for the American Right Wing: An Analysis of the Social Science Record, 1955-1987*. Princeton, N.J.: Princeton University Press, 1992. Synthesis of scholarly research on the American Right from the 1950's to the 1980's as well as an explanation of the right as a defender of nineteenth century values.

Hoeveler, J. David, Jr. *Watch on the Right: Conservative Intellectuals in the Reagan Era*. Madison: University of Wisconsin Press, 1991. Analysis of conservative thought and major conservative intellectuals in the United States in the 1970's and 1980's.

Lipset, Seymour Martin, and Earl Raab. *The Politics of Unreason: Right Wing Extremism in America, 1790-1970*. New York: Harper & Row, 1970. An examination of rightist movements and their followers in the United States.

William V. Moore

Cross-References

Activist Politics, p. 7; Citizen Movements, p. 248; Conservatism, p. 419; Feminist Politics, p. 682; Gay and Lesbian Politics, p. 732; Grassroots Politics, p. 797; Keynesianism, Monetarism, and Supply-Side Economics, p. 1032; The Left and the Right, p. 1079; Neo-Conservatism, p. 1281; Political Correctness, p. 1441; Protest Movements, p. 1621; Radicalism, p. 1661; Religion and Politics, p. 1685; The Republican Party, p. 1699.

NIETZSCHE'S POLITICAL PHILOSOPHY

Field of study: Political philosophy

Known primarily as a philosopher, Friedrich Nietzsche was a student of government who formulated a theory that those who are psychologically and intellectually most suited should rule. It was his idea that the ruling class would select itself on the basis of desire and drive.

Principal terms

MASTER MORALITY: Nietzsche's term for an ethical system based on the exercise of individual power, rather than power from consensus

MORALITY: quality of correct conduct

NAZISM: German political system from 1933 to 1945

SLAVE MORALITY: Nietzche's term for an ethical system based on democratic principles that reward meekness and compliance

ÜBERMENSCH (OVERMAN): Nietzsche's term for the higher state to which an individual should aspire—a state in which a person masters himself or herself and is fit to rule

Overview

The German philosopher Friedrich Nietzsche (1844-1900) brought to the world a new way of viewing the elements that control people. By studying the times in which he lived, he concluded that accepted concepts of morality were based on falsehoods. With the traditions of the Christian church and the philosophies such as those of Arthur Schopenhauer and John Stuart Mill supporting growing theories of sympathetic pity for others, Nietzsche felt that the world was tending toward rule by the weak. He felt the new concepts of representative and participatory government were rapidly driving Europe toward a time when it would be ruled by those who he felt were least fit to govern.

The power of European aristocracies was mostly lost in the revolutions of the seventeenth and eighteenth centuries. The popular feelings against the excesses of the autocracies that had prompted these revolutions remained to foster a natural reaction against aristocratic rule in Europe. Slowly, even the monarchies were becoming partners with the people. In this trend Nietzsche saw danger, since government was no longer by the best—the aristocracy. Instead it was becoming rule by those most able to secure the consent of the unlettered and weak commoners. Believing that there is inherent in humankind a "slave" and a "master" mentality, he set about to describe the advantages of government by the "master." Of the "slave" class and its influence on society Nietzsche wrote: "Too long have we conceded to them that they are right, these little people; so that in the end we have also conceded them right. Now they teach: 'Good is only what little people call good.'"

To correct this, Nietzsche saw the need for a strong and able leader, a superior man whom he called the *Übermensch* (superman). This man would have the will to lead, to be a master rather than a slave. He would rule on the basis of expediency and need, instead of on the morality of the Judeo-Christian religions and those who embraced their precepts without necessarily embracing their theology. Weakness, meekness, and suffering were no longer to be virtues of leadership. Instead, Nietzsche foresaw a world ruled by an aristocracy of leaders of superior will and training.

Nietzsche's search for a comprehensive philosophy of ethics led him to develop a new theory of government because he believed that no political system can exist apart from, or in opposition to, the ethnical culture of the people under its rule. Nietzsche was well educated for his task. He attended the universities of Bonn and Leipzig, concentrating on philology—the study of written records. He did so well at Leipzig that he was given a professorship at the age of twenty-four at the University of Basel, where he studied Greek philosophy and the work of Arthur Schopenhauer.

One of Nietzsche's first published essays, *The Use and Abuse of History* (1874), sets the tone for his developing political philosophy. It attacks "historicism"—the use of history as a guide and regulator of the present and future. It also attacks Georg Wilhelm Friedrich Hegel's view that present-day humankind was the completion and greatest development of history. In Nietzsche's view, history shows that humankind is incomplete and that history is not only incomplete but cyclical. He begins with the animal, whose view of its world is entirely nonhistorical. Because animals forget each moment as it passes, they cannot learn from their history nor plan for the future. Humankind, by contrast, is a prisoner of its past and of the awareness of the passage of time that such awareness brings. A complete reliance, however, upon the past to be a model for the future is unhealthy.

In *Twilight of the Gods* (1888) Nietzsche lists what he calls the "Four Great Errors" made by humans. The first is confusing cause and effect, which springs from ignorance. Particular sources of this error abound in religion. For example, if one elaborately worships a god and prospers, it is said that one enjoys good fortune as a result of one's goodness. Nietzsche counters that people may be able to worship elaborately because they are already wealthy.

The second error is that of false causality. During his era, science seldom spanned the disciplines of learned people, let alone those of little education. It was thus easy to accept plausible but erroneous connections between cause and effect. In particular Nietzsche argues that religion has given us a belief that every event is controlled by a deity or "spirit." Not only does this delusion delay the acquisition of corrected knowledge, it allows humankind to shift responsibility from itself to the unseen powers that move it.

The third error is that of imaginary causes. One deduces causes from their observed results. In ignorance, we tend to construct elaborate and internally consistent histories for what we observe. Again, religious traditions contribute most often to this error. Good feelings are thought to be produced by good relationships with the deity, when the actual goodness or its opposite may be entirely due to random but explainable causes. Many people are crippled in their expression of initiative by the false idea that their past actions have produced poor results because they offended the deity.

Finally, Nietzsche considers the error of free will. To pardon the deity for ills which befall humankind, it is common to blame them on the fact that the deity has given humans the power to do themselves harm without also allowing them the solace of believing that the good things that befall them are also partly attributable to their initiative. To Nietzsche, these four interdependent "errors" make history as it is perceived by the uneducated a faulty tool with which to manufacture a future.

In the absence of absolute and independent sources of information, Nietzsche admits that history has three positive uses. The first is monumental history, which provides man with models of great men and events on which he can aspire to pattern his own life. We recognize many who are "heroes" or "statesmen" on whom we attempt to pattern our individual lives. There is also antiquarian history—the store of records and traditions that maintain in man his love and reverence for his cultural past. From this comes the classical art tradition, wherein even "primitive" works of the past are viewed as excellent and taken as models for current work. Finally there is critical history, which allows man to judge his past efforts and learn to avoid them in his future. This is the history of critics of governmental policy, who can select situations from the past that bear similarities to the present. With care they can select those "pasts" in which their personal "predictions" for the present are borne out.

What most concerns Nietzsche is the abuse of these histories. Monumental history can hinder man's aspirations by setting for him unattainable standards. Antiquarian history might make models of ideas that stultify. Finally, critical history, as man's fear of "re-creating" his past is diminished, may allow him to destroy too much that may be useful.

A danger to studying the philosophy of history is the natural desire of enlightened men to make a science of everything that can be studied. In this man often "discovers" more history than actually exists by seeking or inventing relationships and proofs that are spurious but plausible. The earlier the period being studied, the greater this danger is, since man's sense of time diminishes as the remoteness from the present increases.

Nietzsche identifies several dangers in relying too strongly upon history. One danger in applying history to governmental issues is the conclusion that people have somehow "arrived" as spectators, unable to make "their own history." As a result they are content with doing nothing. Creativity is thus stalled and the taking up of tasks that still may be accomplished is discouraged. Humankind degenerates in this situation.

Another real danger to people of their own history is the imagined constraints that history places on them. If they see their present as a reflection of what happened before, perhaps several times, they tend to fear that they will be unable to produce a new result. Making history into a science worsens that effect, since the scientific historians tend to mold accounts of similar events of the past to resemble each other more than was the case. Humankind looks at the "identical" periods of the past and surrenders to what it feels is inevitable.

Nietzsche believed that if the present resembles the past at all, it is in being the beginning of unlimited possibilities, unconstrained by historical models. *The Use and Abuse of History* ends on this positive note, that humanity can not only take a different path into the future, but also direct the future in ways perhaps never before realized.

Another of Nietzsche's early essays, *Human, All-Too-Human* (1878), argues that humankind's traditions and horizons are transitory, that a "new" history may be written, using what is of value from historical studies to "design" a perfected future. In this essay, Nietzsche draws on the histories that he has just attacked for examples of excellence buried in humanity's less than excellent past. From this he derives a system of government based on an aristocracy. In order for an aristocracy to retain power, it must have either the consent of the governed, in which case it falls when the governed cease to consent, or it must be strong enough to appear invincible. Nietzsche suggests that the consent of the governed is always available because in all societies there exists a "slave" morality. Arising from early humankind's herd morality, this is a mental set that glorifies the weak and meek. It is a pivotal part of the Christian ethic, which tells us—as in the Sermon on the Mount—that the powerless and surrendering masses will achieve immortality. By inference, the strong and grasping are thus doomed, to eternal punishment.

Nietzsche also calls this slave morality a "priest" morality, in which he says the priests maintain the slave morality for their own benefit. He acknowledges that there are virtues to the slave morality, which produces compassion. An integral part of Judeo-Christo-Islamic tradition, it is the root of most ethical systems and affects the establishment of nearly all social-welfare establishments in the Western nations. To replace this attitude is not Nietzsche's aim, but rather to bring a rule and order to the herds. What is lacking, and what Nietzsche hopes will be supplied, is a ruling class not only able and willing to accept the challenge of ruling, but which contains within itself the seeds of perpetuating this rule.

Applications

In order to get the world's attention in this elaboration of his ethical schemes, Nietzsche published *Also Sprach Zarathustra* (*Thus Spake Zoroaster*). The title alludes to the founder of the Zoroastrian religion, whose writings may have had some effect on Nietzsche, but the name is borrowed primarily to add a mystical and antiquarian air to the essay. Nietzsche published *Also Sprach Zarathustra* in sections during the 1880's when he was nearing the period of madness that would become the final chapter of his life. At the time, few copies were printed and his sister withheld the last part from the public, fearing that Nietzsche might be prosecuted for blasphemy because of the book's anti-Christian slant. Three years after Nietzsche was sequestered as entirely insane, the last part was finally released.

Zarathustra attacks all religious and ethical traditions that are based on the idea that strength is evil—an idea arising from the fact that many strong leaders in history were cruel and corrupt. Nietzsche therefore argued that selection of a ruler, the *Übermensch* (overman), must be done with care. He and the people over whom he reigns must be freed of the "sickness" of the Christian structure, which inverts the Nietzschean concepts of "strength is good" and "weakness is evil." Despite the alarmed reactions of his detractors, Nietzsche's *Übermensch* was not some super-political figure derived from the Teutonic tradition, nor was he even in existence. In fact, Nietzsche argued that there must be a search for the type of leaders who are fit to rule.

Nietzsche defines as fit to rule those who desire power. Without such desire, there can be no firmity of purpose to sustain a rule by this new aristocracy—the rule of the strong. So long as the world's political culture is ruled by the Christian ethic of ennobling the weak, no *Übermensch* can arise. He cannot spring from a democracy because democracy is a rule of the weak. How, then, can man find his *Übermenschen*? It is not so difficult: *Übermenschen* will arise when there is both a will to have them rule and a will in them to accept power. Nietzsche does not describe the actual selection process, except in general terms. Society must first be divided into producers (farmers and merchants), officials (soldiers and functionaries), and rulers. Rulers cannot come from the producers, who, in order to be effective, must be narrow of vision and single-mindedly directed to their tasks. Nor will the officials be successful rulers; the task of maintaining armies and other bureaucracies is a menial one, and one that is less successfully carried out as the practitioners grow in vision and intellectual curiosity.

Nietzsche's rulers, then, will be the same as Plato's. They will be aristocrats, maintaining their numbers by election of the best. Their power will most likely be hereditary, with limited election from outside to refresh the breed. As births are arranged, the ruling class will, by its conscious efforts, continually improve. Nietzsche's concept of the *Übermensch* gave many the idea that he was proposing a supernatural successor to humankind. So prevalent was this misconception that Nietzsche followed *Zarathustra* with *The Anti-Christ* (1888), partly to explain that he was not looking for an evolved superman, but a selected, normal if excellent, mortal.

Context

None of *Zarathustra* was received with much notice for many years. Scholars and theologians were aware of it, but its impact on the world of thought was minimal. In the early part of the twentieth century the Western world was torn by war, and those who aligned against the Germans confused Nietzsche's *Übermensch* with the "strongman" concept of the Prussian leaders Otto von Bismarck and Wilhelm II. Meanwhile, a curious use was found for Nietzsche's work during World War I. His sister, Elizabeth, an active anti-Semite, had many copies of *Zarathustra* distributed to the German soldiers in the battlefields, hoping thereby to inspire them to ruthlessness. This was a vain effort; the troops were too occupied and ignorant of philosophical concerns to be much influenced.

In the period between the world wars, Nietzsche was cited as support for the many philosophical cults that follow any global political upheaval. With the rise of Nazism in Germany, Adolf Hitler's concept of a "super-race" was confused with Nietzsche's *Übermensch* and anyone outside of Germany showing support for Nietzsche's views was liable to be attacked. In addition, his sister's strenuous efforts to bring his works to Hitler's personal attention were said by those outside of Germany to show a "tie" to Hitler's politics. Nietzsche was, however, anything but an anti-Semite. Hitler could hardly have been encouraged in his anti-Semitism by Nietzsche's strongly positive views on Jewish contributions to culture and family life.

After Hitler's regime fell, outside interest in Nietzsche faded. Some philosophers still refer to his work when introducing philosophical concepts that attack the Judeo-Christian traditions, allowing Nietzsche to take the blame. His main legacy to the world of philosophy is helping to free that field from the support and control by the church. The notoriety attending his works as a result of their shocking attack on the fabric of European religious tradition for a time made his philosophy popularly read. His voice emboldened many to think of a world not guided by the morality of Judeo-Christian scriptures, even if they eventually rejected his principles. In time, however, the shock faded and with it popular interest in his writings.

Bibliography

Castrell, Alburey. *An Introduction to Modern Philosophy in Seven Philosophical Problems*. 2d ed. New York: Macmillan, 1963. Addresses the problems of theology, metaphysics, epistemology, ethics, politics, history, and esthetics from the viewpoints of a score of ancient and modern philosophers.

Durant, Will. *The Story of Philosophy: The Lives and Opinions of the Greater Philosophers*. New York: Garden City, 1927. Detailed history of philosophical thought from Plato to John Dewey.

Hollingdale, R. J. *Nietzsche*. London: Routledge and Kegan Paul, 1973. Interpretation of Nietzsche's works in relation to his life and surrounding world events. Addresses the myths manufactured about Nietzsche in relation to Nazism.

Nietzsche, Friedrich. *The Portable Nietzsche*. Edited by Walter Kauffman. New York: Penguin, 1959. Selection of Nietzsche's best-known works with historical and philosophical annotations and chronologies.

_____. *The Use and Abuse of History*. Translated by Adrian Collin. New York: Liberal Arts Press, 1957. Annotated translation of Nietzsche's 1874 work on historicism.

Strauss, Leo, and Joseph Cropsey. *History of Political Philosophy*. Chicago: Rand McNally, 1963. Discussion of religious leaders and philosophers from Plato to Dewey.

Loring D. Emery

Cross-References

Autocracy and Absolutism, p. 127; Cult of Personality, p. 477; Dialecticism, p. 540; Elitism, p. 591; Existentialism, p. 642; Fascism and Nazism, p. 656; Oligarchy, p. 1344; Plato's Political Philosophy, p. 1396; Political Philosophy, p. 1505; Postmodernism, p. 1570; Succession, p. 1909; Vico's Political Philosophy, p. 2103.

NOMADIC PEOPLES' GOVERNMENTS

Field of study: Comparative government

Patriarchy, rule by the eldest males of a kinship group, has been the most common government for nomadic peoples. Nomads have created larger governmental organizations, such as confederacies and empires, but those larger states have been comparatively short-lived.

Principal terms

CHIEF: leader of a nomadic tribe, usually a senior male who rules with the advice of other elders

CLAN: extended association of tribes based on real or imagined descent from a common, usually male, ancestor

NOMADIC SOCIETY: society without a fixed residence that moves from place to place, generally on a seasonal basis

PATRIARCHY: family-based system of rule dominated by the oldest males

PATRIMONIAL-BUREAUCRATIC: system of government within nomadic empires in which all state offices derive from the ruler's household

SHAMAN: holy man or woman believed to have special powers, including ability to commune with the gods or spirits of the ancestors

Overview

Extensive nomadic empires such as those of the Turco-Mongol rulers Genghis Khan in the thirteenth century and Tamerlane in the fourteenth century were rare. For the most part, nomadic governments have been relatively small and personal. They were rooted in an extension of ideas about families composed of people related biologically or by marriage, to include the wider kinship networks of tribes and clans. The vocabulary of nomadic government involves father, brother, cousin, mother, and wife. In practice, that kinship often was imagined rather than based on actual blood ties. Recognizing another group as long-lost brothers or cousins, however, provided the basis for alliances between tribes.

Nomadic ideas of kinship almost invariably were based on descent from male ancestors. Women played a role when they were married off to cement cooperative agreements between one tribe and another. Likewise, children could turn to their mothers' relatives for help in times of trouble. Women probably acted as behind-the-scenes councilors. Some nomadic groups, the Turkish-speaking tribes of Central Asia, for example, preserved legends about female warriors, but women's place in nomadic governments usually was not prominent.

The premier place afforded males stemmed from the frequency of war in nomadic societies. The need to expand or defend pasture lands, wells, and waterholes made fighting a common part of life. Poetry and song of nomadic peoples as different as the Cheyenne and the Arabs praised male heroism, horsemanship, skill with weapons, and knowledge of tactics. Amerindians, Turks, and others even referred to their warriors with terms that roughly translate into the English word "braves." When not actually engaged in warfare, nomads were likely to be involved in complicated political negotiations among themselves and with their neighbors that likewise emphasized abilities that males, in theory, possessed.

Nomadic groups were subject to rapid swings between extremes of fragmentation and unity. Since every male in a tribe or clan believed that he was a descendant of the group's founder, each asserted equality with any chief. If a leader seemed arbitrary or arrogant, individual families could break away easily. Because of that, chiefs had to have great political wisdom to keep their bands together.

One way in which several tribes could form an alliance was through their common attachment to a holy place. Known as amphictyonies, such confederations acted in unison to defend each other or extend their influence over a wider area. The Hebrew Bible, in the books of Joshua and Judges, contains an account of such a process. Israel was divided into twelve tribes, each bearing the name of its founder. Although they lived in different areas, the tribes were united by their reverence for the Ark of the Covenant, a symbol of their attachment to the same God. The custodians of the Ark, known as judges, were able to influence, but not command, the behavior of the different tribes. The last of the judges, Samuel, was influential in establishing a monarchy for the Israelites. This was an indication of great political sagacity, because many people in the various tribes did not want to have kings over them.

Religious figures often appeared as advisers to chiefs and emperors. Shamans were men, and occasionally women, who were subject to possession by gods and spirits. Once in a trance, a shaman could grant special powers to a would-be chief guaranteeing him support from the spiritual world. Even when nomads adopted a scriptural religion such as Christianity or Islam, shamans, in the form of priests or mystics, retained an important place in their societies. Their powers were often feared as much as respected. Most of the world's nomadic emperors undertook their rule with a religious sanction.

In the sixteenth century, the tomb-shrine of a Muslim saint-mystic, Safi ud-din (d. 1334 C.E.), located near Tabriz in northwestern Iran, was the focal point for the emergence of an imperial state. Many different Turkish tribes inhabited that part of Iran and neighboring eastern Anatolia. They made frequent pilgrimages to the tomb and revered Safi ud-din's descendants, who were its guardians. In the early 1500's, one of those descendants, Ismail, welded the cavalry supplied by those tribes into an effective army, with which he conquered much of Iran and founded the Safavid Dynasty.

Individual charismatic leaders, such as Ismail, could also create confederacies and empires. Such leaders might begin their careers as successful warriors who inspired their own tribe. They then might extend a tribe's wealth and power by conquering neighboring groups. After a victory, a skillful conqueror would distribute the booty among his followers. He might also use it to attract new adherents to his cause. In the final stage, a nomadic empire invades settled territory and captures its cities. Once that has been accomplished, a patrimonial-bureaucratic empire may appear. In such a government, all officials are members of the imperial household. Indeed, governors and other high officers come from the imperial family.

Nomads have seldom employed inheritance customs such as primogeniture: the principle that a first-born male inherits all of his father's estate. Rather, by a process known as tanistry, all the males in the imperial clan gather their followers and fight for the throne. The most able soldier usually emerges as the leader. If wars of succession are prolonged and battles for leadership prove too costly, the government will lose its coherence. Nomadic empires also can disintegrate when nomads who conquer agricultural peoples intermarry with the local population. Over the course of a few generations, warriors abandon their nomadic heritage. As with the heirs of Genghis and Tamerlane, the empire melts away as the conquering nomads become much like their agrarian subjects.

Applications

Genghis Khan's life and career may be used to illustrate how one nomadic government developed from familial-tribal beginnings into one of history's most extensive empires. Genghis, whose name originally was Temüjin, was born into a Mongolian-speaking tribe living in Central Asia close to the borders of China. The area was inhabited by both Mongolian- and Turkish-speaking peoples. The empire that Temüjin eventually created was composed of people using those languages and was, therefore, Turco-Mongol.

Temüjin's father was a chief who was killed by the rival Tatar tribe when Temüjin was still a child. Temüjin's mother took her children and fled to the hills and forests in order to save their lives. In his youth, Temüjin lived a precarious existence. Lacking the support of a tribe, he wandered about, and collected a few other braves who were similarly displaced and disinherited. That group formed a quasi tribe completely loyal to their surrogate patriarch, Temüjin.

Temüjin eventually took back the headship of his own tribe. He then set about crushing the Tatars who had murdered his father. While he distributed the enemy's goods to friends and family, he dealt leniently with anyone who submitted to his commands. Having the loyalty of his own clan as well as his own band of warriors, Temüjin began conquering the rest of the tribes living in Central Asia.

In the twelfth century, Central Asia was both wild and civilized. Its nomadic peoples were known for their military prowess. They were able to steer a charging horse with their knees while using their hands to discharge arrows from a powerful bow compounded of strips of animal bone and wood. At the same time, Mongols lived between the civilizations of Perso-Islamic West Asia and Chinese-dominated East Asia. They were well acquainted with the traditions of those areas. The people Temüjin united already had a taste for the luxury goods produced by their neighbors. Even poor nomads in Genghis' time wore silk undergarments, because they worked on the caravans that carried this valuable fabric along the famous "Silk Road" connecting China to the Middle East and Europe.

Christians, Muslims, Buddhists, Confucians, and Taoists were all present in Central

Asia. Temüjin was interested in all of their religions. He continued to rely, however, on his own religious traditions in which "The Great Blue Sky," a Mongolian name for God, was central. According to legend, the sky god chose Temüjin for a sacred mission: to bring peace to the world and give it a set of fair laws under which all peoples could live peacefully. The name Genghis Khan itself was a title Temüjin acquired that meant "Universal Lord."

Mongol perceptions of Temüjin's mission differ from those of people living in the present. Many contemporary people look upon Genghis as a bloodthirsty barbarian whose soldiers burnt, raped, and slaughtered their way through Eurasia. His armies did cause death and destruction, but in the twelfth and thirteenth centuries, Genghis was famous for the good government and peace that he brought. He was not a barbarian, but a model ruler. His forces struck both East and West, entering the civilized sections of China and Iran. Turco-Mongol policy was clear and simple. Upon approaching a city, the commander of the army ordered the populace to submit immediately or suffer the consequences. Those who surrendered were treated with care. The Mongols understood the value of craftsmen, and they often took metalsmiths, stone carvers, and weavers back to their Central Asian homeland. Any opposition was, by contrast, met with pitiless slaughter. The Mongols did not engage in cruelty for sadistic reasons; rather, it was a matter of policy. If one's present enemies were annihilated in the most vicious way possible, then one's future enemies might well give up without a fight.

While other nomadic empires disappeared soon after the deaths of their founders, Genghis' political achievement lasted for nearly one hundred years. Before his death, Genghis nominated his third son, Ogatai, as his successor. His three other sons had already received command of one or another region of the Mongol empire. A grand council of the Mongol leaders, the *quriltai*, ratified Ogatai as khan.

At Ogatai's death in 1241, his son Güyük was not able to consolidate his power immediately. For almost five years, the empire was controlled by Ogatai's widow acting as regent, a rare instance of a woman having public power. Güyük's accession in 1246 caused descendants of Genghis' other sons to prepare for a fight. Güyük's death in 1248 from alcoholism, an affliction suffered by many Mongol leaders, forestalled that battle.

At Güyük's death, the descendants of Genghis' youngest son, Tolui, took over the grand khanate, decimating the families of his other sons. Mangu was the first great khan of the Toluid house. Hülagü, Arigböge, and Kublai were the other sons of Tolui. Hülagü had undertaken the conquest of Iran, Iraq, and Syria. He was content to manage his newly acquired principality, and his successors became known as the Il-Khans, meaning subordinate khans. The "Golden Horde" that occupied the Caucasus and the Russian steppe did not challenge the emergence of Kublai as Great Khan after Mangu's death. Only Arigböke attempted to displace his brother, and he failed. Kublai directly controlled the Chinese sections of the Mongol empire, with his brothers acknowledging his supremacy.

Under Kublai and his brothers, the Mongol state came under the increasing influence of Chinese and Persian bureaucrats who had gravitated to the rulers of Genghis' house. According to legend, a Chinese scholar had informed one of the Mongol leaders that an empire may be conquered from horseback, but it cannot be ruled from horseback. Gradually the process of building a patrimonial-bureaucratic state got underway.

During the initial conquests, a few Mongol chiefs had advocated the extermination of all peasants they encountered. While nomads understood the importance of the craftsmen who produced the cloth and metal goods they enjoyed, they believed that farming merely got in the way of grazing their herds. From the start, however, Mongol leaders tried to prevent the senseless slaughter of the peasantry. They saw that agriculture provided a steady source of nourishment and revenue. To manage the collection of taxes, they hired Persian and Chinese scholars to design their governmental systems. These scholars were considered the khan's private secretaries. Their power rested, therefore, not on the official posts they held, but on their personal loyalty to the khan and his equally personal trust in them.

The agrarian civilizations of China and Iran began to absorb their Turco-Mongol conquerors. In the West, Uljaitu (d. 1316), the great-grandson of Genghis, became a Muslim. Kublai became more and more identified as a traditional Chinese emperor, the Son of Heaven. Shortly after the death of Kublai, Mongol rule in China ended. In Iran, Turks and Mongols were absorbed by the indigenous population.

During the Mongol-dominated age, West and East were united as they had never been before. Chinese and Indian goods reached Europe during the age of the Crusades, but the spices or cloth arrived indirectly, transported by Asian merchants. During the reign of Kublai, Marco Polo, a Venetian trader, and his uncles traveled throughout the Middle East and Asia under a safe conduct pass issued by Kublai Khan, establishing a direct link with Europe. Many other European merchants must have done the same thing, but no record of their journeys has survived, as did Marco's. The Polos were astounded by the wealth of the Asian lands they traversed. Their experience had an enormous impact on history. When Christopher Columbus set out in search of Cathay (China), Japankuo (Japan), and India, one of the books that inspired his quest was that of Marco Polo. In that way, the Mongols inadvertently contributed much to the shape of the modern world.

Context

Control of herds of animals that provide food, transport for durable goods such as tents, and mounts useful in battle are the bases for the nomadic way of life. Nomads were once found on almost every continent. Population growth and the emergence of technological societies have steadily reduced the number of nomadic peoples. Until the second half of the twentieth century, nomads had found niches in a variety of locales. They were cattle herders in East Africa; the Bedouins of the Arabian desert had flocks of sheep and goats as well as herds of horses and camels; the Laplanders followed the reindeer; the Amerindians of the North American plains found the vast numbers of wild bison a resource nearly as reliable as domesticated stock.

Nomads usually have lived at the borders of agricultural regions. Nomads first appeared about 3000 B.C.E., just after the emergence of the earliest agrarian civilizations. Civilization and nomadism developed in tandem. Since they can only carry a few household goods, nomads always have depended on town-dwellers to supply them with metal goods such as cooking pots, tools, and weapons. In return, nomads supplied the city people with surplus meat, skins, and wool from their herds. Far from being stereotypical barbarians, nomads had extensive first-hand knowledge of civilized life, including an awareness of the sophisticated governmental systems of city-states and empires. Nomads became involved with those larger state systems, either by entering their employ as soldiers, or by establishing their own conquest states in civilized regions.

Bibliography

Allsen, Thomas T. *Mongol Imperialism: The Policies of the Grand Qan Mongke in China, Russia, and the Islamic Lands, 1251-1259.* Berkeley: University of California Press, 1987. Fine study that shows how well organized the Mongol state was.

Barth, Fredrik. *Nomads of South Persia: The Basseri Tribe of the Khamseh Confederacy.* Boston: Little, Brown, 1961. Interesting study of the lifestyle of a particular nomadic group.

Donner, Fred M. *The Early Islamic Conquests.* Princeton, N.J.: Princeton University Press, 1981. Following the death of the Prophet Muhammed (632 C.E.), Arab merchants led Bedouins in the creation of an extensive empire.

Morgan, David. *Medieval Persia, 1040-1797.* New York: Longman, 1988. Brief but thorough account of the interactions of nomads and sedentary peoples in Iran.

_____. *The Mongols.* Oxford: Basil Blackwell, 1986. Original sources as well as contemporary scholarship; provides a readable account of Mongol history.

Nelson, Cynthia, ed. *The Desert and the Sown: Nomads in the Wider Society.* Berkeley: Institute of International Studies, University of California, 1973. Case studies of nomadic groups in several geographical regions.

Rossabi, Morris. *Khubilai Khan: His Life and Times.* Berkeley: University of California Press, 1988. Highly readable study of the most famous Mongol ruler of China.

Stearns, Peter N., Michael Ada, and Stuart B. Schwartz. "Nomadic Challenges and Civilized Responses." In *World Civilizations: The Global Experience.* New York: HarperCollins, 1992. Overview of nomadic life in all portions of the globe.

Gregory C. Kozlowski

Cross-References

American Indian Governments, p. 59; Asia: Politics and Governments, p. 108; Charismatic Leadership, p. 209; Empires and Empire Building, p. 597; Force, p. 712; Government Types, p. 785; Hegemony, p. 817; Islam and Government, p. 994; Religion and Politics, p. 1685; Tribal Government, p. 2027.

NOMINATION PROCESSES

Field of study: Politics

General election voting to select holders of public offices is preceded by the campaigns of the parties' candidates, who are chosen by the nomination process. A nomination is often tantamount to election, since the partisan outcome of an election is often a foregone conclusion.

Principal terms

CAMPAIGN: a personal campaign is a series of operations by an individual aspirant for a party's nomination; a party campaign is a series of operations by a party's nominee in a general election

CONVENTION: meeting of delegates or members to choose a nominee or nominees for a political party; also known as committee or caucus

ELECTOR: person who is qualified to vote in an election or electoral college

ELECTORAL COLLEGE: set of delegates who choose the holder(s) of office(s)

ELECTORATE: set of persons who are qualified to vote in an election

GENERAL ELECTION: regular election to choose the holder or holders of an office or offices; the word "general" is often omitted

NOMINEE: political party's official candidate for office

POLITICAL PARTY: organization with nominees for offices

PRIMARY ELECTION: election to choose a nominee or nominees; the word "election" is often omitted

PROPORTIONAL REPRESENTATION: electoral system in which a party's proportion of seats is approximately the same as the proportion of votes it received

Overview

Electoral processes in the United States culminate in general elections or electoral college voting. General elections and electoral college voting are preceded by the party campaigns of the parties' nominees. The selection or nomination of the parties' candidates or nominees is the culmination of the nomination process. A primary election or party convention is the usual mechanism for selecting a party's nominees. Primaries or conventions are preceded by the personal campaigns of aspirants to party nominations. These personal campaigns are also part of the nomination process. A personal campaign for a party's nomination may begin long in advance of the primary or convention that selects the party's nominees. Politicians have been known to focus their entire careers on acquiring their party's nominations for particular offices. Consequently, it is often impossible to date the beginning of any particular nomination process.

The nomination process is a sifting process. For each legislative or executive office, a plethora of aspirants is winnowed to a few names on the general election ballot or before the electoral college: the major parties' nominees plus any independents. This reduction in numbers is useful for the nominees and for the electorate or electoral college. A nominee acquires a party label, its official endorsement, a certain standing, and organized support. The elector has a simpler choice, a policy guideline, and decision criteria.

The nomination process is structured by a country's electoral system. There are a variety of electoral systems, since no electoral system is perfectly democratic, resulting in a variety of nomination processes.

For seats in a legislature, an elector usually votes either for individual nominees or a list of party nominees. Individual nominees are common in systems of single-member districts; party lists are more common in systems of proportional representation. Both systems are used concurrently to elect the members of parliament in some countries. For example, half of Germany's Bundestag (Diet) is elected from party lists and half from single-member districts.

A safe seat is one that is almost certain to be won by a particular party in successive general elections; receiving that particular party's nomination thus is tantamount to being elected to the seat. Safe seats occur in systems of proportional representation, for example, in elections for the Australian Senate. Australia's Labor Party and the coalition of Liberal and National (Country) parties are almost certain to win two seats each in each state; the real contest is over the fifth seat. Safe seats occur also in systems of single-member districts, as in the "Solid South" of the United States. From about 1880 to 1950, Democratic Party nominees were almost certain to win in the former Confederate states.

For any given office, in any given election, it may be obvious in advance that a particular party's nominee is going to win, as in the Federal Convention of Germany. The Federal Convention is the electoral college that elects the president of Germany. The convention is composed of the members of the Bundestag plus an equal number of members of the state legislatures (who are selected to reflect the parties' proportions of state legislators). Since its partisan composition is known in advance, its outcome is often known in advance. When there is a majority party or majority coalition, its nominee is almost certain to be elected by the Federal Convention. A particular nomination is tantamount to election in such circumstances.

The nomination process is often the decisive stage in the electoral process for executive as well as legislative office(s). General elections and electoral colleges, in effect, often ratify the obvious outcome of the nomination process.

Nominations usually are bestowed by political parties by means of primary elections or party conventions, sometimes called committees or caucuses. There are exceptions. Mexico's Institutional Revolutionary Party (PRI), for example, empowered its incumbent president to choose the party's nominee for president of Mexico. Mexico's presidency has been, for most of the twentieth century, a safe seat for the PRI.

Primary elections are a legacy of the early twentieth century Progressive Movement in the United States. Before the advent of primaries, nominees were chosen by indirect election rather than direct election. For presidential nominations, the multitiered system of indirect elections was such that each major party held precinct meetings to elect delegates to a city or county convention, city or county conventions elected delegates to a state convention, state conventions elected delegates to the national convention, and the national convention elected the party's nominee for U.S. president. If a state party organization gained control of any stage of that process, then it controled the subsequent stages in its state. A direct election by the people was possible only at the first stage of this process, the precinct meeting.

Progressives supported the adoption of primaries as a way to decrease the power of party organizations and to increase the power of ordinary voters in the United States. Primary elections were not adopted elsewhere in the twentieth century, except as an occasional expedient.

U.S. primaries were created by the laws of the states and vary from state to state. Some states use primaries for some offices and conventions for other offices. For victory in a primary, some states require only a plurality; others require a majority or a stipulated minimum plurality, with a runoff election or a party convention if no candidate wins the primary election. Some states require that an elector be registered in advance for a particular party to be allowed to vote for a candidate for that party's nomination. Some states allow any elector to vote for a candidate for any party's nomination for any given office, but not for more than one candidate for a given office.

Despite the variety of rules, one result became standard as primaries spread from state to state in the twentieth century: Each state party organization lost control of its party's nomination process. Party slates—lists of nominees for various offices prepared by local political machines—gradually disappeared from most places.

Conventions are used to select a party's nominee(s) in many countries. These conventions may be regulated by law, as in Germany, or not, as in Britain. Members of a convention are party activists, not ordinary citizens. A party's organization—its officers, employees, politicians, and active members—are likely to control its convention. This influence is usually obvious in systems of proportional representation, where a party's convention leadership is expected to propose a party list, subject to amendment by the party convention. A party organization's influence is often transparent in systems of single-member districts, as in Britain's Conservative Party: A Conservative constituency party organization has the responsibility for selecting the party's nominee in its district, and the party's national headquarters has the power to veto the nomination of any unsuitable aspirant.

Careers, campaigns, and parties are affected by the character of the nomination process. Individualistic careers are facilitated by primary elections; personal campaigns in primary elections are quite public, focused on mass electorates. Party-focused or organizational careers are facilitated by party conventions; personal campaigns for party nominations are rather private, focused on few people. A party's nominees are more likely to hang together if the party organization controls the nomination process, which is more likely with conventions than with primaries.

Consequently, the degree of party solidarity is affected by the choice between a primary and a convention as the nomination process.

Applications

Legal trends in the twentieth century have been to recognize parties and to regulate the nomination process. Nominations were bestowed by parties but, legally, parties were unknown to the law in many countries; party affiliations of nominees, for example, were not listed on the ballot in Great Britain until 1970. Historically, nominations were bestowed as if parties were private clubs. Laws regulated the public general elections but not the private nomination process. "White primaries," for example, permitted only whites to vote in primaries in the South of the United States. Democratic Party nominations were tantamount to election, so blacks were disfranchised for all practical purposes. White primaries were finally outlawed by the U.S. Supreme Court in 1944.

Perhaps nothing in democracies so embodies the essence of politics as the nomination process. Often the law is circumvented or exploited by ambitious candidates and political parties.

Electoral laws vary not only from country to country, but also from the upper house to the lower house in some countries. In Australia, for example, the Senate is elected, state by state, by proportional representation. The House of Representatives is elected, district by district, by preferential voting, a system in which electors rank all the candidates on the ballot.

Australia's party system and preferential voting occasionally create an unusual nomination process. A nominee is elected if he or she receives a majority of the first preferences. If three nominees are on the ballot and no nominee receives a majority of first preferences, then the nominee with the fewest first preferences is eliminated, and his or her votes are allotted to the candidates who were listed as second preference on those ballots. There is then a majority winner, barring a tie. The Liberal and National parties have preferred to support a single nominee against the Labor Party. Occasionally, they fail to agree about whether that nominee should be Liberal or National. This causes no great difficulty if the seat is a safe seat for the coalition: Both parties nominate candidates and "exchange preferences," that is, urge their supporters to rank their nominees as 1 and 2. Thus, the general election also serves as a primary election to choose the coalition's nominee, Liberal or National.

Primaries cannot be scheduled quickly, but conventions can. This difference is sometimes important for nomination processes. From the time a general election is scheduled to the time it occurs, for example, is only a few weeks in Great Britain. Within such a tight schedule, a convention has practical advantages over a primary election.

Australian party organizations preselect candidates because (among other things) the exact timing of general elections is usually unknown. Legal restrictions on party nominees do not apply to preselected candidates, because they are not party nominees. When a general election is scheduled, the preselected candidate is nominated by a hastily convened convention. Legal restrictions apply to these party nominees. The nomination process, with prospective candidates, is the same in Britain.

Preselected candidates are political realities but legal nonentities. This discrepancy imparts in many countries a certain unreality to conventional descriptions of the nomination process. Personal campaigns and expenditures of aspirants for preselection are scarcely discussed; party campaigns and expenditures, from official nomination to general election, are often described as if they were the only campaigns and expenditures. The total duration of a candidate's campaigning and the total amount of a candidate's expenditures are routinely understated in conventional reporting.

The nomination process is about political power and political control: control of candidates, control of parties, control of elections, control of office holders, control of official policies. Political control by a party organization is facilitated by indirect elections rather than direct elections, by conventions rather than primaries in the nomination process.

A political machine is a party organization with relatively complete political control. Nominations are controlled by a political machine, if a party's nominees are routinely an approximation of the population, in terms of race, religion, and other characteristics. Indeed, the entire electoral process is controlled by a political machine, if the elected legislators are routinely an approximation of the population, as in the parliament of the former Soviet Union. Primary elections only achieve such representative results by chance.

Context

Presidential nominations in the United States shifted in law and practice, from conventions to primaries in the twentieth century, as primary elections were grafted onto the parties' national conventions. Party nominations continued to be bestowed officially by party national conventions; but this became a matter of form, not substance, after the selection of delegates to national conventions had shifted from state party conventions to state primary elections. This conversion of the convention system into a primary system was gradual, and has remained incomplete in the twentieth century: An old-style convention might still occur, but only if no clear winner emerged in a party's state primaries.

Old-style national conventions had brokered outcomes, which were negotiated among power brokers. A famous example was the Republican National Convention in 1920. That year state party conventions were widely used to elect state delegates to the parties' national conventions. State primaries existed in several states, but these primaries were often advisory; state delegates were rarely mandated to vote for a particular candidate. These state primaries scarcely figured in the personal campaign of Senator Warren Harding. His personal campaign was pitched towards the prospective powerbrokers at the national convention, who made their decision in a smoke-filled room at about 2 A.M. His nomination was a classic example of old-style convention politicking.

New-style national conventions have foregone conclusions, determined by antecedent primaries. The first example was the Democratic National Convention in 1960. By 1960, state primaries were widely used to elect state delegates to the parties' national conventions. These primaries were not merely advisory; state delegates often were mandated to vote for a particular candidate. With hindsight, 1960 was a pivotal transitional year for personal campaigns by presidential aspirants; but at the time, the best tactics were somewhat obscure. Senator Lyndon Johnson and some other aspirants chose to conduct an old-style campaign focused on prospective powerbrokers at the Democratic National Convention. Senators John Kennedy and Hubert Humphrey chose to try a primary route to their party's presidential nomination. Senator Kennedy's decision to campaign in primaries was designed in part to demonstrate that a Roman Catholic could be electable. He won sufficient primaries to come to the convention with a commanding lead, received his party's nomination, and won the presidential election. This decisively changed the presidential nomination process.

Bibliography

Arrow, Kenneth J. *Social Choice and Individual Values.* 2d ed. New York: John Wiley, 1963. This mathematical monograph is a classic analysis of electoral systems. The mathematics is advanced—so advanced that the author himself made a mistake and failed to prove his major theorem in the first edition (1951), as he admitted in his preface to the (corrected) second edition (1963).

Key, V. O., Jr. *Southern Politics in State and Nation.* New York: Alfred A. Knopf, 1949. The classic treatise on the "Solid South" in the United States, written just before the South ceased to be solid.

Lakeman, Enid, and James D. Lambert. *Voting in Democracies: A Study of Majority and Proportional Electoral Systems.* London: Faber & Faber, 1955. Descriptive analysis of electoral systems. Real examples are described in some detail. Various editions are available.

Michels, Robert. *Political Parties: A Sociological Study of the Oligarchical Tendencies of Modern Democracy.* Translated by Eden and Cedar Paul. Glencoe, Ill.: The Free Press, 1958. Classic analysis of leadership influence in political parties. The author coined the celebrated Iron Law of Oligarchy: Who says organization, says oligarchy. Published in various editions; published originally in 1915.

Russell, Francis. *The Shadow of Blooming Grove: Warren G. Harding in His Times.* New York: McGraw-Hill, 1968. This book describes, among other things, the smoke-filled room that led to Senator Harding's nomination by the Republican National Convention in 1920. The popular accounts of that nomination are corrected in some details, but confirmed in most essentials.

White, Theodore H. *The Making of the President: 1960.* New York: Atheneum, 1964. Describes the primary campaign that led to Senator Kennedy's nomination by the Democratic National Convention in 1960.

Thomas W. Casstevens

Cross-References

Delegates, p. 501; Elections, p. 578; Political Machines and Bosses, p. 1468; Political Party Conventions, p. 1492; Political Party Roles, p. 1499; Political Representation in the United States, p. 1525; Presidential Elections in the United States, p. 1596; Primary Elections, p. 1603; Voting in History, p. 2116; Voting Processes, p. 2123.

NONALIGNED MOVEMENTS

Field of study: International government and politics

The Nonaligned Movement is a political coalition of more than one hundred nations, mostly from the Third World. Since its inception in 1961, the movement has worked to end colonialism, neocolonialism, racism, and bloc politics, reduce global inequality, and create a new international economic order.

Principal terms

COLD WAR: period of conflict and competition between the United States and the Soviet Union which lasted more than four decades after World War II

CONTAINMENT: post-World War II U.S. policy of halting the expansion of communism and Soviet influence

NEOCOLONIALISM: control of Third World nations by industrialized rich nations, through indirect means such as economic domination and the cooption of local elites

NEW INTERNATIONAL ECONOMIC ORDER: Third World demand for reforming the existing international economic system, including trade, aid, and investment relationships

NONALIGNMENT: principle of foreign policy that emphasizes independence from and nonattachment to the competing power blocs

NORTH-SOUTH RELATIONS: relations between the industrialized countries of the West, plus Japan, and the developing nations of Asia, Africa, Latin America, the Middle East, and the Caribbean

SOUTH-SOUTH COOPERATION: economic cooperation among developing nations

Overview

The Nonaligned Movement (NAM) is a collective movement of the Third World states in world politics, dominated by the newly independent nations of Africa and Asia. The former Yugoslavia was the only European state that has played an important role in NAM, although a few small European countries have participated as members, observers, or guests at its summit meetings. The NAM membership has quadrupled since its inception, from 25 in 1961 to 109 in 1994, making it the second most extensive organization in the world after the United Nations and its subordinate organizations. It is a grouping of extremely diverse states, representing more than two billion people living on four continents, having different languages, histories, cultures, religions, ideological persuasions, and political, social, and economic systems.

The Nonaligned Movement represents the solidarity of the less powerful small and medium-sized states in world affairs. NAM is concerned with reducing structural inequality in the international system and emphasizes different aspects of this problem at its summit meetings of heads of member states. It has concentrated on issues such as decolonization and independence, antiracism, world peace and disarmament, economic development, creation of a new world order, and antibloc politics. The nonaligned countries share a commitment to a set of guiding principles enunciated by its summit conferences since 1961: peace and disarmament, especially the reduction of tensions between the major powers; independence, including self-determination for colonial peoples and equality between all races; economic equality, restructuring the existing international economic order, particularly with respect to inequality between rich and poor nations; cultural equality, restructuring the world information and communication order, and opposing cultural imperialism and the Western monopoly of information systems; and universalism and multilateralism through strong support for the United Nations system. The Nonaligned Movement has also condemned apartheid, Zionism, and bloc policies that perpetuate the division of the world into blocs.

Nonalignment as a collective movement in world politics is distinct from nonalignment as a principle of foreign policy in individual countries. It is possible that the policy of a nonaligned country on an international issue, such as the Soviet invasion of Afghanistan, may not be in harmony with the general view of the movement. As an instrument of foreign policy, nonalignment originated in the late 1940's in India. Unlike the policy of neutrality of a nonbelligerent country during a general war, nonalignment, as conceived by Jawaharlal Nehru, was an activist foreign policy without joining any power bloc or military alliance—multilateral, bilateral, or regional. In the late 1950's Nehru worked closely with Tito of Yugoslavia and Gamal Nasser of Egypt to develop a common approach to nonalignment. These three leaders were later joined in their efforts by Kwame Nkrumah of Ghana and K. S. Sukarno of Indonesia. Each of these leaders emphasized a certain aspect or dimension of nonalignment: Nehru emphasized peace and political independence; Tito was for peace and equidistance between major powers; and Nkrumah, Sukarno, and Nasser opposed colonialism, neocolonialism, and racism. The movement was thus shaped by these founding leaders' vision and outlook on world politics and the role of the newly independent states in it. These themes were to become the underlying principles of the Nonaligned Movement.

The Nonaligned Movement is not a bloc bound by any kind of international agreement. It has no constitution, permanent headquarters, or secretariat, nor does it have a cohesive ideological framework of its own. Over the years the movement has developed a democratic, nonhierarchical, inclusive administrative and organizational structure, which allows it to function coherently and effectively. It operates through summit conferences, an official spokesperson, and a coordinating bureau.

The summit meeting of heads of state or government, hosted by a member country, is the most important institution of the NAM. To date, ten summits have been held: in Belgrade, 1961; Cairo, 1964; Lusaka, 1970; Algiers, 1973; Colombo, 1976; Havana, 1979; New Delhi, 1983; Harare, 1986; Belgrade, 1989; Jakarta, 1992. The eleventh summit was scheduled to take place in Colombia in 1995. The host country, which assumes the role of Chair, makes a significant commitment of its diplomatic and bureaucratic resources and exerts a powerful influence on the movement. Specialized tasks, however, are carried out by functional bodies or expert groups appointed at the summit. Since the Lusaka Conference, the Chair has been the official spokesperson or leader of the movement and maintains contacts among other member states, ensures continuity, and carries out the decisions, resolutions, and directives of the conference. This gives the leader of the host country international visibility and influence. The Chair lobbies as a bloc in the United Nations. The coordinating bureau maintains working contact with NAM members at the United Nations and serves as an intermediary organization to carry out movement activities between summit meetings.

The method of decision making followed by the movement is one of consensus. Working through many levels of decision making—starting with a working group of officials, then moving to the levels of ambassadors and ministers, and finally to the heads of state or government—the movement has maintained a high degree of cohesiveness on difficult problems in world affairs, despite the diversity of its membership.

Applications

The Nonaligned Movement has been a dynamic force in world politics since its inception. It has continuously changed in response to changing international realities. In the 1960's, the movement was preoccupied with political independence, self-determination, and Cold War politics. It sought to reduce the level of conflict in East-West relations. At its first three summit meetings, the movement focused on eliminating colonialism and neocolonialism, including the decolonization of South Africa and the right of the Palestinian people to their homeland. At the Fourth Summit, however, focus shifted to issues of global inequality and to creation of a new international economic order. Since membership in the movement had increased to seventy-five by the early 1970's—more than two-thirds of the U.N. members—the movement began to be a coalition influencing world politics, especially at the United Nations. U.N. secretary general Kurt Waldheim's address to the Fourth Summit in Algiers indicated recognition of the movement as a major force in world politics.

The movement's espousal of economic activism and its adoption of a radical orientation to the existing international economic arrangements in the 1970's was the most significant development in its history. The 1973 Algiers Summit emphasized the issue of Third World underdevelopment resulting from inequities inherent in the existing international economic system, which was dominated by the developed Western nations. Supported by the solidarity of movement members, particularly the action of the Organization of Petroleum Exporting Countries to quadruple the price of oil, the Chair, President Houari Boumedienne of Algeria, called the Sixth Special Session of the General Assembly of the United Nations in April and May, 1974, which passed the Charter of Economic Rights and Duties of States and the Declaration of the Establishment of a New International Economic Order. These economic concerns were further articulated at the Fifth and Sixth summits in 1976 and 1979. The economic demands contained in the NAM documents have been translated into programs of action by the U.N. Conference of Trade and Development (UNCTAD), which has been dominated by the nonaligned countries since it was founded in 1964. The movement thus has succeeded in focusing world attention on the issues of global inequality and developing methods to transfer wealth from rich to poor nations.

Under the leadership of India's Prime Minister Indira Gandhi, there was some moderation in the 1980's of the radical stand the movement had taken in the 1970's. At the Seventh Summit, held in New Delhi in 1983, the movement softened its criticism of the West and advocated a multilateral framework, including both capitalist and socialist industrialized states, for resolving economic crisis in the Third World. Similarly, at the Eighth and Ninth summit meetings, the movement refrained from using anti-West or anti-United States rhetoric. It proposed practical and constructive ways of addressing the Third World problems of finance, foreign debt, technology transfer, foreign trade, and adequate supply of food.

The end of the Cold War in 1989 and the disintegration of the Soviet Union in 1991, however, brought into question the relevance of the movement in the 1990's. At its Tenth Summit, in 1992, the nonaligned nations decided that the movement should continue. Thereafter, it has tried to remain relevant by recasting its role as a Third World pressure group in world politics. The foreign ministers of nonaligned nations, meeting in their eleventh conference in Cairo in 1994, declared that responding to the changes in international relations was the movement's most important challenge. In the post-Cold War era, the movement has shifted from political to economic concerns, such as the external debt of Third World nations, the revitalization of North-South dialogue, the adverse effects of the passage of the Uruguay round of trade talks in 1994 on poor Third World nations, and South-South economic cooperation. The movement has continued to call for restructuring and democratization of the management of international economic relations.

Context

The Nonaligned Movement developed in the context of Cold War politics when the world was polarized into two ideological and military blocs. The origin of the movement can be traced to the Bandung Conference, which met in April, 1955, in the capital city of Indonesia, to discuss common concerns of the newly independent nations of Asia and Africa. Led by India's Prime Minister Nehru, the twenty-nine states participating at the conference expressed their opposition to joining one bloc or the other and advocated the principle of nonalignment—staying out of great power rivalry. Nonalignment was thus the policy of refusing to join a military alliance in order to protect one's independence. The pursuance of such a policy, the nonaligned believed, would moderate tensions of the Cold War and help maintain peace in the world. Nonalignment was a pragmatic foreign policy, because it allowed the newly independent nations to remain on good terms with countries belonging to the two power blocs, and to seek economic, technical, and other assistance from both. After nonalignment was transformed into a collective movement and a permanent organization in

1961, the movement carried on the anticolonialist and anti-imperialist spirit of Bandung.

The movement represents the interests of its members, which are a highly diverse group. Small and medium-sized newly independent states in the Third World, who generally lack experience in bilateral and multilateral diplomacy, have found their participation in the movement beneficial. Since NAM conducts its politics mostly within the United Nations, joining the movement has allowed these countries to acquire expertise in multilateral diplomacy. NAM has also given the nonaligned, who lack the traditional attributes of power, visibility, and, in the case of movement leaders such as Algeria, Ceylon (now Sri Lanka), and Zimbabwe, influence in international affairs. NAM has advanced the interests of certain groups of states. The Africans, for example, succeeded in focusing the attention of the international community on the political situation in southern Africa, obtaining worldwide economic sanctions against South Africa, and ultimately saw South Africa expelled from the United Nations. The Arabs' advocacy of the rights of the Palestinian people in their struggle against Israel has also been taken up by the organization. Such collective efforts of the nonaligned have brought results: democratic elections and majority rule in South Africa in 1994, and the possibility of negotiated settlement of the Palestinian problem following the signing of the Arab-Israeli Accord in 1993.

In the 1990's, the movement attracted Latin American states in greater numbers. In the wake of the resurgence of democracy in the region, most Latin American states sought a nonaligned foreign policy independent of the United States. The selection of Colombia as the host and leader of the 1995 Summit Meeting was indicative of the growing interest of Latin American states in the movement.

The U.S. response toward the movement has been influenced by its overall global strategic considerations. It has fluctuated between periods of indifference and neglect to periods of confrontation and attempted rapprochement. During the 1960's, when the United States followed the policy of containment, it labeled nonalignment as an immoral, shortsighted policy, and generally neglected the movement. The radicalization of the movement in the 1970's under the leadership of Algeria, and the anti-American rhetoric of the nonaligned, especially in the United Nations, brought sharp reaction and rebuttals from the United States. During this period, the United States became disillusioned with the United Nations, perceiving the world body to be dominated by the nonaligned states, which constituted more than two-thirds of the General Assembly. In the late 1970's, President Jimmy Carter began to emphasize human rights in U.S. foreign policy and made efforts toward improving relations with the nonaligned. President Ronald Reagan, however, gave low priority to the nonaligned and the movement, and continued to complain about the "tyranny of the majority" in the United Nations, despite the moderate stand taken by the movement on many international issues of the 1980's.

The end of the Cold War and the disintegration of the Soviet Union changed international relations fundamentally in the 1990's, providing a new opportunity for improved relations between the United States and the nonaligned. In the 1980's, the movement had moderated its stand on many global issues, but in the 1990's, under the pragmatic leadership of President Suharto of Indonesia, it began to redefine its role as a spokesman for the Third World interests. There were indications of increased cooperation between the United States and NAM, as evidenced by the first ever joint resolution in the United Nations cosponsored by the two in the fall of 1993.

NAM continues to play an important role within and outside of the United Nations. Upon NAM's initiative, the United Nations declared the 1990's the Decade for the Eradication of Colonialism. Foreign ministers from NAM and the European Union have started meeting regularly to discuss international problems, which indicates a recognition of the movement's new role. With the leadership of the movement being passed on to Colombia in 1995, Latin American states are becoming more active in the organization. NAM is a truly international movement, which is poised to take a significant place in world politics in the 1990's and beyond.

Bibliography

Brands, H. W. *The Specter of Neutralism: The United States and the Emergence of the Third World, 1947-1960*. New York: Columbia University Press, 1989. Detailed historical study of U.S. relations with the three architects of the policy of nonalignment—India, Yugoslavia, and Egypt—with special focus on the decision-making elites in Washington, D.C.

Jackson, Richard L. "The United States and the Non-aligned Movement." *Review of International Affairs* 37 (February-May, 1986). Perceptive analysis of the changing U.S. response—negative to confrontational to rapprochement—to the nonaligned movement.

Leonhard, Alan T., ed. *Neutrality: Changing Concepts and Practices*. Lanham, Md.: University Press of America, 1988. Provides an analysis of the policy of neutrality of small European states such as Switzerland, Sweden, Finland, and Austria.

Liska, George. *Nations in Alliance: The Limits of Interdependence*. Baltimore: The Johns Hopkins University Press, 1962. Argues that smaller powers have sought to gain some influence in world politics through the policy of nonalignment.

Millar, T. B. "Alignment and Nonalignment Revisited: A Western Perspective." *The Nonaligned World* 2, no. 3, (July-September, 1984). Perceptive analysis of the implications of the alignment and nonalignment for the nonaligned states in world politics.

Singham, A. W., and Shirley Hune. *Non-Alignment in an Age of Alignments*. London: Zed Books, 1986. In-depth study of the nonaligned movement, covering the first seven Summit Conferences from 1961 to 1983.

Willetts, Peter. *The Non-Aligned Movement: The Origins of a Third World Alliance*. London: Frances Pinter, 1978. Provides a quantitative analysis of the external behavior of the nonaligned states, especially the coalition and the breakup of the coalition within the nonaligned movement.

Sunil K. Sahu

Cross-References

Alliances, p. 47; Hegemony, p. 817; Imperialism, p. 889; Nationalism, p. 1268; North Atlantic Treaty Organization, p. 1332; Self-Determination, p. 1796; Superpowers and World Politics, p. 1916; United Nations, p. 2045; World Political Organization, p. 2186.

NONPARTISAN POLITICAL ORGANIZATIONS

Field of study: Politics

Nonpartisan groups are interest groups that do not affiliate with any political party. Nonpartisan groups illustrate the uneasy relationship that exists between the institutions that link citizens to their government in a democratic society—interest groups and political parties.

Principal terms

FACTION: group of individuals with shared traits or common interests
INTEREST GROUP: organized group of individuals that seeks to influence public policy
NONPARTISAN: free from party affiliation, association, or designation
NONPARTISAN SLATING GROUPS: organizations that recruit, nominate, finance, and campaign on behalf of a slate of candidates in a nonpartisan election
PLURALISM: theory of government that argues that numerous groups are competing for widely scattered resources in the U.S. political system
POLITICAL ACTION COMMITTEE (PAC): special committee set up to collect and spend money for political campaigns
POLITICAL PARTY: group of voters, activists, candidates, and government officials who identify with a party label and seek to elect to public office individuals who run under that label

Overview

The relationship between interest groups and political parties in the United States has always been an uneasy one. While interest groups are organized groups of individuals who seek to influence public policy, political parties are larger groups that organize under a party label and try to elect candidates to public office. Although these definitions may seem to be distinct, political parties and interest groups perform similar functions. Both institutions give citizens a chance to participate in politics and feel connected to government. Both help candidates get elected to office by participating in campaigns. Both seek policy goals by influencing government officials.

Nonpartisan groups want to make it clear that there are differences between these institutions. Nonpartisan groups are interest groups that do not seek to promote one political party over another. Groups such as the League of Women Voters and Common Cause adamantly declare that they are nonpartisan. These groups seek to work with officials in both parties, including state legislators, members of Congress, and the White House. This gives them access to both parties so they can gain support for their interests.

The nonpartisan tradition is entrenched in U.S. politics. The Framers of the Constitution, including James Madison, recognized that political parties were inevitable but still warned against the dangers of factions. Political parties were not mentioned in the

Constitution, but did form and eventually developed into massive political machines in many U.S. cities. These machines led people to associate political parties with corruption, because identifying with a particular party helped citizens to get jobs and other city services. In reforming U.S. politics, Progressives in the 1890's sought to eliminate this corruption by making local and county elections nonpartisan; political parties would not endorse candidates and partisan labels would be removed from election ballots. Progressives also supported the women's suffrage movement, which eventually won for women the vote in 1920. These two activities together spawned some of the first nonpartisan groups.

The uneasy relationship between political parties and interest groups can be seen by looking at these early nonpartisan groups. Some nonpartisan groups found themselves competing with partisan groups for members. Such was the case with the League of Women Voters (LWV), a group of women that formed in 1919 to increase women's participation in politics. Members of the league believed that citizens should be informed and participate in the political process. From the start, the league competed against many women's divisions in state and local party organizations, such as the New Jersey Republican Women's Club.

Other groups started out as nonpartisan organizations but quickly were incorporated into the political parties. Such was the fate of several farmers' groups that formed in the early 1900's. In Minnesota, South Dakota, and North Dakota, farmers created the Nonpartisan Political League and the Farmers' Alliance to fight for changes in insurance, tax laws, and the operation of mills and grain elevators. Unlike early farming associations, these nonpartisan groups were explicitly political; their strategy was to support candidates in both parties' primaries. The farmers believed that nonpartisanship could force the Republican Party to listen to their interests if they could show political power in elections. In 1916, the Nonpartisan League successfully elected a number of candidates. By the 1920's, however, many of these groups had disbanded and became factions within the major political parties, instead of remaining as interest groups.

Still other nonpartisan groups found themselves creating organizations that had a partisan bias in their membership. This was the fate of the National Municipal League, an early advocate for structural reform in U.S. elections, believed that local elections should be nonpartisan. Its efforts were successful; as of the 1980's about 70 percent of all U.S. cities relied on nonpartisan elections. The NML, however, also realized that politics could be chaotic if party labels were removed from the ballot without some preparation. It solved this problem by advocating nonpartisan slating organizations that would recruit, nominate, finance, and campaign for candidates in the nonpartisan elections. Slating groups began to appear in numerous cities, including San Antonio, Dallas, Cincinnati, Chicago, and Phoenix.

Typically known as Good Government associations, these organizations perform many of the functions of political parties, but in nonpartisan elections. Such groups, however, may have a distinct partisan bias toward the Republican Party. Slating organizations' staff members usually come from civic associations, which typically are upper- or middle-class, white, and male. The candidates selected thus tend to serve the interests of the Republican Party. Moreover, nonpartisan elections also lower voter turnout, thereby making it less likely that minorities and lower-income voters will come to the polls. This also favors the Republican Party. Many political scientists have therefore concluded that nonpartisan elections have a distinct partisan bias.

These early nonpartisan groups show the uneasy relationship that exists between political parties and interest groups. This uneasy relationship continued into the 1990's. The fact that most interest groups are not partisan does not mean that they are not political. Nonpartisan interest groups may engage in functions that are considered the domain of the political parties, including endorsing candidates and giving money to campaigns.

In endorsing candidates, many nonpartisan groups select candidates that represent their interests. These candidates may come from any political party. To help determine which officials should be selected, several interest groups, such as Americans for Democratic Action and the American Conservative Union, have created rating scales for members of Congress. These scales typically rate the member from zero to one hundred, depending on how consistently the member has voted with the interest group.

Some nonpartisan groups have given money to political party candidates. Interest groups tend to give to candidates who will support their views and who are likely to be in office. This means not only that incumbents receive more money than challengers, but also that interest groups will often give to candidates from both parties. Although nonpartisan groups may claim that these donations are nonpartisan, they still may have a partisan bias. The Sierra Club, for example, is active in giving to congressional candidates through its political action committee, the Sierra Club Committee on Political Education, created in 1976. This environmental group's leaders firmly state that it is a nonpartisan organization, yet the Sierra Club has supported more Democrats than Republicans, since Democrats tend to be closer to the Sierra Club on environmental issues. In fact, the Sierra Club has attempted to recruit its own Republican candidates to answer the charge from Republicans that the club is partisan.

Nonpartisan groups have certain advantages. For example, they can gain access to government officials from all political parties and ideologies. This gives them more potential supporters in government, since they are not limited to one political party.

Applications
To examine the contrasts among nonpartisan groups, one can look at the nonpartisan activities of Common Cause, the League of Women Voters, and the Machinist Non-Partisan Political League (MNPL). All three groups engage in political activities and claim they are nonpartisan, but are very different in terms of how they view their role in politics. They show that when looking at interest groups, nonpartisanship is often a matter of degree, not an absolute certainty.

The most nonpartisan of these organizations is Common Cause, created in 1970 after John Gardner placed an advertisement in *The New York Times* seeking members for ten dollar donations. The main objective of Common Cause is to achieve good government, which it defines as one that is democratic and free of corruption. Common Cause refuses to participate in election campaigns and has no connection with any political party. Such rigid nonpartisanship at times poses problems. Because of its desire to remain independent, Common Cause cannot share in the rewards of predictable alliances with other political groups, such as money, information, and access to government officials. It further denies itself access to government officials by refusing to engage in electoral politics. Common Cause has to work much harder to be heard, because it does not help elected officials with their campaigns. This can sometimes leave it isolated politically. In 1989, for example, Common Cause lost many potential allies when it strongly criticized senators who voted against campaign finance reform. Perhaps because of this, Common Cause was not able to persuade enough senators to vote favorably on campaign finance to override a veto by President George Bush.

Common Cause's nonpartisanship is not typical of interest groups. Most nonpartisan groups follow a pattern similar to the Machinist Non-Partisan Political League. The most partisan of the three organizations considered here, it was founded by the International Association of Machinists, a labor organization, in 1948. Its original goals were to give one million dollars in voluntary contributions to educate members and to publicize the voting records of members of Congress. Although the MNPL claims to be nonpartisan, its contributions definitely have a Democratic bias. The MNPL gives mostly to congressional Democrats and has supported mostly Democratic presidential candidates, including Lyndon B. Johnson in 1964 and George McGovern in 1968.

Between these two extremes is the League of Women Voters. This organization has been nonpartisan since its inception in 1919, but plays a greater role in electing candidates to office than does Common Cause. The league does not endorse candidates nor does it help candidates with their campaigns; instead, it emphasizes voter education.

The LWV performs two primary services for citizens. First, it conducts voter registration drives to encourage citizens to vote. The LWV creates television advertisements, places signs in neighborhoods, and sets up voter registration clinics to encourage people to participate. It also has supported legislation that would help voters to register, such as the Motor Voter Bill in 1993, which enables voters to register when they collect their driver's license.

Second, the LWV seeks to inform voters about political candidates, with the understanding that an informed voter is a better voter. To make it easier for voters, the league is divided into local, state, and national levels. In 1988, there were 1250 local leagues, 53 state leagues (in the fifty states, the District of Columbia, Puerto Rico, and the Virgin Islands), and 1 national league. The local and state leagues are responsible for publishing nonpartisan information about the candidates in local, county, and state newspapers. This information usually appears one to two weeks before election day. The LWV also sponsors political debates at all levels of government, starting with congressional debates in 1922. The league is probably most famous, however, for its sponsorship of presidential debates. In 1952, it sponsored its first presidential debate when it asked the major contenders to make a joint appearance before its convention in front of a nationally televised audience. Since that time, the League has held numerous presidential debates, including the first televised debate in 1960 between Richard Nixon and John F. Kennedy, and the 1988 debate between Michael Dukakis and George Bush.

Context

Many factors have encouraged the development of nonpartisan groups in the U.S. political system. U.S. citizens often have distrusted political parties, even during the days of the adoption of the Constitution. Political parties are sometimes viewed as huge organizations that try to encompass so many diverse groups and interests that any distinction between the two major American political parties, the Democrats and the Republicans, is lost. Historically, the two major parties have been labelled jokingly as "Tweedledee" and "Tweedledum," signifying that they are one and the same. Political machines also have left their impact: Political parties have been criticized as instruments of corruption because of the days when political parties bought votes, stuffed ballot boxes, and arranged for jobs for party members.

While many people distrust political parties, interest groups realize that they are an essential part of U.S. politics. Interest groups understand that political parties help to organize the electorate and give many citizens a chance to identify with the government. More important, they realize that political parties control significant political resources, including money, grassroots organizations, and party labels. Nonpartisan politics allows interest groups a way to associate with the political parties and perform some of their functions, but without limiting their politics in the future. Interest groups ranging from Common Cause to the Machinist Non-Partisan Political League have sought the benefits of nonpartisanship, while maintaining the relationships with government officials that are necessary to achieve their interests.

Just as important to the growth of nonpartisan groups, however, has been the fact that any interest group or political party in U.S. politics must participate in a pluralistic political environment. In a pluralistic system, resources are so widely scattered that many groups compete for influence over the fate of those resources. On almost any public policy issue, whether it is public welfare, civil rights, or health care, numerous interest groups and political parties are in competition, trying to convince public officials to promote their interests. Under such a system, interest groups often are reluctant to engage in any long-term coalitions, with other interest groups or with political parties. Nonpartisan groups thus fit naturally into a system of pluralism, because they help interest groups retain the benefits of being interest groups, while serving some of same functions that political parties perform. As these groups compete for some of the same resources, and also for the attention of the electorate and government officials, the end result is that in a pluralist system such as the United States, interest groups will tend to be strong when political parties are weak, and vice versa.

Such is not the case in other democracies that have political parties and interest groups. In many democracies, the relationship between these two types of organizations is strong, with political parties and interest groups often serving more narrow programmatic interests. Although organized interests play a substantial role in helping elect candidates to office in the United States, their links to parties as institutions are weaker than elsewhere. There is much evidence to support this conclusion. Not only do fewer interest groups say that they are close to political parties in the United States, but also political parties are not seen as critical factors in interest group policy-making. U.S. interest groups in general are less likely to consult party officials on policy matters or invite party members to national strategy meetings. Most interest groups rely heavily on legislative staff, whether in Congress or in the state legislatures, because the staff provides the best access to government officials, not the political party organizations.

For all these reasons, then, nonpartisan groups can be seen as a natural complement to both interest groups and political parties in the United States. They are the end result of an uneasy relationship between these two important political organizations.

Bibliography

Gaston, Herbert Earle. *The Nonpartisan League*. Westport, Conn.: Hyperion Press, 1975. Case study of an early attempt to organize a nonpartisan organization.

Hawley, Willis D. *Nonpartisan Elections and the Case for Party Politics*. New York: Wiley Press, 1973. One of the few books that examines nonpartisan politics in detail, although mostly at the state and local level.

Key, V. O. *Politics, Parties and Pressure Groups*. 2d ed. New York: Thomas Y. Crowell, 1947. Classic work on political parties and interest groups, which discusses the differences between political parties and interest groups.

Lee, Eugene C. *The Politics of Nonpartisanship: A Study of California City Elections*. Berkeley: University of California Press, 1960. Often-cited book that examines nonpartisan elections by looking at eighty-eight cities in California.

Schlozman, Kay Lehman, and John T. Tierney. *Organized Interests and American Democracy*. New York: Harper & Row, 1986. Excellent overall reference on interest groups; chapter nine examines the relationship between political parties and interest groups.

Young, Louise M. *In the Public Interest: The League of Women Voters, 1920-1970*. New York: Greenwood Press, 1989. Provides a case history of one prominent nonpartisan group, the League of Women Voters.

Jan Carol Hardt

Cross-References

Aging and Politics in the United States, p. 35; City Government in the United States, p. 266; Elections, p. 578; Interest Groups, p. 936; Political Parties, p. 1485; Two-Party Systems, p. 2033; Voting in History, p. 2116; Woman Suffrage, p. 2141.

NORTH ATLANTIC TREATY ORGANIZATION

Field of study: International government and politics

Founded in 1949 to serve as a deterrent to possible Soviet aggression in Western Europe, the North Atlantic Treaty Organization (NATO) is an alliance of North American and Western European countries that are committed to working together to maintain peace and security within the international system.

Principal terms

COLLECTIVE SECURITY: mutual agreement among a group of nations that if one of them is attacked by another, the others will all defend the one that has been attacked

COLLECTIVE SELF-DEFENSE: basis for an alliance among nations, all of whom pledge to aid any member that is attacked by a nonmember country

INTEGRATED MILITARY STRUCTURE: union of military forces from different countries into a single fighting force, through cooperative strategy, training, and equipment management

NORTH ATLANTIC COUNCIL: the most important institution within NATO; consists of representatives from each member country and makes consensual decisions

PEACEKEEPING OPERATION: use of neutral military forces to maintain or restore peace in an area of conflict

SECRETARY-GENERAL: principal spokesman for NATO and its primary mediator in disputes among member countries

Overview

At the conclusion of World War II in Europe, the United States moved rapidly to demobilize its military forces. The Soviet Union, an ally of the United States in the struggle against Nazi Germany, did not. Instead, between 1947 and 1949, the Soviets took advantage of their continued military presence to install local governors in a number of Eastern European countries, to blockade the U.S., British, and French sectors of occupied Berlin, and to threaten the sovereignty of Greece, Turkey, and Norway.

In response both to Soviet actions and to perceived Soviet intentions in the years immediately following the war, the United States and its recent allies moved to form an alliance to deter any aggression by the Soviet Union toward the industrialized democracies of Western Europe. By the late summer of 1949, twelve countries had signed and ratified the North Atlantic Treaty. This agreement called for the creation of a North Atlantic Council, consisting of representatives from all parties to the treaty. In the fall of 1949, the North Atlantic Council established the North Atlantic Treaty Organization, more commonly known by its acronym, NATO.

NATO is a permanent security and political alliance of independent countries that have a common interest in promoting and maintaining international peace and security. Its members are primarily, but not exclusively, concerned with the protection of their own peace and security within the international system, and they embrace the principles embodied in the Charter of the United Nations. The organization operates on the principle of collective self-defense, meaning that if any member of the alliance is attacked by a nonmember country, then all members will come to its assistance. By joining NATO in 1949, the United States entered a standing alliance for the first time in its history and it pledged to tie its own security and defense to that of its transatlantic allies.

The original twelve members of NATO are Belgium, Canada, Denmark, France, Iceland, Italy, Luxembourg, The Netherlands, Norway, Portugal, the United Kingdom, and the United States. Greece and Turkey joined in 1952, the Federal Republic of Germany in 1955, and Spain in 1982. In 1995, the total number of member states in NATO stood at sixteen. Its headquarters are located in Brussels, Belgium.

The most powerful body within NATO, the North Atlantic Council meets in permanent session, most often at NATO headquarters. Each member country has one representative on the council. The person who represents a particular country can vary. When the council convenes at the summit level, for example, the heads of state or heads of government of member countries usually represent their countries. The council typically meets at least twice yearly at the ministerial level, when the foreign or defense ministers of the various countries make up the council. Most often, however, the council consists of the permanent representatives from member countries who normally hold the rank of an ambassador.

The significance of the North Atlantic Council lies in the policy decisions that it makes and the rules of NATO's operation that it establishes. The council makes its decisions on the basis of consensus and unanimity, meaning that all of its members' representatives must agree on an issue before it can adopt a decision. Once it adopts a decision, however, all the other institutions and structures within NATO—both military and civilian—must support it as creations of the council. Likewise, the national governments of member countries, as parties to the North Atlantic Treaty, must accept and uphold council decisions.

The secretary-general of NATO, who is chosen by the North Atlantic Council, heads the International Secretariat, the bureaucracy within NATO, and chairs the council's meetings. The secretary-general is responsible for implementing council decisions and providing council members with expert advice and information. The secretary-general also plays the highly visible role of principal spokesman for NATO in its external relations and is the organization's primary mediator in disputes among member countries.

As an alliance concerned with defense and security, NATO must address how the various military forces of its member countries will come together to fight effectively if ever they are required to do so. Through cooperation and collaboration in the areas of strategy, training, and equipment, NATO has sought to unite the military forces of its member countries into an integrated military structure.

NATO's Military Committee is charged by the North Atlantic Council with the responsibility of organizing and heading the alliance's integrated military structure; it is the highest military authority within the alliance. Member countries send representatives to sit on the committee. As with council meetings, the officials who represent their countries on the committee can vary. At least twice a year, for example, the national chiefs of staff from member countries compose the committee. The national chiefs of staff elect a committee chairman, who normally serves a three-year term. When the national chiefs of staff are not present, the committee is made up of permanent military representatives appointed by their home governments.

The Military Committee provides expert guidance to the North Atlantic Council on military questions and oversees subordinate military commands. The two major NATO commands subordinate to the committee are the Allied Command Europe and the Allied Command Atlantic, each of which is headed by a supreme allied commander who reports to the committee. The commander's role is to determine the force requirements necessary to defend his area of responsibility, to develop plans for the defense of that area, and—when necessary—to carry out these plans through the deployment and exercise of force.

Not all the member countries of NATO participate in the alliance's integrated command structure. In 1966, President Charles de Gaulle of France withdrew his country's forces because of concerns related to the loss of French sovereignty over its national military forces. For similar reasons, Spain does not participate. The small island nation of Iceland does not participate in the integrated command structure because it maintains no national military forces.

Applications

In July, 1991, the Warsaw Treaty Organization (or Warsaw Pact), the rival alliance system to NATO led by the Soviet Union, dissolved. The following December, the Soviet Union itself ceased to exist. The threat of Soviet aggression and expansionism had served as the justification for NATO's existence since its inception in 1949. After the dramatic events of 1991, NATO sought to carve out new niches and justifications for its continued existence in the absence of the Soviet threat.

One role that NATO has taken on in the post-Cold War era has been to work closely with other international organizations, such as the United Nations (U.N.), which engage in peacekeeping operations and collective security measures. Peacekeeping operations involve the use of military forces, at the request of the parties to a dispute, to maintain or restore peace in areas of conflict. Peacekeeping forces must remain neutral and back neither side in any dispute. Collective security measures also involve the use of military forces. Instead of remaining neutral, however, military forces engaging in collective security measures come to the assistance of one particular side in a dispute—the side that has been the victim of aggression.

Within the United Nations, the Security Council—whose five permanent members include the United States, the United Kingdom, France, Russia, and China—makes decisions regarding the implementation of peacekeeping operations and collective security measures. All five permanent members of the Security Council must agree to either type of action before they can take place. One case involving U.N. peacekeeping operations and collective security measures in which NATO played a role was the civil war in Bosnia-Herzegovina.

In the winter of 1992, the republic of Bosnia-Herzegovina declared its independence from Yugoslavia. The government that made this declaration was led by Muslims, who constituted just one of the three major ethnic groups who populated Bosnia-Herzegovina. The other groups are Bosnian Serbs and Bosnian Croats. Both groups, particularly the Serbs, were unhappy with the declaration of independence. By the spring of 1992, a civil war had erupted in Bosnia-Herzegovina, pitting the country's three major ethnic groups against one another.

The United Nations responded to the civil war in Bosnia and the atrocities being committed in the country by dispatching a peacekeeping force to the country to distribute humanitarian assistance and to try to moderate the conflict. The U.N. Security Council also passed a number of resolutions designed to stop the war. These resolutions authorized an economic embargo and naval blockade to prevent Serbia and Montenegro—the two remaining republics that constituted Yugoslavia—from supplying military assistance to the Bosnian Serbs. They also mandated an international embargo on the trade of weapons to parties within Bosnia-Herzegovina; created a no-fly zone over the country to prohibit any military aircraft from engaging in bombing attacks; and established safe havens within Bosnia-Herzegovina where the use of military force was to be forbidden.

To help enforce its resolutions and protect its peacekeeping forces, the U.N. Security Council asked NATO for military assistance, which the North Atlantic Council agreed to provide. Beginning in late 1992, NATO forces engaged in operations designed to implement the U.N. Security Council resolutions calling for an arms embargo and a naval blockade and economic embargo of Serbia and Montenegro. In April, 1993, NATO accepted responsibility for enforcing the no-fly zone. In June the U.N. Security Council authorized NATO to mount air strikes against combatants in the civil war that assaulted U.N.-designated safe havens. Before an air strike could take place, however, the Security Council required that both the U.N. secretary-general and the North Atlantic Council grant approval.

In carrying out its commitments to the United Nations, NATO used military force for the first time in its forty-four year history in the spring of 1994. In March NATO warplanes shot down four Bosnian Serb jets that violated the no-fly zone. In April NATO bombers attacked Bosnian Serb forces in retaliation for attacking the Muslim enclave of Gorazde, an area that had been designated a safe haven.

Context

During the Cold War, NATO was the most powerful international security organization in the world and the one charged with the defense of democratic Europe. NATO has been joined in the post-Cold War era by an increasing number of international organizations that are concerned with European security. Two of the most important of these are the Conference on Security and Cooperation in Europe (CSCE) and the Western European Union (WEU).

The Conference on Security and Cooperation in Europe was established by the Helsinki Final Act of 1975, an international agreement between the communist and noncommunist states of Europe, the United States, and Canada. Originally, the CSCE did not function as an international organization but as a series of meetings between representatives of the parties to the Helsinki Final Act. In 1990, in accordance with the provisions of the Charter of Paris for a New Europe, the CSCE was institutionalized by its members. An international secretariat was created and the new organization was charged with responsibility for conflict prevention, cooperative security, and the advancement of democracy and human rights in Europe.

In late 1994 the CSCE had fifty-three members and was the only international organization devoted to the promotion of European security that included all European countries as members. Like NATO, the CSCE makes decisions on the basis of consensus among its members. The organization's international secretariat is located in Prague, the capital of the Czech Republic.

Because the CSCE has no armed forces under its command, it lacks the military capability to enforce its policy decisions. To remedy this problem, the CSCE has turned to NATO to serve as its agent of implementation and enforcement. In December, 1992, NATO and the CSCE reached an agreement that NATO could assist the CSCE in support of any peacekeeping operations and collective security measures to which the members of both organizations agreed.

The Western European Union was originally established in May, 1955. The 1992 Maastricht Treaty on European Union designates the WEU as the security and defense organization of the European Union, an international organization which is devoted to the integration of the economic, social, foreign, and security policies of the major European democracies. In late 1994 members of the WEU included Belgium, France, Germany, Greece, Italy, Luxembourg, The Netherlands, Portugal, Spain, and the United Kingdom. Denmark, Greece, and Ireland maintained observer status, and Iceland, Norway, and Turkey were associate members. Observer status is granted by the WEU to members of the European Union that have not yet joined the organization. Associate membership is granted on request by the WEU to members of NATO. In 1993 the headquarters of the WEU were situated in Brussels, Belgium.

The WEU functions as a European regional defense organization that cooperates closely with NATO. In early 1994 NATO and the WEU reached an agreement on the concept and implementation of a Combined Joint Task Force (CJTF). The CJTF concept allows for the use of NATO forces and equipment by the WEU when members of both organizations agree to it. The CJTF makes it possible for NATO assets to come under the command of the WEU in the pursuit of policy goals common to the two organizations.

Since the collapse of the Soviet Union and the advent of the post-Cold War era, NATO has engaged in self-examination and refocused its mission from one based only on collective self-defense to one that includes peacekeeping and collective security. The organization has also moved to establish procedures to add new members in the future, including countries that were once a part of the Soviet alliance system.

Bibliography

Feld, Werner J. *The Future of European Security and Defense Policy*. Boulder, Colo.: Lynne Rienner, 1993. Focuses on the changing role of NATO in post-Cold War Europe, addressing issues concerning the cooperation of NATO with other European security organizations, such as the West European Union and the Conference on Security and Cooperation in Europe.

Henderson, Nicholas. *The Birth of NATO*. Boulder, Colo.: Westview Press, 1983. Provocative memoir of a former British participant in the critical months of negotiation leading up to the signing of the North Atlantic Treaty in 1949.

Kaplan, Lawrence S. *NATO and the United States*. Boston: Twayne, 1988. Authoritative history of the relationship between the United States and NATO.

Kaplan, Lawrence S., et al., eds. *NATO After Forty Years*. Wilmington, Del.: Scholarly Resources Books, 1990. Collection of essays examining NATO's accomplishments and shortcomings. The chapters covering the various types of relationships NATO's members have had with one another and NATO's role in the post-World War II world are particularly well done.

North Atlantic Treaty Organization. *NATO Handbook*. Brussels: NATO Office of Information and Press, 1992. Official NATO publication which details the organization's membership, structure, and operational procedures. The text offers insights into what NATO perceives its role to be in the post-Cold War era. The appendix contains a chronology of the alliance's evolution. NATO's information service *NATO Review*, also publishes a bimonthly journal that contains articles on issues of international peace and security written by key policymakers and academicians. Available free of charge, the *Review* is an invaluable source of current information regarding issues facing the Atlantic community.

Samuel E. Watson III

Cross-References

Alliances, p. 47; Armed Forces, p. 89; Conflict Resolution, p. 397; Geopolitics, p. 759; Hegemony, p. 817; Military Structure, p. 1198; National Security, p. 1261; Peace, p. 1390; Superpowers and World Politics, p. 1916; Supranational Government Institutions, p. 1922; Treaties, p. 2020; World Political Organization, p. 2186.

OCHLOCRACY

Field of study: Political philosophy

A hypothetical form of government described by the Greek philosopher Aristotle, an ochlocracy is a system in which every member of a community contributes equally to its governing. Such a government would have no designated rulers or agents of representation.

Principal terms

ANARCHY: absence of rule or law

ARISTOCRACY: rule by a minority who consider themselves the most fit to rule

AUTONOMY: self-rule of a community or defined polity

CONSTITUTION: written or unwritten contractual agreement under which a government operates

MONARCHY: rule by one person, typically selected by heredity or arranged marriage

OLIGARCHY: system of government controlled by a small minority

PLUTOCRACY: oligarchic system in which the ruling minority is chosen on the basis of wealth

TOWN MEETING: the practice of ochlocracy, in which all citizens of a town meet, discuss issues, and decide on a course of action

TYRANNY: rule by single person maintained in office by force and given to arbitrary conduct

Overview

Aristotle examined all the forms that government could take with the same meticulous methodology that he applied to his other studies. His principal work on the subject, *Politics*, is a systematic exploration of the subject. In *Politics*, he asks the question: "On what principle should political power be distributed?" He lists six possible constitutions of government. Three he calls good: monarchy, aristocracy, and limited democracy. Three are bad: tyranny, oligarchy, and extreme democracy.

This last form of government, extreme democracy, Aristotle called "ochlocracy" from the Greek *ochlos*, meaning "mob," and *-cracy*, meaning "rule." Although ochlocracy may be translated as "mob rule" or "anarchy," government as ochlocracy is potentially much more benign. Aristotle, while aware it had limitations, examined the possibilities of the ochlocratic system.

One advantage to ochlocracy is that it meets all objections of exclusion. No one can claim to be left out. Disenfranchised peoples may find leaders to organize them into antigovernment movements. Governments must either include everyone or devise an equitable system of representation for subgroups, which is often impossible. Ochlocracy defuses this ticking bomb of revolution.

Another advantage of ochlocracy is that it brings the broadest possible personal experience to the governing process. Since people derive economies from division of labor, task specialization is the logical result. Talents become available that may not be included in a "representative government." In an ochlocracy, people of all walks of life participate in government. In other forms of government, only people of certain specialties may gain political power.

One such specialty is the politician. Those who are so skilled find niches in all governments and cooperate to exclude less politically able members. This is a strong argument for the dilution of politicians' strength by others not similarly talented. As government grows in complexity it begins to address issues that are not its business. This expansion justifies bureaucratic growth and its attendant burden on the populace. Ochlocracy avoids this; the size of a government is limited to the total population, so expansion is impossible.

According to Aristotle, the poor are destined to be the ruling class in a democracy, the wealthy in an oligarchy. So long as an oligarchy has the consent of the governed it is workable, but pressures on a society as a result of war, crop failure, or population growth may leave the poor with no relief but revolution. Ochlocracy, by avoiding economic division in government, negates the issue of rich and poor.

Finally, government by the whole prevents the concentration of government into a clique as a result of the ruling group's preferment of those sympathetic to itself. In modern democratic republican governments, for example, the ruling group uses public funds to support those allied with its interests, therefore restricting government to those it permits to be candidates. In an ochlocracy political clout is meaningless; every citizen is a successful candidate.

Aristotle next offers his criticism of ochlocracy, listing its problems and limitations in turn. One severe limitation on ochlocracy is the burden of communication. A body cannot act in concert unless its members are informed of the deliberations and decisions of its members. In even the smallest "state"—the household—the act of hearing a question and deciding its disposition is not always possible for all of its members.

That ochlocracy was even considered by Aristotle is a tribute to the influence that Plato's *Republic* had on political thought. Plato's ideal government was one of small states; he felt that a limit to the population of a state was necessary to make it governable at all. In his *Laws*, the companion piece to his *Republic*, he fixed the ideal population of a state at 5,040. This tiny number, scarcely a large township, cannot avoid interference from others without a degree of isolation impossible in modern population centers. Even in Plato's time city populations numbered many times his ideal number.

Aristotle assumed that the size limitations placed on a republic by Plato had no scientific basis; the maximum population might be very much larger if limiting factors were eased by scientific and political progress. Still, the upper limit of size is soon reached beyond which the process of direct democracy falters. With modern means of communication it might be extended directly to all people who use a common language and to those who do not by a mutually agreed system of interpretation. In Aristotle's and Plato's time, however, such a communication system would be quite limited.

Other limitations to the ochlocratic system are apparent in the context of modern government. An ochlocracy in a modern state would be vulnerable because of its diversity. Ties of ethnicity, history, hereditary occupation or past political experience form homogeneous groups larger than the 5,040 of Plato. Including all these groups produces a state composed of many differing groups with disparate agendas. In the United States, for example, those of the Northeast cannot be expected to place the concerns of those of California before their own.

Allocation of tax money for public institutions, laws affecting commerce, and environmental legislation tend to divide people of the disparate regions. In regions of sparse population, for example, popular support is weak for limitations on individual wealth that are instituted to preserve environmental quality. Forcing a solution upon a populace not noticeably affected by the problem is unpopular.

Aristotle addressed this difficulty directly. He recognized the obvious differences in people; the wealthy, the poor, the landed, the landless, the tradesman, the farmer, the free, the enslaved. The slave population, in Aristotle's time, was a large fraction of the total population. Some consideration had to be given to the rights of slaves, not only to avert civil unrest but also to respond to humanitarian impulses. This leads to the question of who constitutes the "everyone" that make up the ochlocracy.

One may set people outside the constitution, as the United States Constitution once did. It counted each slave as a fraction of a person. While women were counted as whole persons, neither they nor slaves had a role in the government. Ownership of land, special taxes, and literacy tests were all criteria for participation in "democracy."

Aristotle concludes that ochlocracy is impractical. He does, however, maintain that the concept of a broad base for the constitution of a government is desirable. He predicted that a too-narrow constitution of representatives in a republic would lead to a self-serving and inefficient government. This prediction has been proven to be correct in modern republics.

Applications

From the examinations that Aristotle and other philosophers made of the question of which form of government is best grew a search for a workable compromise between the ochlocratic and oligarchic extremes. In the myriad ways in which people govern one another, both extremes are extant. There are many oligarchies in which an elite rule; the governments of most democracies today are based on small and self-perpetuating cliques of specialists whose talent is for being returned to office whenever term limits are not imposed.

There are also ochlocracies today. While at its inception the United Nations was proposed as a democracy, it is a sort of ochlocracy, with the members being nations and not individuals. There are some checks on the freedom of the United Nations to act as an ochlocracy; for example, veto option was granted the five victor nations of

World War II. In most issues, however, the one-entity-one-vote principle gives the smallest and newest emerged nation equal representation in voting with a superpower. This representation is extended to even splinters of an older nation that has been divided by civil war. In the many ways that it suffers the disadvantages of, and boasts the advantages of, Aristotle's ochlocracy, the United Nations is an ochlocracy.

The concept of consensus applies to other organizations also, particularly those of business and industry. In traditional industrial culture, management of a firm was often in the hands of a hereditary aristocracy. For efficiency this has given way to an oligarchy consisting of a board of directors and a large horizontal structure of administrative officers and managers. These leaders are developed by a series of merit-influenced promotions from within the ranks.

In this otherwise logical and ability-driven system, there is an irrational human need to establish the oligarchy as infallible. Any weakness in a leader's image leads to a weakening of political position, lessening the loyalty of his or her underlings and even imperilling his or her continuance as a member of the oligarchy.

This "no mistakes" management culture fosters the practice that every decision of importance be reviewed by the entire management team and even the immediately lower levels of authority. This has the ostensible purpose of bringing more experience to the decision, an advantage to ochlocracy mentioned by Aristotle. It also allows for a wide distribution of accountability if a decision subsequently is found to be faulty. The breadth of the decision process allows the top leaders to say, with a semblance of truth, that there was a consensus behind a mistake even if the consensus was forced by political strength of the dominant members. This process has been expanded in a concept called "participatory management," in which inclusion in decisions is ostensibly extended to all workers in order to weaken the power of a labor union.

Another institution that resembles an ochlocracy is the jury. A defendant on trial for a crime may ask that his or her case be weighed by a jury. Furthermore, this jury must by law be made up of the defendant's peers, not an elite group inclined to be biased against the defendant. The criminal court system in the United States demands that a conviction be allowed only if there exists no reasonable doubt of the defendant's guilt. In most states, a jury must reach a unanimous consensus in order to convict. In its features of people of different social background and status working together as equals either to reach a consensus or agree to disagree, a jury resembles an ochlocracy.

Other, smaller systems are extant that use ochlocratic methods. Often social clubs make selections from candidates for enrollment on the basis of a committee composed of every person with any interest in the outcome. The one characteristic all successful ochlocracies seem to have in common is small size; none approaches the 5,040 citizens of Plato's state.

Context

The ochlocratic system is of no foreseeable use in governing large entities because of communication problems, impossibility of maintaining homogeneity, and risks of corruption of the uninformed. It provides a framework, however, for the study of political systems. Consensus dynamics and the effects of specialization on democratic processes are readily studied in small, controlled groups such as industrial management and "governments" such as the United Nations.

There are also small groups in which a consensus is vital and the role of authority is secondary. Simultaneous-activity sports (such as soccer) are best played when almost complete autonomy is afforded the individual players on the playing field consistent with the rules of the game.

Similarly, in medical emergencies away from permanent treatment facilities, the responding mobile teams often act effectively as a body without any conscious direction by a leader. Experience has shown that this works quite well despite the unstructured appearance of the procedures. It must be recognized, however, that these teams have had a rigid and formalized set of procedures, known from experience to be most effective, drilled into them. They are acting without a leader, but they are not arguing toward a consensus on what to do while a patient lies bleeding on the ground.

Some local governance is conducted by town meetings in which all adult residents of a town are allowed to hear and speak on issues affecting the town's government. In these assemblies, no issues affecting national or state functions such as taxation, defense, or entitlements are discussed. Only a group that has autonomy can enjoy true ochlocracy; still, these town meetings come close to the model of ochlocratic government.

One type of application of ochlocracy is the think tank or brainstorming session. A problem is posed to a group of people who bring a wide variety of experience to the issue. In order to allow the widest range of talent and freedom to bear on the problem, the rules of the session forbid criticism of the first fruits of the individual approaches toward a solution to the problem. Later, with consensus and supporting information for the most likely possibilities, the choices are progressively narrowed to a few from which a selection is usually made on the basis of economics and logistics.

Bibliography

Aristotle. *Aristotle's Politics*. Translated by Benjamin Jowett. New York: Modern Library, 1943. Important in this translation is an expended table of contents that uses the philosopher's own organization for the sections.

Durant, Will. *The Story of Philosophy*. Garden City, N.Y.: Garden City Publishing, 1927. Historical account of philosophical thought from Plato to John Dewey.

Ebenstein, William. *Great Political Thinkers*. New York: Holt, Rinehart and Winston, 1960. Thoroughly annotated collection of readings of the philosophers and religious leaders from Plato to Freud.

Sabine, George. *A History of Political Theory*. New York: Holt, Rinehart and Winston, 1961. History of political thought, beginning with the city-state before Plato and extending through the Reformation to the fascist and socialist states at the outset of World War II.

Schmandt, Henry, and Paul Steinbicker. *Fundamentals of Government*. 2d ed. Milwaukee, Wis.: Bruce, 1963. Treatise on the elements and types of government and their relationship to the current governments of modern states.

Strauss, Leo, and Joseph Cropsey. *History of Political Philosophy*. Chicago: Rand McNally, 1963. Discussion of the political thought of religious leaders and philosophers from Plato to Dewey, including John Calvin and Martin Luther.

Loring D. Emery

Cross-References

Aristocracy, Oligarchy, and Plutocracy, p. 78; Aristotle's Political Philosophy, p. 83; Buddhism and Government, p. 152; The City-State, p. 272; Class Conflict, p. 331; Equality and Egalitarianism, p. 630; Oligarchy, p. 1344; Plato's Political Philosophy, p. 1396; Pluralism, p. 1402; Political Participation, p. 1479; Polity, p. 1545; Populism, p. 1551; The State, p. 1878; Town Meetings, p. 1993.

OLIGARCHY

Field of study: Political philosophy

Oligarchies, or governments by the few, have been the subject of an ancient and continuous debate among political philosophers about whether they provide good and stable governments, or tyrannous and corrupt ones.

Principal terms

ARISTOCRACY: government by a class of the rich, the noble or well-born, or the learned

BOURGEOISIE: middle class, which gained political importance in capitalist societies of the Western world after the mid-nineteenth century

DEMAGOGUE: leader who gains support through false promises, lies, and appeals to prejudice

DEMOCRACY: government that features direct participation of the citizenry in politics

ELITES: small, dominant, informal, but not necessarily unchanging, groups directing governments and other organizations

MONARCHY: rule by a king or queen

REPUBLICAN: government conducted through representative institutions

TIMOCRACY: a government in which civil and political honors are distributed according to wealth and honor

Overview

Oligarchy is a system of government in which power is confined to the few. Since the term was coined in ancient Greece, political philosophers have debated whether oligarchies can provide virtuous and stable governments, or whether they inevitably become tyrannical and corrupt.

Although most such debates have concerned European experiences with oligarchies, later twentieth century analyses have examined oligarchical rule in the U.S. South, Latin America, medieval China, and modern sub-Saharan Africa. Many of these studies have ranged beyond oligarchical government to include for example, the role of oligarchies in international banking and international corporations, parliaments and diets, political parties, and trade unions. Oligarchies, or oligarchical tendencies, in fact, have been identified in most institutions. By the late twentieth century, when there was a growing emphasis on egalitarianism throughout the world's developed societies, studies tended to depict oligarchies in negative terms. Oligarchies increasingly have been perceived as the degenerate phase of aristocracy, corruptions of democracy, adjuncts to totalitarianism, or the perversion of elites.

In ancient Greece, however, the word *oligarchia* did not have negative connotations. From the sixth through the third centuries B.C.E., most Greek cities and city-states were governed at some time by oligarchies. This was true even of the numerous Greek cities where the long-term political trend was toward forms of democracy and equality, at least among persons who were ranked as citizens. The ancient Greeks, therefore, not only evolved theories about oligarchies, but also had a wealth of practical experience with oligarchical rule. Fragments of the Boeotian constitution discovered between 1906 and 1934, for example, provide an important outline of the structure and functions of a Boeotian oligarchy under the general leadership of Thebes from 446 to 386 B.C.E. As Boeotia's largest city, Thebes dominated a confederation of ten other cities, among them Orchomenus, Thespiae, and Chaeronea; Thebes itself was governed by a widely based oligarchy of its own. Because membership in the oligarchy was dependent on property qualifications, it was confined to the wealthy, although the acquisition of sufficient property presumably opened a way into the oligarchy for those previously denied entrance. The exclusion of tradesmen and menial laborers for ten years after they had acquired sufficient property indicated that the property qualifications were also based on general conservative principles. Within both the Theban and Boeotian oligarchies there was a striving for equality, and public service was regarded as an unpaid duty. Even those who were not members of the Theban oligarchy, and thus were ineligible to exercise political rights, were accorded citizenship with full civil rights.

Although Athens has been remembered for its early attainment of a radical democracy among its citizens, it also was governed by an oligarchy after Athenian military failures in Sicily during the Peloponnesian Wars (413 B.C.E.). Amid this crisis, ten senior statesmen (the poet Sophocles among them) were empowered to supervise the course of events. These ten men constituted the leadership within a group of thirty who eventually drafted new constitutional proposals. At the same time, the oligarchs had suspended the Athenian constitution and had launched a reign of terror against their opponents. Participation in the oligarchy was open only to those who were wealthy enough to serve without jeopardizing their livelihoods, while other political rights were restricted by property qualifications to about five thousand well-to-do citizens.

Ancient Greek philosophers and political thinkers drew mixed conclusions about whether oligarchies were good or bad and whether they produced more or less stability than did monarchies or democracies. Aristotle, for example, believed that the best form of government for Greek city-states was a combination oligarchy and democracy. In his cyclical theory of government, he held that there were three virtuous forms of government—monarchy, aristocracy, and constitutional democracy—and three bad, or unstable, forms, each of which was a degeneration of a good form. Thus tyranny was a corruption of monarchy; oligarchy was a corruption of aristocratic rule; and democracy was a corruption of constitutional democracy.

Neither individually nor collectively were Greek thinkers of one mind about oligarchies. For them, oligarchy had both good and bad points. Seldom, however, was it considered to be an ideal form of government when unmixed with other forms. Herodotus, for example, when asked to render advice on a new government for Persia, reviewed the case favoring oligarchies. He noted oligarchs' rejection of democracy because the masses were violent, ignorant, irresponsible, and prone to develop cliques that ended in tyranny, and he also noted their denunciations of monarchies as capricious. Oligarchs claimed that they were responsible persons who used their wealth for public service, while allowing citizens a broad array of liberties. In view of these observations, Herodotus argued that the best guarantee of freedom and order lay with monarchy.

Since modern political philosophy owes so much to the political philosophers of ancient Greece, divisions over the character and tendencies of oligarchies have been perpetuated. In the seventeenth century, for example, Thomas Hobbes identified monarchy, aristocracy, and democracy as the three classical forms of government. Hobbes believed that monarchy represented the best form of government, whereas oligarchy simply defined aristocracy as its enemies saw it. John Locke, a late seventeenth century advocate of democracy, had little use for oligarchical rule.

The rise of totalitarian states, notably the Soviet Union, Italy, and Germany, during the 1920's and 1930's, revitalized discussions about oligarchy. As the triumphant leader of the Russian Revolution (1917-1920), Vladimir Ilich Lenin candidly explained that command of the Russian state and control over the country's means of production by the Communist Party rightly placed governing authority in the hands of an oligarchy. Even more obvious was the oligarchical nature of the Soviet's "collective leadership" that dominated the post-Stalin era from 1953 until the creation of the Russian Federation in 1989. In both Fascist Italy and Nazi Germany, despite differences in the characters of their regimes, totalitarian ideologies equated forceful control over the state and society and the best interests of the entire population with the aims and actions of oligarchical leadership. Much the same type of oligarchic rule characterized governance in the People's Republic of China after 1949.

Stimulated by the upheavals produced by Fascism, Nazism, Stalinism, and Chinese Communism, as well as by renewed interest in the bureaucratization of life in developed societies, Western political philosophers have extended their analyses of oligarchy beyond government systems. Italian economist and sociologist Vilfredo Pareto, among others, analyzed the rise and decline of elites, while Robert Michels, building on related ideas of Gaetano Mosca, proposed an "iron law of oligarchy" characteristic of all organizations.

Applications

For twentieth century political philosophers, political scientists, and sociologists, questions of whether oligarchies, either in theory or practice, are good, bad, or simply inevitable, have led them to seek answers by analyzing a wide spectrum of institutions and organizations.

Seminal work along these lines sprang from studies produced by early twentieth century European thinkers and scholars such as Pareto, Mosca, and Michels, whose work, although independent of one another, showed many similarities. Robert Michels' life and thought, in particular, provide insights into how and why his investigations of nongovernment oligarchies developed and led to the formulation of his iron law of oligarchy.

Michels was born into the tolerant, easy-going but declining bourgeoisie of Cologne, Germany, in 1876. His family was pro-French, Catholic, pacifist, and anti-Prussian. They opposed the style of aggressive capitalism that characterized German industrialization during the late nineteenth century. Educated in England, Paris, Munich, and Leipzig, Michels earned his doctorate at the Halle University in 1900. Idealistic, he soon became a socialist, and at times a revolutionary syndicalist. Because of his politics, for years he was denied the academic posts that he sought, and earned his living by producing a stream of articles on social reform, socialism, women's rights, art, and French, German, and Italian politics.

In 1911, Michels published *Zur Soziologie des Parteiwesens in der modernen Demokratie* (the sociology of modern democratic parties), which was translated into English as *Political Parties*. One section of this work dealt with the oligarchical tendencies of organizations. Disillusioned by his experiences in socialist organizations, in which struggles for power, asocial actions, and egotism seemed to him to work no differently than they did in government or industry, Michels declared that organization equated with oligarchy. This oligarchic tendency, he argued, operated as a sociological law wherever politics, in the broadest sense, was at work. In his view, the psychology of organization itself, the tendency of leaders to organize themselves and consolidate their interests, the gratitude of followers toward leaders, and the general passivity of the masses, all inevitably produced oligarchy.

Michels' major observations concerning oligarchy were by no means novel. Pareto previously had observed that history revealed elites to be a constant presence in political life. Whether governments were monarchic, aristocratic, or democratic, a ruling class invariably was present. Michels also drew upon Mosca's criticisms of Marxist beliefs that elites or oligarchies—rulers—would be swept away by the empowerment of the working classes. Michels, like Mosca, doubted that Marxist socialists would show different instincts than those of the propertied classes once they were charged with responsibility for administering capital belonging to the people's state. Where Michels' work differed significantly from that of Pareto and Mosca, however, was in the wealth of detail he employed to sustain his thesis. Michels amassed his evidence and formulated his criticisms from close observation of the workings of the Catholic church hierarchy, the Prussian Army, democratic political parties, Marxists, and a variety of socialist groups. From these empirical studies, he concluded that the majority of humankind, through what to him was a cruel quirk of history, were destined to submit to the rule of a small minority of people drawn from their own midsts, to serve as a pedestal for the weight of oligarchy. While there were few oligarchical governments in developed societies by the last half of the twentieth century, oligarchies apparently flourished in nearly all of their organizations.

Context

As a form of government, oligarchies satisfied many of the political requirements of ancient Greek cities and city-states. This was especially the case between the sixth and the third century B.C.E., when Greek cities were divesting themselves of traditional monarchies and tyrannies in favor of more broadly based governments that acknowledged the citizenry's desires for an expanding range of civil and political liberties. Oligarchies were an especially attractive change from monarchies when oligarchs dedicated their abilities, time, and wealth to public service and acted responsibly. Oligarchy likewise had been a popular and stable form of government when it was blended into varieties of Greek democracy as a balancing force. It was just such a blend that Aristotle had praised as the best type of government for the Greek city-state. There is no doubt that creation of oligarchies sometimes was a signal of crises: the suspected decline of a city, or the exigencies of the Peloponnesian War. More often, the prevalence of Greek oligarchies in city-states such as Thebes, Sparta, and Athens was an important sign of their economic growth and prosperity. The fact that they eventually succumbed to more democratic forms of government or to the imposition of Persian or Roman imperial rule was no indication that they had not served useful purposes.

By the seventeenth and eighteenth centuries, however, oligarchic government had taken on negative connotations in the writings of Western political philosophers. Oligarchies, whether those of John Calvin's Geneva, the Roman Catholic church, Cromwell's England, the Tory Party from 1714 to 1760, or the early American colonies and, later, states, all appeared to be hindrances to the major political currents of their times. Oligarchy was interpreted as the corruption of aristocratic regimes, or as antiliberal or antidemocratic. By the twentieth century, the open institution of an oligarchical government would have been anathema in most Western societies. The notable exceptions to this, of course, were the totalitarian governments that arose in Hitler's Nazi Germany, Mussolini's Fascist Italy, and Lenin's and Stalin's Russia, each of which proved to be an ephemeral regime. Where oligarchic government persisted, as in Caribbean or South American states—as juntas, for example—or in the collective leadership of the post-Stalinist Soviet Union or the People's Republic of China, they were apt to be identified with a transient phase of underdevelopment or to be perceived as the last remnants of totalitarianism.

That twentieth century political thinkers such as Michels, Mosca, or Pareto should then discover that overt oligarchy, which had all but vanished as a type of government, existed throughout nearly all other organizations—including democratic political parties, trade unions, business corporations, religious hierarchies, and voluntary associations—was an ironic twist. Oligarchies have lived on as an integral and inevitable part of handling power and responsibilities within increasingly bureaucratized human organizations.

Bibliography

Aristotle. *The Politics of Aristotle*. Translated by Ernest Barker. Oxford, England: Clarendon Press, 1948. Clearly written, scholarly study by an outstanding classicist. Extensive discussions of Aristotle's and Plato's views on oligarchies as they functioned in Crete, Carthage, and Athens, including the strengths and weaknesses of oligarchical governments.

Colley, Linda. *In Defiance of Oligarchy*. Cambridge, England: Cambridge University Press, 1982. Scholarly, clearly presented study describes the political battles of the British Tory Party against England's ruling Whig oligarchy from 1714 to 1760. Good working picture of an eighteenth century oligarchy in a nation considered to be free.

Kern, Robert, ed. *The Caciques*. Albuquerque: University of New Mexico Press, 1973. Excellent series of essays covering modern oligarchical politics and the system of *caciquismo* (rule by chiefs) in Mexico, Brazil, Peru, and other Latin American countries. Excellent for comparative purposes.

Meier, Christian. *The Greek Discovery of Politics*. Translated by David McLintock. Cambridge, Mass.: Harvard University Press, 1990. Superb analysis of the Greek concepts and practices of oligarchies. Introduces the Greek conception of politics into which oligarchies were fitted.

Mitzman, Arthur. *Sociology and Estrangement*. New York: Alfred A. Knopf, 1973. Easily read study of the lives and work of three sociologists of Imperial Germany, including Robert Michels. Includes an extended discussion of Michels' background and his theory of the "iron law of oligarchy." Includes much material on Pareto and Mosca.

Moore, J. M., trans. *Aristotle and Xenophon on Democracy and Oligarchy*. Berkeley: University of California Press, 1975. Essential for serious readers on oligarchy. Presents the Boeotian and Athenian constitutions and interprets their meaning in clear and extensive commentaries. A rare chance to view ancient oligarchies through documents.

Sabine, George H. *A History of Political Theory*. 3d ed. New York: Holt, Rinehart and Winston, 1961. Clearly written, standard work. Good introduction to Plato and Aristotle on oligarchies, which places them in context.

Sealey, Raphael. *A History of the Greek City States, ca. 700-338 B.C.* Berkeley: University of California Press, 1976. Clear scholarly study of Greek politics, especially useful for analyses of the oligarchical leadership of various Greek leagues.

Clifton K. Yearley

Cross-References

Aristocracy, Oligarchy, and Plutocracy, p. 78; Aristotle's Political Philosophy, p. 83; Caste Systems, p. 203; Church Government, p. 241; The City-State, p. 272; Democracy, p. 513; Elitism, p. 591; Fascism and Nazism, p. 656; Marxism-Leninism, p. 1155; Nietzsche's Political Philosophy, p. 1300; Plato's Political Philosophy, p. 1396; Political Myths and the Philosophies of Mosca and Pareto, p. 1474.

ONE-PARTY SYSTEMS

Field of study: Politics

In one-party political systems, a single party dominates the governmental land-scape, getting its members placed in all or most of the important political offices. There are two types of one-party systems: "formalized" (or authoritarian) and "one-party dominant" (or pluralistic). The differences between them are subtle, but important.

Principal terms

DOMINANT PARTY: political party in a political system that controls more public offices than any others or that is the only operating party in the system

FORMALIZED SYSTEM: form of one-party system in which the only party allowed to exist freely and legally is the dominant party

ONE-PARTY DOMINANT SYSTEM: form of one-party system in which multiple parties are legal and allowed to compete for power, but one party enjoys sustained and overwhelming support

PUBLIC POLICY: favored course of action, presumably in the public interest, sought by politicians and parties during their control of government

SPOILS: favors and material rewards, such as jobs or special political treatment, that a party in power may give to loyal members

Overview

One-party systems are those in which a single party represents the only effective means by which individuals may participate in government. In the United States, when thinking of parties in politics, it is typical to think in terms of a two-party system; Democrats and Republicans. In a system of one-party government, however, there is no such competition. The platform of the party and the policies of the government become virtually indistinguishable.

In one-party systems, the party performs routine functions as in a two-party or multiparty system. It puts its members up for election to office, establishes rules and procedures for operation of the party, establishes a platform of policies it will pursue, and provides its members with political spoils.

In some systems, additionally, the party may have demanding, restrictive admissions tests for membership. Not all dominant parties in one-party systems use such restrictive membership devices. Those in formalized one-party systems are much more likely to use them than are those in one-party dominant systems. In order to understand the different types of one-party systems, it is crucial to understand the distinctions between formalized one-party and one-party dominant political systems.

In formalized one-party systems, other parties are illegal. Other parties might "mislead" the country if they are allowed to exist or compete with the dominant party for power. As such, they are considered undesirable to injurious to a sense of "the public good," and the dominant party, through the passage of laws and the use of government's police power, keeps the opposition from forming or running candidates for office.

A well-known example of the formalized one-party system is the former Soviet Union with its powerful Communist Party of the Soviet Union (CPSU). The first leader of this party, Vladimir Lenin, led a successful revolution in 1917 against the ineffective successor to an old monarchical system in Russia. After seizing power, Lenin declared that in order to correct the wrongs of the previous government, the society must work toward achieving communism. According to Lenin, the CPSU, because of its commitment to communist principles, was the only political party that could lead Russian society toward that end. In 1920, the communist-controlled legislature of the Soviet Union labelled other parties subversive and prohibited their existence by law. The pros and cons of Lenin's approach are certainly debatable, but the Soviet experience is a classic case of a formalized one-party system.

One-party dominant political systems, on the other hand, are those in which other parties are allowed to exist and compete for power, but one party consistently dominates the competition and holds firmly to its control of government. This tends to occur when the party is able to build its power from a number of bases; these bases may include popular appeal, constitutional mechanisms, patronage, divisions in opposition strength, and political repression. Voters and politicians often feel that they have no practical alternative to joining or supporting the party in such a system. A classic example of a one-party dominant political system is Mexico's Institutional Revolutionary Party, whose uninterrupted hold on power during the twentieth century has not been matched elsewhere in the world. Longer-lived than the Soviet Communist Party, the Institutional Revolutionary Party has maintained itself not only through patronage, support from interest groups, legal mechanisms, repression, and fraud, but also from popular support and an "if-you-can't-beat-'em, join-'em" appeal to those seeking office.

Whether a party system follows the formalized or one-party dominant model, the advantages and disadvantages are essentially the same. There are two basic advantages for the ruling party in a one-party system: Policy-making is easier and long-range policy is highly stable. The disadvantages are that dominant parties in such a system tend to be more hierarchical and elitist, and that there is a lack of competing interests and views from which voters may choose. The reason that easier policy-making conditions exist is that political parties in control of government may simply enact their policy preferences. This is a much easier task when there are no other parties to offer an alternative point of view. The dominant party has little or no concern about opposition in a one-party system, so it can fulfill its goals more with less dissent. The long-range political policy of one-party governments is also much more stable than in other systems, because the dominant party is unlikely radically to change its viewpoint over time. There are few questions about what the government will do to address problems or issues, because the party in power has a history of dealing with similar problems.

The two disadvantages of a one-party system have to do with the values of democracy, which holds that opposing viewpoints, accessibility, and freedom of choice are important elements in any governmental system. If citizens cannot choose their preference between two or more parties' plans for the country, can democracy truly exist? In one-party systems, the dominant party tends to be both hierarchical and elitist. In other words, it is a very closed organization with a rigid chain of command from the top of the party down to the individual members. It does not welcome or accept every citizen who wishes to participate in party affairs, because there are a limited number of spoils that it can offer to its members. The second major disadvantage is that there is a lack of competing interests and views in forming political policy, because the dominant party has no opposition. What if the dominant party pursues a policy that is injurious to the government or its people? In a one-party system, the chances of preventing bad policy that an opposition party's criticism may provide are reduced or eliminated.

Applications

Examples of one-party systems are not hard to find, in either the formalized or party-dominant forms. Formalized systems have historically existed in communist regimes, such as the former Soviet Union or the People's Republic of China, where the government's and the people's political needs are presumably fulfilled by a single political party. The dominant party is seen as the complete representative of the people's will and welfare, and by definition, any party opposed to the dominant party is therefore opposed to the people. As such, opposition parties are prohibited, labelled as dangerous to social order.

One-party dominant systems are also plentiful, though in contrast to formalized systems, they do allow political opposition. Japan, for example, was ruled by the Liberal Democratic Party steadily from 1955 to 1993, despite the existence of other organizations such as the Japan Socialist, Communist, Democratic Socialist, and Clean Government parties. In Sweden, the Social Democratic Party has ruled almost continuously since 1932, and Israel was ruled by the Labor Party from the time of its formal recognition as an independent country in 1948 to the late 1980's. In the United States, during the Era of Good Feelings (1817-1823), the Democratic Party effectively disposed of its competition of the time, the Federalist Party. Federalists suffered from a perception that they were a party of wealthy elites, and during the War of 1812, their sympathies were uncomfortably pro-British. Democrats controlled almost all major national and state political offices by 1816, and it was clear that the Federalist Party would no longer be able to offer a viable alternative to Democratic power. This one-party system was relatively short-lived; in the 1830's, a group calling itself the Whig Party began running candidates against Democrats and winning some elections. The Whigs ultimately suffered the same fate as the Federalists, making way for the formation of the modern Republican Party. While the Whigs were more successful than the Federalists at challenging Democratic power, it is nevertheless true that for a time in early American history, the Democrats enjoyed a one-party dominance over

U.S. government. Since the time of the formation of the Republican Party, American national politics have occasionally favored one party or the other, but have not drifted back into a clear period of one-party dominance.

Although American national politics have not recently experienced one-party dominance, different states or regions of the country have not been free from it. Even into the late twentieth century, there have been states classified as one-party dominant, because of the persistent and overwhelming advantage enjoyed by either Democrats or Republicans in a state's government. Perhaps the most notable of these one-party subsystems is the American South, which as a region has historically exhibited a high degree of loyalty to the Democratic Party. At one time, Democratic dominance was such that the winner of the Democratic party primary was considered the winner of the general election for office, because Republicans either did not run any candidates, or the candidates they ran were patsies. Beginning in the 1960's, however, with the advent of modern civil rights legislation, the South's loyalty to the Democratic Party began to wane; in the modern day, most scholars seem to agree that the South now more closely reflects the true two-party competition of American national politics.

Whether a political system assumes the formalized one-party form or one-party dominant form, the party in such a system will behave roughly the same. Free of the worries that come from political challenge, it will establish policies and principles on which laws and rules of order will be based. It will emphasize the altruism and importance of the party to the welfare of the people and will hold itself out as an organization that all should wish, but that not all will be allowed, to join. Those who aspire to political office will be either obliged or required to join the party—even if it means an abandonment of their personal views—because the only way to get elected in such a system is to belong to the party, and it will not welcome those who come in sporting an attitude of change or dissent.

The party may also use its current political power to increase its future prospects for success through the passage of laws or the adoption of policies favorable to itself. Through spoils, election law, use of state-owned media, and other means, parties in power may seek to stay in power.

In summary, while dominant parties in one-party systems enjoy several advantages that stem from their unchallenged positions, it is true that voters suffer a lack of real choice under such a system. The dominant party may become complacent or uncaring in the fulfillment of its governmental duties, because it does not have to worry about being "thrown out" for doing a bad job. Ultimately, the desirability of a one-party system may boil down to the question of whether efficiency or democracy is more desirable.

Context
One-party systems are not new; they existed, in a sense, as far back as when the first political societies were formed. In modern times, one-party dominance has been based more on themes of ideology than on class distinction. It has, nevertheless, played an important part in the history of superpowers and developing nations alike.

One-party systems are likely to exist in countries in which one of two conditions is present: Under revolutionary or post-revolutionary conditions, the victorious side is likely to consolidate its hold on power by prohibiting or discouraging opposing political movements. Another condition under which single-party dominance may develop is one in which a single political party has been able to build upon early successes to create an intense loyalty to itself. The dominant party may use its political power to make laws that are advantageous to itself in such a system, but, if constitutional protections are in place, it cannot legally outlaw other parties, nor prohibit them from participating in the electoral process.

Sociologists have suggested that one of the prerequisites for holding power is the attempt to eliminate or minimize the threat from other powerseekers. As long as it is in the nature of parties to seek power, it seems likely that the more successful ones will do what they can to create or perpetuate a one-party system of governance. Be it through revolution or popular control of the ballot box, establishing dominance is a rule of party politics.

Bibliography

Heard, Alexander. *A Two-Party South?* Chapel Hill: University of North Carolina Press, 1952. Excellent discussion of the development of a one-party system in the American South and the conditions that led to its breakdown.

Key, V. O. *Politics, Parties, and Pressure Groups.* 3d ed. New York: Thomas Y. Crowell, 1952. Explains why parties form, why they exist, how they work, and how they strive to establish dominance in the American political system.

Marx, Karl, and Friedrich Engels. *The Communist Manifesto.* Translated by Samuel Moore. New York Labor News, 1948. Provides a logical, rigorous philosophical justification for formalized one-partyism.

Pempel, T. J., ed. *Uncommon Democracies: The One-Party Dominant Regimes.* Ithaca, N.Y.: Cornell University Press, 1990. Details the development of one-party dominant systems in allegedly multiparty democratic countries. Considers party strategy, underlying social conditions, and dominant party prospects for the future.

Riordon, William L. *Plunkitt of Tammany Hall.* New York: Alfred A. Knopf, 1948. Beginning students of party studies will appreciate its brevity, clarity, humor, and colorful description of an important period in American political history. An account of how a one-party dominant machine gets and stays that way.

John C. Kuzenski

Cross-References

Chinese Communism, p. 223; Communist Parties, p. 377; The Democratic Party, p. 520; Fascism and Nazism, p. 656; Marxism-Leninism, p. 1155; Mexico: Politics and Government, p. 1179; Multiparty Systems, p. 1235; Political Parties, p. 1485; Political Party Roles, p. 1499; The Republican Party, p. 1699; Revolutionary Parties, p. 1731; Russian Political History, p. 1770; Two-Party Systems, p. 2033.

SURVEY
OF
SOCIAL
SCIENCE

ALPHABETICAL LIST

CATEGORY LIST

HISTORY OF GOVERNMENT AND POLITICS

INTERNATIONAL GOVERNMENT AND POLITICS

LAW AND JURISPRUDENCE

RELIGION AND GOVERNMENT

TYPES OF GOVERNMENT